Job Shop Lean

Job Shop Lean
An Industrial Engineering Approach to Implementing Lean in High-Mix Low-Volume Production Systems

Shahrukh A. Irani

Routledge
Taylor & Francis Group

A PRODUCTIVITY PRESS BOOK

First published 2020
by Routledge

52 Vanderbilt Avenue, New York, NY 10017
and by Routledge

2 Park Square, Milton Park, Abingdon, Oxon, OX14 4RN

Routledge is an imprint of the Taylor & Francis Group, an informa business
© 2020 Taylor & Francis

ISBN: 978-0-367-47225-2 (hbk)
ISBN: 978-1-4987-4069-2 (pbk)
ISBN: 978-1-003-03418-6 (ebk)

Typeset in Garamond
by codeMantra

This book is dedicated to my late parents, Ardeshir Irani and Freni Irani, who embodied moral values, kindness, generosity, decency, humility, and love for the family.

Contents

Foreword

Let me state up front that, properly planned and led, Job Shop Lean is guaranteed to impact the bottom line of any high-mix low-volume (HMLV) manufacturer!

Except for bombs and bullets, modern supply chains for the Department of Defense are often characterized as being fraught with HMLV orders. With tremendous pressure to be fiscally responsible, the Department of Defense, like industry, has been implementing an array of techniques and tools for reducing cost and order sizes to the bare minimum based on customer pull from the warfighter. In 2000, while pulling together a portfolio of manufacturing technology projects for meeting the needs of the US forging industry and the Defense Logistics Agency, I recruited Dr. Shahrukh Irani to participate in the Forging Industry Association Department of Defense PRO-FAST Program's Forging Defense Manufacturing Consortium. My specific intent was that he investigate, develop, test, and deploy the Production Flow Analysis and Simplification Toolkit (PFAST) software that his team was developing to serve as the foundation for implementing Job Shop Lean.

Working closely with Dr. Irani over several years, he and his team implemented PFAST in several custom forges that support the Department of Defense. This was accomplished by placing interns in forges and having the students "Lean out" their manufacturing facilities using his Job Shop Lean methodology that PFAST helped to implement. With support from the host company and hands-on mentoring by Dr. Irani, the interns helped to pilot Job Shop Lean at custom forges in Connecticut, Ohio, Texas, Oregon, and California.

Contrary to other authors of front matter (Forewords, Prefaces, Acknowledgments, etc.) that appear in books on Lean, I will not waste your time citing content that is referenced later in between the covers of this treasure chest of practical Lean concepts for HMLV manufacturers. Suffice it to say, Dr. Irani and his interns made substantive contributions to the forges with respect to key metrics established by each of those host forges. Their customer-driven metrics included reduction of work in process, reduction of product flow distances, reduction in inventory, grouping of machines into work cells, efficient factory layouts and detailed work station design to optimize operator movements. Details are available in the many case studies included in this book. Better yet, instead of reading the case studies, go to these forges and talk to their leadership. You will easily see that it was their leadership, driven by their conviction that Job Shop Lean was a good fit in their custom forge shops, that helped them to achieve impressive bottom line results!

If you are an HMLV manufacturer, especially a small-to-medium job shop, my challenge to you and your management team is simple: Invoke a variant of my Rule of Teams to implement Job Shop Lean in your enterprise – *We work as teams to provide value via customer-focused processes that we are empowered to improve using Lean.*

Jon D. Tirpak, PE, FASM
Chief Engineer
Sabattis, LLC
974 Casseque Province
Mount Pleasant, SC 29464
Phone: 843-480-5784
Email: JonTirpak@att.net

Testimonial

As a company, we initiated a Lean journey in 2015 to eliminate waste, improve communications, and increase efficiency in the process from delivering a fit-for-purpose quote to a customer to being paid for our completed work. In the midst of that journey, we recognized our manufacturing mindset needed to change from the standard high-volume low-mix to our true DNA, which is low-volume high-mix.

Todd Chretien, our Director of Manufacturing, found Dr. Irani (and Job Shop Lean). Together they began to study and examine the possibility of changing the way our machine shop processed jobs. Based on their work, we tested the 'cell' concept and realized very encouraging results. Todd and Dr. Irani worked with the team to completely re-layout our machine shop into seven manufacturing cells. The shop began to change physically and culturally. The change was slow and steady. But the result has been countless efficiency gains that have revolutionized the shop and inspired the personnel.

Our journey continues as we drive towards implementing Job Shop Lean throughout the manufacturing, assembly, and testing processes at multiple locations. We have shared our findings with other internal and external manufacturing facilities. The opportunities to improve are truly endless, and we are excited about what we have done and will do in the future.

A huge thank you to Dr. Irani and the students from the Department of Industrial Engineering at the University of Houston for their help throughout this process.

Ed Smith
Vice President
Superior Completion Services
Houston, Texas
https://superiorenergy.com/

Acknowledgments

In 1999, during one of our conversations, Prof. Blaine Lilly (Department of Mechanical and Aerospace Engineering, The Ohio State University) held up his copy of *Lean Thinking* by James Womack and Daniel Jones and asked me, "Have you read this book?"

Prof. Rajiv Shivpuri (Department of Integrated Systems Engineering, The Ohio State University) was a faculty colleague, friend, and mentor at The Ohio State University. He introduced me to Jon Tirpak and recommended me for inclusion in the team of Principal Investigators for the Forging Defense Manufacturing Consortium.

Jon Tirpak (Executive Director of the Forging Defense Manufacturing Consortium) funded my research on Job Shop Lean from 2004 to 2012. Per his "Golden Rule"[1] for annual renewal of funding, every year I had to pilot Job Shop Lean in one of the custom forge shops that were members of the Forging Defense Manufacturing Consortium.

Dr. Jin Zhou, Dr. Heng Huang, and Dr. Smart Khaewsukkho were the three doctoral students whose outstanding research contributed to the development of the Production Flow Analysis and Simplification Toolkit (PFAST) software.

Prof. Rajiv Ramnath (Department of Computer Science & Engineering, The Ohio State University) and his graduate students, Thomas Mampilly and Dustin Hoffman, partnered with my team to produce the commercial version of the PFAST software.

Hannes Hunschofsky (Head of Engine Division, Hoerbiger Corporation of America) gave me the once-in-a-lifetime opportunity to implement Job Shop Lean in their facility located on Milby Street, Houston, TX.

Todd Chretien (Director of Manufacturing, Superior Completion Services) is leading a customized do-it-yourself implementation of Job Shop Lean in

---

[1] Whoever has the gold makes the rules.

their in-house machine shop. Superior Completion Services began their Job Shop Lean journey in June 2018. Having worked with Todd for over a year, I am convinced that, for Job Shop Lean to be implemented successfully, it *must* be led by an executive who studies it, masters it, implements it, then teaches it to his/her team before stepping aside so they can "take it from there". Todd is the reason and inspiration that I completed the remaining chapters in this book!

While I cannot name every one of them, I wish to thank the 1,000+ members of the now-defunct online chat group, JSLEAN, that I created and moderated from 2001 to 2012. Our numerous arguments were fueled by my epiphany that the Lean tools based on the famous Toyota Production System were archaic and had limited use for HMLV manufacturers. But those same arguments convinced me that I needed to work in industry and produce results to prove that Job Shop Lean was not academic mumbo jumbo like the peer-reviewed papers that I had published in research journals. It is said, "Those who can, do; those who cannot, teach" and "Those who can, do; those who cannot, consult". I offer this book as humble evidence that a researcher and teacher *can* leave academia to become a consultant. By leaving academia to work in industry, I finally became an Industrial Engineer (IE) who puts theory into practice and is able to learn from failure.

While I cannot name every one of them, I wish to thank the hundreds of IE students I taught at The Ohio State University from 1996 to 2012. In each course that I taught, my students had to suffer through a demanding team-based industry project that required them to apply in the real world what I taught in the classroom.

I am grateful to my precious family – Gulnar (wife), Anosh (son), and Arnaz (daughter) – for their care, love, patience, and understanding as I slogged through the past 3 years to write this book.

Beyond my immediate family, I always had the support of my brother (Vispi) and his family (Perses, Farah, and Freyana).

Last, but not the least, I am grateful to the Taylor & Francis Group editorial team of Michael Sinocchi, Katherine Kadian, Todd Perry and Sofia Buono who helped to make this book a reality.

Author

Shahrukh A. Irani, PhD, is the President of Lean and Flexible, LLC, a consulting company that delivers advisory, training, and implementation services focused on Lean for HMLV manufacturing (aka Job Shop Lean). Currently, he teaches a two-semester project-intensive course on Lean Manufacturing in the Department of Industrial Engineering at the University of Houston. From 2012 to 2018, he was the President of the Houston Senior Chapter of the Institute of Industrial and Systems Engineering. From 2012 to 2014, he worked as the Director of IE Research at Hoerbiger Corporation of America, Inc. (HCA), Houston, TX. In that position, he gained invaluable industry experience by undertaking projects to demonstrate the viability of Job Shop Lean in HCA's HMLV manufacturing facilities. From 1996 to 2012, he was an Associate Professor in the Department of Integrated Systems Engineering (ISE) at The Ohio State University (OSU). His research at OSU produced Job Shop Lean, a comprehensive methodology to adapt Lean for HMLV small and medium enterprises (SME). Also, his research team at OSU developed the PFAST software that facilitates the implementation of Job Shop Lean. During his sixteen years at OSU, he received the Outstanding Faculty Award for excellence in teaching from the ISE department's graduating classes of 2002, 2003, 2004, 2005, 2006 and 2009, and the 2002 Charles E. MacQuigg Outstanding Teaching Award from the College of Engineering. For 1999–2001 and 2001–2003, he served as the Director of the Facilities Planning and Design (FAPAD) division of the Institute of Industrial Engineers. In 1996, he was voted Young Engineer of the Year by the Minnesota Federation of Engineering Societies and the Minneapolis Chapter of the Institute of Industrial Engineers. Dr. Irani is the Editor of the *Handbook of Cellular Manufacturing Systems* (1999, John Wiley).

Chapter 1

About This Book

The Genesis of Job Shop Lean

This book has extracted the relevant theory out of many books, validated it through industrial implementation, and developed a formal methodology – Job Shop Lean – to implement Lean in any HMLV (high-mix low-volume) manufacturing facility. As early as the 1960s, the British knew that the major part of their discrete parts manufacturing industry was concerned with production in medium and small batches of a variety of components (Gallagher and Knight, 1973). To address the challenges of HMLV manufacturing, the British used *Group Technology* (GT), a technique for identifying and bringing together related or similar components in a production process in order to take advantage of their similarities to gain the inherent economies of flow line production. However, the scope and scale of implementation of GT in the UK varied with the variety of components being made, the volumes of production, the stability of demand, and most importantly, the manufacturing processes required to make them. By discovering similarities between parts, GT impacted design and manufacturing functions such as parts standardization, machine design, process planning, cost estimation, fixture design, and CAD (Computer Aided Design).

GT revolutionized the design of manufacturing facilities. Typically, custom manufacturing facilities tended to be functionally organized whereby equipment of the same type was co-located in departments ("process villages"). GT helped to transform these job shops into facilities whose equipment was organized into manufacturing cells. *Cellular Manufacturing* (CM) is an application of the GT concept to reconfigure and design the layout of any HMLV facility. CM involves processing a collection of similar parts on a dedicated group of machines or manufacturing processes. A *Manufacturing Cell* can be defined as "an independent group of functionally dissimilar machines, located together on the floor, dedicated to the manufacture of a family of similar parts". A *Part Family* can be defined as "a collection of parts which are similar either because of geometric shape and size or because similar processing steps are required to manufacture them". It is preferable that a cell be dedicated to producing a single part family, that each part family be produced completely within its cell, and that the different cells in a facility have minimum interaction with each other.

In 1963, Prof. John Burbidge introduced his method – Production Flow Analysis (PFA) – to reorganize an entire manufacturing facility into manufacturing cells (Burbidge, 1963). PFA can segregate a large number of seemingly diverse components into families by grouping parts with similar sequences of manufacturing operations into clusters (aka part families). In this book, PFA is the method of choice for part family formation and cell design, which serve as the starting point to implement Job Shop Lean.

GT and CM could be used to design large vertically integrated facilities as a network of cells producing families of components that are routed to assembly lines (or cells) producing product families! When the final assemblies are exploded into the subassemblies and components that are used to build them, these subassemblies and components can be segregated into families based on their design and manufacturing similarities. These part families can be produced in separate manufacturing cells. As early as 1925, this idea of cells dedicated to producing different families of parts that were supplied directly ("point of use") to different stations on the assembly line had been implemented by a US company, Jones and Lamson Machine Company, to build a range of turret lathes (Flanders, 1925).

The Toyota Production System (and Lean) Gave GT/CM a New Lease of Life

The introduction of GT into an organization can fundamentally affect both the overall structure and the internal operation of all departments, and its long-term effects should therefore be considered before starting a major project. It will not only change the pattern of the working day for most employees in the firm, but also involve them in a new way of thinking (Gallagher and Knight, 1973).

While hundreds of books have been written on the Toyota Production System (TPS), it is the book written by the person who led its implementation at Toyota, Taiichi Ohno, that truly explains the heart and soul of the system (Ohno, 1988). Similarly, if one desires to read a book written by the person that led a company-wide implementation of GT, then the book by Gordon Ranson (1972) describes the implementation of GT at Serck Audco Valves. Ranson's book describes benefits gained from GT that assembly facilities like Toyota attribute to the TPS! In addition, two other books summarize GT implementations by numerous other British manufacturers (Jackson, 1978; Burbidge, 1979).

GT seeks to identify and group together similar parts to take advantage of their similarities in manufacturing and design. GT has been practiced around the world for many years as part of good engineering practice and scientific management. Originally, GT was defined as "a method of manufacturing piece parts by the classification of these parts into groups and subsequently applying to each group similar technological operations" (Mitrofanov, 1966). A modern definition of GT is "the realization that many problems are similar, and that by grouping them, a single solution can be found to a set of problems, thus saving time and effort" (Shunk, 1985). This definition captures the true essence of GT that the population of entities or activities in a manufacturing system, or sub-system, can be replaced by a smaller number of families. However, the most general definition of GT is that "it is a manufacturing philosophy which identifies and exploits the underlying proximity of parts and manufacturing processes" (Ham, 1985). The manufacturing concept of *part family* is analogous to the statistical concept of clusters. Part families have been exploited in numerous areas of design and manufacturing such as Variety Reduction, Standardization, Flexible Machine Design, Cost Estimation, Variant Design, and Computer-Aided Process Planning (CAPP).

Without a doubt, GT failed to sustain the attention of industry. GT may have fallen out of favor with manufacturers as early as the 1970s. Possibly because the *thinking* which is at the core of the TPS (and Lean) was not known to the pioneers of GT and CM at that time! In contrast, Lean took the entire world of business by storm. I believe that it was champions like Taiichi Ohno (who invented the TPS) and James Womack (who founded the Lean Enterprise Institute) who ensured that the power of the TPS (and Lean) was recognized. Their efforts paid off! Lean has been widely adopted in manufacturing, service, government, distribution, healthcare, banking, etc. In fact, there is no business that would not benefit from adopting Lean!

This book seeks to rejuvenate GT and recommend it to HMLV manufacturers in the 21st century. I think that the same barriers that GT proponents could not overcome in the 1960s and 1970s could be overcome today. In Table 1.1, I have suggested how each of the barriers that hindered the adoption of GT/CM in the 20th century could be overcome today in the 21st century by adopting appropriate practices of the TPS, Industry 4.0, commercially available technology enablers and software tools, decision support and knowledge creation using machine learning and Artificial Intelligence, etc.

Table 1.1 How Past Barriers to GT Implementation Can Be Eliminated Today

Barrier to GT Implementation	How the Barrier Could Be Dissolved
Cells are susceptible to crippling stoppages due to machine breakdowns, operator absenteeism, etc.	• But so would any other manufacturing system be susceptible to the same disturbances! It is good business strategy to "stress test" a cell and to make it robust and resilient to shocks. For example, a co-leader should be groomed for the cell to accommodate the leader's absence due to vacation, illness, family emergencies, resignation, or firing. • Total Productive Maintenance (TPM) requires that routine maintenance checks be done on a bottleneck machine. And if preventive maintenance is needed, it is done outside of production hours. The cell members do this as part of their duties since their performance metrics would be affected if the machine failed catastrophically during a production shift!
Cells are inflexible if changes occur in the composition of its part family, product demand fluctuates, technology changes, etc.	• The Sales and Marketing representative who is charged with getting business for the cell must do due diligence to bring in work from customers who need the parts made in the cell. • During the design phase, simulation analyses should be done to determine how many machines should be assigned to a cell to withstand ≈15% fluctuations in demand. Beyond that, there is no other recourse but to use overtime or outsource the extra work to a vendor. • Technology changes do not occur overnight. It is the responsibility of company management to anticipate technology changes that could obsolete the machines and processes (and parts produced) in the cell.

(Continued)

Table 1.1 (*Continued*)   How Past Barriers to GT Implementation Can Be Eliminated Today

Barrier to GT Implementation	How the Barrier Could Be Dissolved
Pre-existing locations of immovable machines ("monuments") do not favor the implementation of cells	• Water Spiders who have up-to-date knowledge of the production schedules for these machines help to move orders to/from these machines to other machines in the facility on a JIT basis. • If any cell requires use of a monument, the other machines in that cell are moved into close proximity to it. • Equipment builders are willing to design down-sized/right-sized machines that are simple and dedicated to the specific product (or product family) which allows the smaller machines to be placed inside the cell (Source: Why Boeing Is Big on Right-Size Machine Tools. https://www.mmsonline.com/articles/why-boeing-is-big-on-right-size-machine-tools).
Cost of changing the existing layout in order to implement cells	• A new accounting approach like Lean Accounting encourages quantification of the cost savings from waste elimination. • A new accounting approach like Throughput Accounting encourages quantification of the increase in sales when throughput is increased at bottleneck work centers.
Upgrading of accounting and administrative systems	With the emergence of *Lean Accounting* and *Throughput Accounting*, there is widespread awareness that traditional accounting methods make it hard to justify implementing what is guaranteed to benefit the complete enterprise – Lean!
Training that employees need to be given so they are able to work in a cell	• Then give them the training they need! The benefits will be tenfold greater than the costs incurred. Investing in a well-trained and motivated workforce will keep paying back for years to come! • Every company that is recognized for successfully implementing Lean gave every one of their employees training on the fundamentals of Lean (Lean 101). • Toyota continues to use the TWI (Training Within Industry) program to develop their supervisors and line employees.

(*Continued*)

Table 1.1 (*Continued*)   How Past Barriers to GT Implementation Can Be Eliminated Today

Barrier to GT Implementation	How the Barrier Could Be Dissolved
	• Read Mike Rother's *Toyota Kata* (McGraw-Hill, 2010) or David Mann's *Creating a Lean Culture* (Productivity Press, 2014) to understand the value of workforce training, development, and engagement to ensure the successful implementation of Lean.
Upgrading of shop scheduling	Switch off the MRP engine that resides in your ERP (Enterprise Resource Planning) system. Instead, bolt on a finite capacity scheduling tool like Preactor (www.Preactor.com), TACTIC (www.waterloo-software.com), or Schedlyzer (www.optisol.biz). Else use a rough-cut scheduler like CSuite (http://www.factoryphysics.com/quick-flow-benchmarking).
Maintaining high machine utilization	• Toyota and Eliyahu Goldratt popularized the notion that high machine utilization is a poor performance metric because it does not guarantee increased sales of finished products. • Toyota's use of a simple metric like Takt Time that is displayed on electronic counters mounted above their assembly lines drives a factory-wide awareness to do whatever it takes to maintain line output to match the Takt Time. • Toyota pioneered numerous practices, such as Chaku-Chaku, Setup Reduction, Jidoka, TPM, and Poka-Yoke, that help to maximize available equipment capacity. • Eliyahu Goldratt's TOC guides managers to maximize utilization of only the bottleneck (or bottlenecks) in their facility and allow the non-bottlenecks to remain idle, if necessary.
Resistance to change from employees	The same resistance is met when implementing Lean. But enough is now known about Toyota's methods to involve employees in finding solutions to their problems and making the changes that are necessary.

(*Continued*)

Table 1.1 (*Continued*) How Past Barriers to GT Implementation Can Be Eliminated Today

Barrier to GT Implementation	How the Barrier Could Be Dissolved
Resistance to change from managers	• The same resistance is met when implementing Lean. But enough is now known about Toyota's methods to have their future executives start on the floor and come up through the ranks, all the time learning in complete detail the work that is being done and the workers doing that work. Thereby, they develop into "Lean leaders". • Most managers try to run their factories from their offices. If they choose not to be fully aware of their factory operations, their resorting to "managing with PowerPoint slides and Excel reports" is guaranteed to fail.
Identification of machine groups and part families	• Modern ERP packages ought to carry the data that is required for GT/CM studies. If they do not, or the data is inaccurate, then that manufacturer needs to fix that problem! • Statistical packages such as SPSS and Minitab include Cluster Analysis and other algorithms that can be used for part family formation and cell design. • Specialized software like PFAST can also be used for part family formation and cell design. • Sometimes expertise with Excel matched with the experience of employees is sufficient to identify the important part families! Lean teaches us that the employees on the floor often have the best answers to the problems they face. Management simply needs to involve them in the problem-solving process! • If it is any consolation to the practitioner, even academics have struggled for years to find good algorithms and software tools for part family formation and cell design. • The modern-day explosion in commercially available Machine Learning and Artificial Intelligence software is the reason for excitement that this age-old barrier can be overcome.

(Continued)

Table 1.1 (*Continued*)   How Past Barriers to GT Implementation Can Be Eliminated Today

Barrier to GT Implementation	How the Barrier Could Be Dissolved
Absence of part/product families	• I find this hard to believe, especially having worked in custom forge shops, machine shops, foundries, etc. over the years. • The literature on GT shows that the concepts of GT and CM have been applied successfully in all discrete manufacturing sectors of industry.
Redesign of "misfit" parts and processes	• Experienced Manufacturing Engineers have access to modern tools such as Value Analysis, Design for Manufacturing and Assembly (www.DFMA.com), Product Configurators, Product Lifecycle Management, and Variant Design. • Take inspiration from the *Five Why's* questioning process to tackle any problem that we have learned from Toyota. The Five Why's questioning process is such a simple yet effective approach to get a cross-functional team thinking about how to redesign a part or its router so it can be produced faster, better, and cheaper using only the machines inside a cell.

What This Book Teaches

This book seeks to rejuvenate GT/CM and recommend it to HMLV manufacturers in the 21st century. I think that the same barriers that GT/CM users could not overcome in the 1960s and 1970s could be overcome today. Job Shop Lean is an approach to implement Lean in HMLV manufacturing facilities. Job Shop Lean integrates the TPS with GT/CM. GT/CM was used as an enterprise transformation strategy in the 1960s by an HMLV manufacturer in the UK, Serck Audco Valves (Ranson, 1972). GT/CM "fell off the radar" by the 1970s. In contrast, TPS thrived and evolved into Lean (Womack and Jones, 2003) mainly due to the efforts of the Lean Enterprise Institute (www.Lean.org). If you have read Taiichi Ohno's book on TPS (Ohno, 1988) and Ranson's book on GT/CM (Ranson, 1972), it will become clear that TPS has eliminated the obstacles that caused GT/CM to fail. The significant overlap between TPS and GT/CM cannot be missed! GT/CM provides all the tools to replace the "misfit" Lean tools in the right-hand column of Table 1.2.

Table 1.2   Lean Tools That Will (or Will Not) Work in Most Job Shops

Tools That Will Work in Most Job Shops	*Tools That May Not Work in Most Job Shops*
Strategic planning	Value Stream Mapping (VSM)
Top-down leadership	Assembly line balancing
Employee involvement	One-piece flow cells
5S	Product-specific Kanbans
Total Productive Maintenance (TPM)	First In First Out (**FIFO**) Sequencing at work centers
Setup reduction (SMED)	Pacemaker scheduling
Error-proofing (Poka-Yoke)	Inventory supermarkets
Quality at source	Work order release based on pitch
Visual controls/visual management	Production based on level loading (Heijunka)
Product and Process standardization	Mixed model production with Takt Time
Single-function (inflexible) machines	**Single-function (inflexible) machines**
Jidoka	Plan For Every Product (PFEP)
Right-sized machines	
Standard work	

In my opinion, for Job Shop Lean to be implemented in HMLV environments, it is sufficient to use the same five-step process for implementing Lean aka *Principles of Lean* (Womack and Jones, 2003; **Source:** https://theleanway.net/The-Five-Principles-of-Lean). Here are some key offerings of this book:

■ It teaches strategies for material flow reduction and simplification, especially the implementation of work cells, as a basis for guiding efforts to eliminate waste and delays that increase customer wait time.

■ A GT/CM production system is ideal for HMLV manufacturing. A cell (i) has a Value Stream focus because all the parts (or products) produced in it start and finish inside the cell, (ii) has a team-based work environment, and (iii) can be managed as a business using standard performance metrics. Since it will not be possible to transform an entire factory into stand-alone cells, the constraints that prevent cell implementation promote a process of Continuous Improvement. Each constraint that was identified becomes the focus of one or more projects to dissolve it.

■ It devotes a chapter to the tools of *PFA*. One of the PFA tools – *Product-Process Matrix Analysis* – helps to identify families of parts with similar/identical routings in a product mix that could contain 100's, even 1,000's, of active part numbers.

■ It devotes a chapter to *Product Mix Segmentation*. It is important to segment the product mix based on Volume, Revenue, and Demand History into two categories: (Runners, Repeaters) and Strangers. That helps to design a layout for the manufacturing facility that has two areas: One area has a Cellular Layout to produce parts that are ordered often in high-to-medium quantities; the other area has a standard Functional Layout, possibly with flexible equipment, to produce parts that are produced infrequently, usually in small lot sizes.

■ It devotes a chapter to a practical approach to scheduling a cell that incorporates Lean, TOC (Theory Of Constraints), and academic Scheduling Theory. Effective operations scheduling is a much-needed but much-ignored requirement for managing an HMLV facility! The misplaced confidence in Material Requirements Planning (MRP) has to end. In addition to this chapter on scheduling, another chapter surveys additional practices/systems, such as Water Spiders[1] and real-time communications, that make it possible to know the status of any active order on a shop floor where 100's of orders could be in process.

■ It devotes a chapter to improvement projects that were done by employees to implement their own ideas.

■ It encourages every HMLV manufacturer seeking to implement Lean to engage with students and faculty from a local university.

Reading Plan for This Book

In order for the reader to navigate his/her way through this book, Table 1.3 provides a summary of the key takeaways from each chapter.

---

[1] Please do a Google search on the Japanese word "mizusumashi" whose English translation is "water spider" or "whirligig beetle".

Table 1.3   Key Takeaways from Each Chapter in This Book

Chapter #	Takeaways from the Chapter
2	• Why Lean is necessary but insufficient for HMLV manufacturers • How a job shop operates differently from an assembly line • Examples of small and medium-size job shops in different sectors of industry • Review of the (five) Principles of Lean (**Source:** https://www.lean.org/WhatsLean/Principles.cfm) • How Job Shop Lean implements the Principles of Lean in job shops by focusing on (i) Product Family Formation, (ii) Factory Layout, and (iii) Pull Scheduling under Capacity Constraints • Example of a Job Shop Lean implementation using Industrial and Systems Engineering (ISE) software tools to implement the Principles of Lean
3	This chapter consists of the *Job Shop Lean Assessment Tool* that helps any HMLV manufacturer to determine if they should/should not invest in implementing Job Shop Lean.
4	This chapter establishes that the first step in a successful implementation of Job Shop Lean is that the existing factory layout be evaluated and redesigned to optimize material flow. Inefficient material flow is a major reason for waste creation and delivery delays. Three principles of optimal material flow (Design For Flow (DFF)) are offered to guide the design of a FLean (Flexible and Lean) factory layout. Viable strategies for implementing each of the three DFF principles are offered.
5	How to design factory layouts based on the principles of DFF? This chapter provides an overview of the method of PFA, which can be used to improve material flow (i) in an entire factory, (ii) a single shop (or building) inside the factory, (iii) a single cell, or (iv) a single machine.
6	How to implement the method of PFA? This chapter provides an overview of the PFAST software that helps to implement each of the four phases of PFA: Factory Flow Analysis, Group (or Shop Flow) Analysis, Line (or Cell Flow) Analysis, and Tooling (or Machine-level Flow) Analysis.
7	This chapter explains that job shops should not limit themselves to the traditional layout choices (Functional and Cellular) when they build a new facility or re-layout an existing facility. The Functional Layout is inefficient, whereas the Cellular Layout is inflexible. For successful implementation of Job Shop Lean in any HMLV manufacturing facility, it is essential that their facility layout be FLean. Hybrid Cellular Layouts are FLean because they combine the advantages of the traditional Functional and Cellular layouts.

(Continued)

Table 1.3 (*Continued*)   Key Takeaways from Each Chapter in This Book

Chapter #	Takeaways from the Chapter
8	This chapter explains in detail how the PFAST software is used to design all of the layouts discussed in Chapter 7.
9	This chapter explains how the outputs produced by PFAST are used to implement several Lean Advisory Tools to optimize material flow in a job shop that produces 100's of active products with dissimilar routings. PFAST uses the standard data that is used in any facility layout and material flow analysis project. The Lean Advisory Tools that can be implemented using PFAST are as follows: 1. LAT A: Waste Assessment in the Current State 2. LAT B: Product Mix Segmentation 3. LAT C: Feasibility Analysis for CM 4. LAT D: Cell Layout 5. LAT E: Design of Hybrid Cellular Layouts 6. LAT F: Product Mix Rationalization 7. LAT G: Revision of Manufacturing Routings 8. LAT H: Evaluation of Current and Proposed Layouts. In special cases, additional Lean Advisory Tools that have been implemented using PFAST are 1. Investing in multi-function equipment to reduce the number of machines in every cell 2. Training a Water Spider to coordinate material flows between all the machines and support services specific to a virtual cell.
10	Job Shop Lean focuses on the elimination of waste and production delays in the material flows at every level of a typical manufacturing enterprise. Chapter 5 introduced the method of PFA to analyze and simplify flow at different levels of a manufacturing enterprise. Chapter 6 introduced the PFAST to implement PFA. This chapter presents real-world examples of how software tools like PFAST, STORM, and SGETTI (www.Sgetti.com) were used to implement all four stages of PFA: Factory Flow Analysis, Group (or Shop Flow) Analysis, Line (or Cell Flow) Analysis, and Tooling (or Machine-level Flow) Analysis.
11	Can Job Shop Lean be taught in any ISE curriculum? This chapter provides the syllabi for the ISE courses (three undergraduates and one graduate) that I taught at The Ohio State University to develop a cadre of ISE students who would be able to implement Job Shop Lean.

(Continued)

Table 1.3 (*Continued*)   Key Takeaways from Each Chapter in This Book

Chapter #	Takeaways from the Chapter
12	This chapter introduces the SGETTI (www.Sgetti.com) software for visualization-aided analysis of material flows at different levels of a typical manufacturing enterprise. SGETTI, in combination with other commercially available software like MINITAB (https://www.minitab.com/en-us/) and FLOW PLANNER (https://www.proplanner.com/solutions/material-logistics-planning/flow-planner/), will replace PFAST in due course of time.
13	Segmenting the product mix is one of the Lean Advisory Tools to reduce and simplify material flow in a job shop and was discussed earlier in Chapter 9. This chapter discusses how to implement several methods for segmenting the product mix of any HMLV manufacturer into Runners, Repeaters, and Strangers.
14	Implementation of cells is one of the Lean Advisory Tools to reduce and simplify material flow in a job shop and was discussed earlier in Chapter 9. This chapter explains how to determine the correct layout shape for a cell that has to produce a family of products with dissimilar routings.
15	This chapter is a case study that complements Chapter 14. It describes the valuable lessons that were learned from implementing a single Make-To-Order machining cell in a large machine shop that produced both metallic and nonmetallic compressor parts.
16	Implementation of cells is one of the Lean Advisory Tools to reduce and simplify material flow in a job shop and was discussed earlier in Chapter 9. What if the Product-Process Matrix Analysis of the product mix shows that there is considerable machine sharing between different cells? Especially when some of those shared machines are monuments that simply cannot be placed inside any cell (such as heat treatment or shot peening)? This chapter suggests a viable portfolio of projects to eliminate (or reduce) the need for any cell to send its parts to other cells or monuments or shared machines (such as a Coordinate Measuring Machine).
17	In the right-hand column in Table 1.2 of this chapter (Chapter 1) are listed a number of Lean Tools ideally suited to assembly lines that will not work in most job shops. This chapter offers a comprehensive (but not exhaustive) Job Shop Lean toolkit that has proven effective in a variety of HMLV manufacturing facilities.

(Continued)

Table 1.3 (*Continued*)   Key Takeaways from Each Chapter in This Book

Chapter #	Takeaways from the Chapter
18	This chapter explains how to utilize the tools in the Job Shop Lean toolkit discussed in Chapter 17 to systematically implement each of the (five) Principles of Lean in any custom fabrication shop.
19	The fourth Principle of Lean is *Establish pull: As flow is introduced, let customers pull value from the next upstream activity.* How does one implement this principle in a job shop and not an assembly line? This chapter provides an in-depth discussion on flow shop and job shop scheduling using the academic scheduling software, LEKIN.
20	This chapter is a case study that complements Chapter 19. It describes the use of a commercial finite capacity scheduling software, Schedlyzer (www.Optisol.biz), to schedule a stand-alone Make-To-Order machining cell that produced drop-in orders for compressor parts needed repair crews in the field.
21	This chapter is a step-by-step tutorial on following the (five) Principles of Lean to implement Job Shop Lean using software tools like PFAST, SGETTI, MINITAB, FLOW PLANNER, SCHEDLYZER, PREACTOR, etc. The following steps are explained: 1. Product-Process Matrix Analysis to identify part families and the group of machines that will be co-located in a cell to produce each part family 2. Identification of exception operations and shared machines that result in inter-cell flows or machine duplication 3. Determination of capacity requirements for each cell (Capacity Requirements Planning) 4. Allocation of shared machines to each cell (Machine Allocation Analysis) 5. Design of the layout of each cell (Intra-Cell Layout) 6. Design of the overall layout of the facility (Inter-Cell Layout) 7. Operations scheduling in each cell (Intra-Cell Scheduling) 8. Operations scheduling for the inter-cell flows in the entire facility (Inter-Cell Scheduling) In practice, the Job Shop Lean tools described in Chapters 17 and 18 could be utilized to reduce the inter-cell flows due to shared machines that are not monuments in a multi-cell facility layout.
22	This chapter describes the variety of projects that were done in the Shipping department of Hoerbiger Corporation of America, Houston, TX, in partnership with ISE students.

(Continued)

Table 1.3 (*Continued*) Key Takeaways from Each Chapter in This Book

Chapter #	Takeaways from the Chapter
23	This chapter describes the implementation of Job Shop Lean by Ulven Forging Inc.
24	This chapter describes the implementation of Job Shop Lean by G&G Mfg. Co.
25	This chapter describes the implementation of Job Shop Lean by Hoerbiger Corporation of America, Houston, TX.
26	This chapter describes a variety of educational and training resources on Job Shop Lean.
27	This chapter explains how to use the method of Value Network Mapping (VNM) instead of Value Stream Mapping to implement Job Shop Lean in machine shops, custom fabrication shops, and other job shops.
28	This chapter provides some guidance and advice to executives and middle managers tasked with implementing Job Shop Lean. It complements the list of management books listed in the section titled *What This Book Does Not Teach* in this chapter.

Appendices for Select Chapters in This Book

Several chapters have *Appendices* that could not be included in this book due to page restrictions set by the publisher. Table 1.4 provides a detailed list of the Appendices associated with each chapter in this book. This material is an essential complement to this book. Appendices for all chapters are available for download at https://www.crcpress.com/9781498740692.

Table 1.4 Appendices for Select Chapters in This Book

Chapter #	Appendices in the Chapter
1	1. A Chronological Bibliography on GT
2	1. Literature on Job Shop Lean
4	1. Guidelines for Designing a Good Factory Layout 2. A Detailed Checklist to Evaluate Any Factory Layout 3. A Lean Checklist to Evaluate Any Factory Layout
9	1. Detailed Explanation of Each Lean Advisory Tool (LAT)

(Continued)

Table 1.4 (*Continued*)   Appendices for Select Chapters in This Book

Chapter #	Appendices in the Chapter
11	1. Syllabus for Undergraduate Course on Process Analysis and Improvement 2. Syllabus for Undergraduate Course on Facilities Design 3. Syllabus for Undergraduate Course on Production Control and Scheduling 4. Syllabus for Graduate Course on Job Shop Lean
12	1. PFA Using a Flow Diagram: The Simple Case of a Single Routing 2. Does a Hospital Operate like a Job Shop or an Assembly Line? 3. Design of Lean Hospitals by Combining Data Mining and Visualization of Patient Flow Routes
14	1. Original Source of Data for This Exercise 2. Original Outputs in the PFAST Analysis Report for the Exercise 3. A Modified Multi-Product Process Chart to Visualize Many Different Routings Simultaneously 4. Hybrid Flow Shop Layout for the Cell 5. Evaluating Different Shapes for a Multi-Product Multi-Machine Cell Using STORM
15	1. Design of the Manual Packings Cell (MPC) Using PFAST and Storm 2. Checklist for Implementing a Manufacturing Cell 3. Support Systems for a Flexible and Lean (FLean) Manufacturing Cell 4. Final Presentation to Management for Approval to Implement the Cell
16	1. Implementing Job Shop Lean When Cells Are Infeasible 2. Quick-Read Guide on Product-Process Matrix Analysis 3. (PowerPoint Presentation) Cell Formation Using Product-Process Matrix Analysis 4. (Research Paper) Extended PFA 5. Quick-Read Guide on Product-Routing Cluster Analysis 6. (PowerPoint Presentation) Cell Formation Using Product-Routing Cluster Analysis 7. Classification of Work Centers Based on their Suitability for Duplication in Multiple Cells 8. (Example from Actual Project) Classification of Work Centers Based on their Suitability for Duplication in Multiple Cells

(*Continued*)

Table 1.4 (*Continued*)   Appendices for Select Chapters in This Book

Chapter #	Appendices in the Chapter
17	1. Overcoming the Challenges of Implementing Lean in Any HMLV Machine Shop
19	1. Fundamentals of Job Shop Scheduling 2. Fundamentals of Flow Shop Scheduling 3. A Simple Case of Sequencing and Scheduling a Flow Shop Cell with Capacity Constraints 4. Finite Capacity Scheduling: Helping the Job Shop to Promise Delivery Dates That Can Be Met
24	1. Free Online Sources of Information on Implementing Lean in CNC Machine Shops
25	1. Examples of Kit Carts Implemented in Different Companies
27	1. Value Stream Mapping of a *Complete* Product
28	1. Informative Books on the TPS

Supplementary Reading for Select Chapters in This Book

Several chapters have *Supplementary Reading*. Table 1.5 provides a detailed list of the Supplementary Reading associated with each chapter in this book. This material is mainly intended for faculty (and practitioners) who may wish to develop lectures and seminars (or workshops) for instructional (or training) purposes.

The *Supplementary Reading* for this book is available on a flash drive that is being sold separately by the author. If the reader is interested in pricing information for purchasing this flash drive, he/she should contact the author by email (ShahrukhIrani1023@yahoo.com) or by phone (832-475-4447). The price for the flash drive includes cost of materials and postage to any zip code in the United States. For any other country, the unit price will change depending on US postal rates for that country. Sale of the flash drive is conditional on the buyer providing a proof-of-purchase for their copy of this book.

Table 1.5 Supplementary Reading for Select Chapters in This Book

Chapter #	Supplementary Reading
8	1. Quick-Read Guide on Product-Process Matrix Analysis 2. Quick-Read Guide on Product-Routing Cluster Analysis 3. Design of a Cellular Layout for an Entire Facility 4. PFA: A Tool for Designing a Lean Hospital
11	Final Reports for Student Projects: 1. (Final Presentation for Internship) Bula Forge & Machine 2. (MS Non-Thesis Project Report) Enginetics Aerospace 3. (Final Presentation for Internship) Guardian Automotive 4. (MS Non-Thesis Project Report) Hirschvogel 5. (Final Presentation for Internship) Horton Emergency Vehicles 6. (Final Presentation for Internship) Maritime Castings Repair Facility 7. (MS Non-Thesis Project Report) OSU Medical Center 8. (Independent Study Project Report) Trafficware 9. (Final Presentation for Internship) Trinity Forge 10. (ISE532 Course Project Report) UniPrint 11. (Final Presentation for Internship) Xunlight
12	1. Presentations on Using Spaghetti Diagrams for Material Flow Assessment 2. Exercise on Waste Identification: Entire Factory 3. Exercise on Waste Identification: Single Cell 4. Fundamentals of Process Analysis and Improvement 5. An IE Instructor's Guide to Teach Process Analysis and Improvement Using the Toast Kaizen Video 6. Case Study on Process Improvement 7. Case Study: Implementing the Quick-Start Approach for Job Shop Lean at Ulven Forging Inc. 8. Case Study: Implementing the Quick-Start Approach for Job Shop Lean at Bula Forge & Machine Inc.
13	1. Product Mix Segmentation Using PQ Analysis 2. Product Mix Segmentation Using PQ$ Analysis 3. Product Mix Segmentation Using PQR$ Analysis 4. Product Mix Segmentation Using PQT Analysis
	CASE STUDY: "C-Cells" – Productivity Techniques for Job Shops
19	1. Scheduling an M-machine Flow Shop to Minimize Makespan 2. An IE Student's Study Guide for Bottleneck Scheduling Using TOC 3. Introduction to Flow Shop Scheduling 4. Case Study on Flow Shop Scheduling 5. Scheduling a 5-Machine Flow Shop 6. [Solution Key] Releasing Orders to a Cell with Capacity Constraints

(Continued)

Table 1.5 (*Continued*)   Supplementary Reading for Select Chapters in This Book

Chapter #	Supplementary Reading
24	CASE STUDY: Implementation of Job Shop Lean at Hardy Machine & Design Inc.
26	1. How to Develop a Video and Self-Study Guide on Waste Elimination 2. Instructional Materials for the *Toast Kaizen* Video 3. Instructional Materials for the *Single Piece Flow*© Simulation 4. Instructional Materials for the *Stamping Out Chaos*© Simulation 5. A Step-by-Step Approach for Implementing Job Shop Lean 6. Instructional Materials for the *Job Shop Lean*© Simulation
27	1. Value Stream Mapping: A Foundation Step for Lean Manufacturing 2. Value Stream Mapping from an IE Viewpoint: Ideas for Enhancement and Extension 3. Value Stream Mapping from an IE Viewpoint 4. Evaluation of the Value Stream Mapping Icons for Use in Job Shop-Type Facilities 5. VNM: Visualization and Analysis of Multiple Interacting Value Streams in Job Shops 6. Value Stream Mapping of a Complete Product 7. Integration of Lean Thinking and TOC in a Custom Forge Shop

What's Next?

I intend to continue expanding this book. Potential avenues could be (i) starting a blog on my website (www.LeanandFlexible.com), (ii) posting additional chapters on my website (www.LeanandFlexible.com), (iii) activating my *Lean and Flexible* group on LinkedIn, and (iv) writing another book which will have only case studies on Job Shop Lean, industry applications of Sgetti, software tools for implementing GT, etc.

Software to Implement Job Shop Lean

Table 1.3 makes it amply clear that the implementation of Job Shop Lean requires a full-blown implementation of the method of PFA to streamline material flow at all levels of the manufacturing facility (Factory, Shop, Cell, and Machine). Unfortunately, the PFAST (Production Flow Analysis and Simplification Toolkit) software that was developed to implement PFA is no longer sold commercially. Table 1.6 provides the current commercial

Table 1.6   Commercial Software to Implement Job Shop Lean

Task	Commercial Software to Perform this Task
Time and motion study	• ProPlanner (*Website*: https://www.proplanner.com/solutions/assembly-process-planning/time-studies/) • Timer Pro (*Website*: www.acsco.com) • OTRS10 (*Website*: https://shinkamanagement.com/time-study-software/)
Part family formation	• JMP (*Website*: https://www.jmp.com/en_us/home.html) • Minitab (*Website*: https://www.minitab.com/en-us/) • PFAST • Sgetti (*Website*: https://www.sgetti.com/)
Factory layout	• Flow Planner (*Website*: https://www.proplanner.com/solutions/material-logistics-planning/flow-planner/) • PFAST • Sgetti (*Website*: https://www.sgetti.com/) • SIMOGGA (*Website*: http://www.amia-systems.com/)
Process and system simulation	• FLEXSIM (*Website*: https://www.flexsim.com/) • SIMCAD (*Website*: https://www.createasoft.com/) • SIMIO (*Website*: https://www.simio.com/index.php)
Master scheduling	• DBR+ (*Website*: https://www.demanddriventech.com/) • Infor ERP VISUAL Easy Lean (*Website*: https://www.visualbusiness.net/easy-lean. An online video about this ERP system with its own FCS module can be viewed at https://vimeo.com/37543399. Also, a Functional Overview of INFOR ERP VISUAL can be downloaded at http://www.infor.com/shared_resources/14397/articles/visual-functional-overview.pdf.)
Finite capacity scheduling	• Preactor (*Website*: https://www.plm.automation.siemens.com/global/en/products/manufacturing-operations-center/preactor-aps.html) • Tactic (*Website*: http://www.waterloo-software.com/) • Schedlyzer (*Website*: https://optisol.biz/)
Machine monitoring and manufacturing execution systems	• FactoryWiz (*Website*: https://factorywiz.com/) • Forcam (*Website*: https://www.forcam.com/en) • MachineMetrics (*Website*: https://www.machinemetrics.com/) • Merlin (*Website*: http://www.memex.ca/company/)

software to perform some of the core tasks to implement the (five) Principles of Lean. If you have questions, please do not hesitate to contact me at ShahrukhIrani1023@yahoo.com or 832-475-4447.

What This Book *Does Not* Teach

GT cells are highly susceptible to disruptions such as the ones discussed in Table 1.1. Their long-term health can be ensured by implementing the standard Lean tools listed in the left-hand column of Table 1.2. The operators in a cell must have the training and be granted some autonomy to manage their cell. Supervisors, plant managers, etc. who impact the cell must also be trained. Upper management must be committed to and have prior experience in implementing GT cells. They must engage and incentivize their employees to embrace and be a part of the new work culture (and challenges) that cells are guaranteed to create.

I believe that Lean provides a complete plan for building the management and support systems to ensure the success of a GT implementation. Toyota showed that respect for people, leadership that rose from the ranks and knows the work being done by their subordinates, worker empowerment, hiring new employees who can internalize the PDCA (Plan-Do-Check-Act) process for problem-solving, etc. help to create a world-class organization! If you are an executive who is desirous of leading the implementation of Lean in your facilities, I urge you to read the management-oriented books on Lean listed in the next section.

Management-Oriented Books on Lean

Bahri, S. 2009. *Follow the Learner: The Role of a Leader in Creating a Lean Culture*. Lean Enterprise Institute, Inc.

Bahri, S. 2016. *The Lean Dentist: Establishing One-Piece Flow in Patient Treatment*. Lean Enterprise Institute, Inc.

Byrne, A. 2013. *The Lean Turnaround: How Business Leaders Use Lean Principles to Create Value and Transform Their Company*. McGraw-Hill.

Byrne, A. 2016. *The Lean Turnaround Action Guide: How to Implement Lean, Create Value and Grow Your People*. McGraw-Hill.

Emiliani, B, Stec, D., Grasso, L. & Stodder, J. 2017. *Better Thinking, Better Results: Case Study and Analysis of an Enterprise-wide*

Lean Transformation. Weathersfield, CT: Center for Lean Business Management.

Harada, T. 2015. *Management Lessons from Taiichi Ohno: What Every Leader Can Learn from the Man Who Invented the Toyota Production System.* McGraw-Hill Education.

Koenigsaecker, G. 2013. *Leading the Lean Enterprise Transformation.* CRC Press.

Lancaster, J. & Adams, E. 2017. *The Work of Management: A Daily Path to Sustainable Improvement.* Lean Enterprise Institute, Inc.

Lane, G. 2010. *Mr. Lean Buys and Transforms a Manufacturing Company: The True Story of Profitably Growing an Organization with Lean Principles.* CRC Press.

Ohno, T. 1988. *Toyota Production System: Beyond Large-Scale Production.* Productivity Press.

Ohno, T. 2012. *Taiichi Ohno's Workplace Management: Special 100th Birthday Edition.* McGraw-Hill Education.

Tarvin, P. 2016. *Leadership & Management of Machining: How to Integrate Technology, Robust Processes and People to Win!* Hanser Publications.

Tena, J.A., Castro, E. & Priolo, R. 2017. *Follow the Learner: Eliminating Waste to Get Closer to Your Customer.* Lean Enterprise Institute, Inc.

Appendices

Appendices for this chapter are available for download at https://www.crcpress.com/9781498740692.

References

Burbidge, J.L. (1963). Production flow analysis. *The Production Engineer,* 742–752.

Burbidge, J.L. (1979). *Group Technology in the Engineering Industry.* London, UK: Mechanical Engineering Publications Ltd.

Flanders, R.E. (1925). Design, manufacture and production control of a standard machine. *Transactions of ASME,* 46, 691–738.

Gallagher, C.C. & Knight, W.A. (1973). *Group Technology.* London, UK: Butterworth.

Gettelman, K.M. (1971, November). Organize production for parts not processes. *Modern Machine Shop,* 50–60.

Ham, I., Hitomi, K. & Yoshida, T. (1985). Group Technology: Applications to Production Management. Hingham, MA: Kluwer-Nijhoff Publishing.

Harmon, R.L. and Peterson, L.D. (1990). *Reinventing the Factory.* New York, NY: McGraw-Hill.

Irani, S. A. (2001, March). Software solves identity crises for parts from "big" families. *Lean Advisor,* 3–6.

Jackson, D. (1978). *Cell System of Production: An Effective Organization Structure.* London, UK: Business Books Ltd.

Miltenburg, J. (1995). *Manufacturing Strategy.* Portland, OR: Productivity Press.

Mitrofanov, S. P. (1966). Scientific Principles of Group Technology. London, UK: National Lending Library for Science and Technology.

Ohno, T. (1988). *Toyota Production System: Beyond Large-Scale Production.* Portland, OR: Productivity Press.

Ranson, G.M. (1972). *Group Technology: A Foundation for Better Total Company Operation.* London, UK: McGraw-Hill.

Rother, M. & Shook, J. (2009). *Learning to See.* Cambridge, MA: Lean Enterprise Institute (www.lean.org).

Shunk, D.L. (1985, April). Group technology provides organized approach to realizing benefits of CIMS (Computer Integrated Manufacturing Systems). *Industrial Engineering,* 17 (4), 74–76, 78.

Womack, J.P. & Jones, D.T. (2003). *Lean Thinking: Banish Waste and Create Wealth in Your Corporation.* New York, NY: Free Press.

Chapter 2

Introduction to Job Shop Lean

Lean Is Necessary for Every Manufacturer but ...

The goal of a manufacturer is to reduce the total time that a customer must wait from the time that they place their order to the time that they receive their order free of defects. *Waste* is any activity performed by the manufacturer that adds a delay to the time that the customer must wait and adds a cost to the price that the customer must pay. There are *Seven Types of Waste* that result in administrative, manufacturing, distribution, and other delays – Overproduction, Waiting, Overprocessing, Scrap and Rework, Transportation, Operator Motion, and Inventory. Henry Ford pioneered the development of the tools for eliminating waste such as Just-In-Time (JIT), Parts Standardization, Motion Efficiency, and Process Simplification. But it was Toyota that made cost reduction through waste elimination the foundation for their revolutionary Toyota Production System (TPS) (Ohno, 1988) that thrives in all their facilities distributed across the globe to this day!

... Lean Is Also Insufficient for Many Manufacturers

To satisfy a customer, a manufacturer must fulfill three goals – Quality, Cost, and Delivery. Lean limits many manufacturers with its focus on cost reduction through waste elimination. In contrast, Theory Of Constraints (TOC) is a competing manufacturing strategy that sets three goals for any manufacturer: *Maximize Throughput, Reduce Inventories,* and *Reduce Operating Costs.* Say a manufacturer has set a price of $X on an order and it takes the manufacturer Y days to deliver the order to the customer. The manufacturer achieves a Throughput of (X/Y) $/day by completing that order. Thereby, TOC *Maximizes Throughput* by eliminating the delays in completing those orders that have a higher value. *Throughput* is what keeps any manufacturer in business! Plus TOC accomplishes waste elimination by pursuing the two goals of *Reduce Inventories* and *Reduce Operating Costs.*

Lean further limits many manufacturers because of the tools used to implement Lean. These tools were primarily developed to improve the performance of (inflexible) assembly lines. Every Toyota facility is engaged in **low**-mix **high**-volume assembly of *only* automobiles. Toyota does not make refrigerators and bicycles on any of their automobile assembly lines! An assembly line that uses a conveyor to move a product (or product family) through a fixed sequence of workstations is simply not flexible enough to make 100's of different products with dissimilar manufacturing routings. Figure 2.1 compares the assembly line and the job shop on two criteria, Production Volume (QUANTITY) and Product Variety (MIX). These two manufacturing systems are at opposite ends of the spectrum of manufacturing systems (see ex. Miltenburg, 1995; p. 41).

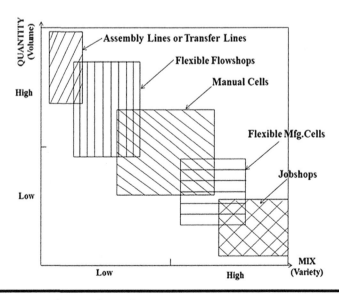

Figure 2.1 Spectrum of manufacturing systems.

How a Job Shop Differs from an Assembly Line

An assembly line and a job shop are radically different manufacturing systems. A job shop is a **high**-mix **low**-volume (HMLV) manufacturer. Some of the characteristics of a typical job shop that make its production system radically different from the TPS are as follows:

- It fulfills orders for a diverse mix of 100's, sometimes 1,000's, of different products.
- Manufacturing routings differ significantly in their equipment requirements, setup times, cycle times, lot sizes, etc.
- The facility has a Functional Layout; i.e., the facility is organized into departments ("process villages") such that each department carries equipment with identical/similar process capabilities.
- Demand variability is high.
- Production schedules are driven by due dates.
- Due dates are subject to change.
- Production bottlenecks can shift over time.
- Finite capacity constraints limit how many orders can be completed on any given machine on any day.
- Order quantities can range from low to high.
- Lead times quoted to customers must be adjusted based on knowledge of the production schedule.
- The diverse mix of equipment from different manufacturers makes operator training, maintenance, etc. more challenging than for an assembly line.
- It is a challenge to identify the part families in the product mix.
- Customer loyalty is not guaranteed.
- It is necessary to be able to serve different markets. In fact, a job shop must deal with the tendency for their product mix to alter as their customer base changes or they hire new sales and marketing staff who bring with them their past business contacts from new sectors of industry.
- It could be a challenge to recruit and retain talented employees with a strong work ethic, a desire to learn on the job and get cross-trained to operate different machines.
- There are limited resources for workforce training.
- It is hard to control the delivery schedule and quality of suppliers.
- It is hard to negotiate the due dates set by customers.
- Production control and scheduling is more complex.

A job shop is possibly the hardest HMLV facility to design and manage. Given the many differences listed above, rather than just imitating Toyota, it was decided to develop a *suitable* approach to implement Lean in any HMLV facility.

An Assembly Line Is Inflexible Compared to a Job Shop

Like any other manufacturer, even a job shop has to eliminate waste. So Lean is necessary for any job shop but far from sufficient! In order to achieve Quality, Cost, and Delivery for a variety of products made for a large number of customers, a job shop *must also* have processes and systems that make it flexible. *Process Flexibility* exists when the available resources (machines, people, tools, etc.) and systems can make a variety of parts with different specifications. *Setup Flexibility* exists when individual assets can rapidly change over from making one part to a different part. *Routing Flexibility* allows for the same part to be made using any one of several different routings. *Mix Flexibility* is the ability to simultaneously process a large variety of parts requiring different materials, vendors, tolerances, etc. *Volume Flexibility* accommodates variability in the order quantities for the same, or different, parts/products. This variability increases when the same facility seeks to produce parts/products in different phases of their life cycle, such as ramp-up, production, end-of-life, or prototype. Finally, *Facility Flexibility* requires that the entire facility could be reconfigured quickly if changes in mix and/or volume occur. In addition, if equipment is mobile, then it reduces transportation delays when, after every operation in its routing, a product must be moved to another machine at a different location in the facility.

High-Mix Low-Volume Manufacturers with Job Shop-Like Manufacturing Facilities

All HMLV manufacturers will surely benefit by implementing Lean, regardless of the fact that they produce a large number of different components or assemblies. There are savings to be gained by cutting the costs due to all forms of waste that exist in their production systems. Job Shop Lean focuses on only the following HMLV manufacturers that have job shop-like operating conditions in their facilities:

- Machine shops, forge shops, fabrication shops, foundries, stamping facilities, etc.
- Feeder shops that make the machined parts, fabricated subassemblies, injection molded parts, etc. for the assembly lines in vertically integrated Make-To-Order (MTO) factories that build tanks, ships, jet engines, excavators, cranes, furniture, etc.
- Remanufacturing facilities.
- Maintenance, Repair, and Overhaul (MRO) facilities.

Any manufacturer with an SIC (Standard Industrial Classification) Code that is 20xx, 23xx, 24xx, 25xx, 31xx, 34xx, 35xx, 36xx, 37xx, 38aa, or 39xx will usually be a discrete manufacturer of a variety of components and custom assemblies. Their manufacturing environment will have the operating characteristics of a job shop.

Primary Focus of Job Shop Lean

Job Shop Lean focuses on two major differences between most HMLV manufacturers and Toyota:

Difference #1 (Facility Layout): The first major difference between an HMLV manufacturer and Toyota is that if you walk through any HMLV facility, you will find that forklifts (not conveyors) are the dominant material handling equipment in use. *That is because they have a facility layout that cannot produce a large mix of products with 100's, often 1,000's, of different routings without also producing waste* (Irani, 2001). That is because HMLV manufacturers have been advised since time immemorial that, in order for them to be flexible, the best facility layout to have is a Functional Layout. A Functional Layout consists of many departments where each department contains equipment of similar or identical processing capabilities. Examples of such departments are Press, CNC (Computer Numerical Control) Turning, CNC Milling, Grinding, and Inspection. Unfortunately, this choice of layout results in a chaotic material flow in the facility. For example, Figures 2.2 and 2.3 display the material flows in two forge shops that produce 100's of different forgings for defense and aerospace customers. Figure 2.4 displays the material flow in a machine shop for a sample of ≈125

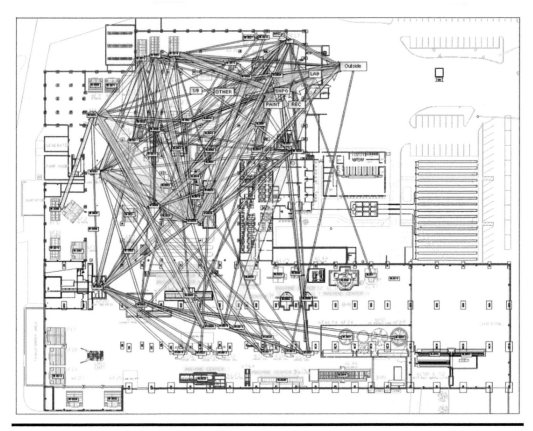

Figure 2.2   Material flow network at a Department of Defense (DOD) supplier.

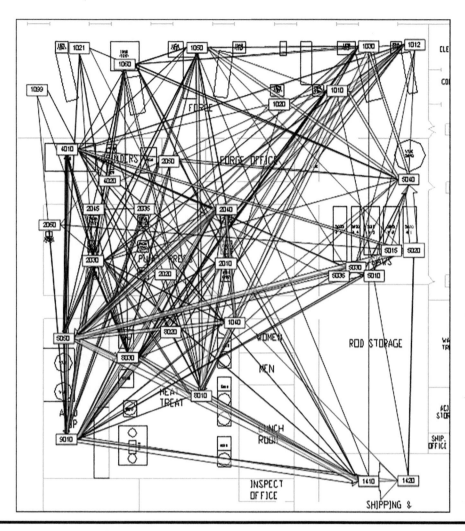

Figure 2.3   Material flow network at a Defense Logistics Agency (DLA) supplier.

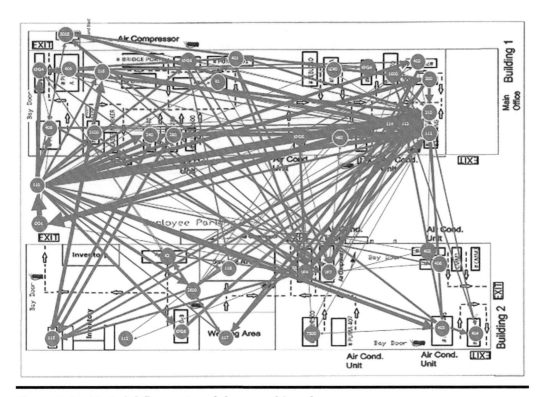

Figure 2.4 Material flow network in a machine shop.

different parts made for different customers. Figure 2.5 displays the material flow in a fabrication facility that builds industrial scales used to weigh eighteen-wheeler trucks.

Also, in a Functional Layout, large distances separate the work centers used for consecutive operations required to make any product. This automatically results in batch production which, in turn, causes significant queueing delays at those work centers that are bottlenecks. Table 2.1 provides empirical evidence that the WIP (work-in-process) between consecutive processes grows as the distance between them increases (Harmon and Peterson, 1990). When two processes are adjacent, as in assembly line or a manufacturing cell, it is possible to achieve one-piece flow. But, as that proximity is eliminated, invariably batch production is preferred, large containers are used to hold a batch of parts, heavy (and slow) material handling equipment is needed to carry these containers, etc. And, with production scheduling being done by an MRP (Material Requirements Planning) system that discourages real-time communications between consecutive processes, the waste of waiting also results.

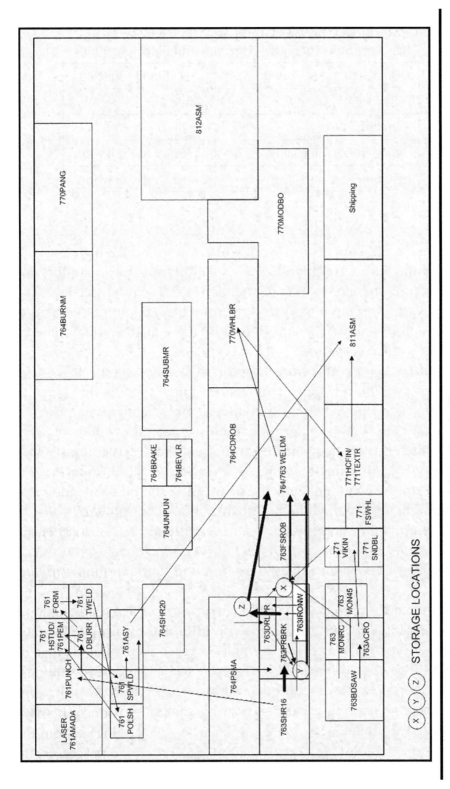

Figure 2.5   Material flow network in an MTO fabrication facility.

Table 2.1 Empirical Evidence That WIP between Consecutive Processes Grows as Distance between Their Locations Increases (Harmon and Peterson, 1990)

Distance to the Next Process	Handling Lot Size
Adjacent	Single unit
Across the aisle	Unit load
Other end of the facility	At least 1 hour of work
In another facility	At least 1 day of work

In summary, the Functional Layout will always produce high levels of at least five of the Seven Types of Waste – WIP, queues, transportation, overproduction, and operator motion (Gettelman, 1971) – in any facility. The other two wastes – scrap/rework and overprocessing – do not depend on the layout of the facility. They are caused by the equipment and manufacturing processes currently in use.

Difference #2 (Production Scheduling): The second major difference between an HMLV manufacturer and Toyota is that it is easier to practice Pull Scheduling in an assembly facility where FIFO (First In First Out) flow of orders is naturally enforced by the conveyor lines on which the products move through assembly. In contrast, the majority of HMLV manufacturers have relied on ERP (Enterprise Resource Planning) systems which use an MRP engine for production planning, operations scheduling, and shop floor control. *MRP cannot plan production and schedule operations subject to finite capacity! MRP cannot synchronize parallel production of components that go into the same subassembly if they have different production (or supplier) lead times!*

Given the batch-and-queue workflow that is a result of the Functional Layout of an HMLV facility, the reliance on MRP will further produce many of the Seven Types of Waste. For example, overproduction is due to reliance on MRP-generated forecasts, WIP is due to batching of several orders to reduce setup time losses, and queues form when too many orders are released for production under the standard assumption of an MRP system that capacity is infinite.

A Standard Process for Implementing Lean

The Lean Thinking Process is a simple five-step process for the implementation of Lean proposed by James Womack and Daniel Jones (Womack and Jones, 2003). It is implemented as follows:

1. *Identify value:* Specify value from the standpoint of the end customer by product family.
2. *Map the value stream:* Identify all the steps in the value stream for each product family, eliminating whenever possible those steps that do not create value.
3. *Create flow:* Make the value-creating steps occur in a tight sequence so the product will flow smoothly toward the customer.
4. *Establish pull:* As flow is introduced, let customers pull value from the next upstream activity.
5. *Seek perfection:* As value is specified, value streams are identified, wasted steps are removed, and flow and pull are introduced. So return to Step 1 to begin the process again and continue until a state of perfection is reached. In this state, perfect value is created with no waste.

Unfortunately, while the process may be universally applicable, many of the Lean tools that are used to implement the Lean Thinking Process are unsuitable for implementing Lean in HMLV environments. That is because of the two differences between HMLV manufacturers and Toyota that were discussed earlier. Table 2.2 lists my personal assessment of how well the popular Lean tools would work in the most challenging HMLV facility, a job shop.

The tools in the left-hand column of Table 2.2 will also work in HMLV environments. *Top-down Leadership* and *Employee Involvement* are essential in just about any business or manufacturing facility. Even job shops need *Standard Work Instructions* to minimize the impact on setup times due to the variety of process plans, setup procedures, tooling packages, material sizes, gauges, etc. And I know of no business that has not profited by empowering and training employees to control *Quality At Source. Setup Reduction* is equally important in any business. Notice how the professional chefs on Food Network shows glide around their kitchens to get anything they need as soon as they need it? *Single-function (Inflexible) Machines* appears in both columns because simple machines are easy to learn, use,

Table 2.2 Lean Tools That Will (or Will Not) Work in Most Job Shops

Tools That Will Work in Most Job Shops	Tools That May Not Work in Most Job Shops
Strategic planning	VSM
Top-down leadership	Assembly line balancing
Employee involvement	One-piece flow cells
5S	Product-specific Kanbans
Total Productive Maintenance (TPM)	FIFO sequencing at work centers
Setup reduction (SMED)	Pacemaker scheduling
Error-proofing (Poka-Yoke)	Inventory supermarkets
Quality at source	Work order release based on pitch
Visual controls/visual management	Production based on level loading (Heijunka)
Product and process standardization	Mixed model production with Takt Time
Single-function (inflexible) machines	**Single-function (inflexible) machines**
Jidoka	Plan For Every Product (PFEP)
Right-sized machines	
Standard work	

set up, operate, and maintain when incorporated into assembly lines. Toyota pioneered the concept of right-sized machines but Boeing took the idea to a new level![1] In the case of CNC machine shops, it is commonplace to see a (flexible) multi-function equipment that performs different operations to complete parts in a single setup. Yet, it is also standard practice to position drill presses and other simple manual single-function machines next to a CNC lathe or CNC mill to perform secondary operations.

Next let us discuss the tools in the right-hand column of Table 2.2. I personally believe that these tools will have limited use in HMLV environments. And that is due to the two major differences between HMLV manufacturers and Toyota discussed earlier – *Facility Layout* and *Production Scheduling*. Numerous IE (Industrial Engineering) textbooks and research papers on these two subjects describe methods and tools that can replace the Lean tools with tools suitable for job shops.

---

[1] Zelinski, P. (2006). Why Boeing is big on right-size Machine Tools. *Modern Machine Shop.* www. mmsonline.com/articles/why-boeing-is-big-on-right-size-machine-tools.

Adapting the Lean Thinking Process to Implement Job Shop Lean

The Lean Thinking Process could be easily adapted for HMLV manufacturing by replacing the Lean tools in the right-hand column of Table 2.2 with GT/CM tools for HMLV manufacturing. As a practicing IE, I have structured later chapters in this book to explain how Steps #1 and #2 can be implemented using Group Technology (Flanders, 1925; Gallagher and Knight, 1973; Ranson, 1972) methods, Step #3 can be implemented using Facility Layout methods, and Step #4 can be implemented using Production Scheduling methods. The Womack–Jones process for implementing Lean would be modified as follows:

- *Step #1 Identify value:* In an assembly facility, a few products are produced in high volumes on assembly lines. So, it is relatively easy to select a product (or family of product variants) to be a Value Stream. But in the case of machine shops, forge shops, foundries, and numerous other HMLV manufacturers, it is unrealistic to consider each component to be a Value Stream when the product mix consists of 100's, maybe 1,000's, of different parts. **How would Step #1 be modified to implement Job Shop Lean?** First, using Volume, $ales, Routing Similarity, and Sales History of the different products, the use of *Product Mix Segmentation* will partition the entire product mix into three different segments – Runners, Repeaters, and Strangers. Next, using the routings of the parts included in the Runners and Repeaters segments of the product mix, the use of *Production Flow Analysis (PFA)* (Burbidge, 1963, 1979)[2] will allow us to group parts with similar/identical routings into part families. *Each part family is analogous to a Value Stream.*
- *Step #2 Map the value stream:* *Value Stream Mapping* (VSM) is essentially a manual method. It is incapable of mapping all the routings in a single product family, let alone 100's or 1,000's of dissimilar routings in any job shop's product mix. **How would Step #2 be modified to implement Job Shop Lean?** *Just do not use VSM!* Sure, if the routings of all the parts in a part family are identical, then a single VSM could represent the entire family. Else, if there are differences in the routings

---

[2] *Classification and Coding* is an alternative method for part family formation that uses design and manufacturing attributes of the parts to form part families.

of the parts in the part family, then a Value Network Map (VNM) could be developed to aggregate many streams into a single map. *VNM is capable of mapping a large family of similar Value Streams. It can capture the interactions between different streams that use common resources.* I use VNM only if a facility is producing a final product as well as the components and subassemblies that go into that product.

■ *Step #3 Create flow: Continuous Flow* can happen only in an assembly line. A *One-Piece Flow Cell* is essentially a low-mix high-volume assembly line. But this type of material flow would be rare in any HMLV facility, except to make a product (or products) for which they have a Long Term Agreement with the customer. **How would Step #3 be modified to implement Job Shop Lean?** Cells are the foundation and building blocks of Job Shop Lean. Each cell is designed to operate like a "mini-job shop" that has to produce any combination of products in a large product family. None of these products necessarily has to be produced under a Long Term Agreement. So, with the daily mix of products changing and different due dates for in-process orders, the cell may not exhibit a perfect one-piece flow. Still, *due to the proximity between the different machines/workstations in the cell*, it is easy to move small batches of parts between machines by hand, on wheeled carts, on short roller conveyors, or using a Gorbel crane. A manufacturing cell must be capable of operating autonomously, like the amoeba and paramecium which are single-cell self-sufficient organisms. *Inside a cell, Job Shop Lean and Lean become one!* All the Lean tools listed in the left-hand column of Table 2.2, such as cross-training of the employees, 5S, SMED, TPM, Poka-Yoke, and Standard Work, ensure that the cell can operate as a self-sufficient business unit whose operations are not disrupted by defective materials, machine breakdowns, long setups, absenteeism, poor communications with suppliers and customers, etc. After Step #3 is fully implemented, one part of the job shop will consist of cells, with each cell being dedicated to a product family. The remainder of the job shop will produce orders for spare parts, prototypes, and one-off orders.

■ *Step #4 Establish pull:* All the Lean tools for Production Planning and Control, Operations Scheduling, and Shop Floor Control listed in the right-hand column of Table 2.2 are suited for assembly-line production and are based on a Make-To-Stock (MTS) inventory model. **How would Step #4 be modified to implement Job Shop Lean?** Unlike an assembly line, the typical job shop does not have a fixed production rate ("Takt Time") that drives their daily schedule. That is because their order mix and schedule for releasing orders tend to change daily! The typical job shop is a MTO business where orders are pulled into production based on actual demand, with each order having a due date for delivery to its customer. Some of the tools that have been successfully used to implement Pull Scheduling in (MTO) job shops are *Constraint Workload Analysis, Finite Capacity Scheduling (FCS), Manufacturing Execution Systems (MES), Water Striders, Constant WIP (CONWIP),* and *Electronic Scheduling Boards.*

■ *Step #5 Seek perfection:* It is somewhat easy to improve an assembly facility using the method of *VSM* (Rother and Shook, 2009). A Takt Time can be calculated for each assembly line on which 100's, maybe 1,000's, of automobiles of the same model will be assembled during the course of the year. **How would Step #5 be modified to implement Job Shop Lean?** First, by finding part families based on analysis of the Runners and Repeaters segments in its product mix. Next, by implementing a cell to produce each part family. As more and more cells are implemented in the same facility, some of the major challenges that will arise are (i) being able to place inside each cell all the equipment it needs to be self-sufficient, (ii) ensuring that the order pipeline for the part family assigned to each cell is sustained, (iii) convincing employees to get cross-trained to run different machines in the same cell, and (iv) changing the mindset of management to allow the cell operators to manage their cell. Luckily, the revolutionary TPS has provided us solutions to these challenges that led to the demise of GT and CM in the United States and Europe in the 1960s!

A Comprehensive Approach for Implementing Job Shop Lean

Figure 2.6 presents a flowchart for an approach that is based on the Womack–Jones process for implementing Lean. Each iteration of the process shown in Figure 2.6 is expected to yield a stand-alone flexible manufacturing cell to produce a part family.

In practice, several real-world constraints will need to be "broken" to ensure that each cell can be implemented! For example, operators will

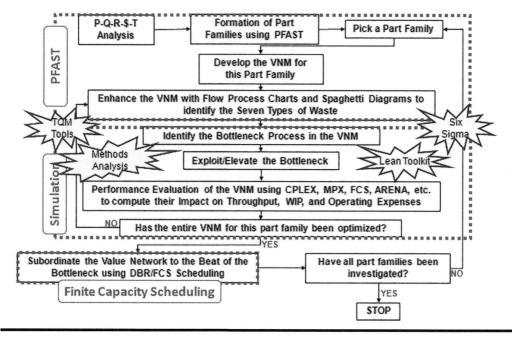

Figure 2.6 A Comprehensive Approach for implementing Job Shop Lean.

need to be trained to operate multiple machines in a cell. Or an incentive program will be needed to ensure that the cell's team strives to become a cohesive autonomous team. It could very well be that some of the constraints are unbreakable! For example, raw material is single-sourced from another country and cannot be purchased on a JIT basis. Or, in the case of heat treatment furnaces, they simply cannot be placed inside a cell next to a CNC grinder. It is unrealistic to expect an HMLV facility to be completely converted into a Cellular Layout. Therefore, a job shop will end up being divided into at least two areas: one area consisting of flexible manufacturing cells with each cell dedicated to a product family and another (separate) area where the spare parts, prototypes, and one-off orders will be produced. By dividing the facility into these two areas, the benefits that are gained are as follows:

1. The cells enable on-time delivery, first time quality, teamwork, and other related benefits.
2. Only a small portion of the same business needs to be managed as a complex job shop.

Illustration of the Comprehensive Approach for Implementing Job Shop Lean

This section illustrates key results from different steps in the Comprehensive Approach for implementing Job Shop Lean. The standard five-step Womack–Jones process is followed, except that the tools used to implement each step are different.

*Steps #1 and #2 Identify **and** Map a Value Stream:* With nearly 600 part numbers being produced in this facility, *Product Mix Segmentation* was necessary to select a reduced sample of important parts to focus on. Figure 2.7(a) shows the use of PQ Analysis (P = Products, Q = Demand) to segment the product mix *only* on the basis of production volume. This divides the product mix into two segments – **high** volume and **low** volume. Alternatively, Figure 2.7(b) shows the use of PQ$ Analysis (P = Products, Q = Demand, $ = Revenue) to segment the product mix by *simultaneously* considering *both* Quantity (Q) *and* Revenue ($). This method segmented the HMLV manufacturer's product mix into two segments: Segment #1 is that portion of the product mix that accounts for at least 80% of total production quantity *and* 80% of total revenue; Segment #2 is the remainder of the product mix.

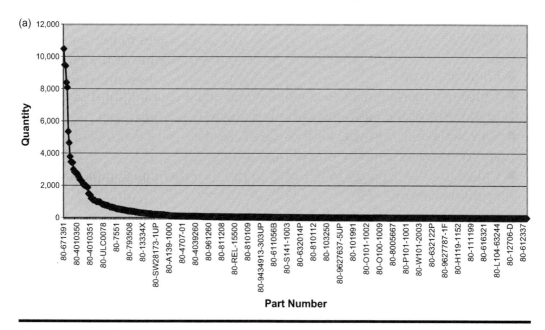

Figure 2.7 Product Mix Segmentation with (a) PQ analysis.

(Continued)

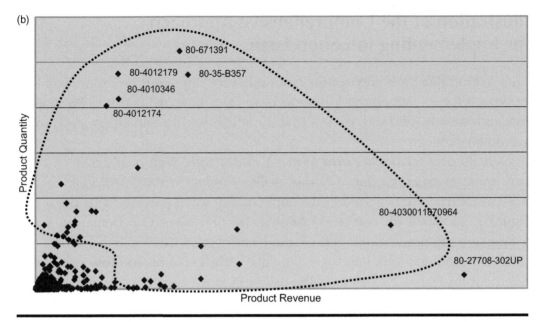

(b)

Figure 2.7 (CONTINUED)   Product Mix Segmentation with (b) PQ$ analysis.

What does one do about the remainder of the product mix that was ignored? There is no single cookie-cutter answer. This is where each company's leadership team can exercise their creativity to develop innovative strategies such as:

■ Eliminate them.
■ Outsource their manufacture while remaining a supplier for those parts in the eyes of the customers who buy them.
■ Seek additional business for those parts so they can become Repeaters and be produced in any one of the existing cells.
■ Utilize unused capacity in the cells to produce them during the second or third shifts.

Next, the routings of those parts included in Segment #1 must be analyzed to identify potential part families that could be produced in manufacturing cells. This can be done using one of the PFA algorithms – *Product-Process Matrix Analysis* – to identify the part families and machine groups that will constitute the flexible manufacturing cells. Each cell would be dedicated to a product family. The algorithm produces the matrix shown in Figure 2.8 where each part family and its corresponding machine group appear as a block of 1's. Figure 2.8 *is a matrix and not a VSM.*

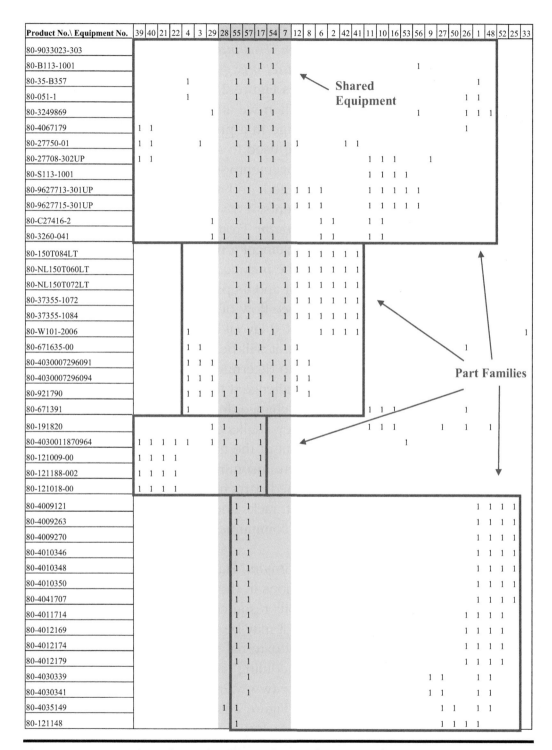

Figure 2.8 Formation of part families and manufacturing cells.

Still, this matrix is a visualization of numerous different Value Streams. Each family of parts is a Value Stream. This matrix representation of all the potential part families in the product mix guides the implementation of Job Shop Lean! What else does Figure 2.8 show? Those machines which are required in many cells! When we attempt to solve this machine sharing problem, we essentially engage in a process of CI (Continuous Improvement)! Different ideas can be used to solve this problem. To evaluate and later implement each improvement idea, a team will need to be formed, several kaizen events scheduled, and actions taken to implement the ideas developed during those events.

Step #3 Create Flow in the Value Stream: From the matrix in Figure 2.8, a single block of 1's is selected to implement a manufacturing cell. This block shows the machines that must be included in the cell and the parts that will be made in that cell. The cell and its part family are equivalent to a Value Stream. To achieve delay-free flow of all orders made inside the cell, it is important to develop a detailed layout and operational policies to operate the cell. Prior to cell layout, it will be necessary to compute the workload and capacity requirements to determine the equipment requirements for the cell. This could be a challenge if the composition of the part family and demand of its parts could change during the lifetime of the cell! Figure 2.9 illustrates that one of the key challenges when implementing this step is the design of the detailed layout of the manufacturing cell. Layout design includes consideration for where incoming materials will be staged, where outgoing containers with finished parts must be placed so they can be moved to the Shipping department, racks and other storage options for tools, WIP, gauges, inspection tables, communication boards, ergonomics and safety, etc.

Step #4 Establish Pull in the Value Stream: Having implemented the cell, it is required to schedule daily operations in the cell subject to customer due dates and the availability of various resources such as machines, material, labor, tooling, and fixtures. Also, it may be necessary to coordinate the schedule of the cells with those of external shared resources and the vendors that supply the cell. "Pull Scheduling" is best done using a commercial FCS software tool like Preactor (www.Preactor.com) to generate the schedule and display its Gantt Chart (Figure 2.10) on large computer screens distributed at several locations on the factory floor. Unlike MRP, an FCS tool will NOT release orders into the cell if it cannot be completed by its due date. Corrective actions will have to be taken first, a new feasible schedule generated and only then would the same order be released for production in

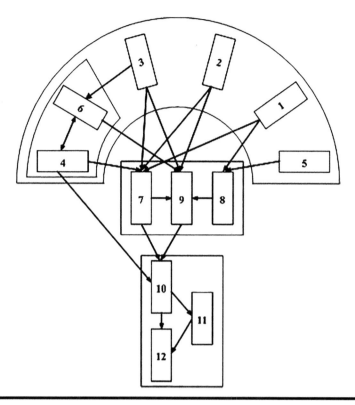

Figure 2.9   Cell layout designed for a flexible machining cell.

the cell. An ERP system would download into Preactor the firm orders and their due dates quoted to customers. The schedule generated by Preactor would then be released to the shop floor. In addition to Preactor, two other FCS products are Tactic (www.Waterloo-Software.com) and Schedlyzer (www.Optisol.biz). Although not a scheduling tool, CSuite from Factory Physics, Inc. (www.factoryphysics.com) offers rapid modeling technology that can quickly simulate and optimize extremely large supply chains. Unlike other supply chain simulators, CSUITE considers finite capacity as well as randomness within production and inventory.

As the schedule executes, its progress would be monitored with an MES tool that can be used for Shop Floor Control. FACTORYVIEWER is the commercial MES that is bolted onto PREACTOR. A competing MES is FORCAM (www.FORCAM.com).

Computer-aided scheduling may play a major role in the successful implementation of Job Shop Lean. But any computer-generated schedule can be disrupted by the vagaries of the dynamic shop floor. Say that the operator

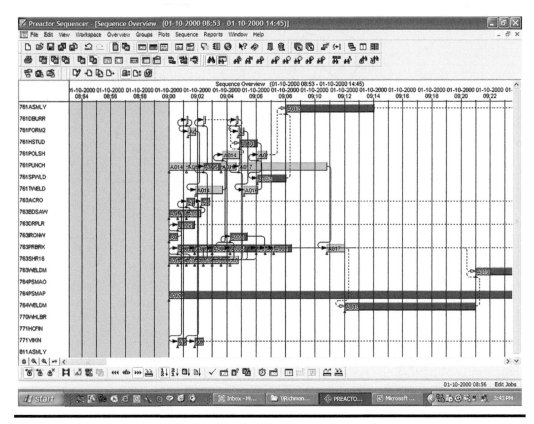

Figure 2.10 Finite capacity schedule displayed as a Gantt Chart.

who must start a job on a machine at 8:30 a.m. on Tuesday decides to take a break. Or he falls sick and does not show up for work that day. Or he finds that he is missing a tool. Or he is waiting for a setup person to set up his machine. A schedule can also be disrupted by machine breakdowns, vendor delivery failures, scrap or rework, etc.

Appendices

Appendices for this chapter are available for download at https://www.crcpress.com/9781498740692

References

Burbidge, J.L. (1963). Production flow analysis. *The Production Engineer*, 42(12), 742–752.

Burbidge, J.L. (1979). *Group Technology in the Engineering Industry*. London, UK: Mechanical Engineering Publications Ltd.

Flanders, R.E. (1925). Design, manufacture and production control of a standard machine. *Transactions of ASME*, 46, 691–738.

Gallagher, C.C. & Knight, W.A. (1973). *Group technology*. London, UK: Butterworth.

Gettelman, K.M. (1971, November). Organize production for parts not processes. *Modern Machine Shop*, 46, 50–60.

Harmon, R.L. & Peterson, L.D. (1990). *Reinventing the Factory*. New York: McGraw-Hill.

Irani, S. A. (2001, March). Software solves identity crises for parts from "big" families. *Lean Advisor*, 3–6.

Jackson, D. (1978). *Cell System of Production: An Effective Organization Structure*. London, UK: Business Books Ltd.

Miltenburg, J. (1995). *Manufacturing Strategy*. Portland, OR: Productivity Press.

Ohno, T. (1988). *Toyota Production System: Beyond Large-Scale Production*. Portland, OR: Productivity Press.

Ranson, G.M. (1972). *Group Technology: A Foundation for Better Total Company Operation*. London, UK: McGraw-Hill.

Rother, M. & Shook, J. 2009. *Learning to See*. Cambridge, MA: Lean Enterprise Institute. www.lean.org.

Womack, J.P. & Jones, D.T. (2003). *Lean Thinking: Banish Waste and Create Wealth in Your Corporation*. New York: Free Press.

Chapter 3

Is Job Shop Lean Right for You?

Are you interested in implementing Job Shop Lean in your company? If yes, would you like to receive a quick no-charge assessment whether your production system is a good fit for this approach? If yes, please complete this survey and mail it to: Dr. Shahrukh A. Irani, Lean & Flexible, llc, 4102 Pensacola Oaks Lane, Sugar Land, TX 77479. Else you can scan it and email it to ShahrukhIrani1023@yahoo.com. I am pleased to provide this pro bono service to a reader of my book! ☺

Job Shop Lean Assessment Tool

Toyota is a *low*-mix *high*-volume manufacturer of a *limited variety* of *similar assemblies*. Compared to Toyota, would you say that you are a *high*-mix *low*-volume (HMLV) manufacturer of a *large variety* of *dissimilar components*?

☐ Yes
☐ No

Several performance measures, such as Order Flow Time, Inventory Dollar Days (Work-In-Process Inventory), and $ **S**hipped per **Day (Throughput), focus on the** speed with which an order is shipped to and paid for by a customer **(Cash Flow Velocity). Now, Lean recommends to focus on the elimination of the Seven Wastes (Overproduction,**

Waiting, Transportation, Overprocessing, Inventory, Operator Motion, and Scrap/Rework). Can the impact of Waste Elimination be measured using Cash Flow Velocity?

☐ Yes
☐ No

Does your product mix consist of 100's, maybe 1,000's, of different components whose routings are dissimilar?

☐ Yes
☐ No

If **you answered "Yes", have you analyzed the product mix to find the groups of components with identical or similar manufacturing routings (aka "component families")?**

☐ Yes
☐ No

If **you know your component (or product) families, have you exploited this knowledge for:**

Your Response	Application of Part Family Knowledge
☐ Yes ☐ No	Creation of flexible work instructions for an entire part family
☐ Yes ☐ No	Selection of flexible automation
☐ Yes ☐ No	Generation of quotes
☐ Yes ☐ No	Estimation of standard costs and times
☐ Yes ☐ No	Reduction of setup times when the same machine has to be changed over many times
☐ Yes ☐ No	Design of tooling families to plan tool magazine layouts for CNC (Computer Numerical Control) machines
☐ Yes ☐ No	Standardization of part designs (Variety Reduction)
☐ Yes ☐ No	Rationalization of product mix
☐ Yes ☐ No	Cross-training of employees
☐ Yes ☐ No	Automation of office processes

What is the current method for production control, operations scheduling, and shop floor control?

- ☐ Enterprise Resource Planning (ERP) without Finite Capacity Scheduling (FCS)
- ☐ ERP with FCS
- ☐ Drum-Buffer-Rope aka CONstantWIP (CONWIP)
- ☐ Level Loading (Heijunka)
- ☐ Others _____

Characteristics of Your Manufacturing Operations:

Your Response	*Characteristic*
☐ Yes ☐ No	Our product mix consists of several business segments, e.g., Runners, Repeaters, One-Offs, etc.
☐ Yes ☐ No	We see our product mix change every year
☐ Yes ☐ No	Our product mix has a large number of products with dissimilar routings
☐ Yes ☐ No	Average Order Flow Time (= Ship Date – Start Date) is high
☐ Yes ☐ No	The value of inventory (Finished Goods, WIP (work-in-process), and Raw Materials) as a % of Sales is high
☐ Yes ☐ No	Lead Times quoted to customers are based on current Order Flow Times
☐ Yes ☐ No	Performance metrics are not based on Throughput, Operating Cost, and Inventory
☐ Yes ☐ No	Vendor lead times are high, their deliveries are unpredictable, and quality rejects are common
☐ Yes ☐ No	Limited work has been done to standardize products, and processes for our entire product mix

Concerns about Factory Layout, Material Handling, and Shop Floor Logistics:

Your Response	Concern
☐ Yes ☐ No	The material flow in the facility is chaotic
☐ Yes ☐ No	We could not manually map all the routings of our entire product mix
☐ Yes ☐ No	The layout of the facility "just happened over time" as the business grew
☐ Yes ☐ No	There is significant material handling activity involving fork lifts, bridge cranes, etc.
☐ Yes ☐ No	There is significant walking around by employees having to search for tools, chat with friends, move product from their machines to other machines, search for material handling equipment to move orders that they have completed, etc.
☐ Yes ☐ No	We have a functional layout with equipment of the same or similar processing capabilities being co-located in one area
☐ Yes ☐ No	We have not explored how to implement manufacturing cells to produce families of parts
☐ Yes ☐ No	Product is moved on pallets and/or large storage containers for any inter-operation transfer
☐ Yes ☐ No	There is no visual Line Of Sight (LOS) for order progressing between key work centers
☐ Yes ☐ No	We have no knowledge of how much floor space in our current facility is wasted
☐ Yes ☐ No	Our layout is not flexible to handle changes in product mix and/or production volumes
☐ Yes ☐ No	We plan to re-layout the entire factory or portions of it
☐ Yes ☐ No	We plan to add a new building to expand the existing facility
☐ Yes ☐ No	We plan to move and relocate into another facility
☐ Yes ☐ No	We plan to build a new facility and relocate into that facility
☐ Yes ☐ No	We plan to add new equipment or replace existing equipment

Methods for Production Planning, Operations Scheduling, and Shop Floor Control:

Your Response	Method
☐ Yes ☐ No	Our Sales department pushes orders into production regardless of WIP levels
☐ Yes ☐ No	Our ERP system lacks good data especially BOMs (Bill Of Materials), Routers, Standard Times, etc.
☐ Yes ☐ No	Orders are released into production without good knowledge of available capacity, especially at system bottleneck(s)
☐ Yes ☐ No	We rely on our ERP system to produce a daily schedule based on infinite capacity
☐ Yes ☐ No	We have an end-of-month frenzy to meet shipping revenue goals
☐ Yes ☐ No	We have to "search and find" to track down an order when a customer calls
☐ Yes ☐ No	Our on-floor tracking and inventory control of tooling and shop consumables is poor
☐ Yes ☐ No	Many work centers have significant number of orders in queue waiting to be processed
☐ Yes ☐ No	Too many setup changes occur due to repeated schedule changes

Practices on the Shop Floor:

Your Response	Practice
☐ Yes ☐ No	We have no formal program to reduce setup times on bottleneck equipment
☐ Yes ☐ No	We do not have a preventive maintenance schedule for our key equipment
☐ Yes ☐ No	Orders are released without complete paperwork
☐ Yes ☐ No	The use of 5S (Sort, Shine, Set, Standardize, Sustain) in the office and in the factory is limited primarily to housekeeping
☐ Yes ☐ No	Each work center maintains a white board that tracks key metrics (Safety, Quality, Delivery, Inventory and Productivity aka (SQDIP))
☐ Yes ☐ No	Employee performance in any work center is measured using Efficiency and Productivity
☐ Yes ☐ No	Machine operators rely on the Inspection department to check the quality of their work

Measures of Management Involvement and Employee Engagement:

Your Response	Measure
☐ Yes ☐ No	The Owner, VP Operations, Plant Manager, etc. visit the floor often
☐ Yes ☐ No	Employees can do problem-solving using Five Why's, Ishikawa Diagrams, etc.
☐ Yes ☐ No	Managers, supervisors, and employees have daily morning huddles
☐ Yes ☐ No	Employees take extended breaks, start the shift late, end the shift early, etc.
☐ Yes ☐ No	Employees wait for their supervisors to tell them which orders to work on
☐ Yes ☐ No	Employees submit their ideas for improvement to management

Would you be interested in learning the following practices/tools suitable for implementing Lean in high-mix low-volume (HMLV) environments?

Practice/Tool	Description
☐ Yes ☐ No	Value Network Mapping
☐ Yes ☐ No	Product Mix Segmentation
☐ Yes ☐ No	Design for Flow
☐ Yes ☐ No	Part Family Formation using Routings
☐ Yes ☐ No	Part Family Formation using Group Technology
☐ Yes ☐ No	Multi-product Manufacturing Cells
☐ Yes ☐ No	Hybrid Cellular Layout (aka Mixed Mode Facility Layout)
☐ Yes ☐ No	Shop Floor Control using Water Striders
☐ Yes ☐ No	Product Mix Rationalization
☐ Yes ☐ No	ERP with Finite Capacity Scheduling
☐ Yes ☐ No	MES (Manufacturing Execution System) for Asset Monitoring
☐ Yes ☐ No	Setup Reduction using Tooling Families
☐ Yes ☐ No	Flexible Work Instructions using Part-Process Families
☐ Yes ☐ No	Variety Reduction across Multiple Product Bills Of Materials

Chapter 4

Design For Flow (DFF): The Essential Foundation for Job Shop Lean

---

A Tribute to Manufacturing Pioneers of the Past

Job Shop Lean is based on the ideas and work of several manufacturing pioneers and industry consultants whose work on Group Technology (GT), Cellular Manufacturing (CM), and the Toyota Production System (TPS) is available in the open literature. Their ideas and implementation experiences are the building blocks for adapting Lean for high-mix low-volume (HMLV) manufacturing environments. In this introductory section of the chapter, I would like to discuss the core concepts of Job Shop Lean that were derived from the writings of those pioneers.

Focus on reducing the time it takes to complete an order: Figure 4.1 was obtained from a research paper (Merchant1975).[1] Quoting from his paper "...when the life of the average workpiece in batch-type metal cutting production shops is analyzed, only about 5% of its time is actually spent on machine tools and, of that 5%, only about 30% is actually spent as productive time in removing metal (or 1.5% of the overall time spent in the shop)... One of the greatest areas of improvement in the productivity of metalworking manufacturing (is) by reduction of time of parts in process in the shop, and thus of the resulting extremely high inventory of unfinished parts on

---

[1] This paper is available online and can be obtained by Googling "M. Eugene Merchant, The future of CAM systems".

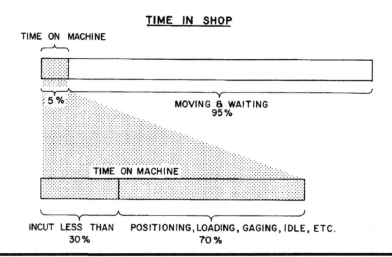

Figure 4.1   Life of the average workpiece in the average (batch-type production) shop. (*Source*: Merchant, 1975.)

the shop floor, and of finished parts waiting for others in process so assembly can proceed. It is evident from Figure 4.1 that this inventory could potentially be reduced by up to 90%. Resulting reduction of indirect capital, labor costs and improvement of productivity could be enormous... The 30% machine utilization indicated by Figure 4.1 must be combined with the fact that the average machine spends approximately 50% of its time waiting for parts to work on (because of the 95% time in transit shown in Figure 4.1)...".

Management must provide employees opportunities to participate in decision-making: Figure 4.2 was obtained from the same paper (Merchant, 1975). Quoting from his paper "...employers are now clearly recognizing the human need for the nature of work to be such as to assure the worker of deep satisfaction from performing it (as well as freedom from unpleasant or harmful conditions)... As shown in Figure 4.2, while the so-called hygiene factors of a job i.e. company policy and administration, supervision, work conditions, salary, etc. can cause *dis*satisfaction if they are not satisfactory, they can do little to provide on-going job satisfaction. Instead, such satisfaction derives from the adequacy of so-called motivating factors of a job i.e. opportunity for achievement, recognition, responsibility, advancement, growth, etc. The major feature of jobs which provide such opportunities is participation in decision-making...[2]".

---

[2] History and current knowledge suggest that Toyota has utilized the Training Within Industry (TWI) program to develop their employees, encourages employees to modify their working environments by engaging in short-duration problem-solving events ("kaizen"), and allows assembly line operators to shut down the entire line if they find product defects or line equipment malfunctions.

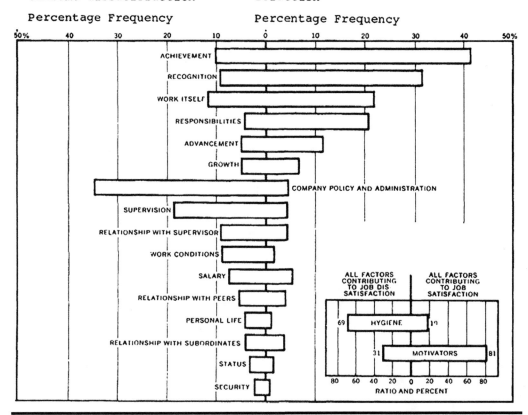

Figure 4.2   Factors that influence employee satisfaction/dissatisfaction with their jobs. (*Source:* Merchant, 1975.)

A manufacturing cell has the potential to (1) *reduce the time it takes to complete an order,* (2) *create a team-based work environment for the employees who work in it, and* (3) *increase job satisfaction through decision-making:* Figure 4.3 was obtained from the same paper (Merchant, 1975). Quoting from his paper "...the layout and organization of a factory and its manpower and equipment on a part-family and product-line basis (rather than on a functional basis) provides immediate economic benefits from decreased manufacturing lead time, decreased inventory of parts in process and increased job satisfaction of workers... Figure 4.3 illustrates one of the cells utilizing NC (Numerical Control) for producing a family of box-like parts used in avionics equipment. By going to Cellular Manufacturing, Ferranti Ltd. of Edinburgh has reduced the throughput time of parts in process by a factor of ≈5".

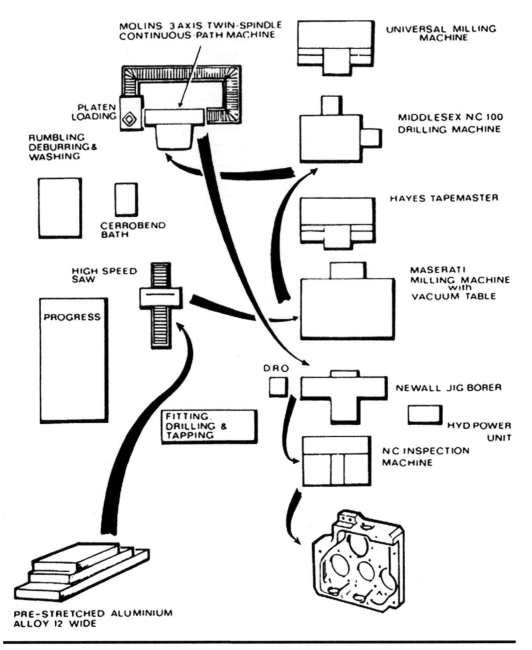

Figure 4.3   An advanced GT NC manufacturing cell implemented by Ferranti.
(*Source*: Merchant, 1975.)

Shigeo Shingo, who consulted for Toyota, supports the "alteration of plant layout so that little or no transport is required…by (having) machines laid out to correspond to the product processing flow". Quoting from his book (Shingo, 1989) "…layout improvement is a fundamental precondition for setting up the **flow** so crucial to the Toyota Production System…traditional plant layout has led people to assume that painting should be carried out in painting shops and presswork in press shops… Although this has long been a blind spot of production management, re-examination of these old assumptions will bring about a revolution in thinking and facilitate the discovery and implementation of many powerful new ideas… Instead of arranging departments by type of machines (e.g., press department or lathe department), consider the following arrangements:

- *Single Process Line:* For month-long production of a single product and a single model in large quantities.

- *Common Process Line:* When production of a single product is not sufficient for a month's continuous flow but products A, B, C, and D have processes in common that can be arranged in a continuous flow.
- *Similar Process Line:* Products A, B, C, D, E, and F have some but not all of their processes in common, so only partial lines can be formed of those common processes.

At Toyota, the Common Process Line is used most frequently". Surprisingly, on Page 102 of his book, Shingo writes "In general, however, many plants have fewer common process factors and must adopt the similar process arrangement". I contend that it is not necessary to adopt a Functional Layout even when the product mix does not allow the implementation of pure cells. Modern factories have hybrid layouts that are a combination of Process and Product layouts, as discussed in a later chapter on *Hybrid Cellular Layouts.*

A good factory layout is a must for every manufacturing facility: Taiichi Ohno, the chief architect of the TPS, recognized the importance of a good factory layout in his book (Ohno, 1988). He makes several statements that indicate he recognized the importance of a factory layout as he developed the TPS:

- (Page 11) "I was manager of the machine shop at the Koromo plant. As an experiment, I arranged the various machines in the sequence of machining processes".
- (Page 33) "We realized that the (Kanban) system would not work unless we set up a production flow that could handle the Kanban system going back process by process".

- (Page 54) "Toyota's main plant provides an example of a smooth production flow accomplished by rearranging the conventional machines after a thorough study of the work sequence".
- (Page 54) "It is crucial for the production plant to design a layout in which worker activities harmonize with rather than impede the production flow".

- (Page 100) "By setting up a flow connecting not only the final assembly line but all the processes, one reduces production lead time".

- (Page 123) "When work flow is properly laid out, small isolated islands do not form".

- (Page 128) "The first aspect of the TPS…means putting a flow into the manufacturing processes… Now, we place a lathe, a mill and a drill in the actual sequence of the manufacturing processing…".

Flow: The Essential Foundation for Job Shop Lean

Kiyoshi Suzaki, who consulted for Toyota, has devoted an entire chapter (Chapter 4 *Developing Flow on the Production Floor*) in his book (Suzaki, 1988). Quoting from his book "…the importance of factory layout has not been addressed in spite of the significant waste often associated with badly planned layouts…the impact on a company's performance from improving the layout can be substantial… **Flow refers to the movement of material through the plant**. It assumes that material will not be stagnant at any point in time from the receiving of raw material to the shipping of finished products… Problems such as a process-oriented layout (Functional Layout), line imbalance, machine breakdowns, long setup or tool-change time, machine breakdown, quality problems, and labor absenteeism cause interruptions that disrupt a steady flow of production in a factory…".

Any HMLV manufacturer seeking to implement Job Shop Lean should invest in designing, and changing as necessary, their factory layout in order to achieve Flow. Appropriately, all constraints that hinder Flow help to determine Continuous Improvement (CI) projects to improve factory operations using other TPS/Lean tools such as Error Proofing, Quality At Source, Total Productive Maintenance, Workforce Engagement, and Setup Reduction.

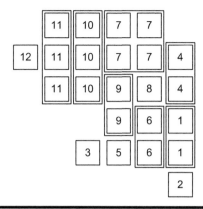

Figure 4.4   Functional Layout.

This approach is in stark contrast to the conventional wisdom of undertaking a large portfolio of kaizens[3] to eliminate the Seven Types of Waste (see Figure 4.8). This approach is equivalent to "CI-A-Mole[4]"! Instead, by taking actions to improve Flow by attacking the root cause for the Moving and Waiting wastes (and delays that significantly increase the total time that any order spends in the factory), cost reduction due to elimination or reduction of occurrences of the Seven Types of Waste is guaranteed! Besides cost reduction, the ability to quote shorter Lead Times to customers could bring in new business.

As Figures 4.1 and 4.7(b) clearly suggest, the greatest wastes in the typical factory are due to Moving and Waiting. *And the root cause for these two wastes (Moving and Waiting) is the factory layout, especially if it is a Functional Layout!* The majority of HMLV manufacturers that are machine shops, forge shops, fabrication shops, etc. usually have a Functional Layout. A Functional Layout like the one shown in Figure 4.4 consists of many departments where each department contains equipment of similar or identical processing capabilities. For example, in Figure 4.4 all three Machine #11's are co-located and adjacent to each other. So are all four Machine #7's, and so on.

Since time immemorial, HMLV manufacturers have preferred a Functional Layout for their factories. For example, a machine shop will have departments like CNC (Computer Numerical Control) Turning, CNC Milling, Grinding, Inspection, Assembly, and so on. Unfortunately, this choice of

---

[3] A kaizen is a concerted 5-day event that engages a team to plan and implement a tangible improvement in their workplace.

[4] *Source*: https://en.wikipedia.org/wiki/Whac-A-Mole.

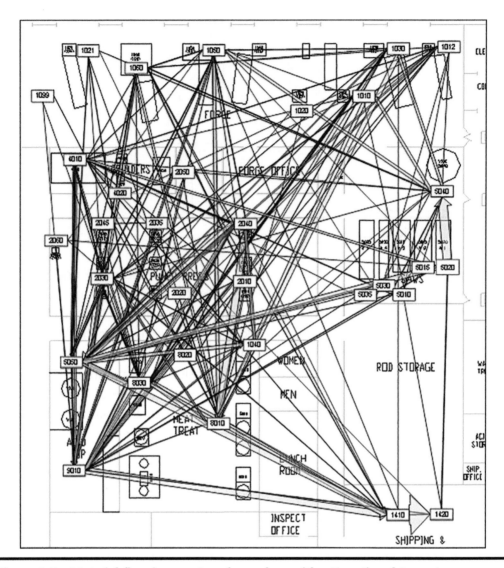

Figure 4.5   Material flow in a custom forge shop with a Functional Layout.

layout for any HMLV factory will invariably lead to a chaotic material flow in their facility that is hard to manage. Figure 4.5 displays the material flow in a custom forge shop that has a Functional Layout and produces ≈500 different forgings for defense and aerospace customers.

In contrast to the Functional Layout in Figure 4.4, Figure 4.6 is a Cellular Layout that is essentially a rearrangement of all the machines in the layout of Figure 4.4 into three separate cells. *Each cell is comprised of different machines extracted from several departments in the Functional Layout.* For example, Cell #2 contains machines drawn from Department #s 1, 6, 7, 9, and 10. Each of

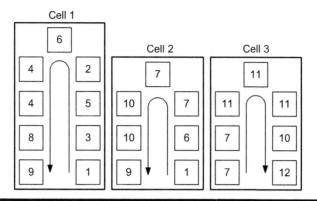

Figure 4.6 Cellular Layout.

the three cells has been designed with the machines in it arranged in such a way that the parts produced in that cell will travel the least distance between operations with minimum backtracking. To illustrate Ohno's statement about "arranging the various machines in the sequence of machining processes", let us assume that a part with the routing 3→5→2→6→4→8→9 has to be produced in the two alternative layouts shown in Figures 4.4 and 4.6. Take a pencil and trace this routing in Figure 4.4 by connecting Machine #3 to Machine #5 to Machine #2…and so on. Repeat the process for Cell 1 in Figure 4.6 because it contains all the machines required to make this part. In which case do you think that the part will travel less distance and have machine operators positioned closer to each other so they can communicate on issues concerning quality, schedule changes, etc.? This is why the implementation of Job Shop Lean always commences with implementing any and all factory layout changes that will improve Flow!

Flow Delays and the Seven Types of Waste

Instead of making Waste Elimination a primary goal, an HMLV manufacturer ought to focus on achieving Flow by first and foremost revising the layout of their factory. That will automatically result in waste elimination too! Figure 4.7a is a Flow Diagram that shows the flow path of a single forging produced in the same custom forge shop featured in Figure 4.5. Each arrow connects two departments where consecutive operations in the routing for the forging are performed. In the case of every arrow in the Functional Layout, the travel distance is greater than the 3 ft (at most 6 ft)[5] that the

---

[5] This is the typical distance that separates two adjacent machines that are co-located in a cell.

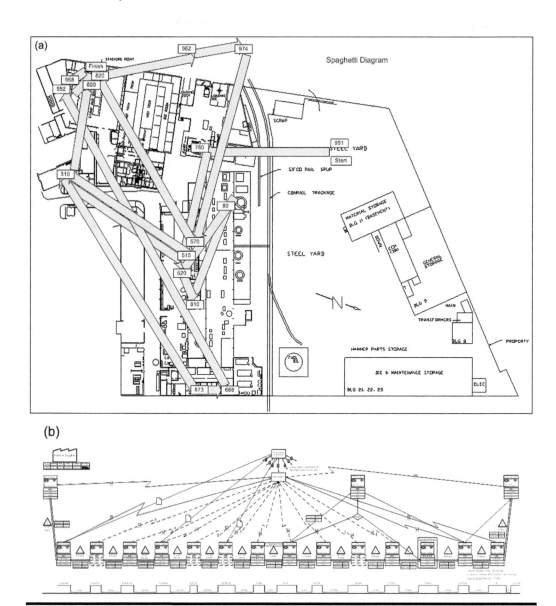

Figure 4.7   (a) Flow path of a single forging produced in the custom forge shop in Figure 4.5. (b) Value Stream Map to complement the Flow Diagram in Figure 4.7(a).

operator of a machine should walk to deliver a part (or product) that they worked on to the operator of the next machine. Why does a Functional Layout have large distances separating consecutive operations in any part's routing? Assume that the forging has one operation in Department X and the next operation in Department Y. In both departments, it has to go to a specific machine. Either department contains other machines with processing capabilities that are similar (or identical) to the particular machine used

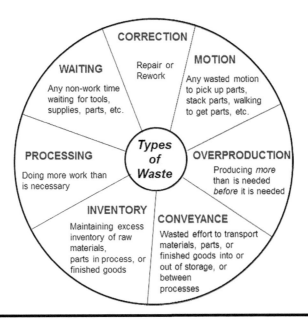

Figure 4.8   Seven Types of Waste. (*Source*: www.systems2win.com/LK/ lean/7wastes.htm.)

by this forging. So, since either department has a significantly large area, a large distance separates the machine in Department X and the machine in Department Y that both process the forging.

Figure 4.7(b) shows the Value Stream Map[6] that was prepared to accompany the Flow Diagram in Figure 4.7(a). Travel time is a function of travel distance! So it was not surprising that analysis of the VA (value-added) versus NVA (non-value-added) times in the map in Figure 4.7(b) yielded a VA Ratio (Total Labor Hours ÷ Flow Time) ≈18% for this par-ticular forging! This means that 82% of the time that this forging spent in the forge shop was due to *avoidable* delays caused by the Seven Types of Waste shown in Figure 4.8. At least five of the Seven Types of Waste shown in Figure 4.8 (Inventory, Waiting, Conveyance/Transportation, Overproduction, and Operator Motion) can be directly attributed to a Functional Layout. The other two wastes shown in Figure 4.8 – Correction (or Scrap/Rework) and Overprocessing – are not directly caused by the layout of the facility. They are the result of the manufacturing processes, the equipment used to make the product(s) and the skills of the employ-ees who operate the equipment.

---

[6] Rother, M. & Shook, J. (2009). *Learning to See: Value Stream Mapping to Create Value and Eliminate Muda*. Cambridge, MA: Lean Enterprise Institute Inc. www.Lean.org.

The Seven Types of Waste are equivalent to costs and delays that inflate the Production Cost and Flow Time for an order, respectively. This was known many years ago and is corroborated in Figure 4.1 that was published in a research paper (Merchant, 1975). Comparing Figures 4.1 and 4.8, each of the Seven Types of Waste has a **Cost** ($) and **Delay (**minutes, hours, or days**)** associated with it! Figure 4.1 shows that 95% of the time it took to complete a part was due to delays caused by two of the Seven Types of Waste – Moving and Waiting! Next consider just the 5% time spent on the machines:

1. Thirty percent of that time was VA time because machines were actually cutting metal to produce a finished part! Effectively, only 1.5% (0.05*0.30 = 0.015) of the total Time in Shop was spent on cutting metal to produce a finished part. But what if even the time spent in cutting metal included delays due to Overprocessing Waste (e.g., the cycle time was longer than it should have been) or Overproduction Waste (e.g., the batch size was inflated due to Safety Stock and/or Scrap adjustments)?
2. Seventy percent of that time was NVA time spent on activities such as loading/unloading, gauging, positioning, waiting, etc. that are equivalent to Operator Motion Waste.

Finally, in the Functional Layout there is limited communication between the operators who work in two different departments even when departments are adjacent to each other.[7] In the absence of real-time communications between departments, blind reliance is placed on a production schedule that is usually produced by the MRP (Material Requirements Planning) engine embedded in the ERP (Enterprise Resource Planning) system. MRP, which implicitly assumes a batch-and-queue production system, lacks any and all ability to produce a feasible daily production schedule for the factory floor! So, a Functional Layout combined with the use of a scheduling methodology that encourages a batch-and-queue production flow creates the wastes (and delays) of (i) Waiting, (ii) Operator Motion and Equipment Idle Time due to increased number of unplanned setup changes, and (iii) Overproduction because large batches are encouraged to keep machine utilization high!

---

[7] Unless an operator in one department leaves their machine to go over and talk to an operator in the other department (which is Operator Motion Waste and idles both their machines)!

Quick-and-Dirty Estimation of the Monetary Value of Any Waste and/or Flow Delay

Convert travel distance into Work-In-Process (WIP) cost: As the distance between the locations of any two consecutive operations increases, the WIP between consecutive processes tends to grow, as summarized in Table 4.1. Quoting from their book (Harmon and Peterson, 1990) "If successive processes are immediately adjacent, a single unit is moved at a time, as in assembly line. If the next process is across the aisle, the handling lot size is a unit load. If the next process is across the plant, the handling lot size is, at least an hour's supply of product because more frequent collection is impractical. If the next process is in another plant, the handling lot size is at least one day's production…".

Quoting again from (Harmon and Peterson, 1990) "…(since) the WIP (Work In Process) between processes will be, at least one half the handling lot size, (there are) potential orders-of-magnitude differences in WIP levels based on the layout". It is easy to convert the travel time between consecutive processes into WIP using classical Inventory Theory. In Figure 4.9, the base of the inventory triangle represents the time it takes for a batch (= Handling Lot Size) produced by the "supplier process" to be taken away to the "customer process". The height of the triangle represents the Handling Lot Size. As the distance that separates the "supplier process" and the "customer process" increases, the base of the triangle will increase because the "supplier process" will produce parts for a longer duration until the material handler returns after having dropped off the previous lot. This will increase the height of the triangle (= Handling Lot Size). Since the minimum inventory between the two processes is 0 and the maximum inventory between the two processes is the Handling Lot Size, the WIP between the two processes is at least half the Handling Lot Size.

Convert WIP into Transportation Cost: Typically, an hourly rate is used to cost the use of any material handling equipment, assuming that an

Table 4.1 Relationship between Handling Lot Size and Travel Distance in Any Layout

Distance to the Next Process	Handling Lot Size
Adjacent	Single unit
Across the aisle	Unit load
Other end of the facility	At least 1 hour of work
In another facility	At least 1 day of work

Source: Harmon and Peterson (1990).

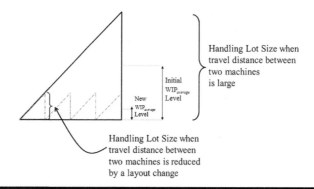

Figure 4.9 Relating WIP and handling lot size.

employee operated it throughout the period of use. With reference to Table 4.1, once the Handling Lot Size is a unit load or larger, it needs a large container to hold it. To move that large (and heavy) container, a bulky material handling equipment such as a forklift or bridge crane is needed. In practice, either type of handling equipment travels at slow speed. Also, it takes time to find the forklift or bridge crane to transport a unit load from a "supplier process" location to a "customer process" location. So, if a large travel distance is involved, the actual cost of transportation will be (Hourly Rate)*(Wait Time+Move Time) instead of only (Hourly Rate)*(Move Time).

Convert Flow Time to WIP: Despite its simplicity, Little's Law makes it easy to justify converting an existing Functional Layout into a Cellular Layout because that will reduce the Flow Time for any order. The theoretical form of Little's Law is as follows: $L_q = \lambda W_q$, where L_q is the average number of customers in a line who are awaiting service, λ is the arrival rate of customers that are seeking service, and W_q is the average wait time for a customer in the line before he/she gets served. Little's Law can be adapted to convert a reduction in Flow Time due to layout improvements into a reduction in WIP. If L_q = WIP, λ = Throughput, and W_q = Flow Time (the average time that a unit of product sends in the facility), then WIP = Throughput * Flow Time. For example, assume that 25 units/day are being produced (= Throughput) in the current facility layout and that it takes 5 days (Flow Time) to complete one unit. In this case, the WIP = 125 units. Say that the Flow Time for a unit is reduced to 1 day by moving all the machines needed to produce it into a work cell. Now, the WIP = 25 units. Clearly, by speeding up the product's flow in the facility, the cost of carrying the order as WIP inventory gets reduced.

Convert the Costs of VA/NVA Activities and Flow Delays into a Cash Flow Diagram: In the case of a single product, a Value Stream Map (Rother and Shook, 1999), such as the one shown in Figure 4.10, effectively converts all

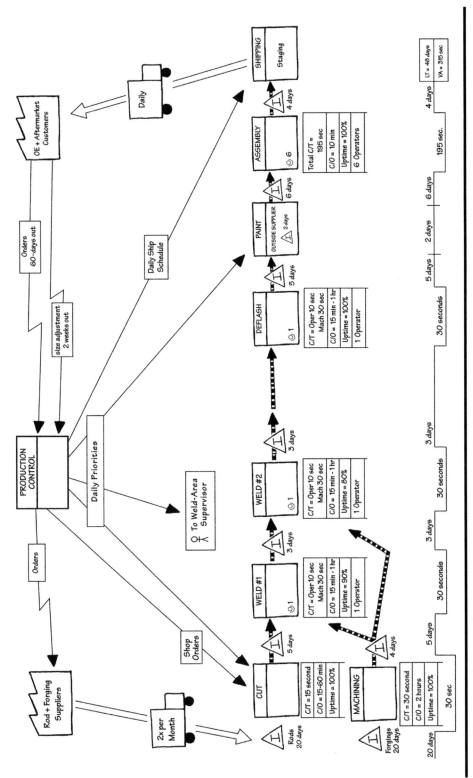

Figure 4.10   Value Stream Map. (*Source:* Rother and Shook, 1999.)

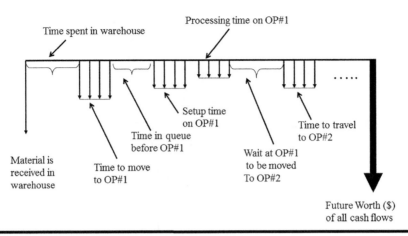

Figure 4.11   CFD incorporating all the VA and NVA activities in a Value Stream Map.

VA and NVA activities corresponding to the Seven Types of Waste into times. Each of these times can be used to calculate an approximate cost for the corresponding VA or NVA activity. For example, in Figure 4.10 the timeline at the bottom of the map shows that the VA time for a unit of product was 315 seconds whereas the Flow Time was 48 days. But how much money was invested to produce this unit of product and what did the company lose because that unit of product was (incomplete) WIP for 48 days? If we produce a Cash Flow Diagram (CFD), like the one shown in Figure 4.11, then the cash flow for each VA and NVA activity, such as setup, processing, waiting, and travel, and the carrying cost of inventory due to waiting in queues, batch production, and batch transportation can all be captured in the CFD. Using Discounted Cash Flow (DCF) techniques and a suitable Compound Interest Rate, we could reduce the entire series of cash flows in the diagram to a (single) Future Worth value. This Future Worth could be compared with the selling price that the customer pays.

Therefore, it is possible to use a time-based financial metric to quantify the savings from (i) reduction of material flow delays and (ii) elimination of NVA activities to produce each unit of product that flows through a facility.

Design for Flow: Principles for Factory Layout Design to Achieve Flow

Tompkins et al. (2003) state that "…effective flow within a department involves the progressive movement of materials, information or people between workstations… Planning for effective flow requires the

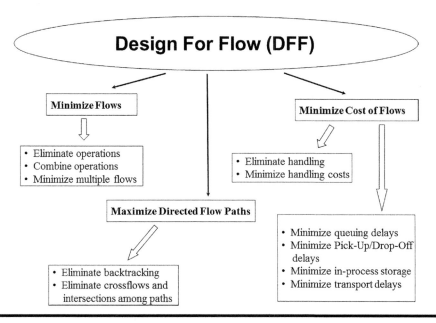

Figure 4.12 Principles of design for flow.

consideration of flow patterns and flow principles…". Figure 4.12 presents a framework – Design For Flow – for the principles they developed that should guide the design of any factory layout:

1. *Minimize flow:* Flow becomes necessary only when two or more different work centers are required to produce a product. Minimizing flow represents the work simplification approach to material flow. This approach includes:

    a. Eliminating flow by planning for the delivery of materials, information, or people directly to the point of ultimate use and eliminating intermediate steps.

    b. Minimizing multiple flows by planning for the flow between two consecutive points of use to take place in as few movements as possible, preferably one.

    c. Combining flows and operations wherever possible by planning for the movement of materials, information, or people to be combined with a processing step.

    Table 4.2 lists some strategies for designing a factory layout to minimize flows.

Table 4.2   Strategies to Minimize Flows

- Use Value Engineering to eliminate non-essential features of parts (or products)
- Adopt new multi-function manufacturing technology to produce parts (or products) in fewer steps
- Design manufacturing routings to have the least number of operations ("process razing")
- Deliver material to point of use (and eliminate off-site storage in a warehouse)
- Decompose the factory into a connected network of flowlines and cells, as shown in Figure 4.13[a]
- Process parts or subassemblies in parallel
- Combine several transfer batches being sent to the same work center into a single unit load
- Eliminate "misfit" routings that need operations external to their host cell by rationalizing the product mix to eliminate those parts (or products)
- Eliminate "misfit" routings that need operations external to their host cell by replanning their routings to absorb the external operations into the host cell (if capable machines are available inside the cell)
- Prevent proliferation of new routings by using Variant Process Planning to modify existing routings for similar parts/products that were made in the past
- Release orders to the floor by limiting the daily workload on bottleneck machines to ≈80%–85% of theoretical available capacity[b]; thereby, with fewer orders in process, there will be fewer unit loads on the factory floor that will need to be moved

[a] In some cases, in the case of small products, such as a motor, I observed a product-focused factory that included both parts machining and final assembly being done by a single operator!

[b] At least stop relying on the MRP engine embedded in the ERP system! The initial foray into Finite Capacity Scheduling could start with the Drum-Buffer-Rope method of scheduling. Later, if sufficient data is available in the ERP system, a full-blown FCS tool like Preactor, Tactic, Schedlyzer, or nMetric could be explored.

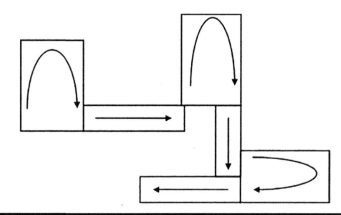

Figure 4.13   Factory decomposed into network of flowlines and cells.

2. *Maximize directed flow paths:* A directed flow path is an uninterrupted flow path progressing directly from origin to destination. An uninterrupted flow path is a flow path that does not intersect with other paths. Congestion occurs due to interruptions in flow when flow paths intersect. A directed flow path progressing from origin to destination is a flow path with no backtracking (which would increase the length of the flow path). Figure 4.14 gives examples of Forward vs. Backtrack vs. Cross flows in any facility layout and classifies these flows as good, bad, or acceptable.

Table 4.3 lists some strategies for designing a factory layout to maximize directed flow paths.

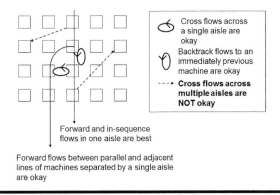

Figure 4.14   Classification of flow directions.

Table 4.3   Strategies to Maximize Directed Flow Paths

- Design an overall factory layout using the **complete** Assembly Operations Process Chart based on (i) the BOM[a] of a standard product and (ii) other product BOMs for necessary product variants that are ordered frequently by customers
- Break up departments to duplicate machines of the same type at multiple locations to prevent backtracking, as shown in Figure 4.15, e.g., instead of a Functional Layout, and explore a Hybrid Flow Shop layout, as shown in Figure 4.16(a), instead of a classical Flow Shop layout, as shown in Figure 4.16(b)
- Cascade flowlines with common machines by positioning them adjacent to each other, as shown in Figure 4.17; thereby, with adjacent flowlines or cells having common equipment, if demand fluctuations create a workload between cells, then orders could simply flow across the aisle that separates the flowline that lacks capacity to the adjacent flowline that has capacity available on the appropriate common resources
- Reduce the length of flowlines by giving them U, W, S, or other curvilinear shapes, as shown in Figure 4.18

[a] Bills of Materials.

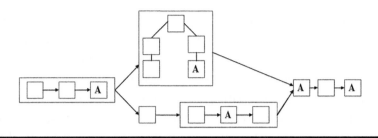

Figure 4.15 **Duplicating machines of the same type at multiple locations to prevent backtracking.**

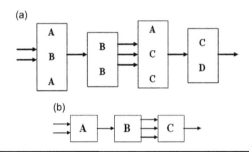

Figure 4.16 **(a) Hybrid Flow Shop Layout. (b) Flow Shop Layout.**

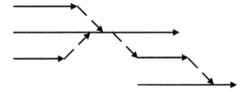

Figure 4.17 **Cascading flowlines.**

Figure 4.18 **Flowlines with U, W, and S shapes.**

3. *Minimize the cost of flow:* The cost of flow depends on a variety of factors, such as volume and weight of the products being moved, the distance of travel, the method for material handling, the speed and frequency of travel, the quantity of product being moved per trip, etc. For example, the least cost of material handling between two workstations would be when, as soon as one unit of product is completed at one workstation, it is automatically ejected from that workstation

into a short and inclined chute (or a roller conveyor). It rolls down the conveyor and reaches the operator at the next workstation which is adjacent. Gravity is free and available 24/7! Tompkins et al. (2003) view this principle from either of the following two perspectives:

a. Minimize handling that requires walking, manual travel, and motions by an operator.

b. Eliminate manual handling by mechanizing or automating flow to allow workers to operate their equipment or perform other VA tasks that have been assigned to them.

In addition to the above ideas listed in Tompkins et al. (2003), poor shop floor communications between the individual work centers, material handlers, and the Production Control and Scheduling office (or department) can increase the costs of flow. Large distances of separation between two work centers often cause (i) work completed at any work center to become WIP at that work center because the material handler did not arrive immediately to pick it up and move it to the next work center and/or (ii) work completed at any work center becomes WIP at the next work center because, at the time that the material handler delivered the work to the next work center, that work center already had a large queue of WIP to work on. Therefore, large travel distances between consecutive operations help to increase the costs due to (i) material handling, (ii) WIP inventory carrying costs, and (iii) queuing delays.

Table 4.4 lists some strategies for designing a factory layout to minimize cost of flows.

Role of Product Design and Manufacturing Engineering

Every IE (Industrial Engineering) textbook on *Facilities Planning and Material Handling* has initial chapters that discuss how decisions made by Product Designers and Manufacturing Engineers transform into the charts and input data for software to design facility layouts, analyze material flows, balance assembly lines, determine machine requirements for high-mix work cells, etc. Every successful effort to (i) eliminate parts, (ii) combine parts in a product's BOM (Bill Of Materials), or (iii) eliminate or combine operations in a routing would reduce part (or product) travel. Less material movement equates to better Flow! Here are some examples of how product designers, manufacturing engineers, cost estimators, machinists, and equipment builders could reduce the need to move a part (or product) in any factory:

Table 4.4 Strategies to Minimize Cost of Flows

• Have a linear, L, U, S, Z, or other curvilinear contour for every material flow path
• Minimize travel distances for heavy/large unit loads
• Discourage the "make-and-fill" mindset of batch production by adopting material handling practices such as
  o Utilize gravity to move materials
  o Limit the number of large wire mesh containers, pallets, etc. that are in use on the factory floor
  o Reduce the volume of material handling trips that require bulky and slow material handling equipment
  o Use handling equipment like tuggers that can do milk runs; thereby, multiple unit loads can be hooked up in a train that visits multiple locations along a travel route to pick up or drop off orders
  o Increase communications between equipment operators and material handlers by implementing Lean practices such as wide-area electronic display boards, daily huddles in every shift to share WIP status, etc.
  o Determine specific locations on the factory floor where shared material handling equipment will always remain parked when not in use

o Establish Standard Work Instructions (SWI) to select containers and material handling equipment to move these containers, at least for products that are frequently produced • Prevent WIP buildup at individual machines by minimizing the floor space allocated to each machine's footprint • Place buffer inventories at bottleneck work centers to balance consecutive operations with unequal workloads • Expand the role of each material handler to include expediting; thereby, each handler will have access to the daily schedule and can expedite orders per the schedule, as he/she roams the factory floor in a tugger[a]

[a] *Source:* http://nwcpe.com/wp-content/uploads/2014/10/The-Water-Spider-Position-by-Tom-Fabrizio.pdf. For additional information, please Google "water strider, Toyota".

■ *Inside-out product assembly:* Keep the product variation as far to the end of the assembly process as possible. If many variants of the same product have to be built, keep standard modules and components on the inside and "bolt on" special features and options on the outside.

■ *Avoid monuments:* Avoid designing components or subassemblies that require a new or unique process that will have to be shared by multiple product lines, due to the cost of the equipment.

■ *Batch early:* If processes that necessitate batching (plating, painting, heat treatment, drying/aging, electroplating, etc.) are absolutely necessary, try to design products where these batch processes can be used as early as possible. Nothing is worse than having an operation in the middle of an assembly line that has to be sent to a vendor for processing!

■ *Standardize modules and components, not necessarily products:* Offering a broad mix of products or mass customization of a base product design gives competitive advantage. So, reducing product Stock Keeping Units (SKUs) may not be a good idea. However, reducing module and component SKU'sshould be a core strategy (especially for aftermarket and MRO (Maintenance, Repair, and Overhaul) business segments).

■ *Challenge every tolerance:* Nothing is worse than holding tolerances that are not necessary because that always requires a sophisticated process that may have to be outsourced or a machine that requires to be operated by a highly skilled operator. Tolerances should be assigned using established standards and input from floor employees.

■ *Shorten manufacturing routings:* Eliminate or combine operations in manufacturing routings wherever the opportunities present themselves. Reducing the number of VA steps to make a part will automatically reduce the number of NVA activities (load/unload, wait, material handling to move the part, etc.) associated with each VA operation.

■ *Inspect at source:* Every time that an entire batch of parts processed on any machine has to be sent to a separate Inspection department because the operator is not responsible for ensuring the quality of the part, the possibility of scrap/rework exists. Could the operator be trained (and trusted!) to inspect their own work for defects? If not, then could an inspector be dispatched from the Inspection department to the machine when the operator raises a flag signaling the need for FPI (First Piece Inspection)? Every time that a scrapped part has to be replaced, the delays and costs of an entire cycle of NVA activities are repeated and added to the Flow Time and Production Cost, respectively, for that part!

■ *Reduce variety of tooling:* Every unique feature allowed in a part or product's design requires the creation of a new tool. But there are significant costs associated with maintaining each and every tool kept in a tool crib. *So the first priority should not be to do a 5S kaizen to organize the tool crib!* Instead, the first priority should be to use GT to create a sortable database of all tools currently in use and undertake Variety Reduction with that data.

■ *Touch 100 times:* A part (or product) is designed ONCE but may be produced a 100 times! Think of material handling and orientation for every operation done on each unit, especially if it is heavy and has to be manually handled. What about all the transfers in and out of different storage containers that are used for transportation inside the factory vs. to a vendor vs. to the final customer?

How to Assess If a Factory Layout Is Designed for Flow

The three Appendices for this chapter are assessments used to evaluate an existing facility layout. Of the three assessments, the Appendix *A Lean Checklist to Evaluate Any Factory Layout* is the best. It is highly recommended because it includes a wide range of **specific** and **well-established** operational practices that are embedded in the Toyota Production System.

An Approach for Designing a Factory Layout to Achieve Flow

The next chapter will introduce the method of Production Flow Analysis (PFA) to design the layout of any HMLV factory to achieve Flow. Recall some of the statements that Taiichi Ohno, the chief architect of the TPS, made in his book:

1. "I was manager of the machine shop at the Koromo plant. As an experiment, I arranged the various machines in the sequence of machining processes".
2. "The first aspect of the TPS...means putting a flow into the manufacturing processes... Now, we place a lathe, a mill and a drill in the actual sequence of the manufacturing processing...".
3. "Toyota's main plant provides an example of a smooth production flow accomplished by rearranging the conventional machines after a thorough study of the work sequence".
4. "By setting up a flow connecting not only the final assembly line but all the processes, one reduces production lead time".

PFA is perfectly aligned with Ohno's ideas for factory layout design. If any HMLV manufacturer has up-to-date and accurate data, then PFA will **certainly** help to design a layout based on the material flows that are unique to **that** HMLV manufacturer's factory.

How to Achieve Flow If the Factory Layout *Cannot* Be Changed

Several industry practitioners sent excellent review comments after they received the first draft of this chapter. A common theme in their comments was, "What if a layout change is not possible or inappropriate? Then how to achieve Flow in my factory?" Table 4.5 presents the reviewers' comments and my responses to each comment.

Table 4.5 Overcoming Barriers to Achieving Flow

Reviewer's Comment	Reviewer #1 Response to Comment
I suggest you elaborate on how to deal with requirements that force batching. We build electronic parts, and our customers require (that) we send our assemblies to an outside lab for X-ray. They also insist on date codes which form lots. The bottom line (is that) batching is never good, and we would all like to have single-piece flow. However, many of us are required by our customers to batch. Thus we need tools to better plan for those conditions.	• Batching is an absolute must in the case of outside operations or when customers demand lot integrity. • Single-piece flow is achievable if you produce a low variety of products on assembly lines. But, in any job shop, there is almost always workload imbalance between the different operations in any routing. So, my approach is to try to transform an existing factory layout into cells. Only within a cell can a realistic alternative to single-piece flow be attempted – Transfer Batch Flow. Although not comparable to single-piece flow on an assembly line, at least a Transfer Batch is a fraction of the Order Batch Size! • How to implement Flow when dealing with an external vendor, such as painting, coating, blasting, wash tank, polishing, heat treatment, etc.? Single-piece flow is out of the question! Essentially you hold a buffer of orders for the vendor to pull from (so they are never starved of work) **AND** the vendor holds a buffer that you pull from (so you are never starved of work). • Do you use an effective scheduling system or rely on your ERP system to determine start dates for orders, generate daily schedules, etc.? If not, make a start and explore the Drum-Buffer-Rope method of scheduling bottlenecks and controlling the release of orders into production. • Can you get a commitment from the vendor on Lead Time and Quality? When you outsource, vendor quality is critical if you are a one-off HMLV manufacturer! If your customer has ordered a batch of five large high-precision shafts, and your heat treater delivers a batch in which one of the five pieces is defective, there goes your On-Time Delivery performance with your customer if they want a lot of five pieces to be delivered to their dock! Else, in the absence of any control on a vendor's quality and delivery, you will be stuck with an external system constraint that will frequently perturb your in-house schedule. ☺

Table 4.5 (Continued) Overcoming Barriers to Achieving Flow

Reviewer #1	
Reviewer's Comment	*Response to Comment*
The other condition that presents a challenge is the sharing of expensive equipment which cannot be dedicated to a single work cell. In some cases, the process step could be outsourced.	• There is no miracle solution for this one, short of establishing a daily production schedule that distributes available capacity on the expensive equipment across multiple jobs received from different work cells. Establish at least one morning huddle so all cell leaders communicate their schedule to the work center leader for the expensive equipment. • Go all out to maximize machine utilization on this equipment by starting a Total Productive Maintenance program for it. Have your CI team to see *The Goal* video so they can learn a systematic way to increase VA utilization of such equipment!

Reviewer #2	
Reviewer's Comment	*Response to Comment*
I do not think that the chapter sufficiently covers the solutions to problems encountered by job shops with variable loads, many routings, custom designs, etc. Especially in job shops/HMLV operations with very large high-precision parts such as <my client>. These (parts) invariably require overhead cranes/forklifts to load/unload and move parts. This dictates to some extent the flow and layout options.	• In the case of a machine shop that produces large high-precision parts, the idea of *Virtual Cells* may be appropriate. Shop floor communications could compensate for a poor layout. Could a machine operator signal a material handler when they have completed a job? Could a water strider ply the entire facility? Implementing VCs (Virtual Cells) needs the full cooperation of the shop employees and the material handler's functioning as water striders. But you will need to identify the part families in your client's product mix to implement this approach. • The next chapter in this book describes the method – *PFA* – that can be used to implement cells to address the problems of variable loads and routings. • In my experience, most job shops/HMLV manufacturers do not invest the necessary time, effort, and resources to plan the initial layout of their facility. Nor do they do a good job for subsequent layout changes that invariably must be made because machines are replaced, product mix changes, etc. over time. I have yet to see a Spaghetti Diagram of any client's facility that showed a streamlined material flow network!

(Continued)

Table 4.5 (*Continued*) Overcoming Barriers to Achieving Flow

	Reviewer #2	
Reviewer's Comment	*Response to Comment*	
I absolutely agree that combining operations reduces handling, WIP, etc. But this can also create a bottleneck machine, which being expensive and large with dedicated foundations, is not easily duplicated or moved.	You are right! The pros and cons of introducing multi-function flexible automation will have to be based on a simulation study to determine throughput and WIP in the two cases.	
I agree with your view of having inspectors move out to the job, *if required*, rather than moving the job to them. But if they can conduct the inspection at the machine, then so can the operator which eliminates this need. However, with large high-precision parts, several features are not possible to be inspected at the machine, such as geometric tolerances and bore pitches. I have yet to find any portable equipment with sufficient Gage R&R (Repeatability and Reproducibility). So, reluctantly, I am faced with using an expensive CMM[a], which many suppliers demand be placed on a special foundation in an enclosed temperature controlled environment (which then causes all manner of problems with regard to flow and delays).	In my previous job, the material flow to/from different cells to the CMM was a problem. Given the high skill requirements to operate the CMM, even the availability of the CMM operator contributed to queue buildup outside the air-conditioned room in which the CMM was housed.	

(*Continued*)

Table 4.5 (*Continued*)   Overcoming Barriers to Achieving Flow

Reviewer #2	
Reviewer's Comment	*Response to Comment*
Your chapter also makes recommendations for all operations to be retained in-house, but for our supplier (WT) this could be impractical regarding certain heat treatment and coating processes which require special facilities. Also bringing them in-house in a high-precision machining environment causes all sorts of problems with cross contamination/layout options as you probably witnessed at our supplier, WT.	You are right! In the case of WT, we produced a Flow Diagram for the product that had the greatest number of orders last year. Okay, this is just one product and they make many other variants of that product (as was noted when we toured the warehouse). Still, a Value Stream Map is a good start! Knowing how expensive it is to move "dirty" processes such as Grinding, Spray, Mask, Polishing, and Welding, their locations could have been better planned when the factory was being built. Now it is going to be expensive to relocate any of those departments or position them adjacent to high-precision equipment.
In the case of our supplier, WT, routings do not exist! So PFA is impractical. I think that it may be possible to design generic/parametric routings.	• Routings and BOMs are to a custom manufacturer what DNA is to the identity of a human being. So WT needs to invest time, effort, and resources to produce these routings for their different products, especially they are implementing a new ERP system. • A routing is produced based on the part drawing. Concerning your idea about designing generic/parametric routings, have you considered using the Opitz Classification and Coding (C&C) system to generate routings using Variant Process Planning? There are two books *Group Technology at Work* and *Capabilities of Group Technology* that contain an excellent collection of articles on manufacturing planning using a C&C system. Both books have been edited by Nancy Lea Hyer.

(Continued)

Table 4.5 (Continued) Overcoming Barriers to Achieving Flow

Reviewer #2	
Reviewer's Comment	*Response to Comment*
1. I do not think that the chapter covers sufficiently the solutions to problems encountered by job shops. It needs more focus on the real problems which job shops face. 2. I still believe that flow should be the goal, but within the practical limitations imposed by operating in a job shop environment.	This chapter lays the foundation for the rest of this book which gets into the details that you seek. For example, a later chapter in this book titled *How Cell Formation Drives the Implementation of Job Shop Lean* discusses strategies that extend beyond factory layout. There are two Strategy Maps that offer realistic if the factory layout cannot be organized completely, or even partially, into cells: • **Strategy Map #1** discusses what to do when a cell cannot have one or more machines it needs ("Shared Machines") because there are not enough to "go around" • **Strategy Map #2** discusses what to do when cells have to send work to external Monuments (including outsourced services)
Reviewer #3	
Reviewer's Comment	*Response to Comment*
I read with interest that the chapter was "grounded on the three principles of Design For Flow". Woollard had defined 18 (and I had reduced it to four based on the early writings of Carpenter, Sorensen, Flanders, and others) as described below: 1. The first step in organizing for flow is to put the processes in sequence.... which creates another set of problems because they are usually not balanced in terms of cycle times	• Frank George Woollard's work may have inspired Ohno.[b] In January 2009, Lean Management historian and author, Prof. Bob Emiliani, published a 55th Anniversary Special Edition of Woollard's 1954 book, *Principles of Mass and Flow Production*, which also includes his 1925 paper "Some Notes on British Methods of Continuous Production" and commentary and analysis of Woollard's work by Dr. Emiliani. • Job Shop Lean assumes that a typical HMLV facility does not operate like any assembly facility. In particular, a cell in the typical HMLV facility has the operational characteristics of either a flow shop or a job shop, but never as an assembly line! Please see Figure 4.16a and b earlier in this chapter. These HMLV manufacturing systems usually produce many orders having different due dates, order lot sizes,

(Continued)

Table 4.5 (*Continued*)   Overcoming Barriers to Achieving Flow

Reviewer's Comment	Response to Comment
2. The second step in organizing for flow is to synchronize the sequential process steps…collecting 3–5 sequential steps that can be organized for flow creates a cell…the cell emerges from your efforts to synchronize the processes. 3. The third step in organizing for flow is balancing the work content for a flow cell to emerge. 4. The fourth step in organizing for flow is balancing the demand pace. Some of this can be done internally by work scheduling, but the most influential department is Sales & Marketing (S&M). Their job should be to load the inbound side to a define capacity in daily buckets, not monthly or quarterly quotas. That sort of goal setting for S&M drives hockey stick production demands. If S&M loads production to 100%, this will stress the production system, as most can only reliably deliver a maximum of about 80% of capacity. Although, stressing production will drive the need for improving the system.	setup and cycle times on the machines they use, etc. Therefore, I do not use the Assembly Line Balancing methodology that you propose in Steps #1–#4. Specifically, in Step #4, instead of "balancing the work content", which is essential for an assembly line, the operation of a high-mix cell is best done by releasing orders into the cell *if and only* (i) the workstation with the heaviest workload is not loaded beyond its available capacity in any shift and (ii) the orders can be completed by their due dates, or with minimum lateness. • Regarding Step #4, a later chapter in this book discusses practical scheduling methodology by integrating Lean, Theory Of Constraints, and scheduling theory. It discusses how to load an HMLV cell to determine the set of orders that should be released for production without exceeding available capacity on the bottleneck machine in the cell. Most HMLV manufacturers use a thumb rule like (Customer Due Date − Fixed Lead Time = Start Date) to determine start dates for jobs with no consideration at all for reality − Capacity is finite not infinite! Their reliance on an ERP system which assumes infinite capacity ensures that far more work is released into their factories than what can be completed. The thumb rule invariably results in workload spikes in the day-by-day production plan that forces reliance on overtime and expediting costs to rush completed orders to their customers.

[a] Coordinate Measuring Machine.

[b] *Sources:* (1) https://en.wikipedia.org/wiki/Frank_George_Woollard; (2) Emiliani, M.L & Seymour, P.J. (2011). Frank George Woollard: Forgotten pioneer of flow production. *Journal of Management History, 17*(1), 66–87.

Conclusion

"Flow" refers to the movement of material throughout a factory. It assumes that material will not be stagnant at any point in time from the receiving of raw material to the shipping of finished products. *The essential foundation for implementing Job Shop Lean in any HMLV factory is to make each and every justifiable factory layout improvement that improves Flow.* This chapter stressed that designing a good factory layout will simultaneously impact On-Time Delivery and Waste Elimination. It offered three principles (Design For Flow) on which the layout of any factory ought to be based: (i) minimize flows, (ii) maximize directed flow paths, and (iii) minimize cost of flows. Specific strategies to implement each principle were presented. The three Appendices for this chapter are different assessments that could be used to evaluate how well a current factory layout achieves Flow.

Appendices

Appendices for this chapter are available for download at https://www.crcpress.com/9781498740692

References

Apple, J.M. (1977). *Plant Layout and Material Handling.* New York: John Wiley.

Harmon, R.L. & Peterson, L.D. (1990). *Reinventing the Factory.* New York: The Free Press.

Merchant, M.E. (1975). The future of CAM (Computer Aided Manufacturing) systems. *International Workshop on Managing Requirements Knowledge, Proceedings of the National Computer Conference*, New York, NY, pp. 793–799.

Ohno, T. (1988). *Toyota production system: Beyond large-scale production.* Portland, OR: Productivity Press.

Rother, M. & Shook, J. (1999). *Learning to See: Value Stream Mapping to Add Value and Eliminate Muda.* Boston, MA: Lean Enterprise Institute. www.Lean.org.

Shingo, S. (1989). *A Study of the Toyota Production System from An Industrial Engineering Viewpoint.* Portland, OR: Productivity Press.

Suzaki, K. (1988). *The New Manufacturing Challenge: Techniques for Continuous Improvement.* New York: The Free Press.

Tompkins, J.A., White, J.A., Bozer, Y. A. & Tanchoco, J.M.A. (2003). *Facilities Planning.* New York: John Wiley.

Chapter 5

Overview of Production Flow Analysis (PFA)

Achieving Flow in any high-mix low-volume (HMLV) factory is essential for implementing Job Shop Lean. Flow can be achieved in the entire factory by redistributing the existing manufacturing equipment into manufacturing cells after considering all the different paths along which materials flow in the factory. The locations of all support departments would also have to be revised. However, per the first principle of Design For Flow, prior to implementing any layout changes in any factory, all efforts must be made to reduce the chaotic material flows in that factory. How does one know that the material flows in a factory are chaotic? Table 5.1 lists some of the symptoms of chaotic material flows in a factory.

Table 5.1 Symptoms of Chaotic Material Flows in a Factory

• Large travel distances between consecutive operations in any routing
• Perceived shortage of floor space for factory expansion
• High levels of WIP (work in process) and finished product inventory
• High-order throughput times
• Significant queuing and material handling delays
• Significant material handling activity
• Poor order tracking capability
• Highly un-patterned material flow ("Spaghetti Diagram")
• Inefficient communications between work centers

Table 5.2 Causes of Chaotic Material Flows in a Factory

• Building architecture
• Locations of manufacturing departments
• Locations of support services and utilities
• Points of access between departments
• Shortage of space for factory expansion
• Process plans for making parts and products
• Variety of routings
• Current manufacturing technology
• Current material handling equipment
• Current storage systems for WIP
• Current communication systems being used on the shop floor
• Outsourced operations (and delivery performance of vendors)
• Absence of scheduling based on resource constraints

Table 5.2 lists some of the causes for chaotic material flows in a factory.

Production Flow Analysis (PFA)

Production Flow Analysis (PFA) (Burbidge, 1971) is a systematic methodology for the comprehensive design of a factory that originally relied on manual methods for machine grouping, part family formation, cell formation, and layout design. If viewed in a larger context, PFA can also be used to implement the principles of Design For Flow and plan a new layout for any work system within a factory. PFA can be used to analyze and improve Flow in different work systems that exist at different levels in any factory, such as around a single machine, in a single cell, in a machine shop, in a tool crib, in the tool magazine of a machining center, between departments or shops in the entire factory, between all cells and support departments housed in a building, etc.

Stages for Implementing Production Flow Analysis

When applied to a single factory, PFA is typically implemented in four stages:

1. Factory Flow Analysis (FFA)
2. Group Analysis (GA)
3. Line Analysis (LA)
4. Tooling Analysis (TA).

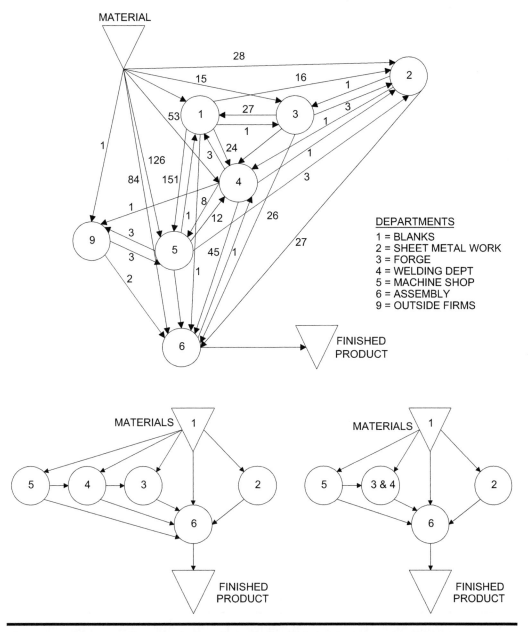

Figure 5.1 Factory Flow Analysis. (*Source*: Burbidge, J.L. (1971, April/May). Production flow analysis. *The Production Engineer*, 50, 139–152.)

At each stage, PFA achieves material flow reduction for a progressively reducing portion of the factory.

In FFA (Figure 5.1), flows between shops (or buildings) are analyzed. In addition, if parts are observed to backtrack between any of the shops, these flows are eliminated by a redeployment of equipment. FFA may often be

PART/PRODUCT

MACHINE/WORKSTATION

	K48251A	L48388B	L48267E	M44276F	M44193M	L47693	M48185C	M44276D	E48595	E34267	E12204	E12288	E47697	K47782	E48586	K34596	E33494	M48265D	K44276C	M45691D	M45869B	M48306H	K34098A	E7392	E46364	E33295	K45199	K43590	M61592	E18694
DMT(3)		X							X		X	X	X										X		X		X	X		X
DM(3)			X	X			X				X		X			X	X	X					X			X	X	X	X	
PG			X			X										X	X	X	X											
DXY(3)	X	X	X													X							X				X	X	X	
P&GR					X																									
PGR											X														X					
PGH																														
PGG																				X	X				X					
P&G									X	X	X	X	X	X								X	X			X	X	X	X	X
RP																								X						
PGB				X									X	X						X	X				X					
W&P	X								X														X				X	X		
WG3													X																	

COMPONENT - MACHINE CHART. INITIAL RECORD. FORGE.

PART/PRODUCT

MACHINE/WORKSTATION

	L48267B	K34596	M48265D	E34494	K48519M	L47238	E7392	K484098A	K48559	M61592	M48195C	E42267D	E34260	E18699	E17995	M48366	K48266	L48388H	M45691A	M45691D	M48266B	K42251	E46364	E46228	E33295	E18698	M47693	E33298	M48566	M47693F
PG	X	X	X	X	X	X																								
DM 3/1	X	X	X	X																										
DXY 3/1	X	X																												
RP							X																							
P&G								X	X	X	X	X	X	X	X	X	X	X	X										(X)	
DMT 3/2								X	X	X			X		X			X												
DM 3/2								X	X	X	X		X	X																
DXY 3/2								X	X	X	X						X	X												
W&P								X	X	X		X						X												
WG3														X																
PGG																			X	X					X					
PGB																			X	X	X	X	X		X					
PGR																								X	X					
DMT 3/3																											X	X	X	
DM 3/3																											X	X		
P&GR																														X

GROUP-1 / FAMILY - 1 (machines PG, DM 3/1, DXY 3/1, RP)
GROUP-2 / FAMILY - 2 (machines P&G, DMT 3/2, DM 3/2, DXY 3/2, W&P, WG3) — ONE "EXCEPTION" (circled X)
GROUP-3 / FAMILY - 3 (machines PGG, PGB, PGR, DMT 3/3, DM 3/3, P&GR)

COMPONENT - MACHINE CHART. AFTER FINDING FAMILIES AND GROUPS

Figure 5.2 Group Analysis. (*Source*: Burbidge, J.L. (1971, April/May). Production flow analysis. *The Production Engineer*, 50, 139–152.)

redundant for a factory that essentially is a single machine shop, forge shop, or fabrication shop.

In GA (Figure 5.2), flows inside a shop in a larger vertically integrated factory, such as the machine shop or fabrication shop, are analyzed. GA analyzes operation sequences of the parts being produced in the shop to identify manufacturing cells. Loads are calculated for each part family to obtain the equipment requirements for each cell. Each cell is usually assigned all the equipment necessary to satisfy the complete manufacturing requirements of its part family. However, due to environmental considerations or the high cost of buying new equipment, a cell may not get the equipment it needs. In that case, inter-cell material flows or even flows involving outside vendors will **have** to be allowed. These flows are obstacles to Flow and necessitate compromise solutions because they can be expected in just about every factory.

In LA (Figure 5.3), Flow inside a single cell is improved. The goal is efficient transportation of products with minimum material handling and travel by operators. A linear or U-layout is designed to arrange the machines in the cell. The routing of each part assigned to the cell and the frequency of use of each routing are used to develop the cell layout.

In TA, the principles of GA and LA are integrated with attributes of the parts, such as their shape, size, material, tooling, fixturing, etc. at a single machine (Table 5.3). TA involves activities such as setup reduction, organized storage of tools, standardization of tools, creation of tooling packages for repeated jobs, improvement of the ergonomics of loading/unloading heavy products, tools and dies on/off the machine, etc. TA helps to schedule the cell by identifying families of parts with similar operation sequences, tooling, and setups. It seeks to sequence parts on each machine and to schedule all the machines in the cell to reduce setup changeover delays that increase the time to complete an order.

TA also helps to increase available machine capacity on the bottleneck work center in a cell. This can be done using Time and Motion Study, Methods Analysis, and Setup Reduction (Shingo, 1989). How can Flow be improved at an individual machine by reducing idle time on the machine, such as a stamping press, forging press, heat treatment furnace, or cleaning tank? During the setup cycle of any machine, the machine remains idle for some time because the operator is moving to/from different locations around the machine while getting the machine ready to process the next job. By measuring the Flow of the machine operator as he/she moves between different pairs of locations around the machine, a machine layout can be developed to reduce Operator Motion Waste. Figure 5.4(a) displays the movements of the operator around a cold forging press throughout a setup cycle **before** any layout improvements were made around the press. Figure 5.4(b) displays the movements of the same operator **after** layout improvements were made around the press.

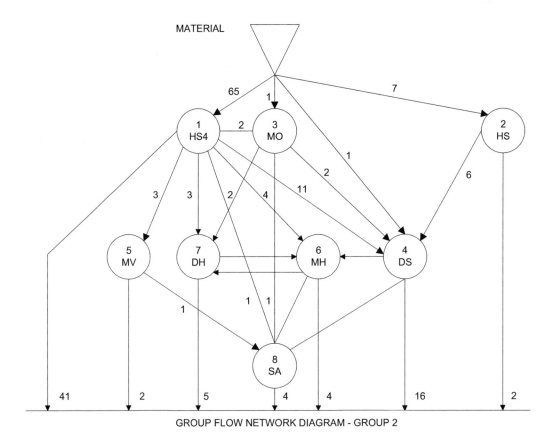

GROUP FLOW NETWORK DIAGRAM - GROUP 2

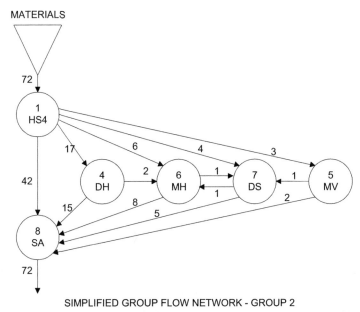

SIMPLIFIED GROUP FLOW NETWORK - GROUP 2

Figure 5.3   Line Analysis. (*Source*: Burbidge, J.L. (1971, April/May). Production flow analysis. *The Production Engineer, 50*, 139–152.)

Table 5.3 Tooling Analysis

	Digit 1	Digit 2			Digit 3	Digit 4	Digit 5	Digit 6	Digit 7	Digit 8	
		Dimension				*Matching with*					
		3 Jaw Chuck									
	Method of Holding	*Bore Dia. φ*	*Overall*	D_w	*L*	*Special Attachments*	*Boring Tool Carrier*	*Quadruple Single-Point Tool Holder*	*Material*	*Surface Accuracy*	
0	3 Jaw chuck outer			<40	L/D_w < 0.1	w/o	w/o	w/o	GG-formed	Rough turned ▽	0
1	3 Jaw chuck inner	42 φ	160	41–100	L/D_w < 0.5	Axial copying	Boring, counter-sinking, reaming, tapping.	Uniform cutting, w/o accuracy.	ST-formed	Fine turned ▽▽	1
2	4 Jaw chuck	60 φ	250	101–200	L/D_w up to limit of chuck	Face copying	Only outer turning.	Uniform cut, or staggered cut, with accuracy, simple boring up to 48 φ.	NE-formed	Outer fit	2
3	Spring collet	80 φ	315	301–400	Shafts < 500	2 Axis copying	1 with 2	Outer shaping, chamfering, inserting with form tool, not copying.	GG-cut off	Inner fit (+ outer)	3

(Continued)

Table 5.3 (Continued) Tooling Analysis

	Digit 1	Digit 2 Dimension — 3 Jaw Chuck Bore Dia. φ	Digit 2 Overall	Digit 2 D_w	Digit 3 L	Digit 4 Special Attachments	Digit 5 Boring Tool Carrier (Matching with)	Digit 6 Quadruple Single-Point Tool Holder	Digit 7 Material	Digit 8 Surface Accuracy	
	Method of Holding										
4	Mandrel or arbor	80 φ	400	401–500	Shafts 500–10,00	Conical surface tapering ± 12°	Shaping, etc. with form tool; with 3; not copying.	3 with 4	ST-cut off	Positional accuracy	4
5	Jig or fixture	125 φ	500	501–1,000	Shafts 1–2 m	Steep cone	Inner shaping inserting chamfering; with 3; copying.	Shaping, inserting chamfering with form tool; copying.	NE-cut off	Polishing	5
6	Between center			>1,000	Shafts 2–5 m	Short thread milling	Inner and outer at the same time	5 with 2 & 1 or 3	GG-bar	Knurling, etc.	6
7	Chuck-center				Shafts >5 m	Threading with lead screw		6 with back tool holder	ST-bar		7
8	Steadies					Thread with copying			NE-bar		8
9	Eccentric (face plate)					Unround copying		Automatic cycle with 4th & 5th digits	Non-metal		9

Source: Gallagher, C.C. & Knight, W.A. (1973). *Group Technology*. London, UK: Butterworths.

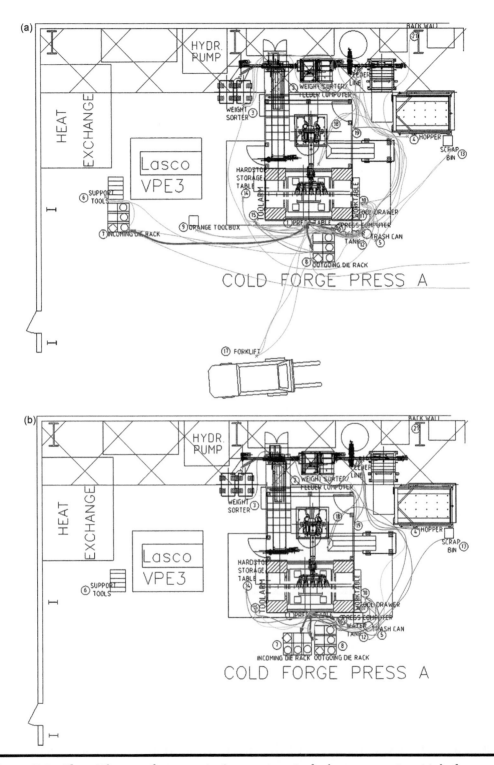

Figure 5.4 **Flow Diagram for operator's movements during press setup (a)** *before* **and (b)** *after* **layout improvements.**

Software to Implement PFA

Quoting from a research paper (Merchant 1975) "…In the Netherlands, the Metals Institute of TNO is developing and testing in industry, a computer-based software system for automatic classification of parts into group technology families and automatic layout of factories into group technology cells based on those families…". We could not obtain this software back in 1999 when we started developing the methodology to implement Job Shop Lean at The Ohio State University. So my team of doctoral students (Dr. Heng Huang, Dr. Jin Zhou, and Dr. Smart Khaewsukkho) and I developed the PFAST (Production Flow Analysis and Simplification Toolkit) software. This academic software continues to be used today to implement Job Shop Lean in HMLV manufacturing facilities that are willing to invest in factory layout changes. PFAST will be discussed in the next chapter.

Data Needed to Implement PFA

PFA is perfectly aligned with Ohno's ideas for factory layout design to achieve Flow at any level in any factory. That is because the PFA algorithms for material flow analysis use data that implicitly conveys the logical flow of material as follows:

1. The Assembly Precedence Diagram for a product shows the order in which parts and sub-assemblies are delivered to different stations on an assembly line that builds the final product.
2. The manufacturing routing to produce each component that goes into the final product shows the exact sequence in which different machines are used to make it.

If an HMLV manufacturer has the above data and it is up-to-date, then PFAST could **certainly** be used to design the layout of any cell, shop, or their entire factory. For example, recall some of the statements that Ohno made describing his approach to factory layout:

- (Page 11) "I was manager of the machine shop at the Koromo plant. As an experiment, I arranged the various machines in the sequence of machining processes".

■ (Page 128) "The first aspect of the TPS...means putting a flow into the manufacturing processes...Now, we place a lathe, a mill and a drill in the actual sequence of the manufacturing processing...".

The flow of any component is going to be determined by its routing. Table 5.4 presents the sequence of operations required to produce a forging in a custom forge shop. In an ideal situation, there would be perfect Flow of this forging if the equipment in the forge shop was laid out such that the work centers were arranged in a U, S, or L shape per the sequence of operations in the table.

Table 5.4   Routing for a Forging Produced in a Custom Forge Shop

Operation No.	WC No.	Name of Work Center (WC)
1	951	TEST STOCK OR LAB RELEASE
2	760	SAW 36 IN ABRASIVE
3	510	BLAST – ROTO
4	810	COAT – DIP
5	80	20000 # HAMMER #2089 or #3585
6	510	BLAST – ROTO
7	310	MACHINING –CNC
8	673	SOLUTION TREAT 2
9	666	PRECIP TREAT 4/16
10	952	TEST FORGE
11	520	BLAST – TABLE
12	310	MACHINING –CNC
13	800	INSPECT
14	962	TO OUTSIDE WORK (going out)
15	974	FROM SONIC TEST (coming back)
16	570	PICKLE
17	958	NDT MICRO
18	952	TEST FORGE
19	820	STAMP

Conclusion

"Flow" refers to the movement of material throughout a factory. It assumes that material will not be stagnant at any point in time from the receiving of raw material to the shipping of finished products. PFA can be used to improve Flow in any work system within a factory, such as a single machine, in a single cell, in a machine shop, in a tool crib, in the tool magazine of a machining center, between departments or shops in an entire factory, within a building, between all cells and support departments in a machine shop, etc.

References

Burbidge, J.L. (1971, April/May). Production flow analysis. The Production Engineer, 50, 139–152.

Merchant, M.E. (1975). The future of CAM (Computer Aided Manufacturing) systems. International Workshop on Managing Requirements Knowledge, Proceedings of the National Computer Conference, New York, 793–799.

Shingo, S. (1989). *A Study of the Toyota Production System from an Industrial Engineering Viewpoint.* Portland, OR: Productivity Press.

Chapter 6

Overview of Production Flow Analysis and Simplification Toolkit (PFAST)

Production Flow Analysis (PFA) provides an effective framework for analyzing the material flows at different levels of resolution in a factory. Historically, the four stages of PFA were implemented manually. That limited the detection and elimination of many instances of chaotic material flows in the existing factory. Therefore, PFAST (Production Flow Analysis and Simplification Toolkit (PFAST) was developed to implement a variety of computer algorithms (Figure 6.1) that help to partially automate the manual PFA methods. Thereby, the implementation of PFA can be done for large datasets in significantly shorter periods of time. Most of the algorithms in PFAST are versatile, and can be used to automate different stages of PFA, as shown in Table 6.1. Essentially, PFAST is an academic software that combines algorithms implemented in (i) facility layout software like FactoryFLOW (www.plm.automation.siemens.com) and Flow Planner (www.proplanner.com/en/products/flow_planner/) and (ii) statistical analysis software like SAS (www.SAS.com) and Minitab (www.Minitab.com). For example, if you Google "Cluster Analysis Freeware", you will find software available online that is equivalent to two of the PR Analysis (Product-Routing Analysis) modules in PFAST – PR Analysis I and PR Analysis II – that help to determine the machine groups and part families to form manufacturing cells.

PFAST could help to evaluate the strategic benefits of numerous strategies for material flow simplification to support Lean Manufacturing, as shown in

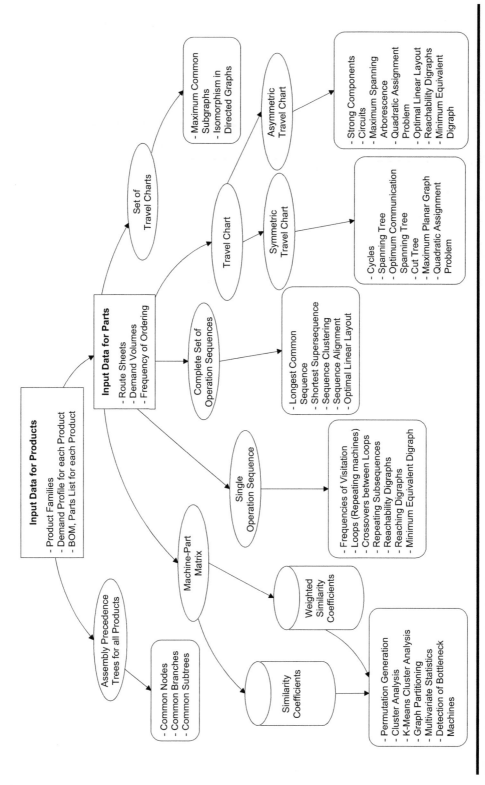

Figure 6.1 Algorithms in PFAST.

Table 6.1   Algorithms to Automate Different Stages of PFA

Algorithm	FFA (Factory Flow Analysis)	GA (Group Analysis)	LA (Line Analysis)	TA (Tooling Analysis)
Pareto Analysis	a	a	a	a
Sorting	a	a	a	a
Cluster Analysis		a		a
String or Digraph Clustering	a	a	a	a
Graph Partitioning		a		
Traveling Salesman Problem		a		a
Quadratic Assignment Problem	a	a	a	a
Maximum Spanning Arborescence, Maximum Spanning Tree, and Maximum Weight Planar Graph	a	a	a	a
Strong Components	a		a	

ᵃ Stage in which algorithm is used.

Table 6.2. Since PFAST uses three types of input data: operation sequences, machine-part matrices, and From-To charts, it could be used for a variety of projects dealing with material flow analysis and simplification. Examples of these projects are listed in Tables 6.3–6.5.

Table 6.2   Using PFAST for "Lean" Factory Design

- Value Network Mapping (VNM) for multiple interacting value streams
- Consolidation of buildings and departments
- Strategic duplication of equipment among departments
- Formation of manufacturing cells and focused factories
- Design of a network of material handling aisles
- Modification of process plans and product designs
- Systematic investment in flexible manufacturing cells
- Choice of subcontracted operations and/or parts
- Reduction of variety of routings in the part mix
- Elimination of parts that complicate the flow network
- Enhancement of flexibility in routing products to utilize non-bottleneck machines

Table 6.3 Using PFAST for Material Flow Analysis

- Descriptive statistics for routing data based on PQ Analysis, PQ$ Analysis, and PQR$ Analysis (P = Product, Q = Quantity, R = Routing, $ = Revenue)
- Descriptive statistics for material flow network in a facility
- Grouping of similar routings
- Detection of redundant variety in routings
- Identification of "misfit" (or outlier) routings
- Analysis of in-house vs. subcontracted material flows
- Elimination or reduction of poorly utilized material flow paths
- Detection of flow backtracking in routings
- Detection of flow backtracking in material flow network
- Detection of cross flows among aisles in the facility
- Detection of recurrent combinations (or sequences) of operations in routings
- Evaluation of current vs. desired flexibility of existing manufacturing equipment
- Creation of alternative routings for key products

Table 6.4 Using PFAST for Cellular Manufacturing

- Feasibility assessment for implementation of manufacturing cells using SICGE (Special, Intermediate, Common, General, Equipment) classification of the machines
  - o Shared machines that will be required in several cells
  - o Parts whose routings contain *only* unshared machines
  - o Parts whose routings contain *only* shared machines
  - o Parts whose routings contain *both* unshared and shared machines
- Specific number of cells that could be implemented
- Parts that could not be produced in cells due to complexity of their routings
- Composition (machine group and part family) of each cell
- Complexity (number of different machines and parts) of each cell
- Homogeneity analysis of the part mix based on routing similarities
  - o Parts that do not belong to any cell
  - o Parts whose routings span more than one cell
  - o Parts with "exception" (or outlier) operations external to their host cell
  - o Parts that could be produced in more than one cell
- Duplication of equipment required in two or more cells
- Alternatives for the number and composition of the cells due to shared machines
  - o For a fixed number of cells
  - o For a variable number of cells
- Analysis of the stability of cell compositions due to changes in part mix
- Prioritization of Integrated Product and Process Design (IPPD) in order to eliminate inter-cell flows, exception operations, and capacity sharing between cells
- Support of kaizen events for detailed planning of each cell
  - o Capacity Requirements Planning
  - o Machine allocation and load balancing, especially if inter-cell flows involved

(*Continued*)

Table 6.4 (*Continued*)   Using PFAST for Cellular Manufacturing

> o Capital investment for purchase of new machines and technology upgrades
> o Layout, material handling, and scheduling of *intra-cell* part flows
> o Layout, material handling, and scheduling of *inter-cell* part flows
> o TOC analyses of capacity-constrained machines in each cell
> • Support of what-if analyses to evaluate strategies to eliminate inter-cell flows
> o Redesign the parts to eliminate exception operations
> o Combine cells that require common machines
> o Subcontract, even eliminate, parts with exception operations
> o Buy extra machines to distribute among competing cells
> o Purchase multi-function centers to replace 2–3 machine sets in one or more cells
> o Put shared machines in a centrally located *Common Facilities* cell
> o Reroute operations on bottleneck machines to alternative machines in the cells
> o Design the overall facility layout to minimize inter-cell transfer delays
> o Speed up the material handling between the cells using visual signals
> o Adopt priority scheduling rules for parts that require inter-cell flows

Table 6.5   Using Other Software for Design and Performance Analysis of a Pilot Cell

> • Selection of the family of parts to produce in the cell
> • PQ Analysis and PQ$ Analysis of the "business" assigned to the cell
> • Capacity requirements for the cell
> • Machine requirements vs. actual allocations made to the cell
> • Exception operations that cannot be done inside the cell
> o Machines that could not be assigned to the cell due to insufficient workload
> o *Monuments* that are external to the cell
> o Support services that are external to the cell
> • Inter-cell flows
> o Due to exception operations
> o Due to machine overloads caused by fluctuations in customer demand
> o Access to identical machines in other cells when internal breakdowns occur
> o Access to identical machines in other cells where operators with similar skills work
> • Line, U, or S layout for the cell using STORM and PFAST software tools
> • Flow Diagram for the cell
> • Current and Future State VNM for the cell using Visio and Factory Flow software tools
> • Performance evaluation of the cell using simulation software tools like SIMIO and FLEXSIM
> • Operations scheduling for the cell using PREACTOR or TACTIC scheduling software tools

Table 6.6   Using PFAST for Generic Facility Layout

- Pareto analysis of parts using multi-criterion sampling
- Sorting of parts to identify those with identical routings
- Design of a block layout for a factory site, building, department, or shop
- Design of a flowline or U-layout for a cell
- Design of non-traditional layouts
  - o Hybrid Cellular Layouts
  - o Cascading Cells
  - o Modular Layouts
  - o Virtual Cellular Layouts
- Strategic duplication of equipment in several shops or departments
- Strategic consolidation of shops or departments
- Design of a flexible layout using multiple samples of routings
- Design of a network of material handling aisles

Chapter 7

Functional, Cellular, and Hybrid Cellular Layouts for Any Job Shop

Functional Layout vs. Cellular Layout

In a typical high-mix low-volume manufacturing facility, such as a machine shop, forge shop, fabrication shop, and mold-making shop, there is a very high probability that they have a Functional Layout (Figure 7.1). The Functional Layout has advantages such as high machine utilization at work centers and high flexibility in allocating operations to alternative machines in any work center. However, it has disadvantages

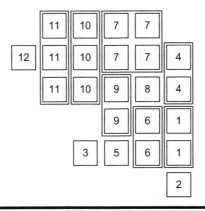

Figure 7.1   Functional Layout.

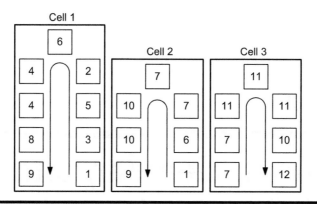

Figure 7.2   Cellular Layout with three cells.

such as high-throughput times, high WIP (work-in-process) levels, and complex order tracking.

The implementation of Lean Manufacturing usually includes changes in the factory layout, especially the implementation of one or more manufacturing cells. A Cellular Layout (Figure 7.2) has advantages such as low lead times and low WIP levels. However, high machine utilization is not guaranteed in all cells. Also, in case of machine breakdowns and changes in demand or product mix, a cell designed to produce a single part family is inflexible and unsuitable for reconfiguration.

A Cellular Layout Is Not a Panacea!

High-mix low-volume manufacturers, especially job shops, are ill-advised to undertake a complete reorganization into a Cellular Layout based on specific part families, unless the customer base, part mix, and order volumes for the cells will be stable in the long term. Significant changes in product mix and/or order quantities are usually the downfall of a Cellular Layout. In fact, many job shops keep their Functional Layout and rely on daily production meetings, expeditors, and other firefighting strategies to progress and track orders! Even more importantly, advances in computer-aided factory management using Enterprise Resource Planning (ERP) systems, Finite Capacity Scheduling (FCS), and Manufacturing Execution Systems (MES) can be integrated to manage a group of machines that are not co-located physically in a cell.

Design of Flexible and Lean (FLean) Layouts for Job Shops

A Functional Layout is flexible but promotes batch-and-queue production. A Cellular Layout is inflexible but enables single-piece flow. Can the layout of any high-mix low-volume manufacturing facility be **both** Flexible **and** Lean (FLean)? This chapter describes a variety of Hybrid Cellular Layouts (HCLs) that (i) exploit the knowledge of families of parts with similar/identical routings *and* (ii) avoid total reorganization of the existing Functional Layout into a Cellular Layout. *An HCL is intermediate between a Cellular Layout and a Functional Layout.* All HCLs for a factory are developed under the assumption that the product mix of the factory has been analyzed to discover the part families that are the basis for cell formation. However, during the layout design phase, creative strategies are used to place the shared machines as if they had been retained in functional departments ("process villages"). It is designed by integrating different strategies for facility layout design, such as (i) some machines will be grouped into cells, (ii) some of its functional departments will be retained as-is, (iii) some of its functional departments will be split and distributed at two or more locations across the factory, and (iv) some machines will be grouped into partial cells (aka Layout Modules), etc.

Table 7.1 shows the routing of each product in a hypothetical facility that consists of 12 machines and produces 19 products. Figures 7.1 and 7.2 show a Functional Layout and a Cellular Layout with three cells to produce a sample of parts in Table 7.1, respectively. With reference to the cells shown in Figure 7.2, Machines #1, #6, #7, #9, and #10 have been duplicated in several cells. This physical duplication of identical machines into cells destroys the flexibility obtained by having all machines of a shared type in a functional group, as in a Functional Layout. HCLs attempt to avoid this physical separation of machines that must be shared by two or more cells.

Hybrid Cellular Layouts

Cellular Layout with reorientation of cells (Figure 7.3): Here, by a simple 90° rotation of Cell 2, all machines of types #1 and #7 are located physically adjacent to each other, as if in a Functional layout, even as the original allocation of machines to cells is retained. Hence, in case of machine breakdowns or demand changes, parts could still be transferred quickly among machines of the same type.

Table 7.1 Operation Sequences of Products

Product #	Sequence	Production Quantity
1	1→4→8→9	2
2	1→4→7→4→8→7	3
3	1→2→4→7→8→9	1
4	1→4→7→9	3
5	1→6→10→7→9	2
6	6→10→7→8→9	1
7	6→4→8→9	2
8	3→5→2→6→4→8→9	1
9	3→5→6→4→8→9	1
10	4→7→4→8	2
11	6	3
12	11→7→12	1
13	11→12	1
14	11→7→10	3
15	1→7→11→10→11→12	1
16	1→7→11→10→11→12	2
17	11→7→12	1
18	6→7→10	3
19	12	2

Cellular Layout with reorientation and reshaping of cells (Figure 7.4): This is a more complicated case of an HCL since it was generated by a reorientation as well as change of shape of one or more cells. Instead of retaining the U (or rectangular) shape for all cells, cells are allowed to have L (or S) shapes, which allows more machine types *that would otherwise have been distributed among the cells* to remain co-located in functional groups.

Cellular Layout with S-shaped flowlines (Figure 7.5): This layout for embedding functional groups in a Cellular Layout is similar to Figure 7.4. A Flowline Layout was developed for each of the cells. Next, the cells were

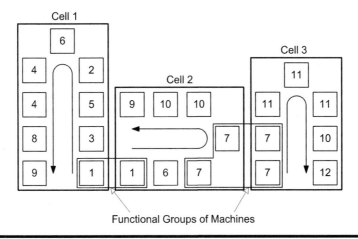

Figure 7.3   Cellular Layout with reorientation of cells.

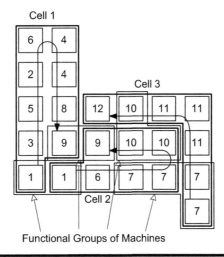

Figure 7.4   Cellular Layout with reorientation and reshaping of cells.

arranged in parallel to minimize inter-cell flows. Finally, their linear shapes were modified into S-shapes to group identical machines into functional groups.

Hybrid Flow Shop Layout (Figure 7.6): In this layout[1], the machines are allocated into several groups of machines and the groups are arranged in a line. However, unlike a traditional manufacturing cell, each group of machines does not process a family of parts. Rather, it can perform one or more consecutive operations occurring in the operation sequence of almost

---

[1] This HCL is similar to a Mixed Model Value Stream.

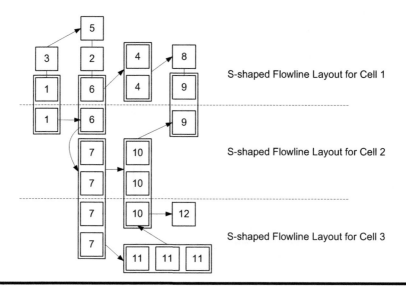

Figure 7.5   Cellular Layout with S-shaped flowlines in parallel.

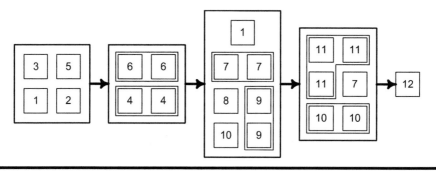

Figure 7.6   Hybrid Flow Shop Layout.

every part. In a Flow Shop, the routing of every product is identical to the sequence of machines that comprises the linear layout of the flow shop. In this HCL, only the pair of operations, 7 → 4, in the routings of Parts #2 and #10 cause flow to backtrack in the layout. Otherwise, if every part routing in Table 7.1 is mapped onto the layout shown in Figure 7.6, then the travel route of each part for consecutive operations either (i) connects two consecutive groups of machines or (ii) bypasses a group to connect to a group of machines that is further along. If an additional Machine # 4 could have been purchased and allocated to the third stage in Figure 7.6, then zero backtracking would have existed in this layout.

Virtual Cellular Layout (Figure 7.7): The layouts in Figures 7.3–7.6 demonstrate the basic objective of HCLs to minimize the number of machine types that cannot be retained in functional departments when a Functional Layout

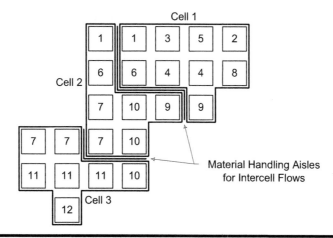

Figure 7.7   Virtual Cellular Layout.

is changed to a Cellular Layout. The goal is to have the benefits of part family-based manufacturing without necessarily co-locating machines into (rigid and inflexible) cells. In the Virtual Cellular Layout, machines shared by several cells can be retained in functional groups if the cells are located adjacent to each other. This adjacency of the cells allows the machines in any cell to be "virtually co-located" with a designated material handler moving all parts in that particular family among the different machines in the cell. Even though the shared machine types are located in functional groups, their setups can remain dedicated to a particular family of parts matched with a specific manufacturing cell.

Cellular Layout with a remainder cell (Figure 7.8): This layout eliminates the machine duplication problem experienced with a Cellular Layout. One

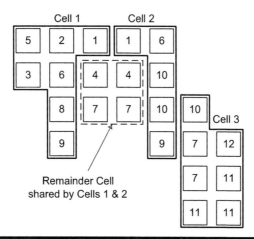

Figure 7.8   Cellular Layout with a remainder cell.

or more shared machine types are kept in a Remainder Cell accessible to all the cells that need to share these machines. The original compositions of Cells 1 and 2 (Figure 7.2) were relaxed to facilitate flows of parts through the Remainder Cell. Machines in the Remainder Cell were arranged using standard methods for the design of a Functional Layout.

Cascading cells (Table 7.2): This layout depends on the similarity of routings of parts in different families. The cells are designed such that simple parts with short routings are produced in the simpler cells and complex parts with long routings are produced in larger, more complex cells. There is no inter-cell movement for any part. *Every part must be completed in just one cell!* Significant machine duplication, possible requiring the purchase of additional machines, is usually necessary to implement this layout.

Table 7.2 Cascading Cells

Part Numbers	Cell Composition
12, 13, 17, 19	7 → 11 → 12
14, 15, 16	1 → 7 ↔ 11 → 12 10
10	4 ↔ 7 8
1, 4	1 → 4 → 7 → 9 8
2, 3	1 → 4 ↔ 7 9 2 8
18	6 → 7 → 10
5, 6	1 → 6 → 10 → 7 → 9 8
7, 11	6 → 4 → 8 → 9
8, 9	3 → 5 → 6 → 4 → 8 → 9 2

⬇ shows the cascading of a simple cell into a more complex cell.

Conclusion

High-mix low-volume manufacturers, especially job shops, ought not to undertake a complete reorganization into a Cellular Layout where each cell is designed to make a specific part family. Significant changes in the customer base, part mix, and order volumes for each of the cells are usually the downfall of a Cellular Layout. A Cellular Layout is inflexible but enables single-piece flow. A Functional Layout is flexible but promotes batch-and-queue production. An HCL is intermediate between these two traditional facility layouts! Any HCL is capable of being **both** Flexible **and** Lean (FLean) because it is designed using a fusion of strategies for facility layout design.

Conclusion

Chapter 8

Designing Functional, Cellular, and Hybrid Cellular Layouts for Any Job Shop Using PFAST

Background[1]

What is a job shop? A job shop is just one type of high-mix low-volume (HMLV) manufacturing facility that produces small batches of a variety of custom products that require a unique setup and sequencing of process steps. Examples of job shops include a wide range of businesses like a machine shop, a single machining center, a forge shop, a fabrication shop, an automobile repair shop, a commercial print shop, a hospital, etc. These businesses deal in customization and relatively small production runs, not volume and standardization. In the job shop, similar equipment or functions are grouped together in a Functional (aka Process) Layout, such as all Drill Presses in one area and all Grinders in another area. When an order arrives in the job shop, it will travel throughout the various areas of the facility according to a pre-defined sequence of operations. Not all jobs will use every machine in the plant. Jobs often travel in a jumbled routing and may return to the same machine for processing several times. The job shop has the most flexibility in making a variety of products to meet customer quality and service standards. As customers request repeat jobs and as volumes grow, the job shop may group machines into work cells to process batches of like jobs.

---

[1] Source: www.inc.com/encyclopedia/job-shop.html

Is the Functional Layout *Really* the Best Layout for a Job Shop?

Recall from an earlier chapter where several authors(Merchant, 1975, Ohno, 1988, Shingo, 1989) were quoted as saying that a Functional Layout ought to be replaced with a Cellular (or Product) Layout. In particular, Shigeo Shingo, who consulted for Toyota, wrote in his book (Shingo, 1989) "...Instead of arranging departments by type of machines (for example, press department or lathe department), consider the following arrangements:

- *Single process line:* For month-long production of a single product and a single model in large quantities.
- *Common process line:* When production of a single product is not sufficient for a month's continuous flow but products A, B, C, and D have processes in common that can be arranged in a continuous flow.
- *Similar process line:* Products A, B, C, D, E, and F have some but not all of their processes in common, so only partial lines can be formed of those common processes...".

So what should be the basis for determining which of the above arrangements (or combination of arrangements) suggested by Dr. Shingo gives the best layout for a particular job shop? The answer lies in a thorough analysis of (i) the routings of all the products that are produced by the job shop, (ii) the order volumes (and revenues earned) by each product, (iii) the cost of distributing identical (or similar) pieces of equipment in several locations, (iv) the feasibility of implementing manufacturing cells, (v) the infeasibility of relocating certain equipment such as a heat treatment furnace, etc.

Fundamental Challenge of Designing a "Best Fit" Layout for Any Job Shop

In the case of any assembly line in a factory, every product that is built on that line follows a fixed routing which is the sequence of workstations in the assembly line. But the product mix of a job shop invariably involves many different routings due to the variety of products that they choose to make. That is the nature of their business! Unfortunately, a job shop could be making 100's if not 1000's of different components. Each component's routing could be identical or similar or totally different from the routings of other components that are produced in the same facility! For example, two components may have "similar" routings because (i) they visit the same sequence of *departments* such as TURN→MILL→GRIND, but (ii) neither component gets processed on the same *type of machine* in each of the three departments.

Designing Alternative Layouts for Any Job Shop Using PFAST

How to analyze the complex material flow in any job shop whose layout must "fit" hundreds of different routings? Production Flow Analysis (PFA) can analyze material flows in HMLV factories, especially job shops. This chapter explains how, if the routings of all the products produced by a job shop and additional data needed for a standard facility layout project are available, then the PFA algorithms available in the academic software PFAST (Production Flow Analysis and Simplification Toolkit) could analyze the routings to determine a "best fit" layout for the job shop.

The overall structure of the analyses performed by PFAST is shown in Figure 8.1. In this chapter, the focus will be on how to use the different PFAST outputs to design a Functional Layout, a Cellular Layout, and Hybrid Cellular Layouts (HCLs) intermediate between the Functional and Cellular Layouts using data for a hypothetical 12-machine, 19-part machine shop.

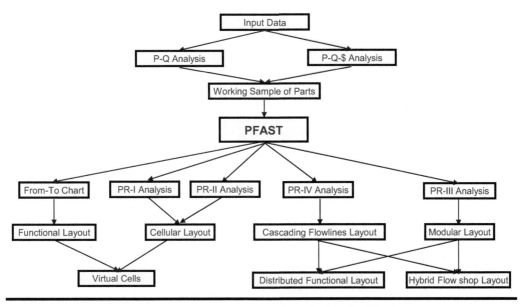

Figure 8.1   Overall framework for using PFAST to design facility layouts.

Input Data

The PQR$ (P = **P**roduct Name/Number, Q = Annual Production **Q**uantity, R = Manufacturing Routing, $ = Annual **$**ales/Revenue) information that is needed for each part is shown in Table 8.1. For example, for Part No. #1, the Annual Production Quantity is 10,642 and the Annual Revenue earned from selling that quantity of the part is $31,336. The Manufacturing Routing for Part No. #1 consists of four operations – Op #1 is performed on Machine #1, Op #2 is performed on Machine #4, Op #3 is performed on Machine #8, and Op #4 is

Table 8.1   PQR$ Data for the Job Shop

Part No.	Qty	Revenue	Op 1	Op 2	Op 3	Op 4	Op 5	Op 6	Op 7
Part 1	10,642	31,336	1	4	8	9			
Part 2	4,270	21,300	1	4	7	4	8	7	
Part 3	1,471	10,901	1	2	4	7	8	9	
Part 4	4,364	25,774	1	4	7	9			
Part 5	5,013	1,580	1	6	10	7	9		
Part 6	4,679	36,069	6	10	7	8	9		
Part 7	5,448	47,776	6	4	8	9			
Part 8	5,339	50,339	3	5	2	6	4	8	9
Part 9	9,117	48,784	3	5	6	4	8	9	
Part 10	8,935	37,774	4	7	4	8			
Part 11	7,100	68,153	6						
Part 12	8,611	60,272	11	7	12				
Part 13	9,933	39,903	11	12					
Part 14	3,824	19,258	11	7	10				
Part 15	1,359	7,800	1	7	11	10	11	12	
Part 16	1,235	8,562	1	7	11	10	11	12	
Part 17	8,581	44,074	11	7	12				
Part 18	3,963	23,137	6	7	10				
Part 19	2,309	3,012	12						

Table 8.2 Attributes for Each Machine Type

Machine No.	Area Requirements	No. Available	Purchase Price	Mobility
1	2,000	2	N/A	N/A
2	1,000	1	N/A	N/A
3	1,000	1	N/A	N/A
4	2,000	2	N/A	N/A
5	1,000	1	N/A	N/A
6	2,000	2	N/A	N/A
7	4,000	4	N/A	N/A
8	1,000	1	N/A	N/A
9	2,000	2	N/A	N/A
10	4,000	4	N/A	N/A
11	3,000	3	N/A	N/A
12	1,000	1	N/A	N/A

performed on Machine #9. In addition, information for every type of machine/equipment that features in the routings is needed, such as area requirements, the ease of relocation (Mobility), and the cost of duplication (Purchase Price), as shown in Table 8.2. The last two attributes of each machine (Mobility, Purchase Price) help to answer the following two questions, respectively: (i) Would it be exorbitantly expensive to relocate that piece of equipment? (ii) Could additional units of the equipment be purchased at reasonable expense? Attribute #2 is often a major constraint when changing a Functional Layout into a Cellular Layout. Several families of products may use the same machine. So, if management desires that each part family's cell has the necessary number of machines of that type in order to operate independently from the other cells, more machines of that type may need to be purchased.

Product-Quantity Analysis (PQ Analysis)

If the number of routings in the complete product mix being produced in a job shop is large, say 1,000 or more parts, then it may be necessary to select a representative sample of parts to focus on. This selection of a smaller set of products is known as Product Mix Segmentation. It helps to focus the implementation of Job Shop Lean on a manageable number of parts. Not only does this reduce the time to do the data analysis, but it also reduces the time that has to be spent to collect detailed data for the fewer parts included in the sample chosen. PFAST uses two sampling techniques – PQ Analysis (Product-Quantity Analysis) and PQ$ Analysis (Product-Quantity-Revenue Analysis) – to extract a smaller sample of parts from a large product mix. Assume that one or more part families are discovered in this sample. Next, the remainder of the product mix can be "seeded" with representative parts from each part family discovered in the sample. Now, if the rest of the product mix is ana-lyzed, either new part families will be found or the pre-existing ones discov-ered in the sample will have more identical/similar parts added to them.

The classical approach for Product Mix Segmentation is PQ Analysis, also known as "Pareto Analysis" or "ABC Analysis" (in the field of Inventory Control and Management). The underlying logic of PQ Analysis is that, if any facility layout is designed to ensure the efficient flow of only those parts that are produced in the largest quantities, then the costs of material han-dling, WIP (work-in-process), queuing, labor, and material handling equip-ment maintenance could be minimized. Also, the production lead times of those parts will be significantly reduced since the layout will be modified to improve the flow of those products. PQ Analysis sorts the parts in order of decreasing Production Quantity. Parts that are produced in high quantities will appear earlier in the sorted sequence of Part #s, whereas parts produced in low quantities will appear towards the end of the sorted sequence of Part #s. PQ Analysis usually shows that less than 20% of the entire product mix in a job shop is responsible for more than 80% of the total production volume.

How to Do PQ Analysis

1 Draw a horizontal axis (X) that represents the products, according to their production quantities, ordered from the largest to the smallest (Figure 8.2).
2 Draw a vertical axis (Y) that represents annual production quantity.
3 Construct a bar graph based on the production quantity of each part.
4 Construct a line graph of the cumulative production quantities.
5 Draw a line on the Y axis from the point that represents a certain percent-age, say 80%, of the total production quantity to intersect the line graph, and then drop a line from that point of intersection to the X axis. This line separates the important parts (to the left of the vertical line) that will

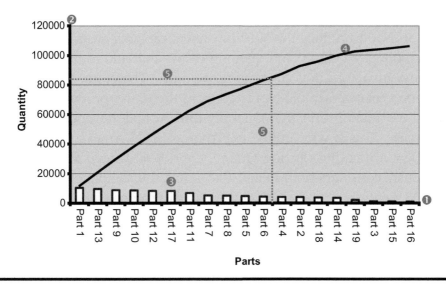

Figure 8.2   PQ Analysis.

be included in the sample from the remaining ones in the product mix (to the right of the vertical line) that will be excluded from the sample.

How to Use PQ Analysis

PQ Analysis is used for Product Mix Segmentation based on Annual Production Quantity only. As shown in Figure 8.2, 11 out of the 19 parts account for 80% of the total production quantity. These 11 parts are considered more important than the remaining 8 parts. Since the size of this example dataset is rather small, we will work with the entire product mix of 19 parts. In most real-world Job Shop Lean implementation projects, it has been our experience that this step to extract a sample is usually necessary. It engages the employees and managers in discussions that result in actions that eventually benefit factory operations.

Product-Quantity-Revenue Analysis (PQ$ Analysis)

PQ$ Analysis is a dual-criterion approach for Product Mix Segmentation that is a better alternative to the single-criterion approach of PQ Analysis. Using PQ Analysis, a sample of parts with high production quantities will be selected to represent the entire product mix of a job shop. However, the ultimate goals of implementing Job Shop Lean are (i) to make money by producing parts on-demand and delivering them to customers by specified due dates and (ii) to reduce the WIP inventory carrying costs by eliminating material handling, batching, and queuing delays that add to the manufacturing costs and in-factory flow times of those parts. Therefore, it is imperative that the representative sample extracted from the entire product mix considers **both** the Annual Production Quantity **and** Annual Revenue Earnings of all the parts. This is why, unlike PQ Analysis, PQ$ Analysis (**P** = **P**art or **P**roduct, **Q** = Annual Production **Q**uantity and **$** = Annual **$**ales/Revenue) simultaneously considers both Q and $ to select the sample of parts.

In a PQ$ Analysis scatter plot, all the parts in the product mix are mapped in two dimensions. The X axis of the scatter plot represents Annual Production Quantity (or Volume) and the Y axis of the scatter plot represents Annual Revenue, or vice versa. If we split each axis into two zones – Low and High – then the entire part mix could essentially be split into four segments – (High Volume, High Revenue), (Low Volume, High Revenue), (High Volume, Low Revenue), and (Low Volume, Low Revenue). This scatter plot is helpful for breaking up the job shop's entire product mix into two segments – "Cats and Dogs" ("Strangers") and "Cash Cows" ("Runners" and "Repeaters"). Thereby, given that most job shops have limited resources to invest in Continuous Improvement projects, they can focus on reducing the costs of wastes and delays in the fulfillment of orders for mainly those products contained in the "Cash Cows" segment of their product mix.

How to Do PQ$ Analysis

1 Draw a horizontal axis (X) that represents Annual Production Quantity (Figure 8.3).
2 Draw a vertical axis (Y) that represents Annual Revenue.
3 Plot each part on the graph based on its (Annual Production Quantity, Annual Revenue) values.
4 Determine the threshold values on both the Revenue and Quantity axes to segregate products with High/Low Revenue and High/Low Quantity, respectively. To determine the location of Q on the X axis, do a PQ Analysis and determine the last product to be included in the sample of products that accounts for ≈80% of the Total Quantity Produced. At the point on the X axis that represents this product's Q value, draw a vertical line. Products with high values of Q will lie on or to the right of this line; products with low values of Q will lie to the left of this line.

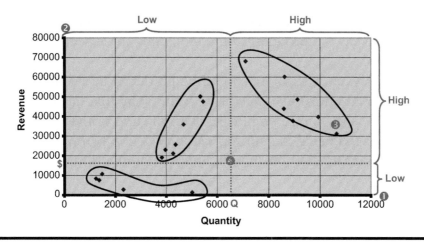

Figure 8.3   PQ$ Analysis.

Similarly, to determine the location of $ on the Y axis, do a P$ Analysis and determine the last product to be included in the sample of products that accounts for≈80% of the Total Revenue Earned. At the point on the Y axis that represents this product's $ value, draw a horizontal line. Products with high values of $ will lie on or above this line; products with low values of $ will lie below this line. Thereby, the PQ$ Analysis scatter plot consists of four quadrants. Each quadrant represents one of the following segments of the job shop's product mix:

– (High Quantity, High Revenue)
– (Low Quantity, High Revenue)
– (Low Quantity, Low Revenue)
– (High Quantity, Low Revenue).

How to Use PQ$ Analysis

The parts in each quadrant of the PQ$ Analysis plot constitute a product mix segment. For example, in Figure 8.3 there are three groups of parts based on Quantity and Revenue:

■ The (High Volume, High Revenue) segment consists of parts 1, 9, 10, 11, 12, 13, and 17
■ The (Low Volume, High Revenue) segment consists of parts 2, 4, 6, 7, 8, 14, and 18
■ The (Low Volume, Low Revenue) segment consists of parts 3, 5, 15, 16, and 19.

Products in the (Low Quantity, Low Revenue) segment constitute the "Cats and Dogs", whereas the products in the remaining three segments constitute the "Cash Cows".

Theoretically, each segment should be produced in a different area of the factory, should utilize manufacturing technology that has the appropriate flexibility, should hire employees with the appropriate skillset, and should be managed using the appropriate production planning and control system! **Realistically**, the job shop could manage the different segments as follows:

1. The parts in the (High Volume, High Revenue) segment could be produced using standard practices of the Toyota Production System.
2. The parts in the (High Volume, Low Revenue) segment could be produced using a two-bin Kanban system.
3. The parts in the (Low Volume, High Revenue) segment could be produced using a strict Make-To-Order policy with stringent Quality Control to prevent scrap. The best skilled employees and most productive machines would be used to produce orders for those parts. Setup Reduction kaizens would be done repeatedly so setups on these machines could be changed "on a dime". If necessary, the use of overtime would allow the job shop to quote competitive lead times to win orders for these parts.
4. The parts in the (Low Volume, Low Revenue) segment would be targeted for elimination.[2] However, if the customers who order those parts are also ordering parts in any of the "Cash Cow" segments then the low (or no) margins earned from producing orders for those parts may just have to be tolerated. Or perhaps prices could be negotiated to lose less on orders for these parts?[3]

---

[2] The owner of a fabrication job shop in Columbus, Ohio, had this to say about eliminating the parts in this segment, "We happily recommend to our customers to contact our competitors and ask them to make those parts instead of asking us! Thereby, the quality problems and shop floor disruptions caused by orders for those parts are passed on to our competitors".

[3] The owner of a job shop in Mt Vernon, Ohio, that produces custom plastic lenses, mirrors, and domes for safety, security, transportation, and solar applications had this to say about pricing a one-time order, "I roll the costs of special tooling, scrap/rework, overtime, etc. into my quote. Even then the customer comes back to me! That is because they know from past experience working with me on larger orders that they are guaranteed quality and a competitive due date for delivery. I have a full-time employee dedicated to producing and monitoring my daily production schedule. She is especially vigilant when a one-time order is released into the shop."

From-To Chart

The From-To Chart is a chart that shows the volumes of material flow between all pairs of departments in a Functional Layout (or all pairs of machines in a cell). It captures the cumulative volume of material flow between any pair of departments (in a Functional Layout) that is contributed by all the parts in the job shop's product mix whose routings contain that pair of machines. For any two departments, the chart will have two cells in the From-To Chart that capture the aggregate material flow in either direction between the two departments. For example, in Figure 8.4, the flow from Machine #7 to Machine #8 is 6,150 and the flow from Machine #8 to Machine #7 is 4,270.

How to Create a From-To Chart

1 For each part (or product) in the product mix being produced in the job shop, obtain its (i) routing and (ii) production quantity (Figure 8.4).
2 Identify all machines (or workstations) that feature in these routings and verify their locations in (i) the layout of the job shop and (ii) the plant list.
3 Enter all the machines identified into the columns of the From-To Chart in any sequence. These columns are the "TO" machines.
4 Enter all the machines identified into the rows of the From-To chart, preferably in the same sequence. These rows are the "FROM" machines.

To

MACHINE	1	2	3	4	5	6	7	8	9	10	11	12	3
1		1471		19276		5013	2594						
2				1471		5339							
3					14456								
4							19040	43751					
5		5339				9117							
6				19904			3963			9692			
7				13205				6150	9377	7787	2594	17192	
8							4270		36696				
9													
10							9692				2594		
11							210167			2594		12527	
12													
4													

Figure 8.4   From-To Chart

5 For each routing, decompose the sequence of machines into consecutive "From-To" pairs of machines. Enter the production quantity for that part into each cell in the From-To Chart that corresponds to a From→To pair of consecutive machines. For example, in Table 8.1 Part #12 has the operation sequence 11→7→12 and a production quantity of 8,611. This sequence can be decomposed into two "From-To" pairs: 11→7 and 7→12. The pair of operations 11→7 corresponds to the cell in the From-To chart at the intersection of (From) Row #11 and (To) Column #7. Enter "8611" in that cell. Similarly, the pair of operations 7→12 corresponds to the cell in the From-To chart at the intersection of (From) Row #7 and (To) Column #12. Enter "8611" in the corresponding cell in the From-To Chart for the 7→12 pair.

6 Repeat Step 5 for each of the routings selected in Step **1**.[4]

7 After the flows for the entire product mix have been entered, sum all the entries in each cell in the From-To Chart to obtain the aggregate material flow between that directed pair of machines in the job shop. For example, according to Table 8.1, the "From-To" pair 11→7 appears in the routings for Parts #12, #14, and #17. Therefore, the aggregate material flow from Machine #11 to Machine #7 is calculated as the sum of the production quantities of the three parts, i.e., 8,611 + 3,824 + 8,581 = 21,016.

How to Use the From-To Chart

Design of a Functional Layout: PFAST uses the From-To Chart as input to generate a Functional Layout (Figure 8.5). In a Functional Layout, all machines of the same functional capability are grouped and co-located into "departments" or "process villages". When the material flows contained in the From-To Chart are superimposed on the current facility layout with the thickness of the arrows representing the flow volumes, a Spaghetti Diagram (or Flow Diagram) results. Notice in Figure 8.5 that many flows (like the flow from Machine #6 to Machine #4) "jump over" intermediate departments; i.e., they are not located across from each other separated by a common

---

[4] In the case of Parts #11 and #19, there will be no entry in this From-To Chart, unless you include the Raw Material Stores (as the first operation in either part's routing) and Finished Goods (as the last operation in either part's routing).

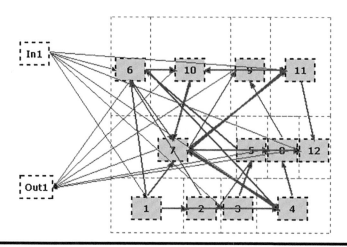

Figure 8.5   Functional Layout.

material handling aisle. So an order being processed in one department cannot quickly flow across the aisle to the other department. Like this inter-department flow, several flows are bound to occur between non-adjacent departments that do not share a common aisle in any Functional Layout that is designed using a From-To Chart.

In theory, we could try to eliminate those operations in product routings that resulted in an inter-departmental material flow between non-adjacent departments in a Functional Layout. Alternatively, to eliminate any inter-departmental material flow that occurred between non-adjacent departments, we could duplicate machines to create partial cells that were located *either* at the "FROM" machine **or** at the "TO" machine connected by that flow. **In practice**, if a job shop decides to persist with a Functional Layout, this still provides opportunities to implement flow improvement strategies based on the third principle of Design For Flow (Minimize the cost of flows). Recall the Industrial Engineering way to work improvement – *eliminate* work else *reduce* work else *simplify* work! The feasibility of eliminating or reducing the material flows between non-adjacent departments in a Functional Layout will depend completely on the particular products being produced, the particular machines involved, the facility constraints and, above all, the budget that the management provides to make the improvements. Unfortunately, there is no cookie-cutter nor a silver bullet solution to a problem that is best solved on a case-by-case basis!

Instead of using PFAST, you could input the From-To Chart in Figure 8.4 to a standard facility layout software like STORM, and it will produce a

Functional Layout for the entire facility, like the one shown in Figure 8.5. The algorithms internal to any of the available commercial software tools will place departments with the highest traffic volume adjacent to each other.[5]

Product-Routing Analysis Type I (PR-I Analysis) and Product-Routing Analysis Type II (PR-II Analysis)

PR-I Analysis (aka Product-Process Matrix Analysis) and PR-II Analysis (aka Hierarchical Cluster Analysis) are the primary methods for part family formation and machine grouping to create the manufacturing cells that help to convert a Functional Layout into a Cellular Layout. In fact, PR-I Analysis was first used by Prof. J. L. Burbidge, the inventor of PFA, to implement a Cellular Layout for a crane manufacturing facility! PFAST integrates PR-I Analysis and PR-II Analysis for visualization-aided determination of the machine-part compositions of different cells.

How to Do PR-I Analysis

1 (Figure 8.6) Construct the Initial 0–1 Matrix. This is a binary matrix representation of all the routings listed in Table 8.1 that comprise the hypothetical machine shop's product mix. The PR-I Analysis algorithm analyzes this matrix to form part families (and machine groups). Typically, the number of machines tends to be much less than the number of parts. Therefore, the Part #s are listed in the rows of the matrix, and the Machine #s listed are listed in the columns of the matrix.

2 Check the routing for each part. Identify the machines required to produce each part and enter 1's in the corresponding cells in the matrix. Each "1" in the matrix links a Part # to a particular Machine # that occurs one or more times in the part's manufacturing routing. For example, according to Table 8.1, the routing of Part #1 contains Machines #1, #4, #8, and #9. Therefore, in the row for Part #1, the cells in the matrix that are at the intersection of that part's row with the columns for those four machines are filled with 1's.

---

[5] In fact, the same software tools could be used to design the layout of an individual manufacturing cell or a shadow board for tools used to assemble a variety of products!

The Initial 0–1 Matrix is the basis for rough-cut identification of machine groups and part families which are the basis for the design of manufacturing cells. Unfortunately, the Machine #s and the Part #s are randomly listed in the columns and rows of the matrix, respectively. Therefore, it is highly unlikely that this matrix will immediately suggest the potential clusters of machines and parts.

Next, using the 0–1 matrix shown in Figure 8.6, compute Similarity Coefficients for all pairs of parts as follows:

$$S_{IJ}^{P} = \frac{N_{IJ}^{M}}{N_{II}^{M} + N_{JJ}^{M} - N_{IJ}^{M}}$$

where

S_{IJ}^{P} = Similarity between Parts I and J

N_{IJ}^{M} = Number of machines used by both Parts I and J

N_{II}^{M} = Number of machines used by Part I only

N_{JJ}^{M} = Number of machines used by Part J only

Similarly, using the 0–1 matrix shown in Figure 8.6, compute Similarity Coefficients for all pairs of machines as follows:

$$S_{KL}^{M} = \frac{N_{KL}^{P}}{N_{KK}^{P} + N_{LL}^{P} - N_{KL}^{P}}$$

where

S_{KL}^{M} = Similarity between Machines K and L

N_{KL}^{P} = Number of parts processed by both Machines K and L

N_{KK}^{P} = Number of parts processed by Machine K only

N_{LL}^{P} = Number of parts processed by Machine L only

1 (Figure 8.7) Construct the Final 0–1 Matrix. Using the matrix of Similarity Coefficients for parts, resequence the initial permutation of parts in Figure 8.6 such that each pair of consecutive parts has a high value for their Similarity Coefficient. In Figure 8.6, the parts appeared in the sequence Part #1→Part #2→Part #3→... Part #18→Part #19. However, in Figure 8.7, the

	m1	m2	m3	m4	m5	m6	m7	m8	m9	m10	m11	m12
Part 1	1			1				1	1			
Part 2	1			1			1	1				
Part 3	1	1		1			1	1	1			
Part 4	1			1			1		1			
Part 5	1					1	1		1	1		
Part 6						1	1	1	1	1		
Part 7				1		1		1	1			
Part 8		1	1	1	1	1		1	1			
Part 9			1	1	1	1		1	1			
Part 10				1			1	1				
Part 11						1						
Part 12							1				1	1
Part 13											1	1
Part 14							1			1	1	
Part 15	1						1			1	1	1
Part 16	1						1			1	1	1 .
Part 17							1				1	1
Part 18						1	1			1		
Part 19												1

Figure 8.6   Initial 0–1 Matrix

new permutation of parts is Part #8→Part #9→Part #5→... Part #13→Part #19. Similarly, using the matrix of Similarity Coefficients for machines, resequence the initial permutation of machines in Figure 8.6 such that each pair of consecutive machines has a high value for their Similarity Coefficient. In Figure 8.6, the machines appeared in the sequence Machine #1→Machine #2→Machine #3→...Machine #11→Machine #12. However, in Figure 8.7, the new permutation of machines is Machine #2→Machine #3→Machine #5→... Machine #11→Machine #12. Using the new permutations for parts and machines, rewrite the Initial 0–1 Matrix (Figure 8.6) to form the Final 0–1 Matrix (Figure 8.7).

How to Do PR-II Analysis

1 In Figure 8.7, unlike Figure 8.6, at least two blocks of 1's can be observed along the diagonal of the matrix. Each block of 1's represents a potential cell. Also, the 1's outside either block indicate machines shared between the cells or exception operations that necessitate inter-cell (INC) flows. Next, in Figure 8.7, the "inverted tree" structure extending to the left of the Final 0–1 Matrix that provides an alternative visualization for representing the clusters of parts (aka part

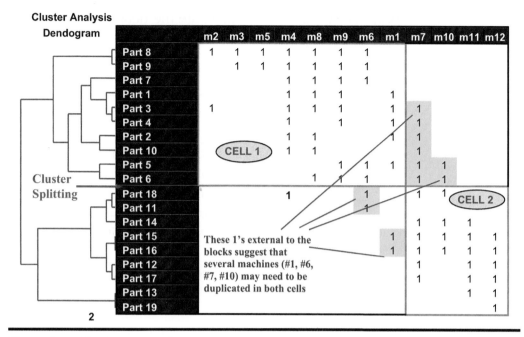

Figure 8.7   Final 0–1 Matrix

families) is a Cluster Analysis dendrogram In the permutation of parts in the Final 0–1 Matrix that was produced using PR-I Analysis, the clusters of parts are not easy to recognize from the linear ordering of the parts. In contrast, the dendrogram displays the formation of families of parts in a hierarchical precedence, based on commonality of machines in their routings. In addition, the hierarchical structure of the dendrogram helps to vary compositions of the different part families (and corresponding machine groups) that will constitute the cells. This automatically helps to vary the number of cells that could be implemented in a Cellular Layout.

PR-II Analysis can be done using a commercial Statistical Analysis package like Minitab or SAS. You can input the matrix of Similarity Coefficients for parts to the software to obtain the dendrogram that displays the part families. Else, you can input the matrix of Similarity Coefficients for machines to the software to obtain the dendrogram that displays the machine groups. However, if you produced the Final 0–1 Matrix using the two permutations of machines and parts obtained from the dendrograms generated by commercial packages, the machine-part groups of 1's along the diagonal of the matrix may not be as clear-cut.

2 PFAST uses a proprietary algorithm to generate the dendrogram shown in Figure 8.7 as follows:

1. Start by treating each part as a cluster.
2. Next, in the matrix of Similarity Coefficients for parts, find the two clusters that have the highest value for Similarity Coefficient in the entire matrix.
3. Draw a horizontal line from each of the two clusters to intersect the vertical line that corresponds to the value of this Similarity Coefficient. This merges the two clusters into a new cluster.
4. Recalculate the Similarity Coefficients in the matrix. The similarity between two clusters is calculated as the average similarity between all pairs of parts in the two different clusters.
5. Repeat Steps 2~4 until all the parts have been grouped into a single cluster.

The rearrangement of the Initial 0–1 Matrix into the Final 0–1 Matrix using PR-I Analysis and PR-II Analysis will show every family of parts that uses similar or identical combinations of machines as "blocks" of 1's that appear along the diagonal of the matrix. Each block in the final matrix consists of a set of consecutive rows (a part family) and consecutive columns (a machine group). For any block of 1's in the final matrix, the corresponding group of machines could be co-located to implement a manufacturing cell. Depending on the particular part mix being analyzed, the final matrix could quickly suggest whether a Cellular Layout is suitable for the facility, or whether an HCL would be a better alternative. For example, splitting the Cluster Analysis dendrogram in Figure 8.7 between Parts #6 and #18 generates two part families:

■ Part Family 1 consists of Parts #8, #9, #7, #1, #3, #4, #2, #10, #5, and #6.
■ Part Family 2 consists of Parts #18, #11, #14, #15, #16, #12, #17, #13, and #19.

Next, by eye-balling the matrix to identify the group of machines for each of the two part families formed earlier, we can identify the group of machines that will constitute each of the two cells that were formed:

■ Cell 1 consists of Machines #2, #3, #5, #4, #8, #9, #6, #1, #7, and #10.
■ Cell 2 consists of Machines #7, #10, #11, and #12.

In Figure 8.7, the 1's outside the blocks are "external operations" that could necessitate (i) putting machines of the same type(s) in two or more cells or (ii) INC flows of parts from one cell that does not have a particular machine to another cell that has that machine. In Figure 8.7, we can see that, if we desire to implement two cells, then Machines #1 and #6 will also be required in Cell #2, and Machines #7 and #10 will also be required in Cell #1. Unless these machines are duplicated in both cells, INC flows will occur that are not easy to coordinate and will be disruptive to operations in both cells. Cells with overlapping machine requirements between different part families can be expected in job shops and other Make-To-Order manufacturing facilities that make a large variety of products in low-to-medium quantities.

In practice, various strategies can be used to eliminate the INC flows, such as distributing the existing machines of each type among several cells or acquiring[6] extra machines of a type that is needed in several cells. Alternatively, in Figure 8.7, instead of placing the cut-off line between the two cells between Parts #6 and #18, it could have been placed between Parts #11 and #14. That would have eliminated the need to duplicate Machine #6 in both cells. Unfortunately, it would make one of the part families (and the cell to produce all the parts in it) much larger. Larger cells (and teams) are harder for one person to manage effectively.

How to Use PR-I Analysis and PR-II Analysis

When it is desired to replace a Functional Layout with a Cellular Layout, PR-I Analysis and PR-II Analysis will show how many different machines (or other manufacturing resources) will be required in multiple cells. If the overlap in machine requirements among the potential cells is insignificant and does not involve expensive machines, then a Cellular Layout is feasible. The cells could be independent or at most there could be minor INC flows. In the case of machine sharing between cells, either of two decisions must be taken: (i) Duplicate each machine in every cell where it is required or (ii) "starve" certain cells by not allocating them sufficient number of machines of any type. In the latter case, some cells will have to send their parts to other cells that have the machines they need. These INC flows delay parts from being completed on time by their host cell.

---

[6] This is where the "Purchase Price" column in Table 8.2 plays a key role.

Design a Cellular Layout with independent cells: Based on Figure 8.7, if it is desired to form two independent cells with no INC flows of parts between them, then Machines #1, #6, #7, and #10 must be duplicated in both cells. The parts assigned to each cell's part family are known. So, for each cell, a From-To Chart can be generated from the routings of its part family and input to a facility layout software like STORM. STORM will do the number-crunching and assign the different machines in the cell to appropriate locations in order to design a U-shaped layout for each cell. Next, by superimposing their routings on the cell layout, the material flow in either cell can be visualized, as shown in Figure 8.8. Does Figure 8.5 display a more orderly material flow, or does Figure 8.8?

Design a Cellular Layout with INC flows (Figure 8.9): In this layout, we only duplicate Machine #7 in Cell 1, because 6 out of the 10 parts in Family 1 require this machine. As shown in Figure 8.9, there are INC flows, caused by sharing of Machines #1, #6, and #10 between the two part cells. Each cell retains a U-shaped layout. Does Figure 8.5 or 8.9 display a more orderly material flow? Does Figure 8.8 or 8.9 display a more orderly material flow?

Product-Routing Analysis Type IV (PR-IV Analysis)

Compared to the traditional representations of the 0–1 Machine-Part Matrix (PR-I Analysis) and Cluster Analysis dendrogram (PR-II Analysis), PR-IV Analysis visualizes part families and material flows in a manufacturing facility differently. Unlike PR-I Analysis and PR-II Analysis, which use Similarity Coefficients to form part families, PR-IV Analysis groups parts into families based on the similarity of their routings. Routings, not 0–1 matrices, determine the material flow paths of all the products produced in an HMLV facility. In the binary matrix representation of PR-I Analysis, the binary coding of the routings loses the actual path along which the part will flow through a sequence of machines (or work centers). PR-IV Analysis overcomes that traditional shortcoming of the matrix representation by modeling each part routing as a hypothetical flowline cell that is dedicated to the production of that part. Now, instead of a 0–1 matrix with machines listed in the columns of the matrix and parts listed in the rows of the matrix, only the parts are listed one below the other in the rows of the matrix. This helps to simulate a factory floor with manufacturing flowlines placed side-by-side. Each flowline is dedicated to production of

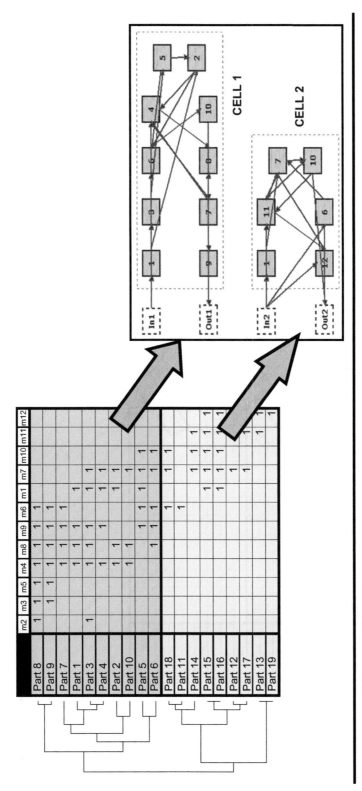

Figure 8.8 Cellular Layout with no INC flows.

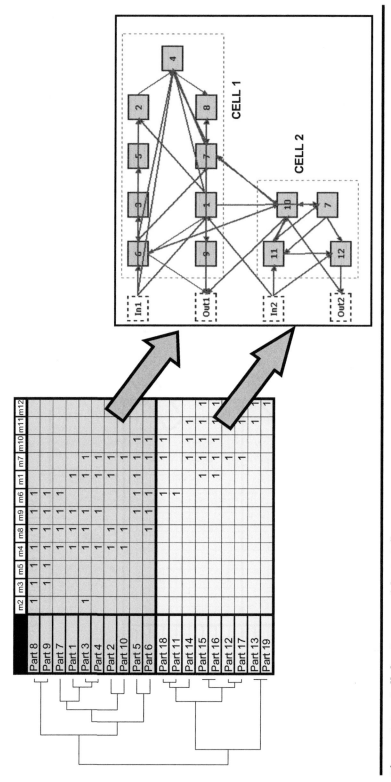

Figure 8.9   Cellular Layout with INC flows.

a single part. However, the PR-IV Analysis algorithm "shuffles and rear-ranges" these flowlines in such a way that flowlines for parts with identical or similar routings are placed adjacent to each other. Thereby, if an order is loaded on a flowline whose machines are busy, then that order could potentially be loaded on an adjacent flowline that may have machines of the same type with available capacity.

How to Do PR-IV Analysis

1 Construct a table with each row containing the sequence of operations for a particular part (Figure 8.10). The columns are simply numbered 1, 2, 3, ...

2 The PR-IV Analysis algorithm automatically resequences the ordering of the parts in the column labeled "Part No.". Each machine in the routing of a part is placed in one of the columns. For example, in the case of Part #18, Machine #6 is placed in Column #4, Machine #9 is placed in Column #9, and Machine #10 is placed in Column #10.

Part No.	1	2	3	4	5	6	7	8	9	10	11	12	13	14
Part 11				6										
Part 18				6					7	10				
Part 14								11	7	10				
Part 12								11	7			12		
Part 17								11	7			12		
Part 13								11				12		
Part 19								2				12		
Part 15	1					7	11	10	11			12		
Part 16	1					7	11	10	11			12		
Part 5	1			6				10	7				9	
Part 6				6				10	7			8	9	
Part 10				4					7		4	8		
Part 2	1			4					7		4	8		7
Part 4	1			4					7				9	
Part 3	1		2	4					7			8	9	
Part 1	1			4								8	9	
Part 7				6	4							8	9	
Part 8	3	5	2	6	4							8	9	
Part 9	3	5		6	4							8	9	

Figure 8.10   PR-IV Analysis

How to Use PR-IV Analysis

Unlike Figure 8.7, Figure 8.10 implicitly assumes that all parts start in a Raw Materials Store (RMS) on the left, move through the factory from left to right and terminate in a Finished Goods Store (FGS) to the right. Machine #3 or #1 will be located side-by-side to the right of the RMS. Next, some parts will go to Machine #7 or #6 or #4 or #2 or #5. **In theory**, if some of the machines (Machines #7, #10, #11, and perhaps #4) could be duplicated in at least two separate locations in the factory, then all parts would flow without backtracking from the RMS to the FGS! However, the Machine #7 that occurs in Column #14 probably could not be justified and will require Part #2 to backtrack to Machine #7 elsewhere in the layout.

How to put Figure 8.10 to work? Say for each part produced in the facility, you implement a flowline cell simply by placing the machines that occur in its routing in sequence from left to right in Figure 8.10. If you did the same and implemented a separate flowline to produce each part, you surely could not afford to buy that many machines! Instead, what if you placed side-by-side those flowlines that produce parts with identical or similar routings? This would allow an entire part family to be produced on a single flexible flowline whose layout conforms with the logical material flow for the entire part family!

With reference to Figure 8.10, you would start with just Machine #6 to initiate a machining flowline on the shop floor. But then you could only make Part #11. Next, you would expand this 1-machine flowline into a 3-machine flowline with three machines (Machines #6, #7, and #10) sequenced as follows: 6→7→10. This flowline could now produce Parts #11 **and** #18. Next, if you expanded the 3-machine flowline by placing Machine #11 side-by-side with Machines #6 and #10 side-by-side with Machine #12, this new flowline could also make Parts #12, #17, #13, and #19. Next, if we add Machine #1 at the front of the flexible flowline then the cell could make Parts #15 and #16 too. Stop! The part family for the flowline that you are currently building ought **not** to include any more parts.

Next, starting with the routing for Part #5, start building another flexible flowline for the second part family.

PR-IV Analysis is used to design HCLs that are part-Functional Layout and part-Cellular Layout, such as Cascading Flowlines, Modular Layouts, and Hybrid Flow Shops. The Cascading Flowline Layout (CFL) shown in Figure 8.11 is a layout where the two cells are "virtual". Although each of

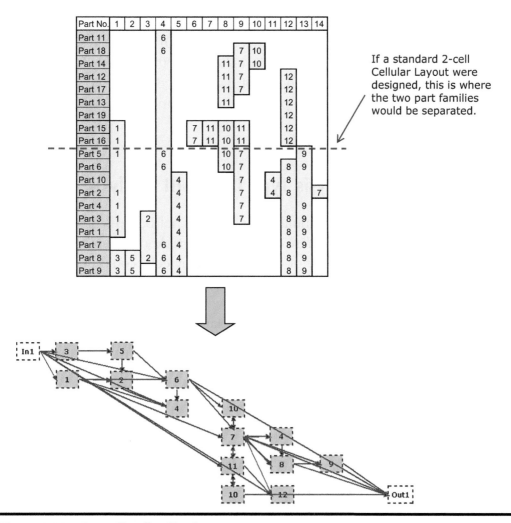

Part No.	1	2	3	4	5	6	7	8	9	10	11	12	13	14
Part 11				6										
Part 18				6				7	10					
Part 14						11	7	10						
Part 12						11	7					12		
Part 17						11	7					12		
Part 13						11						12		
Part 19												12		
Part 15	1					7	11	10	11			12		
Part 16	1					7	11	10	11			12		
Part 5	1			6				10	7				9	
Part 6				6				10	7		8		9	
Part 10					4				7	4	8			
Part 2	1				4				7	4	8			7
Part 4	1				4				7				9	
Part 3	1		2		4				7		8		9	
Part 1	1				4						8		9	
Part 7				6	4						8		9	
Part 8	3	5	2	6	4						8		9	
Part 9	3	5		6	4						8		9	

If a standard 2-cell Cellular Layout were designed, this is where the two part families would be separated.

Figure 8.11   Cascading flowline layout.

the two cells has a clear-cut part family to produce, the two cells do not have a U-layout. Instead, they have a linear layout and have been placed side-by-side. Thereby, if there is at least one of each of the following machines in both cells – Machines #1, #6, #7, #10, and #11 – those machines are co-located, as if they were in a "process village" in a Functional Layout. Thereby, if the demand in one cell increases, or decreases, then the parts in the overloaded cell could "cascade" into the adjacent cell where the same machines may have free capacity. Since the CFL allows easier machine sharing between cells, it is more flexible than a traditional Functional Layout or Cellular Layout. The CFL can accommodate variations in volume and/or product mix without major factory layout changes. In contrast, the Functional Layout (Figure 8.5) would remain chaotic and wasteful like before. And, the Cellular Layout (Figures 8.8 and 8.9) would have to be reconfigured if the demand for parts in either or both families changed. Also, due to changes in the INC flows of parts between the two cells, shop floor personnel will have to take pains to monitor and progress the completion of those parts.

Product-Routing Analysis Type III (PR-III Analysis)

In the case of many HMLV manufacturers, it may not be possible to implement a true Cellular Layout where each cell is capable of completely processing a family of parts. Some of the reasons why cells could not be implemented are:

1. The manufacturer is reluctant to invest large amounts of money to relocate all manufacturing equipment into a cell (or cells). For example, in the semiconductor industry, the "recipe" (routing) for producing a chip could contain 100+ operations. Also, the typical semiconductor fab has a Functional Layout and usually costs billions of dollars to build. So, instead of major rearrangement of manufacturing equipment, a fab might agree to group and co-locate some equipment.
2. The manufacturer does not focus on a single sector, such as Oil & Gas or Mining or Aerospace. Thereby, the variety of parts they make is too high, and it is hard to identify families of parts with similar routings. Also, if parts in the same family are not ordered with common due dates and/or orders for them do not repeat, then it is not advisable to implement cells.
3. The manufacturer sends many parts to outside vendors because those processes could not be absorbed into a cell. For example, in the case of a mold manufacturer, 9 of the 11 machined parts that comprised a mold were being sent to outside suppliers for Heat Treat, Anodize, and DLC (Diamond-Like-Carbon) Coat processes.
4. The manufacturer has in-house processes that cannot be moved into a cell. For example, in the case of a forge shop, the Forging Presses and Heat treatment furnaces cannot be absorbed into a cell.

How to implement Job Shop Lean in a facility that does not convert to a Cellular Layout? The answer lies in using PR-III Analysis to find sub-strings of operations that occur with high frequency in a large number of rout-ings. The machines that occur in these sub-strings could be grouped and co-located into partial cells (aka Layout Modules). Thereby, even if entire routings cannot be grouped into families, at least those routings will have in common one or more sub-strings of operations that repeat across sev-eral routings. Now, if these operation sub-strings can be grouped using Cluster Analysis (PR-II Analysis), then the machines in each cluster could be co-located and managed by one or more cross-trained operators.

How to Do PR-III Analysis

1 Compare all pairs of routings in Table 8.1 to find common sub-strings of operations that occur in two or more of the original routings (Figure 8.12).
2 Do a Cluster Analysis (PR-II Analysis) of these operation sub-strings.
3 For each cluster of sub-strings, aggregate them into a From-To Chart and generate a Layout Module (aka partial cell) for the machines in that cluster.

For example, with reference to Figure 8.12, the machines in the Layout Module M1 could be arranged in a flowline layout as follows: $\boxed{1 \& 6} \rightarrow \boxed{4 \& 8} \rightarrow \boxed{7 \& 9}$ and the machines in the Layout Module M2 could be arranged in a flowline layout as follows: $\boxed{1 \& 6} \rightarrow \boxed{10} \rightarrow \boxed{7 \& 11} \rightarrow \boxed{12}$. Did you notice that Machines #1, #6, and #7 repeat in both of these partial cells, as they did in the two cells in Figure 8.7?

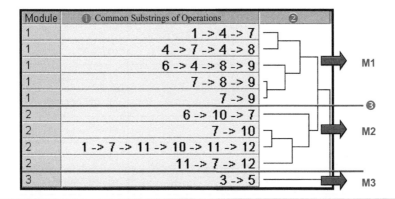

Figure 8.12 Partial cells (aka layout modules).

How to Use PR-III Analysis

Design of a Modular Layout: In a Functional Layout, if a part has to follow its manufacturing routing, then between every pair of machines, it will move in the traditional batch mode between two different departments. In the case of a Modular Layout, each module can be treated as a single machine or partial cell (if it contains two or more machines). Next, it is necessary to produce a From-To Chart that shows the aggregate flows between different modules. So the original routings for the parts in Table 8.1 must be rewritten to show the sequence in which each part visits different Layout Modules, as shown in Table 8.3. For example, the module M1 consists of Machines #1,

Table 8.3   Re-Expression of the Routings in Table 8.1 Using Layout Modules

Part No.	Sequence of Modules	Previous Routing
1	M1	(1→4→8→9)
2	M1→7	(1→4→7→4→8)→(7)
3	1→2→M1	(1)→(2)→(4→7→8→9)
4	M1	(1→4→7→9)
5	1→M2→9	(1)→(6→10→7)→(9)
6	M2→M1	(6→10→7)→(8→9)
7	M1	(6→4→8→9)
8	M3→2→M1	(3→5)→(2)→(6→4→8→9)
9	M3→M1	(3→5)→(6→4→8→9)
10	M1	(4→7→4→8)
11	6	6
12	M2	(11→7→12)
13	M2	(11→12)
14	M2	(11→7→10)
15	M2	(1→7→11→10→11→12)
16	M2	(1→7→11→10→11→12)
17	M2	(11→7→12)
18	6→M2	(6)→(7→10)
19	12	12

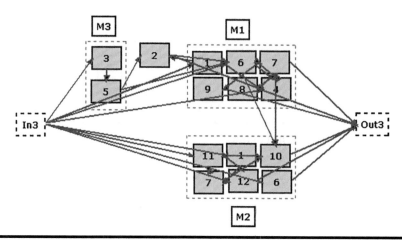

Figure 8.13   Modular Layout.

#4, #6, #7, #8, and #9. So the routing of Part #1 is just M1. Therefore, compared to moving from one machine in some department to another machine in another department in a Functional Layout, Part #1 would flow completely within a single module in a Modular Layout. The machines in each module could be operated by a single cross-trained employee, or at least fewer employees than there are machines. So, at least within each module, one-piece or small batch flow could occur as in a traditional cell. Due to the smaller sizes of the different modules in a Modular Layout, the typical travel distance between two modules will be shorter than if the travel were to occur between two departments in a Functional Layout. Does Figure 8.5 display a more orderly material flow, or does the Modular Layout in Figure 8.13?

Design of a Hybrid Flow Shop Layout: Imagine yet another layout for a machine shop or a fabrication shop that is neither Cellular nor Functional! Unlike the Modular Layout (Figure 8.13), a Hybrid Flow Shop Layout (Figure 8.14) is a strict linear arrangement of the Layout Modules. Thereby, as was observed in the case of CFL in Figure 8.11, all parts produced in the facility will follow a unidirectional flow path, starting from Receiving (IN) on the left and ending in Shipping (OUT) on the right. There could be some by-pass flows between non-adjacent modules. The key difference between a Flow Shop and a Hybrid Flow Shop is that the latter could have two or more different machines co-located in any stage of the shop. For example, in Figure 8.14, Stage #1 contains Machines #1, #2, #3, and #5. In a traditional Flow Shop, all of those machines would have been of any one type (#1 or #2 or #3 or #5). Between any two consecutive stages of the HFL, the WIP queued at each module could be better organized for visual management and prioritization.

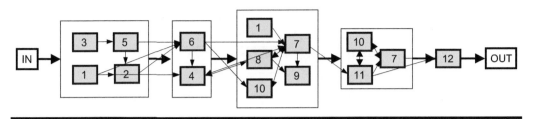

Figure 8.14   Hybrid Flow Shop Layout.

Conclusion

HMLV manufacturers, especially job shops, ought not to undertake a complete reorganization into a Cellular Layout where each cell is designed to make a specific part family. Significant changes in the customer base, part mix, and order volumes for each of the cells are usually the downfall of a Cellular Layout. *Unlike a Cellular Layout (which is inflexible and promotes single-piece flow) and a Functional Layout (which is flexible and promotes batch-and-queue production), any HCL is intermediate between these two traditional facility layouts!* An HCL is **both** Flexible **and** Lean (FLean). That is because an HCL is designed using a fusion of strategies for facility layout design such as (i) some of its machines will be grouped into cells, (ii) some of its functional departments will be retained as-is, (iii) some of its functional departments may be split and distributed at two or more locations across the factory, (iv) one or more machines may be drawn from each of two or more functional departments and grouped into partial cells (aka Layout Modules), etc.

Supplementary Reading

The document titled *Quick Read Guide on Product-Process Matrix Analysis* is a detailed description of PR-I Analysis.

The document titled *Quick Read Guide on Product-Routing Cluster Analysis* is a detailed description of PR-II Analysis.

The PowerPoint presentation titled *Design of a Cellular Layout for an Entire Facility* is the solution key for a facility layout design exercise that uses an expanded version of the data provided in Table 8.1.

The PowerPoint presentation titled *Production Flow Analysis: A Tool for Designing a Lean Hospital* opened my eyes to the tremendous possibilities for using PFA to design hospitals based on the Lean/Job Shop

Lean concepts. We took the data reported in this paper – Karvonen, S., Korvenranta, H., Paatela, M. & Seppala, T. (2007). Production flow analysis: A tool for designing a Lean Hospital. *World Hospitals and Health Services*, 43(1), 28–31 – and significantly expanded the insights on the layout design for the new hospital being designed using the PFAST outputs generated for that same data.

References

Merchant, M.E. (1975). The future of CAM (Computer Aided Manufacturing) systems. *International Workshop on Managing Requirements Knowledge, Proceedings of the National Computer Conference*, New York, pp. 793–799.

Ohno, T. (1988). *Toyota Production System: Beyond Large-Scale Production*. Portland, OR: Productivity Press.

Shingo, S. (1989). *A Study of the Toyota Production System from an Industrial Engineering Viewpoint*. Portland, OR: Productivity Press.

Chapter 9

How Data Mining Guides Various Production Flow Simplification Strategies

Earlier, we explained how the various outputs in a Production Flow Analysis and Simplification Toolkit (PFAST) Analysis Report can be used to design a Functional Layout or a Cellular Layout or Hybrid Cellular Layouts (HCLs) for any high-mix low-volume manufacturing facility. An HCL is intermediate between the traditional Functional and Cellular Layouts for any facility. Figure 9.1 shows the typical sequence of usage of various PFAST outputs.

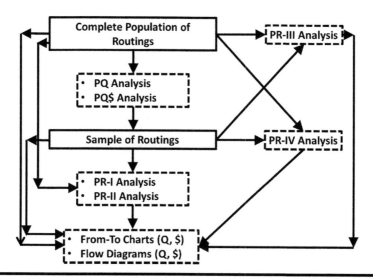

Figure 9.1   Typical sequence of usage for various PFAST outputs.

Variety of Flow Simplification Strategies Enabled by PFAST

Ulven Forging Inc., a custom forge shop, was the first job shop where we did an industry project to:

1. Validate PFAST in a real-world setting.
2. Implement Job Shop Lean.
3. Utilize a full-time IE (Industrial Engineering) intern to support the implementation of Job Shop Lean.

That work was done in 2004 and is described in a later chapter *Implementation of Job Shop Lean in a Forge Shop*. Since then we have executed many projects for different high-mix low-volume manufacturers that expressed interest in implementing Job Shop Lean. Every one of them agreed to first and foremost convert their factory layout to a Cellular Layout to the extent that it was possible and financially justifiable.

What we have learned from these projects is that a layout change is not the only strategy to reduce and simplify material flow in any high-mix low-volume manufacturing facility! Instead, different combinations of the PFAST outputs

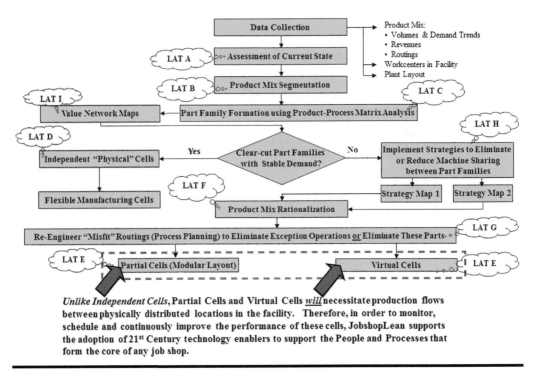

Unlike *Independent Cells*, Partial Cells and Virtual Cells <u>*will*</u> necessitate production flows between physically distributed locations in the facility. Therefore, in order to monitor, schedule and continuously improve the performance of these cells, JobshopLean supports the adoption of 21st Century technology enablers to support the People and Processes that form the core of any job shop.

Figure 9.2 Flowchart for using different LATs to implement Job Shop Lean.

help to offer a variety of flow reduction and simplification strategies to each HMLV manufacturer. Each of these specific strategies to simplify and streamline the existing material flows in a high-mix low-volume manufacturing facility using some combination of PFAST outputs is called a Lean Advisory Tool (LAT), as shown in Figure 9.2. Figure 9.2 also shows the typical sequence in which the LATs are implemented to improve flow in any high-mix low-volume manufacturing facility that wishes to implement Job Shop Lean.

The Appendix for this chapter provides a detailed explanation for each LAT using the relevant section in a workbook titled *Lean Advisory Tools for Job Shops*. Each section in the workbook explains one of the many different LATs that can be implemented using one or more of the outputs in the PFAST Analysis Report.

Management Actions Based on LAT-Aided Recommendations

Figure 9.3 provides a visual comparison of the material flow network in the Current and Modular Layouts that was proposed due to the existence of monuments that prevented the implementation of a true Cellular Layout.

The final recommendations for factory layout changes were to implement (i) a cell for the machines used to produce Part Family #1 and (ii) several Layout Modules (Partial Cells) for the machines used to produce Part Families #2 and #3. Ulven Forge Inc.'s implementation team evaluated and ranked each of the recommendations based on cost and time savings, feasibility, affordability, and ease of implementation. The following changes were made:

- An additional processing area was created in the Drop Hammer building (Machines #7 and #11) where Cleaning, Finishing, Packaging, and Shipping (Machine #55) were consolidated. This reduced order flow times and increased throughput.
- The 158-ton Trim Press (Machine #12) was replaced by a 440-ton press that was positioned next to the 5,000 lb. Hammer (Machine #7) to form an Upset Forging cell. This eliminated the transportation of large forgings to a distant 350-ton Trim Press (Machine #5). Also, a 350 kW Induction Heater (Machine #3 or #16) and conveyor were purchased and co-located in the cell. *There is about $8 million in Total Revenue flowing from Machine #7 to Machine #12, as shown in the $-type From-To Chart (Page A3 in LAT A).*

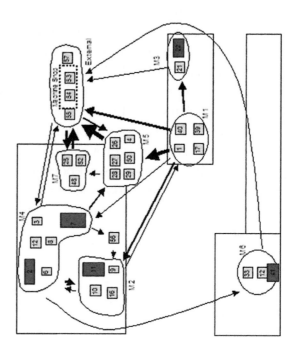

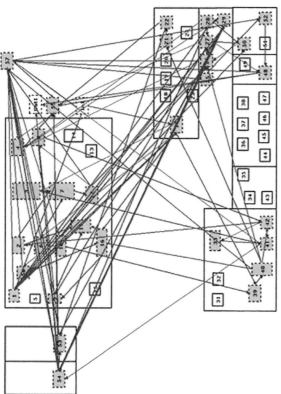

Figure 9.3 Material flow networks in Current Layout vs. Modular Layout.

- A new 2.5″ Upsetter (Machine #40) was purchased and positioned next to the 3,000 lb. Hammer (Machine #11) to form an Upset Forging cell. The benefits included a reduction in part travel distance and increased throughput at the Hammer. *There is about $2 million in Total Revenue flowing from Machine #40 to Machine #16, as shown in the $-type From-To Chart (Page A3 in LAT A). Also, Machines #16, #11, and #10 constitute one of the Layout Modules (16→11→10) that were identified, as shown in the PR-III Analysis dendrogram (Page E2 in LAT E).*
- The 1.5″ Upsetter (Machine #56) was replaced with a faster machine for shearing the same size of bar stock and positioned next to the 700-ton Press (Machine #1) to form an Upset Forging cell. With its faster upsetting/forging cycle time, it drastically increased throughput at the 700-ton press.
- An overhead crane was installed at the 5,000 lb. Hammer (Machine #7) to reduce piston change-out time, reduce die key tightening time, and improve product flow in the area.
- A portable Marvel Hacksaw (Machine #17) and 1.5″ Bar Shear were acquired.
- In their machine shop, a CNC (Computer Numerical Control) mill was acquired and positioned next to the EDM (Electric Discharge Machining) machine to reduce outsourcing costs and lead times because the company could make its own die sets.
- A new Magnaflux test machine was purchased and installed. This eliminated costs and reduced lead times associated with outside testing.

Appendices

Appendices for this chapter are available for download at https://www. crcpress.com/9781498740692

Supplementary Reading

The LATs are a precursor to a suite of apps that are being developed to replace PFAST. The workbook titled *Lean Advisory Tools for Job Shops* was developed to explain each of the different LATs that can be implemented using the PFAST Analysis Report. The data used in the PFAST Input File is from the first Job Shop Lean project that we did at a custom forge shop, Ulven Forging Inc.

Later in the book, we will introduce a Spaghetti Diagramming app, Sgetti, which combines and automates the manual work that has to be done to implement some of the LATs using the PFAST outputs, such as LAT A (Waste Assessment in the Current State) and LAT H (Evaluation of Current and Proposed Layouts).

Chapter 10

Improving Flow at *Any* Level in a Factory

Introduction

Production Flow Analysis (PFA) is an effective sequential strategy for analyzing the material flows at different levels in a single factory. Typically, PFA is implemented in four stages:

1. Factory Flow Analysis (*FFA*)
2. Group Analysis (*GA*)
3. Line Analysis (*LA*)
4. Tooling Analysis (*TA*).

Each stage in PFA seeks to improve the flow in a progressively smaller area of the factory. First, *FFA* evaluates the flows between shops (or buildings) in the factory to eliminate wastes due to transportation, communication delays, use of large containers for WIP (work-in-process), and use of bulk-handling material handling equipment to move the large containers over large distances. Next, *GA* evaluates the flows in *each* shop (or building) within the factory to implement manufacturing cells that will produce families of parts with identical (or similar) routings. Then, *LA* evaluates the flows between machines in *each* cell inside a shop. The layout of a cell is designed for efficient inter-machine material handling, multi-machine tending by any

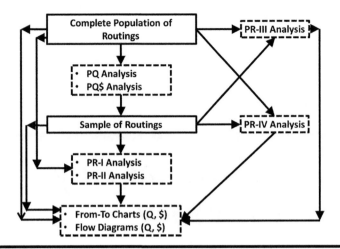

Figure 10.1   Typical sequence of usage for data mining algorithms in PFAST.

operator, and minimum wasted operator movements. Finally, *TA* evaluates the flows at *each* machine in a cell to optimize the workstation layout for ease of machine operation, parts inspection, rapid setup activities (machine loading/unloading, tool changes, fixture changes, machine cleanup), etc.

This chapter gives examples of how PFA can be used to analyze and improve flow at different levels of a factory, such as Factory, Shop, Cell, or Machine. The examples are intended to illustrate that PFA can be used to improve flow in any high-mix low-volume work system, regardless of the size and scope of that system. All that is needed to use PFA to simplify material flow in any work system is (i) a complete list of different "products" that are produced in it, (ii) a complete list of "work centers" that are used to make the products, (iii) a "routing" for each product that clearly shows the sequence in which different work centers in the system are used to produce the product, and (iv) a measure of importance/significance of each product. This data is effectively summarized using the acronym "PQR$" (P = Products, Q = Quantities, R = Routings, $ = Revenues[1]). PFA is implemented using the PFAST (Production Flow Analysis and Simplification Toolkit) software, which semi-automates the manual methods of PFA. It is the versatility of the suite of algorithms in PFAST that allows its use to implement all four stages of PFA depending on the size and scope of the work system in which flow has to be improved. PFAST processes the PQR$ data provided by any high-mix low-volume manufacturing facility using the different data mining algorithms shown in Figure 10.1.

---

[1] In more advanced studies, T = Time is considered with Q = Quantities to determine the frequency with which each product is produced, especially if it was ordered many times and not just once.

Examples of Factory Flow Analysis

Fabrication and Assembly of an Industrial Scale: Figure 10.2(a) shows the Indented Bill Of Routings for the complete product assembly. Figure 10.2(b) shows the Operations Process Chart for the complete product. The chart was produced from the Indented Bill Of Routings but also required interviews with key shop floor employees who were familiar with the complete product build process. The routings that were input to PFAST were developed from the Operations Process Chart. The improved layout for the factory that is shown in Figure 10.2(d) was developed mainly from the PR-IV Analysis (aka Product-Routing Analysis Type IV) shown in Figure 10.2(c) and the From-To Chart in the PFAST Analysis Report. For the purpose of comparison, Figure 10.2(e) shows the existing layout for the factory.[2]

Fabrication and Assembly of a Duct Assembly: In this project, we assisted an aerospace and defense supplier. First, we emailed them the case study described earlier in Figures 10.2(a–e) and explained the methodology for designing a facility layout using PFA. They provided the PFAST Input File for a multi-component duct assembly that also needed several outsourced operations. We ran the data through PFAST and emailed them the PFAST Analysis Report. Next, we followed up with a couple of conference calls to explain to their Lean implementation team how to utilize the PR-IV Analysis and From-To Chart to recognize part families and work centers connected by heavy traffic flow, respectively. Figure 10.3(a) shows the initial paths (and distances) that the product traveled in the factory. Figure 10.3(b) shows the new paths (and distances) that the product traveled in the factory after layout changes were made. Table 10.1 shows the results that they reported to us in return for our pro bono assistance.[3]

Make-To-Order Fabrication of Pipes: In this project, we assisted a high-mix low-volume pipe fabricator. We used PFAST to design the factory layout shown in Figure 10.4. In this proposed layout, we had two Cells and two Layout Modules (aka Partial Cells) but left *untouched* the Process Layout for the rest of the facility. We recommended that the two cells be immediately implemented. However, we did *not* recommend that the two Layout Modules be implemented because (i) there were too many machines in either module

---

[2] In the case of an assembled product, it is necessary to develop composite routings that connect the routings of the (1) component to (2) the subassembly it goes into to (3) the final product.

[3] PFAST was developed as part of a research contract that had been awarded to The Ohio State University by the Department of Defense. Such pro bono projects helped to please our sponsors above and beyond what they expected! ☺

(a)

```
15:44:14                                                              PAGE:     1
FUNCTION: MBIL                  MULTI-LEVEL BILL INQUIRY              07/21/1999

    PARENT: 2158002065-A        DESC: 2158,●,20K,5X7,4KD
        RV:         UM:EA       RUN LT:       1   FIXED LT:   3
      PLNR: 3KB                 PLN POL: N              DRWG: TC202034

      LEVEL     PT                       C PARTIAL                    Q M LT    SCR
    1...5...10 USE SEQN COMPONENT        T DESCRIPTION       QTY UM T B OFF    PCT

       1        0   010 WC[R]811ASMLY    R ASSEMBLY, F/S      1.5 HR I M    0   0.0
       1        0   900 TB201990         N 2158,FRAME,CS,       1 EA I M    0   0.0
        2       0   010 WC[R]763WELDM    R WELD,MANUAL WE      .5 HR I M    0   0.0
        2       0   020 WC[R]770WHLBR    R SHOTBLAST,WHEE      .1 HR I M    0   0.0
        2       0   030 WC[R]771HCFIN    R PAINT,HEAVY-CA      .5 HR I M    0   0.0
        2       0   900 T201972-4300     P ANGLE,CS,7GAX2       2 EA I M    0   0.0
         3      0   010 WC[R]763SHR16    R SHEAR 16'          .01 HR I M    0   0.0
         3      0   020 WC[R]763PRBRK    R FORM,PRESS BRA     .01 HR I M    0   0.0
         3      0   900 MZ1304010054     N SHEET,7GAX48.7   11.96 LB I B    0   0.0
        2       0   900 T201972-6700     P ANGLE,CS,7GAX2       2 EA I M    0   0.0
         3      0   010 WC[R]763SHR16    R SHEAR 16'          .01 HR I M    0   0.0
         3      0   020 WC[R]763PRBRK    R FORM,PRESS BRA     .01 HR I M    0   0.0
         3      0   900 MZ1304010054     N SHEET,7GAX48.7   18.63 LB I B    0   0.0
        2       0   900 TA201974         N 2158,BEARING,L       4 EA I B    0   0.0
        2       0   900 TB201971         P 2158,FRAME COR       4 EA I M    0   0.0
         3      0   010 WC[R]764WELDM    R WELD,MANUAL WE     .15 HR I M    0   0.0
         3      0   900 TB201970         P 2158,FRAME COR       1 EA I M    0   0.0
          4     0   010 WC[R]763SHR16    R SHEAR 16'          .01 HR I M    0   0.0
          4     0   020 WC[R]761PUNCH    R STRIPPIT            .1 HR I M    0   0.0
          4     0   030 WC[R]763PRBRK    R FORM,PRESS BRA     .02 HR I M    0   0.0
          4     0   900 MZ1301010034     N PLATE,1/4X72X1   10.05 LB I B    0   0.0
         3      0   900 TN201973         N 2158,BUMPER,CS       2 EA I B    0   0.0
       1        0   900 TB600364-1       N LC,745,10K,5KD       4 EA I B    0   0.0
       1        0   900 TC201989-1       N 2158,PLAT,MT,2       1 EA I M    0   0.0
        2       0   010 WC[R]763WELDM    R WELD,MANUAL WE     2.5 HR I M    0   0.0
        2       0   020 WC[R]770WHLBR    R SHOTBLAST,WHEE      .1 HR I M    0   0.0
        2       0   030 WC[R]771HCFIN    R PAINT,HEAVY-CA     .75 HR I M    0   0.0
        2       0   900 MZ0901020056     N NUT,3/4-10,HEX       4 EA I B    0   0.0
        2       0   900 T201962-6544     P CHAN,CS,1/4X2.       1 EA I M    0   0.0
         3      0   010 WC[R]763SHR16    R SHEAR 16'          .01 HR I M    0   0.0
         3      0   020 WC[R]763PRBRK    R FORM,PRESS BRA     .02 HR I M    0   0.0
         3      0   900 MZ1301010034     N PLATE,1/4X72X1   43.41 LB I B    0   0.0
        2       0   900 T201963-6431     P CHAN,CS,1/4X2.       3 EA I M    0   0.0
         3      0   010 WC[R]763SHR16    R SHEAR 16'          .01 HR I M    0   0.0
         3      0   020 WC[R]763PRBRK    R FORM,PRESS BRA     .02 HR I M    0   0.0
         3      0   900 MZ1301010034     N PLATE,1/4X72X1   68.12 LB I B    0   0.0
        2       0   900 T201965-4738     P CHAN,CS,1/4X2.       1 EA I M    0   0.0
         3      0   010 WC[R]763SHR16    R SHEAR 16'          .01 HR I M    0   0.0
         3      0   020 WC[R]763PRBRK    R FORM,PRESS BRA     .02 HR I M    0   0.0
         3      0   900 MZ1301010034     N PLATE,1/4X72X1   50.19 LB I B    0   0.0
        2       0   900 T201966-4738     P CHAN,CS,1/4X2.       1 EA I M    0   0.0
         3      0   010 WC[R]763SHR16    R SHEAR 16'          .01 HR I M    0   0.0
         3      0   020 WC[R]761PUNCH    R STRIPPIT            .02 HR I M    0   0.0
         3      0   030 WC[R]763PRBRK    R FORM,PRESS BRA     .03 HR I M    0   0.0
         3      0   900 MZ1301010034     N PLATE,1/4X72X1   50.19 LB I B    0   0.0
        2       0   900 TA201967         P FLAT,CS,3/4X3X       2 EA I M    0   0.0
         3      0   010 WC[R]763BDSAW    R SAW,BAND SAW       .01 HR I M    0   0.0
         3      0   020 WC[R]771VIKIN    R SHOTBLAST,VIKI     .01 HR I M    0   0.0
         3      0   900 MZ1307010089     N FLAT,3/4X3X20'    10.9 LB I B    0   0.0
        2       0   900 TA201968         P 2158,STIFFNR W       2 EA I M    0   0.0
         3      0   010 WC[R]763BDSAW    R SAW,BAND SAW       .01 HR I M    0   0.0
         3      0   020 WC[R]763ACRO     R MACHINE,ACROLO     .01 HR I M    0   0.0

                     *** continued on next page ***
```

Figure 10.2   (a) Indented Bill of Routings (IBOR) for the complete product.

(Continued)

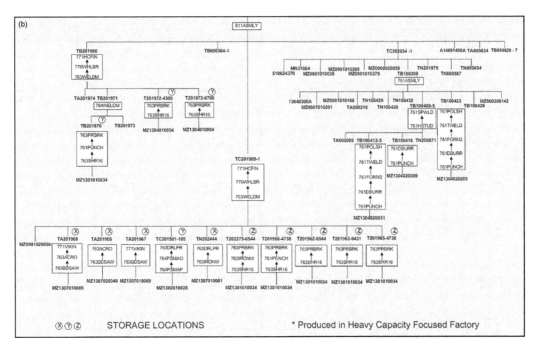

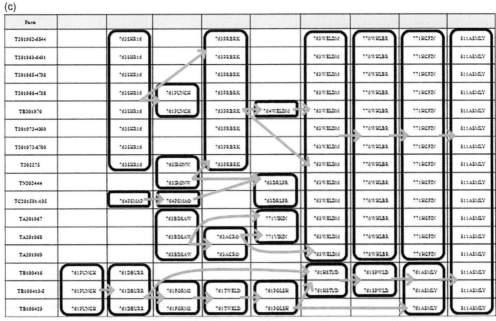

Figure 10.2 (CONTINUED) **(b) Operations process chart for the complete product. (c) PR-IV analysis of the routings in the operations process chart.**

(Continued)

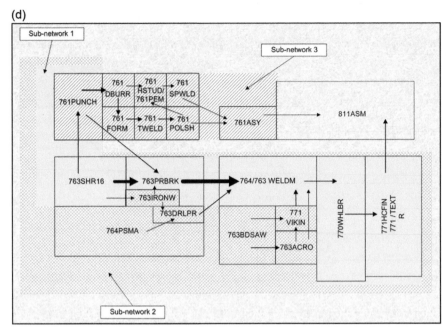

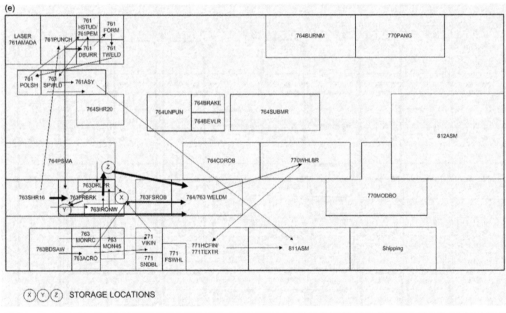

Figure 10.2 (CONTINUED) **(d) Proposed layout for the factory. (e) Existing layout for the factory.**

and (ii) it was more important that they "right-size" the single large washing line (Work center #825) which was a monument located in the center of the facility. "Right-sizing" required them to replace it with multiple washing stations (or smaller washing lines catering to different pipe geometries and size ranges). Otherwise, the WIP and queuing delays caused by this bottleneck work center could not be reduced.

In addition, the "long tail" in the PQ Analysis produced by PFAST indicated that (i) they were offering an extremely diverse catalog of products and (ii) they were accepting many orders of very small quantities[4] which resulted in numerous setups on the shop floor.

Also, the From-To Chart contained too many machines in the routings! This was because parts with similar, sometime identical routings, contained different Machine #s even when those machines were from the same functional group. Consequently, the PR-I Analysis matrix was sparse and the usual blocks of 1's representing part families were not recognizable.

Other recommendations that we made to this pipe fabricator were (i) the complex material flow in the existing factory layout would not be impacted significantly by investing first in an extensive re-layout of the factory, (ii) they should form an internal team to rationalize their product mix which would eliminate the large number of "Cats and Dogs" (or Strangers) for which their sales people were accepting orders, and (iii) they should "scrub" their routings to make them more amenable for a future analysis using PFAST.

Examples of Line Analysis

Welding Cell: In this project, the same aerospace and defense supplier referenced in Figure 10.3(a) and (b) provided another PFAST Input File for a large number of weldments produced for aircraft engines. We ran the data through PFAST. The PR-I Analysis indicated that the sample of routings corresponded to a single homogeneous part family because they were mostly identical or similar. So the project's goal reduced to designing the layout of a cell that would produce the entire family of weldments. There was no need to find part families! We emailed the complete PFAST Analysis Report to the aerospace and defense supplier with instructions on how to use only the From-To Charts and Flow Diagrams in the PFAST Analysis Report. They implemented the welding cell layout shown in Figure 10.5.

---

[4] Naturally, the small orders had small profit margins!

(a)

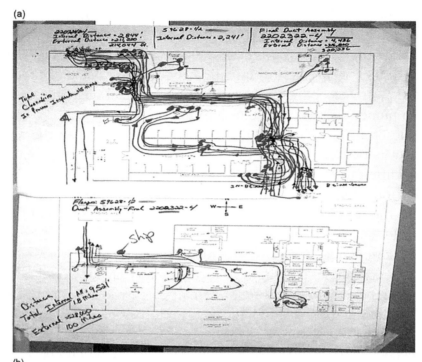

(b)

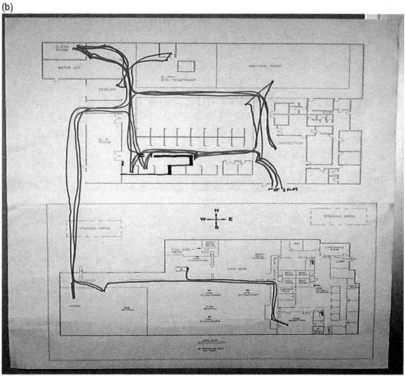

Figure 10.3 Travel distances for the duct assembly in (a) the initial. Travel distances for the duct assembly in (b) the new layouts

Table 10.1 Impact of Layout Changes on Key Performance Metrics for Duct Assembly

Metric	Before Layout Changes	After Layout Changes	% Reduction
Lead time	7 weeks	3.5 weeks	50
Cycle time	8 hours	6 hours	25
Part travel	2,450 ft	1,578 ft	36
Walking	3,150 ft	1,578 ft	50
WIP	360 pcs	200 pcs	44

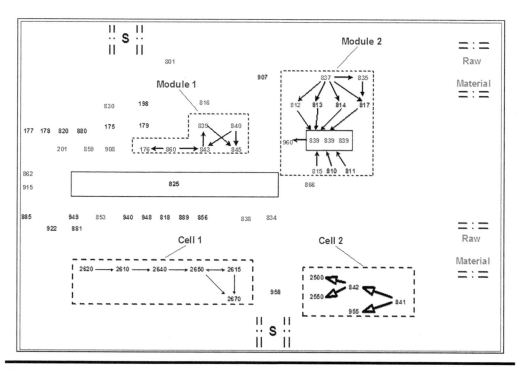

Figure 10.4 Hybrid layout for pipe fabrication job shop.

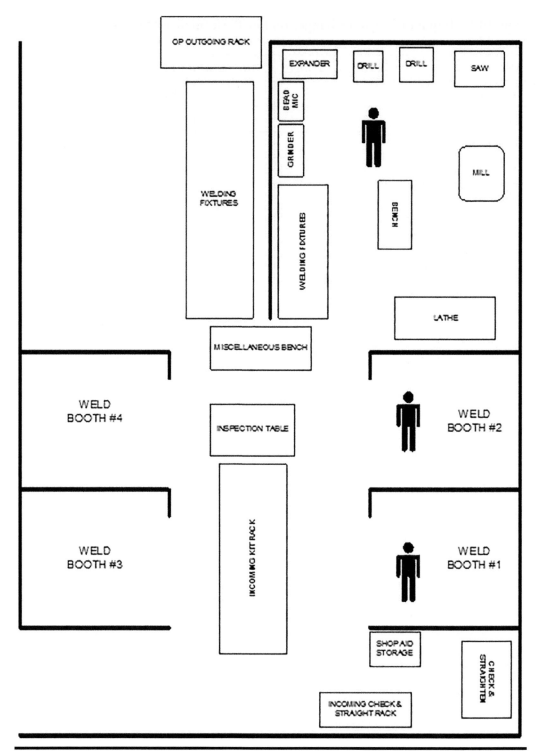

Figure 10.5　Layout for welding cell.

Unfortunately, since the weldments were used in fighter jet airframes, ITAR (International Traffic in Arms Regulations) rules prevented them from providing us specific data on financial benefits or other KPI (Key Performance Indicators) improvements gained from implementing the cell. However, we have reproduced the following comments that they made about the cell:

■ Co-located machines, equipment, tooling, and processes help to minimize parts transportation and waiting.
■ Emphasis is on FLOW!
■ Eliminated wasteful steps that impede the speed at which parts can flow through the assembly process.
■ Created a visual workplace that is self-explaining, self-regulating, and self-improving.
■ Waste has no place to hide!

The above comments did not come as a surprise because Cellular Manufacturing and Lean go hand-in-hand!

Grinding Cell: In this project, we designed a layout for a finishing cell in an investment casting (lost wax) job shop. The PFAST Input File contained the routings and Annual Volumes for upwards of 500 different castings. Only the From-To Charts and Flow Diagrams generated by PFAST were used to produce the Spaghetti Diagram for the Current cell and block layouts for the proposed cell layout, as shown in Figure 10.6. The proposed layout significantly reduced travel distances between most pairs of machines with significant volume of traffic flowing between them. Prior to the cell implementation, we organized a 5S event which helped to eliminate trash, broken furniture, and other clutter on the floor.

The castings were heavy. So they were pushed on floor-mounted roller conveyor segments that connected the workstations in the cell. In the new layout, we reduced the lengths of the different segments to achieve (1) FIFO (First In First Out) flow between the workstations and (2) limit how many castings would be in process at any given time inside the cell. Initially, there was considerable resistance to this idea both from the management and from the employees who worked in the cell. However, it was only a matter of time before they saw the WIP in the cell reduce as they pulled work into the cell to match the available manpower and realistic throughput limits of the cell.

The shortened conveyor segments *also* improved the material handling ergonomics and safety conditions in the cell. Previously, every cell operator tried to maximize the number of castings he/she processed without any

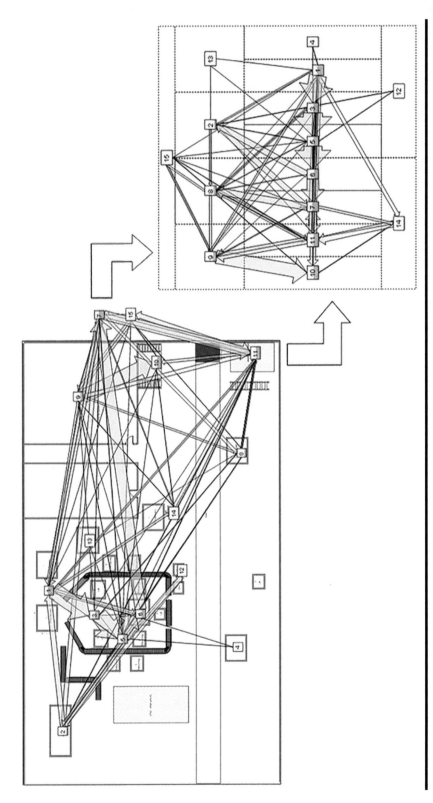

Figure 10.6 Spaghetti diagrams for current vs. proposed layouts for the grinding cell.

concern for the productivity of the other operators. In the new cell, no castings could be put on the floor if the conveyor segment leaving a workstation was full. This stopped the practice of lifting a heavy casting off the conveyor and putting it on the floor in order to start working on the next casting!

Examples of Tooling Analysis

Cold Forging Press WorkStation Layout: Setup time on any machine includes the time that the machine remains idle because the operator is moving to/ from different locations around the machine to perform activities required to run the next job. Figure 10.7(a) displays the movements of the operator around a cold forging press throughout a setup cycle. This was *before* any improvements were made in the operator's workspace around the press. Figure 10.7(b) displays the movements of the same operator after layout changes were made. Here is how PFA was used in this project. First, the sequence of steps performed by the machine operator during a complete setup cycle was determined. The location at which each step was performed was also noted. Next, this information was input to PFAST, which converted the single routing into a From-To Chart. The chart showed the frequency of trips between any pair of locations that the operator visited consecutively during a press setup, as shown in Figure 10.7(c). The thick (or thin) arrows in the Flow Diagram are a visual estimate of high (or low) frequency of moves between any two locations. The Q-type From-To Chart produced by PFAST was input to the STORM software for facility layout. Figure 10.7(d) illustrates how the STORM software was used to approximate a circular location grid with the press at its center. The theoretical layout for the press' workspace that STORM produced was given to the operator who "massaged" it to accommodate real-world constraints that the software failed to consider.

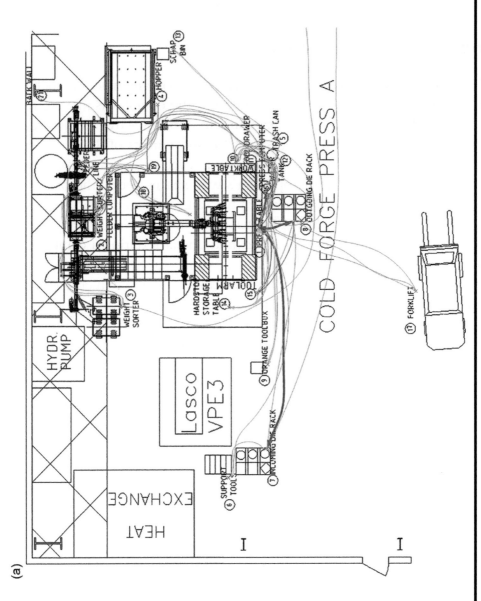

Figure 10.7 (a) Flow diagram for operator's movements during press setup before layout improvements.

(Continued)

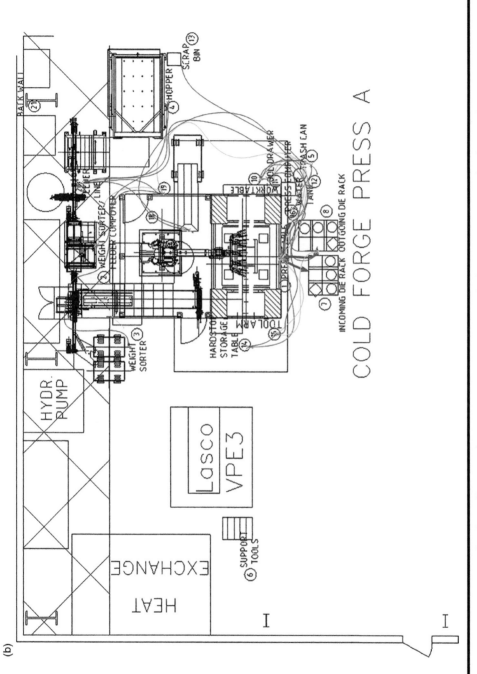

(Continued)

Figure 10.7 (CONTINUED) ((b) **Flow diagram for operator's movements during press setup** *after* **layout improvements.**

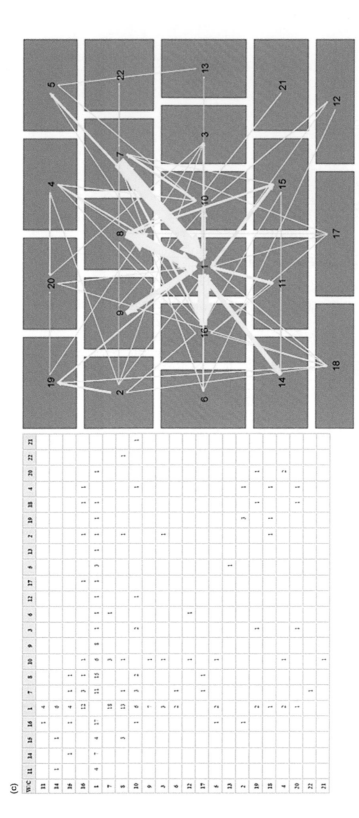

Figure 10.7 (CONTINUED) (c) From-To chart and flow diagram for operator's movements produced by PFAST.

(*Continued*)

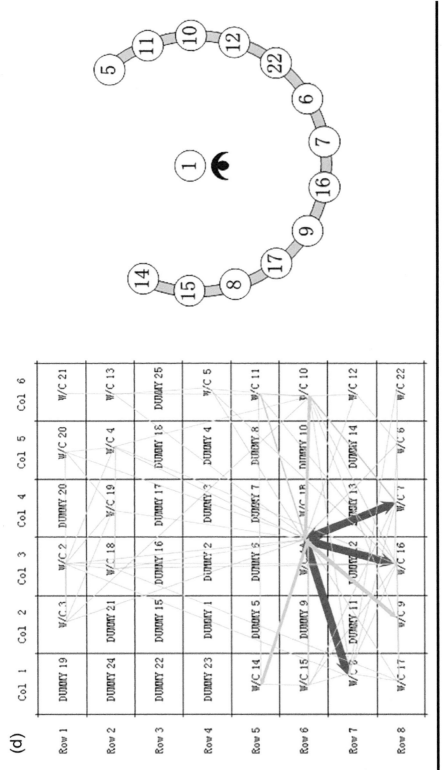

Figure 10.7 (CONTINUED) (d) STORM-generated layout vs. actual layout that was implemented.

Conclusion

PFA can be used to analyze and improve material flow in any high-mix workflow system, regardless of whether the "material" is products, people, tools, etc. If the workflow system is a traditional factory that manufactures and assembles products, then the workflows could be improved at different levels, such as the entire factory, a single shop in the factory like the machine shop, a single cell inside a shop, or a single machine inside any cell. All that is needed to use PFA to simplify material flow in any work system is (i) a complete list of the different "products" that are produced in the system, (ii) a complete list of "work centers" that are used to make the products, and (iii) a "routing" for each product that clearly shows the sequence in which different work centers in the system are used to produce the product. This data for each product is effectively summarized using the acronym "PQR$" (P = Products, Q = Quantities, R = Routings, $ = Revenues[5]).

---

[5] In more advanced studies, T = Time is also included with Q = Quantities to better clarify the frequency with which each product is produced.

Chapter 11

Industry Applications of Production Flow Analysis by IE Students

A Tribute to My Students

I feel privileged to have taught and mentored the students whose reports and presentations have been included in this chapter. They put into practice what they had learned in class in such an impressive fashion! The work they did is clear evidence of their own abilities and work ethic. I pray that all of them are successful and happy in their professional lives as Industrial Engineers (IE).

IE Tools Ought to Replace the Lean Tools

There is consensus in the Lean community that the Lean tools alone are never going to sustain a Lean implementation. That is because **nothing** can compensate for the lack of support from upper management! Still, compared with the many manual and computer-aided tools that IEs use, the manual pencil-and-paper Lean tools are incapable of solving complex problems. So, it is not just the lack of support from upper management that has prevented industry from reaping the full benefits from implementing Lean. It is also the over-reliance on simple manual tools and the rejection of far more powerful tools because "Toyota does not use them" (or did not use them in the previous century!).

Replacing "Textbook IE" with "Toyota IE"

While the Lean tools have their shortcomings, the IE that is underlying them is superior to the archaic IE that is taught in textbooks. Most IE textbooks contain no examples of how the IE concepts, methods, and tools they teach were actually put to work in the real world! Table 11.1 provides a blunt personal assessment of the differences between the IE that is taught in the classroom and the Toyota-style IE that is the backbone of Lean. Starting around 1999, I began complementing the mainstream textbooks I was using for IE courses that I was teaching at The Ohio State University with books on Lean. Since I had never worked in industry, the latter books were my only "look into the mind of Toyota". That is how I started blending the "Textbook IE" with the relevant "Toyota IE".

Courses That Merged the Classroom and the Factory Floor

Being a full-time IE faculty at The Ohio State University, I was unable to work full-time in industry to learn how practitioners were implementing Lean. For the same reason, I was unable to personally spearhead the adoption of my advanced research on Job Shop Lean. But the same could not be said for my students, both undergraduate and graduate! They were in a better position to work in industry and assess whether what I taught them in my classes worked in practice. So, I revamped all the courses I taught by **blending** Lean, IE, and OR (Operations Research) as follows:

1. I requested to be allowed to teach three core classes in the undergraduate curriculum – *Process Analysis and Improvement, Facility Layout,* and *Production Control and Scheduling* – and a graduate elective where I could teach the emerging BoK (Body of Knowledge) on *Job Shop Lean*. Each of these course syllabi appears in an Appendix for this chapter.
2. In each of the undergraduate courses, I replaced the outdated IE with the appropriate "Toyota IE" and related Lean tool(s).
3. In any course, if there was an OR model or computer algorithm to computerize the pencil-and-paper Lean tool, I would teach that too.
4. All four courses had a mandatory industry project that required students to work in teams at a local company that had agreed to host one or more teams.

Table 11.1 Some Differences between Academic and Hands-On (Toyota-Style) IE

IE Taught in Textbooks	IE That I Attribute to Toyota
• OR model is taught without explanation of what it takes to obtain the values for coefficients, upper and lower bounds, assumptions that may compromise the feasibility of implementation in industry, etc. • OR model makes assumptions and simplifications in the actual problem in order to realize a solution • OR model is taught out of an academic textbook with no case studies to demonstrate industrial application of the model	• Projects that are done are those which company leadership understands and supports ("I'd rather do what I understand instead of what is too complicated and tough to implement") • As the developer of the solution(s), be sure to work side-by-side with employees who will be affected by the solution(s) and ensure that they accept/implement the solution(s) • It is okay to solve many small problems for which radical changes will not be necessary (neither an OR model)
Students are recommended to go to the College of Business for courses on Lean Leadership, Change Management, Culture Change, Workforce Motivation, etc.	• Know, or at least be acutely aware of, the importance of soft skills to effect change • Gain acceptance for one's ideas by building trust among employees that changes will not be harmful to them
• Learning happens almost exclusively in the classroom • Industry relevance of course material is primarily delivered with, for example, Harvard Business Review case studies • Industry projects in a course are viewed by students as "being too much work" • Co-ops and internships never have faculty engaged/partnered with the students • Capstone Design project, which is done at the end of the program of study, is usually the only time when learning occurs by immersion in industry	• "Stand on the X" for hours and watch work being done in the area where improvement is sought • Go talk to the employees to find out the problems and their root causes on one's own – see for yourself, learn for yourself • Work, and problems related with doing it, is best learned by doing it oneself

(Continued)

Table 11.1 (Continued) Some Differences between Academic and Hands-On (Toyota-Style) IE

IE Taught in Textbooks	IE That I Attribute to Toyota
• Industry experience is not a requirement to teach IE courses • An engineering degree, let alone an IE degree, is not a requirement to teach IE courses • Sabbatical leave is not taken to gain industry experience but to do academic research to produce journal publications	• Have the ability to work side-by-side with line workers and supervisors is essential • Engage with employees and encourage them to implement their ideas for improving the product they make, the equipment and tools they use, their workplaces, etc.
Course on Methods Analysis and Time Studies	
Methods Analysis is an afterthought in the core curriculum	• Any and all work can be decomposed into value-added, non-value added and necessary-but-non-value-added elements • Cost reductions that do not eliminate employees can be achieved simply by eliminating the Seven Types of Waste in the entire organization • The ability/skill to recognize the Seven Types of Waste is best learned from co-ops, internships, and industry projects (at least never solely in a classroom)
Methods Analysis is done using archaic methods such as Flow Process Charts and Man-Machine Charts	Methods Analysis is done using more effective tools such as Value Stream Mapping, Standard Work Instructions, and 3Ps (Production, Preparation, and Process)

(Continued)

Table 11.1 (*Continued*) Some Differences between Academic and Hands-On (Toyota-Style) IE

IE Taught in Textbooks	*IE That I Attribute to Toyota*
Course on Facilities Planning	
The leading textbooks do not have a single case study to demonstrate that subject matter in them has practical application	• Teach the OR underlying the manual Lean tools such as Value Stream Mapping, Spaghetti Diagrams, U-shaped cells, Water Striders, etc. • Term project requires that students do a team-based project in industry where they must demonstrate how they applied what is being taught every week
Course on Production Planning and Control	
The Economic Order Quantity (EOQ) model for inventory control is taught as a calculus problem	• Utilize setup reduction to make setup time (and cost) insignificant when making lot size decisions • Make-To-Order policy – do not batch produce assuming significant setup time and put excess inventory in stock
The Economic Production Quantity (EPQ) model for inventory control is taught as a calculus problem	The EPQ model for inventory control provides the science underlying the ultimate goal of Single-Piece Flow in any work environment
Material Requirements Planning	• Generate a level-loaded mixed model production plan • Design flexible lines with minimal setup change times to adapt to product mix changes

(Continued)

Table 11.1 (*Continued*)   Some Differences between Academic and Hands-On (Toyota-Style) IE

IE Taught in Textbooks	IE That I Attribute to Toyota
• Heuristic scheduling of job shops with zero transfer delays • Finite Capacity Scheduling • ERP (Enterprise Resource Planning) • MES (Manufacturing Execution System)	• Reduce the large job shop to a network of smaller autonomous work cells • Utilize rough-cut shop loading strategies such as Drum-Buffer-Rope, three-bin Kanban locations, Bottleneck Loading, etc. • Have morning huddles with employees to assign job priorities • Allow firefighting and expediting as long as the customer is happy • Customers do tolerate tardiness, suppliers will dictate delivery dates, machines will fail, employees will fall sick – yet, it is amazing what good supervisors and cooperative employees can do when they are asked to "move heaven and earth"
Every possible OR optimization approach – Traveling Salesperson Problem, Queuing Theory, Mixed Integer Programming – has been used to schedule and sequence jobs on the single capacity-constrained machine	• Show how setup reduction and product variety reduction help to minimize the need for setup-dependent sequencing of jobs

(Continued)

Table 11.1 (*Continued*)   Some Differences between Academic and Hands-On (Toyota-Style) IE

IE Taught in Textbooks	IE That I Attribute to Toyota
• Lot sizes are based on queuing theory (which implicitly assumes batch production) • Schedules are generated in a back office away from the shop floor	• Design the layout to place consecutive pairs of work centers in close proximity with each other • Production rate of "supplier work center" is controlled by "customer work center" using physical or electronic signals (kanbans) • Visual monitoring of buffer inventories between work centers • "Go See" scheduling to replenish on-hand inventories of different products (like when the cooks in the kitchen come out to replenish food in various dishes at a Chinese buffet)
• A course on Manufacturing Processes course is absent from the core curriculum • Manufacturing Processes courses offered in other departments do not cover the topics of interest to IEs	• Add the Manufacturing Processes course back into the curriculum • Add a second course – Mfg. Eng. – that teaches IE-related aspects of Lean such as standardization, setup reduction, error-proofing, automation, Total Productive Maintenance, Lean automation, right-sized equipment, 3P, etc.
PowerPoint presentations are the de facto mechanism for reporting on any project	• A3 Report • PowerPoint slides are presented only if and when more details are needed

Programs for an IE Department to Engage with Industry[1]

Every industry project that a team of students did in any course helped me to assess whether what I was teaching was applicable in industry. However, the course projects were just one way in which the students and I learned if the blend of Lean, IE, and OR that I was teaching them worked in practice. In addition to the courses, I leveraged all of the co-curricular and extra-curricular programs to engage with industry that a strong IE department, such as the one at The Ohio State University, gives its students and faculty:

- Independent Study Projects
- Senior Capstone Design Projects
- Undergraduate Honors Theses
- Masters Non-Thesis Projects
- Masters Theses
- Internships
- Sponsored Research Grants
- Consulting
- Workshops
- Presentations to industry attendees at the Annual Job Shop Lean Conference.

All of the above programs allowed me to work with a large number of students who applied what I taught them in my courses during the industry projects that had been assigned to them. Each project yielded a close-out report or presentation that helped to assess if the **blend** of IE, Lean, and OR was theory that worked in practice.

Appendices

Appendices for this chapter are available for download at https://www.crcpress.com/9781498740692.

---

[1] If you would be interested in receiving an electronic copy of a report that provides details about the scope, deliverables, and cost for each of the programs in the Industry Outreach and Engagement portfolio of an IE department, please email me at ShahrukhIrani1023@yahoo.com.

Supplementary Reading

This chapter showcases some of the presentations and reports that were prepared by IE students for the projects they did in industry. Some of the projects were done for one or more of the core courses on IE that I taught them. Others were done as internships I arranged for them at companies interested in implementing Job Shop Lean. Table 11.2 gives details about each project that was done by different students for different courses that I taught at The Ohio State University.

Table 11.2   Details about Projects Done by Different Students

Sponsor Company	Student(s) Who Did the Project	Brief Description of the Project
Bula Forge & Machine Inc.	Bryan Wang	This presentation titled Results and Experiences from Implementing the Quick-Start Approach to Job Shop Lean in a Custom Forge Shop describes the work that Bryan did during his internship.
Enginetics Aerospace	Po-Hua Tseng	This Masters Non-Thesis Report titled *Designing a Flexible and Lean Manufacturing Facility using a Large Representative Sample of Different Parts* describes the work that Po-Hua did during his internship at a commercial and defense aerospace manufacturer.
Guardian Automotive	Alwyn Aliwarga	This presentation titled *CSM/Lean* (CSM = Common Sense Manufacturing) describes the work that Alwyn did during his internship to complement and enhance a company's ongoing implementation of Lean with relevant IE and Job Shop Lean practices.
Hirschvogel Inc.	Alwyn Aliwarga	This presentation titled *Learning to See and Seeing the Whole Using Value Network Mapping* describes the work that Alwyn did at a Tier 1 forging facility for his Master of Science degree in IE. He demonstrated that a Lean implementation in a high-mix high-volume facility can be done without using Value Stream Mapping. The Masters Non-Thesis report that Alwyn wrote based on this work is included.

(Continued)

Table 11.2 (*Continued*) Details about Projects Done by Different Students

Sponsor Company	Student(s) Who Did the Project	Brief Description of the Project
Horton Emergency Vehicles	Alwyn Aliwarga	This presentation titled *Project Review: Back-End Facility Design* describes the work that Alwyn during his internship to streamline the flow of a large variety of parts that were produced in a Fabrication Shop. This shop was the "back end" of a single assembly line that built a variety of ambulances. It was ideally suited for the implementation of Job Shop Lean because it had to produce different kits of parts that had to be delivered per a timed schedule to different stations in the assembly line.
Maritime Castings Repair Facility	Dan Gallo	This presentation titled *Implementing Job Shop Lean in a Casting Repair Facility* describes the work that Dan did during his internship to implement Job Shop Lean in a captive machine shop adjacent to a foundry owned by the same company. The Final Report that was submitted to the agency that funded our work is included.
OSU (Ohio State University) Medical Center	Nirikshina Gowd	This Masters Non-Thesis Report titled *Equipment Flow Analysis (EFA) and Application of Lean Principles in Hospital Operations* describes the work that Nirikshina did for her Master of Science degree in IE. She used the method of Production Flow Analysis to analyze the availability and utilization of patient transport equipment in a large hospital complex subject to factors such as the layout of the Medical Center, volumes of patient flows between and within buildings, communications between dispatchers and patient transporters, etc.
Trafficware	Ashwin Justus Amol Musale Azhar Nawaz	This Independent Study Project Report titled *How to Speed Product Flow in the 980X Controllers Cell* describes the work that Ashwin, Amole, and Azhar did during their co-curricular project to get hands-on IE experience. They supported one of my consulting projects to improve throughput in a manual assembly cell.

(Continued)

Table 11.2 (*Continued*)   Details about Projects Done by Different Students

Sponsor Company	Student(s) Who Did the Project	Brief Description of the Project
Trinity Forge	Nathan Huffmann John Schott	This presentation titled *Process Analysis to Improve Tooling Management in a Custom Forge Shop* describes the work that Nathan and John did during their internship in a custom forge shop. Their project focused on the preparation, transportation, post-use put-away and storage of forging dies and related tooling that had to be sent to different forging presses in the forge shop. In the words of the VP of Trinity Forge, "What an eye opener this Lean Tooling project has been. This project will affect tooling movement (in our shop) for years to come".
UniPrint	Natalie Dexter Emilie Hehl Colleen Lorencen	This report titled *An IE Student's Guidebook for Facility Assessment and Redesign using Job Shop Lean Best Practices* describes the work that Natalie, Emilie, and Colleen did to apply what they were taught in the two courses on *Facility Design* and *Production Control and Scheduling* that I taught in the same quarter. Quoting from Page 1 of their guidebook, "This document has been created to serve as a guidebook that will demonstrate how to successfully evaluate a facility through the use of Lean Manufacturing, Theory Of Constraints and other Industrial Engineering techniques".[1]
Xunlight Corporation	Alwyn Aliwarga	This presentation titled *Xunlight Operational Improvements: Facility Design* describes the work that Alwyn did during his internship in the Module Assembly area of a low-volume hi-tech start-up assembly facility.

[1] After the quarter ended, the team volunteered to continue working with UniPrint to implement some of their recommendations.

Chapter 12

Production Flow Analysis Using Metrics-Aided Visual Assessment of Material Flow Diagrams

A *Different* Strategy to Reduce Both Waste and Lead Time

Planning for effective flow in any system, regardless of whether it is the entire factory (or hospital) or a single machine in the factory (or Operating Room in the hospital), requires the consideration of flow principles and flow patterns. Effective flow involves the progressive movement of materials, information, people, etc. between workstations without delays due to the use of slow material handling equipment, large distances of separation between many pairs of "supplier → customer" work centers, late arrivals of orders to work centers, etc.

In a previous chapter, we had presented the following three principles of *Design For Flow* that guide the design of any factory layout:

1. *Minimize flow:* Flow becomes necessary only when two or more different work centers are required to produce a product. Minimizing flow represents the work simplification approach to material flow. This approach includes the following:

a. Eliminating flow by planning for the delivery of materials, information, or people directly to the point of ultimate use and eliminating intermediate steps.

b. Minimizing multiple flows by planning for the flow between two consecutive Points Of Use (POU) to take place in as few movements as possible, preferably one.

c. Combining flows and operations wherever possible by planning for the movement of materials, information, or people to be combined in a processing step.

2. *Maximize directed flow paths:* A directed flow path is an uninterrupted flow path progressing directly from the origin to destination. An uninterrupted flow path is a flow path that does not intersect with other paths. Congestion occurs due to interruptions in flow when flow paths intersect. A directed flow path progressing from origin to destination is a flow path with no backtracking (which would increase the length of the flow path). Forward, Backtrack, and Cross flows in any facility layout can be considered to be good, acceptable, and bad, respectively.

3. *Minimize the cost of flow:* The cost of flow depends on a variety of factors, such as volume and weight of the products being moved, the distance of travel, the method for material handling, the speed and frequency of travel, the quantity of product being moved per trip, etc. For example, the least cost of material handling between two workstations would be when, as soon as one unit of product is completed at one workstation, it is automatically ejected from that workstation into a short and inclined chute (or a roller conveyor). It rolls down the conveyor and reaches the operator at the next workstation which is immediately adjacent to the work center that just processed the product. Gravity is free and available 24/7! This principle can be viewed from either of the following two perspectives:

a. Minimize handling that requires walking, manual travel, and motions by an operator.

b. Eliminate manual handling by mechanizing or automating flow to allow workers to operate their equipment or perform other value-adding tasks that have been assigned to them.

In addition, poor shop floor communications between the individual work centers, material handlers, and the Production Control and Scheduling office (or department) can increase the costs of flow. Large distances of separation between two work centers often cause (i) work completed at any work center to become work-in-process

(WIP) at that work center because the material handler did not arrive immediately to pick it up and move it to the next work center and/or (ii) work completed at any work center becomes WIP at the next work center because, at the time that the material handler delivered the work to the next work center, that work center already had a large queue of WIP to work on. Therefore, large travel distances between consecutive operations help to increase the costs due to (i) material handling, (ii) WIP inventory carrying costs, and (iii) queuing delays.

Assembly Line vs. Job Shop Layouts

In the typical Toyota factory, every product flows through the same sequence of workstations on any one of their automobile assembly lines. These workstations are connected by a conveyor that runs under the floor (or is ceiling-mounted). The "single-piece flow" of products from one workstation to the next workstation in a FIFO (First In First Out) sequence is a fundamental advantage that only an OEM (Original Equipment Manufacturer) like Toyota enjoys. Sadly, this fundamental advantage of linear material flow in the factory is not enjoyed by the 1,000's of machine shops, forge shops, fabricators, etc. who cannot adopt assembly line manufacturing!

In the typical machine shop or forge shop or fabrication shop, their products cannot be produced on assembly lines. By default, the facility layout in any of these manufacturing facilities tends to be a Process/Functional Layout. That is a bad choice of layout for any high-mix low-volume (HMLV) manufacturer! In a Process Layout, the travel distance between each pair of consecutive operations in any product's routing is large enough to prevent "single-piece flow" (Transfer Batch Size = 1). This automatically results in the batch-and-queue mode of production that will **surely** result in material flow that produces significant amounts of the Seven Types of Waste **daily**. By default, any waste helps to inflate the Lead Time quoted for delivery of any order.

Bad Facility Layouts Automatically Produce Waste

The core philosophy underlying the Toyota Production System (TPS) is the pursuit and elimination of the *Seven Types of Waste* (**T**ransportation, **I**nventory, **M**otion, **W**aiting, **O**verproduction, **O**verprocessing, and **D**efects

aka **TIMWOOD**) in any and every aspect of the Toyota enterprise.
Quoting from Toyota's website, "(The *Toyota Production System* is) a production system which is steeped in the philosophy of the complete elimination of *all* waste imbuing all aspects of production in pursuit of the most
efficient methods". But we have entered the 21st century where the customer wants the manufacturer to make **what** he/she wants **when** he/she
wants it for **how much** he/she wishes to pay! So, a HMLV manufacturer
must be judicious about emulating the manufacturing practices of a repetitive assembly line manufacturer like Toyota! *If the manufacturing facilities
of the majority of US manufacturers operate more like job shops*, why should
they be designed, operated, and managed as if they were repetitive assembly lines?

If a HMLV manufacturing facility has a Process/Functional layout, then it
automatically generates significant amounts of Seven Types of Waste **daily**
as explained below:

1. *Transportation:* When the travel distance between two consecutive
   work centers that process a batch of product increases, material handling costs will also increase. That is because the labor consumed and
   usage of material handling equipment for transferring each batch of
   product between the two work centers will increase.

2. *Inventory:* When two consecutive work centers that process a batch
   of product are separated by a large distance, each unit produced at
   the "supplier" work center cannot be immediately transferred to the
   next location, the "customer" work center. The operator at the "supplier" work center will produce a large batch of parts before signaling the material handler to come and take the batch of parts to the
   "customer" work center. Thereby, until the time that the entire batch
   is completed at the "supplier" work center and moved to the "customer" work center, the WIP during that period of time grows from 0
   to the size of the batch. According to *Little's Law*, if the average time
   to complete an order (aka, Order Flow Time) increases and production volumes remain steady, then WIP inventory in the system will
   increase.

3. *Motion:* It is common practice for a machine operator to also do the
   work of a material handler. First, he/she goes looking for the forklift truck (or pallet jack or crane) that is needed to pick up and move
   the batch that he/she completed to the location of the next operation. Having found the material handling equipment, he/she returns

to his/her machine. Next, he/she picks up the container(s) holding the batch and walks to the location of the next operation. Having completed the delivery, he/she leaves the material handling equipment at the location that they just visited and walks back to his/her machine. But, as is usually the case, if he/she meets one or more friends during the return walk, then he/she spends some time to "shoot the breeze" with each friend!

4. *Waiting:* Even after a batch of parts is completed at a machine, it usually takes time for the material handler who is responsible for moving the batch to arrive, pick up the batch, and move it to the next location. What about the time it took him/her to find the material handling equipment that he/she needed? Even after the batch is delivered to the next location, it may have to wait for batches received from other machines that will be processed earlier because those batches arrived earlier. Also, it is often the case that, when two work centers are far apart, the material handlers tend to make fewer trips between them which results in Waiting delays.

5. *Overproduction:* In the typical HMLV factory, the layout tends to be a Process/Functional layout where similar/identical equipment is co-located in a department. Production control and scheduling are done using the ERP (Enterprise Resource Planning) system. Even if there are morning huddles and daily gemba walks by management, there is limited communication between the supervisors and operators who work in different departments *throughout* any shift. Given this near-total absence of real-time communications throughout any shift, blind reliance is placed on a production schedule that is usually produced by the ERP system. **Unfortunately**, the typical ERP system uses an MRP (Material Requirements Planning) engine to schedule production. Thereby, MRP encourages the production of large batches because (i) it assumes that capacity is infinite, (ii) it tends to aggregate orders for the same product whose due dates are far apart in order to reduce number of setups and increase machine utilization, and (iii) it relies on demand forecasts to plan production. It is no surprise that Taiichi Ohno, the father of the TPS, rejected the suggestion to adopt MRP software when he was designing his universally embraced production system.

6. *Overprocessing:* Every time that a product has to be transported from one machine to another, the question arises whether that operation on a different machine is **really** necessary. In fact, many of

the modern-day advancements in Product Design, Manufacturing Processes, Manufacturing Equipment, etc. seek to minimize the number of steps in a product's manufacturing routing that must be performed on different machines! For example, Additive Manufacturing and Multi-function Machining Centers combine operations required to produce a complete/final product which eliminates transportation steps.

7. *Defects (scrap or rework):* If one-piece flow from a current operation to the next operation is not feasible, then an operator could end up producing and moving an entire batch of defective products to the next operation. When the operator at the next location rejects the entire batch, even if the batch is not scrapped, the cost of rework is surely incurred! Imagine how much more this cost and delay would increase if that same batch was sent to a centrally located Inspection department? Again, it is not surprising that the TPS is built on respect for **and** trust in their employees who are well-trained and whose workmanship ensures high FTT (First Time Through) quality of the parts they produce.

Production Flow Analysis of *Any* Material Flow System Using Spaghetti Diagrams

In its traditional form, a Spaghetti Diagram (also referred to as a Flow Diagram or Material Flow Map by Industrial Engineers) shows the actual path traveled by any part produced in a facility. The path is traced on a current layout of the facility by drawing a line to connect the locations of the machines visited by the part per the sequence of processing steps specified in the part's routing. Practitioners often refer to a Flow Diagram as a "Spaghetti Diagram" because, if each routing in a large sample of routings were a noodle that was stretched and tied around each machine per the sequence of machines specified in the routing, the resulting material flow in the facility would invariably look chaotic like a bowl of spaghetti. Even if a single diagram were drawn that displays the material flow in the current layout of **any** manufacturing or service work system, it is guaranteed to point out opportunities to make beneficial improvements in the layout, material handling, communication, and other aspects of that system. The individual (or kaizen team) using the diagram will **surely** have their "Aha!" moments to discover opportunities for flow improvement.

It is easy to understand why the Flow Diagram is a hugely popular tool in the toolkit of Lean and/or Six Sigma practitioners. Most of them tend to work on projects to improve flow in low-mix high-volume systems, as in assembly systems. Due to the low variety of products being produced *repetitively* in an assembly system, there is a small number of different routings that need to be mapped. So, even if several Flow Diagrams had to be drawn, they would not take much time to generate. And the conclusions drawn them will surely impact flow in the entire assembly system! For example, one of the Appendices for this chapter presents all the ideas for reducing the total distance traveled by a single forging being produced in a custom forge shop. All of the ideas to reduce the total time to complete that forging, the total labor cost of moving that forging, etc. were obtained simply from visual analysis of the Spaghetti Diagram. It was generated by connecting step-by-step the locations of the operations that appeared one-by-one in the routing of that forging onto the current layout of the forge shop.

Motivation

If Spaghetti Diagrams are used to evaluate material flow in HMLV work systems involving 100's of different routings, the "pencil-and-paper" option for drawing one (or more) Flow Diagrams and sole reliance on visual diagnosis of the diagram(s) will prove to be a nightmare! That is because the manual approach for generating a Flow Diagram has significant shortcomings: (i) It takes considerable time to map a significant number of product routings, (ii) it will take equal (if not more!) time to generate a diagram for each and every change that is made in the current layout of the system, and (iii) if a significant number of product routings are to be mapped, the resultant diagram will surely become too "messy" for visual diagnosis.

This chapter introduces a software tool, **Sgetti**, which has the potential to make any and every manually drawn Spaghetti Diagram a thing of the past. The app can easily handle the complexity of mapping a large number of different routings and overcome the tedium of doing the same by hand! **IF** the routings that would be used to draw any diagram manually could be entered into an Excel spreadsheet as a sequence of steps, then Sgetti makes it unnecessary to have to manually draw a Spaghetti Diagram and modify/manipulate it repeatedly to evaluate different layout options!

An earlier chapter (Chapter 5) described how Production Flow Analysis (PFA) helps to analyze and improve material flow at four levels of the typical manufacturing enterprise – Factory, Shop, Cell, and Machine. But what if we were to generalize the application of PFA and aspire to improve flow in any HMLV work system that displays a complex material flow map? Sgetti can be applied to a broad range of material flow systems! The only requirements for using Sgetti to visualize the material flow map for a high-mix work system are that:

1. The system has a large number of different "machines".
2. The system has a layout that clearly shows all the "machines" in different locations.
3. The system produces a variety of "products" with different "routings".
4. Each "routing" could be manually traced in the current layout.

Based on the above analogy, the flow of any number of different "materials", such as products, tools, people, documents, etc., in various work systems could be visualized by suitably defining the "products", "machines", and "routings" for that work system. Table 12.1 lists examples of high-mix work systems that could be visualized using Flow Diagrams generated by Sgetti.

Table 12.1 Work Systems That Can Be Visualized with the Sgetti App

Work System	Product	Machine	Routing
Factory	One or more assembled products that are comprised of components and subassemblies	Buildings in the factory that house one or more departments	• Complete BOM (Bill Of Material) of each product • Sequence in which the final product visits different departments • Sequence in which each subassembly visits different departments • Sequence in which each component that goes into a subassembly or a final product visits different departments

(Continued)

Table 12.1 (*Continued*)   Work Systems That Can Be Visualized with the Sgetti App

Work System	Product	Machine	Routing
Shop	• Subassemblies, especially if welding is done to produce large fabrications • Single/individual components	• Work centers • Individual pieces of process equipment (saws, lathes, mills, CMMs, etc.)	• BOM of each (complete) sub- assembly • Sequence in which each subassembly visits different work centers or individual machines • Sequence in which each component visits different work centers or individual machines
Cell	• Subassemblies, especially if welding is done to produce large fabrications • Single/individual components	Individual pieces of process equipment (saws, lathes, mills, CMMs, etc.)	• Sequence in which each subassembly visits different machines • Sequence in which each component visits different machines
Machine	• Subassemblies, especially if welding is done to produce large fabrications • Single/individual components	• Locations around the machine that are visited (or controls on the machine that are adjusted) during each step of the setup cycle • Tools and fixtures that are used (or loaded/unloaded) for each operation performed on the machine	Sequence in which all the tasks are done to complete a process, such as machine setup
Office	Documents	• People • Departments	Sequence in which a document is touched by different people (or departments)

(Continued)

Table 12.1 (*Continued*)   Work Systems That Can Be Visualized with the Sgetti App

Work System	Product	Machine	Routing
Hospital	Patient	Departments that provide care/ treatment to different patients	Sequence in which the patient visits (or is visited by personnel from) different departments
Kitchen	Any activity such as cooking a meal, hosting a lunch meeting, baking a cake, hosting a Thanksgiving dinner, etc.	Items stored in all cabinets, the refrigerator, drawers, etc.	Sequence in which the different locations in the kitchen were visited to get the necessary items required for each activity
Buffet	Plate filled by a customer on each visit to the various buffet stations	Food container that holds a specific food item on the buffer menu	Sequence in which different food containers were visited and the items in them were scooped into his/ her plate
Grocery store	A customer	The aisle where a class of grocery item is stored, e.g., cereals	The shortest travel path that connects all the aisles in which the different items in the customer's grocery list are stored

How Does a Spaghetti Diagram Expose Poor Material Flow in *Any* Facility Layout?

Do travel distances separate pairs of work centers that are consecutively used often? In a Spaghetti Diagram, if a From-To Chart is computed for the entire product mix and the flows in this chart are then mapped on the current layout, then a bad layout will exhibit long thick arrows between pairs of work centers that have high volumes of material flow between them.

Are the majority of work locations with heavy traffic between them located close to each other? This can be assessed by eyeballing the diagram and counting the number of pairs of work centers that are connected by long thick arrow.

Is there a continuous flow along a linear or curvilinear path, or do the lines look like "a tangled pile of noodles"? This can be assessed by following the routings of parts that have the highest individual volumes of flow.

Is there heavy bi-directional traffic in one or more material handling aisles (or corridors)? This can be assessed by eyeballing the flow directions of different arrows with respect to one or more vertical (or horizontal) material handling aisles.

Is there considerable cross traffic? Cross traffic in a facility layout is where flow path(s) of one or more part(s) intersect each other. A good facility layout should display few intersecting paths to prevent congestion and safety hazards, especially if heavy-duty material handling equipment operating in aisles that cross each other were to collide.

Is there a considerable backtracking? Flow backtracking in a facility layout is where material flow in a material handling aisle occurs in both directions. This is undesirable due to the congestion that results when the material handling equipment (or employees) traveling in one direction must wait for the material handling equipment (or employees) moving in the other direction to pass. Also, if a unidirectional material handling system, such as a conveyor, is in use, then, once a product is released by any work center, that product will have to go to the end of the line, come back on a reverse conveyor, and then reenter the line in order to access the work center again.

If large multi-component fabricated products are made in the facility, does the facility have a POU layout? This can be assessed by looking at the flow arrows that connect components and/or subassemblies in consecutive levels of the IBOM (Indented Bill Of Materials) or IBOR (Indented Bill of Routings).

Is LOS (Line Of Sight) lacking between key pairs of locations in the facility layout? The LOS between any two locations is either "0" (Absent) or "1" (Present). That is because light travels in a straight line! If LOS = 1 between two work centers, then, if a line is drawn between their two locations in the facility layout, it will not go through any (obstructing) columns, walls, machines, etc. in the layout. An unobstructed LOS between two work centers would allow their operators to visually communicate to each other about the production status of orders, the status of their machines especially if either one is broken down or about to be shut down for preventive maintenance, if either is going on break, if either needs help to setup their machine, etc.

Is there significant In/Out flow at shared work centers, especially those work centers that are monuments? Shared work centers are those that tend to be used by a large number of parts from several part families.

Monuments are immovable work centers that cannot be relocated. Or at least it would cost an arm and a leg to relocate any monument in the existing facility! In the Spaghetti Diagram, if (i) there are many flows coming to (or going away from) any such work center or (ii) flow arrows of unequal lengths (especially the thick arrows that represent high traffic flows) connecting it to other work centers in the facility, then the existing facility layout does not have good material flow.

Are shared work centers and monuments correctly located in the current facility layout? This can be assessed by eyeballing the diagram.

Does the facility have the correct layout? If the facility currently has a Process Layout, then *expect* the Spaghetti Diagram to invariably show a chaotic material flow! Since time immemorial, HMLV manufacturers, especially job shops, have been misled to believe that organizing their equipment into process-based groups gives them flexibility. But that is only as far as being able to run a particular job on any of several machines available within a particular department! Thereafter, if the job must visit another functional group of machines where it will be loaded on one of several machines, then significant travel and waiting delays get added to its Time To Ship. Is it any surprise that the TPS rejects the Process Layout which is synonymous with the much-despised batch-and-queue mode of production?

Should one or more manufacturing cells be implemented? If it is desired to implement a manufacturing cell to produce a family of parts with identical (or even similar) routings, then a Spaghetti Diagram will easily show how much the equipment that must be co-located into a cell is currently distributed all over the facility.

How could a Spaghetti Diagram help to determine where in the facility a cell should be located to minimize the cost of moving all the machines it needs to that location? First mark the locations of all the machines that will go into the cell on the current layout of the facility. Then, seek an available location that, on the average, is closest to the current locations of all the machines that will go into the cell.

Could a single multi-function flexible machine be purchased that would replace two or more existing machines? A machining center is a single multi-function machine that is capable of replacing two or more existing machines. Sometimes this is good and sometimes this is inadvisable. For example, in the case of machine shops and fabrication shops, if a single flexible machine could combine or eliminate two or more existing machines, that would free up employees and reduce travel distances (and times), the number of setups, the number of inspections, the number of tool changes, etc. In one of our past projects with an aerospace precision machine shop, we were able to evaluate if the flexible machining center that they were buying to replace two existing machines would simplify material flow in their shop. Their Spaghetti Diagram highlighted the poor material flows between the machines it would replace and the rest of the shop.

Case #1 Usefulness of Manually Drawn Spaghetti Diagrams: Facility Re-Layout

A Spaghetti Diagram does a visual rendering of the material flow in the current layout of a facility that *immediately* suggests opportunities to improve the material flow, starting with re-layout of the entire facility or certain portions of the facility. The layout changes are bound to improve the material flow. In turn, that is bound to eliminate waste. In turn, that is bound to reduce the average delivery time for any order. Figure 12.1(a) shows the initial path that was followed by a product assembly (and the distance it traveled through the factory). In contrast, Figure 12.1(b) shows the simpler path that the product traveled after factory layout changes improved material flow in the factory. Just by *visually* comparing the two diagrams, one can expect that the new layout of Figure 12.1(b) scored higher on all the metrics that were used to compare it with the old layout of Figure 12.1(a). Table 12.2 confirms the significant improvements in material flow that were reported by the client after they implemented the new layout.

Case #2 Usefulness of Manually Drawn Spaghetti Diagrams: Patient Care Cell

Quoting from a book[1] on hospital layout design "…In pre-admission testing, at first people could not see anything to change or fix. But when we mapped out a Spaghetti Diagram of the patient's experience, we realized that the patients had to stop in 16 different places, on four different floors, over 2 days, to get through their day surgery… (The team) transformed a space in the existing clinic into a one-stop shop for pre-admission testing. Now patients can register in the clinic lobby as soon as surgery is deemed necessary.

---

[1] Grunden, N. & Hagood, C. (2012). *Lean-Led Hospital Design: Creating the Efficient Hospital of the Future*. New York: CRC Press, pp. 122–123.

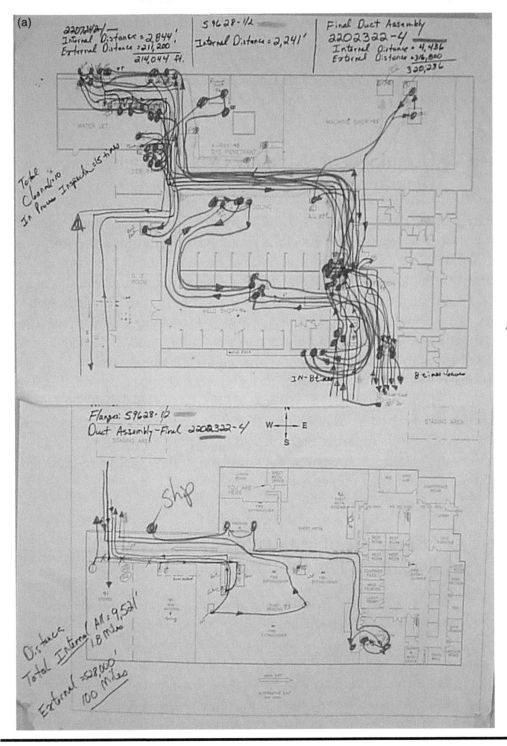

Figure 12.1   Spaghetti Diagram for product assembly – (a) before layout changes.

(Continued)

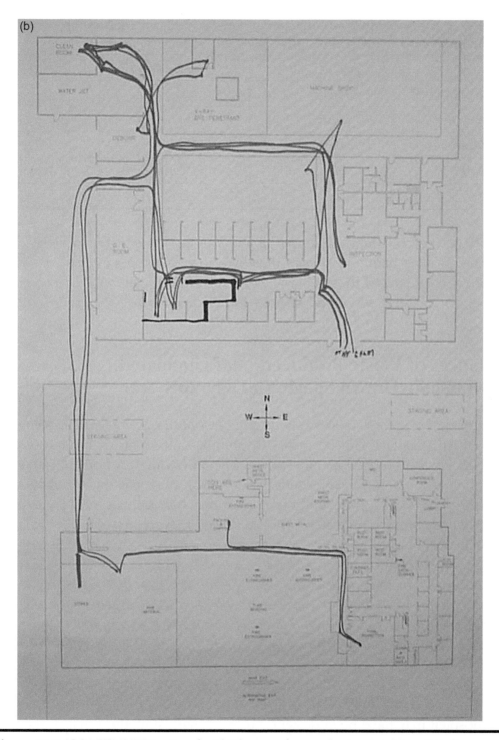

Figure 12.1 (CONTINUED)   Spaghetti Diagram for product assembly – (b) after layout changes.

Table 12.2   Impact of Layout Changes on Key Performance Metrics for Product Assembly

Metric	Before Layout Changes	After Layout Changes	Reduction (%)
Lead time	7 weeks	3.5 weeks	50
Cycle time	8 hours	6 hours	25
Part travel	2,450 ft	1,578 ft	36
Walking	3,150 ft	1,578 ft	50
WIP	360 pcs	200 pcs	44

Lab, EKG, and pre-admission testing of all kinds are done then and there… We have worked hard to eliminate silos. We view everything as one continuous, horizontal path of the patient… Our new building will focus on process, deliberately defining service adjacencies for quick access…".

Instances of Waste Produced (Not Eliminated!) by Manually Drawn Spaghetti Diagrams

Instance #1: Figure 12.2 shows a hospital layout that was designed using a Spaghetti Diagram. This particular diagram is called a String Diagram because it was produced manually using strings of different colors. In the diagram, each string may represent the flow path of (i) patients, (ii) doctors, (iii) clinicians, (iv) support staff, (v) medications, (vi) supplies, (vii) equipment, (viii) information, and (ix) visitors (including vendors), etc. Now, the **same** hospital layout must be flexible and reconfigurable to allow all of these flows throughout the hospital to execute quickly, cheaply, and safely. *Unfortunately, by the time that five, ten or at most fifteen flow pathways of just patients with different ailments are mapped using different colored strings, you can be rest assured that the clutter in the diagram will be excessive and visualization of material flow to guide design of the hospital layout will cease to be effective.* I did a Google search and found that it costs $800,000,000 to build a certain hospital (*Source*: www.quora.com/How-much-does-it-cost-to-build-a-hospital). Does it worry you that the layout of this hospital may have been designed using a manual method that oversimplifies **and** completely ignores the reality that the hospital's layout should be designed for flexibility, based on consideration of a few thousand flow paths taken by patients, doctors, staff, etc.?

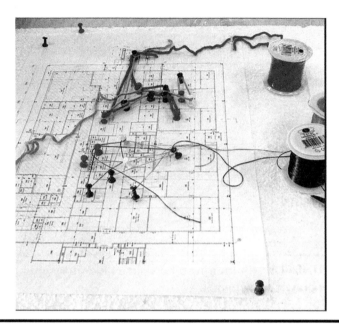

Figure 12.2 Hospital layout design using a Spaghetti Diagram produced with colored strings.

Instance #2: Figures 12.3(a) and (b) show two different layouts for a medical diagnostics laboratory that were evaluated *manually* using Spaghetti Diagrams that were produced using pencil and paper. The team (or individual) produced the two diagrams by following a person (or persons) in real time with a clipboard in hand and used a pencil to connect the chronological

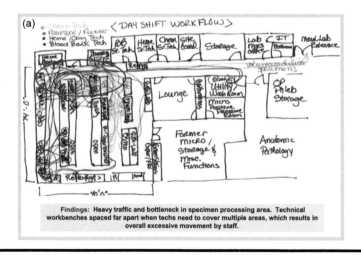

Figure 12.3 (a) Improved flows.

(Continued)

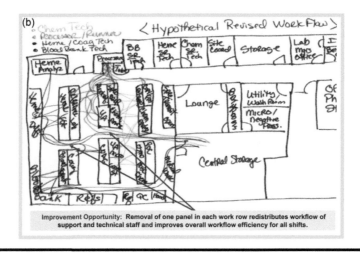

Figure 12.3 (CONTINUED) **(b) Improved flows in a laboratory visualized using a Spaghetti Diagram drawn using pencil.**

sequence of points that he/she (or they) visited during the observation period on the laboratory layout. Does it worry you that the layout of this medical diagnostics laboratory may have been designed by tracking and mapping too small a sample of different people and/or laboratory specimens?

Instance #3: Value Stream Mapping (VSM) is a manual Lean tool often used in conjunction with Spaghetti Diagrams to document material and information flows for a single product (or product family). A VSM, like the one shown in Figure 12.4, is produced manually using pencil and paper or Post-It notes or a computer-aided drawing package like Visio. It may be possible to manually produce a VSM for an assembly line that makes one product, or a family of similar products that can be produced on the same line. *Unfortunately, the developers of VSM (Mike Rother and John Shook) state in their bestseller book **Learning To See** that "... (when) any value streams have multiple flows that merge...draw such flows over one another...but do not try to draw every branch if there are too many. Choose the few components first, and get the others later if you need to...just draw the flow for one or two main materials".* So they are as good as admitting that there is no manual method to identify one or more groups of Value Streams that are similar (or identical). Let alone being able to draw them on an 11×17 sheet of paper in a manner that does not produce a Spaghetti Diagram that cannot be read and diagnosed!

It is impossible to use VSM to map the large number of different patient flows that occur in a hospital day in and day out! But, it is important to know if the Value Stream for a diabetic patient who is over the age of

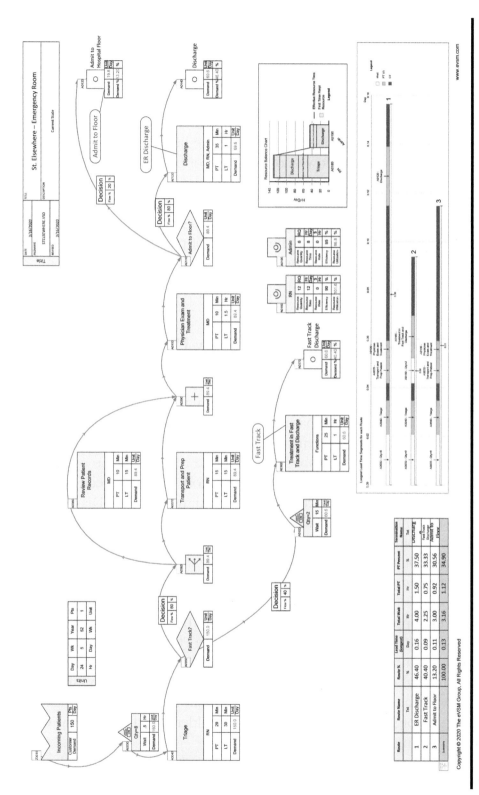

Figure 12.4   Example of a VSM in health care. (Source: https://evsm.com/sites/default/files/v8help/qhcex.pdf).

seventy and is coming in for chest pains goes through departments that are common to the Value Stream for a heart surgery patient because those two patients will be competing for shared resources (*Source*: http://theleanway-consulting.com/rethinking-value-streams-in-healthcare/)! Now consider the case of the University of Texas MD Anderson Cancer Center which focuses on treatment of cancers. The sheer *variety of cancers* that they treat makes them a job shop and not an assembly line in the health care industry! So, if they decide to improve the flow and treatment of breast cancer patients who visit the departments of Chemotherapy, Radiology, and Lab Testing, would those departments also not deliver the same speed and quality of care given to patients with other forms of cancer who visit those same departments? Could a VSM even display the network of patient flow pathways for just the different types of breast cancer (*Source*: www.cancercenter.com/breast-cancer/types/)!

Major Challenges of Generating Flow Diagrams by Hand

Just a single multi-component product assembly will take considerable time to map. Figure 12.5 is the Flow Diagram for a single fabricated product that is comprised of three major subassemblies. Each subassembly is assembled from a different kit of components that are produced in-house. Some components are common to two subassemblies. The routings of the components and subassemblies used twenty-two different work centers spread all over the factory. Imagine using pencil and paper to draw the Flow Diagram for all the components and subassemblies in any large and complex product, such as a car, commercial airliner, or aircraft carrier!

Even when the routings of a few (≤15) different components (or tools, people, documents, etc.) are mapped, the Flow Diagram becomes cluttered and "unreadable". The (visual) readability of a Flow Diagram is essential for identifying opportunities to improve flow in the high-mix work system being studied! For example, Figure 12.6(a) is the Flow Diagram for a family of 38 parts produced in a manual machining cell. Can you infer anything from that (messy) diagram? Similarly, Figure 12.6(b) shows a computer-generated Flow Diagram for a custom forge shop that gave us the routings for 500+ different forgings they supplied to shipbuilders for the US Navy. Can you infer anything from that (messy) diagram?

To evaluate every idea for changing the existing layout to improve flow suggested by a Flow Diagram, a new diagram will need to be manually generated.

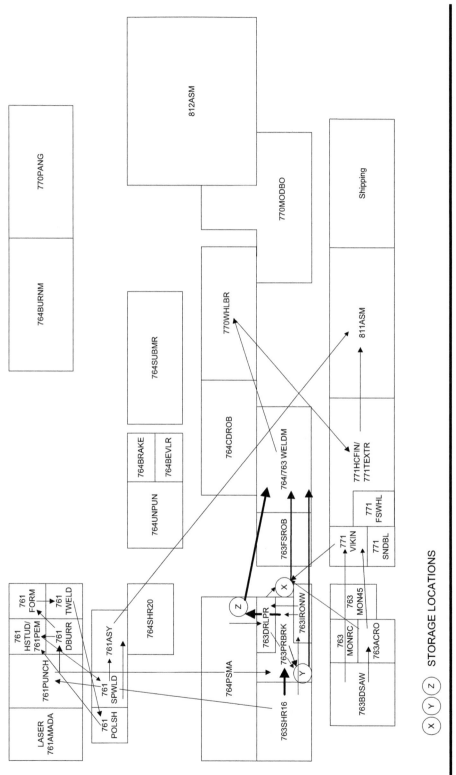

Figure 12.5   Flow Diagram for all the components and subassemblies to produce a fabricated product.

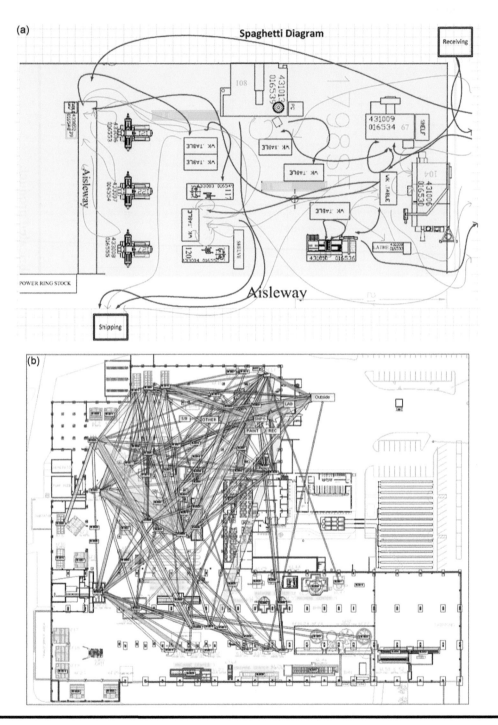

Figure 12.6   Flow Diagram for (a) a large part family produced in a machining cell and (b) 500+ different forgings produced in a custom forge shop.

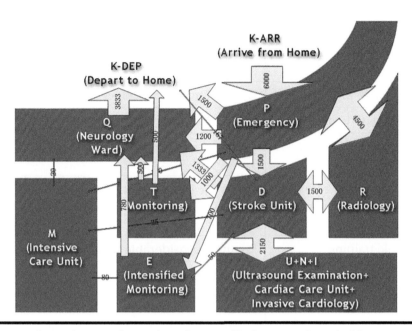

Figure 12.7   Flow Diagram for patient flow traffic in a new hospital layout.

Figure 12.7 is the Flow Diagram for a sample of 20 different patient care pathways with varying patient volumes recorded for each pathway. In this case, all the pathways were consolidated into a single From-To Chart. It was hard enough to produce just the one diagram for a layout based on the STORM software that uses a heuristic optimization algorithm. Now imagine redrawing this diagram manually every time with arrows of different thicknesses **whenever** the mix of care pathways is changed and/or the patient volumes in one or more care pathways changes from one quarter to another!

There Is No Reason for Spaghetti Diagrams to Be Hand-Drawn in the 21st Century!

A Spaghetti Diagram could be produced to visualize in aggregate the flow paths of (i) 100's of different parts, (ii) a specific sample of parts drawn from a large population, (iii) all the parts and subassemblies that go into a single product, and (iv) all the parts and subassemblies that go into a group of products, etc. But, if they had to do it manually, no CI (Continuous Improvement) team in an HMLV manufacturing facility will ever agree to do this! Table 12.3 compares the pros and cons of producing Spaghetti Diagrams by hand versus using an app like Sgetti.

Table 12.3   Comparison of Spaghetti Diagrams Produced by Hand versus Computer

Hand-Drawn	Computer-Generated
Easy and quick to produce	Easy and quick to produce
Effective for 5 (10–15) routings	Effective for 100's of routings
Paper, pencil, and string are cheap	Commercial software is expansive
Tedious to redraw for every change in routings, layout, product mix, etc.	This is the key merit of a software tool!
Requires little training	Requires considerable training
Visual assessment of good/bad material flow is empirical	Assessment of good/bad material flow can be: • Visual • Quantitative: Simple metrics such as LOS Efficiency (LOSE), Total Travel Distance, etc. • Quantitative: Sophisticated metrics such as throughput WIP, Queues at Work Centers, etc.

Case Study: Design of a Lean Hospital Layout

There are easily 1000's of different material flow pathways in any hospital because the "material" could be patients, doctors, staff, equipment, medications, supplies, etc. *Unfortunately, hospital architects cannot design flexible and adaptable hospital layouts because they **do not have** a tool to undertake a comprehensive material flow analysis of a large population of diverse material flow pathways. This section describes a study that was done where the material flow mapping app, Sgetti, was used to design the layout of a new hospital based on a detailed analysis of different patient flow paths.*

Earlier, I had done an extensive search of the literature on "Lean Hospitals", "Lean in Health Care", etc. to investigate if the concept of Cellular Manufacturing had been explored in the design of hospital layouts. To my happy astonishment (and satisfaction!), I came across **one** paper[2] where the authors had used PFA to design the layout of a new hospital using many different flow pathways (aka routings in the manufacturing world) of different categories of patients who would be cared for in that hospital.

---

[2] Karvonen, S., Korvenrata, H., Paatela, M. & Seppala, T. (2007). Production flow analysis: A tool to design a lean hospital. *World Hospitals and Health Services*, 43(1), 28–31.

Please visit https://vimeo.com/88779268 to access the PowerPoint presentation that describes the full details of the original study that doctoral student, Ms. Shijie Huang, and I did to replicate, verify, **and** extend the original work that the authors describe in their seminal paper.

Why was a "Lean Hospital" given an "unLean" layout that makes it very expensive to execute the "single patient flow" that is essential for patient care? Figure 12.8(a) shows the list of departments in the new hospital. The very word "department" supports my contention that hospital layouts, like machine or forge shops, have their resources organized by function into "silos" or "process villages". That is the fundamental reason why almost every patient in a hospital has to be transported from one location to the other in order to receive the care that they need to be restored to health. A Functional Layout results in batch-and-queue production which is a production mode that the TPS rejects.

Figure 12.8(b) lists the different routings followed by patients diagnosed with different disorders that each required different departments to be visited in a certain sequence. For example, in the case of PRN #1 (KPRPQK), 1,200 patients first arrived from HOME and were admitted to the EMERGENCY. Next they were sent to RADIOLOGY after which they were sent back to EMERGENCY. Then they were sent to the NEUROLOGY ward from where they went back HOME. In stark contrast to PRN #1, which had only six steps, look at PRN #20, which had fifteen steps but only eight patients with that medical condition were admitted to the hospital. Which patients are in greater danger of "falling through the cracks" if the new hospital is designed to be "efficient" like an (inflexible) assembly line which only produces a few types of automobiles in large quantities?

Figure 12.8(c) is the From-To Chart developed using the raw data in Figure 12.8(b). Every cell in this chart aggregates the patient flow volumes between that pair of departments that occur consecutively in different care pathways. This asymmetric matrix is the basis for determining the thicknesses of the different flow arrows shown in the Bubble Diagrams for the different hospital layouts that were generated and evaluated using Sgetti.

In addition to the From-To Chart of Figure 12.8(c), Sgetti can use several other representations of the raw data in Figure 12.8(b), such as 0–1 Product-Process Matrix and Modified Multi-Product Process Chart. The use

Code for the Processing Unit	Process
D	Stroke Unit
E	Intensified Monitoring
I	Invasive Cardiology
K	Home
M	Intensive Care Unit
N	Cardiac Care Unit
P	Emergency
Q	Neurology Ward
R	Radiology
T	Monitoring
U	Ultrasound Examination

	Process Route Number (PRN)	Number of Patients
1	KPRPQK	1200
2	KPK	1000
3	KPRPEQK	700
4	KPRPDRDUDQK	517
5	KPRPK	500
6	KPRPTQK	500
7	KPRPDRDUDQK	333
8	KPRPDRDUDUDQK	258
9	KPTK	500
10	KPRPDRDUDUDK	167
11	KPRPMEQK	80
12	KPRPDRDUDIDQK	67
13	KPRPDRDUDUDIDQK	33
14	KPRPDRDYDNDQK	33
15	KPRPDRDUDEDQK	33
16	KPRPMQK	20
17	KPRPDRDUDUDNDQK	17
18	KPRPDRDUDUDEDQK	17
19	KPRPDRDUDMDQK	17
20	KPRPDRDUDUDMDQK	8
	Total Number of Patients	**6000**

Figure 12.8   a) List of departments in the hospital. b) Different flow pathways followed by patients with different disorders.

(Continued)

of these representations is essential if it is desired to replace the existing Process Layout with a Cellular Layout or layouts that combine the features of these two well-known layouts, such as Virtual Cells, Partial Cells, Cascading Flowlines, and Hybrid Flow Shops.

FROM		D	E	I	M	N	P	Q	R	T	U	Home (K)
								TO				
	D		50	100	25	50		1000	1500		2000	500
	E	50						780				
	I	100										
	M	25	80					20				
	N	50										
	P	1500	700			100		1200	4500	1000		1500
	Q											3500
	R	1500					4500					
	T							500				500
	U	2000										
	Home (K)						6000					

Incorrect Numbers?

Figure 12.8 (CONTINUED)   c) From-To Chart for patient flow traffic between various pairs of departments.

Comparison of Alternative Hospital Layouts Using Sgetti

Figure 12.9(a) shows the departmental adjacencies in Layout #1, which was the initial layout that was designed for the new hospital using the From-To Chart in Figure 12.8(c).

Figure 12.9(b) shows the reduction in the "Flow Change" metric that was computed by the Sgetti app for Layout #2, which had different departmental adjacencies compared with Layout #1.

Figure 12.9(c) shows the reduction in the "Flow Change" metric that was computed by the Sgetti app for Layout #3, which had different departmental adjacencies compared with Layout #1.

Figure 12.9(d) shows the reduction in the "Flow Change" metric that was computed by the Sgetti app for Layout #4, which had different departmental adjacencies compared with Layout #1. Layout #4 demonstrates the "stack concept" for the layout of a hospital that is built in a crowded city. This particular layout assumes that all material flow occurs along elevator shafts in a central column and that at most two departments are placed on each floor.

Figure 12.9(e) shows the increase in the "Flow Change" metric that was computed by the Sgetti app for Layout #5, which had different departmental adjacencies compared with Layout #1. Layout #5 demonstrates an "eight-shaped" layout of a hospital that is built in the suburbs where the availability of land allows an open space design. This particular layout assumes that all

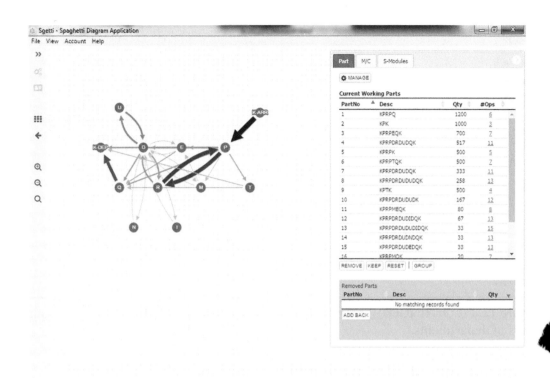

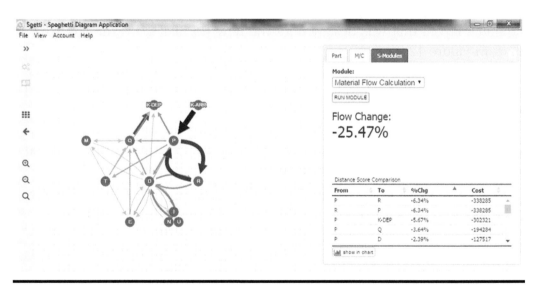

Figure 12.9   a) Bubble Diagram for layout #1. b) Bubble Diagram for layout #2 that reduced material flow in layout #1 by 25.47%.

(*Continued*)

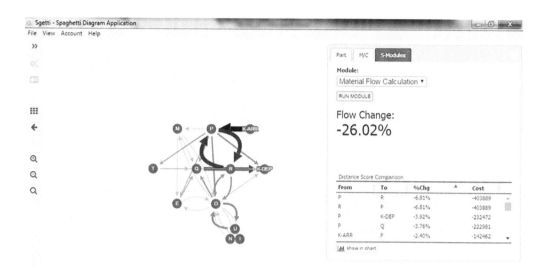

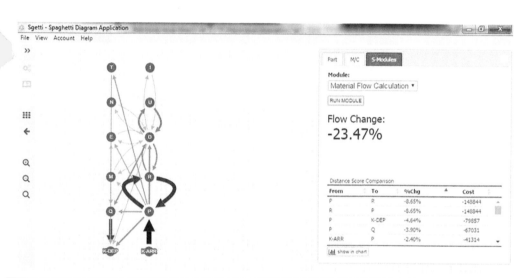

Figure 12.9 c) Bubble Diagram for layout #4 that reduced material flow in layout #1 by 23.47%. d) Bubble Diagram for layout #5 that increased material flow in layout #1 by 1.03%.

(Continued)

resources and support systems will be housed at the center of each of the two circles that each represent a cluster of departments. Unfortunately, the "Flow Change" metric indicates that this layout has the worst material flow of the four alternative layouts that were generated.

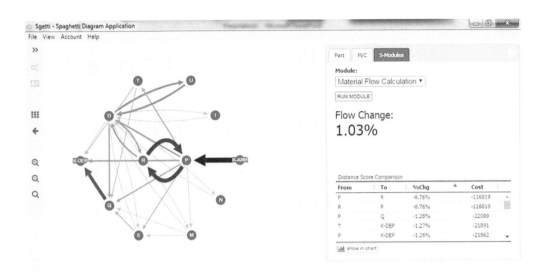

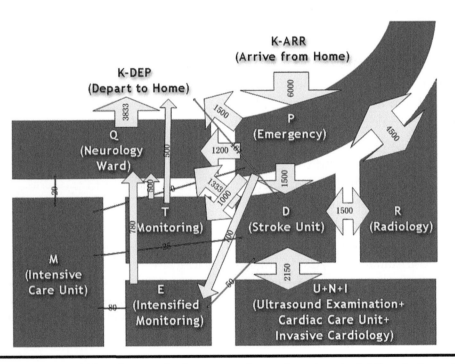

Figure 12.9   e) Bubble Diagram for layout #3 that reduced material flow in layout #1 by 26.02%. f) Block layout for the new hospital layout based on layout #2.

Figure 12.9(f) shows the (hypothetical) layout for the new hospital that was designed by sizing and shaping the different departments in Layout #2 to reflect the approximate areas that were assumed for the different departments in the new hospital.

Advantages of Material Flow Mapping with Sgetti

Sgetti will prevent at least one meaningless CI event: When any HMLV manufacturer undertakes to implement Lean, they will surely conduct numerous *kaizen*[3] events. When implementing Lean, it is common practice to have **at least one** CI event that involves *manually* (i) developing a VSM for one product (or product family) and (ii) developing one or more Spaghetti Diagrams for the same product (or product family) to understand how that product (or product family) flows through the entire facility, possibly to/from one or more vendors. I will state unequivocally that for any HMLV manufacturer to conduct an event with this scope is a waste of time and money. Why? Because (i) a VSM assumes a repetitive (and stable) assembly line (or process) that ignores the dynamics of factory floor operations in HMLV facilities and (ii) a Spaghetti Diagram for a single product (product family) could ignore the sharing of resources (machines, labor, materials, etc.) with other products (or product families) not considered during the event. What does such a kaizen event cost? My ball park estimate for the cost of such an event is $75,000 (ten employees, 5 days each, 10 hours per employee per day @ $150/hour = $75,000). Plus, if it is facilitated by an external consultant, then add at least another $10,000–$20,000 to the cost of the event!

Sgetti is fast: Sgetti is the first app in a suite of apps that are being developed to complement the knowledge and experience of the employees who work on CI teams at HMLV manufacturing and service companies. Sgetti will eliminate the tedious and error-prone work that one or more members of the team would do for hours to produce a Spaghetti Diagram or VSM. Imagine **manually** drawing (and redrawing!) one Spaghetti Diagram after another, especially with arrows of different thicknesses (or colors), **every time** that a layout change was suggested or the mix of care pathways (and/or the patient volumes for any of those care pathways) was changed!

Sgetti can provide the complete material flow map for any large-scale HMLV material flow system: In the Lean Hospital case study discussed earlier in the chapter, Sgetti would have helped the authors to design and evaluate a large number of alternative layouts for the new hospital. According to their paper, the authors used a small sample of **only 20** different patient care pathways with varying patient volumes recorded for each pathway.

---

[3] Kaizen is a Japanese word ("kai" = change, "zen" = good) that refers to any improvement, one-time or continuous, large or small, in the same sense as the English word "improvement". I equate "kaizen" to "CI".

I would have expected them to take into consideration a much larger sample of patient care pathways to design the new hospital's layout! *But, if the authors manually produced all the tables and diagrams for their paper, then I can fully understand why they did not collect data for a few hundred more patients with a wider range of ailments.*

Sgetti can compare different material flow maps by combining visualization and numerical scoring: Any CI team tasked with designing a new facility layout or mapping a product's Value Stream will have talented employees who have the expertise and experience to "read" a Spaghetti Diagram or the VSM that accompanies it. Any member (or members) of the team could visually compare the Spaghetti Diagrams for different competing layouts and say something like, "Of all layouts proposed for the new facility, the material flow in Layout #X has the best material flow!" But, will the executive (or business owner) who is going to write the check to finance the implementation of that layout be satisfied with that justification? I seriously doubt that he/she will be satisfied with that answer. Instead, he/she will ask the team to (i) to determine a shortlist of two, at most three, alternative layouts, then (ii) do a detailed spreadsheet analysis of those layouts to compare their operating costs, throughput performance, floor space requirements, communications flow with the front office, etc. Sgetti would provide the **metrics-aided** visualization of different Spaghetti Diagrams so all members of the team could see, measure, and compare the material flow efficiencies of all layouts in order to determine the "Final Three" layouts to evaluate in more detail.

Sgetti puts the "team" into the efforts of a CI team: Let us consider the case of a CNC (Computer Numerical Control) machine shop that wants to finalize the design of the layout for a new building. They seek a layout design for that building that has much better material flow compared with the chaos that exists in their current facility layout. Sgetti will allow rapid evaluation of ideas/inputs from **some or all** of the following individuals who are impacted by a facility layout: (i) Owner/President, (ii) Consultant, (iii) Architect, (iv) VP, $ales, (v) VP, Operations (or Plant Manager), (vi) Turning Department Supervisor, (vii) Milling Department Supervisor, (viii) CMM (Coordinate Measuring Machine) Department Supervisor, (ix) Shipping/Receiving Department Supervisor, (x) Maintenance Manager, (xi) Material Handler, (xii) Tool Crib Manager, and (xiii) Intern (or Senior Capstone Design team from a local IE (Industrial Engineering) department) tasked with designing the layout alternatives and evaluating their performance using a simulation software like SIMIO (www.simio.com) or FLEXSIM (www.flexsim.com). Needless to say, a smaller team is going to call the shots on the final layout decision. But, Sgetti would allow any person who makes a suggestion to see how it would affect the flow in the current best layout with a few mouse clicks. Whenever an expensive and long-term change is being made for the better, it is absolutely advisable that all employees feel that their suggestions were considered. With Sgetti being used to evaluate different alternatives for the shop layout, the Owner/President of this CNC machine shop would have to pay for pizza and soda to have **just one** lunch meeting with all key stakeholders in their conference room!

Conclusion

This chapter explained the many ways in which a Material Flow Map (aka Spaghetti Diagram or Flow Diagram) can show the many opportunities for improving material flow in any work system, such as a machine shop, hospital, grocery store, or work bench. An app like Sgetti, which is able to map the flow in any large multi-product material flow system and uses metrics-aided visualization to assess any changes in the system configuration, easily outdoes the current manual approach to drawing these maps. Perhaps the most powerful feature of this app is that it requires a minimal amount of data to provide useful diagnostics and lays the foundations for future use of more data-intensive commercial alternatives like *Flow Planner, VIP-PLANOPT,* or *SIMOGGA.*

Appendices

Appendices for this chapter are available for download at https://www.crcpress.com/9781498740692.

Supplementary Reading

Folder #1 (Presentations on Spaghetti Diagrams) contains the following files:

1. There are two versions of the same presentation that describes an earlier version of the Sgetti app. Sgetti app was used to generate a slew of Flow Diagrams to explore layout improvements in a CNC

machine shop that is housed in two buildings separated by a parking lot. Unfortunately, the two webinars (Webinar #1 was hosted by *Exact JobBOSS* and Webinar #2 was hosted by *Invistics Corporation*) based on these presentations that had been posted online have been taken down.

Folder #2 (Waste Identification in Entire Forge Shop) contains the following files:

1. The PowerPoint presentation titled *Facility Walkthrough: The KISS Approach to Lean Assessment of a Value Stream* is part of a lecture in the ISE540 course that I taught at The Ohio State University. The lecture sought to show IE undergraduates different examples of the Seven Types of Waste that add delays to the total time it took to produce a forging in a large custom forge shop. **The "master slide" is Slide #4.** The slide shows the Spaghetti Diagram for the path that the forging took through the custom forge shop. See the presentation in slideshow mode. Click on any active button when you mouse over it to display the photograph linked to that button. A photograph displays any one of two categories of waste: (i) Those wastes that can be observed at any machine (or work center) and (ii) Those wastes that occur during transportation from one machine (or work center) to another machine (or work center). I took the photographs as I walked through the facility visiting the different work centers in the sequence that they appeared in the Spaghetti Diagram! For the sake of comparison, the Flow Diagram shown in Figure 23.6 of Chapter 23 resulted when the routings of all 530 different forgings that were produced by this custom forge shop were mapped on the same facility layout! Use Slide #5 for additional discussions on waste identification.

Folder #3 (Waste Identification in Forging Cell) contains the following files:

1. The PowerPoint presentation titled *Design of a Forging Cell for One-Piece Flow Using Value Stream Mapping* was part of a lecture that showed IE undergraduates the different examples of the Seven Types of Waste that occur when a component is produced in a single manufacturing cell. See the presentation in slideshow mode. **The "master slide" is Slide #2**. As you mouse over the travel path for the part in Slide #2, you will be able to click on the photographs that we took at different locations in the Current State of the cell where we observed

waste as we walked the routing of the forging from start to finish. Could you compute a cost (or delay) for each instance of waste? Slide #3 shows the VSM. Slide #4 shows the cell layout that we designed to eliminate batching, operator motion waste, etc.

Folder #4 (Process Analysis and Improvement) contains the following files:
1. The PowerPoint presentation titled *Fundamentals of Process Analysis and Improvement: An Industrial Engineer's Approach for Analyzing and Improving Any Work That We Do* is one of the core lectures in the ISE540 course that I taught at The Ohio State University. I find it interesting that I taught how to use a Spaghetti Diagram and a Flow Process Chart in tandem. My emphasis (unfortunately!) was on the material handling steps contained in a process and not the actual value-adding operations in the process. **In stark contrast**, Toyota focuses on creating a Standard Work Instruction that describes a process in its entirety. The Spaghetti Diagram only helps to design the layout of the work space in which the process is executed. It shows all the material handling delays that result in poor work balance between the different workstations where the value-adding steps are performed. With modern-day software for VSM, such as eVSM, I think that the Flow Process Chart and the VSM can be combined into one chart.
2. (*Source*: Groover, M.P. (2007). *Work Systems and the Methods, Measurement and Management of Work*. Upper Saddle River, NJ: Pearson Prentice Hall) This presentation is based on a chapter (Chapter 8 *Introduction to Methods Engineering and Operations Analysis*) that teaches how an IE would undertake to improve a kaizen event to improve a process such as setup reduction on a machine.
3. (*Source*: Groover, M.P. (2007). *Work Systems and the Methods, Measurement and Management of Work*. Upper Saddle River, NJ: Pearson Prentice Hall) This presentation is based on a chapter (Chapter 9 *Charting and Diagramming Techniques for Operations Analysis*) that teaches some of the IE charting and diagramming techniques that have been modified or enhanced in the TPS. In particular, if you carefully study pages 235–245 in the chapter, you will find that Toyota(Lean) tools are very similar to these classical IE tools (Flow Diagram, Flow Process Chart, Right-Hand/Left-Hand Activity Chart, Worker-Machine Chart, Operations Chart) described in those pages! If you would like to receive a list of older IE textbooks that explain in

detail how Process Analysis and Improvement is influenced by Product Design, Process Engineering, Machine Design, Work Instructions, etc. (and vice versa too!), please email me at ShahrukhIrani1023@yahoo.com.
4. (*Source*: Rother, M. (2010). *Toyota Kata: Managing People for Improvement, Adaptiveness and Superior Results*. New York: McGraw-Hill) This appendix (*Appendix 2 Process Analysis*) is an **excellent** case study that describes how to use VSM in combination with Assembly Line Balancing to clearly determine where to focus process (or system) improvement efforts to improve system (or process) performance, how much to improve a particular step in the process, etc.

Folder #5 (Instructor's Guide on *Toast Kaizen*) contains the following files:
1. The classic video, *Toast Kaizen: Introduction to Continuous Improvement and Lean Principles*, shows a loving husband preparing a slice of toast for his loving wife. Albeit a simple process, it provides a very good example for teaching Process Analysis and Improvement by **integrating** Lean and IE. Still, I was very underwhelmed by the video and felt that it completely ignored how IE methods could complement/supplement how a "Lean Thinker" identifies the Seven Types of Waste in any process. For starters, besides measuring the Job Completion Time, the video did not explain how to quantify the Seven Types of Waste. Nor does it even mention how, per the Theory Of Constraints (TOC), the starting point for process improvement should have been the system's bottleneck. The challenge of determining whether the toaster or the butter was the system bottleneck was quietly eliminated by thawing the butter well in advance! Plus it fails to even mention the use of Activity Sequencing and Scheduling in order to determine the best sequence in which to execute the different steps in the process. Given the many shortcomings of the video, I decided to develop this comprehensive Instructor's Guide that an IE teacher could use if they decide to use this video in any course on Lean, Work Study, or other similar subject.

Folder #6 (Case Study on Process Improvement) contains the following files:
1. This article titled *Focusing on the Process to Ensure Success* appeared in The Fabricator. *Monozukuri* means "having a state of mind, the spirit to produce not only excellent products but also have the ability to constantly improve the production system and its processes". Isn't that similar to the fundamental goal of Lean Thinking? That **any** manufacturer

(or service provider) who teaches and trains every employee and manager of theirs to document and/or map, analyze, and improve each and every process that they execute at work daily will surely best their competition!

Folder #7 (Quick-Start Implementation of Job Shop Lean at Ulven Forging Inc.) contains the following files:

1. This PowerPoint presentation titled *A Quick-Start Approach for Implementing Job Shop Lean* describes the work that Meina Tanzil, an IE graduate student from The Ohio State University, did when she worked as a full-time intern for 3+ summer months at SIFCO Forging Group. Here is a detailed breakdown of the different sections in the lecture:

   i. *Slide #1:* The *Quick-Start Approach for (Implementing) Job Shop Lean* uses a Spaghetti Diagram developed from the routing of a single product to improve flow for the entire product family that it belongs to.

   ii. *Slide #2:* This slide is self-explanatory.

   iii. *Slide #3:* This slide is self-explanatory.

   iv. *Slide #4:* This flowchart describes the *Comprehensive Approach for (Implementing) Job Shop Lean* in any machine shop, forge shop, fabrication shop, etc.

   v. *Slide #5:* **This is the Master Slide for the entire presentation**. The flowchart describes the step-by-step implementation of the *Quick-Start Approach for (Implementing) Job Shop Lean*.

   vi. *Slide #6:* These are the steps *Collect Sales Data* and *Obtain all Routings/Bill of Routings* in the flowchart shown in Slide #5.

   vii. *Slide #7:* This is the step *Pick a Part Family with Highest Contribution* in the flowchart shown in Slide #5. If you click on the hyperlink *Input File* embedded on this slide, you will see one of the PFAST outputs used to segment the product mix. If you click on the hyperlink *Dendogram* embedded on this slide, you will see one of the PFAST outputs used to form part families.

   viii. *Slides #8–#9:* This is the step *From This Part Family, Pick a Part (or Parts) with Same Routing* in the flowchart shown in Slide #5. Part Family #2 is the part family from which the forging was chosen and used to develop the Flow Diagram.

   ix. *Slide #10:* This slide shows a portion of the routing for the forging. Next, it was necessary to obtain an up-to-date CAD (Computer-Aided Design) drawing of the existing layout of the forge shop showing each and every step in the routing of the forging (Receiving of Bar Stock, the work center associated with each operation in the routing, Shipping of Forging). All that remained was to "connect the dots" and map the part's forging on the current layout of the forge shop.

x. *Slide #11:* This is the step *Generate the Flow Diagram for the Part (or Parts)* in the flowchart shown in Slide #5 to map the part's forging on the current layout of the forge shop.

xi. *Slide #12:* This is the step *Evaluate the Flow Diagram to identify Flow Delays, ..., Absence of LOS*, etc. in the flowchart shown in Slide #5.

xii. *Slides #13–#15:* These slides are related to Slide #12. They list the observations that the intern made while executing the step *Evaluate the Flow Diagram to Identify Flow Delays, ..., Absence of LOS, etc.* in the flowchart shown in Slide #5. She spent several consecutive days actively tracking the flow of an in-process order for the particular part that was the focus of the study. Her observations, which have been documented on the *Part Flow Tracking* slides, indicate the magnitude of the production delays experienced by the order (and wastes that added to the costs of fulfilling the order).

xiii. *Slide #16:* This is the step *Create a Flow Process Chart to Identify Flow Delays and Eight Types of Waste* in the flowchart shown in Slide #5. If you click on the hyperlink *Flow Process Chart* embedded on this slide, you will see the variety and significant number of non-value-added steps that were observed in the production flow path of this particular order.

xiv. *Slides #17–#18:* These are the steps *Create the Value Stream Map for Detailed Evaluation of the Flow Diagram and Compute Value-Added* Ratio in the flowchart shown in Slide #5. Since the Flow Diagram had already given us considerable information on the delays and wastes in the material flow portion of the VSM, we used this particular VSM to gain insights on the production control and communication flows between the office and the shop floor. It is never a good sign when there is total reliance being placed on an ERP system to schedule shop operations!

xv. *Slides #19–#32:* These are the steps *Help to Identify the Bottleneck and Perform TOC Analysis at the Bottleneck* in the flowchart shown in Slide #5. In a custom forge shop, given that forging is the main value-creating process, the internal bottleneck tends to be at the Press Shop! ☺ Thereby, eliminating waste in that shop became the goal for the duration of the internship! Poor workplace organization was quickly identified as being a major reason for the occurrence of the Eight Types of Waste in the shop! If you click on the hyperlink *5S* embedded on Slide #24, you will see the slide deck that we used to train the shop employees so they could take the first step to streamline the flow of work at and around the forging presses.

xvi. *Slides #33–#42:* During the training session that she conducted for the employees in the Saw department and Press Shop, the intern taught Waste Elimination as follows: (i) First, she displayed a specific instance of each type of waste, (ii) then, she asked the employees *Why?* They thought that this waste was produced, and (iii) finally, she encouraged the employees to brainstorm *How?* They could eliminate that waste with least time and effort.

xvii. *Slides #43–#44:* This is the step *Identify and Prioritize Strategies for Improvement* in the flowchart shown in Slide #5. The employees who attended the 5S training and some of the managers involved in the project gathered in a room. The intern wrote each idea that was discussed and approved by the group on a Post-It note and posted it on a grid (X axis = High/Low Cost of implementing the improvement idea, Y axis = High/Low Impact of implementing the improvement idea). The team then guided the intern to position each Post-It note on the grid based on their approximate determination of values for the Cost and Impact of that idea!

xviii. *Slides #45–#47:* This is the step *Project Schedule to Implement Recommendations in Order of Priority* in the flowchart shown in Slide #5. The most significant decision that resulted from this internship was that SIFCO Forging Group decided to hire a full-time Lean Manager who would take responsibility for the long-term implementation of Lean in that facility.

xix. *Slides #48–#54:* These slides describe General Findings and Suggestions beyond the improvement ideas that the employees came up with. In particular, Slide #54 refers to the project that was suggested to study throughput at the Heat Treatment furnaces (whose energy bills were significant!).

xx. *Slide #55:* This slide describes Future Work that was not a high priority at that time.

2. The other folder (Hyperlink Files) contains the files that display when you click on the hyperlinks in the main presentation.

Folder #8 (Quick-Start Implementation of Job Shop Lean at Bula Forge & Machine Inc.) contains the following files:

1. This PowerPoint presentation titled *Experiences and Results from a Job Shop Lean Pilot Project in a Custom Forge Shop* describes the work that, Bryan Wang, another BuckIE graduate student from The Ohio State University, did when he worked as a full-time intern for 3+ summer months at Bula Forge & Machine Inc. located in Cleveland, OH. Like the other custom forge shops (Ulven Forging Inc. and SIFCO Forge Group) that partnered with us on this federal grant managed by the **Advanced Technology Institute**, Bula Forge & Machine Inc. is a HMLV SME (small and medium enterprise). Bryan went above and beyond his core responsibility during the internship which was to implement the *Quick-Start Approach to Job Shop Lean* at Bula Forge & Machine Inc. In addition, he (i) developed an in-house curriculum on Lean that he taught to all the members of Team Bula and (ii) made a **video** that summarized the work that he did during his internship and includes interviews with different members of Team Bula. The video includes:
    i. An introduction to Bula Forge & Machine Inc.
    ii. The first reactions to Lean from members of Team Bula when Bryan started his internship and what the same individuals said about Lean when his internship ended
    iii. How Bula Forge & Machine Inc. started their Lean journey by hiring an IE intern through the LEAP (Learn → Earn → Apply → Practice) Internship Program at The Ohio State University
    iv. Comments on the overlaps *and* differences between (Toyota)Lean and Job Shop Lean
    v. Guidance on how to adopt, adapt, or replace methods and tools of the TPS when dealing with the unique challenges of implementing Lean in the HMLV environment of a small family-owned job shop
    vi. Guidance on how to integrate VSM and TOC to identify and prioritize improvement projects to eliminate waste and production delays in a job shop
    vii. Structure and content of the Lean training on the fundamentals of Lean that all members of Team Bula were able to put to immediate use in their forge shop
    viii. Results and benefits achieved from implementing Lean in a job shop that were reported from this LEAP internship
    ix. Barriers and challenges to implementing Lean in a job shop that were learned from this LEAP internship

Bibliography

Apple, J.M. (1977). *Plant Layout and Material Handling.* New York: Pearson Education Inc./Prentice Hall.

Burbidge, J.L. (1996). *Production Flow Analysis for Planning Group Technology.* New York: Oxford University Press Inc.

Daita, S.T., Irani, S.A. & Kotamraju, S. (1999). Algorithms for production flow analysis. *International Journal of Production Research*, 37(11), 2609–2638.

Irani, S.A. & Huang, H. (2003). Manufacturing facility compaction by machining function combination. *Transactions of the ASME (ASME Journal of Manufacturing Science and Engineering)*, 125(4), 740–752.

Irani, S.A., Zhang, H., Zhou, J., Huang, H., Tennati, K.U. & Subramanian, S. (2000). Production Flow Analysis and Simplification Toolkit (PFAST). *International Journal of Production Research*, 38(8), 1855–1874.

Muther, R. (1973). *Systematic Layout Planning.* Boston, MA: Cahners Books.

Stephens, M.P. & Meyers, F.W. (2010). *Manufacturing Facilities Design and Material Handling.* Hoboken, NJ: Pearson Education Inc./Prentice Hall.

Tompkins, J.A., White, J.A., Bozer, Y.A. & Tanchoco, J.M.A. (2010). *Facilities Planning.* Hoboken, NJ: John Wiley.

Zhou, J. & Irani, S.A. (2003). A new flow diagramming scheme for mapping and analysis of multi-product flows in a facility. *Journal of Integrated Design and Process Science*, 7(1), 25–58.

Chapter 13

Product Mix Segmentation

Acknowledgment

This chapter is based on a series of articles written by Tim Heston, Senior Editor on the editorial staff of *The Fabricator* magazine (https://www. thefabricator.com/). Thank you, Tim!

Author's Note

If a reader wishes to receive the original drafts of the articles that I submitted for publication to *The Fabricator* magazine, please contact me at ShahrukhIrani1023@yahoo.com or 832-475-4447.

Part 1 of 5: Analyzing Products, Demand, Margins, and Routings

Abstract: Unlike the Toyotas of the world, a typical job shop manufactures a diverse mix of products (P) with different routings (R) produced in various quantities (Q) with varying revenue and profits ($) and demand repeatability (T). These parameters for each product in the product mix of a job shop enable a PQR$T Analysis that can uncover the reality of a job shop's current state.

Most job shop managers operate multiple businesses under one roof. Such high-mix, low-volume (HMLV) operations use the ***same*** business strategy, the ***same*** suppliers, the ***same*** facility layout, the ***same*** production scheduling, and the ***same*** equipment, all for what amounts to several different businesses.

Unlike Original Equipment Manufacturers and top-tier suppliers, which generally produce product lines in a relatively low-mix, high-volume (LMHV) environment, job shops struggle to develop rules and guidelines to rationalize their business and standardize processes, materials, policies, tools, routings, setups, and so forth. This is all completely understandable, given their diverse product mix. For this reason, they send disparate products, some high-volume, some low-volume, some repeat, and some one-offs, through the same network of manufacturing processes.

A typical lean implementation in a job shop starts with selecting a few products produced per a long-term agreement. Takt Times are calculated, one-piece-flow cells are designed, and Kanban lot sizes are determined – but then what? It is true that a job shop can implement flow production for a portion of its product mix, but what about the rest of its product mix? This is why product mix segmentation is so important.

A typical job shop, the polar opposite of the Toyotas of the world, manufactures a diverse mix of products (P) with different routings (R) produced in various quantities (Q) with varying revenue and profits ($) and demand repeatability (T). These parameters for each different product make up a PQR$T Analysis, a comprehensive data analysis tool that job shops can use to do a product mix segmentation. This ultimately helps the job shop identify the various "businesses", from somewhat predictable repeat work to fabricated prototypes, and it is knowingly (or maybe unknowingly) operating under its roof.

The PQR$T Analysis separates products that produce high revenue or (ideally) profits from those that do not; i.e., high-value jobs are treated differently than low-value jobs. It also breaks up the product mix per their routings, i.e., those with identical/similar routings that belong to a product family and those that do not.

Defining Product Mix

Job shops can process 100's or even 1,000's of different products a year, and classifying them can be a monumental challenge. Here, the PQR$T Analysis can help. Specifically, PQT Analysis relates a product's quantity and demand repeatability (Q and T) by defining *Runners*, *Repeaters*, and *Strangers*.

A *Runner* is a product or product family that has sufficient volume for a dedicated facility or manufacturing cell to produce them. This does not mean that such facilities or cells need to be used continuously because few job shops manufacture such volumes. Instead, these runners may justify a cell or facility that is used as-needed and, most important, *is not shared with any other product or product family.*

A *Repeater* represents repeat work, but volumes are not high enough to dedicate a cell or facility to produce them. Repeaters are scheduled for production in regular intervals. For instance, tool room personnel may know that a certain die is needed each Tuesday morning. Suppliers get used to that regular order, setup resources are made ready, fork lifts may be standing by to move them to/from presses, and so on.

A *Stranger* is a product or product family with low or intermittent volumes. These are fitted into the schedule around the regular slots dedicated to repeaters.

From all this, the final PQR$T Analysis creates a multidimensional data plot that can reveal much about an HMLV operation. Volume/quantity and demand repeatability (Q and T) are analyzed for Runners, Repeaters, and Strangers. Products are also grouped into those producing high or low profit margin (or revenue). Finally, routings (R) are analyzed for both products that are part of a product family and those that are not.

Benefits of PQR$T Analysis

Why bother with such an analysis? It is because it can uncover inefficiencies and identify the core strengths of an HMLV manufacturing operation. If a job shop manager knows exactly what makes the most money and what does not, and why, he can use this for immediate improvements as well as long-term planning.

When it comes to immediate improvements, the analysis can help managers set up flexible fabrication cells for the Strangers in the product mix, with flexible, quick-setup machines. Another cell (or even a separate area) could be dedicated to produce spares or repair items, while another could be dedicated to prototype work. Having a dedicated prototype area would help managers identify and analyze emerging and new business that might eventually end up in the production area.

The analysis also can aid business negotiations. For instance, one job shop may not be able to make high margins on certain work because the work is outside the shop's core competency. After analysis, a manager would know that these Strangers, or even Runners, are not helping the company grow. But that does not mean these jobs would not benefit other job shops in the same geographic area. Why not swap these jobs with these other shops that may be able to benefit from work that fits their core competence, workforce skills, manufacturing technology, and supplier capabilities? It is about competing through cooperation. If a manager has concrete data revealing what makes money for the company and what does not, he can negotiate with competitors and swap jobs with similar revenue. What may be unprofitable for one shop may be very profitable for another, depending on the equipment and processes each job shop has on their floor. Of course, a manager could end up with a bad deal unless he has the necessary intelligence, and here is where PQR$T Analysis comes into play. It lets the business data do the talking, instead of relying on well-worn strategies like waste elimination that have run their course.

Part 2 of 5: Analyzing Product Mix and Volumes – Useful but Insufficient

Abstract: For job shops, the traditional PQ Analysis (Product Quantity Analysis) method misses the sweet spot. The method can be used to segment the product mix of a job shop based on the annual production volume for each product, which helps determine the type of layout best suited for each product segment. However, the tool may be insufficient for a job shop because it does not consider varying margins, revenues, routings, and repeatability of various jobs.

PQR$T Analysis builds on the traditional PQ Analysis, a method for product mix segmentation that OEMs and top-tier manufacturers have embraced for years to plan their lean implementation. Typically, PQ Analysis identifies two distinct segments in a manufacturer's product mix based on production volume alone: those products that are in the HMLV segment and those products that are in the LMHV segment. The "high-mix" is assumed because typically the "long tail" of the product mix contains a large number of products, each of which is produced in small quantities. The "low-mix" is assumed because typically only a few products account for the majority of the total production volume.

The production system designed for one segment is *not* going to be optimal for the other segment. In fact, the use of PQ Analysis encourages a job shop to utilize Value Stream Mapping (VSM), a Lean tool that is fundamentally incapable of analyzing the HMLV segment of the job shop's product mix. For example, the HMLV environment calls for short production runs, whereas the LMHV environment calls for long production runs, and this significantly affects a number of manufacturing choices, such as

- The number of different setups performed consecutively
- The time an operator requires to learn and unlearn a specific task
- The stability of equipment or process parameters during machine operation
- The type and extent of cross-training required for employees who will work in different cells
- The diversity of work assigned to a particular employee
- The extent of flexible versus dedicated automation that must match the diversity of products being produced
- The amount of inspection and automated process control for any task
- Methods for production planning and control
- Methods for inventory control and buffer management
- Methods for operations scheduling
- Methods for supply chain management.

The PQ Analysis Curve

The PQ Analysis method can be used to segment the product mix based on the annual production volume of each product. This helps determine the type of layout best suited for each segment: flowline, job shop, cellular, or some combination of these basic layouts. The typical PQ Analysis curve for an HMLV facility will show, at the left end of the curve, relatively few products being produced in large quantities. These products are best produced on single- or multi-product production lines, or in product-focused cells. The right end of the same curve will show many different products being produced in small quantities that tend to be manufactured in a process, or departmental, layout, often referred to as a *job shop layout*.

Understanding the shape of the PQ Analysis curve is an essential starting point for any job shop implementing Lean. A shallow PQ Analysis curve, which implies that the various products are being produced in similar quantities, suggests a process/functional layout for producing the entire product mix. A deep curve shows that the company's product mix involves a high variety of quantities. These can be grouped into two or more product segments that ideally should be produced in separate production areas, each with a different layout.

You determine whether the PQ Analysis curve is shallow or deep using three ratios. First, use the 80-20 Rule (Pareto Law): The first 20% of the total number of products accounts for 80% of the total (or aggregate) quantity. If the product mix does not meet the condition of this 2:8 ratio, then check for 3:7 (30% of product mix accounts for 70% of total quantity) and then, finally, the 4:6 ratio. A ratio that increases in value from 0.25 to 0.67 indicates that the product mix is *not* dominated by a few high-volume *Runners*, i.e., a product or product family that has sufficient volume for a dedicated facility or manufacturing cell. Instead, it may contain a number of medium-volume repeaters and low-volume strangers. *Repeaters* represent repeat jobs with volumes not high enough to dedicate a facility or cell, while *Strangers* have low or intermittent volumes. A product mix that falls into the 4:6 ratio would likely involve much variety and small lot sizes.

Sample Analysis

Consider Figure 13.1, which relates a job shop's 79 part numbers to quantities for individual orders (on the left vertical axis) and aggregate quantities for an entire group of part numbers (on the right vertical axis) produced during a certain time period.

The graph indicates that only a portion of part numbers are tied to the majority of the total number of parts that the shop produces. The aggregate quantity curve starts low on the left and rises sharply because this shop produces 800,000 pieces in total of about eight or nine different parts that could be classified as "high volume". After this point, the aggregate quantity curve rises less steeply until about 1.6 million on the aggregate quantity axis. That is the "medium-volume" portion of the curve. From there, the curve rises gradually until the total number of parts that the shop produces is reached (in this case, 1,766,478). This shows the common scenario for almost all job shops: The majority of part numbers in their product mix are

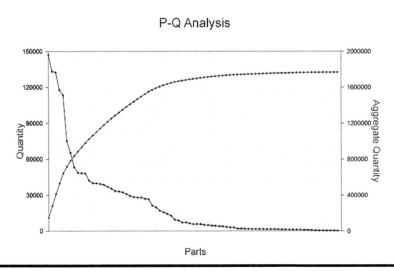

Figure 13.1   The PQ Analysis graph relates a job shop's 79 part numbers to per-order quantity (left axis) and aggregate quantity (right axis).

produced in low volumes; i.e., their PQ Analysis curve will have a short torso and a long tail.

Figure 13.2 shows the parts sorted in order of decreasing quantity. Specifically, we need to determine what portion of the shop's 79 part numbers make up 80, 70, and 60% of the operation's aggregate quantity. Since part numbers cannot be divided in half, you will notice that some calculations result in the closest percentage possible to 60, 70, and 80. So in this case, 13 part numbers (16% of the entire product mix of 79 part numbers) account for *60%* of the total aggregate quantity, 17 part numbers (21% of 79) account for *69%* of the total aggregate quantity, and 23 part numbers (29% of 79) account for *80%* of the total aggregate quantity. This produces the following ratios: 16:60, 21:69, and 29:80, as shown in Figure 13.2.

So is this job shop an LMHV shop, an HMLV shop, or some combination of the two extremes? The numbers show that it is a combination of the two extremes. For the analysis, we use the 4:6, 3:7, and 2:8 ratios as guides. The 16:60 ratio is not close to the 4:6 ratio, but the 21:69 and 29:80 ratios are somewhat close to 3:7 and 2:8, respectively. Although this shop does have a significant percentage of part numbers tied to low volume, its medium- and high-volume parts represent the majority of what the shop actually produces. So in this case, we chose to divide the product mix into two segments, one consisting of the top 23 parts (corresponding to the 29:80 ratio line in Figure 13.2) and the other consisting of the remaining part numbers that are produced in significantly lower volumes.

No.	Part	Quantity	Agg. Qty.	Agg. Qty. (%)	
1	80-671391	147000	147000	8.3	
2	80-4012179	133070	280070	15.9	
3	80-35-B357	132314	412384	23.3	
4	80-4010346	117614	529998	30	
5	80-4012174	113400	643398	36.4	
6	80-671635-00	75012	718410	40.7	
7	80-4030339	65198	783608	44.4	
8	80-4030341	53200	836808	47.4	
9	80-051-1	48580	885388	50.1	
10	80-B113-1001	48132	933520	52.8	
11	80-121018-00	47950	981470	55.6	
12	80-4041707	42000	1023470	57.9	
13	80-4009263	39886	1063356	60.2	
14	80-S113-1001	39732	1103088	62.4	**16:60**
15	80-4030011870964	39256	1142344	64.7	
16	80-4010350	38500	1180844	66.8	
17	80-9033023-303	36848	1217692	68.9	
18	80-121148	35350	1253042	70.9	**21:69**
19	80-4012169	33362	1286404	72.8	
20	80-4009270	32900	1319304	74.7	
21	80-121188-002	32200	1351504	76.5	
22	80-4009121	30800	1382304	78.3	
23	80-121009-00	29288	1411592	79.9	
24	80-4035149	28252	1439844	81.5	**29:80**
25	80-3249869	28014	1467858	83.1	
26	80-4011714	28000	1495858	84.7	
27	80-191820	26866	1522724	86.2	
28	80-4067179	26502	1549226	87.7	
29	80-4010348	21000	1570226	88.9	
30	80-4010351	19600	1589826	90	
31	80-4011725	16800	1606626	91	
32	80-27750-01	15428	1622054	91.8	
33	80-27377	14112	1636166	92.6	
34	80-4010349	12600	1648766	93.3	
35	80-4030007296094	9240	1658006	93.9	
36	80-27708-302UP	8540	1666546	94.3	
37	80-121189	7014	1673560	94.7	
38	80-4010352	7000	1680560	95.1	
39	80-4030007296091	6356	1686916	95.5	
40	80-C27416-2	5614	1692530	95.8	
41	80-4009262	5600	1698130	96.1	
42	80-4035144	5600	1703730	96.4	
43	80-921790	4914	1708644	96.7	
44	80-4003111	4900	1713544	97	
45	80-C46806-1	4354	1717898	97.2	
46	80-4012213	4144	1722042	97.5	
47	80-4059989	3850	1725892	97.7	
48	80-551500	3724	1729616	97.9	
49	80-121387	3220	1732836	98.1	
50	80-3260-041	2828	1735664	98.3	
51	80-ULC0200	2800	1738464	98.4	
52	80-NL150T060LT	1764	1740228	98.5	
53	80-C55581	1750	1741978	98.6	
54	80-522500	1652	1743630	98.7	
55	80-NL150T072LT	1540	1745170	98.8	
56	80-C558-1	1526	1746696	98.9	
57	80-3260-0980	1512	1748208	99	
58	80-4030007296090	1456	1749664	99	
59	80-C27416-1	1456	1751120	99.1	
60	80-4012212	1400	1752520	99.2	
61	80-4039260	1400	1753920	99.3	
62	80-150T084LT	1344	1755264	99.4	
63	80-37355-1072	1204	1756468	99.4	
64	80-9627714-301UP	1078	1757546	99.5	
65	80-9627713-301UP	1050	1758596	99.6	
66	80-9627712-301UP	1022	1759618	99.6	
67	80-9627715-301UP	1022	1760640	99.7	
68	80-9627716-301UP	1022	1761662	99.7	
69	80-37355-1084	952	1762614	99.8	
70	80-D8097	756	1763370	99.8	
71	80-A37353	728	1764098	99.9	
72	80-NL150T084LT	644	1764742	99.9	
73	80-W101-2006	462	1765204	99.9	
74	80-S113-1004	364	1765568	99.9	
75	80-G121-1002	280	1765848	100	
76	80-3260-503	182	1766030	100	
77	80-4030007296089	168	1766198	100	
78	80-NL150T096LT	168	1766366	100	
79	80-NL150T120LT	112	1766478	100	

Figure 13.2 The PQ Analysis shows input data for a shop's 79 part numbers and their quantities, as well as the three ratio lines used to segment the product mix.

Putting PQ Analysis to Work

Such an analysis can help focus data collection efforts. Job shops are complicated operations producing many products. This often makes Continuous Improvement (CI) efforts difficult, time-consuming, and costly, because collecting data for all products is … well? … difficult!

Say that managers want to reduce material handling costs, standardize storage containers, and improve shop floor communications between machine operators and material handlers. This would require data collection to generate VSMs, Flow Process Charts, and Material Handling Analysis charts as part of a larger Systematic Handling Analysis (SHA) initiative. Using the PQ Analysis, the improvement team could quickly select one or more products from the high-volume segment and leave the low-volume products for future investigation.

Material handling cost boils down to the total time workers spend moving the material between two locations. The time is a function of travel distance between the locations and the number of trips made between them (which is directly proportional to volume). In other words, the high-volume segment of products probably has the highest contribution to material handling costs. Working with only the high-volume segment, as identified in the PQ Analysis, the improvement team could produce a From-To Chart to identify work centers (W/C) that frequently process part numbers in the high-volume segment.

Managers also can use the PQ Analysis to implement an inventory control policy that is suitable for each of the two segments (HMLV and LMHV). Inventory control for the LMHV Runners could be done using supermarkets and Kanban-based replenishment. In fact, if product families (based on common raw materials, sizes, or shapes) exist within that segment, then the improvement team could implement dedicated storage locations, use common containers and handling devices, and implement other inventory control measures. In contrast, inventory control for the HMLV segment of parts would be done using a pure Make-To-Order strategy with zero on-hand inventories for these parts. In turn, a Make-To-Order strategy would necessitate the use of finite capacity scheduling (FCS) based on due dates instead of the standard pull scheduling or MRP (Material Requirements Planning) scheduling approaches.

Limitations of PQ Analysis

While this approach may be a starting point, job shops should not stop here. The reason is that PQ Analysis does not consider the R (routings), $ (margin), and T (demand repeatability) of the product mix. As we have shown, the PQ Analysis method places importance on high-volume products. But for a job shop, a high-volume job may provide significant revenue and volume (Q), but at low margins ($). In fact, it is the R, $, and T information that really helps job shops hit the sweet spot in their business, i.e., accepting complex, high-precision jobs with high-skilled labor content that are produced in low volumes but are highly profitable. Certain job shops tied to the defense and aerospace sectors, for instance, could thrive in any recession because they can fulfill *low*-volume, *high*-margin orders for complex parts.

Part 3 of 5: PQ$ Analysis – Why Revenue Matters in Product Mix Segmentation

Abstract: Fabricators have to look past the traditional PQ Analysis, which may point job shops in the wrong direction. Revenue plays a role when analyzing a job. Instead of focusing on a sample of products selected using a single criterion, Quantity, the PQ$ Analysis (Product Quantity Revenue Analysis) brings Revenue into the equation.

Job shops serve various business sectors that demand different parts or products in specific one-time quantities or annual production volumes. Developing an improvement road map requires managers to analyze this product mix using a multi-criterion approach like PQR$T Analysis. Each criterion used to develop the analysis is critical. Considering only product quantities, as in a traditional PQ Analysis, would produce vastly different results and may point job shops in the wrong direction when it comes to CI and strategic planning to achieve business growth. That is because a traditional PQ Analysis segments the mix of parts (P) based only on their quantities (Q), as is typical in LMHV repetitive production assembly facilities. Unfortunately, such an analysis identifies at most only three product segments: high volume, medium volume, and low volume. The PQ Analysis runs into problems when applied in HMLV manufacturing facilities, especially job shops that produce small batches of high-priced products. The PQ Analysis will always ignore the low-volume products, even though they may bring in significant revenue. At the same time, this analysis may emphasize certain high-volume jobs that are not big moneymakers.

Any business can improve cash flow by completing high-value orders in the shortest period of time and by minimizing the notorious and well-known Seven Types of Waste that decrease profitability of low-volume products that have, or could have, very healthy margins. From the perspective of part flow, three types of operational costs (transportation, work-in-process (WIP), and queuing) increase manufacturing costs. Two of those costs (transportation and queuing) depend heavily on production volumes and container sizes, but WIP costs depend heavily on product value, which is usually reflected in the sales earned from each product.

This is where PQ$ Analysis can help. Instead of focusing on a sample of products selected using a single criterion (Quantity), this analysis brings Revenue into the equation. Most important, it does not just separate the product mix into *three* segments based on volume (low, medium, or high), but into *at least four* segments. For instance, if a shop decides to separate products into high and low categories on *both* criteria (Volume and Revenue), then every product would fall into any one of the following four segments: (High Volume, High Revenue; Low Volume, High Revenue; High Volume, Low Revenue; and High Volume, High Revenue). If a shop was to categorize each of the two criteria for segmentation into three categories (low, medium, and high), then the number of segments would, of course, grow to nine, and so on.

The bottom line is that, unlike PQ Analysis, PQ$ Analysis incorporates how much money parts actually make. And when it comes to running a business, two things matter: the total amount of money made and the speed with which those orders that make the most money are completed and shipped.

The PQ$ Analysis produces a scatter plot, as shown in Figure 13.3. The horizontal axis (X) represents Quantity or Volume, while the vertical axis (Y) represents Revenue or Profit Margin. Every point in the scatter plot represents a particular product. As Figure 13.3 shows, this shop's product mix appears to have only three segments: (Low Quantity, Low Revenue), (Low Quantity, High Revenue), and (High Quantity, High Revenue). The dotted lines on the two axes are threshold values, separating low revenue from high revenue (R*) as well as low from high quantities (Q*). Each quadrant defines a product mix segment that ideally should be managed as a separate business and be produced in a separate area of the facility with a suitable layout, possibly utilizing different manufacturing technology and workforce skills.

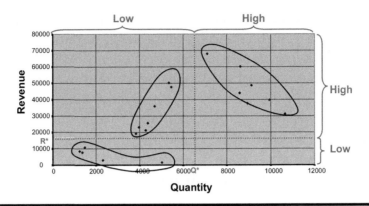

Figure 13.3 The PQ$ Analysis scatter plot shows the product mix of a hypothetical job shop.

The Whole Is Greater Than the Parts

Figure 13.4 shows how a typical job shop would prioritize products based only on quantity. Part numbers that are produced in the highest volumes are placed on top, followed by part numbers with decreasing quantities.

No.	Part	Qty.	Aggregate Qty.	Aggregate Qty. %
1	80-671391	147000	147000	8.3
2	80-4012179	133070	280070	15.9
3	80-35-B357	132314	412384	23.3
4	80-4010346	117614	529998	30
5	80-4012174	113400	643398	36.4
6	80-671635-00	75012	718410	40.7
7	80-4030339	65198	783608	44.4
8	80-4030341	53200	836808	47.4
9	80-051-1	48580	885388	50.1
10	80-B113-1001	48132	933520	52.8
11	80-121018-00	47950	981470	55.6
12	80-4041707	42000	1023470	57.9
13	80-4009263	39886	1063356	60.2
14	80-S113-1001	39732	1103088	62.4
15	80-4030011870964	39256	1142344	64.7
16	80-4010350	38500	1180844	66.8
17	80-9033023-303	36848	1217692	68.9
18	80-121148	35350	1253042	70.9
19	80-4012169	33362	1286404	72.8
20	80-4009270	32900	1319304	74.7
21	80-121188-002	32200	1351504	76.5
22	80-4009121	30800	1382304	78.3
23	80-121009-00	29288	1411592	79.9

Figure 13.4 In a PQ Analysis, products are ranked by quantity, with the highest-volume products on top. The red line indicates the threshold between the high-volume and low-volume segments of the product mix based on the classical 80-20 Pareto Rule.

(Continued)

24	80-4035149	28252	1439844	81.5
25	80-3249869	28014	1467858	83.1
26	80-4011714	28000	1495858	84.7
27	80-191820	26866	1522724	86.2
28	80-4067179	26502	1549226	87.7
29	80-4010348	21000	1570226	88.9
30	80-4010351	19600	1589826	90
31	80-4011725	16800	1606626	91
32	80-27750-01	15428	1622054	91.8
33	80-27377	14112	1636166	92.6
34	80-4010349	12600	1648766	93.3
35	80-4030007296094	9240	1658006	93.9
36	80-27708-302UP	8540	1666546	94.3
37	80-121189	7014	1673560	94.7
38	80-4010352	7000	1680560	95.1
39	80-4030007296091	6356	1686916	95.5
40	80-C27416-2	5614	1692530	95.8
41	80-4009262	5600	1698130	96.1
42	80-4035144	5600	1703730	96.4
43	80-921790	4914	1708644	96.7
44	80-4003111	4900	1713544	97
45	80-C46806-1	4354	1717898	97.2
46	80-4012213	4144	1722042	97.5
47	80-4059989	3850	1725892	97.7
48	80-551500	3724	1729616	97.9
49	80-121387	3220	1732836	98.1
50	80-3260-041	2828	1735664	98.3
51	80-ULC0200	2800	1738464	98.4
52	80-NL150T060LT	1764	1740228	98.5
53	80-C55581	1750	1741978	98.6
54	80-522500	1652	1743630	98.7
55	80-NL150T072LT	1540	1745170	98.8
56	80-C558-1	1526	1746696	98.9
57	80-3260-0980	1512	1748208	99
58	80-4030007296090	1456	1749664	99
59	80-C27416-1	1456	1751120	99.1
60	80-4012212	1400	1752520	99.2
61	80-4039260	1400	1753920	99.3
62	80-150T084LT	1344	1755264	99.4
63	80-37355-1072	1204	1756468	99.4
64	80-9627714-301UP	1078	1757546	99.5
65	80-9627713-301UP	1050	1758596	99.6
66	80-9627712-301UP	1022	1759618	99.6
67	80-9627715-301UP	1022	1760640	99.7
68	80-9627716-301UP	1022	1761662	99.7
69	80-37355-1084	952	1762614	99.8
70	80-D8097	756	1763370	99.8
71	80-A37353	728	1764098	99.9
72	80-NL150T084LT	644	1764742	99.9
73	80-W101-2006	462	1765204	99.9
74	80-S113-1004	364	1765568	99.9
75	80-G121-1002	280	1765848	100
76	80-3260-503	182	1766030	100
77	80-4030007296089	168	1766198	100
78	80-NL150T096LT	168	1766366	100
79	80-NL150T120LT	112	1766478	100

Figure 13.4 (CONTINUED) In a PQ Analysis, products are ranked by quantity, with the highest-volume products on top. The red line indicates the threshold between the high-volume and low-volume segments of the product mix based on the classical 80-20 Pareto Rule.

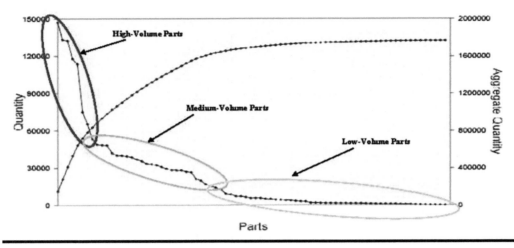

Figure 13.5   The PQ Analysis shows that the shop runs a few high-volume parts and has a "long tail" of various low-volume parts (which is typical for job shops).

The PQ Analysis curve in Figure 13.5 shows that the shop runs few part numbers in high quantities. In fact, most parts run in low quantities, as shown by the long tail that is typical for a job shop's production volumes. The sharp changes in the slope of the curve indicate a potential cutoff point between different product mix segments between low-volume "Strangers", medium-volume "Repeaters", and high-volume "Runners". Using the classical 80-20 Pareto Rule would identify two segments in the product mix: The top 23 part numbers represent the high-volume segment (representing 80% of aggregate volume), and the remaining 56 part numbers represent the low-volume segment.

But what about Revenue? To include that variable, a P$ Analysis using Revenue instead of Quantity as the variable for ranking the parts from highest to lowest Revenue dollars would produce the chart in Figure 13.6. Next, a threshold line is inserted between the "high-revenue" and "low-revenue" segments by using the 80-20 Rule as a guide, grouping the high-value parts that produce 80% of total Revenue. This produces the plot in Figure 13.7.

So will the two samples of parts (the high-Quantity parts from the PQ Analysis and the high-Revenue parts from the P$ Analysis) always include the same parts? Not necessarily! Because either analysis ignores the other criterion completely. In contrast, PQ$ Analysis will produce the (obvious!) scatter plot in Figure 13.8, which suggests that the product mix could be broken into three segments: (High Volume, Low Revenue), (Low Volume, High Revenue), and (Low Volume, Low Revenue).

The part groupings are distinct enough that we could actually just eyeball them to get a general idea of which products should be part of which

No.	Part	Revenue	Aggregate Revenue	Aggregate Revenue %
1	80-27708-302UP	1952230	1952230	8.69
2	80-4030011870964	1618932	3571162	15.89
3	80-27750-01	931854	4503016	20.04
4	80-9033023-303	922670	5425686	24.14
5	80-4067179	757428	6183114	27.51
6	80-4030007296091	757190	6940304	30.88
7	80-35-B357	697298	7637602	33.98
8	80-671391	658560	8296162	36.91
9	80-NL150T060LT	632744	8928906	39.73
10	80-NL150T072LT	591752	9520658	42.36
11	80-150T084LT	587664	10108322	44.98
12	80-4030007296094	574084	10682406	47.53
13	80-3260-041	569842	11252248	50.07
14	80-921790	526120	11778368	52.41
15	80-37355-1072	501774	12280142	54.64
16	80-C27416-2	495992	12776134	56.85
17	80-671635-00	466340	13242474	58.92
18	80-9627713-301UP	462378	13704852	60.98
19	80-37355-1084	447062	14151914	62.97
20	80-W101-2006	445858	14597772	64.95
21	80-9627715-301UP	423766	15021538	66.84
22	80-4010346	379806	15401344	68.53
23	80-4012179	377916	15779260	70.21
24	80-C46806-1	362474	16141734	71.82
25	80-9627714-301UP	360430	16502164	73.43
26	80-4012174	324324	16826488	74.87
27	80-NL150T084LT	281596	17108084	76.12
28	80-121018-00	275716	17383800	77.35
29	80-051-1	255052	17638852	78.48
30	80-4030007296090	234346	17873198	79.53
31	80-121188-002	202860	18076058	80.43
32	80-9627712-301UP	192276	18268334	81.28
33	80-B113-1001	186116	18454450	82.11
34	80-4041707	180180	18634630	82.91
35	80-3249869	179200	18813830	83.71
36	80-4009263	176302	18990132	84.50
37	80-121009-00	171332	19161464	85.26
38	80-3260-0980	157024	19318488	85.96
39	80-C55581	151284	19469772	86.63
40	80-4009121	151228	19621000	87.30
41	80-4010350	148610	19769610	87.96
42	80-121148	143444	19913054	88.60
43	80-4030341	140980	20054034	89.23
44	80-9627716-301UP	139258	20193292	89.85
45	80-G121-1002	138768	20332060	90.47
46	80-D8097	133882	20465942	91.06
47	80-C558-1	131922	20597864	91.65
48	80-4009270	126994	20724858	92.21
49	80-C27416-1	124054	20848912	92.77
50	80-4011725	119448	20968360	93.30

Figure 13.6   For a P$ Analysis, products are ranked by their revenue, with the highest-revenue products on top. The red line indicates the threshold between high-revenue and low-revenue products.

(Continued)

51	80-4030339	117208	21085568	93.82
52	80-191820	100744	21186312	94.27
53	80-4012169	98756	21285068	94.71
54	80-4011714	91560	21376628	95.11
55	80-4010351	86632	21463260	95.50
56	80-4035149	86170	21549430	95.88
57	80-NL150T096LT	83258	21632688	96.25
58	80-S113-1004	70532	21703220	96.57
59	80-4010348	69300	21772520	96.88
60	80-27377	69286	21841806	97.18
61	80-NL150T120LT	68572	21910378	97.49
62	80-3260-503	48342	21958720	97.70
63	80-121189	47348	22006068	97.91
64	80-A37353	47320	22053388	98.13
65	80-4010349	43092	22096480	98.32
66	80-4003111	41216	22137696	98.50
67	80-S113-1001	39732	22177428	98.68
68	80-4030007296089	38892	22216320	98.85
69	80-4012213	34846	22251166	99.01
70	80-4010352	34790	22285956	99.16
71	80-4059989	33306	22319262	99.31
72	80-ULC0200	31556	22350818	99.45
73	80-551500	29050	22379868	99.58
74	80-121387	27720	22407588	99.70
75	80-4009262	27048	22434636	99.82
76	80-4035144	14952	22449588	99.89
77	80-4012212	10682	22460270	99.94
78	80-522500	8428	22468698	99.97
79	80-4039260	6062	22474760	100.00

Figure 13.6 (CONTINUED) For a P$ Analysis, products are ranked by their revenue, with the highest-revenue products on top. The red line indicates the threshold between high-revenue and low-revenue products.

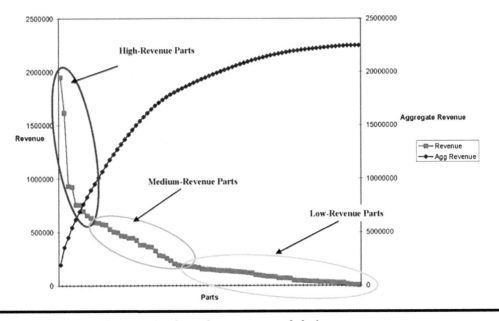

Figure 13.7 The P$ Analysis plot relates parts and their revenues.

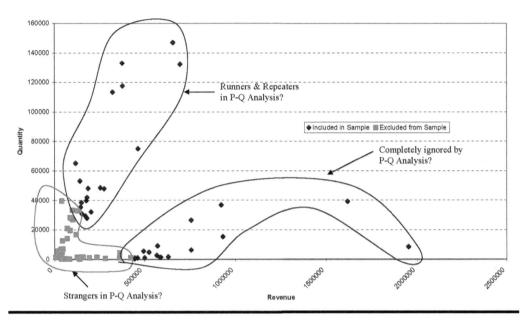

Figure 13.8   The PQ$ Analysis scatter plot shows how PQ Analysis and P$ Analysis were used to determine three segments in the product mix: (High Volume, Low Revenue), (Low Volume, Low Revenue) and (Low Volume, High Revenue).

segment. But to be more precise, we simply locate the point on the scatter plot that represents the product number corresponding to the revenue threshold, R^*, where aggregate revenue reaches 80%, and draw a vertical line. We would do the same with quantity, Q^*, to draw a horizontal line, as is shown earlier in Figure 13.3. Instead of relying on any variant of the 80-20 Rule, Production Flow Analysis and Simplification Toolkit (PFAST) uses a proprietary algorithm that (1) normalizes the original Quantity and Revenue values on a scale [0,1], (2) computes a weighted sum for each product using its normalized values (Q^n, R^n), and (3) ranks/sorts the parts in decreasing order of these normalized values.

Note that if the shop had relied solely on PQ Analysis, it would have ignored products in the (High Revenue, Low Volume) segment. And if the shop had relied solely on the P$ Analysis, it would have ignored the (Low Revenue, High Volume) segment. It is important that job shops remain acutely aware of the fact that, unlike Toyota, reducing costs through waste elimination simply does not make them competitive and ensure long-term growth. They have to be flexible, agile, and reconfigurable in order to fulfill orders for parts that could belong in any of the four segments: (High Volume, Low Revenue), (Low Volume, High Revenue), (Low Volume, High Revenue) and (Low Volume, Low Revenue).

Putting the PQ$ Analysis to Work

So how can the information gained from a PQ$ Analysis guide kaizen events, "big bang" improvement projects, management policies, and strategic planning?

Market Diversification

Figure 13.8 shows that the job shop does not have a single part in the high-revenue, high-quantity quadrant. That is typical because most job shops do not specialize in high-volume, low-mix manufacturing. However, no job shop owner would pass up a long-term contract from a defense prime contractor or OEM to supply a single part (or well-defined part family) that will be ordered on a consistent basis throughout the year, perhaps even for a few years (as is the case in the aerospace sector). In this case, the shop would be well advised to set up a stand-alone cell using the well-known Lean tools such as one-piece flow, U-shaped cell layout, Takt Time, and level-loading.

Operating (Two) Factories within a Factory (Virtual Cells)[1]

Here I have paraphrased Page 27 ("One Business or Two?") in Glenday, I. 2007. *Breaking Through to Flow: Banish Fire Fighting and Increase Customer Service.* Ross-on-Wye, UK: Lean Enterprise Academy Ltd. A manufacturer of hydraulic pipes and couplings produces 2,000 SKUs (Stock Keeping Units), all requiring a 48-hour lead time. The company, however, was finding it increasingly difficult and costly to achieve this lead time. An analysis showed that more than half of sales came from only 92 products, which was less than 5% of the entire product mix. Customers ordered other products infrequently in small quantities, even as single items. Armed with this information, managers decided the company needed two types of factories: a high-volume, repetitive manufacturing facility and a flexible job shop. However, it was not cost-effective to build two factories or even to physically separate the equipment. Instead, managers determined what equipment would be needed for high-volume products in a fixed sequence and painted those machines green. To determine who would run these machines,

---

[1] For an excellent discussion on Virtual Cells in process industries, please see Pages 185–195 ("Virtual Cells") in King, P. L. 2009. *Lean for the Process Industries: Dealing with Complexity.* New York, NY: CRC Press.

managers selected employees based on their work routine preference and gave them green overalls. They painted the remaining equipment beige and selected employees who preferred to tackle difficult and complex operations, including frequent setups and, yes, gave them beige overalls.

Although the equipment and staff intermingled on the floor, each business operated totally differently. The green factory had fixed hours of work, just-in-time (JIT) deliveries, and improvement activities focused on achieving faster cycle times and increased productivity. The beige factory had work hours that varied according to the level of demand each week. Materials were purchased only when required. Improvement activities focused on flexibility and responsiveness. This company succeeded in creating and operating two businesses under the same roof, even if each business had different policies, procedures, and performance metrics.

Supplier Management

No manufacturer wants a dispersed supplier network with long supply chains for any component or subassembly they obtain from outside vendors. High-volume operations with a matching Make-To-Stock inventory policy allow large production batch sizes; thereby, a supplier can be located far from a manufacturer's location. That supplier can make Periodic FTL (Full Truck Load) deliveries on a relatively consistent and predictable schedule despite being located far from the customer's manufacturing plant. Inventory buffers can be maintained at both the outgoing and incoming points in the Value Stream of the outsourced product(s). *In contrast*, the low-volume operations of any job shop, whose daily schedules are constantly disrupted at the whim and fancy of their customers, force them to work with nearby suppliers who can accommodate changes in the mix and lot sizes of orders sent to them.

Purchasing Management

High-revenue, low-volume products that are produced from rare (and expensive!) materials necessitate an "unLean" strategy for raw material purchasing and inventory control, specifically bulk purchase of the raw material(s). For instance, a CNC (Computer Numerical Control) machine shop that produces an aerospace component from titanium, which is not easily available if shipped from, say, China, would keep a close watch on available inventory, supplier lead times, and market prices for that exotic metal. They would purchase the raw material in bulk whereby they would (1) get a quantity discount and (2) earn quantity discounts on bulk buys. Although Lean would consider this "hoarding of inventory" to be wasteful, this strategy makes complete business sense for a defense supplier who produces parts needed to make emergency repairs on legacy weapon systems in the field. In fact, the DoD (Department of Defense) mandates safety stocks for critical components to maintain almost all weapon systems, especially those like the B-52 bombers which are operating many years beyond their original operational lifespan.

Inventory Control: Specific inventory control systems can be used for products in different segments. Consider products in the high-volume, low-revenue segment. These orders could help develop customer relationships. In fact, the same customers may also provide valuable high-revenue orders. Still, why should a job shop focus improvement efforts on large orders that do not make much money? In this case, a shop could outsource low-revenue, high-volume jobs to another manufacturer. All that they would have to do is receive the parts from the subcontractor, label them, and ship them to the end customer. True margins may suffer because the job shop outsources these orders which already have low margins to begin. But the customer goodwill earned from "going the extra mile" provides a long-term payoff. Besides, removing this low-margin work from the shop floor would allow manufacturing capacity to be invested in other parts in the product mix, which would lead to a healthier balance sheet.

Shop Floor Scheduling: A simple practice to facilitate shop floor scheduling could be that the color of the paperwork and containers associated with a high-revenue order are different from the paperwork and containers for the other orders. This way, everybody gives a higher priority to processing high-revenue orders that are waiting in queues at different W/Cs across the facility.

Equipment Purchases: The value and volume of production of different products influence the flexibility and sophistication of the manufacturing equipment used to produce them. High-volume assembly facilities are increasingly embracing "right-sized" automation, i.e., equipment designed for producing a limited range of products in medium-to-high volumes. On the other hand, many job shops struggle to hire and retain skilled equipment operators. Therefore, they prefer to purchase flexible and multi-function machines that can quickly do setup and tool changes or even machines that are capable of lights-out operation during the night shift or during weekends.

Part 4 of 5: Minding Your P's, Q's, R's, and Revenue Too

Abstract: Incorporating the PR Analysis (relating product mix and routing similarities) into a PQ Analysis (relating product mix and quantities) creates the PQR Analysis. Similarly, incorporating PQ$ Analysis (relating product quantities and revenues) with PR Analysis creates PQR$ Analysis. A product mix, quantity, routing, and revenue analysis (PQR$ Analysis) can jump-start a job shop's improvement efforts.

Most job shops, knowingly or unknowingly, operate multiple businesses under one roof. All these "businesses" use the same workforce, the same planning strategies, the same suppliers, the same facility layout, and the same equipment. In reality, job shop managers could split their product mix into two or more segments, and *ideally*, each segment should be allocated a separate area that is run using different management policies, support systems, workforce skills, and operational strategies, including scheduling, purchasing, inventory control, and facility layout. Why? It is because these segments require shared resources, including people and machines, and so when they are merged, they inherently interfere and compete with each other.

As discussed earlier, the PQ Analysis, which relates product mix (P) to associated quantities (Q), is a useful but incomplete method for segmenting the product mix of a job shop. Yes, it is simple to implement on a spreadsheet, and it complements VSM. Unfortunately, even VSM works best in LMHV assembly facilities. In fact, the fundamental concept of VSM is based on the theory of assembly line balancing. And an assembly line simply is not a job shop, and never will be! VSM can map a single or, at best, two or three routings, which is obviously not enough for a job shop. Nor is VSM able to depict an entire family of products with different setups and cycle times for various operations in their routings. Essentially, VSM is a method that misleads job shops into believing that, just because they have a few high-volume products, their entire business can run to the assembly line-like "beat" of repetitious production. And PQ Analysis fails to consider the routing, revenue, stability, and repeatability of demand for a job shop's different products. Although VSM and PQ Analysis complement each other, both are really effective only in LMHV situations and will *incorrectly* focus attention on a small percentage of a job shop's product mix. This is why the PQR$T Analysis can play a valuable role because it reflects the realities job shop managers face. They have to manage a production system that has a diverse product mix (P) with different routings (R) produced in various quantities (Q) with varying revenue and profits ($) and demand stability and order repeatability (T). Analyzing all these factors *together* will help job shop managers see the whole picture.

Analyzing Product Mix Using Quantities and Routings

PQR Analysis is an approach that incorporates a PR Analysis (one relating product mix and routing similarities) into a PQ Analysis. This approach (PQR Analysis) segments a product mix into at least two, three, or more segments. Thereafter, product families in each segment can be produced using a suitable manufacturing system, be it a high-volume cell devoted to a single product, a flexible line devoted to a product family, or a flexible cell that, say, can run unattended overnight to produce a large family of parts, but during the day will produce the remaining low-volume products in the product mix.

Much of the methodology behind PQR Analysis comes from the PFA work of Prof. John Burbidge of Britain, as well as the Group Technology strategies that helped transform numerous job shops in the U.K. into cell-based facilities during the 1970s. These proven approaches for HMLV manufacturing were pioneered by the British, Germans, and Russians (and not Toyota!). The Toyota Production System provides significant value for high-volume, low-mix production. But, of course, a job shop is not Toyota.

PQ$ Analysis is an approach that incorporates revenue into a PQ Analysis.

PQR$ Analysis is a combination of PR Analysis and PQ$ Analysis. Although not as comprehensive as the complete method of PQR$T Analysis, the product-quantity-routing-revenue (PQR$) analysis, unlike the PQ Analysis, will surely not mislead job shop owners when they make decisions about their product mix.

PQR$ Analysis

Consider one job shop that has 530 products whose routings contain 57 pieces of equipment (W/Cs), including equipment available at the shop's suppliers. Like any contract manufacturer, it is easily a complex, highly variable operation. In this example, the company used PFAST to perform the

PQR$ Analysis. However, it is possible to implement these same analytics using Microsoft Excel® or Access®, or even Six Sigma statistical analysis software such as Minitab®.

To start, the improvement team assigns each W/C a number and determines whether the machine is a monument or if it can be relocated (see Figure 13.9). They determine whether the process would be expensive to duplicate if the shop wanted to purchase new machines to minimize shared resources among product mix segments.

The team also produces the information in Figure 13.10, which shows the quantity, routing (with corresponding W/C numbers), and revenue for each product number over a specified period. Figure 13.11 shows the current facility layout with all the W/C locations, including unmovable monuments.

Next the shop does a full-scale PR Analysis (see Figure 13.12), also called a *machine-part matrix clustering* or *product-process matrix clustering*, to analyze all 530 products and their individual routings to assess if there are families of parts using groups of machines that could be moved into manufacturing cells. Think of this analysis as a visualization of all 530 Value Streams without using VSM at all! In this spreadsheet, "1" occurs at every point of intersection where a part number along the

W/C #	DESCRIPTION OF EQUIPMENT	RELOCATABLE?	COST OF DUPLICATION
1	700 TON PRESS	YES	EXPENSIVE
2	5" UPSETTER	NO	EXPENSIVE
3	5000# Area FURNACE	YES	
4	LARGE ROTOBLASTER	YES	
5	350 TON PRESS	YES	EXPENSIVE
6	5" UPSETTER FURNACE	YES	
7	5000# Area HAMMER	NO	EXPENSIVE
8	GRINDING TABLE	YES	
9	60 TON PRESS	YES	
10	150 TON TRIM PRESS	YES	EXPENSIVE
11	3000# Area HAMMER	NO	EXPENSIVE
12	158 TON TRIM PRESS	YES	EXPENSIVE
13	HYDRAULIC BENDER	YES	
14	4" THREADER	YES	
15	4" BELT GRINDER	YES	
16	3000# Area FURNACE	YES	
17	BAND SAWS	YES	
18	200# Area OPEN DIE HAMMER	NO	EXPENSIVE
19	400# Area FURNACE	YES	
20	400# Area OPEN DIE HAMMER	NO	EXPENSIVE
21	600# Area FURNACE	YES	
22	600# Area OPEN DIE HAMMER	NO	EXPENSIVE

Figure 13.9   The company lists its W/Cs and specifies whether the machine can be relocated and whether the process would be expensive to duplicate. This is just a portion of the complete list of 57 W/Cs. The red signifies monuments, which are not practical to move. Highlighted green sections (not shown in this portion of the chart) signify outside processes.

No.	Part	Quantity	Revenue	Routings										
1	80-A37353	728	47320	17	6	2	11	10	29	54	55			
2	80-C27416-1	1456	124054	17	6	2	11	10	29	54	55			
3	80-C27416-2	5614	495992	17	6	2	11	10	29	54	55			
4	80-C46806-1	4354	362474	17	6	2	11	10	29	54	55			
5	80-C55581	1750	151284	17	6	2	11	10	29	54	55			
6	80-C558-1	1526	131922	17	6	2	11	10	29	54	55			
7	80-D8097	756	133882	17	6	2	11	10	29	54	55			
8	80-B113-1001	48132	186116	17	56	57	54							
9	80-4003111	4900	41216	1	57	25	55	48	55					
10	80-4009121	30800	151228	1	57	25	56	48	55					
11	80-4009262	5600	27048	1	57	25	57	48	55					
12	80-4009263	39886	176302	1	57	25	58	48	55					
13	80-4009270	32900	126994	1	57	25	59	48	55					
14	80-4010346	117614	379806	1	57	25	60	48	55					
15	80-4010348	21000	69300	1	57	25	61	48	55					
16	80-4010349	12600	43092	1	57	25	62	48	55					
17	80-4010350	38500	148610	1	57	25	63	48	55					
18	80-4010351	19600	86632	1	57	25	64	48	55					
19	80-4010352	7000	34790	1	57	25	65	48	55					
20	80-4011714	28000	91560	1	26	57	66	48	55					
21	80-4011725	16800	119448	1	57	25	67	48	55					
22	80-4012169	33362	98756	1	26	57	68	48	55					
23	80-4012174	113400	324324	1	26	57	69	48	55					
24	80-4012179	133070	377916	1	26	57	70	48	55					
25	80-4012212	1400	10682	1	26	57	71	48	55					
26	80-4012213	4144	34846	1	26	57	72	48	55					
27	80-4030339	65198	117208	1	27	9	73	48	55					
28	80-4030341	53200	140980	1	27	9	74	48	55					
29	80-4035144	5600	14952	1	28	50	75	48	55					
30	80-4035149	28252	86170	1	28	50	76	48	55					
31	80-4039260	1400	6062	1	28	50	77	48	55					
32	80-4041707	42000	180180	1	57	25	78	48	55					
33	80-4059989	3850	33306	1	26	57	79	48	55					
34	80-4067179	26502	757428	17	39	40	80	57	54	57	55			
35	80-4030011870964	39256	1618932	17	39	40	81	22	53	29	28	4	55	
36	80-150T084LT	1344	587664	17	6	2	82	12	8	42	41	57	55	
37	80-G121-1002	280	138768	17	6	2	83	12	8	42	41	57	55	
38	80-NL150T060LT	1764	632744	17	6	2	84	12	8	42	41	57	55	
39	80-NL150T072LT	1540	591752	17	6	2	85	12	8	42	41	57	55	
40	80-NL150T084LT	644	281596	17	6	2	86	12	8	42	41	57	55	
41	80-NL150T096LT	168	83258	17	6	2	87	12	8	42	41	57	55	
42	80-NL150T120LT	112	68572	17	6	2	88	12	8	42	41	57	55	
43	80-3249869	28014	179200	17	56	1	89	29	26	54	57	48	55	
44	80-121009-00	29288	171332	17	39	40	90	22	55					
45	80-121188-002	32200	202860	17	39	40	91	22	55					
46	80-121189	7014	47348	17	39	40	92	22	55					
47	80-671391	147000	658560	17	16	11	93	26	4	55				
48	80-121018-00	47950	275716	17	39	40	94	22	55					
49	80-121148	35350	143444	1	50	26	95	55						
50	80-121387	3220	27720	17	39	40	96	22	55					
51	80-ULC0200	2800	31556	17	39	40	97	22	55					
52	80-35-B357	132314	697298	17	1	57	98	54	55					
53	80-27750-01	15428	931854	17	39	40	99	41	3	7	12	57	54	55
54	80-37355-1072	1204	501774	17	6	2	100	12	8	42	41	57	55	
55	80-37355-1084	952	447062	17	6	2	101	12	8	42	41	57	55	

Figure 13.10   The spreadsheet shows the input data used for PQR$ Analysis, i.e., quantity (Q), revenue ($), and the routing (R) for each product/part (P). Note: This is just a sample of parts that was extracted from the product mix of 530 part numbers. A complete PQR Analysis would include all 530 part numbers because analyzing the complete population of all product routings does have value, as revealed in the "Narrowing the Analysis" section.

(*Continued*)

56	80-051-1	48580	255052	17	1	26	102	54	55									
57	80-191820	26866	100744	17	16	11	103	26	29	28	27	48	55					
58	80-522500	1652	8428	17	16	11	104	26	29	28	27	48	55					
59	80-551500	3724	29050	17	16	11	105	26	29	28	27	48	55					
60	80-S113-1001	39732	39732	17	16	11	106	57	53	55								
61	80-S113-1004	364	70532	17	16	11	107	57	53	55								
62	80-27708-302UP	8540	1952230	17	39	40	108	9	11	10	39	40	57	54				
63	80-9033023-303	36848	922670	57	54	57	109											
64	80-9627712-301UP	1022	192276	17	6	56	110	11	10	6	7	12	8	54	57	54	53	8	55
65	80-9627713-301UP	1050	462378	17	6	56	111	11	10	6	7	12	8	54	57	54	53	8	55
66	80-9627714-301UP	1078	360430	17	6	56	112	11	10	6	7	12	8	54	57	54	53	8	55
67	80-9627715-301UP	1022	423766	17	6	56	113	11	10	6	7	12	8	54	57	54	53	8	55
68	80-9627716-301UP	1022	139258	17	6	56	114	11	10	6	7	12	8	54	57	54	53	8	55
69	80-3260-041	2828	569842	17	6	2	115	10	29	28	54	57	55					
70	80-3260-0980	1512	157024	17	6	2	116	10	29	28	54	57	55					
71	80-3260-503	182	48342	17	6	2	117	10	29	28	54	57	55					
72	80-671635-00	75012	466340	17	3	7	118	26	4	55								
73	80-4030007296089	168	38892	17	3	7	119	8	4	54	29	4	55					
74	80-4030007296090	1456	234346	17	3	7	120	8	4	54	29	4	55					
75	80-4030007296091	6356	757190	17	3	7	121	8	4	54	29	4	55					
76	80-4030007296094	9240	574084	17	3	7	122	8	4	54	29	4	55					
77	80-27377	14112	69286	17	16	11	123	26	4	55								
78	80-921790	4914	526120	17	3	7	124	8	54	29	28	4	55					
79	80-W101-2006	462	445858	17	6	2	125	33	41	54	57	4	55					

Figure 13.10 (CONTINUED) The spreadsheet shows the input data used for PQR$ Analysis, i.e., quantity (Q), revenue ($), and the routing (R) for each product/part (P). Note: This is just a sample of parts that was extracted from the product mix of 530 part numbers. A complete PQR Analysis would include all 530 part numbers because analyzing the complete population of all product routings does have value, as revealed in the "Narrowing the Analysis" section.

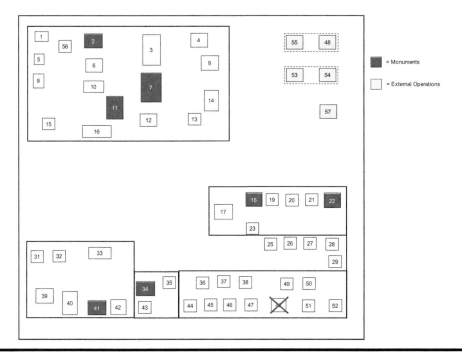

Figure 13.11 The current shop layout shows monuments in red and external operations in green.

PARTS

MACHINES

Figure 13.12 The complete PR Analysis shows routings for all 530 parts in the shop's product mix. Part numbers are on the Y axis, and W/Cs on the X axis. Here, blocks of blue show groups of products with similar or perhaps identical routings that could be grouped into part families. However, the long vertical blue bands running from top to bottom suggest that several part families require many W/Cs, so the improvement team is cautious about implementing too many independent cells.

Y axis (a row in the spreadsheet) is matched with a W/C along the X axis (a column in the spreadsheet). Compact blocks[2] of 1s suggest that part families are present. Note that Figure 13.12 is a 530-line chart miniaturized, so clusters of 1s appear as solid blue blocks.

Narrowing the Analysis

Working with all 530 part numbers at once is not practical for any improvement effort. So from here, the team extracts a smaller sample of part numbers that have significant volume, significant revenue, or share common routings. Here is where analyzing the product mix (P), quantities (Q),

---

[2] Each block is defined by a band of consecutive rows intersected by a band of consecutive columns.

routings (R), and revenue ($) comes into play. This is where the team also uses the PFAST software to replace the traditional PQ Analysis of the entire product mix with a PQ$ Analysis.

Figure 13.13 shows a typical PQ Analysis distribution of production volumes for the product mix of this forging job shop. The left side of the graph shows the few product numbers with high volumes, while the long tail to the right shows numerous jobs with low volumes.

Figure 13.14 brings *revenue* into the mix. As shown, most jobs have low quantities and low revenue. No surprises there! But note the remaining jobs. A few high-quantity jobs produce only moderate levels of revenue, while a significant number of low-quantity jobs produce moderate and even *high* revenue.

Considering both part quantity *and* revenue, the team focuses on products produced in quantities greater than 1,800 and earning revenue of more than $30,000, as shown by the dotted line in Figure 13.14. Initially, only 44 product numbers were included in the sample, which accounts for only about 8% of the total product mix, 68% of the total volume, and 46% of the total revenue. In other words, *almost half* of the company's earnings come from those 44 products. Here is where that original PQR Analysis (Figure 13.12) done for the complete product mix steps back into the picture. Of the 100's of remaining products not included in the sample, 35 have

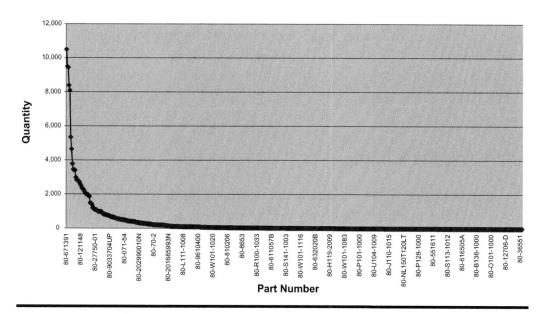

Figure 13.13   The PQ Analysis compares the products based just on their production quantities. Like most job shops, this custom forge shop has a few part numbers with high quantities and a long tail of low-quantity parts.

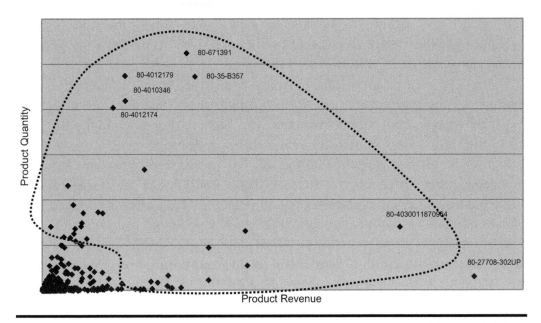

Figure 13.14   The PQ$ Analysis of the entire product mix relates product numbers (P) to both quantities (Q) and revenue ($). The dotted line shows the products the team chose for focusing their improvement efforts. The algorithm for this bi-criterion analysis can easily be programmed in Excel.

routings that are *similar or identical* to a significant number of routings for the 44 products initially selected in the sample. Seeing this, the team decides to include them in the sample selected for improvement, bringing the total number of products to 79. Thereby, the new sample accounts for 15% of the total number of active products, about 74% of the total volume, and about 54% of the total revenue.

Analyzing the Sample

The steps executed till now narrow the analysis and determine which products use similar machines, but they do not truly reveal the complex material flow that plagues the job shop. So from here, the team uses the product mix, quantity, and routing information for the 79 products in the sample to develop a From-To Chart (Figure 13.15). The chart lists the same set of W/Cs in the same sequence on both the X and Y axes. Each routing is broken up into several pairs of from-to segments, i.e., the quantity of products that move *from* one specific W/C *to* another. If the routing of a part consists of a sequence of the following W/Cs (17→6→2→11), then PFAST breaks up that

Q-Type From-To Chart

W/C	8	12	7	3	41	42	50	28	29	53	54	4	26	1	57	25	52	48	55	27	9	22	21	40	39	10	11	16	17	56	6	2	33
8	35336					8008					10108	17220	75012		15428				5194														
12	12577																																
7		11257																															
3			15428																														
41				23436																													462
42							35252				462			8008																		462	
50							35252	80934					35360		36252																		
28											16184	17220	28014		32242																		
29										39256															20706				28014				
53	5194								39256		19811				10154				40096														
54									22134	5194									21250														
4											16184								29797														
26							35360		32242		28014	28470	36580		34372					35350													
1											14064	13277			52151					11839	11839												
57							36252			40096						38920	31722	14641	75880	11839													
25																	38920																
52																		38920	70642														
48																			74167														
55																		67494	35350														
27										39256					11839				12247		11839												
9																											8540						
22																						16172											
21																						16172											
40						15428							26502		8540								16172		22073			8540					
39									20706				19335		40096										8540	8540					5194		
10																											26789	8540					
11									20706																		23864	23345					
16									28014					18089											21219			23345		8540			
17				97146									28014	28014	48132													5194					
56	5194																													76146	34370		
6			5194			462																								5194	5194		
2			8008																													29176	
33					462																						20706						

Figure 13.15 W/Cs are listed both on the X and Y axes in this From-To Chart. The set of "From" W/Cs that appear on the Y axis are identical to and in the same sequence as the "To" W/Cs that appear on the X axis.

routing into the following from-to pairs of W/Cs – 17→6, 6→2, and 2→11. Note that this analysis then has to be repeated for each of the 79 routings in the sample. Not surprisingly, 99.99% of job shops shy away from doing such crucial analysis because of the tedium and inherent error in doing that data mining by hand. For instance, Part No. 80-A37353 has a quantity of 728. The routing starts at W/C 17 and moves to W/C 6, i.e., from the Band Saw to the Furnace before moving to other operations downstream. In this case, the quantity of 728 is inserted where W/C 17 (on the Y axis) and W/C 6 (on the X axis) intersect, as shown in Figure 13.15. When this 728 is added to the quantities from all part numbers flowing between those two machines (17→6), the chart reveals that during a predetermined time period, 34,370 forgings traveled from the Band Saw (W/C 17) to the Furnace (W/C 6).

When the flow volumes and directions between all pairs of W/Cs are super-imposed on the facility layout, with arrow thicknesses proportional to traffic volumes, the result is the Flow Diagram (aka Spaghetti Diagram) in Figure 13.16. The chaos in this diagram is commonly observed in most job shops.

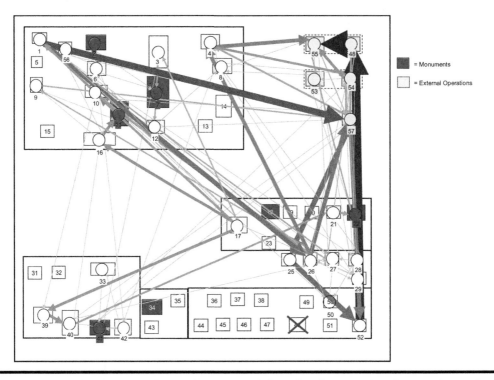

Figure 13.16   The diagram shows the material flow for the sample of parts shown in Figures 13.10 and 13.14. Thicker arrows correspond to larger quantities in the From-To Chart. For this job shop, a VSM could never have captured this aggregate view of the entire material flow network.

Identifying Product Families

After analyzing the part routings using the PR Analysis Type 1 algorithm, which is one of the four complementary cluster analysis algorithms available in PFAST, the team organizes the 79 part numbers into four product families, as shown in Figure 13.17. The clusters of 1s indicate products with similar routings using the same group W/Cs. In Figure 13.11, the blocks colored red correspond to the W/Cs that are monuments, and the blocks colored green correspond to outside operations (vendors and the company's own machine shop located several miles away). Figure 13.17 uses that same color scheme for columns (red for monuments and green for outside processes). Using the results of Figure 13.17, the company compared the four part families with each other and, based on the total quantity (Y axis) and the total revenue (X axis), developed a scatter plot depicted in Figure 13.18. Then, they developed another material flow diagram, as shown in Figure 13.19, which superimposes the material flow diagrams for each of the four part families on each other.

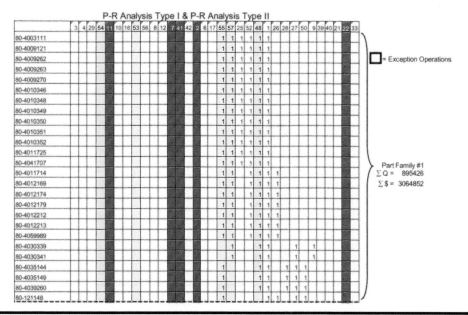

Figure 13.17 The machine-part matrix clustering mirrors the one shown in Figure 13.12, and only this one has just the 79 products derived from the PQ$ Analysis. Green columns signify outside processes; red columns signify monuments. Clusters of 1s show identical or similar part routings. Based on this, the team groups these products into four product families. Note: This matrix derived from the PR Analysis is one of four different types of cluster analysis that can be done using the PFAST software to group parts into families based on how similar their routings are.

(Continued)

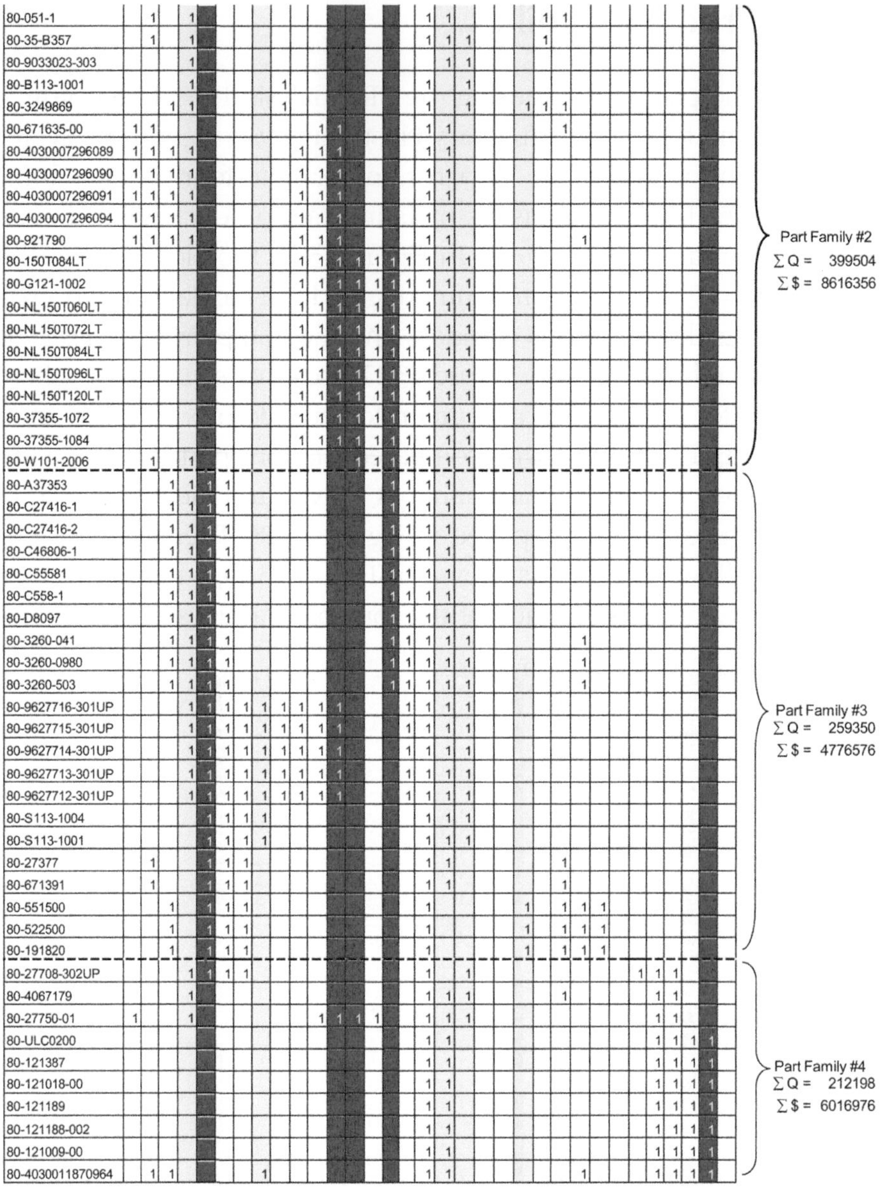
80-051-1
80-35-B357
80-9033023-303
80-B113-1001
80-3249869
80-671635-00
80-4030007296089
80-4030007296090
80-4030007296091
80-4030007296094
80-921790
80-150T084LT
80-G121-1002
80-NL150T060LT
80-NL150T072LT
80-NL150T084LT
80-NL150T096LT
80-NL150T120LT
80-37355-1072
80-37355-1084
80-W101-2006
80-A37353
80-C27416-1
80-C27416-2
80-C46806-1
80-C55581
80-C558-1
80-D8097
80-3260-041
80-3260-0980
80-3260-503
80-9627716-301UP
80-9627715-301UP
80-9627714-301UP
80-9627713-301UP
80-9627712-301UP
80-S113-1004
80-S113-1001
80-27377
80-671391
80-551500
80-522500
80-191820
80-27708-302UP
80-4067179
80-27750-01
80-ULC0200
80-121387
80-121018-00
80-121189
80-121188-002
80-121009-00
80-4030011870964
Part Family #2
ΣQ = 399504
Σ$ = 8616356
Part Family #3
ΣQ = 259350
Σ$ = 4776576
Part Family #4
ΣQ = 212198
Σ$ = 6016976

Figure 13.17 (CONTINUED) The machine-part matrix clustering mirrors the one shown in Figure 13.12, and only this one has just the 79 products derived from the PQ$ Analysis. Green columns signify outside processes; red columns signify monuments. Clusters of 1s show identical or similar part routings. Based on this, the team groups these products into four product families. Note: This matrix derived from the PR Analysis is one of four different types of cluster analysis that can be done using the PFAST software to group parts into families based on how similar their routings are.

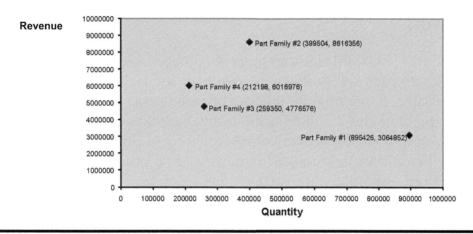

Figure 13.18 The scatter plot identifies how product families compared in quantity (X axis) and revenue (Y axis).

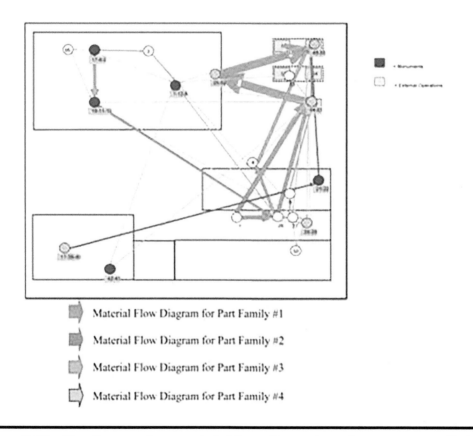

Figure 13.19 The diagram shows material flow after part numbers are grouped into part families. Compare this to the chaos shown in Figure 13.16.

The Payoff

Seeing all this, could this custom forge shop have been organized into four cells with each cell producing a family of similar forgings? Probably not, especially considering the number of monuments needed to produce the part families 2 and 3 (again, see those columns marked in red that run through the clusters of rows that represent the two part families). But at least the first part family could be produced in a dedicated cell. Regardless, the analysis gives a clear picture of the current, albeit complex, state of affairs on the shop floor of this custom forge shop.

At first glance, all this may seem like a lot of effort for not much reward. But this analysis is just a starting point. It gives the improvement team a guide, showing what to tackle first and which ideas would pay off, as well as which ideas to avoid. The custom forge shop discussed in this example moved certain machines to reduce job travel time and purchased other equipment to make material flow more efficiently. Ultimately, these layout changes saved $137,000 a year. That is not a bad return on investment based on a 3-month project done by an intern from The Ohio State University working under my guidance!

Putting the PQR$ Analysis to Work

Limit the "Grunt Work" to Collect Data for CI Kaizens

The PFAST Analysis Report contains outputs that could be used for a range of CI kaizens. Unfortunately, in the case of the typical job shop, a kaizen team usually will not have time to collect relevant data for all products. For example, the team could easily use just the PQ Analysis to segment their product mix into at least two segments: high volume and low volume. Then, using the PR Analysis for *at least* the high-volume segment of the product mix, they could seek product families in that segment. Any product family found in that segment could then be the focus of a kaizen to design and implement a cell. Implementation of a cell is ideal for (i) fostering self-directed teamwork, (ii) developing a plan to cross-train employees to operate all machines in the cell, and (iii) developing the leadership skills of some of the cell operators.

Split the Facility

With part families identified, a job shop could implement one or more cells to produce a family of products with similar routings. For a multi-product family, the cell could be an automated, flexible manufacturing cell capable of producing a family of parts with minimum changes in machine setups. For prototype and one-off high-margin jobs with small lot sizes, the "cell" could be a single machine with secondary operations such as deburring or polishing and cleaning done adjacent to that machine. Especially if the parts are being made using an AM (Additive Manufacturing) process!

Absorb Low-Volume Products into High-Volume Product Families

Based on the PQR$ Analysis, products in the low-volume, high-margin segment can be absorbed into one of the existing product families in the high-volume segment, especially if they share similar routings. CI efforts to improve performance of this manufacturing cell will increase its available capacity, which will enable it to accept more orders for its product family, which in turn will allow the sales team to hunt for new business to produce new parts that fit this cell's product family. A job shop could even purchase another shop(s) if they discover that a significant chunk of their competitor's product mix already fits into their shop's existing product families.

Cull the Product Mix

Conducting the PQR Analysis can help determine whether any low-volume product does not indeed fit into other product families that are being produced in separate cells. If one or more such products are identified, the team can ask some questions: Is this low-volume product ordered by customers who provide high-volume work also? Is it a complex fabrication or prototype that offers high margins? If yes, then that low-volume product is profitable and may be worth keeping. If not, then it may be a product ripe for culling. As one plant manager at a sheet metal job shop once told me, "We gladly fire those customers that send us difficult and low-margin products and ask that they take their business to our competitors. That way we transfer the problems these customers caused us to our competitors!"

Employ Water Spiders to Support Physical or Virtual Cells

Scheduling deliveries of materials to manufacturing cells designed to fulfill orders for product families can be done using one or more material handlers. These people (called *Water Spiders* or *Water Striders* in Lean parlance) could have an expanded role as "virtual cell managers". That is, even though the group of machines that a strider monitors and supplies are dispersed, all those machines constitute a cell that produces a family of parts. So the operators in that cell report to this "manager on wheels". A related practice is that of the "milk run", which is a timed route that is traveled on a repeating schedule by a designated handler.[3]

Co-Opetition between Job Shops[4]

Co-opetition (co-operative competition) is a business strategy that encourages competitors to work together to increase the benefits for all players. By collaborating, competitors benefit by pooling their resources for mutual gain. Say Job Shop #1 identifies low-volume, less profitable products that it wants to cull. But for Job Shop #2, those products may fit into product families that are being produced efficiently in cells. If Job Shop #2 got to produce orders for Job Shop #1's unprofitable products, it could do so with a good profit margin. In fact, Job Shop #1 could be in the same situation and produce profitably the "cats and dogs" in the product mix of Job Shop #2. So, in principle, these two small or medium-size HMLV manufacturers could swap jobs, leaving both manufacturers with more profitable work that better fits their operations. Of course, both shops must ensure that any swapping does not affect their goals of being able to serve diverse markets. The key is for these two job shops to ensure that their new product acquisitions fit the capabilities of their existing (or planned) cells. Here, strategic planning done using PQR$ Analysis could play a central role by helping two competing job shops to cooperate with each other.

---

[3] This method gets its name from the dairy industry practice where one tanker collects milk every day from several dairy farmers for delivery to a milk processing firm. (**Source:** http://www.businessdictionary.com/definition/milk-run.html)

[4] Brandenburger, A.M. & Nalebuff, B. J. (1996). *Co-opetition: A Revolution Mindset That Combines Competition and Cooperation.* New York, NY: Currency Doubleday.

Part 5 of 5: Why a Timeline Analysis of Order History Matters

Abstract: The traditional PQ Analysis may point job shops in the wrong direction. Since PQ Analysis is based on the 80-20 Rule, it fails to consider how many times a product is ordered, the average size and variability in the size of those orders, and the inter-arrival times between consecutive orders. So, if it is desired to do a complete product mix segmentation analysis, then the stability and repeatability of demand over time (the "T" in PQR$T Analysis) for every product in the entire product mix must be taken into consideration. This section of this chapter describes the method of PQT Analysis, which considers the aggregate production volume for each product, the number of orders placed for the product, the quantity associated with each order, etc. PQT Analysis should be used instead of PQ Analysis for identifying Runners (high-volume products in a job shop's product mix that are frequently ordered using Kanbans), Repeaters (medium-volume products in a job shop's product mix that are frequently ordered but their demand lacks a consistent "beat"), and Strangers (low-volume products in a job shop's product mix that are rarely ordered). Analysis of demand variability using PQT Analysis would work even in the case of shops with more than a thousand different part routings.

The traditional PQ Analysis uses the quantity (Q) produced of each product in a manufacturer's list of different products (P) to determine which products are Runners (high volume), Repeaters (medium volume), and Strangers (low volume). Unfortunately, it ignores details about every product's order history, including the number of orders placed, the quantity/size for each order, and the time interval between consecutive orders. Take the case of two products (Product X and Product Y) that had the same (high) production volume (Q) last year. However, a single customer placed a single large order for Product X, whereas demand for the other product (Product Y) came from several really small-quantity orders received during the 52-week horizon. If PQ Analysis were used to segment the product mix, both products would be classified as Runners; however, it is clear that one of them is a Runner (Product Y) and the other is a Stranger (Product X). The reason for this error is because PQ Analysis saw both products as equally important based on the cumulative/aggregate demand for the entire year. *In practice*, because the demand variability (T) of these two products is different, the shop should handle orders for each product differently as follows:

1. For the product ordered many times (Product Y), since each small-quantity order would necessitate a setup and a short production run, the shop may have to scramble to find a different machine, depending on machine availability at that time. Unless all orders for that product could be run on a single machine with quick-change setup or a machine that can run lights out during the night shift?

2. For the product with a single large shipment quantity (Product X), perhaps the order could be split up and run on two or more capable machines. Else one machine could process the entire production run. But how about if the customer had been offered a level-loaded delivery schedule across a multi-week planning horizon? This would be done by splitting the order quantity into several equal-size batches that were delivered over consecutive weeks, which would eliminate the spike in shop workload due to this one-time order.

Time Matters

The PQT Analysis factors in the demand variability with time (T) by considering a product's order history. This changes how a shop determines whether products are Runners, Repeaters, or Strangers. Now, Runners would be products having both high volume and high demand repeatability (or low demand variability); i.e., these are the products that are ordered relatively frequently at predictable intervals. Repeaters would have medium volume and medium demand variability. Strangers would have both low volume and low demand repeatability because they are ordered infrequently at unpredictable intervals. Consider Figure 13.20 that shows the typical "long tail" of a job shop's product mix. The callouts show which parts this shop identified as Runners using PQ Analysis. But this classical Pareto Analysis does not show the whole story because, again, the analysis considers only a product's *aggregate* volume over several consecutive years, not how frequently the orders for that product came in the door throughout that period.

Figure 13.21 brings demand repeatability (T) into the picture, showing the *Number of Pieces Sold* (*Q*) over the different years as well as the *Number of Orders Placed* (*T*) during a given year. Those who are Excel-savvy and

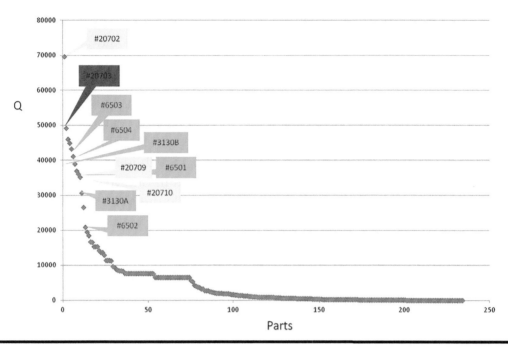

Figure 13.20   The PQ Analysis curve shows a typical job shop's product mix, with a few parts produced in high volume (Runners) and a long tail of parts produced in low-to-medium volume (Repeaters and Strangers). The horizontal axis represents the part numbers, and the vertical axis represents the quantity of each part. The labels show which part numbers the shop classified as Runners using only the PQ Analysis.

P (Part #)	Number of Pieces Sold (Q)					Number of Orders Placed (T)				
	2004	2005	2006	2007	TOTAL	2004	2005	2006	2007	TOTAL
20702	10891	26723	21647	10406	69667	3	6	4	2	15
20703	6174	16139	21208	5696	49217	1	3	4	1	9
9301	16108	29910	0	0	46018	37	62	0	0	99
9302	19416	25496	0	0	44912	43	63	0	0	106
6503	2720	19588	17500	3500	43308	10	55	45	10	120
6504	3244	17883	16800	3150	41077	14	52	43	9	118
3130B	8142	14454	13308	3108	39012	42	72	78	12	204
20709	4940	13574	13910	4556	36980	2	7	6	2	17
6501	6924	9140	17204	2800	36068	14	19	37	8	78
20710	3558	14220	15322	2140	35240	1	6	6	1	14
3130A	5244	10840	11628	2996	30708	32	56	60	16	164
20707	6427	10145	9909	0	26481	3	4	3	0	10
6502	3339	5964	9357	2170	20830	20	37	58	20	135
3127 (3115)	4071	7227	6654	1554	19506	21	36	39	6	102
20701	3179	6093	5905	3339	18516	1	3	2	1	7
6904	3228	6851	6659	0	16738	3	4	2	0	9

Figure 13.21   The partial list of products shows the quantities of products as well as how many times they are ordered during a particular year. Note: This is a partial list extracted from the job shop's complete list of active parts. A complete list could include 100's or even 1,000's of additional part numbers, depending on the size of the job shop or the sample size selected.

would like to put their Six Sigma training to the test could also record the number of pieces associated with each order, since that would give them the complete timeline needed to analyze the order history for every part (or part family) being produced.

Figure 13.21 illustrates a timeline analysis done using a "quick and dirty" PQT Analysis that uses *# of Orders* received over several years as a measure of demand variability. Per the hypothetical example of Product X and Product Y that was discussed earlier, two products with identical annual shipment quantities may both be ordered six times in one year. But one product was ordered once every two months, while the inter-order intervals for the other product had high variability. Ideally, using a week-by-week timeline to record the demand for each product (instead of just a cumulative quantity for each year), the time series analytics available in Excel® or even a statistical analysis package like Minitab® could be used to classify the products as Runners, Repeaters, or Strangers using more sophisticated analytics. Still, the "quick and dirty" PQT Analysis in Figure 13.21 reveals much about reality on this job shop's factory floor. Recall the part numbers labeled as Runners in Figure 13.20. Now look at Figure 13.21. It shows that some of those parts are ordered frequently one year, then only a few times the next year. After evaluating **both** Figure 13.20 **and** Figure 13.21, the shop decided that a Stranger is a part ordered less than 10 times during 2004–2007, a Repeater is ordered 11–50 times during the same period, and a Runner is ordered more than 51 times in those four years. Compared to the PQ Analysis in Figure 13.20, Figure 13.22 shows that PQT Analysis changes how a shop segments its part mix and deals with customers who order parts that are Runners versus those parts that are Strangers. In Figure 13.22, there are *fewer* Runners compared to the number of Runners identified by the PQ Analysis in Figure 13.20. In fact, the shop classified four high-volume products as Repeaters, simply because they were ordered infrequently compared to the rest of the Runners.

Coefficient of Variation as a Metric for Demand Variability

If demand data such as that shown in Figure 13.21 is available for the entire product mix, then the coefficient of variation (CV) could be calculated for each product to quantify the demand variability for that product. Now the PQT Analysis scatter plot featured in Figure 13.22 would be modified to replace "# of Orders" on the X axis with "CV_Q" while retaining "Q" on the

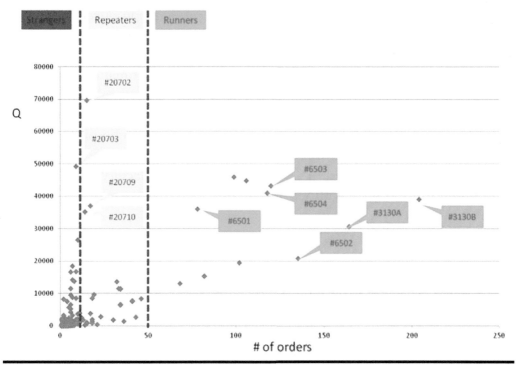

Figure 13.22 **The complete PQT Analysis changes how the shop classifies its Strangers (low volume), Repeaters (medium volume), and Runners (high volume).**

Y axis. For more in-depth discussions on using the CV to analyze demand variability, the interested reader is referred to the following references:

1. Pages 212–215 ("Step 2: Analyze Product Demand Variability") in King, P. L. 2009. *Lean for the Process Industries: Dealing with Complexity.* New York, NY: CRC Press.
2. Pages 264–302 ("Chapter 8: Variability Basics") in Hopp, W.J. & Spearman, M. 2008. *Factory Physics.* 3rd Edition. New York, NY: McGraw-Hill/Irwin.

Putting the PQT Analysis to Work

Important Role of the Sales Department

Any cell with a product family that is composed of Runners and/or Repeaters will have longevity due to sufficient workload from a steady pipeline of work. But a cell that is producing a product family with many

Strangers could be short-lived! Demand for the products produced in that cell may not remain sufficient and steady throughout a year, let alone for two or more consecutive years. Therefore, the sales department *must* work harder to ensure a pipeline of orders for that cell. For that matter, why must any HMLV manufacturer implement cells to produce Strangers in their product mix? For decades, many job shops have operated with their equipment arranged in a standard Process Layout and claimed to be profitable. However, it is strongly recommended that the Strangers in the product mix of any job shop be produced in a separate area of their facility that operates like a traditional job shop without cells.

Operate an Idle Cell Like a Shared Resource

If demand variability for a product family is high, then the cell will (1) run when it has orders and (2) become idle when it has no orders. Unfortunately, accountants do not take kindly to machines and their operators remaining idle, especially *expensive* machines! So, instead of idling a cell until more orders are received for that cell, the knee-jerk decision by management could be to (1) move the employees working in that cell to another cell and (2) move any mobile machines in that cell to another cell. *Instead of dismantling an idle cell*, it may be pragmatic to operate it like a shared resource that processes orders from other cells that need to use some of the machines in that cell. Assuming that the cell's team has a daily morning huddle, the leaders of the other cells would join the meeting. During that meeting, the cell leaders would prioritize orders received from other cells using a suitable priority rule (Earliest Due Date or First-Come-First-Serve) to process the orders in queue that day.

Beware of the Effects of the Learning Curve!

In a typical job shop, much time could elapse between two orders for the same product (or even products in the same product family). Even if both orders had identical routings, some of the machine operators may go through a *Learning Curve*[5] the second time around because they would have to recall how they set up the machine, ran the machine, did FAI (First Article Inspection), etc. the first time they ran that particular part. In fact, even for the simplest of tasks, the Learning Curve guarantees that the cycle

---

[5] **Source:** https://en.wikipedia.org/wiki/Learning_curve.

time for that task will decrease with the number of times that the operator repeats that task. So, even when two dissimilar jobs are run consecutively on the same machine, both the machine and its operator will require time to transition from the current job to the next job. The more an operator gets repeat orders for the same job, the more efficient he/she becomes due to familiarity with the entire system to run that job (raw material, machine, tools, fixtures, gauges, finished product, inspection procedures and documentation, etc.). As the saying goes, "Practice makes perfect". Is it any surprise that one of the universally applicable practices to reduce setup times on the bottleneck machine in any high-mix cell is to try to adjust the daily schedule so similar or identical jobs are run consecutively? **CAUTION!** This does not imply that orders for the same job which are months apart should be aggregated into a single large batch just to save available capacity on the bottleneck machine in *that* week!

Be Flexible in Assessing Each Cell's Performance

Based on the earlier discussion, it is important to recognize that key performance metrics such as the value-added machine utilization, operator productivity, and product quality will be high in a cell whose product family is comprised primarily of Runners and/or Repeaters. In contrast, in a cell whose product family has many Strangers (or is a mixture of Repeaters and Strangers), those same performance metrics could all be negatively impacted due to the *Learning Curve* effect of running consecutively many dissimilar jobs with small lot sizes.

Design Cells with Flexibility to Adapt to Mix and Volume Changes

A stable cell gives the employees who work in it an identity and fosters a spirit of teamwork. They see their goal being to fulfill orders for any and every part in the cell's product family in the right quantity with the right quality at the right time. Management can delegate the responsibility for decision-making to those who work in the cell because it is they who actually fulfill orders from customers! If a cell has longevity, then its employees can be trained to execute the functions that help it to achieve a desired level of Overall Equipment Effectiveness (OEE) for the cell. Unfortunately, demand variability could nullify the ability of a cell to operate autonomously as a business unit. A team cannot form if its membership is always in flux!

Especially during periods when the cell is idle and its employees have been reassigned to other cells. Now it becomes necessary to track, monitor, and ensure that these flexible employees are doing work of consistent quality, regardless of which cell they work in.

So how to design a flexible cell that has a product family with many Strangers (or a mixture of Repeaters and Strangers)? Some of the practices gleaned from the open literature are as follows:

1. Invest in training (and cross-training too!) of the employees working in every cell.[6] Thereby, a cell can have fewer people than machines so that cell staffing is sufficient and adjusted to the varying workloads caused by demand fluctuations. However, it is not easy task to recruit, train, and retain skilled employees capable of working on different machines!

2. Train machine operators to inspect their own work and then hold them accountable for defective work (instead of letting them produce defective parts and pass them on to the Inspection department). Else install a buddy-buddy system so that one machine operator gets his/her work inspected and approved/disapproved by another machine operator working in the cell. Else have a roving inspector who, like a Water Spider, walks around the shop with an essential kit of inspection devices on a mobile cart to inspect parts in any cell on a JIT basis.[7]

3. Utilize a Manufacturing Execution System (MES) like ibaseT (www. ibaseT.com) to digitally provide work instructions, documents, and specifications for any part that is to be produced in the cell on a JIT basis. Examples of commercial software for digital work instructions are Vuforia Expert Capture (www.PTC.com), www.Q2Serp.com, www. VKSapp.com). Assuming that the cell is producing a family of similar (but *not* identical) parts, it will be necessary to develop a *flexible* Standard Work Instruction similar to the ones used to guide assembly

---

[6] In a recent client engagement, the lathe operators in Cell #1 did not wish to learn how to operate the Haas mill, and vice versa. But in Cell #2, one member of the team was running a VT-36 lathe and the Mori Seiki mill. What should management have done in this situation? ☺

[7] In a recent client engagement, the Inspection department assigned an inspector to check the work coming out of Cells #1 and #2. His work table was positioned across the aisle from where these two cells were located side-by-side. And when there was a lull in the cells' workload, this inspector would simply walk back to the Inspection department.

operators on a mixed model assembly line.[8] Think of a flowchart with several decision blocks, each block asking a question in IF-THEN-ELSE format. Each decision block's question asks the operator about a particular design or manufacturing attribute of the part he/she is making. Depending on the particular value of that attribute, the flowchart displays a different sequence of steps to execute next. I have begun doing research on using the Group Technology concept of the *Composite Part* for a part family.[9]

4. Invest in multi-function "smart" manufacturing equipment to mitigate the Learning Curve effect on operators and machines in the cell. These modern-day machines that boast hardware and software that minimize human error due to a changing mix of parts are advertised in trade magazines like *The Fabricator* (www.TheFabricator.com) and *Modern Machine Shop* (www.mmsonline.com).

Analyze Operations Using Industrial Engineering Tools[10]

In a cell that experiences high demand variability, it will be important to quote the jobs run in it using labor and machine-hour rates that have been adjusted for parts with *different* manufacturing complexity, *different* lot sizes, employees with *different* skills, employees with *different* work preferences, etc. Job shop managers may feel intimidated by this challenge, but such challenges can be met by qualified Industrial Engineers who know how to mine

---

[8] To obtain a background for my research, the interested reader could read these papers in the research literature: (1) Dasari, R.V. & Moon, Y.B. (1997). *Analysis of Part Families for Group Technology Applications using Decision Trees. International Journal of Advanced Manufacturing Technology*, 13, 116–124, and (2) Ghosh, T., Modak, M. & Dan, P. K. (2011). *Coding and Classification Based Heuristic Technique for Workpiece Grouping Problems in Cellular Manufacturing System(s). International Transaction Journal of Engineering, Management, & Applied Sciences & Technologies*, 53–72.

[9] A Composite Part is a hypothetical part that includes all of the design and manufacturing attributes that are observed on the CAD drawings of all parts in the family.

[10] In Chapter 28 (Starter Advice for Implementing Job Shop Lean), I reiterate this recommendation in the section *Hire Industrial Engineers.*

an ERP (Enterprise Resource Planning) system or machine monitoring system for data, who know which data analysis methods to use, who know how to engage with employees whose work routines need to be videotaped, etc.[11]

Success Story: History Shows that Cells Can Be Implemented in Job Shops!

Would you be interested in a case study that describes a cell that was implemented to produce the Strangers in the product mix of a job shop? If you would like to receive an electronic copy of the article that is the basis for this section (Berk, D.J. 1982. *"C-Cells" Productivity Techniques for Job Shops*. Production & Inventory Management Review.), please contact me at ShahrukhIrani1023@yahoo.com or 832-475-4447. Note the year of publication of the article! Here are key excerpts from the article:

- Key Japanese manufacturing industries rely on a vast supporting structure of tiny subcontractors to fill their general fabrication requirements. In any typical metal working job shop, that idea can be subcontracted to create "internal subcontractors".

---

[11] For example, in a recent Job Shop Lean implementation, we began by completely rearranging the layout of their in-house machine shop into a Hybrid Cellular Layout with seven cells. After Cell #1 was implemented, it was desired to identify the factors that contributed to significant differences between Standard and Actual machining cycle times on the VT-36 lathes in the cell. First, we videotaped 3–4 hours of uninterrupted operation of the lathe. Then, we used this video to do a Time and Motion Analysis of the human–machine interactions to identify periods when the machining cycle was interrupted. Next, we watched the video together with the machine operator to understand why he "did what he did" that resulted in some of the interruptions. For example, the operator said that when a costly and hard-to-machine material like Inconel was being machined, he would make more passes and stop the machine to do more in-process inspections to ensure part quality. On another occasion, the insert broke which forced the operator to stop the machine, walk to the vending machine in the center of the shop to get a replacement insert, walk back to the cell, swap out the broken insert on the tool holder, re-initialize the CNC program for the repaired tool, and start the cutting cycle again. **This project is one of many projects that were done to implement Job Shop Lean at Superior Completion Services (https://superiorenergy.com/).** Specifically, the PQR$T Analysis method was used to design a Hybrid Cellular Layout for their in-house machine shop. Some of the key factors that influenced the layout design were as follows: (1) The sizes of the parts suggested that the shop be divided into two sections: "Minions Lane" (for small parts) and "Monster Highway" (for big parts); (2) customers did not want to be bothered about the machine shop's capacity constraints; and (3) the shop schedule changed frequently due to uncontrollable external disruptions in the supply chain! Then, to make each cell operate as autonomously as possible, suitable projects were chosen from the exhaustive lists in Tables 3(a) and 3(b) of Chapter 18. If the reader desires specific details about these projects, please get written permission from Todd Chretien, Director of Manufacturing, Superior Completion Services, Houston, TX 77032; Email: Todd.Chretien@SuperiorEnergy.com; Phone: 281-784-5700 x6111.

■ A subsidiary of an American multinational making heavy capital equipment was having production scheduling problems.....Closed-loop MRP had been installed for several years with elaborate capacity planning and shop floor control modules.....Yet the smooth WIP control expected was not happening. Expediting was still intense. Too many shortage lists fluttered around the shop.

■ If a basic maxim of manufacturing is "move the tool to the work, not the work to the tool", then why did people move material around so much, anyway? The conspicuous answer was that the major material removal, cutting, forming, and joining jobs had to be done by big, fixed-installation W/Cs. Workpieces had to be trucked or craned from machine to machine.....All jobs, big or small, flowed through this single fabricating network of machines toward the stockroom. No matter what the nature of the parts, they were all documented by the same type of route-sheet paperwork that determined physical flow. All parts were monitored by the same dispatching system.

■ The characteristics of "big" and "small" jobs merited a closer look. Using the computer for an 80/20 Pareto Analysis, the first step was to define "small" jobs that were the parts at the bottom of the ABC Analysis that, all together, would not consume more than 10% of total direct labor hours in a year.....Roughly half the parts manufactured used 9/10 of direct labor capacity and the other half of the parts used only 1/10.....The "small" parts, 1/10 of total direct work, were responsible for half of the total shop WIP control load.....Suppose this plant stopped making the "small" parts? Zap! Only 1/10 of the direct load gone. But half of the material movement gone; half of the feedback transactions (gone); half of the expediting, the route-sheet maintenance and machine setup conflicts (gone).....But it was not possible to stop making these parts because it was not feasible to purchase them from outside. *However, a next-best solution could be to confine minor parts to some place and method within the plant where they might incur less "burden" than they induced in the plant flow.*

■ Based on the ABC (Value) Analysis that defined the "small jobs", this imaginary place and method was dubbed a "C-Cell". The "C" obviously denoted the low labor-hour stratum of the parts group. The plant employed about 200 direct workers making some 6,000 stocked parts.....Based on the 12-month sales forecast, the ABC Analysis identified the 3,000 lowest labor-content items. Other limits screened out 1,000 original C-Cell parts candidates, so that the new ratio of C-Cell parts to main plant parts was 2:4, or 1:2.

■ Next, the Industrial Engineers established a basic equipment require-ment. This list included relatively low-cost sheet-metal machines, three MIG (Metal Inert Gas) welding sets, a radial drill, a lathe, and a small paint booth. It is significant that operators had been selected and trained so that, within the restricted job mix in the C-Cell, they could handle all the tools. One manager (The Small Job Manager, or "SJM") was appointed…..This cell became the "corner store", virtually a self-contained business. Its SJM rooted out appropriate work for his area. The (twelve) workers assigned to the cell welcomed innovation, thrived as a team. In a compact physical area, they produced a substantial por-tion of total parts requirements. In doing so, they minimized the cost and difficulty of expediting and WIP control…..Through efficient com-munications, the C-Cell did many things efficiently that a small group can achieve, which a large plant complicates as it expands…..Higher throughput in assembly was the key indicator correlated with the C-Cell…..Qualitative improvements included a "tidier" flow of material on the main shop floor, happier foremen, the eventual use of the C-Cell as a skill development center through which other operators were rotated…(and)…a noticeable improvement in the overall shop "frustra-tion quotient" as schedule changes became easier to implement.

Supplementary Reading

These are the original drafts of the articles that describe PQ Analysis, PQ$ Analysis, PQR$ Analysis, and PQT Analysis. I submitted them for publication to Tim Heston, Senior Editor on the editorial staff of *The Fabricator* maga-zine (https://www.thefabricator.com/). Tim used them to write his series of articles for *The Fabricator* magazine.

Conclusion

This chapter described the four elements – PQ Analysis, PQ$ Analysis, PQR$ Analysis, and PQT Analysis – that comprise the PQR$T Analysis approach for segmenting the product mix of any HMLV manufacturer. PQR$T Analysis will ensure a thorough and successful implementation of Job Shop Lean because it will identify at least two (maybe more!) different businesses operating under the same roof. Ideally, a different production system must be designed for each business.

References

Irani, S. A. (2011, June). Analyzing products, demands, margins and routings. *The Fabricator*, 42. thefabricator.com/thefabricator/article/shopmanagement/analyzing-products-demand-margins-and-routings.

Irani, S. A. (2011, August). Analyzing product mix and volumes: Useful but insufficient. *The Fabricator*, 36–37. https://www.thefabricator.com/thefabricator/article/shopmanagement/analyzing-product-mix-and-volumes-useful-but-insufficient.

Irani, S. A. (2011, October). Minding your P's, Q's, R's – and revenue too. *The Fabricator*, 64–67. https://www.thefabricator.com/thefabricator/article/shopmanagement/minding-your-p-s-q-s-r-s-and-revenue-too.

Irani, S. A. (2011, December). PQ$ Analysis – Why revenue matters in product mix segmentation. *The Fabricator*, 42–44. https://www.thefabricator.com/thefabricator/article/shopmanagement/pq-analysis-why-revenue-matters-in-product-mix-segmentation.

Irani, S. A. (2012, February). Why a timeline analysis of order history matters. *The Fabricator*, 48–49. https://www.thefabricator.com/thefabricator/article/shopmanagement/why-a-timeline-analysis-of-order-history-matters.

Chapter 14

Determining the Correct Layout Shape for a High-Mix Machining Cell

Origin of Manufacturing Cells

Group Technology (*GT*) is a method of classification of manufactured parts (or assemblies) into groups (or families) that have similar manufacturing routings, design attributes, materials, quality specifications, etc. Knowledge of these groups can be exploited in a variety of activities such as facility layout, machine design, fixture design, tooling standardization, variant design, cost estimation, feature-based process planning, etc. GT has been practiced around the world for many years since the 1960s as part of sound engineering practice and scientific management.

Cellular Manufacturing (CM) is an application of GT to factory reconfiguration and shop floor layout design. Cells are often implemented in high-mix low-volume (HMLV) manufacturing facilities, including job shops, to gain most of the operational benefits of flowline production. A *manufacturing cell* is "an independent group of functionally dissimilar machines, located together on the shop floor, dedicated to the manufacture of a part family". A *part family* is "a collection of parts which are similar either because of geometric shape and size or because similar processing steps are required to manufacture them". In order for a cell to be dedicated to the production of a single part family, it must have the necessary equipment, flexibility to produce a variety of parts, cross-trained employees, autonomy to make personnel decisions, reliable quality and deliveries from vendors, and complete (plus timely) response from external support departments, such as Maintenance, Purchasing, Production Control, etc.

Figure 14.1 shows a U-shaped cell for producing three (different) product families in a sheet metal shop. It originally appeared as Exhibit 6.23 in Chapter 6 *Improving Processes for Productivity Gains* of the book by Suzaki, K. (1987). *The New Manufacturing Challenge: Techniques for Continuous Improvement.* New York,: The Free Press. ISBN 0-02-932040-2. According to Suzaki, "...quite a few people think of their shops as job shops, and this is typically so in a sheet metal shop. By conducting PQ Analysis and Process Route Analysis, however, we often find this is not the case...". With reference to the U-shaped cell, Suzaki states that "...with this arrangement, a good combination of machine capacity utilization and operator's time utilization was achieved while preserving a smooth material flow...". Additional advantages of a U-shaped cell (or line) are improved process synchronization, improved material transfer, elimination of in-process inventory achieved by One-Piece Flow production, and reduction in the number of operators required to monitor and operate the machines in the cell.

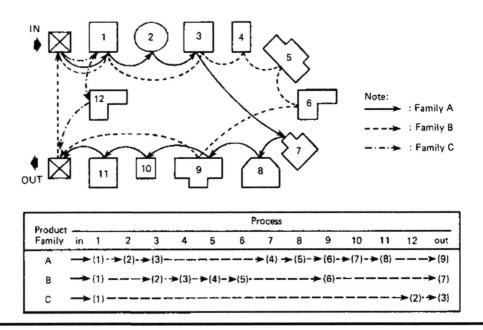

Figure 14.1   Flow diagram for multiple products being produced in a cell.

The First Enterprise-Wide Implementation of Cells

Starting in 1959, Serck Audco Valves, a UK manufacturer of industrial stop valves and actuators, began reorganizing their entire manufacturing enterprise using GT and CM as a foundation. This enterprise transformation was led by Gordon Ranson. In his book[1] (Ranson, 1972), Mr. Ranson wrote "As a practitioner with some twelve years' experience of this technique (GT), the definition which I think most clearly describes GT is as follows: *The logical arrangement and sequence of all facets of company operation in order to bring the benefits of mass production to high variety, mixed quantity production*". Many other contemporary HMLV manufacturers in the United Kingdom followed in the footsteps of Serck Audco Valves. During the period 1961–1967, Serck Audco Valves reported the following improvements in company performance using GT and CM (Burbidge, 1979)[2]:

Metric	Performance
Sales	Up by 32%
Stocks	Down 44%
Ratio of stocks/sales	Down from 52% to 22%
Manufacturing time	Down from 12 to 4 weeks
Overdue orders	Down from 6 to 1 weeks
Output per employee	Up about 50%
Capital investment	Cost recovered four times by stock reduction alone

Interestingly, the benefits of GT and CM reported in Burbidge's book published in 1979 are comparable to those attributed to the Toyota Production System (aka Lean) for repetitive high-volume assembly.

Serck Audco Valves began their implementation of GT/CM by transforming the Functional Layout of each of their machine shops into a Cellular Layout. The Functional Layout has advantages such as high machine utilization and high flexibility in allocating parts to alternative machines in any department (aka process village or work center) whenever any batch of parts

---

[1] Ranson, G.M. (1972). *Group Technology: A Foundation for Better Total Company Operation.* London, UK: McGraw-Hill.

[2] Burbidge, J.L. (1979). *Group Technology in the Engineering Industry.* London, UK: Mechanical Engineering Publications, pp. 109–114. ISBN 0852984022.

arrives for processing. However, it has disadvantages such as high stock-to-dock order flow times, high work-in-process (WIP) levels, poor quality control, and difficulty in locating orders. The Cellular Layout has advantages such as lower stock-to-dock order flow times, lower WIP levels, and better quality control. However, it has disadvantages such as inflexibility to significant mix and volume changes, major production shortfalls due to machine breakdowns, and management's reluctance to give sufficient autonomy to the team running a cell, especially in union shops. Perhaps the biggest disadvantage of this layout is that it requires duplication of the same equipment in two or more cells.

Role of Production Flow Analysis in the Design of a Cell Layout

In Figure 14.1, the number of products being produced in the cell is only three. So, it is easy to manually map and visually compare the routings of the product families to determine (i) commonality of machines in the different process routes and (ii) the appropriateness of the U shape for the cell layout. Despite the differences among the three routings, it is possible to arrange the machines into a single U-shaped "super sequence" of machines. *Notice that all three product families assigned to this cell (or line) have only one common process, Process #1.* Product Families A and B have *only three* processes in common, Product Families A and C have *only one* process in common and Product Families B and C have *only one* process in common. Despite the three routings being dissimilar, Figure 14.1 clearly demonstrates that, if the workstations in this line were arranged in the sequence 1 → 12, then except for "machine-hopping" (bypass flows), the cell layout would "fit" the manufacturing routings of all three product families. Further, if different segments in the line are bent into U or S shapes at appropriate points, then every inter-machine move in the process route of any of the three product families would occur between machines *physically* located adjacent to each other.

The analysis of the product routings (aka Process Sequence Analysis) discussed in the previous paragraph was done manually! What if the Process Sequence Analysis had to be done manually and/or visually for 25 different routings? For 100 different routings? For 1,000 different routings? The task would be very time-consuming, cumbersome, and error-prone. The PFAST (Production Flow Analysis and Simplification Toolkit) does these analyses rapidly and effectively. Thereby, computer-aided Process Sequence Analysis would allow the Lean practitioner to spend more time on creative problem-solving to develop a detailed layout of the multi-product multi-machine cell. For example, with reference to the U-shaped line in Figure 14.1, Suzaki states that "…The complexity associated with machine-hopping is resolved by using a traffic-light concept i.e. the operator should follow the machines with green lights and skip the operation of those with yellow lights…". But would such a system work in a multi-product cell with twenty-five or more different routings that do not fit into a single linear flow path?

Principles to Guide Planning for Effective Flow in a Cell

In Chapter 3 *Flow, Space, and Activity Relationships* of the book[3] by Tompkins et al. (2003), the authors state that "…effective flow within a department involves the progressive movement of materials, information or people between workstations… Planning for effective flow requires the consideration of flow patterns and flow principles…". The authors list the following principles that result in effective flow:

1. *Minimize flow*: Flow becomes necessary only when two or more different work centers are required to produce a product. Minimizing flow represents the work simplification approach to material flow. This approach includes:
   a. Eliminating flow by planning for the delivery of materials, information, or people directly to the point of ultimate use and eliminating intermediate steps.
   b. Minimizing multiple flows by planning for the flow between two consecutive points of use to take place in as few movements as possible, preferably one.
   c. Combining flows and operations wherever possible by planning for the movement of materials, information, or people to be combined with a processing step.

   In addition, the use of Process Engineering, Value Analysis, Design for Manufacture and Assembly, etc. to eliminate processing steps in any process route will *automatically* reduce the number of material handling steps involved.

---

[3] Tompkins, J.A., White, J.A., Bozer, Y.A. & Tanchoco, J.M.A. (2003). *Facilities Planning*. New York: John Wiley. ISBN 0-471-41389-5.

2. *Maximize directed flow paths*: A directed flow path is an uninterrupted flow path progressing directly from origin to destination. An uninterrupted flow path is a flow path that does not intersect with other paths. Congestion occurs due to interruptions in flow caused due to intersections between flow paths. A directed flow path progressing from origin to destination is a flow path with no backtracking (which would increase the length of the flow path).

3. *Minimize the costs of flow*: The cost of flow depends on a variety of factors, such as volume and weight of the products being moved per trip, the distance of travel, the method for material handling, the speed and frequency of travel, the quantity of product being moved per trip, etc. For example, the least cost of material handling between two workstations in a cell would be when, as soon as one unit of product is completed at one workstation, it is automatically ejected from that workstation, and drops into a short and inclined chute (or onto a roller conveyor) that exploits gravity to convey the item to the next (adjacent) workstation. This principle can be viewed from either of the following two perspectives:

   a. Minimize handling that requires walking, manual travel and motions by an operator.

   b. Eliminate manual handling by mechanizing or automating flow to allow workers to spend full time on equipment operation or other value-adding tasks that have been assigned to them.

   In addition, poor shop floor communications between the individual work centers, material handlers, and the Production Control and Scheduling office (or department) can increase the costs of flow. Large distances of separation between two work centers often cause (i) work completed at any work center to become WIP at that work center because the material handler did not arrive immediately to pick it up and move it to the next work center and/or (ii) work completed at any work center to become WIP at the next work center because, at the time that the material handler delivered the work to the next work center, that work center already had a large queue of WIP remaining to be processed. Therefore, large travel distances between consecutive operations help to increase the costs due to (i) material handling, (ii) WIP inventory carrying costs, and (iii) queuing delays.

Impact of Travel Distance between Workstations in a Cell

The popular strategy of *One-Piece Flow* could be easily achieved in a cell layout due to the short transfer distances between adjacent workstations. Small transfer batch sizes (or handling lot size) increase the transportation requirements. But, since the short travel distances allow the use of cheap handling methods such as push carts, roller conveyors, chutes, etc. that have small storage capacity, they can potentially reduce WIP inventory. In their book,[4] Harmon and Peterson (1990) provide a convincing illustration of the impact of material handling distance on inventory. The authors state "…If successive processes are immediately adjacent, a single unit is moved at a time, as in an assembly line. If the next process is across the aisle, the handling lot size is a unit load. If the next process is across the plant, the handling lot size is, at least an hour's supply of product, because more frequent collection is impractical. If the next process is (in) another plant, the handling lot size is at least one day's production. As the WIP between processes will be, at least one half the handling lot size, we see potential orders-of-magnitude differences in WIP levels based on the facility layout…". **In order to achieve *One-Piece Flow*,** unless two machines are next to each other, the operator of the first machine cannot finish one part and immediately hand it over to the operator of the next machine.

Characteristics of a Good Cell Layout

In Chapter 5 *Cell Layout Planning* of the book[5] by Hales and Anderson (2002), the authors list the following common characteristics of Lean (or "waste-free") cell layouts that are influenced by the physical/spatial design of the cell layout:

- Output of each operation is adjacent to the input of the next.
- Close placement and orientation of machines allows one operator to run several machines.
- When the U-shape flow pattern is appropriate, the first and last operations should be adjacent so the same operator can perform both.

---

[4] Harmon, R.L. & Peterson, L.D. (1990). *Reinventing the Factory.* New York: The Free Press.
[5] Hales, L.H. & Andersen, B. (2002). *Planning Manufacturing Cells.* Dearborn, MI: Society of Manufacturing Engineers. ISBN 0-87263-549-X.

- There is one-piece (or single-piece) balanced flow and material handling between operations.
- Where part characteristics permit, there is container-less flow between operators with operators performing the material transfers.
- Where part characteristics permit, there is the use of chutes and slides for incoming parts to compress space and avoid the need for containers and their handling.
- Overhead handling equipment is used where appropriate to reduce aisle space requirements.
- There is flexibility for rapid and easy rearrangement of the cell.
- Raw materials and incoming parts are stored close to points of use and are easily obtained by operators.
- Parts or materials stockrooms or "supermarkets" are close to the cells that they supply.
- In multi-cell layouts where one cell feeds another, the output point of the upstream cell should be next to or nearby the input point for the downstream cell. The output point of the last cell in a processing sequence should be close to the shipping docks or to where its "internal customer" operates.

Further, the authors state that "…the major goal of a cell layout is to minimize the distances that must be traveled by the products and the operators within the cell between operations, or between operations and various support service areas within the cell. In addition to the flow of materials, 'other-than-flow' considerations are always present, as they are in any layout design. However, in a cell layout, such considerations may be treated as modifying factors or practical limitations after the preliminary flow-based arrangement has been achieved…".

Basic Flow Patterns in a Cell

In Chapter 5 *Cell Layout Planning* of the book by Hales and Andersen (2002), the authors state that "…when all parts and materials flow in process sequence, (then) progressive flow patterns – straight-thru, U-shape (or circular) and L-shape – can be used between and within cells. When significant backflow is present, … the comb or spine layout is often appropriate… Most guidebooks on Lean Manufacturing and many Japanese authors insist that every cell should be a U-cell. However, your authors respectfully disagree with this 'mandatory' U-shape rule. The use of systematic planning methods on hundreds of cells of many different types has taught us that each flow pattern has its benefits and limitations. In fact, the best approach is often to prepare two or more layouts deliberately using different basic flow patterns. By evaluating the merits of each, the planner will often arrive at a better final layout than if only one flow pattern has been considered...".

Using the Roman Alphabet to Determine the Correct Shape for a Cell Layout

There are three principles of Design For Flow (DFF) – Principle #1: Minimize flow, Principle #2: Maximize unidirectional flow, and Principle #3: Minimize the cost of flow. If the shape of the layout of a cell is designed based on these principles, then the cell will achieve the following *desired* performance objectives for any cell:

1. Maximize One-Piece Flow between every pair of machines with significant volume of material flow occurring between them.
2. Minimize the total number of non-adjacent pairs of machines in the cell with material flow occurring between them.
3. Minimize the total volume of Backtrack and Cross Flows between adjacent (or non-adjacent) pairs of machines in the layout.
4. Minimize the Total Travel Distance.

The U shape is popular for the layout of any high-volume assembly cell because it is a line bent into a U. All products produced in an assembly cell usually follow the same sequence of steps with some "machine-hopping" (aka bypass flows) allowed! But, unlike the linear flow in an assembly line (or cell), there is no guarantee that a U-shaped layout is the best fit for the flow pattern in a multi-product multi-machine high-variety low-volume job shop cell. In the case of a job shop cell, we will *never* know at the outset that the U shape, or any other variants of the U shape, such as L, N, Z, or S, is *always* the best arrangement for the machines! Therefore, it is a challenge to determine which letter (or combination of letters) of the alphabet – A, B, C, D, E, F, G, H, I, J, K, L, M, N, O, P, Q, R, S, T, U, V, W, X, Y, Z – offers the best shape for the layout of a job shop cell.[6]

---

[6] In general, we will assume that a cell will have a *single* IN location and a *single* OUT location for staging incoming parts and outgoing parts, respectively.

Despite there being twenty-six letters in the Roman alphabet, it is not necessary to evaluate all twenty-six letters of the alphabet to select the best location grid to utilize in STORM (or any other block layout optimization software)[7] to evaluate a particular shape for a cell layout. Several alphabets are identical (or similar) in shape and could be grouped into one or more of the following "alphabet shape clusters":

- {C, D, G, J, L, O, P, Q, U, V}
- {B, E, F, M, T, W, Y}
  - E, F, T, or Y are "droopy"[8] versions of each other.
  - M and W are "droopy" versions of E.
- {N, S, Z}
- {A, H, I, K, R, X}

The above clusters of alphabets are not set in stone and can be modified to yield a different set of clusters. However, these clusters suggest that there is a variety of shapes beyond just the U shape that could better fit the material flow pattern implicit to the routings of a large sample of dissimilar products being produced in a job shop cell!

Motivation

This chapter illustrates the combined use of material flow visualization using a Spaghetti Diagram, Process Routing Analysis using the PFAST software, and facility layout design using the STORM software. The goal is to determine the best layout shape for a multi-product multi-machine manufacturing cell, like the multi-product cell shown in Figure 14.1. Should every cell's shape be a U? In this chapter, we work through an exercise that uses a data set that was originally presented in Chapter 3 *Processing Line Approaches* of the book[9] by Sekine and Arai (1992). In their book, the authors present data "...from Company O which uses a machining line to process its products... A PQ

---

[7] An alternative to STORM would be (i) Sgetti, (ii) PLANOPT (www.planopt.com/index.html), (iii) SIMOGGA (www.amia-systems.com/), and (iv) SPIRAL (www2.isye.gatech.edu/~mgoetsch/Spiral.html) or FLOW PLANNER (www.proplanner.com/en/products/flow_planner/).

[8] The best way to describe "droopy" is when the branches of a palm tree wilt due to lack of water, go limp, and sag while the tree trunk remains straight and upright.

[9] Sekine, K. & Arai, K. (1992). *Kaizen for Quick Changeover: Going beyond SMED*. Cambridge, MA: Productivity Press. ISBN 0-915299-38-0.

Analysis shows that Company O is also a wide-variety small-lot production company... In gathering the data via a process-route analysis, (the authors) studied 13 product types that were selected from a total of 32...". For complete details about this exercise reproduced from the Sekine and Arai book, please refer to that book. However, the authors do not present any analysis or results to suggest that they actually designed a layout for that machining line/cell. In their book they simply state "...(Based on PQ Analysis), the production *line* is currently a wide-variety small-lot production *line*... Try to work out the families on your own. Make no more than three families... There are only two NC lathes, LB15 and LB20, and there is only one Upright MC and one NC for Screw Holes. No new equipment may be added...". **Therefore**, we decided to analyze the same data that the authors provide in their book using PFAST and STORM to try to answer the fundamental question:

1. Does a linear, L-shape, U-shape, S-shape or Z-shape best fit the flow pattern in this multi-product multi-machine job shop cell?
2. **OR**, does some other shape for the cell layout better fit the flow pattern for the set of products assigned for production to this cell?

Input Data File for Production Flow Analysis

Table 14.1 presents information about the products being produced in the cell. The columns **Product No.**, **Product Name,** and **Routings** are reproduced as-is from Sekine and Arai. However, the values in the *Quantity* column have been modified from the original values reported by the authors. Further, the values in the *Revenue* column do not appear in Sekine and Arai and were randomly generated in order to complete the standard input data requirements of PFAST.

Table 14.2 lists the machines in the cell.

Figure 14.2 shows the standard Multi-Product Process Chart representation of the routings in Table 14.1.

Design of a Cell Layout

Figure 14.3(a) shows the Q-type (Q=Quantity) From-To Chart for the cell that was generated by PFAST using the data in the **Routings** and **Quantity** columns in Table 14.1.

Table 14.1　Information about the Products Being Produced in the Cell

Product No.	Product Name	Quantity	Revenue	Routings					
1	Slider A	40	10,000	6	9	10	11	12	
2	Slider B	45	25,000	4	6	9	10	11	12
3	Press Brace	80	50,000	5	8	9	10		
4	Bracket #1	15	5,000	4	7	9	10		
5	Table	100	30,000	3	7	10	12		
6	Damper	20	10,000	1	7	9	10		
7	Bracket #2	30	5,000	1	8	9	10		
8	Support	30	20,000	4	7	9			
9	Housing	70	40,000	2	7	9			
10	Flange	15	20,000	2	9				
11	Shaft	10	10,000	3	9	10	12		
12	Base	90	35,000	3	6	4	10	12	
13	Spacer	75	45,000	4	6	4	10	12	

Table 14.2　Description of Machines in the Cell

M/C #	Machine Name	No. Available
1	NC lathe (LB15)	1
2	NC lathe (LB20)	1
3	Horizontal mill (M)	1
4	Upright mill (VM)	1
5	Compact mill (BM)	1
6	Upright MC (6VA)	1
7	NC for screw holes (TNC)	1
8	Marker (MRK)	1
9	Drilling machine (B)	1
10	Manual operations (MAN)	1
11	Honing (H)	1
12	Grinder (G)	1

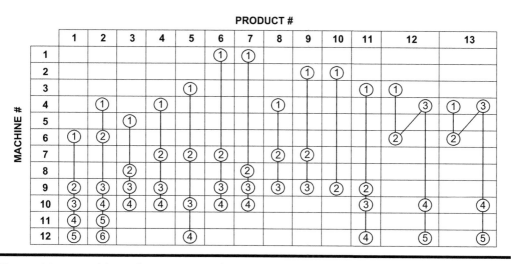

Figure 14.2   Multi-product process chart representation of the routings.

(a)

W/C	4	6	3	7	9	10	12	11	2	5	8	1
4	x	120		45		165						
6	165	x			85							
3		90	x	100	10							
7				x	135	100						
9					x	240						
10						x	275	85				
12							x					
11							85	x				
2				70	15				x			
5										x	80	
8					110						x	
1				20							30	x

(b)

W/C	3	6	4	7	9	10	12	11	2	5	8	1
3	x	35000		30000	10000							
6		x	80000		35000							
4		70000	x	25000		80000						
7				x	75000	30000						
9					x	115000						
10						x	120000	35000				
12							x					
11							35000	x				
2				40000	20000				x			
5										x	50000	
8					55000						x	
1				10000							5000	x

Figure 14.3   (a) Q-type and (b) $-type From-To Charts.

Figure 14.3(b) shows the $-type ($=Revenue) From-To Chart for the cell that was generated by PFAST using the data in the **Routings** and **Revenue** columns in Table 14.1.

Now let us produce our first layout for the cell!

Since there is only one of each of the machines available in this cell, the problem of distributing (or duplicating) any machine at multiple locations in the cell does not arise. In that case, (i) (*if using Sgetti*) we can use the Q-type From-To Chart in Figure 14.3(a) to generate the layout or (ii) (*if using STORM*[10] *or PLANOPT*) we can use the Q-type From-To Chart in Figure 14.3(a) as the **Flow Matrix** and the $-type From-To Chart in Figure 14.3(b) as the **Cost Matrix**. Since we had access to STORM, we chose Option #2.

Linear Layout

The linear layout produced by STORM for the cell which had the lowest value for the total weighted travel distance is shown below:

4	6	3	7	9	10	12	11	2	5	8	1

On the linear layout shown above, draw an arrow for each of the material flows in the From-To Chart of Figure 14.3(a) by connecting the "From" machine (in the row for that cell) to the "To" machine (in the column for that cell).

Study the Spaghetti Diagram.

Now answer the following questions:

■ Does the cell layout maximize One-Piece Flow between every pair of machines with significant volume of material flow occurring between them?
■ Does the cell layout minimize the total number of non-adjacent pairs of machines in the cell with material flow occurring between them?
■ Does the cell layout minimize the total volume of Backtrack and Cross Flows between **adjacent** (or non-adjacent) pairs of machines in the layout?
■ Does the cell layout minimize the Total Travel Distance for all parts produced in the cell?

---

[10] An alternative to STORM would be (i) SGETTI, (ii) PLANOPT (www.planopt.com/index.html), (iii) SIMOGGA (www.amia-systems.com/), and (iv) SPIRAL (www2.isye.gatech.edu/~mgoetsch/Spiral.html) or FLOW PLANNER (www.proplanner.com/en/products/flow_planner/).

Based on your answers above, does the cell layout satisfy the *essential* objectives for cell design based on the principles of Design for Flow? **Answer:** ____Yes ____No.

Curvilinear Layout

If you think that a linear layout is not appropriate for this cell, would bending the linear layout into a curvilinear layout, such as L or U or S or Z or Clover Leaf (which is a line bent into multiple U's), be appropriate for this cell? Figure 14.1 is an example of a U layout for a cell. Here is how you may consider where to bend the linear layout at one or more points:

1. Select a flow arrow with high traffic volume whose pair of machines are not adjacent to each other.
2. Bend the portion of the linear layout between those two machines into a U. Within that segment, check for any remaining non-adjacent pairs of machines with significant traffic between them.
3. If you still see material flows between non-adjacent machines, repeat the bending process again.

Below I have shown an example of a curvilinear layout. I chose a 5 × 5 location grid on which I randomly bent the original linear arrangement of machines generated by STORM into several smaller U's:

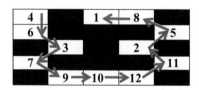

Now please draw **your** curvilinear layout for the twelve machines on the rectilinear grid below:

On the new layout for the cell, draw an arrow for each of the material flows in the From-To Chart of Figure 14.3(a) by connecting the "From" machine (in the row for that cell) to the "To" machine (in the column for that cell).

Study the Spaghetti Diagram.

Now answer the following questions:

■ Does the cell layout maximize One-Piece Flow between every pair of machines with significant volume of material flow occurring between them?

■ Does the cell layout minimize the total number of non-adjacent pairs of machines in the cell with material flow occurring between them?

■ Does the cell layout minimize the total volume of Backtrack and Cross Flows between **adjacent** (or non-adjacent) pairs of machines in the layout?

■ Does the cell layout minimize the Total Travel Distance for all parts produced in the cell?

Based on your answers above, does the cell layout satisfy the *essential* objectives for cell design based on the principles of DFF?

Answer: _____Yes _____No.

At this point, you *may* have concluded that the routings of the parts being machined in this cell are so different that no single sequence of the twelve machines would match all of the routings. So, unlike how an assembly line can be bent into a U shape, it is futile to take a linear ordering of the twelve machines and bend that sequence into a curvilinear layout shape such as an L, U, S, Z, or Clover Leaf shape.

So what could we do next?

M-shaped (or W-shaped) Layout[11]

Given the heuristic layout algorithms available in commercial software tools like STORM[12] and PLANOPT, it is possible to:

---

[11] This grid could be easily created in the STORM software.

[12] Emmons, H., Dale F.A., Khot, C.M. & Mathur, K. (2001). *STORM 4.0: Quantitative Modeling for Decision Support*. Euclid, OH: Lakeshore Communications. ISBN 1-893435-156.

1. Design a location grid for placement of the machines that has a specific shape chosen from any one of the four shape clusters that had been discussed earlier in the chapter, and,
2. Allow the heuristic algorithm to assign the machines to the available locations in the cell layout to minimize total product travel distance.[13]

In Appendix 5 for this chapter, Figure 1 shows that, when different U or S-shaped location grids for the cell layout were provided, STORM produced machine arrangements that had different travel distance scores. Next, let us evaluate a layout shape for the cell that is not based on alphabets that correspond to a line bent into a curvilinear shape. Assign the twelve machines to appropriate locations in the M-shaped (or W-shaped) location grid below. The locations on the grid that appear as ■ represent floor space for the machine operators to stand at their machines or aisles to move product from one machine to another. In order to quickly generate a cell layout, study the From-To Chart of Figure 14.3(a) for large/small values of traffic flow. Next, place those pairs of machines that have heavy traffic flow between them adjacent to each other and those with light traffic flow between them in non-adjacent locations, or even across the aisle from each other. For example, I have placed the three machines that feature at the end of all thirteen routings after studying the flows between the three machines in Figure 14.3(a).

Study the Spaghetti Diagram.
Now answer the following questions:

■ Does the cell layout maximize One-Piece Flow between every pair of machines with significant volume of material flow occurring between them?
■ Does the cell layout minimize the total number of non-adjacent pairs of machines in the cell with material flow occurring between them?

---

[13] PFAST does not have this ability to control the shape of the layout of a cell by varying the location grid for placement of the machines.

- Does the cell layout minimize the total volume of Backtrack and Cross Flows between **adjacent** (or non-adjacent) pairs of machines in the layout?
- Does the cell layout minimize the Total Travel Distance for all parts produced in the cell?

Based on your answers above, does the cell layout satisfy the *essential* objectives for cell design based on the principles of DFF?
Answer: ____Yes ____No.

Are Layout Shapes for Assembly Lines *at All* Suitable for Job Shop Cells?

These are my personal observations but you are welcome to modify this list with your own observations:

1. The twenty-six letters of the Roman alphabet can be grouped into approximately four shape clusters. All letters within a cluster correspond to a particular cell layout shape.
2. It is a mistake to assume that a U layout is the best shape to give a cell layout if a simple visual assessment of the routings of the parts indicates that they are dissimilar.
3. Even if a cell layout shape is a combination of one or more of the four main shapes (one for each cluster of alphabets), the resulting material flow within the cell can be expected to follow the principles of DFF.
4. Any commercial software tool like STORM, SPIRAL, or PLANOPT that uses the From-To Chart as input will generate a Process Layout for the cell. This means that each machine (or work center) will be assigned to one and only one location in the layout. No machine will be duplicated at another location unless that duplication was already captured in the From-To Chart that was used as input. If you would like to discuss how to overcome this major limitation of commercial facility layout software, please email me at ShahrukhIrani1023@yahoo.com.
5. The cell layout should fit the material flow pattern that is implicit to the routings of the products that will be produced in the cell. The material flow pattern for each set of products is unique. No single letter of the Roman alphabet should be assumed for the cell layout shape!

Realistically, the cell layout should be determined using an iterative generate-and-evaluate approach that combines the use of Spaghetti Diagrams, facility layout software, real-world experience, and input from the employees who will work in the cell.

So what could we do next?

Designing a Cell Layout *without* Using a From-To Chart

Poor flow in a cell could be the consequence of (i) two or more different part families being assigned to it in order to have high utilization on one or more common machines in their routings, (ii) one or more parts may not have the desired routings because poor process engineering decisions were made to produce those parts, (iii) the wrong machine may have been chosen to perform a particular operation despite another machine being capable of performing the same operation, and (iv) a group of products with low demand were assigned to the same cell without knowing that they have highly dissimilar routings, etc.

Earlier in the chapter, Figure 14.2 presented the thirteen part routings in the format of a Multi-Product Process Chart. This chart is a classical IE (Industrial Engineering) representation for the different routings of many products being produced in the same facility. Recall that a commercial facility layout software would aggregate all thirteen routings into a single From-To Chart. In stark contrast, PFAST helps to identify clusters of parts whose routings are identical, or at least very similar, and groups them into separate part families. If the sample of products being produced in a cell could be split into two or more families, then that heterogeneity in the product mix assigned to the cell is a problem (or could be a potential problem)!

What if we did not use the From-To Chart and instead used the actual product routings as input? Figure 14.4 is the PR Analysis Type I (aka *Product-Process Matrix Analysis*) output that PFAST produced using the routings in Table 14.1 as input.

Figure 14.5 is the PR Analysis Type II (aka *Product-Routing Cluster Analysis Dendrogram*) output that PFAST produced using the routings in Table 14.1 as input. This output seems to confirm that there are two product families (not one!) that have been assigned to the cell for production. Recall that Sekine and Arai had said "…try to work out the (product) families on your own. Make no more than three families…".

Products	Workcenters											
	11	9	10	12	6	4	3	7	1	8	5	2
10		1										1
9		1						1				1
8		1				1		1				
4		1	1			1		1				
6		1	1					1	1			
7		1	1						1	1		
3		1	1							1	1	
1	1	1	1	1	1							
2	1	1	1	1	1	1						
13			1	1	1	1						
12			1	1	1	1	1					
11		1	1	1			1					
5			1	1			1	1				

Product Family #2

Product Family #1

Figure 14.4 PR Analysis Type I.

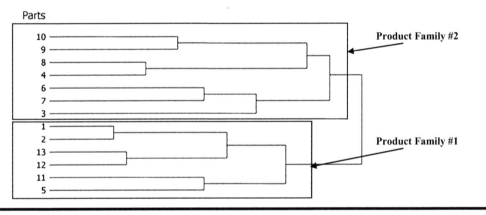

Figure 14.5 PR Analysis Type II.

Based on the analysis of Figures 14.4 and 14.5, the following observations can be made:

1. *Number of product families*: The thirteen products do not constitute a single homogeneous product family. It appears that there are two product families that have been assigned for production to the same cell.
2. *Machine duplication*: Assuming that the parts assigned to the two families are correct, at least Work Centers #4, #9, and #10 **may** need to be duplicated at a second location in the cell layout. Parts from the other part family would visit that location for processing. If there is need for buying one or more machines of the same type, does a budget constraint rule out the purchase of one or more machines of that

type? For example, a second *Drilling Machine* and a second *Upright Mill* may need to be purchased. However, in the case of *Manual Operation* (*MAN*), it could be taught to all cell operators; then an operator would perform that operation at any of the different machines where the parts being worked upon require that operation (aka POU, Point Of Use). There is no need for the *MAN* operation to be at a single location in the cell.

3. *Exception operations*: Assuming that the assignment of parts to the two families is correct, W/C #7 **may not** need to be duplicated at a second location in the cell layout. Only Product #5 in Product Family #1 needs to use that work center; whereas, it is Product Family #2 that clearly has more parts being processed by the *NC for Screw Holes* machine! In the case of any Exception Operation, depending on the cost of the machine, either the extra material handling is allowed or an extra machine is purchased at an affordable price to prevent the extra walking by the operator. Machine duplication is not an absolute must to eliminate the additional product and employee travel that such operations necessitate!

---

1. But is the machine duplication suggested by PR Analysis Type I and PR Analysis Type II really necessary?
2. What if the visual representation of the data makes it appear as if machine duplication is necessary?
3. Could the extent of machine duplication be reduced if the same part families were visualized in the form of a classic Spaghetti Diagram (which maps product routings on the actual layout of a facility?

Figure 14.6(a) is the PR Analysis Type IV (aka *Modified Multi-Product Process Chart, MM-PPC*) output that is produced by PFAST using the routings in Table 14.1.

What are some key differences that you observe between the Multi-Product Process Chart (Figure 14.2) and MM-PPC (Figure 14.6(a))? For example, unlike the random ordering of the thirteen products in Figure 14.2, Figure 14.6(a) displays the product families that appear in Figures 14.4 and 14.5. This allows a rapid and effective visual comparison of (i) routings within a part family as well as (ii) routings in the part family that is immediately adjacent (top or bottom) to a particular family. For a technical discussion on this chart, including a comparison with other

IE charts used for mapping and analyzing multi-product flows, please see Appendix 3 for this chapter.

Figure 14.6(b) shows how multiple occurrences of the same machine in adjacent rows have been enclosed within a bubble. That is because all occurrences inside a bubble could be merged and replaced by a single occurrence of that machine. How does this translate to reducing the need for machine duplication on the actual factory floor? Even if one machine were placed at the location of a bubble, then several products could travel to

Products						
5	3		7	10		12
11	3		9	10		12
12	3	6	4	10		12
13	4	6	4	10		12
2	4	6	9	10	11	12
1		6	9	10	11	12
3	5	8	9	10		
7	1	8	9	10		
6	1	7	9	10		
4	4	7	9	10		
8	4	7	9			
9	2	7	9			
10	2		9			

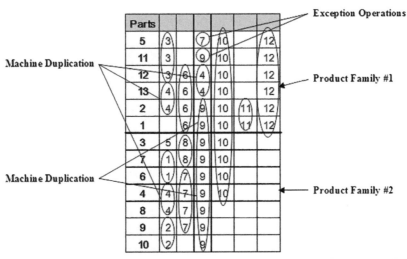

Figure 14.6   a) PR Analysis Type IV. b) Machine sharing between the two product families in the cell.

the location of that particular machine to use it. For example, Part #s 5, 11, and 12 would all visit the same/single Machine #3.

Here are some of the key attributes of the PR Analysis IV output in Figure 14.6(b) that should be taken into consideration to guide the design of the cell layout:

1. The routings of the products are arranged adjacent to each other. Assume that each product has a manufacturing line dedicated to its production. Even if the demand for one product were to decrease or increase, then available capacity on common machines on the line on either side of this product's line could be accessed. For example, Products #1 and #3 belong in different families but the capacity on Machine #9 could be shared between the two families.

2. The set of products assigned to this cell does not constitute a single family. In the figure, we have shown how the set of products can be broken up into two families. Despite two product families having been assigned to this cell, the chart allows us to see which machines are unique to a single family and which machines may need to be duplicated in either cell.

3. With reference to Figure 14.6(b), what would you do to eliminate the impact that the *Exception Operations* have on material flow, transfer of product lots between non-adjacent machines, idle time of operators who must move between non-adjacent locations, etc.?

4. With reference to Figure 14.6b, what would you do to eliminate the need for *Machine Duplication* that is indicated in the MM-PPC? Recall that Sekine and Arai had said "...No new equipment may be added...".

5. With reference to Figure 14.6(b), do you notice that there are *five* "first operation" machines? This is unlike an assembly line/cell where the first station in the line/cell would do the same (single!) operation on each and every product that is produced in the line/cell. How will that impact how you design the "front end" of the cell?

6. With reference to Figure 14.6(b), do you notice that there are *two* "last operation" machines? This is unlike an assembly line/cell where the last station in the line/cell would do the same (single!) operation on each and every product that is produced in the line/cell. How will that impact how you design the "back end" of the cell?

Your Assignment

Given all this information, can you design a layout for the cell that has better flow than was observed in the assembly line layout options that were based on the letters of the Roman alphabet?

Potential Solution for Your Assignment

The Appendices for this chapter discuss the Hybrid Flow Shop Layout that I designed for this multi-product multi-machine job shop cell.

Conclusion

The standard shapes for assembly cells – Line, U, L, N, Z, S, Clover Leaf – may not **at all** be suited for high-variety low-volume non-assembly cells that make a diverse range of parts (or products) with dissimilar routings. Also, due to the theoretical limitations of the algorithms they use, existing commercial layout software packages lack the ability to automatically determine the best shape for a cell layout. So, if it is desired to design a layout that "fits" the material flow corresponding to the routings of the product family to be produced in a high-mix cell, then classical ideas and software for designing the layout of the cell are not up to the task! This chapter described an innovative approach that, instead of using the From-To Chart as input, uses the actual product routings that are aggregated into the From-To Chart. The approach is implemented using the PFAST and SGETTI software tools.

Appendices

Appendices for this chapter are available for download at https://www.crcpress.com/9781498740692.

Chapter 15

Lessons Learned from Implementing the Lean Principles in a Single High-Mix Low-Volume Make-To-Order Compressor Parts Machining Cell

Acknowledgment

This chapter is based on the work that I did when I was the Director of Industrial Engineering (IE) Research at Hoerbiger Corporation of America (HCA) from 2012 to 2014. After an academic career that spanned 22 years, this was my first industry job! It was a golden opportunity given to me by Hannes Hunschofsky, who was then the President of HCA. He invited (and challenged!) me to pilot the implementation of Job Shop Lean in their Houston, TX, facility. This industry job gave me the opportunity to put into practice the research on Job Shop Lean that I did at The Ohio State University. I have learned the hard way that the only way to learn the unique IE that Toyota pioneered is through hands-on implementation. Thank you, Hannes!

Motivation

This chapter describes the lessons I learned from being part of an implementation team that implemented a high-mix low-volume machining cell in a Make-To-Order manufacturing facility that produces compressor parts for field repairs. Unlike a repetitive high-volume automobile manufacturer like Toyota, small and medium-size custom manufacturers (aka Small and Medium Enterprises, SME) usually make a variety of products. Most of these products do not have the volume and repetitive demand to justify producing those products on an assembly line. *However*, by grouping products with similar/identical routings into part families, the aggregate workload on key machines needed to produce a part family could be sufficient over the long term. This would justify the implementation of a FLean (Flexible and Lean) manufacturing cell that will produce any and all parts in the part family.

Background

Group Technology (GT) is a method for classification of manufactured parts (or assemblies) into groups (or families) that have similar manufacturing routings, design attributes, materials, quality specifications, etc. A **part family** is "a collection of parts which are similar either because of geometric shape and size or because similar processing steps are required to manufacture them". Knowledge of these groups can be exploited in a variety of activities such as facility layout, machine design, fixture design, tooling standardization, variant product and process design, cost estimation, feature-based generative process planning, etc. *Since the 1960s*, GT has been practiced around the world for many years as part of sound engineering practice and scientific management.

Cellular Manufacturing (CM) is an application of GT to factory reconfiguration and shop floor layout design. A **manufacturing cell** is "an independent group of functionally dissimilar machines, located together on the shop floor, dedicated to the manufacture of a part family". *Since the 1960s*, cells have been implemented in high-mix low-volume manufacturing facilities, including job shops, to gain most of the operational benefits of flowline production. Due to the diversity of machines in it, a cell is capable of completing all operations required by a family of products, usually with minimum (or no) reliance on outside resources. If a cell is self-sufficient, it produces complete products ordered by customers. This motivates the team of employees working in the cell because they see their work earning revenue for their company. Due to the proximity between different machine operators, the cell fosters teamwork, facilitates quick resolution of quality issues, promotes visual control of WIP (work-in-process) and guarantees shortened lead times. *But there is a downside when the machines and people that support a complete Value Stream are co-located into a cell*! In order for a cell to be dedicated to the production of a single part family, it must have the necessary equipment, flexibility to produce a variety of parts, cross-trained employees, autonomy to make personnel decisions, reliable product quality from vendors, reliable lead times with on-time delivery from vendors, and complete (plus timely) response from other in-house departments, such as Maintenance, Purchasing, Production Control, etc.

Lean Assembly Cell vs. FLean (Flexible and Lean) Machining Cell

A Lean assembly cell is different from an FLean machining cell. Hannes Hunschofsky, my former boss at HCA, coined the buzzword "FLean". For example, an FLean cell that is implemented in a job shop may not allow the perfect one-piece flow that is feasible in an assembly cell. Still, due to the proximity between consecutively used machines, at least small batches of parts can be easily moved between non-adjacent machines on wheeled carts or on short roller conveyors or using jib cranes. In some cases, one-piece flow could also be achieved if one machine operator could coordinate with another machine operator and hand them a part as soon as he/she completes it.

A Manufacturing Cell Is a Value Stream!

The *Principles of Lean* (*Source*: www.lean.org/WhatsLean/Principles.cfm) are a five-step thought process for guiding the implementation of Lean:

1. *Principle #1*: Specify value from the standpoint of the end customer by product family.
2. *Principle #2*: Identify all the steps in the *Value Stream* (*Source*: https://en.wikipedia.org/wiki/Value_stream_mapping) for each product family, eliminating whenever possible those steps that do not create value.

3. *Principle #3*: Make the value-creating steps occur in tight sequence so the product will flow smoothly toward the customer.
4. *Principle #4*: As flow is introduced, let customers pull value from the next upstream activity.
5. *Principle #5*: As value is specified, Value Streams are identified, wasted steps are removed, and Flow and Pull are introduced, begin the process again and continue it until a state of perfection is reached in which perfect value is created with no waste.

Any manufacturing cell implemented in a high-mix low-volume Make-To-Order manufacturing facility *automatically* embodies a Value Stream because:

1. The cell has focus. It produces a family of parts (or assembled products) to fulfill orders received from one or more customers.
2. The cell is (i) flexible enough to produce any and all orders for parts that belong in a specific part family and (ii) Lean because it easily eliminates many of the Seven Types of Waste in its daily operations, especially Transportation, Inventory, and Waiting.
3. The cell employees have to work as a team that is accountable for meeting performance expectations set by management.
4. A cell has the potential to become an Autonomous Business Unit (ABU) within a larger company if it has all required resources available within it (including inspection). How? By empowering the team of employees in the cell to manage day-to-day operations and make decisions about cell scheduling, assigning jobs to different operators, deciding who gets cross-trained on which machines, etc. The team that works in the cell can give top priority to those CI projects that eliminate, or at least mitigate, all the constraints that force the cell to send its orders for processing to external resources, regardless of whether they are vendors or in-house. In particular, the cell should be allowed to communicate directly with their customers concerning changes in delivery dates, questions about part drawings or routers, unforeseen quality problems, etc.[1]

---

[1] The implementation of Virtual Cells needs (i) a reliable daily production schedule and (ii) one or more Water Strider(s) (or Spider(s)) to be responsible for all factory logistics.

Case Study: Design and Implementation of a High-Mix Low-Volume Machining Cell

In the Houston, TX, facility of HCA-TX, the shop floor was loosely organized into seven cells. There were five cells in the machine shop and two cells in the molding department. Except for the QRC (Quick Response Cell), which functioned like a job shop and received orders to produce parts for field repairs on compressors, none of the other four machining cells were self-sufficient. Every one of them had to send their parts out for processing in other areas of the facility! And, of the four machining cells, the Manual Packings Cell (MPC) had a low risk compared with the other four existing machining cells in the facility because the Enterprise Resource Planning (ERP) system showed that it did a relatively lower volume of business. In addition, unlike the MPC, the other four machining cells were in flux for a variety of reasons, such as changes in their product mix, technology upgrades, reduction or replacement of vendors, etc. Therefore, the MPC was the best low-risk candidate for a pilot project to demonstrate the viability of Job Shop Lean in our high-mix low-volume facility. Since HCA-TX management was interested in exploring the merits of Job Shop Lean, they gave their full support for a pilot project to redesign the MPC so it could potentially operate as an ABU. Therefore, we undertook to develop and implement a roadmap to design and implement an FLean machining cell by:

1. Using software tools like PFAST and STORM to map the material flows and design the cell layout.
2. Hiring a full-time IE intern who worked full-time on the project and engaged daily with the cell employees.
3. Involving the in-house Tiger Team which was a group of employees who were responsible for all Lean projects.
4. Involving the in-house IE who provided valuable time study data.
5. Involving the cell employees to implement 5S and ergonomics-related improvements at their machines.
6. Accepting input from the cell employees about the changes that were made in their workplace.
7. Justifying the implementation of the cell to upper management.

As a side note concerning Bullet #1 above, a major takeaway from this project was that software for data analytics is necessary for implementing Job Shop Lean. The software applications that we used significantly enhanced the effectiveness of the decisions made by our team as we had to generate and evaluate several alternative cell layouts. However, software is neither essential nor sufficient! In stark contrast, employee buy-in and management support are *absolutely* essential.

Design of the Manual Packings Cell (MPC) Layout

The overarching objective for redesigning the existing MPC was to co-locate all of its manufacturing equipment so it could operate autonomously. We collected the routings of all the parts that were produced in the MPC during a 5-day week and sorted them in order of decreasing production volumes (PQ Analysis). That was because we wanted to select the top few parts and map their routings on the current layout of the cell to produce the Flow Diagram shown in Figure 15.1. The figure clearly shows the chaotic flows of products into and out of the cell prior to its redesign. In the figure, the flows shown in red represent large values in the From-To Chart and the flows shown in green represent low values. For details about the analyses done

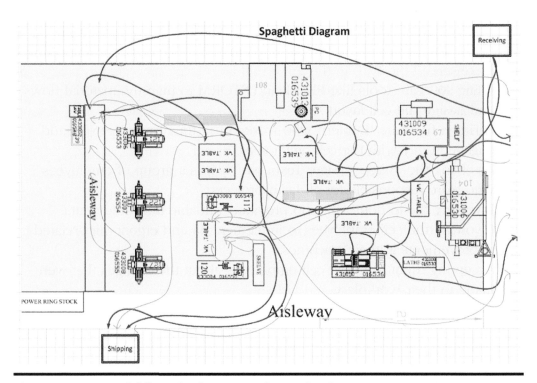

Figure 15.1   Material flows in the current layout for the MPC.

and how their results were translated into the final layout for the cell, please see Appendix 1 for this chapter.

In stark contrast, Figure 15.2 shows the Flow Diagram for the new cell layout that was partially implemented. Some key features of this new layout that we designed for the new cell are as follows:

1. The cell has a classic U-shape which is favored for the typical manufacturing cell. The material flows indicate that this shape fits the flow of products produced in it.
2. The Mori Seiki lathe, which is currently located in another cell (PRR Cell), has been moved into the MPC and positioned opposite the Haas lathe. Both lathes produce the "donuts" from bar stock and are placed in a back-to-back configuration to allow a single operator to attend to both machines. The budget to implement the cell included the purchase of a jib crane that would be positioned between them and be able to reach the location where incoming bar stock would be dropped off by the Receiving department.
3. Three machines that belonged in another cell (PRRC) – ProCut, EZPath, and Mazak VTC – would be moved out of the MPC.

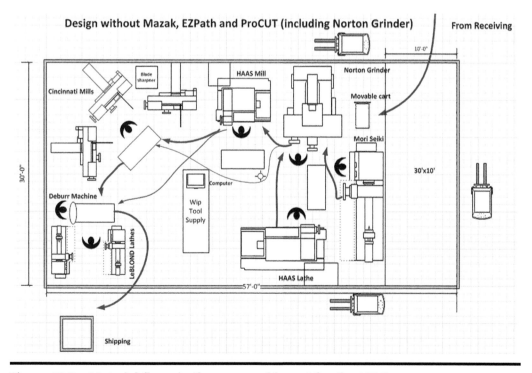

Figure 15.2   Material flows in the proposed layout for the MPC.

The new cell layout reduced the floor space requirements of the MPC almost 50% (from 2,816 to 1,410 sq. ft). This freed-up floor space was eyed for accommodating additional business to be brought from the "mother ship" manufacturing facility in Pompano Beach, FL.

Lessons Learned from Implementing the Cell

Lean Principle #1 provides a sound strategy for implementing Lean: Lean Principle #1 is "Specify value from the standpoint of the end customer by product family". A cell is a factory-within-a-factory whose performance can be measured using the same metrics (Quality, Cost, and Delivery) that are used to measure overall company performance. Except that an FLean machining cell is designed to produce a single product family extracted from the entire product mix. There should be no confusion that, *unlike a Mixed Model flexible assembly line/cell*, an FLean machining cell operates like a flow shop or a job shop!

Bad data will scuttle good software … always! A major takeaway from this project was that computer software is necessary for implementing Job Shop Lean. The new layout for the cell was designed using the PFAST and STORM software tools. The software tools supported and enhanced the effectiveness of the decisions made by the team because they were able to generate and evaluate the alternative layouts that were designed for the cell. Unfortunately, as the preliminary software outputs indicated, the routings for the different parts in the family that we extracted from the ERP system were inaccurate. So we did what Lean Thinkers constantly advise, "Go to the gemba!" The cell employees and machine shop supervisor corrected the routings and even explained to us the differences between the parts. Collecting data in person is an extremely effective and highly recommended learning strategy!

A cell automatically helps to implement Lean Principle #2: Lean Principle #2 is "Identify all the steps in the Value Stream for each product family, eliminating whenever possible those steps that do not create value". Empirical evidence suggests that 95% of the time that an order spends in process in a machine shop is comprised of two of the Seven Types of Waste – Transportation and Waiting (*Source*: www.leaninnovations.ca/seven_types. html). Therefore, only 5% of that time is spent **on** the machines that perform the process steps specified in its routing. The obvious solution for reducing (possibly even eliminating) the wastes of Transportation and Waiting is to implement a manufacturing cell to produce a product (or product family).

But, in order to justify a cell, it is essential to identify and measure the wastes and delivery delays in the timeline of each part being produced in the cell. Use a PQ$ Analysis (P = Product, Q = Quantity, $ = Sales) to identify the part for which to produce (i) a Value Stream Map, (ii) an Extended Value Stream Map showing operations that are external to the cell, (iii) a Process Flowchart, and (iv) a Spaghetti Diagram using the current cell layout! Then use those charts to educate the cell employees about the wastes that they have "been living with" all these years. This will encourage their participation and focus their thinking, time, and energy on designing and implementing a cell that will automatically eliminate significant amounts of waste.[2]

A cell automatically helps to implement Lean Principle #3: Lean Principle #3 is "Make the value-creating steps occur in tight sequence so the product will flow smoothly toward the customer". Cells are the ideal option to implement this principle. Recall that the amoeba and paramecium are self-sufficient single-cell organisms that exist in nature? Similarly, a manufacturing cell is capable of operating autonomously. Inside a cell, the employees can use all the Lean tools, such as cross-training of the cell employees, 5S, SMED, TPM, Poka-Yoke, Standard Work, etc., to operate the cell without having its operations disrupted by scrap or rework, machine breakdowns, long setups, employee absenteeism, poor communications with suppliers and/or customers, etc.

The ERP system might prevent implementation of Lean Principle #4: Lean Principle #4 is "As flow is introduced, let customers pull value from the next upstream activity". A cell is the nearest equivalent to an assembly line. The new cell design was such that all of the operations required to produce its part family were now being done inside the cell. All that was needed to do was to estimate the workload due to orders produced in the cell. We asked the machine operators to guesstimate the workload on their machine due to the batch (or batches) of parts queued at their machine(s). With their years of experience, their guesstimates were really good! **Unfortunately**, the cell received orders per the production schedule set in the corporate ERP system which (i) assumed infinite capacity and (ii) used standard backward scheduling with fixed lead times to determine the release dates to send orders to the cell. How were we going to get a feasible daily schedule released to the cell without modifying the ERP system's parameters set by corporate? Alas,

---

[2] If management desires to expand the waste identification to all parts in the product family being produced in the cell, then the method of Value Network Mapping should be used. It would be a cardinal mistake to manually produce the same set of four maps for each part!

this was not a battle that we wanted to fight because we knew at the outset who would win!

Use the first step in 5S (Sort) as a test of employee buy-in: The power of Lean lies in involving employees to pursue the cost reduction and performance improvement goals for their cell. So, before we moved a single machine to implement the cell, we decided to first "pluck the low-hanging fruits" by making any and all improvements that required no (or minimal) expense. Figure 15.3 shows examples of the housekeeping that was undertaken by (i) the Tiger Team every Wednesday for about 2 hours, and (ii) each employee in the cell with assistance provided to them on an as-needed basis by the graduate IE intern, Dhananjay P. It was amazing to see the quick transformation in the appearance of the cell after **just** the removal of old tables, unused racks, old dust-covered cartons, an unused A-frame cart, boxes filled with old tools and scrapped parts, and an old broken conveyor that served as a table to store WIP.

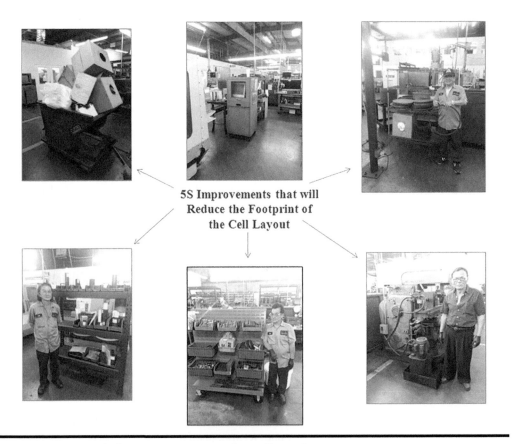

Figure 15.3   Workplace improvements by cell employees.

However, we stressed that all of the kaizens done by the employees had a strategic goal to fit all the machines, support services, and employees in the **least** area without compromising employee safety and ergonomics in their workspace. This automatically reduced the NVA (non-value-added) product travel, material handling, and employee walking. For example, we knew that there would be a certain amount of WIP in the cell. But we did not want that WIP to be stored on pallets on the floor. So we designed storage systems that maximized cube utilization but could be stored under the work tables located in the center of the cell.

Allow employees to show off their efforts (and talents!): Lean can inspire every employee to "take charge of their own work environment". Luong Dam, who operated the three Cincinnati Mills in the MPC, had been with the company for nearly three decades! He quickly realized that we were asking employees to step forward and undertake small changes in their workplaces that would benefit **them** first and foremost. Soon after he saw the *Toast Kaizen* and *5S's at Boeing* videos, one day when we were out on the floor, he called us over and showed us some of the initial housekeeping that he had done to tidy up his area. But there was more to come! He continued working tirelessly with us over a period of 2 weeks to single-handedly rearrange his work center, as shown in Figure 15.4(a) and (b).

*The motivated employees will **surely** come up with innovative ideas!* I had got into the routine of walking through the facility at least once every day just to "press the flesh" with employees working in different areas. But I was also doing in-house benchmarking to see if I could observe good practice in one cell and implement it in the other cells, if possible. Figure 15.5 shows a fixture that had been built by one of our senior multi-talented employees, Phillip N., for another cell (QRC) to store the tools used on their Le Blonde lathes. Well, the MPC also had a couple of those same machines! All that I had to do was to request Phillip to design and fabricate a similar fixture for the MPC. He built it and never asked to be compensated for his time and effort. How much do you think it cost the company besides his time and effort? Such is the power of Lean to motivate and inspire every employee who embraces it!

Follow up every Lean training session with activity in the gemba: To train members of our Tiger Team and the cell employees, I developed a simple simulation to compare and contrast (i) Batch Flow, (ii) Single-Piece Flow, and (iii) Transfer Batch Flow. Also, I used this YouTube video titled *One Piece Flow versus Batch Production – Lean Manufacturing* in that training module (*Source*: www.youtube.com/watch?v=JoLHKSE8sfU). Okay, so we all knew that single-piece flow in a high-mix machining cell that operated in

BEFORE KAIZEN

AFTER KAIZEN

Figure 15.4 Milling work center (a) before and (b) after cell implementation.

a Make-To-Order mode was infeasible. That was because every week the MPC processed a different mix of orders with unique due dates. But had not the cell at least helped to position inter-related machines in close proximity to each other, as in an assembly line (where one-piece flow is guaranteed)? So, during one of the training sessions, we posed this question to the training group, "Can we split up any order batch into (smaller) transfer batches

Figure 15.5 Fixture built for the MPC to store tools.

that could be moved one-after-the-other from the "supplier machine" to the "customer machine"?" Now see what transpired a few days after I had run the simulation and showed the video to the group! When the intern and I were out on the floor, Luong Dam, the employee who ran the three Cincinnati Mills in the MPC, called both of us over to show us what he had implemented between the Haas Mill and the Cincinnati Mills that he operated. Figure 15.6 shows his idea to start pulling just enough pieces off the Haas Mill that he could pack on the arbor used on each of his three mills. Thereby, any order could be split up into two or three sub-batches and each sub-batch runs in parallel on all three mills. To this day, I never lose the opportunity to present Luong Dam's idea to illustrate the integration of (i) cell implementation, (ii) training employees using the single-piece flow simulation, **and** (iii) encouraging those employees to come forward with their own improvement ideas!

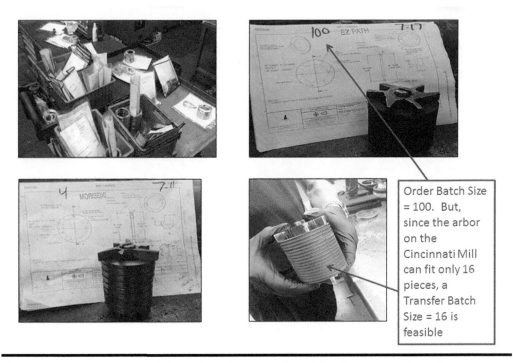

Order Batch Size = 100. But, since the arbor on the Cincinnati Mill can fit only 16 pieces, a Transfer Batch Size = 16 is feasible

Figure 15.6 Transfer batch based on the capacity of the fixture used on the mill.

Implementing Lean Principle #5 Will Take Time! Lean Principle #5 is "As value is specified, Value Streams are identified, wasted steps are removed, and Flow and Pull are introduced, begin the process again and continue it until a state of perfection is reached in which perfect value is created with no waste". Implementing the MPC proved to be a daunting challenge. But that challenge needed to be overcome if the future plan was to redesign the other four "cash cow" cells based on the lessons learned from implementing the MPC. So, we had to clearly know how to overcome the age-old challenges factory transformation by implementing a cellular layout such as (i) being able to place inside each cell all the equipment it needed to be self-sufficient, (ii) ensuring that the order pipeline for the part family assigned to each cell was sustained (else the cell would die), (iii) cross-training employees to run different machines in their cell, (iv) allowing the cell operators to manage their cell, and (v) planning for employee turn-over in the cells due to retirements and other factors, etc. Figure 15.7 pro-vides a map of different tools that have be used either to implement a cell or to improve its performance or to evolve it as its product family, technology, personnel, etc. undergo changes from one year to the next. Depending on the orders placed by its customers, the cell's team would identify appropriate obstacles/needs which, in turn, would determine their choice of tools to use.

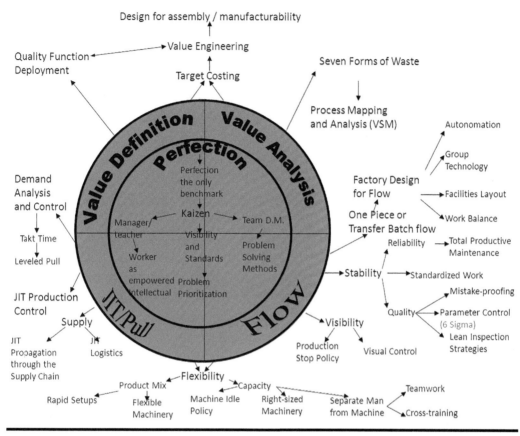

Figure 15.7 Tools of the Toyota production system to implement the lean principles.

Is management willing to let a cell's team operate autonomously? Each cell has the potential to become an ABU within the company. But this will require the team of employees in each cell to be empowered to manage day-to-day operations, to make decisions about scheduling, to assign work to different operators, to decide who gets cross-trained on which machines, etc. The team would determine the CI (Continuous Improvement) projects that should be done to eliminate, or at least mitigate, all the constraints that force the cell to send its orders to external resources, either in-house or vendors. Ideally, each cell should communicate directly with their customers concerning changes in delivery dates, questions about part drawings or routers, unforeseen quality problems, etc. It is my personal opinion that one of the primary reasons why CM, the heart and soul of Job Shop Lean, failed to take root in the early 1960s and 1970s because Western manufacturers did not accept the importance of the management practices of the Toyota Management System (*Source*: https://en.wikipedia.org/wiki/The_Toyota_Way).

Cells are not a panacea for high-mix low-volume manufacturers: Unlike an assembly line (or cell), an FLean cell (i) is flexible enough to produce any and all orders for parts that belong in a specific part family and (ii) utilizes Lean tools to eliminate, to the maximum extent possible, the waste that exists in the Value Stream of each of the parts it produces. **Still**, no job shop is advised to pursue a complete reorganization into FLean cells! It is often the case that the production volumes and demand stability for a part family simply could not justify dedicating equipment, tooling, and personnel to produce that part family in a stand-alone cell. What to do next? Please Google "Virtual Manufacturing Cells" and you will find a slew of research papers written by academics about Virtual Cells (VC). In fact, my doctoral dissertation was inspired by this paper titled *The Virtual Manufacturing Cell* (*Source*: https://ws680.nist.gov/publication/gct_pdf.cfm?pub_id=821359). In this day and age, VC(s) can be implemented by integrating the technology of the "Smart Factory" (aka Industry 4.0) with the novel operational practices of the Toyota Production System. Still, there is no better way to produce a product or provide a service than by physically co-locating the people, equipment, and support services in a work cell!

The cost of implementing a stand-alone cell could pose an insurmountable hurdle or, in the best case, justify a gradual implementation of the cell! The new layout proposed for the cell (Figure 15.2) provided a good start to our implementation efforts. But designing the layout work proved to be the easy part of the project because we used a combination of software tools and employees' input on preferred machining sequences. This reliance on commercial software tools that IEs routinely use in their work is one of the ways in which Job Shop Lean differs from Lean. It may be possible to design the layout of a single cell manually because the data analysis may involve drawing a Spaghetti Diagram for its material flow. But what about the case when the layout of an entire machine shop must be planned? If data sets are so large that they cannot be analyzed manually, why should project personnel refuse to use available software that they are familiar with and have access to just because Lean encourages the manual pencil-and-paper approach?

Next, we had to justify the investments that would be necessary to (i) reposition the machines that were already in the MPC and (ii) move other machines that were currently located elsewhere in the facility into the MPC. Given all the facility-related constraints, our Facilities Maintenance and IE manager (John S.) estimated that a minimum expenditure of about $100,000 would be incurred as detailed below:

- Capital Investment for New Equipment
  - Purchase a Norton Grinder (Estimated Cost = $70,000)
  - Purchase a jib crane for loading/unloading both the Mori Seiki and Haas lathes
  - Purchase new work tables, toolboxes, and cabinets for all machines.
- Relocation of Equipment (Estimated Cost = $30,000)
  - Move Mori Seiki from the other cell (PRRC) into MPC
  - Move Mazak VTC/Mill, ProCut Lathe, and EZPath Lathe out of the MPC into the PRRC.
- Facility Upgrades
  - Relocate and rewire all other machines already in the area occupied by the MPC based on the new floor plan for the cell
  - Resurface the floor.

So why was it decided to incur the extra $70,000 cost of purchasing a Norton Grinder when already a cost of $30,000 was being incurred just to relocate machines into the MPC? Because our intention was to make the MPC self-sufficient like the QRC! A true cell is one which does not send its parts to any shared manufacturing resources elsewhere in the factory.[3] With the Mori Seiki being moved out of the PRRC into the MPC, the only remaining machine(s) needed to make the MPC autonomous would be one (or both) of the Melchiorres located in the CNCPC (CNC Packings Cell). The CNCPC was essentially the CNC counterpart of the MPC! In the Current State, since the Mori Seiki was located adjacent to the Melchiorres, the "donuts" that the MPC started with were (i) machined from bar stock on the Mori Seiki and (ii) ground on the Melchiorres (which are lapping machines!) before being sent to the MPC. It is well known that a lapping machine is ill-suited to perform a grinding operation! Especially when we were using a Norton Grinder to grind parts similar to those being produced in the MPC in the other manual cell, the QRC![4] In the Future State, we wanted to stop the sharing of the Melchiorres by the CNCPC and the MPC because it created inter-cell flows between the CNCPC and the MPC. We wanted to dedicate

---

[3] Though, it is common practice for a cell to send work to vendors when an unexpected spike in demand occurs or a customer drops a rush job!

[4] The redesign of an existing cell presents an excellent opportunity to conduct a kaizen event to make it more efficient and effective. The goal of this event would be to rationalize existing routings in order to eliminate reliance on manufacturing resources external to the cell. The kaizen team could consist of an Industrial Engineer, cell employees, a Manufacturing Engineer from the front office and, if needed, a representative from the machine tool vendor(s).

Table 15.1   Pros and Cons of Implementing Manufacturing Cells

Pros	Cons
Increase in worker satisfaction	Pre-existing machine locations
Reduction of labor turnover/ absenteeism	Employee training needs
Improvement of quality	Upgrading administrative and accounting systems
Better utilization of space	Maintaining high machine utilization
Reduction of WIP	Resistance to change from employees
Reduction of cycle times	Resistance to change from managers
Reduction of setup times	Identification of machine groups and part families
Reduction of labor costs	Absence of production families
Reduction of variable production costs	Redesign of "Misfit" parts and processes

the Melchiorres to processing the orders that were scheduled for production in the CNCPC only!

In hindsight, I ought to have known the perils of doing the Job Shop Lean pilot project on the MPC. In Table 15.1, the left-hand column lists the benefits reported by a wide spectrum of manufacturers who have successfully implemented and sustained cells since the 1960s.[5] Next, what is the problem that tops the list in the right-hand column? Pre-existing machine locations! I guess it took doing the pilot project to realize that no attention had been paid in the past to designing self-contained cells whose teams could operate autonomously without relying on external resources. So, in our case, (i) machines that belonged in the PRRC were located in the MPC and (ii) the MPC had to wait for the CNCPC to send it the pre-machined "donuts" that were its raw materials. Ironically, many of the same problems that are listed in the right-hand column of Table 15.1 have led to the failure of the expansive and expensive Lean Enterprise Transformations that are promised by Lean Thinkers of the 20th century!

---

[5] Askin, R.G. & Estrada, S. (1999). Investigation of cellular manufacturing practices, Chapter 1, in *Handbook of Cellular Manufacturing Systems*, Irani, S.A. (Editor). New York: John Wiley.

Provide management a complete (and honest!) itemization of how the implementation of the new layout for the cell will impact costs and revenues! The $100,000 price tag was just for the initial costs that we were asked to offset in order to justify implementing the first manufacturing cell in our facility! It proved to be an uphill task because the MPC did not get much business, unlike the CNCPC that could boast higher MRR (Metal Removal Rates) and therefore shorter lead times. But we had management's backing to develop a standardized process to design and implement any cell in the future. Assuming that more work could be captured from competitors in the compressor repair business, we presented the following list of projected benefits from implementing the MPC during our final presentation to management:

■ A close comparison of Figures 15.1 and 15.2 will show that the external resource requirements for the cell were reduced to (i) the delivery of raw materials to the cell from the Receiving department and (ii) the removal of finished product from the cell to the Shipping department. This significantly reduced the transportation delays and queuing delays experienced by parts that needed one or more of their operations to be done external to the cell. It was estimated that labor hours wasted every year in moving orders that had to travel out of and back to the cell was reduced by 51 hours.

■ The Line Of Sight Efficiency (LOSE) improved from 0.286 (see Figure 15.1) to 0.714 (see Figure 15.2). One machine operator did not have to walk far to communicate a quality issue or tooling problem to another operator. Or, if one operator wanted to take a break, he could inform the operator of the previous machine to not overproduce beyond a certain number of units during his absence.

■ Two pairs of machines in the cell could each be tended by a single operator. Each operator would spend significantly less time walking between the two machines he was operating.

■ The distance traveled by any order processed in the cell was reduced from 618. to 368 ft. This reduced operator motion waste and allowed for smaller batches of parts to be moved between consecutive machines. Similarly, the total distance traveled by any order from Receiving through to Shipping was reduced from 912 to 523 ft.

■ Order Flow Times, which were as high as 16 days, could be reduced to ≤5 days.

■ The Standard Lead Time quoted to customers could be reduced from 20+ to 10 days.

- The floor space occupied by the cell was reduced from 2,816 to 1,410 sq. ft. The freed-up floor space could be used to add another cell to bring in new business.
- As mentioned earlier, the only two flow segments in the routing of any MPC order that remained external to the cell were (i) delivery of raw materials from the Receiving department and (ii) delivery of finished orders from the cell to the Shipping department. Since the MPC is adjacent to the Shipping department, a natural next project for CI was inspired by the question, "Why does the Receiving department have to be located so far from the MPC? If the Receiving and Shipping departments were co-located in our facility, could their adjacency save considerable labor time spent by employees in both departments having to walk back-and-forth between the two ends of a long thin building?" This project was later assigned during the Autumn 2013 semester to an IE intern from Austria.

Be ready to dot every "i" and cross every "t"! Figure 15.7 in this chapter (and Appendices 2 and 3 for this chapter) give the extent of how much work could be involved to implement just one cell! For example, here are some of the unglamorous IE projects with zero research content that had to be started once we received the go-ahead from management that the MPC could be implemented:

1. *Purchase of new workstations:* The existing workstations were old as in really old! But each cost a pretty penny. But, replacing the existing workstations would serve as a morale booster for the senior employees working in the cell.
2. *Setup reduction:* A no brainer priority!
3. *Ergonomics and employee safety:* The metal slugs that would be machined into the "donuts" supplied to the MPC were produced either on the Mori Seiki lathe external to the MPC or the Haas lathe in the MPC. However, the Receiving department would deliver these (heavy) slugs on pallets that were dropped off a reasonable distance away from either machine. Both machines were operated by female employees. In the case of one of those female employees, she would go looking for a male friend to come and (i) pick up each slug from the pallet, (ii) carry it to the machine, and (iii) load the slug into the chuck using the jib crane.
4. *Cross-training:* Only a couple of the employees in the MPC were cross-trained. Most of them were near retirement. And I was going to

have to convince the ones who only knew how to operate manual WWII (World War II) era machines to learn to operate CNC (Computer Numerical Control) machines? Especially if the MPC got merged into the CNCPC?

5. *Single-piece flow:* Thanks to Luong Dam, the operator of the three (manual) Cincinnati mills, I felt more confident about being able to get all cell employees to buy into this idea. Even if (continuous) one-piece flow was impractical, at least he had implemented the use of transfer batches at the three Cincinnati mills he operated. Could we do the same at the LeBlond lathes? I planned to have the Plant Manager and Machine Shop Supervisor talk to the cell's team about the financial benefits of moving away from traditional batch production inside the cell.

6. *Cell performance measurement:* A cell's team has to be responsible for tracking standard KPIs (Key Performance Indicators) such as Quality, Delivery, Cost, Safety, Inventory, Productivity, etc. Most of the cell employees in the MPC were near retirement. With a classic "command and control" shop floor culture, I knew that it would take months to get the employees in the MPC to report their performance and influence the performance of their colleagues.

7. *Cell scheduling:* One of the other cells had been selected to test our computerized shop floor control system that was an integration of our ERP (SAP), our Finite Capacity Scheduler (Preactor) and our Manufacturing Execution System (FactoryViewer). So the MPC was stuck with the existing "Push Scheduling" system where daily job releases to the cell clearly exceeded the available capacity on the cell's bottleneck (the Haas mill). Plus we would have needed our onsite IE to do the Time Studies that would produce the setup times and cycle times needed by Preactor!

8. *Maintenance:* The MPC had some machine redundancy since there were three Cincinnati mills and two LeBlond lathes. However, there was only one Haas mill and the first operation to be done on all the "donuts" supplied to the cell would be done on either the Mori Seiki or the Haas lathe (not both!). Obviously, any unscheduled breakdown on either the Haas mill or the lathe chosen for the first operation would bring the cell to a standstill. With the decision to load the cell with only 1 day's worth of orders, I decided to approach John S. (who wore three hats – Facilities Management, Maintenance, and IE) to start a plant-wide TPM (Total Productive Maintenance) program.

9. *Water Spider:* Our "mother ship" facility in Pompano Beach, FL, had already trained a couple of employees on each shift to work as Water Spiders. These material movers had situational awareness of the entire facility and, in partnership with our MES, helped to execute and monitor the daily schedule released to the floor by Preactor. If we wanted the MPC to receive raw materials for jobs to be run each day of the week, then we had to start training at least a couple of our current employees. Having worked with him on an earlier project, I knew that I could tap Willie in the Receiving department to undergo training and grow into this new role. But, it was unclear at the time who in the Shipping department was best suited for this new position that would support factory logistics.

*Despite having spent 22 years in academia, I did not have **any** industry experience related to the undergraduate courses that I taught and in implementing Lean!* In hindsight, I should have worked in industry for at least 3–5 years to gain the implementation experience that is essential to teach those courses. Toyota-style IE is a very unique flavor of IE that can only be learned over many years of employment at/by Toyota. Alas, employment at Toyota is not something that a typical IE faculty like me can have on their resume. Nor did my academic department have an educational partnership with Toyota as does the University of Kentucky. Alas, there is no concealing the fact that Toyota-style IE works, whereas the same cannot be said about the majority of what is taught in most IE curricula in the US! For example, a glaring omission in my department's IE curriculum was that we did not teach the employee engagement and leadership skills that influence the success (or failure) of each and every CI project done in industry.

Another obstacle to learning Toyota-style IE was that in every undergraduate IE course I taught, I was expected to use the textbook that was popular in other recognized IE departments. Unfortunately, those textbooks had been written by author(s) who also had no industry experience and were schooled in the traditional IE which became obsolete with the emergence of the Toyota Production System.

However, the biggest obstacle to my learning Toyota-style IE while in academia was that the majority of my time and energy was spent in publishing peer-reviewed papers in academic research journals. These journals promote research that does not translate into practical methods that address (and actually solve!) age-old problems that exist in industry.

Conclusion

Numerous invaluable lessons were learned from undertaking to redesign an existing machining cell. And that was for just one cell! It was as if all the processes, systems, constraints, etc. that are crucial for operating an entire facility had to be reengineered for a small portion of that facility! So, if and when you plan to improve an existing cell or implement a new cell, please be sure to reference this chapter to know how much work may need to be done to implement that cell.

Appendices

Appendices for this chapter are available for download at https://www. crcpress.com/9781498740692.

Bibliography

Hales, H.L. & Anderson, B. (2002). *Planning Manufacturing Cells*. Dearborn, MI: Society of Manufacturing Engineers.

Hyer, N.L. & Wemmerlov, U. (2002). *Reorganizing the Factory: Competing through Cellular Manufacturing*. Portland, OR: Productivity Press.

Irani, S.A. (Editor). (1999). *Handbook of Cellular Manufacturing Systems*. New York: John Wiley.

Irani, S.A. (2017). *JobshopLean: Adapting Lean for Small and Medium High-Mix Low-Volume Manufacturers*. Sugar Land, TX: Lean & Flexible, LLC.

Lee, R.N. (Editor). (1992). *Making Manufacturing Cells Work*. Dearborn, MI: Society of Manufacturing Engineers.

Suri, R. (1998). *Quick Response Manufacturing: A Company-Wide Approach to Reducing Lead Times*. Portland, OR: Productivity Press.

Chapter 16

How Cell Formation Drives the Implementation of Job Shop Lean

Implementing Lean in Job Shops

Lean has its roots in the revolutionary Toyota Production System (TPS). However, an automotive assembly line is a *low*-mix *high*-volume production system. So, regardless of the popularity and well-known success of TPS (and Lean), many strategies and tools that work for Toyota are ill-suited to *high*-mix *low*-volume (HMLV) environments that operate like job shops, such as forge shops, machine shops, fabrication shops, etc. However, it *may* be feasible to implement Toyota-style Lean in a Make-To-Order facility that assembles a range of standard product variants from kits of parts that are built from well-defined and stable part families that they repeatedly produce in-house. Examples of these products are furniture, toys, garden appliances, etc. whose manufacturer has been lost to low-wage countries such as China and Mexico.

Unlike any of Toyota's assembly facilities, a job shop is a much more complex HMLV production system that cannot be improved using only the Lean tools of the TPS. Job Shop Lean is a different approach for implementing Lean that was developed to conquer the complexity of any HMLV production system.

1. First, as shown in Table 16.1, it is important to separate the well-known Lean tools into two sets: those that *are* suited for a job shop and those that *are not* suited for a job shop.
2. Next, as shown in Table 16.2, the collection of Lean tools listed in the left-hand column of Table 16.1 must be expanded by replacing the tools in the right-hand column of Table 16.1 with computer-assisted IE (Industrial Engineering) tools.
3. Finally, as shown in Figure 16.1, if to this expanded toolkit are added (i) the management skills needed to successfully manage the dynamic environment of a job shop and (ii) the workforce capabilities needed to successfully work in the dynamic environment of a job shop, the result is the core set of best practices that have ensured the successful implementation of Job Shop Lean in different HMLV environments.

Table 16.1 Lean Tools That Will (or Will Not) Work in Job Shops

Tools to Use	Tools to Avoid
Strategic planning	Pencil-and-paper problem-solving
Top-down leadership	Value Stream Mapping
Gemba walks by managers	Assembly line balancing
Employee engagement	One-piece flow cells
Workplace design with 6S	Product-specific Kanbans
Total productive maintenance (TPM)	FIFO (First In First Out) sequencing of orders
Setup reduction (SMED)	Pacemaker scheduling
Error-proofing (Poka-Yoke)	Inventory supermarkets
Quality at source	Work order release based on pitch
Visual workplace	Production based on level loading
Product and process standardization	Mixed model production with Takt Time
Right-sized flexible machines	Right-sized inflexible machines
Standard work	Pull-based production scheduling
Continuous problem-solving	Manual scheduling with whiteboards

Table 16.2 A Viable Combination of Lean Tools and IE Tools to Implement Job Shop Lean

Waste Elimination	Work Simplification	Facility Layout
Material handling analysis	Cellular manufacturing	Group technology
Storage systems	Workstation design	Visual management
Process standardization (standard work)	Bottleneck equipment utilization	• Production planning • Capacity requirements analysis • Operations scheduling • Shop floor control • Order progress tracking • Etc.
Flexible automation	Setup reduction	Product mix segmentation
Variety reduction	Factory logistics using Water spiders and mobile communications	Information flow analysis

- **"4H" Leadership**
  - Leads by example (Involved! Engaged!)
  - In-depth knowledge (A jobshop ≠ An assembly line)
  - Uses TOC & Lean & Six Sigma & Software & Technology & ... (Lean is *far from* sufficient!)
  - Value ~~Stream~~ Network Mapping
- **Motivated Workforce**
  - Waste elimination of day-to-day work is second nature (Self-critiquing)
  - Multi-skilled /Team-oriented
  - IT-savvy & Eager for Mass Collaboration (Cafeteria Talk? Kaizen teams? Idea boards? Wikis? Online chat groups?)
- **Product Mix Segmentation**
  - M³ (Mixed Mode Manufacturing) Facility (Runners/Repeaters/Strangers)
- **Independent Cells**
  - Manufacturing Focus through Part Families (Group Technology)
  - Flexibility through Multi-function Automation

- **Partial Cells and Virtual Cells**
  - IT-enabled communications
  - ERP *with* FCS *and* MES
  - Virtual Cells/Distributed Teams
  - Water Strider = Material Handler + Expeditor (= Cell Manager On Wheels!)
  - Real-time Order Tracking (RFID, ADC, 2-way Radio Communications, "Spycams" on constraint w/c's, Cell phones that read bar codes and allow cussing, ... and more)
  - etc.
- **Process Standardization**
  - Variety Reduction
  - Design For Manufacture
  - Value Analysis
  - Computer-Aided Process Planning
- **Unconventional Thinking**
  - Order bartering with competitors ("Goodness Of Fit")
  - No shame in firefighting (Just do it efficiently!)
  - Risk management under uncertainty

Figure 16.1 Core set of Job Shop Lean best practices.

Flow: The Essential Foundation for Job Shop Lean

The essential foundation for implementing Job Shop Lean in any HMLV facility is the design of a good factory layout that facilitates delay-free material flow. Kiyoshi Suzaki, who consulted for Toyota, has devoted an entire chapter (Chapter 4 *Developing Flow on the Production Floor*) in his book to this topic (Suzaki, 1988). Quoting from his book "The importance of factory layout has not been addressed in spite of the significant waste often associated with badly planned layouts. The impact on a company's performance from improving the layout can be substantial. *Flow refers to the movement of material through the plant.* It assumes that material will not be stagnant at any point in time from the receiving of raw material to the shipping of finished products. Problems such as a process-oriented layout (Functional Layout), line imbalance, machine breakdowns, long setup or tool-change time, machine break-down, quality problems, and labor absenteeism cause interruptions that disrupt a steady flow of production in a factory". Therefore, any HMLV manufacturer seeking to implement Job Shop Lean should invest in modifying their factory layout as necessary (and feasible!) in order to achieve Flow.

Cells: The Essential Foundation for Achieving Flow

The first enterprise-wide implementation of cells was done in the mid-20th century! Starting in 1959, Serck Audco Valves, a UK manufacturer of industrial stop valves and actuators, began reorganizing their entire manufacturing enterprise using GT (Group Technology) and CM (Cellular Manufacturing) as a foundation. This enterprise transformation was led by Gordon Ranson. In his book (Ranson, 1972), Mr. Ranson wrote "As a practitioner with some twelve years' experience of this technique (Group Technology), the definition which I think most clearly describes GT is as follows: *The logical arrangement and sequence of all facets of company operation in order to bring the benefits of mass production to high variety, mixed quantity production*". Many other contemporary HMLV manufacturers in the UK followed in the footsteps of Serck Audco Valves. During the period 1961–1967, they reported the following improvements in company performance using GT and CM (Burbidge, 1979):

Metric	Performance
Sales	Up by 32%
Stocks	Down 44%
Ratio of stocks/sales	Down from 52% to 22%
Manufacturing time	Down from 12 weeks to 4 weeks
Overdue orders	Down from 6 weeks to 1 week
Output per employee	Up about 50%
Capital investment	Cost recovered four times by stock reduction alone

Not surprisingly, the benefits of GT and CM reported in Burbidge's book published in 1979 are comparable to those achieved by implementing the TPS (aka Lean) in repetitive high-volume assembly environments.

Serck Audco Valves began their implementation of GT/CM by transforming the Functional Layout of each of their machine shops into a Cellular Layout. Figure 16.2 shows the existing Functional Layout for a hypothetical machine shop that has twelve departments and produces nineteen different parts listed in Table 16.3. The Functional Layout has advantages such as high machine utilization and high flexibility in allocating parts to alternative machines in any department (aka process village or work center) whenever any batch of parts arrives for processing. However, it has disadvantages such as high stock-to-dock order flow times, high WIP (work-in-process) levels, poor quality control, and difficulty in locating orders.

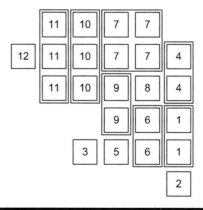

Figure 16.2   Functional Layout.

Table 16.3 Routings and Production Data for a Hypothetical Machine Shop

Part No.	Qty	Revenue	Op 1	Op 2	Op 3	Op 4	Op 5	Op 6	Op 7
			Routing (Sequence of Operations)						
Part 1	10,642	31,336	1	4	8	9			
Part 2	4,270	21,300	1	4	7	4	8	7	
Part 3	1,471	10,901	1	2	4	7	8	9	
Part 4	4,364	25,774	1	4	7	9			
Part 5	5,013	1,580	1	6	10	7	9		
Part 6	4,679	36,069	6	10	7	8	9		
Part 7	5,448	47,776	6	4	8	9			
Part 8	5,339	50,339	3	5	2	6	4	8	9
Part 9	9,117	48,784	3	5	6	4	8	9	
Part 10	8,935	37,774	4	7	4	8			
Part 11	7,100	68,153	6						
Part 12	8,611	60,272	11	7	12				
Part 13	9,933	39,903	11	12					
Part 14	3,824	19,258	11	7	10				
Part 15	1,359	7,800	1	7	11	10	11	12	
Part 16	1,235	8,562	1	7	11	10	11	12	
Part 17	8,581	44,074	11	7	12				
Part 18	3,963	23,137	6	7	10				
Part 19	2,309	3,012	12						

Figure 16.3 shows a Cellular Layout with three cells that was designed for the same shop. *Each cell was designed to produce a subset of the 19 parts listed in* Table 16.3. The Cellular Layout has advantages such as lower stock-to-dock order flow times, lower WIP levels, and better quality control. However, it has disadvantages such as inflexibility to accommodate significant changes in product mix and volume, major losses in available capacity due to unexpected machine breakdowns and management's reluctance to give sufficient autonomy to every team working in a cell, especially in union shops.

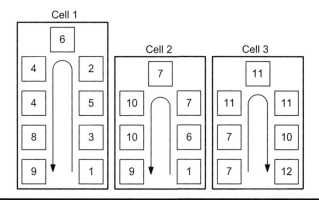

Figure 16.3   Cellular Layout.

Cells: The Foundation for a Comprehensive Approach to Implementing Job Shop Lean

Figure 16.4 presents a flowchart for a comprehensive approach for implementing Lean in job shops and other HMLV manufacturing facilities. At the core of this iterative process is the expectation that a job shop (i) will

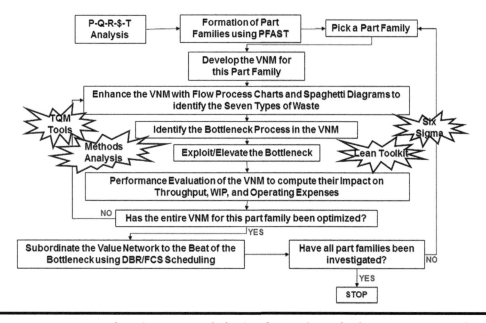

Figure 16.4   Comprehensive approach for implementing Job Shop Lean. *Note:* **The acronym "VNM" stands for Value Network Map. A VNM, unlike a Value Stream Map, is an aggregation of many similar, but not identical, Value Streams. Each Value Stream corresponds to one of the many parts that constitute the part family being produced in a cell.**

identify the stable part families in its product mix and (ii) will implement a manufacturing cell to produce each part family. To implement the process, the existing facility layout, which is usually a Functional Layout, must be transformed into a Cellular Layout. If the proposed approach in Figure 16.4 is implemented correctly, then a job shop will typically end up being divided into at least two *separate* facilities, with one facility having a Cellular Layout and the other facility having a Functional Layout. Subsequently, the stream of projects to eliminate the constraints that prevent the complete conversion to cells will constitute a Continuous Improvement Program (CIP) to support the cells! In theory, each iteration of the process shown in Figure 16.4 will result in the implementation of a stand-alone cell that is dedicated to producing a part family. In reality, numerous constraints will arise that could prevent implementation of any cell. Some constraints could be broken (Example: Operators could be cross-trained to operate multiple machines in a cell) and some constraints may remain unbreakable (Example: Heat treatment furnaces cannot be placed inside a cell next to a CNC (Computer Numerical Control) grinder).

Cells: A Driver for Implementing a Continuous Improvement Program (CIP)

Perhaps the biggest disadvantage of a Cellular Layout is that it requires duplication of the same equipment assets in two or more cells. For example, notice that the machines from the departments 1, 6, 7, 9, and 10 in the Functional Layout in Figure 16.2 have been distributed among two or more cells in the Cellular Layout in Figure 16.3? This *Machine Sharing Problem* is almost always encountered when transforming a Functional Layout into a Cellular Layout. But there is a way to exploit this problem to drive a systematic and comprehensive CIP!

In order to identify the part families and the group of machines that will constitute the cell to produce any part family, it will be necessary to use the method of Product-Process Matrix Analysis.[1] The Initial 0–1 Matrix shown in Figure 16.5(a) converts the original part routings in Table 16.3

---

[1] This method was first utilized by Prof. John L. Burbidge, the inventor of Production Flow Analysis, for identification of part families and machine groups in the fabrication shop of a crane manufacturing facility!

into a matrix with Part #s in the rows and Machine #s in the columns. Each cell in the matrix which contains "1" links a particular Part # to a particular Machine # that occurs one or more times in the routing of that part. For example, the routing for Part #1 is 1→4→8→9. Therefore, in Figure 16.5(a), in the row for Part #1, a "1" occurs in the columns for "m1", "m4", "m8", and "m9". This matrix does not show potential groups of machines and parts that are the basis for implementing manufacturing cells in job shops. However, when the same matrix is manipulated by reordering the rows and columns, it produces the Final 0–1 Matrix in Figure 16.5(b).

This new matrix reveals the potential for implementing two cells provided that some machines can be duplicated in both cells. Each block in the final matrix, which is defined by a set of consecutive rows, represents a family of parts that could potentially be produced by putting the appropriate group of machines into a manufacturing cell. For example, in Figure 16.5(b)

Form Product Families: Initial Matrix

INITIAL MATRIX

	m1	m2	m3	m4	m5	m6	m7	m8	m9	m10	m11	m12
Part 1	1			1				1	1			
Part 2	1			1			1	1				
Part 3	1	1		1			1	1	1			
Part 4	1			1			1		1			
Part 5	1					1	1		1	1		
Part 6						1	1	1	1	1		
Part 7				1			1		1	1		
Part 8		1	1	1	1	1		1	1			
Part 9			1	1	1	1		1	1			
Part 10				1			1	1				
Part 11						1						
Part 12							1				1	1
Part 13											1	1
Part 14							1			1	1	
Part 15	1						1			1	1	1
Part 16	1						1			1	1	1
Part 17							1				1	1
Part 18						1	1			1		
Part 19												1

Figure 16.5   a) Initial 0–1 matrix.

(Continued)

Form Product Families: Final Matrix

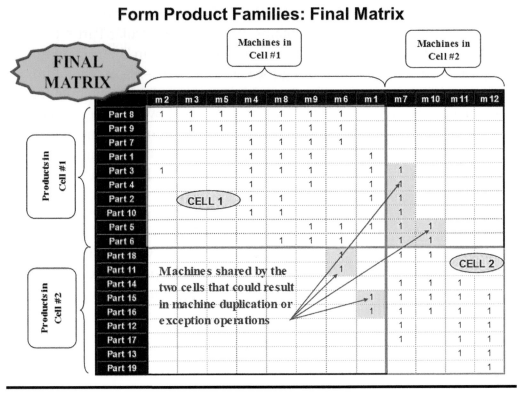

	m2	m3	m5	m4	m8	m9	m6	m1	m7	m10	m11	m12
Part 8	1	1	1	1	1	1	1					
Part 9		1	1	1	1	1	1					
Part 7				1	1	1	1					
Part 1				1	1	1		1				
Part 3	1			1	1	1		1	1			
Part 4				1		1		1	1			
Part 2				1	1			1	1			
Part 10				1	1				1			
Part 5						1	1	1	1	1		
Part 6					1	1	1		1	1		
Part 18									1	1		
Part 11							1					
Part 14									1	1	1	
Part 15								1	1	1	1	
Part 16								1	1	1	1	1
Part 12									1		1	1
Part 17									1		1	1
Part 13											1	1
Part 19												1

Figure 16.5 (CONTINUED)   b) Final 0–1 matrix.

we can see that two cells can be formed: Cell 1 consists of machines 2, 3, 5, 4, 8, 9, 6, 1, 7, and 10, **whereas** Cell 2 consists of machines 6, 1, 7, 10, 11, and 12.

But, if we desire to implement two cells, then machines 1 and 6 must also be placed in Cell #2, and machines 7 and 10 must also be placed in Cell #1. Unless these machines are duplicated and assigned to both cells, inter-cell flows will occur that are not easy to coordinate and will be disruptive to operations in both cells. **Alternatively**, instead of drawing the cutoff line between Part #6 and #18 in Figure 16.5(b), we could have drawn it between Parts #11 and #14. That would have eliminated the need to duplicate Machine #6 but it would make one part family (and its cell) much larger than the other part family.

As Figure 16.5(b) illustrates, it is rare that any HMLV factory will be amenable to a complete reorganization into a Cellular Layout with standalone independent cells! **When** cells are infeasible, **then** *appropriate* projects should be executed to eliminate the constraints. These projects should be driven by the goal to eliminate the need for inter-cell flows between cells in order to utilize (i) machines with idle time located in other cells or (ii) expensive machines that could not be put in every cell that needed them or (iii) monuments like Heat Treatment that must be absolutely kept outside any cell. Figures 16.6(a) and (b) present maps of strategies that can be used to reduce, preferably eliminate, the need for any cell to send the parts it produces to external resources. Notice that both maps display strategies that will require use of the proven Lean tools in the left-hand column of Table 16.1! A CIP that is implemented using these two strategy maps will be effective and profitable in any HMLV manufacturing facility.

A Portfolio of CI Projects to Implement Job Shop Lean

To date, this short list of projects has always produced results. Of course, it has produced its fair share of misfires and failures too. Fortunately, every failure highlighted mistakes in the problem-solving and implementation phases of the project that were avoided in future client engagements.

1. *Involve the company leadership:* Too often, the President/Owner of the company and the VP Operations (sometimes even the Plant Manager!) take a hands-off attitude towards the implementation of Lean. Big mistake! Not only should these individuals participate in the day-to-day efforts of the workforce and in-house CI team tasked with the Lean implementation, they should demonstrate commitment. What should these key individuals do to ensure the success of a Lean implementation? For starters, they could take gemba walks, hold a monthly town hall meeting, and make "Attaboy, keep it up!" recognition of employees a frequent practice.

2. *Design the overall factory layout:* A Factory Flow Analysis (FFA) using a representative sample of components (or products), especially the Runners and Repeaters in the product mix, is essential. This analysis will yield a Spaghetti Diagram that connects all processing departments such as Raw Material Stores (Receiving), Machining, Fabrication, Inspection, Finished Goods (Shipping), etc., including product flows to/from Suppliers. If the existing layout prevents Flow, then all justifiable equipment moves must be executed, especially if there is a plan to introduce new equipment and/or manufacturing technology into the

(a)

Minimize Inter-Cell Product Flow to Use Capacity on Common Machines

REDUCE WASTE OF AVAILABLE CAPACITY IN ANY CELL

- Reduce fatigue-induced breaks due to material handling
- Reduce scrap and rework
- Reduce absenteeism and overtime
- Absorb external support services into the cell
- Overlap shifts and breaks
- Deploy Water Spider(s) to manage shop logistics involving external machines and support services
- Implement a Variety Reduction Program (VRP) to rationalize and standardize part designs, raw materials, CNC programs, tooling, etc.
- Use methods and technology to reduce capacity wasted in changing tools (pre-set tools, combination tools, automated tool changers, large-capacity tool magazines, resident tools permanently loaded on the machines, tool wear sensing and tool life monitoring, in-process gauging, etc.)
- Use methods and technology to reduce capacity wasted in changing fixtures (quick-change process to change setups, tombstone fixtures, flexible fixtures for families of parts, etc.)
- Use methods and technology to reduce capacity wasted due to unscheduled machine breakdowns and maintenance
- Use cobots (collaborative robots) for parallel operation of 2 or more machines by one operator
- Prevent "Hot Jobs" from being dropped into the schedule on a regular basis
- Group schedule families of parts to reduce setup changeover times
- Move production of prototypes, spare parts and other one-off low-volume orders to a Remainder Cell (or adopt Hybrid Manufacturing that integrates Subtractive and Additive Manufacturing processes)

REDUCE CAPACITY REQUIREMENTS IN ANY CELL

- Eliminate exception operations by redesigning the parts to eliminate redundant features that require machine(s) external to the cell
- Eliminate exception operations by performing those operations on alternative machine(s) inside the cell
- Reduce setup times using Six Sigma methodology (and technology)
- Reduce cycle times using Six Sigma methodology (and technology)
- Reduce the inflation of production lot sizes to compensate for safety stock, forecast errors, scrap, high setup times, queue times, etc.

MINIMIZE BATCH FLOW IN ANY CELL

- Utilize transfer batches, possibly even one-piece flow, to the extent possible
- Eliminate use of large containers and pallets to store WIP between machines
- Use mobile and right-sized carts to hold parts for a single order
- Use gravity racks, chutes, possibly even cobots (collaborative robots), to promote continuous flow of parts between machines
- Adapt U, S, L, W or other curvilinear shapes for the cell layout to allow multi-machine tending by each operator
- Replace existing machines with multi-function centers that can perform multiple operations in a single setup

IMPLEMENT A NON-TRADITIONAL SHOP FLOOR LAYOUT

- Design the shop floor layout to position cells containing identical machines adjacent to each other to retain them in functional departments
- Utilize a Hybrid Cellular Layout ex. Cascading Flowlines? Hybrid Flow Shop? Layout Modules (Partial Cells)? Remainder Cells?
- Operate Virtual Cells that are supported by one or more Water Spiders who are moving batches between the machines that belong in any cell

INCREASE AVAILABLE CAPACITY IN ANY CELL

- Overtime?
- Add a second shift?
- Do lights-out production in third shift?
- Outsource?
- Dedicate existing machines to certain parts and purchase new machines that are more efficient at producing the remaining parts in the cell's part family

RIGHT SIZE THE INSPECTION DEPARTMENT

- Call inspectors to the cell to do First Article Inspection on a JIT basis
- Maintain Statistical Process Control (SPC) charts at key machines
- Utilize error-proofing devices (and technology!)
- Decentralize inspection and cross-train machine operators to check each other's work inside their cell
- Implement mobile inspection workstations that follow a Milk Run schedule to visit each cell on a regular basis

Figure 16.6 Strategy maps (a) #1.

(Continued)

(b)

Minimize Inter-Cell Product Flow To & From External Monuments

IMPLEMENT A MODULAR LAYOUT FOR THE FACTORY	ABSORB SOME MONUMENT(S) INTO THE CELL(S)
• Split the machines in each cell into two groups: Pre-Monument and Post-Monument • Create a layout module (aka "partial cell") for each of the two groups of machines in a cell • Locate both partial cells in proximity to the Monument(s)	• For each cell, determine the process requirements for just the parts being produced in the cell --- For those process requirements, purchase or build a smaller ("right-sized") machine dedicated to the cell • Switch to a radically new "cell-friendly" process ex. Manual Deburring versus Cryogenic Deburring

OUTSOURCE ONE OR MORE MONUMENT(S)	MAXIMIZE THROUGHPUT AT EACH MONUMENT

• Qualify a local supplier to process the parts made in the cell
• Maintain a Pre-Monument buffer of parts and a Post-Monument buffer of parts to ensure production does not stop in the cell
• Communicate status of the Pre-Monument buffer to the Shipping department (and the Post-Monument buffer to the Receiving department)
• Establish a Milk Run for delivery of parts to/by the supplier
• (If appropriate) Schedule the Monument using Pull Scheduling practices suitable for low-mix high-volume production, such as Level Loading and Product-specific Kanbans
• (If appropriate) Schedule the Monument using Pull Scheduling practices suitable for high-mix low-volume production, such as DBR (Drum-Buffer-Rope), CONWIP (CONstant WIP) or POLCA (Paired-Cell Overlapping Loops of Cards with Authorization)
• Utilize the EDI (Electronic Data Interchange) features of the ERP (Enterprise Resource Planning) system to give the supplier visibility into the production schedule for the Monument
• Communicate the production schedule for the Monument to all cell leaders and other support personnel
• Implement an Obeya ("War Room") where the production schedule is discussed and updated regularly by all cell leaders and other support personnel
• Allow cell leaders to swap priority changes in their schedules
	• Re-engineer part designs to eliminate features that require operations to be done on the Monument(s)
	• Group schedule orders for the same part if they have delivery dates in the same week(s)
	• Reduce setup times to facilitate production of a high-mix of parts without batch size restrictions:
	  1. Use SMED (Single Minute Exchange of Dies) methods
	  2. Sequence consecutively those orders that have commonality in setup, processing, inspection, material, etc.
	  3. Organize tooling, fixtures, gauges, etc. for part families into separate carts (or shadow boards or storage locations)
	• If the Monument does not consist of a single machine (ex. shot peening) or a single line (ex. paint line) that processes each and every order, then:
	  1. Dedicate equipment to different segments of the product mix, either by volume or by processing characteristics
	  2. Include Additive Manufacturing or other non-traditional manufacturing processes to gain volume and mix flexibility within the work center
	• Dedicate a Water Spiders to manage the timely transfer of orders from one or more cells to all the Monument(s) in the factory
	• Schedule the Monument(s) work centers using a Finite Capacity Scheduling (FCS) system

Figure 16.6 (CONTINUED) Strategy maps (b) #2 to achieve flow when cells are infeasible.

existing factory. Every equipment move will provide ample opportunities to eliminate waste by implementing the proven Lean tools in the left-hand column of Table 16.1!

3. *Improve Throughput in the Bottleneck Department – Part 1:* This project involves the *Exploit the Constraint* step in the five-step POOGI (Process of Ongoing Improvement) to implement TOC (Theory Of Constraints). It would (i) determine the true capacity utilization of the equipment in the department, and primary reasons why the utilization is ≤80%–85%, (ii) assess if the ERP (Enterprise Resource Planning) system has the relevant data for each equipment that is essential to calculate its daily workload (i.e., setup time, cycle time, scrap rate, OEE (Overall Equipment Effectiveness), etc.), (iii) question the due dates and sequencing rules that influence the order in which jobs are processed, (iv) evaluate the manpower levels in each shift and operator skills that determine job assignments, (v) prevent pre-mature release of jobs to the floor by Sales & Customer Service, etc. This project will provide ample opportunities to eliminate waste by implementing the proven Lean tools in the left-hand column of Table 16.1!

4. *Improve Throughput in the Bottleneck Department – Part 2:* The typical small-to-medium HMLV manufacturer is most reluctant to hear any criticism of their ERP system. Does it not perform HR (Human Resources), Accounting, Purchasing, etc. functions well? So, a baby step towards the potential adoption of an FCS (Finite Capacity Scheduling) add-on to an ERP system is the implementation of the DBR (Drum-Buffer-Rope) method of Pull Scheduling embedded in Eliyahu Goldratt's TOC. In essence, by doing this project you would implement the complete five-step POOGI) to implement TOC. Please visit websites like www.demanddriventech.com/solutions/ddmrp-production-planning-scheduling/ and https://www.visualsouth.com/blog/infor-visual-reviews! An online video of the latter ERP system with its own FCS module can be viewed at https://vimeo.com/37543399. Also, a Functional Overview of INFOR ERP VISUAL can be downloaded at http://www.infor.com/shared_resources/14397/articles/visual-functional-overview.pdf.

5. *Increase order flow velocity with shop floor control:* It is well known that 95% of the total time that the typical order spends on the production floor is non-value-added time, especially waiting and transportation times! This project aims to provide a complete "situational awareness"

of all active orders on the floor to minimize WIP throughout the factory floor. Strategies such as Manufacturing Cells, Water Striders, Order Tracking Board, Mobile Communications, and Daily Morning Huddles will deliver results! Recall what Ohno said "All we are doing is looking at the timeline, from the moment the customer gives us an order to the point when we collect the cash. And we are reducing the timeline by reducing the non-value adding wastes".

6. *Acquire a finite capacity scheduler to schedule operations subject to **finite** capacity constraints:* The typical ERP system that is available commercially uses MRP (Material Requirements Planning) for production planning and operations scheduling. MRP cannot schedule! Stop relying on your ERP system to produce feasible daily production schedules! Please take the first step and visit the websites of FCS system vendors such as www.Preactor.com, www.Waterloo-Software.com, and www.Optisol.biz!

7. *Engage the employees:* The implementation of the projects described earlier will automatically surface opportunities for employees to undertake small CI (Continuous Improvement) projects *within* their work areas. However, rather than giving them generic training on the Lean tools listed in the left-hand column of Table 16.1, it would be preferable to offer customized training to different teams appropriate to the problems/issues that they are tackling.

8. *Convince management to hire industrial engineers:* I was an IE teacher and researcher at a Tier 1 research university in my previous job. Not a single one of my Job Shop Lean projects in industry would have succeeded had I not had one or more IE student interns working full-time at each client site!

Group Technology: An Alternative to Product-Process Matrix Analysis

What if good routings are not available for doing the Product-Process Matrix Analysis that is essential for identifying the part families that are the basis for forming the manufacturing cells to produce them? In that case, GT is an alternative approach for part family formation. Figure 16.7(a) shows a portion of the classical Opitz System for Coding and Classification of machined parts using key part attributes such as dimensions, tolerances, internal and external shape features, surface finish, etc. Using this system, the simple disc-shaped part shown in the inset would be given a GT code of 00110. If a database of GT codes could be generated for the entire product mix of a job shop, it could be analyzed using state-of-the-art data mining and machine learning software tools. How to apply knowledge of part families identified using GT? Figure 16.7(b) shows how the use of a standard set of feature attributes for a part family could help to speed up CAD/CAM (Computer-Aided Design/ Computer-Aided Manufacturing) activities in the front office, produce flow-charts on setup reduction for training cell employees, control customer-specified options when quoting parts that will be produced in the cell, etc. Finally, Figure 16.7(c) presents the gamut of improvement activities that can be done using the database of GT codes for any job shop's product mix.

(a)

Create a GT Database for Entire Product Mix

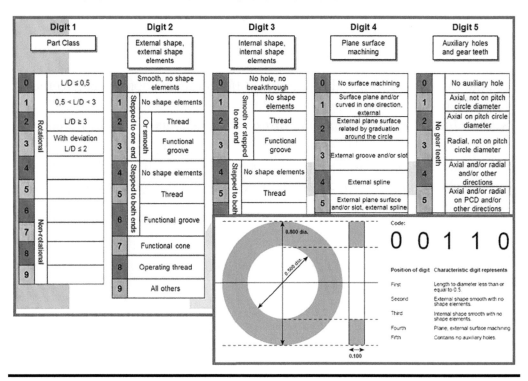

Figure 16.7   (a) The Opitz system for coding and classifying machined parts.

(Continued)

(b)

Example of a GT Application

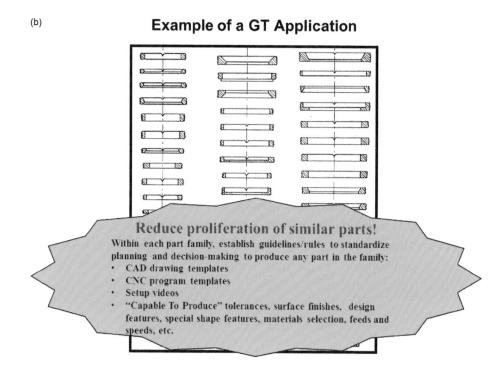

Reduce proliferation of similar parts!
Within each part family, establish guidelines/rules to standardize
planning and decision-making to produce any part in the family:
* CAD drawing templates
* CNC program templates
* Setup videos
* "Capable To Produce" tolerances, surface finishes, design
  features, special shape features, materials selection, feeds and
  speeds, etc.

(c)

Other Applications of the GT Database

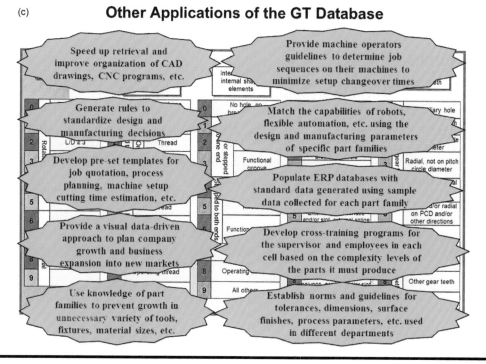

Speed up retrieval and
improve organization of CAD
drawings, CNC programs, etc.

Provide machine operators
guidelines to determine job
sequences on their machines to
minimize setup changeover times

Generate rules to
standardize design and
manufacturing decisions

Match the capabilities of robots,
flexible automation, etc. using the
design and manufacturing parameters
of specific part families

Develop pre-set templates for
job quotation, process
planning, machine setup
cutting time estimation, etc.

Populate ERP databases with
standard data generated using sample
data collected for each part family

Provide a visual data-driven
approach to plan company
growth and business
expansion into new markets

Develop cross-training programs for
the supervisor and employees in each
cell based on the complexity levels of
the parts it must produce

Use knowledge of part
families to prevent growth in
unnecessary variety of tools,
fixtures, material sizes, etc.

Establish norms and guidelines for
tolerances, dimensions, surface
finishes, process parameters, etc. used
in different departments

**Figure 16.7 (CONTINUED)   (b) An example of a GT application. (c) Other
applications of a GT database.**

Conclusion

The key to implementing Lean in any HMLV facility, especially a job shop or Make-To-Order custom fabricator of many product variants, is to overcome the three age-old obstacles that any HMLV manufacturer faces when implementing Lean: (i) How to identify the product families in the product mix? (ii) How to change the factory layout to implement a cell to produce each product family? (iii) How to generate a feasible daily schedule that can be executed, monitored on the shop floor, and updated at the end of each shift prior to the start of the next shift? The TPS (and Lean) has little to offer any HMLV manufacturer that desires to solve these problems. In contrast, Job Shop Lean **first** solves these problems and **then** builds the rest of the production system for any HMLV manufacturer.

Appendices

Appendices for this chapter are available for download at https://www.crcpress.com/9781498740692.

References

Burbidge, J.L. (1979). *Group Technology in the Engineering Industry.* ISBN 0852984022. pp. 109–114.

Ranson, G.M. (1972). *Group Technology: A Foundation for Better Total Company Operation.* London: McGraw-Hill.

Suzaki, K. (1988). *The New Manufacturing Challenge: Techniques for Continuous Improvement.* New York: The Free Press.

Chapter 17

How to Make a Machine Shop Lean *and* Flexible

Acknowledgment

This chapter is based on a presentation I did on September 5–7, 2017 at the Top Shops 2017 Conference hosted by Modern Machine Shop in Indianapolis, IN. The title of that presentation was *Job Shop Lean: How to Achieve Lean and Flexibility in Machine Shops.* Unfortunately, due to unanticipated technical difficulties, the presentation did not go well and I could not do justice to the topic. Therefore, I wrote this chapter based on that presentation and submitted it for publication in *Modern Machine Shop*. Subsequently, the top-notch editorial team of Pete Zelinksi and Jedd Cole at *Modern Machine Shop* used the chapter to develop an abridged article for their magazine – Irani, S.A. (2018, June). 10 Lean Manufacturing Ideas for Machine Shops. *Modern Machine Shop*, 118–134. Their article is available online at www.mmsonline.com/blog/post/10-lean-manufacturing-ideas-for-machine-shops. Thank you, Modern Machine Shop!

Purpose of This Chapter

Given its roots in the 20th-century version of the Toyota Production System (TPS), Lean has yet to advance and adapt for manufacturing in the 21st century. In this century, machines are telling humans what to do, sometimes even outthinking humans! Fortunately, CNC (Computer Numerical Control) machine shops constitute one segment of the US manufacturing industry that has shown a willingness to use technology and data-driven decision support to implement Lean without ignoring the absolute need for a motivated and well-trained workforce. Most of these small and medium-size manufacturers struggles to manage a shop floor where, on any given day, they must manage the flow of anywhere between a few dozen to 100's of products with different routings!

Job Shop Lean was developed to adapt and enhance Lean for implementation in high-mix low-volume (HMLV) manufacturing environments, especially job shops. One of the core requirements of Job Shop Lean is the use of Group Technology and Cellular Manufacturing to reduce and simplify shop floor management in any job shop. Group Technology was first implemented in machine shops as early as the 1960s! Each of those machine shops (i) produced 100's of components with different routings **and** (ii) had a Process Layout where machines with identical/similar capabilities were co-located in departments (or process villages). History will show that, due to the combination of just these two factors, any CNC machine shop has operated in a batch-and-queue production mode. This production mode is the root cause for "management by firefighting" and expediting of orders in *any* machine shop!

Regardless, CNC machine shops have implemented many Lean practices, embraced technology, relied on data analytics to support investment decisions, invested in training to develop talented and motivated employees, etc. So what would be an integrated set of proven best practices of Job Shop Lean that have been, or should be, implemented by a 21st-century CNC machine shop?

A Machine Shop Does Not Operate Like Toyota

Without question, the revolutionary TPS is the gold standard for how any business can pursue cost reduction through waste elimination without headcount reduction. But should an HMLV manufacturer implement Lean the same way as a *low*-mix *high*-volume (LMHV) manufacturer such as Toyota? Never! No Toyota facility makes refrigerators and bicycles on any of their automobile assembly lines. An assembly line that uses a conveyor to move a product (or product family) through a fixed sequence of workstations is inflexible. It could not make other products whose manufacturing routings, Bills Of Materials, and processes used to make the final product are different from those used to make automobiles. Finally, every Toyota assembly line must be just flexible enough only to build a limited variety of automobiles whose annual demand provides sufficient return on investment to justify continued operation of that line.

How a Job Shop Differs from an Assembly Line

An assembly line and a job shop are radically different manufacturing systems. An assembly line is an LMHV manufacturing system. A job shop is an HMLV manufacturing system. Some of the characteristics of a typical job shop that make its production system radically different from the TPS are:

- It fulfills orders for a diverse mix of 100's, sometimes 1,000's, of different products.
- Manufacturing routings differ significantly in their equipment requirements, setup times, cycle times, lot sizes, etc.
- It is a challenge to identify the part families in the product mix.
- The facility has a Functional Layout; i.e., the facility is organized into departments ("process villages") such that each department has equipment with identical/similar process capabilities.
- Demand variability is high.
- Production schedules are driven by due dates.
- Due dates are subject to change.
- Production bottlenecks can shift over time.
- Finite capacity constraints limit how many orders can be completed on any given machine on any day.
- Order quantities can range from low to high.
- Lead times quoted to customers must be adjusted based on knowledge of the production schedule.
- The diverse mix of equipment from different manufacturers makes operator training, maintenance, etc. more challenging than for an assembly line.
- Customer loyalty is not guaranteed.
- It is necessary to be able to serve different markets. In fact, a job shop must deal with the tendency for their product mix to alter as their customer base changes or they hire new sales and marketing staff who bring with them their past business contacts from new sectors of industry.
- It could be a challenge to recruit and retain talented employees with a strong work ethic, a desire to learn on the job, and get cross-trained to operate different machines.

- There are limited resources for workforce training.
- It is hard to control the delivery schedule and quality of suppliers.
- It is hard to negotiate the due dates set by customers.
- Production control and scheduling is more complex.

Why Lean Offers Limited Benefit to Machine Shops

The TPS was designed for assembly plants that produce 100,000's of automobiles. Figure 17.1 compares a machine shop and an assembly plant using two key characteristics of any production system – Production Quantity and Product Mix. Clearly, an assembly plant focuses on LMHV production, whereas a machine shop focuses on HMLV production. Lean being completely based on the TPS, a machine shop cannot expect to realize the complete benefits of Lean by using just tools that are primarily suited for improving operations in an assembly plant.

Lean Tools That Are Unsuitable for Any Machine Shop

Today, nearly every machine shop has realized the gains from implementing one or more of the Lean tools listed in the left-hand column of Table 17.1. In contrast, the Lean tools in the right-hand column of Table 17.1 are

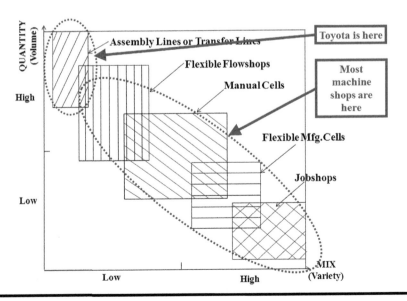

Figure 17.1 Comparison of a machine shop and an assembly plant.

Table 17.1 Lean Tools That a Machine Shop Should Use and Avoid

Tools to Use	Tools to Avoid
Strategic planning	Pencil-and-paper problem-solving
Top-down leadership	VSM
Gemba walks by managers	Assembly line balancing
Employee engagement	One-piece flow cells
Workplace design with 6S	Product-specific Kanbans
TPM	FIFO (First In First Out) sequencing of orders
Setup Reduction (SMED)	Pacemaker scheduling
Error-proofing (Poka-Yoke)	Inventory supermarkets
Quality at source	Work order release based on pitch
Visual workplace	Production based on level loading
Product and process standardardization	Mixed model production with Takt Time
Right-sized flexible machines	Right-sized inflexible machines
Standard work	Pull-based production scheduling
Continuous problem-solving	Manual scheduling with whiteboards

ineffective or inapplicable in any machine shop. They cannot handle the complexity of a Make-To-Order HMLV machine shop, especially if it is a job shop! So what is a Lean machine shop to do to reap additional benefits from implementing Lean? Find and put to effective use a new "Lean toolbox" in which the Lean tools in the right-hand column of Table 17.1 have been replaced with tools that will work!

Group Technology: A Precursor to Lean?

In Table 17.2, the left-hand column lists the *Principles of Lean* (*Source*: www. lean.org/WhatsLean/Principles.cfm) which are a five-step thought process for guiding the implementation of Lean techniques that was originally proposed by James Womack & Daniel T. Jones in their seminal book *Lean Thinking: Banish Waste and Create Wealth in Your Corporation* that was published in 1996. Quoting from the book "The *value stream* is the set of all

Table 17.2 Group Technology Pre-Dates the Principles of Lean by ≈30 Years

Principles of Lean (Circa 1996)	Group Technology (Circa 1967)
Specify value from the standpoint of the end customer by product family	The performance metrics used by the Langston Division of Harris-Intertype Corporation were impacted as follows: • 50% increase in pieces produced per man hour • 20,000 sq. ft of floor space saved in a total machine shop area of 90,000 sq. ft • Time-In-Shop for parts reduced from 30–45 days to 2–5 days
Identify all the steps in the value stream for each product family, eliminating whenever possible those steps that do not create value	• Group the parts into families. • The parts in a family should (i) be about the same size and shape and (ii) should require similar cutting operations, but they need not necessarily all look exactly the same.
Make the value-creating steps occur in tight sequence so the product will flow smoothly toward the customer	• Collect the machines needed to process a family of parts. • Physically arrange the machines according to the process flows of the different parts to create a production line. • Link the machines by a gravity conveyor that routes each container of parts to the next machine specified in their routing. • Each cell is supervised by a foreman who is responsible for the men and machines that have to produce the parts assigned to their cell.
As flow is introduced, let customers pull value from the next upstream activity	• All raw materials (castings, plate, forgings, etc. except bar stock) are stored outside and brought in as needed. • All detailed scheduling, expediting, and material handling for parts being produced on any line were virtually eliminated. Once the raw materials for the parts were released to a line, its foreman took over, and with his group, keeps the workpieces moving until (they) are finished and ready for shipment to assembly or storage. • No posting of individual operations is performed once the part is released for manufacture on a line/cell. • Simplified paper work and administrative systems were developed and implemented to support the cells.

(Continued)

Table 17.2 (*Continued***)   Group Technology Pre-Dates the Principles of Lean by ≈30 Years**

Principles of Lean (Circa 1996)	*Group Technology (Circa 1967)*
As value is specified, value streams are identified, wasted steps are removed, and flow and pull are introduced, begin the process again and continue it until a state of perfection is reached in which perfect value is created with no waste	• After the success of the pilot cell, the entire small-parts shop was completely converted into five lines/cells. • The conversion of the large-parts shop into five lines/cells was begun. • The Vice President (manufacturing) sponsored presentations on the family-of-parts concept to the top managers of other Harris divisions, and encouraged them to consider adopting similar programs.

the specific actions required to bring a specific product (whether a good, a service, or increasingly, a combination of the two) through the three critical management tasks of any business: the *problem-solving task* running from concept through detailed design and engineering to production launch, the *information management task* running from order-taking through detailed scheduling to delivery, and the *physical transformation task* proceeding from raw materials to a finished product in the hands of the customer. Identifying the *entire* value stream for each product (or in some cases for each product family) is the next step in lean thinking…". With reference to "the *physical transformation task* proceeding from raw materials to a finished product in the hands of the customer", the right-hand column in Table 17.2 suggests that Group Technology may have been a precursor to Lean by at least three decades (Gettleman, 1971)!

A Toolkit to Implement Job Shop Lean in the 21st-Century CNC Machine Shop

Segment the product mix: Consider the case of any hospital that is essentially a health care job shop. Isn't the Emergency Department of the hospital operated as a separate hospital-within-a-hospital in order to have short lead times when delivering rapid care to a diverse mix of patients? Similarly, most machine shops choose to make a diverse range of products that differ in their annual production volume, demand pattern, and margin. Based on these three business attributes, a machine shop should segment their product mix into two segments – (Runners + Repeaters) and (Strangers). For parts in the (Runners + Repeaters) segment, batch sizes will tend to be medium or large with many parts having LTA (Long Term Agreements). In contrast, for parts in the (Strangers) segment, batch sizes will tend to be small because orders for these parts tend to be Hot/Rush one-offs, repair, prototype, start-of-lifecycle or end-of-lifecycle. These two segments should be served using **different** business strategies, production systems, CRM (Customer Relationship Management) practices, order fulfillment strategies, etc.

Figure 17.2(a) provides an overview of how to segment a product mix (P) using PQR$T Analysis using any statistical analysis system that has the data analysis capabilities (or even Excel). The segmentation analysis can be done for each of the following axes:

1. Quantity (Q = Production Volume, T = Demand Repetition): PQT Analysis will assign each product to one of three segments – Runners, Repeaters, and Strangers – after considering (i) the total quantity (volume) of the product that was shipped to customers and (ii) the time-based ordering pattern. For instance, was a large quantity of a product ordered only once or the same quantity was purchased in multiple batches over a period of equal monthly (or even weekly) buckets?
2. Mix (R = Routings): PR Analysis will attempt to form part families by clustering parts that have identical/similar routings. While it can be

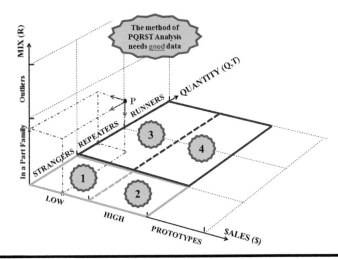

Figure 17.2 a) Product mix segmentation using PQR$T Analysis.

(*Continued*)

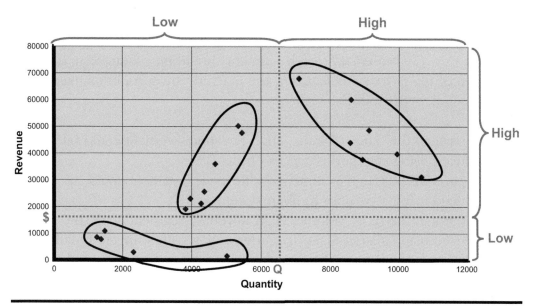

Figure 17.2 (CONTINUED)   b) Example of product mix segmentation using PQ$ Analysis.

expected that a significant portion of the product mix can be assigned to well-defined clusters, many parts will be outliers. The routings of the outliers will need to be "massaged" to fit them into at least one cluster.

3. Earnings ($ = $ales): P$ Analysis will determine if each product is a low (revenue) earner or a high (revenue) earner. Prototypes ought not to be included in the data set that is analyzed.

Figure 17.2(b) shows PQ$ Analysis which is a limited version of PQR$T Analysis. The scatter plot consists of four quadrants. Each quadrant represents one of the following segments of this hypothetical machine shop's product mix: (i) (High Quantity, High Revenue), (ii) (Low Quantity, High Revenue), (iii) (Low Quantity, Low Revenue), and (iv) (High Quantity, Low Revenue). The parts in each quadrant of the PQ$ Analysis plot constitute a product mix segment. In Figure 17.2(b), there are three groups of parts based on Quantity and Revenue:

■ The (High Volume, High Revenue) segment consists of parts 1, 9, 10, 11, 12, 13, and 17
■ The (Low Volume, High Revenue) segment consists of parts 2, 4, 6, 7, 8, 14, and 18
■ The (Low Volume, Low Revenue) segment consists of parts 3, 5, 15, 16, and 19

Products in the (Low Quantity, Low Revenue) segment constitute the "Cats and Dogs", whereas the products in the remaining three segments constitute the "Cash Cows". *Theoretically*, each segment should be produced in a different area of the factory. *Realistically*, the machine shop could manage the different segments as follows:

1. The parts in the (High Volume, High Revenue) segment could be produced using standard practices of the TPS.
2. The parts in the (High Volume, Low Revenue) segment could be produced using a two-bin Kanban system.
3. The parts in the (Low Volume, High Revenue) segment could be produced using a strict Make-To-Order policy with stringent Quality Control to prevent scrap. The best skilled employees and most flexible machines would be used to produce orders for those parts. Setup Reduction kaizens would be done repeatedly so setups on these machines could be changed "on a dime". If necessary, overtime should be used to allow the job shop to quote competitive lead times to win orders for these parts.
4. The parts in the (Low Volume, Low Revenue) segment would be targeted for elimination. For example, the General Manager (GM) of a fabrication job shop in Columbus, Ohio, had this to say about eliminating the parts in this segment, "We happily recommend to our customers to contact our competitors and ask them to make those parts instead of asking us! Thereby, the quality problems and shop floor disruptions caused by orders for those parts are passed on to our competitors". *However*, if the customers who order those parts are also ordering parts in any of the other three segments then the low (or no) margins earned from producing orders for those parts may just have to be tolerated. Or perhaps prices could be negotiated to lose less on orders for these parts? For example, the owner of a job shop in Mt Vernon, Ohio, that produces custom plastic lenses, mirrors, and domes for safety, security, transportation, and solar applications had this to say about pricing a one-time order, "I roll the costs of special tooling, scrap/rework, overtime, etc. into my quote. Even then the customer comes back to me! That is because they know from past experience working with me on larger orders that they are guaranteed quality and a competitive due date for delivery. I have a full-time employee dedicated to generating, executing, and monitoring my daily production schedule. She is especially vigilant when a one-time order is released into the shop."

If the shop currently has a Process Layout, split the shop into a two-shop Hybrid Cellular Layout! In a Process Layout, similar/identical machines are co-located in functional departments (Manual Lathes, CNC Lathes, Manual Mills, CNC Mills, etc.). Any machine shop that has a Process Layout will always operate in a batch-and-queue production mode! Figure 17.3(a) shows the production flow for a sample of 150+ different machined components produced in a CNC machine shop that has a Process Layout. *However,* when implementing the new layout for the shop, split the shop into two shops. With this two-shop layout, a smaller portion of the original shop will need to be managed as a complex job shop. Here is why:

1. In Shop #1, produce orders for parts/products that are in the (Runners + Repeaters) segment of the product mix. Which quadrant(s) in Figure 17.2(b) would constitute this segment? Figure 17.3(b) answers

(a)

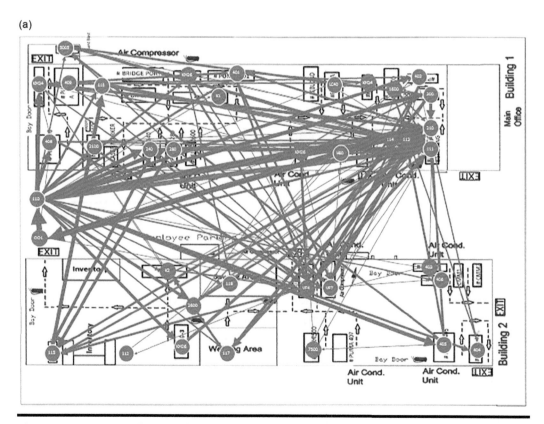

Figure 17.3   (a) Production flow in a machine shop with a process layout.

(Continued)

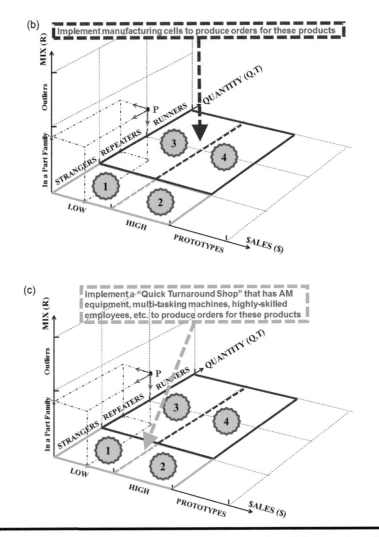

Figure 17.3 (CONTINUED)   (b) Runners and repeaters should be produced in flexible cells. (c) Strangers should be produced in a separate QTS.

this question. This portion of the shop should have a Cellular Layout that consists of several manufacturing cells with each cell dedicated to a product family. Since a manufacturing cell is essentially a mini-job shop, it is both Lean **and** Flexible aka FLean. It is *Flexible* because it is designed to produce all the parts in the part family assigned to it. It is *Lean* because it is designed using the Lean tools that also work in job shops, such as 5S, Single Minute Exchange of Dies (SMED), Total Productive Maintenance (TPM), Poka-Yoke, Employee Cross-Training, Process Improvement (aka Methods Analysis), Design For Manufacture, etc. Each cell provides unquestionable quick response to customer orders, high quality, an environment that fosters teamwork, and order traceability. The performance of each cell and its team members will be measured using metrics, such as on-time delivery, order completion time, scrap and rework costs, inventory turns, savings from kaizens done by employees, etc. Those employees will be assigned to Shop #1 who prefer production runs of mature parts.

2. In Shop #2, produce orders for parts/products that are in the (Strangers) segment of the product mix. Which quadrant(s) in Figure 17.2(b) would constitute this segment? Figure 17.3(c) answers this question. Set up Shop #2 to operate as a QTS (Quick Turnaround Shop) with AM (Additive Manufacturing) machines, flexible automation, multi-tasking machines, machining centers with pallet-changers, multi-skilled and motivated machinists who relish the challenge of producing parts they may not have seen before, etc. that can produce any part in any quantity in a single setup! Those employees will be assigned to Shop #2 who prefer the challenges of one-off manufacture of complex parts and have an intrinsic desire to master new technology. This shop should have a Functional Layout because it is a "remainder job shop". It will produce orders for those parts that do not have sufficient demand to produce them in one of the cells, spare parts, prototypes, one-offs for new customers, rush orders, etc. In this shop, sophisticated practices such as flexible automation could be used side-by-side with mundane practices such as firefighting and overtime, as long as any order completes and ships on time!

Implement a Cellular Layout in Shop #1: In order to implement cells in Shop #1, which will produce the (Runners + Repeaters) segment of the shop's product mix, a Product-Process Matrix Analysis must be done to find clusters of parts/products whose routings are similar/identical. These part ↔ machine clusters are the basis for product families! Figure 17.4(a) shows the (different) product families that were identified in a sample of parts extracted from the product mix of a machine shop. Within any product family, the parts have different shapes. However, each part family could be produced by the group of machines located in the cell where those parts will be produced. Note that an ideal stand-alone cell is one whose entire group of machines are co-located in one area of the shop!

To identify the product families in a large product mix using Product-Process Matrix Analysis, first query the Enterprise Resource Planning (ERP) system to extract the routings of all the parts/products. Next, use

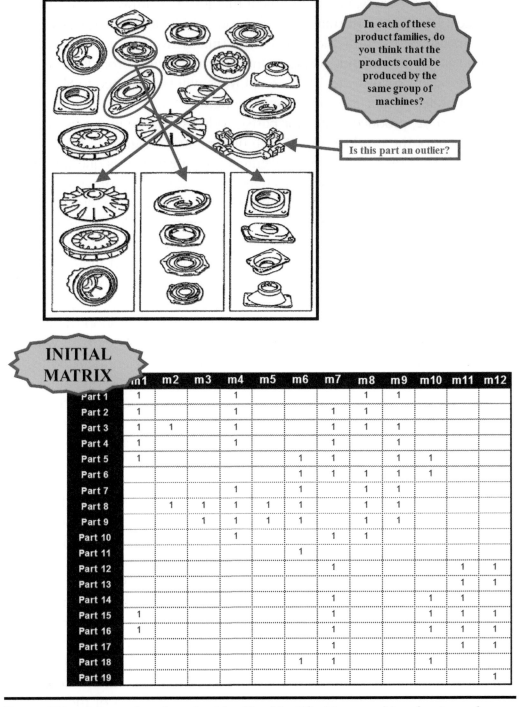

Figure 17.4   a) Examples of product families identified in a machine shop's product mix. b) Initial product-process matrix before grouping to identify part families.

	m1	m2	m3	m4	m5	m6	m7	m8	m9	m10	m11	m12
Part 1	1			1				1	1			
Part 2	1			1			1	1				
Part 3	1	1		1			1	1	1			
Part 4	1			1			1		1			
Part 5	1					1	1		1	1		
Part 6						1	1	1	1	1		
Part 7				1			1	1	1			
Part 8		1	1	1	1	1		1	1			
Part 9			1	1	1	1		1	1			
Part 10				1			1	1				
Part 11						1						
Part 12							1				1	1
Part 13											1	1
Part 14							1			1	1	
Part 15	1						1			1	1	1
Part 16	1						1			1	1	1
Part 17							1				1	1
Part 18						1	1			1		
Part 19												1

(*Continued*)

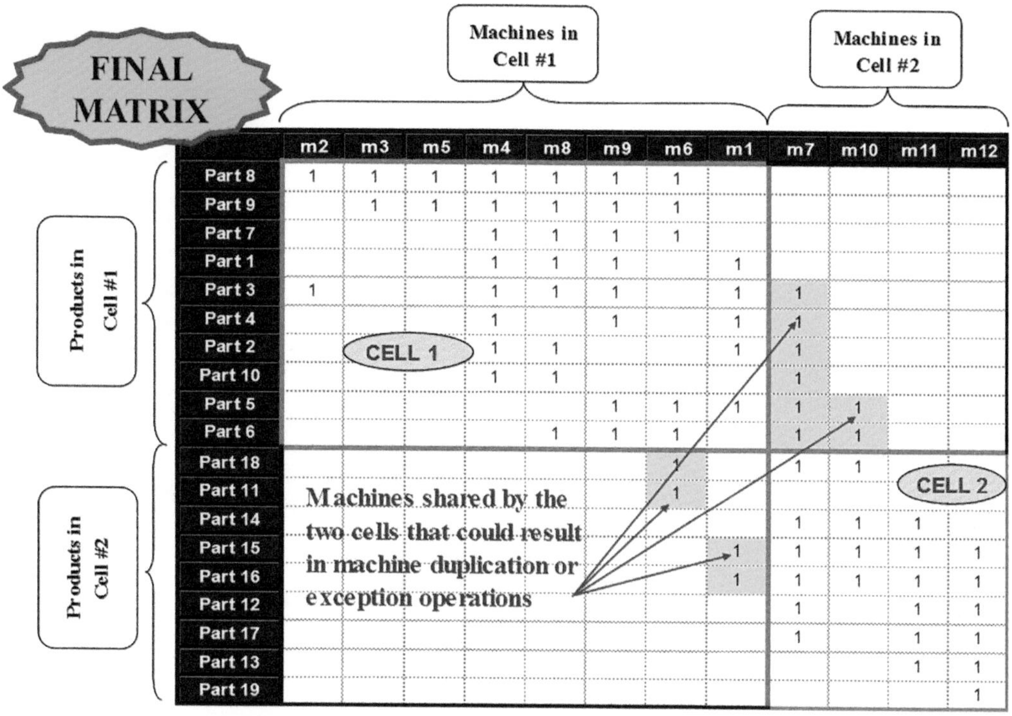

Figure 17.4 (CONTINUED)   c) Final product-process matrix after grouping to identify part families.

these routings to create the Initial Product-Process Matrix, as shown in Figure 17.4(b). Next, use any commercially available data analysis package like Minitab, SAS, or R to manipulate this matrix to get the Final Product-Process Matrix, as shown in Figure 17.4(c). Being a two-dimensional grid, the matrix of Figure 17.4(c) helps to correlate parts that use the same machines and machines that process the same parts. A part family is a cluster of parts whose routings contain similar/identical sets of machines and will appear as a band of consecutive rows in the matrix. Conversely, the cluster of machines that must be co-located in a manufacturing cell to produce those parts whose routings contain the same (or similar) machines will appear as a band of adjacent columns in the matrix. For full details on the calculations that are involved when doing the detailed design of each cell and the overall shop layout, please see Chapter 21 *Classroom Tutorial on the Design of a Cellular Manufacturing System.*

The key to successful implementation of a cell is to co-locate all its machines, personnel, and support services in one area. Figures 17.5(a) and (b) display the material flows for the part family that was being produced in

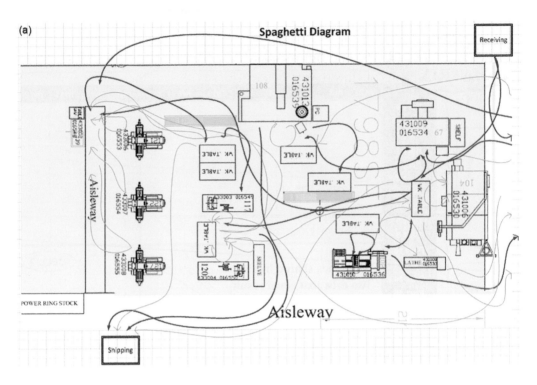

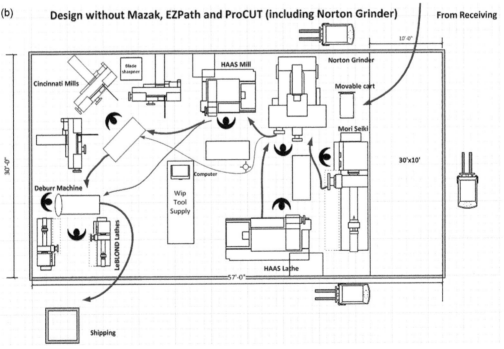

Figure 17.5 **Material flows for a part family (a) before and (b) after implementation of its machining cell.**

a machining cell before and after relayout, respectively. These were the benefits that were reported by the manufacturer that implemented this cell:

- Order Flow Times reduced from 16 to ≤5 days.
- Standard Lead Time quoted to customers was reduced from 20+ to 10 days.
- Annual labor hours spent on material handling personnel who moved parts produced in this cell between the different machines was reduced by 51 hours.
- The U-shape of the cell put machines on the periphery and the tables for cleaning, inspection, etc. in the center. Material flows in the cell in a streamlined counterclockwise fashion.
- The cell's area was reduced from 2,816 to 1,410 sq. ft. With this compact shape of the cell, its operators were forced to prevent work in process (WIP) from accumulating and cluttering up the floor.
- The distance traveled by any order processed in the cell was reduced from 618 to 368 ft. This also allowed each operator to attend to at least two machines without significant walking.
- The LOSE (Line Of Sight Efficiency) improved from 0.286 to 0.714. Any cell employee can assess the progress of any order and quickly communicate with other cell members to progress that order if it is behind schedule.

If a cell is implemented with management's support, it will have the ability to quote short lead times to customers, control the quality of the parts it produces from start to finish and hold down operating costs for the following reasons:

- *Manufacturing focus:* The cell's team can complete and ship any order for any part (or product) in its part (or product) family in any quantity to any customer to reach by an agreed-upon delivery date.
- *Flexibility:* The cell has the manufacturing capabilities and its team has the needed skills/expertise to produce any part (or product) in its part (or product) family.
- *Team-based work ethic:* The cell's team has full authority to execute any number of CI (Continuous Improvement) projects (aka kaizens) to achieve the Key Performance Indicators (KPIs) set by management. The implicit slogan becomes what the Four Musketeers used to scream "One for all, all for one!" Which is why it is extremely important that the

KPIs chosen for the cell are similar to those suggested by Dr. Eliyahu Goldratt – Increase Throughput, Reduce Inventory, and Reduce Operating Expenses.

■ *Accountability:* The cell's team is responsible for achieving their KPIs set by management, such as Delivery, Quality, Cost, Safety, and Productivity Improvement. When any manager or executive wishes to discuss a cell's performance, they just go the location of that cell (instead of taking a gemba walk that touches several departments). If the correct performance metrics are chosen, cell members will not exhibit the selfish/individualistic or elitist behavior that arises when wrong performance measures such as skill-based pay and piece rates are used.

■ *Ownership and autonomy:* Any cell will give a sense of ownership and autonomy to its members because they complete and ship products to their customers. The cell's team has full authority to establish internal cross-training programs for its members, have a say in who gets recruited to work in their cell, partner with other cells to share resources as-and-when-needed depending on the due dates of orders that have to be shipped, communicate directly with customers and suppliers, determine which member does overtime on which days, eliminate absenteeism if it is resulting from morale issues, etc.

Figure 17.6 helps to visualize why a Cellular Layout designed using Product-Process Matrix Analysis helps to align the machine shop's layout with the material flow patterns of each of the part families in their product mix.

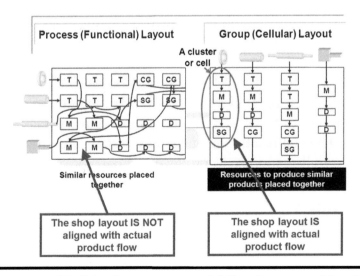

Figure 17.6 Impact of Cellular Layout on material flow in any machine shop.

The foundation for implementing Job Shop Lean is the transformation of the shop's current layout, which is usually going to be a Process Layout, into a Cellular Layout. It is strongly advised that an iterative one-cell-at-a-time process be adopted to design and implement the future Cellular Layout. There is no need to implement all the cells at one shot! The history of Cellular Manufacturing has shown there is a steep learning curve, possibly including resistance to change, when a manufacturer transitions from the existing silo-based batch-and-queue mode of production to the new team-based product family-based mode of production.

The concept of a two-shop Hybrid Cellular Layout for any machine shop is based on real-world experience that (i) never has the Product-Process Matrix Analysis of any machine shop's product mix ever yielded clear-cut clusters of parts and machines and (ii) in the case of some part families, financial and/or technological and/or human resource constraints, their groups of machines cannot be co-located into stand-alone cells that will remain stable for 1+ years. Even if several cells can be implemented in any machine shop, the QTS (Shop #2) that would produce the *Strangers* segment of their product mix will be that part of the shop that will probably not be organized into cells. In fact, that area of the shop could have a Process Layout or Virtual Cellular Layout!

Right-size non-machining processes to absorb them into the cells: In general, machine shops are too focused on improving delivery performance and profitability by acquiring multi-million $ metal-cutting machines. In reality, it is the manual machining processes, such as Saws, the Inspection department and non-machining processes, such as heat treatment, electroplating, coating, washing/cleaning, etc. that are often the root cause for their poor on-time delivery performance and long lead times that they quote to customers. I even saw Shapers in a family-owned CNC machine shop in Houston!

Right-sizing a process that is currently external to a cell, such as Washing, Painting, Deburring, Inspection, etc., would allow it to be brought into the cell. This will have a significant impact on Quality, Production Lead Time, and WIP. Also, it would improve the morale and job satisfaction of the cell personnel since their team's performance will not be affected by the workmanship and schedule priorities of those who work in external departments whose services support all the cells. Figure 17.7 shows a variety of specialized workstations that are in use in different CNC machine shops.

Unfortunately, there are limitations with right-sizing the equipment currently being used in different machine shops. Processes like heat treatment,

Figure 17.7 Right-sized workstations for non-machining support services in machine shops. (*Source*: www.cnccookbook.com/specialized-work-stations-keep-shop-organized/.)

electro-plating, or welding could never be co-located within a cell that has CNC machines! Maybe Deburring could be located in a corner of the cell if it was contained within a sound-proofed chamber having a dust collection system. In some cases, right-sizing could potentially pose a financial challenge. That is because different types of equipment currently co-located in a single department would have to be distributed into each of the cells whose parts need that process. While this eliminates a monument, the cost of designing and building smaller equipment customized for different part families could prove exorbitant!

Maximize throughput in the Inspection department: The Inspection department is often the real bottleneck in a machine shop especially if parts need FAI (First Article Inspection) on a Coordinate Measuring Machine (CMM). Inspection equipment needs to operate in an air-conditioned room. An Inspection department is rarely located in the center of the shop. Instead, it tends to be located at one end of the machine shop, often adjacent to the Shipping department. Shop personnel who work in this department have zero visual connectivity with the rest of the shop, as can be seen in the photographs of Figure 17.8.

- Is any of these Inspectors working in a cell?
- Can Inspection be done on a mobile truck that "drives around" the shop?
- Can there be two (or more) Inspection departments ex. one located in the center of the shop and the other next to Shipping?
- What if Inspection is the Bottleneck?

Figure 17.8 Photographs of the inspection departments in different machine shops.

The Holy Grail for any machine shop should be to eliminate the Inspection department all together and make it a mobile on-demand service delivered JIT (Just-In-Time) to every location. Here is a list of what-if questions that I have posed to the leadership of every machine shop client of mine:

- What if you could right-size CMM machines and other inspection devices to distribute the appropriate inspection capabilities into every one of your cells?
- What if you had roving inspectors who receive electronic requests from machinists to come to their cells to perform FAI?
- What if the CMMs, granite tables, and other equipment in the Inspection department could be placed in an air-conditioned truck that travels around the shop?[1]

---

[1] My inspiration for this idea came from the luxury mobile homes and Red Cross buses that ply the roads.

- What if any of the Machine Monitoring Systems (MMS) on the market (www.FactoryWiz.com, www.MemexOEE.com, www.FORCAM.com, www.MachineMetrics.com) could be used to monitor the CMMs in order to increase their throughput?
- What if the daily schedule of in-process and in-queue jobs in the Inspection department, especially those waiting for FAI, could be displayed on large computer screens mounted at multiple locations in the machine shop?

If the Inspection department is known to be a constant bottleneck, and Water Spiders are in charge of all factory logistics, then the simple but effective method of Pull Scheduling known as Drum-Buffer-Rope could be implemented in lieu of a full-blown commercial Finite Capacity Scheduler (FCS).

Purchase a multi-tasker that replaces two or more machines (or a flexible machining cell that replaces an entire multi-machine cell): "If we are making chips, we are making money" is the mindset of most machine shop owners to this day. Why is metal removal rate the chief driver of a machine shop owner's capital investment choices when he/she should instead utilize Dr. Eliyahu Goldratt's three golden metrics – Increase Throughput, Reduce Operating Expenses, and Reduce Inventory? Unfortunately, this mindset of "keep making chips" often leads to the purchase of expensive new machines that (i) do not alleviate the shop's capacity constraints, (ii) do not increase throughput at their bottlenecks, (iii) waste payroll $ to keep employees busy in non-bottleneck departments, and (iv) do not reduce WIP but simply shift it from one department to another.

Increasing metal removal rates does nothing (absolutely nothing!) to eliminate the significant transportation waste that results when any and every order must travel considerable distance between several departments in the shop in order to be processed on machines specified in its routing. Instead, CNC machine shops ought to invest significant capital in buying multi-tasking machines, any one of which would combine the capabilities of two or more of their existing machines. This would reduce the number of different machines at separate locations that any part must visit! For example, in the case of this family-owned machine shop in Houston that serves several customers in the Oil and Gas industry, the routing for the most complex component they make for a downhole drilling tool assembly is Saw → (Vendor Op) Hole Drilling and Boring → Manual Lathe → CNC Lathe → CNC Mill → Shaper → Inspect → Ship. But they make other components that may have a routing like Saw → Manual Lathe → CNC Lathe → Inspect → Ship or a routing like Saw → CNC Lathe → CNC Mill → Inspect → Ship. Should this shop buy a new CNC Lathe with higher metal removal rates so the Manual Lathes department can be eliminated? Or should this shop buy a multi-function machining center that combines the operations done on the CNC Lathe and CNC Mill? Or should it explore how to eliminate the Shapers by using their CNC mills to cut the internal splines on some of their parts? Having observed the WIP in the three buildings that comprise this machine shop, the CNC Lathes department is not the shop's bottleneck. Plus they have a classic Process Layout! So their purchase of a high-priced CNC Lathe with a faster metal removal rate and in-cut spindle time was not going to reduce their WIP nor help them to quote shorter Lead Times. They could have drastically reduced delivery times by (i) eliminating the Manual Turning department by moving their work to the larger CNC Lathes and (ii) planning for the reorganization of the shop to implement three cells: (Cell #1) CNC Turning only, (Cell #2) CNC Turning → CNC Milling, (Cell #3) CNC Turning → CNC Milling → Spline Cutting.

Instead of their prevailing fixation with metal removal rates and machine utilization, machine shops should buy multi-function machines and systems that combine consecutive operations currently being done on different machines. Especially if those machines are currently located in separate departments, such as CNC Lathes and CNC Mills! By combining machines, the delays due to (i) material handling between several machines, (ii) waiting for material handlers to pick up and move a batch of parts from one machine to another, (iii) producing a large batch instead of splitting the batch into two or more transfer batches, (iv) setup and gauging at each of several machines, and (v) waiting in queue at machines that are shared by multiple part families, etc. are reduced. For example, in the case of the same family-owned machine shop discussed earlier, given the many pallets loaded with turned parts received from the CNC Lathes, their GM was advised to limit new orders released every day to that department, "Are you in the business of keeping your lathe operators busy making parts? Or should you focus on completing and shipping as many parts as you can every day?"

So how does a machine shop plan and decide which new multi-tasking machine or system to buy in order to reduce material flow? By selecting multi-taskers whose flexibility will (i) reduce the total number of individual machines in every cell that currently produces a family of parts and (ii) give the cell the processing capabilities of machines that are currently available only in some other cell or a Common Resource Cell that is accessed by other cells too. The machine shop should first do a Product-Process Matrix

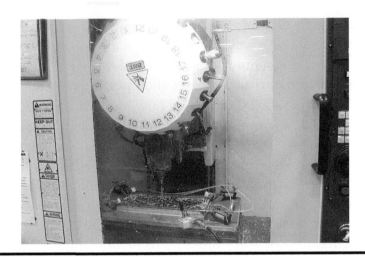

Figure 17.9 Flexible machine that replaced several existing machines in a cell.

Analysis of their product mix to find their part families. Next, for a particular part family, they should draw a Spaghetti Diagram and compute workloads on the different machines in that cell. Using the Spaghetti Diagram (and the Q-type From-To Chart and the PR Analysis Type III outputs from PFAST[2]), they should identify a set of two or three machines that perform consecutive operations that appear in the routings of most parts in the family. Next, for all those operations that would be done on the multi-tasker, prepare the list of specifications (work envelope, axes of freedom, number of tools, in-process gauging, etc.) for all the parts in the part family. Finally, present that list of specifications to the different machine tool vendors who have (or could build for an affordable price) the desired multi-function machine (or system). For example, Figure 17.9 shows a Fanuc Robodrill that replaced a multi-machine cell that produced sealing rings for compressors. In the new one-machine cell that got this compact machining center, the operator had to load the raw material, unload the finished parts, blow away the chips, do final inspection, count the parts, and place them in a tote that was soon sent to the Shipping department.

"Raze" and standardize the routings of all the parts within a part family: The ideal layout for any machine shop would be one where any and every order flows in linear assembly line-like fashion from one end of the shop to the other with minimum backtracking, instead of the chaotic flow seen in Figure 17.3(a) that resembles a bowl of spaghetti. This ambitious goal to eliminate the chaotic material flow in that job shop would be to transform

---

[2] Production Flow Analysis and Simplification Toolkit.

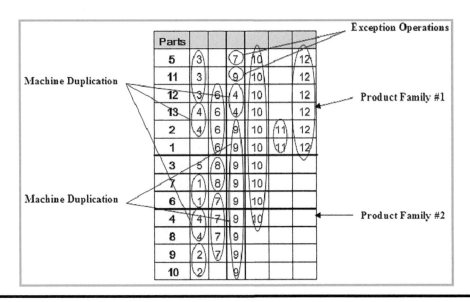

Figure 17.10 Why were these parts with dissimilar routings put in one part family?

its layout into a Hybrid Flow Shop Layout that could be designed using the PR Analysis Type IV output from PFAST. In theory, the new layout would achieve overall linear flow, as observed in a high-mix machining flowline (or flow shop). But, a problem often overlooked by facility layout planners is that the routings may have dissimilarities that can be eliminated! For example, Figure 17.10 shows the routings for a part family assigned for production to a cell. Why were these parts with significantly dissimilar routings even put in one family? Even if the cell to produce all the parts in this family had a U-shaped layout, the as-is routings of the parts will require management of many different material flow paths within the cell.

So, to pursue flow simplification in the shop, a more realistic approach would be to do so one cell a time after "razing" (revising) the routings of all the parts that have been grouped into a part family because they have similar (**not** identical) routings. The "razing" of the routings would be done by asking, "What would it take for two similar routings to be made identical?" First, the routings should be standardized by eliminating the differences in the machines used and the sequences in which the machines are used. Next, operations that are common to many routings should be standardized by eliminating the differences in the fixtures, tools, gauges, etc. used.

Instead of the Make-To-Stock approach for Pull Scheduling, use a Make-To-Order approach for Pull Scheduling: A machine shop typically executes a different schedule every day. Each day's schedule could have a different mix of jobs, the due dates set by the customers for those jobs could be different, the lot sizes of the jobs would probably not be the same, the number of operations could vary significantly across their different routings, the setup times and run times associated with the operations in the different routings would be different, etc. Regardless of all these differences, it is important to issue a **feasible** schedule every day that the shop can execute and complete! Similar to "Pull Scheduling", the schedule should "gate" the release of orders to the shop by loading all the work centers with jobs such that their workload on key resources, especially on the bottleneck(s), does not exceed available capacity constraints (machines, labor, raw materials, dies, etc.).

Unfortunately, it is unrealistic (although not impossible) to manually generate a feasible daily schedule for a machine shop that displays as a Gantt Chart the set of jobs to release into the shop every day after taking into consideration resource capacity constraints, material shortages, changes in vendor deliveries, machine breakdowns, due dates, etc. If a machine shop desires daily Work Order Releases that will not exceed resource capacity constraints, they should not expect their ERP system to do this. The typical ERP system uses an MRP (Material Requirements Planning) or MRP-II (Manufacturing Resources Planning) engine to plan production and schedule operations. MRP assumes infinite capacity, fixed lead times, batch production to reduce setup times, etc. Instead of relying on an ERP system, the logical alternative is to use a commercial FCS that utilizes either the Drum-Buffer-Rope method of scheduling (*DBR+, InforVISUAL EasyLean*) or advanced dispatching heuristics and user-defined rules (*Preactor, Tactic, Schedlyzer*). For example, Figure 17.11 shows the Gantt Chart produced by a commercial FCS (www. Preactor.com) for a fabrication shop that produces industrial weighing scales that weigh the 18-wheeler trucks that ply the US Interstate Highways. In this particular chart, the timelines are for the different work centers in the factory. The Start Time/Finish Times are shown for (i) the final product, (ii) each of the three major subassemblies that comprise the final product and (iii) each of the different components that comprise the kit for each of the three subassemblies. Therefore, a machine shop is best advised to integrate their ERP system with a respectable FCS like Preactor, Tactic, or Schedlyzer.

By transforming their current layout into a Cellular Layout, a machine shop would be using "divide-and-conquer" to effectively schedule several stand-alone mini-job shops instead of one large job shop. Each cell is like a mini-job shop that has a fraction of all the machines in the shop and to process only a fraction of the shop's entire product mix. Ideally, all of the

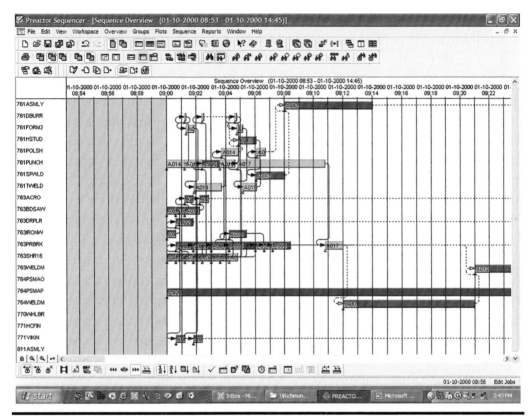

Figure 17.11   Gantt Chart for the daily schedule to produce a large fabricated product.

machines needed to produce any part in its part family will be co-located inside the cell (except vendor operations or true monuments like heat treat that are external to the cell). Who knows, but in the case of a manufacturing cell, there may not even be a need for software to schedule its daily operations! At the daily morning huddle, the cell's team would meet with the production controller. Each cell member would have eyeballed the jobs in process or in queue from the previous day. Being contained within a small area of the shop, a cell facilitates rapid assessment of hours of work in queue at different machines, machine and operator availabilities throughout a shift, etc. The number of new jobs that could be released into the cell that day could be determined by asking the operator of the cell's bottleneck what he/she could realistically hope to complete. The inter-machine proximities and ease of communication between all who work in the cell gives the cell start-to-finish control of the flow of orders it has to process. So, except for unforeseen emergencies, the cell team can make many on-the-fly adjustments in the daily schedule to easily ensure that all jobs are completed and shipped by their due dates. Never underestimate the do-or-die determination of a cell's team to deliver customer service by completing orders with the desired quality at the right time at (or below) cost!

Utilize Water Spiders to manage all shop floor logistics related to executing the daily schedule: Assume that after their ERP system is integrated with a commercial FCS, a machine shop can generate a feasible daily schedule for each cell and for each of the external monuments that are shared by the cells and for each of the support departments (Receiving, Shipping, Inspection, etc.). Next they must publish that schedule to the shop floor, execute it, and at the end of each shift, update the current shop floor status of all active jobs in their ERP. An MES (Manufacturing Execution System) fulfills the role of executing the daily schedule and updating its status in the ERP at the end of each shift. For example, in the Pompano Beach, FL, facility of my former employer, Hoerbiger Corporation of America, given that it is a large (>100,000 sq. ft) facility, they implemented a fully integrated IT system composed of an ERP (SAP), an FCS (Preactor), and an MES (Factory Viewer), as shown in Figure 17.12(a). A full description of this success story is available online at www.lean-scheduling.com/LSI_Case_Studies_Hoerbiger.html and www.preactor.com/Company/News-Articles/Preactor-and-Factory-Viewer-Get-Seal-Of-Approval-F#.Wd4N5VtSy1s.

However, in the case of a single-location HMLV machine shop, especially a small family-owned job shop, it may not be advisable to immediately purchase an MES to complement the FCS that took over scheduling from their ERP system. Instead, small machine shops ought to create the position of Water Spider(s) by freeing up one or more employees on the current payroll. Figure 17.12(b) describes the typical delivery route of a Water Spider in an Assembly Factory. Similarly, Figure 17.12(c) shows the zone of influence of the Water Spider working with (or without) an MES in any CNC machine shop. In a job shop, the job of the Water Spider(s) will combine the work that is typically done by a material handler (who reports to the Plant Manager) and an expeditor (who reports to the Production Controller). Specifically, the Water Spider(s) will handle all shop floor logistics related to moving raw materials, in-process batches, and finished parts between machines as specified in the routers of the different parts. By virtue of being all over the shop floor, the Water Spider(s) have the "situational awareness" needed to execute, monitor, and update the daily schedule that was released to the floor. Whether they can be granted the authority to expedite and execute the daily schedule will depend on the leadership of the specific machine shop.

Manage the Shop with ERP+FCS/APS+MES

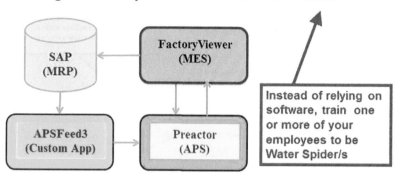

1. Data on Orders/Operations comes from SAP.
2. APSFeed3 augments data with rules to prioritize production of orders, data conversion, and some machine rules added to the SAP data.
3. Preactor uses data from APSFeed3 and scheduling rules to assign and sequence operations to resources.
4. Preactor then publishes schedule to the MES system, FactoryViewer.
5. As operations are executed, data is collected via shop floor terminals and fed back both to Preactor and SAP for updating and perpetuating the scheduling process.

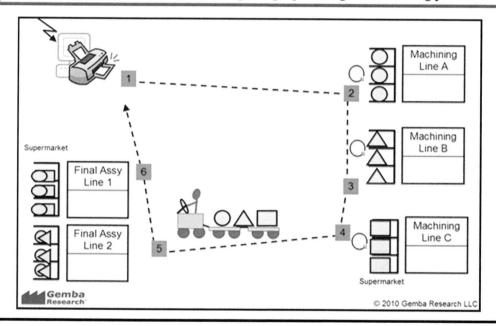

Figure 17.12 a) Manage the shop floor by integrating ERP, FCS/APS (Advanced Planning & Scheduling), and MES. b) Flowchart for daily routine of a Water Spider in an assembly factory. (*Source***: www.qualitydigest.com/inside/twitter-ed/milk-run-vs-water-spider.html.)**

(*Continued*)

Use Water Spider(s) to Support the MES

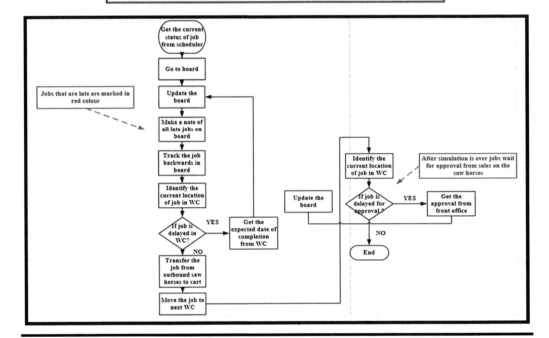

Figure 17.12 (CONTINUED)   c) Utilize Water Spiders with (or without) an MES. d) Flowchart for daily routine of a Water Spider in a machine shop.

In a Job Shop Lean implementation project done at Wear Technology, a CNC machine shop located in McPherson, KS,[3] the two Water Spiders eliminated the previous practice where every employee (including the skilled

---

[3] This article – Danford, M. (2017, July). Lean Manufacturing Begins with Layout, Commitment. *Modern Machine Shop*, 78–86 – is available online at www.mmsonline.com/articles/lean-manufacturing-layout-relies-on-people.

CNC machinists) was responsible for moving the pair of screws that they finished from their machine to the next machine. The typical process for moving a set of screws from one machine to the next involved (i) walking across the shop to fetch the bridge crane and docking it at their machine, (ii) walking around the shop to find a cart on which the screws would be loaded, (iii) returning to the machine to unload the screws off their machine onto the cart, (iv) pushing the cart to the next machine, and (v) returning empty-handed to their machine to wait for their next job. By aggregating all the time that their shop employees wasted being material movers, this machine shop realized significant savings by having just their two Water Spider(s) invest all that non-value-added walking time (aka Waste of Operator Motion)! Figure 17.12(d) shows the flowchart that was developed to explain their daily routine to the two Water Spider(s) at Wear Technology.

Implement an MMS to maximize Total Effective Equipment Performance (TEEP) of those work centers that are the shop's bottleneck(s): *The Goal* is a book (and a video based on it) by Dr. Eliyahu Goldratt that introduces the Theory Of Constraints (TOC). A cornerstone of this theory is the idiom "A chain is no stronger than its weakest link". In the case of a machining cell that produces orders on demand for different parts in a part family, the cell can only complete as many orders as the cell's constraint machine (aka bottleneck) can complete. The cell's bottleneck is that machine which is always having orders in queue (WIP) during each shift while the other machines remain idle. In the case of a cell, it can be assumed that the bottleneck in the cell will not shift with time. Even if it did, the disruptions would be limited to the confines of the cell. Dr. Goldratt proposed a five-step *Process Of Ongoing Improvement* (POOGI) whose first step is to *Exploit the Constraint* in the cell (or the entire machine shop). The focus of this step in the POOGI is to "win back" all the avoidable losses of capacity on the bottleneck machine, such as setup time, idle time due to non-arrival of the next job, machine stoppages due to CNC program errors, unscheduled breaks taken by the operator, time to change broken tools, etc.[4] In order to ensure that the productive utilization of the bottleneck machine is at least 80%, and to ensure that other machines do not suffer unplanned breakdowns, I strongly support the implementation of an MMS like Machine Metrics (www.MachineMetrics.com).

---

[4] Ideally, POOGI is best implemented with the Lean tool of Value Stream Mapping, where a single map helps to identify the wastes, delays, and inconsistencies in the material and information flows for a single product.

With the abundance of MMS on the market (www.FactoryWiz.com, www.MemexOEE.com, www.FORCAM.com, www.MachineMetrics. com), it is possible to do 24/7 monitoring of (i) at least the bottleneck machine(s) in each of the cells and (ii) the monuments in the machine shop. Figure 17.13(a) shows an example of one of the many reports from an MMS that summarizes the capacity losses on a CNC machine. Do you notice that "No Operator" is one of the top three reasons for capacity loss on this particular machine? In contrast, traditional methods such as video-aided machine monitoring or random visits by supervisors project a lack of trust on the part of management. Also, the reports from the MMS, especially the Pareto Analysis chart of how capacity in every 8-hour shift was utilized, can be used to conduct a series of kaizens with the sole purpose of improving value-added utilization of those machines (or multi-machine work centers) in the machine shop that are key to increasing the number of orders it complete daily! In effect, an MMS is ideal for implementing CI using the TOC approach called POOGI, in particular the *Exploit the Constraint* step.

An MMS can also be used to run an effective TPM program to ensure that no individual machines or multi-machine cells fail catastrophically and unexpectedly on any given day. Figure 17.13(b) presents a systematic description of the four categories into which the times recorded by the MMS for different activities performed on any machine during an 8-hour shift can be assigned. TEEP is a performance metric that provides insights as to the true capacity of any manufacturing equipment. It takes into account both Equipment Losses (as measured by Overall Equipment Effectiveness) and Schedule Losses (as measured by Machine Utilization). TEEP = OEE × Machine Utilization = **Availability** × **Performance** × **Quality** × **Utilization**. It is desirable that the TEEP for a cell's bottleneck be around 80%–85%.

Become a machine shop that uses the data in its ERP system to support all kaizen events, morning huddles, and decision-making related to shop floor management: There is a widespread misconception that limits US machine shops from gaining additional benefits from Lean. It is that Lean and ERP are incompatible! The reality is that ERP systems are here to stay, whereas the manual paper-and-pencil tools of Lean will go away with the emergence of data analytics and machine learning. ERP systems can support Lean in three ways: (i) They have the functions/modules to implement Lean projects, (ii) they have the data needed to do Lean projects, and (iii) they can integrate with third-party software to execute Lean practices. Unfortunately, the fundamental shortcoming of contemporary ERP systems is that they do not have up-to-date, complete, and accurate data. In fact, some ERP systems

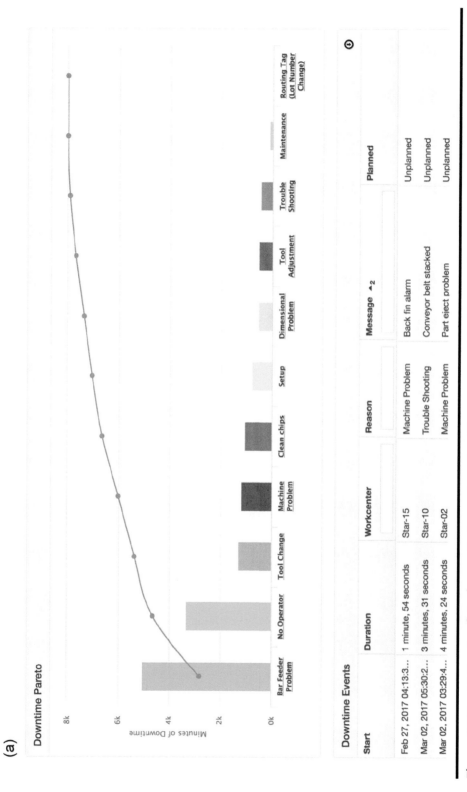

Figure 17.13 (a) Pareto plot of capacity loss categories. (*Source:* www.MachineMetrics.com.)

(*Continued*)

(b)

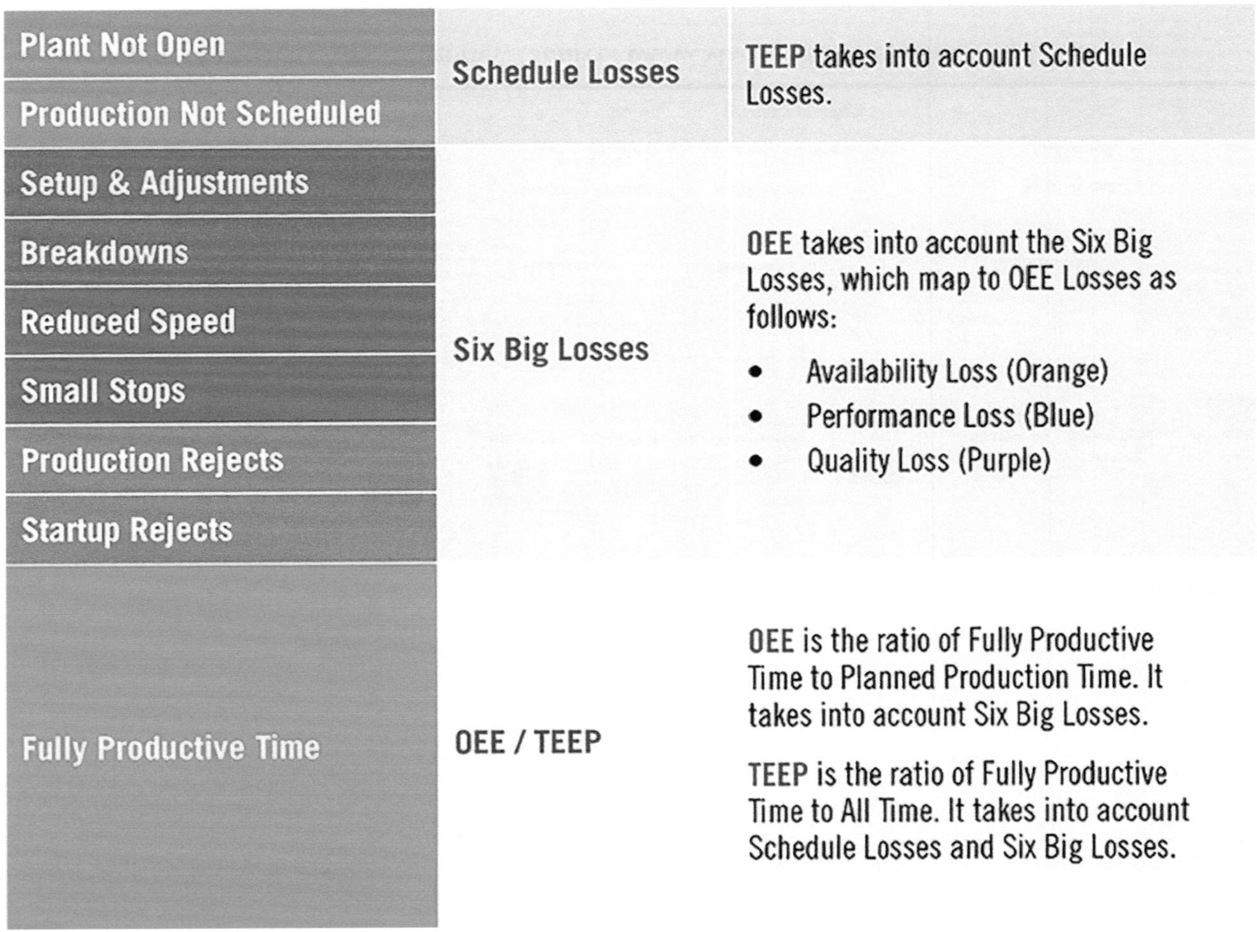

	Schedule Losses	TEEP takes into account Schedule Losses.
Plant Not Open		
Production Not Scheduled		
Setup & Adjustments	Six Big Losses	OEE takes into account the Six Big Losses, which map to OEE Losses as follows:
Breakdowns		• Availability Loss (Orange)
Reduced Speed		• Performance Loss (Blue)
Small Stops		• Quality Loss (Purple)
Production Rejects		
Startup Rejects		
Fully Productive Time	OEE / TEEP	OEE is the ratio of Fully Productive Time to Planned Production Time. It takes into account Six Big Losses.
		TEEP is the ratio of Fully Productive Time to All Time. It takes into account Schedule Losses and Six Big Losses.

Figure 17.13 (CONTINUED) (b) Components of the 8 hours of theoretical available capacity on any machine. (*Source:* www. oee.com/teep.html.)

appear to be Accounting and CRM systems at best! Too often it is the CFO (Chief Financial Officer) and the CIO (Chief Information Officer) who call the shots when selecting an ERP system. What about the COO (Chief Operations Officer) demanding that the ERP system have capable modules for Production Planning, Production Control, Operations Scheduling, Capacity Planning, Shop Floor Control, etc.? Here are some of the questions that a machine shop's leadership team should ask an ERP vendor and challenge them to demonstrate that their ERP can support Job Shop Lean:

1. Can an order be accurately tracked to determine its physical location within the facility or its status at a vendor? And, given the order's current status at any time, can management expect a reliable estimate of its completion date?
2. Can the Water Spider(s) view the daily schedule for all work centers as an electronic Gantt Chart from any shop floor terminal located anywhere in the shop? Can the Water Spider(s) receive an accurate Daily Dispatch list of orders for every shift? Can the Water Spider(s) update the daily schedule in the ERP system in real time out on the shop floor? Can the Water Spider(s) communicate in real time with the office to receive emergency notifications about due date changes, raw material delivery delays, expedite requests for orders (or cancelations) by customers, etc.?[5]
3. Can the ERP system support daily morning huddles on the shop floor or meetings in the conference room by providing data analytics and reports as-needed to support decision-making? Or will some third-party tool for Digital Visual Management, such as www.iObeya.com or https://leankit.com/product/, needs to be purchased and "bolted on" to the ERP?
4. Could each team set up and maintain its own dashboards in readiness for their daily morning huddles? Or when an executive takes a gemba walk and asks them to share details about any aspect of their huddle whiteboard?
5. …and so on.

---

[5] An ERP system must enable real-time communications between the front office, the shop floor, and the Water Spider(s). Together, the ERP system and the Water Spider(s) should achieve the "situational awareness" that is needed so the Shop Floor Control module in the ERP system is up-to-date on status of jobs, machines, tools, employees, etc.

In summary, an ERP system **must** be able to collect, analyze, and synthesize any and all data related to shop floor operations. It **must** be able to transform the data into actionable reports that automate, or at least semi-automate, decision-making by shop employees. Sadly, today much of this decision-making is done during daily morning huddles, or worse, in meetings held in a conference room removed from the shop floor.

Here is a simple challenge to any machine shop that is an advanced adopter of Lean but desires to test if their ERP system can support shop floor operations and business decision-making. They should conduct a kaizen on Value Stream Mapping (VSM) to implement a cell to produce a "cash cow" product family. However, they must use their ERP system to obtain the data to support the kaizen. Some of the tasks they must perform using their ERP system will be as follows:

1. Identify a family of parts instead of selecting one part from the entire product mix with the highest Production Volume or Revenue (or Margin).
2. Create the Current State Map for the part family using data extracted from the ERP system's databases.
3. Create the Future State Map showing how the ERP system would perform all communications (i) on the shop floor and (ii) between the top floor and the shop floor using appropriate technology.

Figure 17.14 shows examples of activities that the ERP system ought to be able to do to enable Value Stream Management (or even daily operation of the cell or virtual cell that embodies a Value Stream).

Rationalize the product mix at the end of every year: At the end of each year, eliminate those products that are losing money aka "Cats and Dogs". For example, the GM of a fabrication job shop in Columbus, Ohio, had this to say about eliminating the parts in this segment, "We happily recommend to our customers to contact our competitors and ask them to make those parts instead of asking us! Thereby, the quality problems and shop floor disruptions caused by orders for those parts are passed on to our competitors". Figure 17.15 illustrates how PQ$ Analysis (P = Products, Q = Production Volume, $ = Revenue or Margin) using a scatter plot generated using Excel can quickly segregate the "Cash Cows" (Runners and Repeaters) from the "Cats and Dogs" (Strangers).

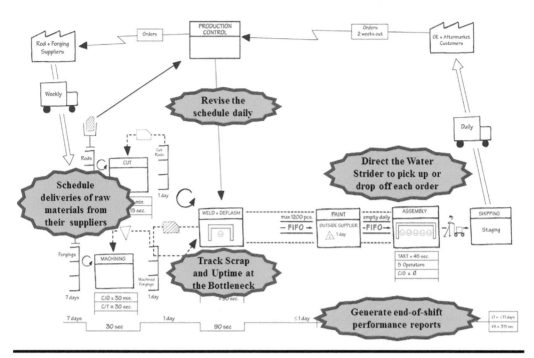

Figure 17.14   How an ERP system ought to support a VSM kaizen.

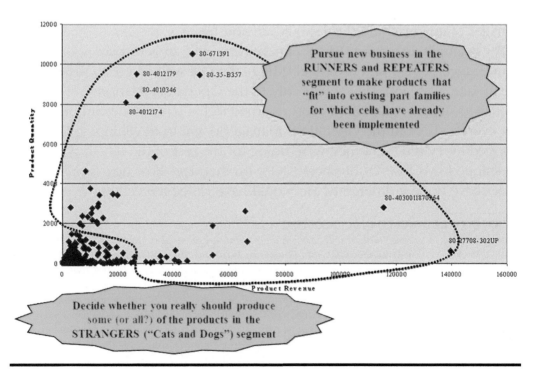

Figure 17.15   Planning product mix rationalization using PQ$ Analysis.

Before Implementing Job Shop Lean, a Machine Shop *Must* Have These Ducks in a Row

The CEO, VP Operations, and Plant Manager should be "4H" leaders[6]: Every executive and manager on the "top floor" needs to demonstrate 4H (Head, Heart, Hands, and Hooves) leadership qualities: (i) They strive to participate in key CI projects; (ii) they engage with their employees as and when their schedule permits; (iii) they have a working knowledge of TOC, Lean, and Six Sigma; (iv) they are adept at risk management under uncertainty; (v) they insist that processes and systems be developed for "efficient firefighting"; and (vi) they do not hesitate to explore cooperative partnerships with competitors, etc. Sadly, in too many machine shops, these individuals take a hands-off attitude and entrust the successful implementation of Lean to the consultant they hired. Big mistake! Not only should these individuals participate in the day-to-day efforts of the workforce and CI team tasked with the Lean implementation, they should demonstrate commitment. Taiichi Ohno, the creator of the TPS, considered every problem to be an opportunity! A leader is constructive (never destructive!) and proactive in how they deal with their subordinates. Table 17.3 lists examples of other essential "4H" leadership qualities that the President/CEO, VP Operations, and Plant Manager of any machine shop should demonstrate.[7]

For example, in a recent client engagement with an aerospace Maintenance, Repair and Overhaul (MRO), the GM walked out to the floor to expedite a late job. He spoke curtly to the Operations Manager, "This job has to ship tonight. Okay?" and returned to his office. One can be sure that everybody from the Operations Manager down to the Shipping Clerk dropped everything that they were doing for the rest of the day to get that job shipped by Close Of Business (COB) on that day! Now how would a 4H leader have done it differently? He would have called a meeting the next day

---

[6] **FURTHER READING: (1)** Byrne, A. (2013). *The Lean Turnaround: How Business Leaders Use Lean Principles to Create Value and Transform their Company.* New York: McGraw-Hill. **(2)** Koenigsaecker, G. (2013). *Leading the Lean Enterprise Transformation.* Boca Raton, FL: CRC Press. **(3)** Byrne, A. (2016). *The Lean Turnaround Action Guide: How to Implement Lean, Create Value and Grow Your People.* New York: McGraw-Hill. **(4-A)** Emiliani, B., Stec, D., Grasso, L. & Stodder, J. 2007. *Better Thinking, Better Results: Case Study and Analysis of an Enterprise-wide Lean Transformation.* Wethersfield, CT: The Center for Lean Business Management. **(4-B)** Lancaster, J. & Adams, E. (2017). *The Work of Management: A Daily Path to Sustainable Improvement.* Boston, MA: Lean Enterprise Institute, Inc. **(5)** Harada, T. (2015). *Management Lessons from Taiichi Ohno: What Every Leader Can Learn from the Man Who Invented the Toyota Production System.* New York: McGraw-Hill.

[7] I strongly urge you to check out the *Two Second Lean* program at this website https://paulakers.net/.

Table 17.3 "4H" Leadership Qualities That Are Desirable in Managers and Executives

"4H" Leadership Quality	How It Should Be Demonstrated
Head	• Be an active learner of Lean. Go ahead and use Google and YouTube to your advantage! Access the considerable (free!) introductory material available online on just about any Lean-related topic like Waste Identification, Gemba Walks, Training within Industry, Problem-Solving Tools, and more! • Teach a couple of classes in the company's in-house Lean Six Sigma training program. Pick a combination of topics like Waste Identification + five Why's + Fishbone Diagram so employees learn what matters to their powers-that-be! • Support a wall paper in the lunch room featuring (i) stellar improvement projects done by employees, (ii) significant issues/concerns being addressed, (iii) growth plans, and (iv) specific problems for which solutions are sought, etc. • Go to the in-house CI team and offer up some of your ideas for improvement. • Develop a habit to *Read → Go Do → Learn → Read More* in order to learn new leadership skills, master effective ways to engage better with employees, convert daily frustrations or on-time delivery failures into opportunities for betterment, etc.
Heart	• Make *Respect for Employees* core to the company's HR policies and programs. • Appreciate employees for their stellar performance with meaningful rewards. Else be creative with "Shout Outs" as they do at restaurants where teams of employees walk up to celebrate a customer's birthday! • Mount a display board in the lobby with an autographed photo of each and every employee of the company. Keep it up to date despite employee departures!
Hands	• Shake hands! Pat backs! Greet employees that walk past during a gemba walk! Be generous with your "Thank You's"! Do the simple things that have a positive impact on employees' morale. • Participate actively in at least a few kaizens, especially those that involve moving equipment, building fixtures, etc. • Be sure to recognize and reward exemplary employees throughout the year instead of only at the end-of-year Christmas Party or Annual Picnic! • Be business-driven with the categories in the Suggestion Program for which employees are rewarded, such as Product Design, Process/Machine Upgrade, Safety and Ergonomics, Community Service, etc.

(Continued)

Table 17.3 (*Continued*)   "4H" Leadership Qualities That Are Desirable in Managers and Executives

"4H" Leadership Quality	*How It Should Be Demonstrated*
Hooves	• Make Gemba Walks and Lean Daily Management (aka Leader Standard Work) a regular routine in order to "feel the pulse" of the shop floor • "Stand on the X" at least once a week by picking a different spot on the shop floor each time to observe daily activities. Note observations and share them with the CI team. Follow up with a Root Cause Analysis (RCA) discussion. Ask the team to submit a Corrective Action Plan (CAP) to address the root cause(s). Make sure that they follow through with the actions they proposed to take. • Lead, or at least participate in, morning huddles of one or two departments every day. • At least once a week, visit any one cell or department. Surprise (in some cases, it may shock) the cell employees while they are at work. Chat briefly with each of them by going to their workstations, instead of having them leave what they are doing to meet you. Ask them about their work! Maybe ask the team leader to describe their progress on one of their ongoing improvement projects?

of the same team that worked to get that late job shipped and brainstormed with them. The goal of that brainstorming session would be to create two diagrams: (i) an Ishikawa Diagram (or Mindmap) to document all the reasons (potential and actual) why that job fell through the cracks and (ii) a Tree Diagram to determine all the actions that would have to be taken to eliminate most of those causes once for all.

Hire a full-time Industrial Engineer (IE) to be the Lean Champion and leader of an in-house CI team[8]: The IE will create, lead, and sustain an in-house team dedicated to CI. An experienced IE can easily master and enhance the methods and tools used to implement any of the buzzword CI strategies like Lean, TOC, Six Sigma, Operational Excellence, etc. If one asks, "How much more can the Lean Tools listed in Table 17.1 of this chapter

[8] **FURTHER READING: (1)** Irani, S.A. (2013, January/February). *The Idea Factory.* Elk Grove Village, IL: Gear Technology, pp. 26–29. **(2)** Irani, S.A. (2013, May). *The Tiger Team: Hear them Roar.* Elk Grove Village, IL: Gear Technology, pp. 36–42. **(3)** Irani, S.A. (2013, November/December). *Educating the Workforce and Management about FLEAN (Flexible and Lean) Manufacturing Cells.* Elk Grove Village, IL: Gear Technology, pp. 82–92.

be enhanced for implementing Job Shop Lean in an HMLV facility?" I would reply, "Significantly, provided you hire an IE".

The importance of training and developing key employees who will be empowered to make improvements on the shop floor and in the front office cannot be stressed enough! People who should be fixtures on the in-house CI team would be the CEO/President (mainly in name), the VP Operations (mainly in name), Plant Manager, IE, and Department Supervisors. The rest of the team should be in flux since employees will come and go after they successfully complete their training **plus** a portfolio of projects in the department where they work.

During my tenure as the Director of IE Research at Hoerbiger Corporation of America, Houston, TX, I had established the following schedule of activities for our in-house CI team:

1. The team met once a week for half-a-day.
2. I taught a problem-solving tool relevant to the project we were working on, often using a relevant video from my personal library.
3. Each member reported the progress they had made on the task(s) they had undertaken for the project we were working on.
4. Our team went to the shop floor to continue work on our (joint) project.

How does a mom-and-pop machine shop create an in-house learning and training program on Lean? In my case, I did not have a large budget to go on a spending spree to acquire professional learning and training resources from Gemba Academy, Tooling U-SME, Greater Boston Manufacturing Partnership, Enna Products Corporation, and other for-profit providers. So here are some tips for creating a viable program on a bare-bones budget:

1. I "dredged" the vast video selection on YouTube to find videos like the ones listed below to enrich and expand an instructional module on any topic:
   a. Lean Workstation (*Source:* www.youtube.com/watch?v=QbNE ev8cxqs)
   b. Lean Manufacturing Cell (*Source*: www.youtube.com/watch?v=AUPji 7L9aSs)
   c. Lean Manufacturing Tour (*Source*: www.youtube.com/watch?v=mqg HUwSaKj8&list=PLBc4f3rCfmO_2ebMtXzmBIcIH9sIRvZ-v)

    d. Watch How a Lean Thinking Company Runs a Morning Meeting (*Source*: www.youtube.com/watch?v=3M6-1e6t6Vc)

    e. Waste Walk With Process Improvement Leaders (*Source*: www.youtube.com/watch?v=146Yn5MV85U)

    f. FastCap CEO's Lean Improvement Walk (*Source*: www.youtube.com/watch?v=3OEePS7Oh_g)

2. I developed several of my own interactive simulations to customize the training specific to our machine shop and mold shop.

3. I developed several half- and one-day workshops on a variety of topics relevant to the training that had to be delivered relevant to the projects that had to be worked on.

4. I found a wealth of case studies and videos on websites like www.MMSOnline.com, www.SEAOnline.com, and www.ProductionMachining.com (especially *Modern Machine Shop*!).

5. I obtained numerous informative articles (sometimes even MS theses!) by Googling key words like "Lean machine shops" or "5S in machine shops".

6. In every instructional module, I complemented the PowerPoint presentation with a video and/or an interactive simulation.

How to make the training 100% relevant to one's **own** machine shop? Some guidelines that I followed to develop the training materials and offer training that our workforce and managers could relate to were (i) I made it relevant to our needs and priorities, (ii) I stressed a hands-on-learn-by-doing mode of instruction, (iii) I appreciated each and every employee that made the effort to **do something** after each training session, and (iv) I limited the additional work (and responsibilities) that each member of the team took on outside of their official job responsibilities.

Establish an active internship program by partnering with the Industrial Engineering and Mechanical Engineering departments at a reputed university: From 1996 to 2012, while I was a faculty in the Department of Integrated Systems Engineering at The Ohio State University (OSU), I managed the LEAP Internship Program. "LEAP" is an acronym for **L**earn, **E**arn, **A**pply, and **P**ractice. This program matched manufacturers who wanted to implement Job Shop Lean with our IE students who had (i) taken the courses that constituted a Job Shop Lean Certificate Program, (ii) impressed me with their performance on the team-based industry projects that were a staple in my courses, and (iii) knew how to utilize the outputs of the PFAST[9] software to implement Job Shop Lean best practices. I firmly believe that IE interns who are mentored by seasoned Lean implementers can achieve measurable results on the projects they do at the companies that recruit them. To this day, even as a professional consultant, I impress upon my client to hire IE interns so I can then teach those students the Toyota-style IE that is rarely taught in most academic departments.

For example, it gives me great pride to present the work of one OSU student, Bryan Wang, who did a summer internship at Bula Forge & Machine (www.bulaforge.com/). Figure 17.16(a) displays the VSM that he developed for a representative forging chosen from a part family identified using PFAST. On the map are posted different projects that he proposed to the forge shop's team tasked with doing a pilot implementation of Lean. The project "Example #2" was chosen for implementation and he guided the team throughout that kaizen. Figure 17.16(b) provides more details about the project plan that he developed for his internship. In addition to his internship work, Bryan also puts together a training program to give the forge shop's team an effective overview of Lean Thinking and teach them some of the core Lean tools that he thought they should all be able to use. Figure 17.17 provides some details about the contents of the lectures that he presented to them. See Bryan's video titled *A Program to Initiate Job Shop Lean at Bula Forge & Machine Inc.* that is posted online (*Source*: https://vimeo.com/91520874). If you would like to read the prize-winning paper titled *The Quick-Start Approach to Job Shop Lean: How to Initiate the Implementation of Lean in a High-Mix Low-Volume Manufacturing Facility* that he submitted for the Student Paper Competition organized by the Lean Division of the Institute of IEs. If you wish to receive a copy of his paper, please request it with an email to ShahrukhIrani1023@yahoo.com).

Develop a MOM (Move Our Money) mindset in all employees[10]: A machine shop should take pains to hire employees who have or will develop some of the following qualities: (i) They self-critique their work to find improvement

---

[9] PFAST helps to analyze and simplify the complex material flow network that exists in any job shop that desires to implement Lean. A job shop easily produces 100's, sometimes 1,000's, of components with different manufacturing routings. Different combinations of PFAST outputs are used to implement strategies to simplify the material flows, such as purchase of flexible automation, product mix segmentation, implementation of stand-alone cells, revision of manufacturing routings, rationalization of the product mix, etc.

[10] **FURTHER READING: (1)** Fisher, K. (2000). *Leading Self-Directed Work Teams: A Guide to Developing New Team Leadership Skills*. New York: McGraw-Hill. **(2)** Mann, D. (2014). *Creating a Lean Culture: Tools to Sustain Lean Conversions*. Boca Raton, FL: CRC Press.

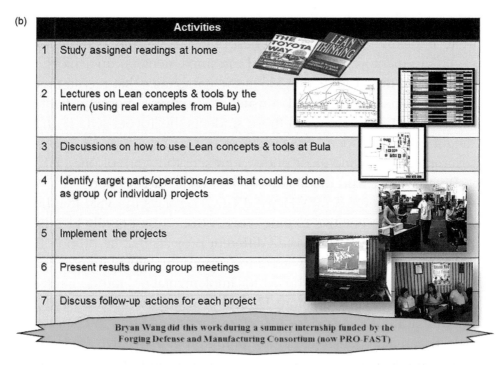

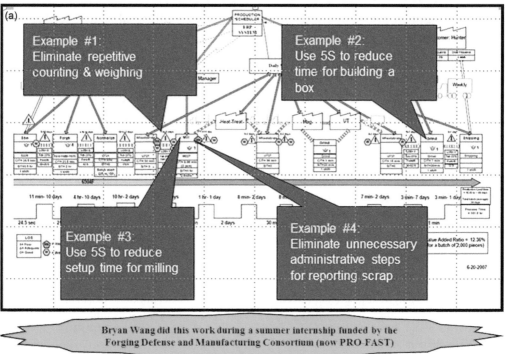

Figure 17.16 (a) Project work that the IE Intern did at Bula Forge & Machine. (b) Project plan for Bryan Wang's Job Shop Lean Internship.

With the intern from OSU as their Facilitator, a group of 10 employees from Bula Forge & Machine, Inc., including the President, Vice-President, Shop Managers, Sales Manager, and department heads of Scheduling, Human Resources, Purchasing, and Engineering, met for 1 hour per week for the first 8 weeks, and added 3 hours in the following 4 weeks.

- Readings of these books followed by discussion: **The Goal, Lean Thinking, The Toyota Way**
- Some additional readings ex. chapters from **Learning to See** and **Toyota Talent**

Bryan Wang did this work during a summer internship funded by the Forging Defense and Manufacturing Consortium (now PRO-FAST)

Figure 17.17   Lean training that the IE intern delivered at Bula Forge & Machine.

opportunities, (ii) they view every day at work as bringing new opportunities to eliminate waste, (iii) they are willing to be cross-trained to broaden their skill set, (iv) they are more team-oriented and less "me first" in their work ethic, and (v) they are self-learners, even if that means "burning the midnight oil", etc. For example, any employee who complains and reports a problem must provide a five Why's chart that captures their "thinking through" about that problem. This is not to say that they should have the solution from the get go. Rather, it is evidence of him/her having stepped back and done the thinking to drive subsequent problem-solving effort by a larger team that might be assigned that problem.

For example, in a recent client engagement, the Operations Manager of an aerospace MRO and I were on the shop floor on the first day of my visit. I observed that orders were piling up at the Pressure Test tank. But there was nobody at that station. In fact, that work center remained idle the entire day! When I arrived the next morning and noticed that the tank was not running yet the number of orders in queue had increased, I naturally asked the Operations Manager, "Where is the operator?" His reply was, "He called in sick". I shrugged my shoulders and returned to the office to continue work on designing their new $6 million facility. But I was not done! Just before lunch, I went back on the floor but this time saw one of the employees who had been doing Bench Work all along now connecting the pneumatic and water lines to test the first order in the Pressure Test tank. Clearly, that person was cross-trained but he had not been told (or did not see the need!) to stop doing Bench Work and move to the Pressure Test tank *until he was told to do so*. I told the GM and Operations Manager that they needed to work together to ingrain a MOM mindset into their workforce. They would not see employees change their behavior overnight! Rather, the Operations Manager would have to use situations such as this one to show employees how they can take the initiative to prevent delays that cause orders to miss shipment dates. Unfortunately, the training that employees in small and medium manufacturing companies get invariably teaches the standard Lean tools for Waste Elimination and Six Sigma tools for Variability Reduction for high-volume repetitive production! **Instead**, they ought to be taught Industrial Engineering methods for time management, problem-solving, job sequencing, reducing machine idle time, calculation of job lateness (or earliness) at the end of each shift, visual communication and reporting, etc.

Hire a qualified and experienced person to manage the Production Planning and Control department: Do you have someone heading the department who has the following credentials "Experienced Director Of Manufacturing with a demonstrated history of working in the manufacturing industry. Strong engineering professional skilled in Operations Management, Production Planning, SAP, Lean Manufacturing, and CI"? These credentials are not hypothetical! Paul Mittendorff, a friend and colleague of mine, has them on his resume. He led the implementation of an integrated system comprised an ERP system, FCS system, and MES at the company where I used to work (*Source*: www.lean-scheduling.com/LSI_Case_Studies_Hoerbiger.html). This integrated system was implemented using a combination of the Lean Tools in the left-hand column of Table 17.1, new tools to replace the tools in the right-hand column of Table 17.1, qualified and motivated people, software, technology, **and** support from the President of the company!

Flexibility: What a Lean Machine Shop Lacks

Lean mostly replicates the manufacturing and management practices of the TPS. Unfortunately, no machine shop operates like an automobile assembly line because no Toyota assembly line needs to be as flexible as a job shop. Not only does a machine shop need to eliminate waste but it must also possess flexibility in all aspects of its operations. Table 17.4 gives examples of some dimensions of flexibility that may, or may not, be possessed by a machine shop that implements Toyota-style Lean.

How to Use the Job Shop Lean Toolkit

Figure 17.4 shows how the Principles of Lean are the basis for a comprehensive approach to implementing Job Shop Lean using different tools in the Job Shop Lean Toolkit. The approach assumes that each Value Stream is a product family. The first four principles are the high-level steps to implement a line or cell or focused factory that will produce that product family. Then the fifth principle says to select the next product family and return to the first principle to start the implementation of the next line/cell/focused factory. Table 17.5 associates each of the tools in the Job Shop Lean toolkit with

Table 17.4   Types of Flexibility That a Job Shop Must Possess

Type of Flexibility	Description
Setup	Individual resources (machines, people, tools, etc.) can be rapidly changed over from producing one part to another
Process	Different combinations of resources (machines, people, tools, etc.) can process a variety of parts having different process requirements
Routing	At least two, maybe more, routings involving different combinations of machines can be used to make the same part
Mix	• The facility can simultaneously process a large variety of parts with different design specifications and process requirements • The facility has the capability to accommodate a significant number of new parts whose routings may not be identical to the existing ones
Volume	• The facility can accommodate high variability in the delivery quantities for the same, or different, parts ordered by customers • The facility can accommodate parts in different phases of their life cycle (prototype, ramp-up, production, end-of-life)
Facility	• The facility can be reconfigured quickly to accommodate changes in mix and/or volume • The facility has many mobile resources that can be relocated and repositioned on demand to accommodate changes in mix and/or volume

Table 17.5   Implementing the Lean Principles Using Job Shop Lean Best Practices

Principle of Lean	Job Shop Lean Best Practice that Implements the Principle
Principle #1: Specify value from the standpoint of the end customer by product family	• Develop an MOM mindset in all employees. • Segment the product mix. • Use Production Flow Analysis (if product routings are accurate) or Group Technology (if CAD drawings are accurate) to identify the product families in the product mix.
Principle #2: Identify all the steps in the value stream for each product family, eliminating whenever possible those steps that do not create value	• Identify the group of machines that will constitute the cell to produce each part family, including external resource requirements of that cell. • "Raze" and standardize the routings of all the parts within a part family.
Principle #3: Make the value-creating steps occur in tight sequence so the product will flow smoothly toward the customer	• If the shop currently has a Process Layout, split the shop into two shops. Next, implement a Hybrid Cellular Layout for the two-shop facility: (i) a Cellular Layout in the shop where the Runners and Repeaters in the product mix will be produced and (ii) a Process Layout in the shop where the Strangers in the product mix will be produced. • Right-size non-machining processes to absorb them into the cells. In addition, make all efforts to right-size and distribute, possibly mobilize, the Inspection department. • Maximize throughput in the Inspection department. • Purchase a multi-tasker that replaces two or more machines in a cell (or a flexible machining cell that replaces the entire multi-machine cell). In essence, try to reduce the total number of distinct physical workstations within a cell that are needed to perform all value-adding tasks to produce parts in the cell.
Principle #4: As flow is introduced, let customers pull value from the next upstream activity	• Instead of the Make-To-Stock approach for Pull Scheduling, use a Make-To-Order approach for Pull Scheduling. In essence, send a feasible daily schedule to each cell, external departments that support all the cells and vendors. • Utilize Water Spiders to manage all shop floor logistics related to executing the daily schedule. • Implement an MMS to maximize TEEP of those work centers that are the shop's bottleneck(s). • Utilize a combination of ERP, FCS, and MES to manage the entire factory using data analytics to support decision-making.

(Continued)

Table 17.5 (*Continued*)   Implementing the Lean Principles Using Job Shop Lean Best Practices

Principle of Lean	Job Shop Lean Best Practice that Implements the Principle
Principle #5: As value is specified, value streams are identified, wasted steps are removed, and flow and pull are introduced, begin the process again and continue it until a state of perfection is reached in which perfect value is created with no waste	• Become a machine shop that uses the data in its ERP system to support all kaizen events, morning huddles, and decision-making related to shop floor management. • Rationalize the product mix at the end of every year. • Ensure that the top floor, especially the COO, VP Operations, and Plant Manager, has "4H" leaders. • Create, nurture, and support an in-house CI team. • Hire a full-time IE to be the Lean Champion and leader of an in-house CI team. • Hire a qualified and experienced person to manage the Production Planning and Control department. • Establish an active internship program by partnering with the Industrial Engineering and Mechanical Engineering departments at a reputed university.

the specific Principle of Lean that it helps to implement in a machine shop and other similar HMLV manufacturing environments.

Conclusion

The TPS was designed for assembly plants that produce 100's of 1,000's of automobiles. Lean is based completely on the TPS. This chapter gives an overview of tools that have helped to implement Job Shop Lean in several small- and medium-size HMLV machine shops. A machine shop should not stop at implementing only the Lean Tools listed in the left-hand column of Table 17.1. Instead, machine shops and all other HMLV manufacturers need to think beyond the TPS and implement Job Shop Lean practices to realize the benefits that they have "still left on the table" by implementing only the Lean Tools. Which they could easily do by using the many new Industrial and Systems Engineering tools that could effectively replace the tools listed in the right-hand column of Table 17.1.

Appendices

Appendices for this chapter are available for download at https://www.crcpress.com/9781498740692

Bibliography

Danford, M. (2010, November). From Job Shop Chaos to Lean Order. *Modern Machine Shop*, 60–67. www.mmsonline.com/articles/from-job-shop-chaos-to-lean-order.

Gettleman, K. (1971, November). Organize Production for Parts: Not Processes. *Modern Machine Shop*, 50–60.

Irani, S.A. (2012a, August). Adapting Lean for High-Mix Low-Volume Manufacturing Facilities. *Gear Technology*, 10–12. www.geartechnology.com/issues/0812x/voices.pdf.

Irani, S.A. (2012b, October). A Quick-Start Approach for Implementing Lean in Jobshops. *Gear Technology*. www.geartechnology.com/issues/1012x/lean-job-shops.pdf.

Irani, S.A. (2017). Implementing JobshopLean. www.leanandflexible.com/implementing-jobshoplean/.

Chapter 18

How to Make a Custom Fabrication Shop Lean *and* Flexible

Acknowledgment

This chapter was inspired by Tim Heston, Senior Editor on the editorial staff of *The Fabricator*. Prior to our conversation regarding the scope of the article, I had presented a core suite of Job Shop Lean best practices for CNC (Computer Numerical Control) machine shops at the Top Shops 2017 Conference hosted by Modern Machine Shop in Indianapolis. The title of my presentation was *Job Shop Lean: How to Achieve Lean **and** Flexibility in Machine Shops*. Tim challenged me to write an article that explained how the Principles of Lean (*Source*: www.lean.org/WhatsLean/Principles. cfm) could be adapted in fabrication job shops and Make-To-Order custom fabrication facilities. Specifically, he asked me to explain how the different practices could be used to implement one or more of the (five) Principles of Lean. The article (Irani, S.A. (2018, August). Remaster the 5 Principles of Lean: How Custom Fabricators Could Focus on Flow, Not Waste. *The Fabricator*, 84–87. www.thefabricator.com/article/shopmanagement/remaster-the-5-principles-of-lean-manufacturing) that was published in The Fabricator is an abridged version of this chapter. Thank you, Tim!

Is *Any* Toyota Assembly Plant *Really* Lean?

Taiichi Ohno, the creator of the Toyota Production System (TPS), said, "The more inventory a company has, the less likely they will have what they need" (*Source*: www.toolshero.com/toolsheroes/taiichi-ohno/). Any Toyota assembly plant operates in a Make-To-Stock (MTS) production mode. This is unavoidable despite their having flexible multi-product assembly lines, level-loaded production of a variety of automobiles on each line, and high commonality of components across different automobile platforms. Recall that the Eight Forms of Waste are Transportation, Waiting, Overproduction, Overprocessing, Operator Motion, Scrap & Rework, Waiting, and Non-Utilized Employee Talent. If it were not for the 1,500[1] Toyota dealership lots spread across the US (*Source*: https://en.wikipedia.org/wiki/Toyota_Motor_Sales,_U.S.A.,_Inc.), one of those wastes – Overproduction aka FGI (Finished Good Inventory) – would exist in abundance at the end of every model year at each and every Toyota assembly plant! A significant number of the 100,000's of automobiles produced every year by each Toyota assembly plant are a sunk cost for Toyota's dealerships who must pay the carrying cost of inventory until they can get rid of them with end-of-year sales promotions.

Waste Elimination *Is Not* a Custom Fabricator's Top Priority

Will any custom fabricator produce a larger quantity of a product than the quantity a customer orders? Will any custom fabricator miss the delivery date that the customer specified? Will any custom fabricator prefer to fill that customer's order from FGI stored for months in their warehouse? I hope not! In the case of any custom fabricator, overproduction waste would eat up valuable capacity on bottleneck resources. In turn, that would waste capacity (machine hours, labor hours, and overtime), inventory (materials, consumables, tools, and end-of-year obsolescence costs), overhead (warehouse staff, electricity, gas, security), and supplier capacity (steel service centers, outside vendors, logistics providers). In turn, that prevents work being done on other jobs that could miss their delivery dates.

---

[1] *Source*: www.toyota.com/usa/operations/.

Minimizing Flow Times *Is* a Custom Fabricator's Top Priority

Taiichi Ohno, the creator of the TPS, said, "All we are doing is looking at the time line, from the moment the customer gives us an order to the point when we collect the cash. And we are reducing the time line by reducing the non-value adding wastes" (*Source*: www.toolshero.com/toolsheroes/taiichi-ohno/). Essentially what Mr. Ohno described is (i) the Flow Time (aka Cycle Time or Throughput Time) of an order (Flow Time = Shipment Date – Start Date) and (ii) the use of Waste Elimination as a strategy to reduce Flow Time. But, in the case of any custom fabricator, does their customer ask them to report how they eliminated waste in the Value Stream(s) of the product(s) they ordered? No! The customer pays their supplier for (i) Price, (ii) Quality, and (iii) On-Time Delivery (OTD) with little, if any, interest in how a supplier achieves those age-old metrics for customer service. The media hype about Lean has misled custom fabricators to focus on "How do we eliminate waste in our operations?" when they should be asking, "How do we improve OTD performance?".

Many Lean Tools *Will Not* Help Custom Fabricators Improve Their OTD Performance

Toyota began development of their famed TPS early in the 20th century. Unfortunately, since the publication of the book *The Machine That Changed the World* in 1990, Lean has misled Make-To-Order manufacturers into believing that waste elimination should be their topmost priority. Unlike Toyota, almost every custom fabricator operates in a Make-To-Order production mode. Even if custom fabricators, shipyards, construction companies, Maintenance, Repair, and Overhaul (MRO) service companies, etc. were 100% successful at implementing Lean, they will never be able to achieve world-class OTD performance beyond the current industry average of 85%–90%. Why? Because all that they will succeed at is implementing the Lean tools that are listed in the left-hand column of Table 18.1! Although those Lean tools will also work in a custom fabrication facility, it is the Lean tools listed in the right-hand column of Table 18.1 that will usually fail if implemented by any high-mix low-volume (HMLV) custom fabricator that seeks to achieve world-class OTD performance.

Table 18.1 Lean Tools That Should (and Should Not) Be Used by Custom Fabricators

Custom Fabricators Can Keep These Lean Tools in Their "Lean Toolkit"	*Custom Fabricators Must Eliminate These Lean Tools from Their "Lean Toolkit"*
Strategic planning	"The Toyota Way" mindset
Top-down leadership	Manual problem-solving sans data analytics
Gemba walks by managers	Value Stream Mapping
Employee engagement	One-piece flow cells
Workplace design with 6S	Product-specific Kanbans
Total productive maintenance (TPM)	FIFO sequencing of orders
Setup Reduction (SMED)	Pacemaker scheduling
Error-proofing (Poka-Yoke)	Inventory supermarkets
Quality at source	Work order release based on pitch
Visual workplace	Production planning using level loading
Product and process standardardization	Mixed model "Heijunka" scheduling
Multi-tasking (= flexible) machines	Right-sized (= inflexible) machines
Standard (but flexible!) work	OEM-style pull production
Continuous problem-solving	Manual scheduling

Assembly Line vs. Job Shop: A Case of *Totally* Different Production Systems

A job shop is the most complex and (almost!) unmanageable production system of all. Figure 18.1 provides the simplest evidence that trying to improve OTD performance of a job shop using tools designed to improve a repetitive assembly line's performance is like fitting a square peg into a round hole! Almost every custom fabricator's facility consists of two types of production systems:

1. The portion of the facility that produces all the components that go into multi-component weldments and/or the final product(s) is a job shop.
2. The portion of the facility that builds the final product(s) by assembling the weldments, components fabricated in-house and purchased

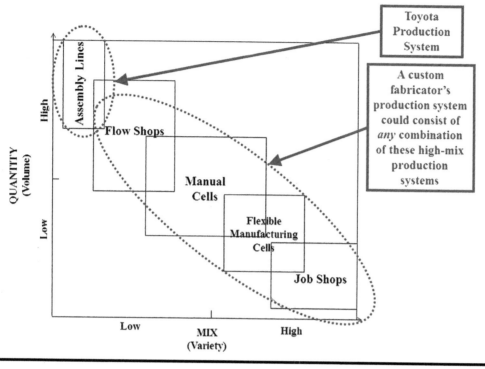

Figure 18.1 Comparison of an assembly plant and a custom fabricator.

components is a flow shop because, despite the high-product variety, the material flow tends to follow the same sequence of steps: Weld → Grind → Shot Blast → Paint → Inspect → Package → Ship.

Therefore, custom fabricators who desire to improve their OTD performance must quit relying on the "TPS" and design "*Their* Production System". But they could do this if and only if they replaced the tools in the right-hand column of Table 18.1 with more capable tools suitable for job shop-type manufacturing.

How Can Custom Fabricators Improve OTD Performance?

Custom fabricators should revisit the original principles of Lean. In their book (Womack, J.P. & Jones, D.T. (1996). *Lean Thinking: Banish Waste and Create Wealth in Your Corporation*. New York: Simon & Schuster), the authors present the Lean Principles which constitute a five-step thought process for guiding the implementation of Lean:

1. *Lean Principle #1:* Specify value from the standpoint of the end customer by product family.
2. *Lean Principle #2:* Identify all the steps in the value stream for each product family, eliminating whenever possible those steps that do not create value.
3. *Lean Principle #3:* Make the value-creating steps occur in tight sequence so the product will flow smoothly toward the customer.
4. *Lean Principle #4:* As flow is introduced, let customers pull value from the next upstream activity.
5. *Lean Principle #5:* As value is specified, value streams are identified, wasted steps are removed, and flow and pull are introduced, begin the process again, and continue it until a state of perfection is reached in which perfect value is created with no waste.

Unfortunately, the Lean Principles are "easy to remember, but not always easy to achieve" (*Source*: www.lean.org/WhatsLean/Principles.cfm). The assembly line, with its single-piece flow and FIFO (First In First Out) sequencing of products and zero pressure to build every order **exactly** to customer specifications (and due dates too!), is ideally suitable for implementing the Lean Principles. In stark contrast, the typical custom fabricator does not operate like an assembly plant. Being a job shop, a typical custom fabricator invariably operates in a batch-and-queue production mode. It is very hard to implement the Lean Principles to improve OTD performance in a custom fabrication job shop by adopting the practices of a low-mix high-volume repetitive production system! Instead, the better strategy would be to accept the fact that a job shop does not operate like an assembly line but implement the same principles using a different set of tools.

Why Lean Principles Are Hard for Custom Fabricators to Implement

Why Lean Principle #1 is hard for a custom fabricator to implement: In order to buffer against the risks of relying on just one or two customers, a custom fabricator chooses to serve customers in several sectors such as automotive, construction, mining, defense, aerospace, medical, etc. Sadly, that does not guarantee customer loyalty. Nor does it produce a predictable mix and arrival rate of orders! In particular, automotive OEMs (Original Equipment Manufacturers) have a reputation for shopping around and pitting one supplier against another to get a better price. And, if having to satisfy a diverse customer base were not enough, a custom fabricator must deal with the tendency for their product mix to alter. This happens when they hire new sales and marketing staff who tap their past business contacts from new industry sectors. In addition to their customers, custom fabricators must handle production instabilities and variability in flow times because they have to deal with their raw material suppliers, outside vendors, equipment suppliers, etc.

Unlike an OEM like Toyota, a custom fabricator does not have clout with its customers. In order to deliver value to its many customers, it must contend with a spectrum of expectations on even the standard metrics of Quality, Cost, and Delivery. Take the metric of OTD! Just about any custom fabricator will admit that it is a challenge to be 100% on time and meet the due dates set by all of their customers. Simply because it is considerably harder to plan production and schedule operations in a job shop than in an assembly plant.

Demand variability in a custom fabricator tends to be high. Few customers agree to the LTA (Long Term Agreements) that are the basis for Pull Production, Level Loading, Mixed Model Production, etc. For any product in a custom fabricator's product mix, (i) the annual demand for the product could be low, medium, or high and (ii) the frequency with which that product is ordered during the year could be low, medium, or high. Due to differences in Volume, Margin, and Demand Pattern, the product mix of a custom fabricator usually consists of three competing segments – Runners, Repeaters, and Strangers. The **same** shop using the **same** production system and the **same** business strategy will be hard-pressed to guarantee OTD for all orders received for products that belong in three different segments.

Why Lean Principle #2 is hard for a custom fabricator to implement: A Value Stream is a product family. Unfortunately, the product families in the product mix of every custom fabricator are not obvious. A custom fabricator fulfills orders for a diverse mix of 100's of different products whose manufacturing routings involve different combinations of machines visited in different sequences. In addition, these routings could differ significantly in their equipment requirements, setup times, cycle times, lot sizes, inspection requirements, vendor operations, etc. It is rare that a custom fabricator will clearly know all their Value Streams because identifying the product families in their (large) product mix remains a daunting computational challenge to this day. Cluster Analysis surely cannot be done using a manual method like Value Stream Mapping! And, despite the availability of commercial statistical analysis software, there are still no robust methods and standard criteria to find clear-cut clusters of products in the product mix of a custom fabricator. Not to mention that the ERP systems of most custom fabricators are notoriously poor at yielding the data that is needed for the statistical analysis tools to do their job!

Why Lean Principle #3 is hard for a custom fabricator to implement: The flow of a product is smooth if and only if all the steps in its routing are performed in sequence on consecutive workstations located in close proximity to each other. Such flow is possible only on an assembly line that produces a very limited range of highly similar products. The limited number of products and high product similarity are among the key reasons why the assembly line is far easier to optimize than a custom fabricator's job shop. Figure 18.9(a) will show the production flow in a Make-To-Order fabrication facility that builds the industrial scales used to weigh the eighteen wheelers that ply the Interstate highways in the US. Not a single Toyota assembly plant will display the crisscross material flow paths as shown in Figure 18.9(a).[2] The chaotic material flow is guaranteed to occur in the typical custom fabricator's facility because that facility will probably have a Process Layout. In this layout, machines with similar/identical capabilities are co-located in functional departments such as Cutting, Bending, Rolling, Machining, Punching, Blanking, Stamping, Deburring, Welding, Painting, Inspection, Assembly, etc. No facility with a Process Layout can expect the value-creating steps in any of its Value Streams to flow smoothly towards the customer! A Process Layout is what causes the batch-and-queue production that the TPS eschews. A Process Layout encourages a "silo mentality" among its many departments because each department tries to maximize their machine and labor utilization. Trying to improve OTD performance with a Process Layout is like searching for the Holy Grail!

Any custom fabricator that wants to drastically improve OTD performance should change the layout of their manufacturing facility from a Process Layout to a Cellular Layout. The impact on the Flow Time of just about any order they produce would reduce drastically! In contrast to a Process Layout, every manufacturing cell in a Cellular Layout (i) has a Value Stream focus (its product family), (ii) has the flexibility to produce any product in the product

---

[2] This Spaghetti Diagram was generated using the Sgetti app for material flow analysis (www.SGETTI.com).

family, (iii) promotes a culture of teamwork, (iv) ensures that every member of the cell's team is accountable to each other and to management, and (v) gives every member of the cell's team a sense of ownership for the end products that they produce for different customers.

Why Lean Principle #4 is hard for a custom fabricator to implement: Pull Scheduling is feasible in any repetitive assembly facility. But it will not work in a Make-To-Order custom fabrication job shop where there is no guarantee for a repeat order for a batch of parts that was just shipped. Production schedules in a custom fabrication facility are driven by due dates. It is hard to negotiate due dates with most customers. Due dates are subject to change. Orders from different customers could be due on the same day because different customers wish to follow *their* production schedules which are based on *their* customers' needs. As if that is not challenging enough, the daily mix of active products seen in the custom fabricator's shop is bound to change from one day to the next day!

Production control and scheduling in **any** job shop is complex. Lead times and delivery dates quoted to customers have to be based on the knowledge of the daily (or weekly) production schedule. Shop bottlenecks can shift over time. Finite capacity constraints limit how many orders can be completed on any given machine on any given day. It is hard to control the delivery schedule and quality of parts sent to (and received from) suppliers. However, the ultimate "stake in the heart" for just about every custom fabricator is their reliance on an ERP (Enterprise Resource Planning) system. Typically, an ERP system uses Material Requirements Planning (MRP) to schedule production. MRP **cannot** do Production Planning and Operations Scheduling because it assumes that capacity is infinite and lead times are fixed. MRP seeks to maximize machine utilization at all work centers, regardless of whether they are bottlenecks or otherwise. MRP assumes that the shop layout is a Process Layout with all identical/similar machines grouped into a single pool. MRP ignores the benefits of using Lean tools that actually help to free up wasted capacity on bottleneck work centers and speed the flow of any order per the sequence of operations in its routing, such as Setup Reduction, Transfer Batch Flow, Error-Proofing, Inspection at Source, etc.

Why Lean Principle #5 is hard for a custom fabricator to implement: Management and culture in a small and medium-sized manufacturing organization are almost completely driven by the personality of the President/ Owner. Also, unlike any OEM like Toyota, a custom fabricator has limited resources for workforce training. In fact, a custom fabricator has to compete against OEMs when they try to recruit and retain talented employees with a strong work ethic, a desire to learn on the job, and interest in being cross-trained to operate different machines. Unfortunately, even though a change to a Cellular Layout has significant benefits, the autonomy that is bred by the working environment of a manufacturing cell could lead to HR nightmares like fallouts among team members, insubordination, go-slow strikes, pay disputes due to multi-skilling, etc. Not every individual likes to (or even wishes to) be cross-trained! Besides, if a cell uses a diverse mix of equipment from different manufacturers, it could make operator training, equipment maintenance, etc. in the cell more challenging than if those same people were working on an assembly line.

Job Shop Lean: How to Implement the Lean Principles in Job Shops

For custom fabricators to achieve world-class OTD performance, they should adopt practices that consider (i) the variety of products that they wish to produce for their customers, (ii) the variability in demand volumes, (iii) the different due dates that their customers set, and (iv) the delivery and quality shortcomings of their suppliers, etc. This can only be done by replacing the Lean tools in the right-hand column of Table 18.1 with tools that would work in job shops and other HMLV manufacturing environments. And that is essentially what Job Shop Lean does simply by implementing the processes, systems, and software used by any Industrial Engineer (IE) who does Work Study & Methods Analysis, Manufacturing Systems Analysis, Supply Chain Management, Production Planning & Inventory Control, Facilities Planning, Material Handling & Factory Logistics, Operations Scheduling, Warehouse Design, Safety Engineering, etc.[3]

Design for Flow: The Foundation of Job Shop Lean

Job Shop Lean is an approach to implement Lean in job shops and other HMLV manufacturing environments that is (i) based upon the Lean Principles, but (ii) focuses on Flow (**NOT** elimination of waste).

---

[3] **FURTHER READING: (1)** Irani, S.A. (2011, February). Continuous Improvement: No One Solution for All. *The Fabricator*, 44–45. **(2)** Irani, S.A. (2012, April). Thinking beyond Lean: 5 Tips for Continuous Improvement. *The Fabricator*, 46–47.

Kiyoshi Suzaki, who consulted for Toyota, has an entire chapter on Flow (Chapter 4 *Developing Flow on the Production Floor*) in his book (Suzaki, K. (1988). *The New Manufacturing Challenge: Techniques for Continuous Improvement*. New York: The Free Press.). Quoting from his book "The importance of factory layout has not been addressed in spite of the significant waste often associated with badly planned layouts. The impact on a company's performance from improving the layout can be substantial. Flow refers to the movement of material through the plant. It assumes that material will not be stagnant at any point in time from the receiving of raw material to the shipping of finished products. Problems such as a process-oriented layout (Functional Layout), line imbalance, machine breakdowns, long setup or tool-change time, machine breakdown, quality problems, and labor absenteeism cause interruptions that disrupt a steady flow of production in a factory".

Therefore, if any custom fabricator expresses interest in implementing Job Shop Lean, the first question I ask them is, "Are you prepared to invest in redesigning and changing your factory layout to the extent that can be financially justified?" In my entire career spanning 22 years in academia and 5+ years in industry, I have never visited or worked with a single job shop or any other HMLV manufacturer that had an efficient and effective factory layout whose design was based on the principles of Design For Flow. This is not an exaggeration! The factory layout, the product mix, the new machines that are purchased, the ERP system – every aspect of a production system **must** be designed for Flow! In the absence of Flow, no custom fabricator will ever achieve the short Flow Times that are a must for world-class OTD performance.

Prerequisites for Any Custom Fabricator Seeking to Implement the Principles of Lean

Change the metrics that drive CI efforts by focusing on OTD performance: Quality, Cost, and Delivery remain important to this day as the primary drivers for customer service. Unfortunately, although any custom fabricator may have a genuine desire to achieve world-class OTD performance, they tend to be led by "old school" executives whose mindset is still driven by efficiency, utilization, and productivity. That mindset must change! And the best way to do it is to introduce more granularity and guidance on how to improve OTD performance without relying on crutches like buying more machines, adding shifts, overtime, expediting, "delivery date creep", etc. Some of the metrics that correlate with actions taken to improve OTD performance are Orders Shipped Late ($), Overtime to Meet End-of-Month Shipping Target, Tardiness (= Actual Ship Date – Original Promise Date) for Orders Shipped Every Week, $ Earned Per Employee, etc. In fact, if the President/CEO of a custom fabricator answers just these three questions below, then I can assess whether their claims of ≈100% OTD performance are coming at an undisclosed (but high!) cost:

1. *Question 1*: Do you determine a start date for any order using the standard method of (Customer Ship Date – Average Lead Time)?
2. *Question 2*: Do you rely on your ERP to schedule your in-house operations and suppliers?
3. *Question 3*: Do you check current schedule status and workload on bottlenecks before you commit to a ship date for a new order?

The Chief Executive Officer, Vice President of Operations, and Plant Manager should be "4H" leaders: Every executive and manager on the "top floor" needs to demonstrate 4H (Head, Heart, Hands, and Hooves) leadership qualities: (i) They strive to participate in key Continuous Improvement (CI) projects; (ii) they engage with their employees as and when their schedule permits; (iii) they have a working knowledge of Theory Of Constraints (TOC), Lean, and Six Sigma; (iv) they are adept at risk management under uncertainty; (v) they insist that processes and systems be developed for "efficient firefighting"; and (vi) they do not hesitate to explore cooperative partnerships with competitors, etc. Sadly, most of these individuals take a hands-off attitude and entrust the implementation of Lean to the consultant they hired. Big mistake! Not only should these executives participate in the day-to-day efforts of the workforce and CI team tasked with the Lean implementation, but also they should demonstrate commitment. What should these key individuals do to ensure the success of a Lean implementation? For starters, gemba walks, a monthly town hall meeting, and frequent "Attaboy, keep it up!" recognition of employees.

For example, in a recent client engagement with an aerospace MRO, the General Manager walked out to the floor to expedite a late job. He spoke curtly to the Operations Manager, "This job has to ship tonight. Okay?" and returned to his office. One can be sure that everybody from the Operations Manager down to the Shipping Clerk dropped everything that they were doing for the rest of the day to get that job shipped by COB (Close Of Business) that day! Now how would a 4H (Head, Heart, Hands, and Hooves) leader have done it differently? He would have called a meeting the next day of the same team that worked to get that late job shipped and brainstormed with them. The goal of that brainstorming session would be to create two diagrams: (i) an Ishikawa Diagram to document all the reasons (potential and actual) why that job fell through the cracks and (ii) a Tree Diagram to determine all the actions that would have to be taken to eliminate most of those causes once for all. Taiichi Ohno, the creator of the TPS, considered every problem to be an opportunity! A leader is constructive (never destructive!) and proactive in how he/she deals with their subordinates.[4]

Hire a qualified and experienced person to manage the Production Planning and Control department: I will assume that the Production Planning and Control department oversees shop scheduling, shop floor control, and all other related functions. This department should be headed by someone with credentials that may look as follows: *Experienced Director of Manufacturing with a demonstrated history of working in the manufacturing industry. Strong engineering professional skilled in Operations Management, Production Planning, SAP, Lean Manufacturing, and CI.* These credentials are not hypothetical! They are on the resume of Paul Mittendorff, a friend and colleague of mine, who is the Director of Manufacturing Systems at Hoerbiger Corporation of America. He led the implementation of an integrated system composed of an ERP system, FCS (Finite Capacity Scheduling) system, and MES (Manufacturing Execution System) at the company where I used to work (*Source*: www.lean-scheduling.com/LSI_Case_Studies_ Hoerbiger.html). World-class OTD performance **can** be achieved using a combination of the Lean Tools in the left-hand column of Table 18.1; new tools to replace the tools in the right-hand column of Table 18.1; people, software, technology, and support from the President of the company!

---

[4] **FURTHER READING: (1)** Byrne, A. (2013). *The Lean Turnaround: How Business Leaders Use Lean Principles to Create Value and Transform Their Company.* New York: McGraw-Hill. **(2)** Koenigsaecker, G. (2013). *Leading the Lean Enterprise Transformation.* Boca Raton, FL: CRC Press. **(3)** Byrne, A. (2016). *The Lean Turnaround Action Guide: How to Implement Lean, Create Value and Grow Your People.* New York: McGraw-Hill. **(4)** Emiliani, B., Stec, D., Grasso, L. & Stodder, J. (2007). *Better Thinking, Better Results: Case Study and Analysis of an Enterprise-Wide Lean Transformation.* Wethersfield, CT: The Center for Lean Business Management. **(5)** Lancaster, J. & Adams, E. 2017. *The Work of Management: A Daily Path to Sustainable Improvement.* Boston, MA: Lean Enterprise Institute, Inc. **(6)** Harada, T. (2015). *Management Lessons from Taiichi Ohno: What Every Leader Can Learn from the Man Who Invented the Toyota Production System.* New York: McGraw-Hill.

Table 18.2   The "First Pass" of Tools Used to Implement Job Shop Lean

Waste Elimination	Work Simplification	Facility Layout
Material handling analysis	Cellular manufacturing	GT
Storage systems	Workstation design	Visual management
Process standardization (standard work)	Bottleneck equipment utilization	• Production planning • Capacity requirements analysis • Operations scheduling • Shop floor control • Order progress tracking • etc.
Flexible automation	Setup reduction	Product mix segmentation
Variety reduction	• Factory logistics • Water spiders • Mobile communications	Information flow analysis

Hire a full-time IE to fill the position of Lean Champion[5]: The IE will create, lead, and sustain an in-house team dedicated to CI. Table 18.2 presents the "first pass" of tools that I typically use for implementing Job Shop Lean in any HMLV manufacturing facility. An experienced IE can easily master and enhance the methods and tools used to implement any of the buzzword CI strategies like Lean, TOC, Six Sigma, Operational Excellence, etc.

Develop a MOM (Move Our Money) mindset in all employees[6]: *A custom fabricator should take pains to hire employees who have or will develop some of the following qualities: (i) They self-critique their work to find improvement opportunities, (ii) they view every day at work as bringing new opportunities to eliminate waste, (iii) they are willing to be cross-trained to broaden their skill set, (iv) they are more team-oriented and* less *"me first" in their work ethic, and (v) they are self-learners, even if that means "burning the midnight oil", etc. Thereby, any employee who complains and reports a problem must provide a five Why's chart that is proof that he/she took pains to think*

[5] **FURTHER READING: (1)** Irani, S.A. (2013, January/February). The Idea Factory. *Gear Technology*, 26–29. **(2)** Irani, S.A. (2013, May). The Tiger Team: Hear Them Roar. *Gear Technology*, 36–42. **(3)** Irani, S.A. (2013, November/December). Educating the Workforce and Management about FLEAN (Flexible and Lean) Manufacturing Cells. *Gear Technology*, 82–92.

[6] **FURTHER READING: (1)** Fisher, K. (2000). *Leading Self-Directed Work Teams: A Guide to Developing New Team Leadership Skills*. New York: McGraw-Hill. **(2)** Mann, D. (2014). *Creating a Lean Culture: Tools to Sustain Lean Conversions*. Boca Raton, FL: CRC Press.

through the problem before reporting it (instead of just complaining about it). This is not to say that they should have the solution from the get go. Rather, he/she should present evidence of him/her having stepped back and done the groundwork that will support subsequent problem-solving effort by a larger team that might undertake to solve that problem with him/her.

For example, in a recent client engagement, the Operations Manager of an aerospace MRO and I were on the shop floor on the first day of my visit. I observed that orders were piling up at the Pressure Test tank. But there was nobody at that station. In fact, that work center remained idle the entire day! When I arrived the next morning and noticed that the number of orders in queue had increased yet the tank was not running, I naturally asked the Operations Manager, "Where is the operator?" His reply was, "He called in sick". I shrugged my shoulders and returned to the office to continue work on designing their new $6 million facility. But I was not done! Just before lunch, I went back on the floor but this time saw one of the employees who had been doing Bench Work earlier in the day now connecting the pneumatic and water lines to test the first order in the queue at a Pressure Test tank. Clearly, that person was cross-trained but he had not seen the need to stop doing Bench Work and move to the Pressure Test tank *until he was told to do so.* For OTD performance to improve, the General Manager and Operations Manager are responsible for ingraining an MOM mindset into their employees. They will not see employees change their behavior overnight! Rather, the Operations Manager would have to use situations such as this one to show employees how they can take the initiative to prevent delays that cause orders to miss shipment dates. **Unfortunately**, the employees in small and medium manufacturing companies that operate like job shops invariably are taught the standard Lean tools and Six Sigma tools for high-volume repetitive production! **Instead**, they ought to be taught TOC and Industrial Engineering methods for time management, problem-solving, job sequencing, calculation of job lateness (or earliness) at the end of each shift, visual communication, progress reporting, etc.

Improve the data in the ERP system in order to conduct the analyses that must be done to support good decision-making[7]: The basic requirement for an effective ERP system is that it must support managers in every department

---

[7] **FURTHER READING: (1)** Plaskett, E. (2018, December). Turning the Page on the Paper Workplace. *Modern Machine Shop*, 56–58. **(2)** Dixon, D. (2004, June). The Truce between Lean and I.T. *Industrial Engineer*, 42–45. **(3)** Sleger, G. (2018, December). MRP Made Easy. *The Fabricator*, 40–43. **(4)** Heston, T. (2017, May). Taming the Chaos: How One Fabricator Built a Truly Scalable Business Model. *The Fabricator*, 48–50. **(5)** Davis, D. (2017, March). Punch Up Your Production: How Having the Right Data Helps Fabricators Boost Overall Throughput. *The Fabricator*, 76–78.

in the entire organization, such as Design & Engineering, Estimation and Quotation, Plant Management, Purchasing, Sales, Shipping/Receiving, Quality Assurance, Production Control & Scheduling, Supply Chain, etc. Any custom fabricator's ERP system should perform at least three functions:

1. Collect, organize, and process data to produce and disseminate reports that support decision-making: For example, during a Current State Assessment to determine if Job Shop Lean was a good fit for their manufacturing operations, the General Manager of Operations in the Tooling Division of a bending equipment manufacturer mined data in their ERP system. He wanted to compare Actual Lead Time vs. Quoted Lead Time for orders received in the two segments of their machine shop's product mix – Repeat and Engineer-To-Order. He produced the two data plots in Figures 18.2(a) and (b). With reference to both figures, if any order falls on the straight line, then the Actual Lead Time = Quoted Lead Time for that order. These two plots helped the management team to quickly recognize that they were doing poorly on OTD performance partly because they were consistently offering their customers shorter Lead Times than they were actually capable of achieving!

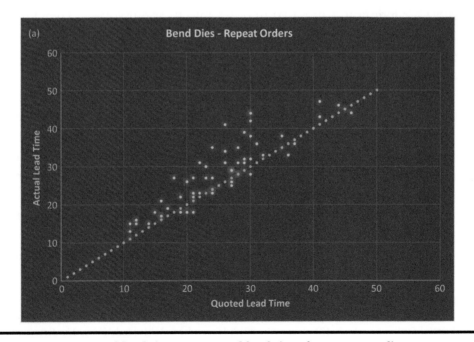

Figure 18.2 **(a) Actual lead time vs. quoted lead time for repeat tooling requests.**

(Continued)

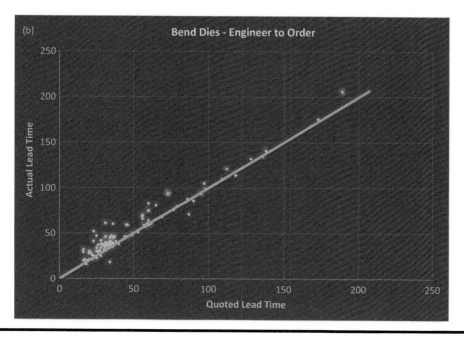

Figure 18.2 (CONTINUED) **(b) Actual lead time vs. quoted lead time for Engineer-To-Order tooling requests.**

2. Utilize that data to support the execution of large-scale CI projects: For example, an MRO fabricator that specializes in "maintenance and repair of engines, Auxiliary Power Units (APU), and airframe systems such as environmental controls, cooling systems, starter ducts, bleed air ducting, and other aircraft pneumatic ducting" was planning to build a new $6 million facility. They wanted help to design the layout for this new facility using the PFAST (Production Flow Analysis and Simplification Toolkit) software. I sent them a PFAST Input File for another project and asked if they could provide me the same data for their operations. By the close of business that day, they had pulled the data from their ERP system and populated the PFAST Input File using which I produced the PFAST Analysis Report for them!

3. Interface with third-party applications that utilize that data: For example, Figures 18.3(a) and (b) display the variety of ductwork up to a ten gauge sheet thickness that is fabricated by a sheet metal shop that builds Heating, Ventilating, and Air Conditioning (HVAC) systems installed in commercial and industrial buildings. Depending on the ductwork layout for an entire floor (or part of a floor) of a building, each type of ductwork has to be produced in different quantities in

(a)

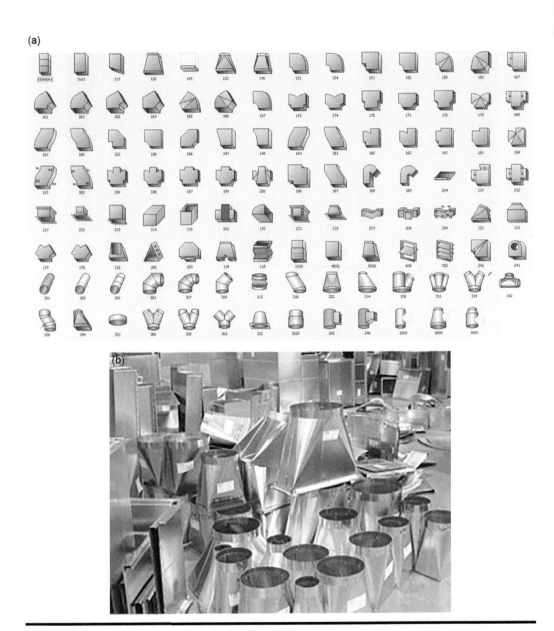

Figure 18.3   (a) CAD drawings of various types of ductwork produced in Atlantic Constructors Inc. sheet metal shop. (b) Pictures of various types of ductwork produced in ACI's sheet metal shop.

combination with matching quantities of other types of ductwork. This sheet metal fabricator has integrated their ERP system with their CAD (Computer-Aided Design) system with a commercial nesting engine to create optimal nests of the blanks that are cut on their Plasma Cutters. Their integrated software suite ensures that the different blanks needed to build a batch of a certain type of ductwork are nested on the same sheet (or consecutive sheets) fed to their Plasma Cutter. As soon as the blanks are shaken loose from the sheet skeleton coming off the Plasma Cutter, the machine operator collects all of the blanks that constitute a kit and places them on one of several "kit-carts". Depending on the type of ductwork, each cart is rolled to the appropriate workstation where the next operation will be performed to produce that type of ductwork. To assist operators at subsequent machines collect all the parts in a kit, the ERP System prints a bar code label for each blank, including a graphic for the ductwork and how the blank will fit on it. The visualization combined with other product identification data on the label was so effective that even I was able to identify and match all the blanks for a batch of one type of ductwork!

Strategies to Improve OTD Performance Using Lean Principle #1

Implement Group Technology (GT) to standardize and codify decision-making at every step in the Value Stream for a fabricated product[8]: "GT is an approach to manufacturing that seeks to maximize production efficiencies by grouping similar and recurring problems or tasks… An important part of GT is the use of a code that, like a library reference system, serves as an index to characteristics in manufacturing, engineering, purchasing, resource planning, and sales to improve productivity in each of these areas." (*Source*: https://hbr. org/1984/07/group-technology-and-productivity) Correct and comprehensive use of GT will mitigate the impact of high variety on production delays that inflate Flow Time. Production delays are bound to happen when there are significant differences in product BOMs, manufacturing routings, material attributes, tooling, gauges, employee skills, etc. of the orders in-process on the shop floor. Some examples of the time-tested applications of GT are:

1. Product Mix Rationalization to eliminate those products in the product mix that are unprofitable based on the analysis of order history for all customers, especially in the Strangers segment.

---

[8] **FURTHER READING: (1)** Gallagher, C.C. & Knight, W.A. (1987). *Group Technology Production Methods in Manufacturing*. Ellis Horwood. **(2)** Colman, R. (2018, August). First Responders Look to Pick Up Speed: New Paradigm Laser Aims to Improve Quoting Turnaround and Part Delivery Times to Drive Business Growth. *The Fabricator*, 98–99.

2. Variant Process Planning to exploit the commonality between past order(s) and a new order in order to reduce the time taken to produce quotes, CAD files, CNC programs, routings, inspection plans, etc. for the new order. For example, the quoting and estimating software tools like SecturaFab® Quoting (https://secturasoft.com/) or the parts nesting software tool like SigmaNest (www.sigmanest.com/products/sigmanest/) demonstrate that the concept and methods of GT have taken root in the fabrication industry.

3. Value Engineering (aka Variety Reduction or Design For Manufacture (DFM)) to eliminate the root causes for the Eight Forms of Waste. Waste is a symptom not a cause. No custom fabricator should make Waste Elimination a strategy for improving OTD performance! (*Source*: http://news.ewmfg.com/blog/what-is-value-engineering).

Segment the product mix into Runners, Repeaters, and Strangers[9]: Any custom fabricator will make a diverse range of products that differ in their annual production volume, demand pattern, and margin. Based on these three business attributes, a custom fabricator should divide and separate their product mix into two segments – (Runners + Repeaters) and (Strangers). For parts in the (Runners + Repeaters) segment, batch sizes will tend to be medium or large with many parts having LTA. In contrast, for parts in the (Strangers) segment, batch sizes will tend to be small because orders for these parts will be Hot/Rush one-offs, repair, prototype, start-of-lifecycle, or end-of-lifecycle. In practice, if a custom fabricator segments their product mix using PQ$ Analysis (P = Products, Q = Annual Production Volume for each product, $ = Annual Revenue Earnings for each product), the segmentation will position each of their products in one of four quadrants: (i) (High Quantity, High Revenue), (ii) (Low Quantity, High Revenue), (iii) (Low Quantity, Low Revenue), and (iv) (High Quantity, Low Revenue).

---

[9] **FURTHER READING: (1)** Heston, T. (2017, March). In Defense of Diversification: How a Defense Fabricator Was Born. *The Fabricator*, 68–70. **(2)** Irani, S.A. (2011, June). Analyzing Products, Demands, Margins and Routings. *The Fabricator*, 42. **(3)** Irani, S.A. (2011, August). Analyzing Product Mix and Volumes: Useful but Insufficient. *The Fabricator*, 36–37. **(4)** Irani, S.A. (2011, October). Minding your P's, Q's, R's – and Revenue too. *The Fabricator*, 64–67. **(5)** Irani, S.A. (2011, December). PQ$ Analysis: Why Revenue Matters in Product Mix Segmentation. *The Fabricator*, 42–44. **(6)** Irani, S.A. (2012, February). Why a Timeline Analysis of Order History Matters. *The Fabricator*, 48–49. **(7)** Heston, T. (2015, November). *How SWOT and Lean Go Together. The Fabricator*, 94–96.

The custom fabricator should use different strategies to fill orders for products in each segment as follows:

1. The parts in the (High Quantity, High Revenue) segment could be produced using standard practices of the TPS.
2. The parts in the (High Quantity, Low Revenue) segment could be produced using a two-bin Kanban system.
3. The parts in the (Low Quantity, High Revenue) segment could be produced using a strict Make-To-Order policy with stringent Quality Control to prevent scrap. The best skilled employees and most productive machines would be used to produce orders for those parts. Setup times should be reduced so these machines could be changed "on a dime". Even overtime should be viewed as a "necessary evil" in order to quote aggressive delivery dates to win orders for these parts.
4. The parts in the (Low Quantity, Low Revenue) segment would be targeted for elimination. But, if the customers who order those parts are also ordering parts in any of the other segments, then the low (or no) margins earned from filling orders for parts in this segment may just have to be tolerated. Or perhaps prices and delivery dates could be negotiated to mitigate the sunk cost on orders for these parts?

Group the parts (or products) into families based on similar/identical routings: If the manufacturing routings of the products are accurate, do a Product-Process Matrix Analysis of the products included in the Runners and Repeaters segment to group the parts (or products) into families based on similar/identical routings. Similarly, do another (separate) analysis to find the part families in the Strangers segment. Figure 18.4(a) shows what the initial matrix for the product mix may look like. Figure 18.4(b) shows the final matrix after the initial matrix was analyzed using PFAST to group parts that used the same (or almost the same) set of machines into a part family. Figure 18.4(b) can be the starting point for an enterprise-wide campaign to improve Flow using the spectrum of improvement strategies that are described later in Tables 18.3(a) and (b).

For example, the sheet metal fabricator whose products are shown in Figures 18.3(a) and b sought to improve the layout of their shop after they are shown in Figure 18.5. The figure shows the material flow paths of a representative sample of different types of ductwork produced frequently in their shop.

(a)

	m1	m2	m3	m4	m5	m6	m7	m8	m9	m10	m11	m12
Part 1	1			1				1	1			
Part 2	1			1			1	1				
Part 3	1	1		1			1	1	1			
Part 4	1				1		1		1			
Part 5	1					1	1		1	1		
Part 6						1	1	1	1	1		
Part 7				1			1	1	1			
Part 8		1	1	1	1		1	1	1			
Part 9			1	1	1		1	1	1			
Part 10				1			1	1				
Part 11							1					
Part 12							1				1	1
Part 13											1	1
Part 14							1			1	1	
Part 15	1						1			1	1	1
Part 16	1						1			1	1	1
Part 17							1				1	1
Part 18						1	1			1		
Part 19												1

(b)

	Machines in Cell #1								Machines in Cell #2			
	m2	m3	m5	m4	m8	m9	m6	m1	m7	m10	m11	m12
Part 8	1	1	1	1	1	1	1					
Part 9		1	1	1	1	1	1					
Part 7			1	1	1	1						
Part 1				1	1	1		1				
Part 3	1			1	1	1		1	1			
Part 4				1		1		1	1			
Part 2		1		1	1			1	1			
Part 10				1	1				1			
Part 5						1	1	1	1	1		
Part 6					1	1	1		1	1		
Part 18							1		1	1		
Part 11							1					
Part 14									1	1	1	
Part 15								1	1	1	1	1
Part 16								1	1	1	1	1
Part 12									1		1	1
Part 17									1		1	1
Part 13											1	1
Part 19												1

Products in Cell #1: Part 8, Part 9, Part 7, Part 1, Part 3, Part 4, Part 2, Part 10, Part 5, Part 6

Products in Cell #2: Part 18, Part 11, Part 14, Part 15, Part 16, Part 12, Part 17, Part 13, Part 19

CELL 1

CELL 2

Machines shared by the two cells that could result in machine duplication or exception operations

Figure 18.4 (a) Initial product-process matrix before cluster analysis to identify part families. (b) Final product-process matrix after cluster analysis to identify part families.

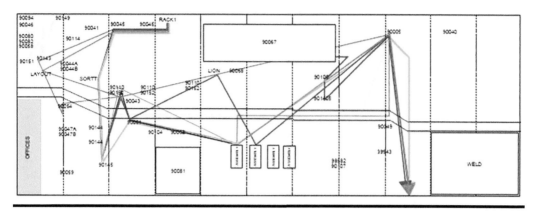

Figure 18.5   Current state of production flow in the sheet metal fabrication shop.

Figure 18.6(a) shows each and every component in the BOM (Bills Of Material) to build a particular type of ductwork that was entered into the PARTS spreadsheet in the PFAST Input File. Figure 18.6(b) lists all the work centers in the layout of the sheet metal shop that is shown in Figure 18.5 that was entered into the WORK CENTERS spreadsheet in the PFAST Input File.

(a)

Part No	Description	Annual Quantity	Revenue
TF-TRA-1	TDC Reducer Top	383	383
TF-TRA-2	TDC Reducer Bottom	383	383
TF-TRA-3	TDC Reducer Right	383	383
TF-TRA-4	TDC Reducer Left	383	383
SF-TRA-1	S/D Reducer Top	296	296
SF-TRA-2	S/D Reducer Bottom	296	296
SF-TRA-3	S/D Reducer Right	296	296
SF-TRA-4	S/D Reducer Left	296	296
TS-NCL-1	TDC Non-Coil Line Straight Duct Top	1	1
TS-NCL-2	TDC Non-Coil Line Straight Duct Bottom	1	1
SS-NCL-1	S/D Non-Coil Line Straight Duct Top	1	1
SS-NCL-2	S/D Non-Coil Line Straight Duct Bottom	1	1
TS-CL-1	TDC Coil Line Straight Duct Top	2245	2245
SS-CL-1	S/D Coil Line Straight Duct Top	1314	1314
TF-90E-1	TDC 90 deg Elbow Top	238	238
TF-90E-2	TDC 90 deg Elbow Bottom	238	238
TF-90E-3	TDC 90 deg Elbow Inside	238	238
TF-90E-4	TDC 90 deg Elbow Outside	238	238
SF-90E-1	S/D 90 deg Elbow Top	121	121
SF-90E-2	S/D 90 deg Elbow Bottom	121	121
SF-90E-3	S/D 90 deg Elbow Inside	121	121
SF-90E-4	S/D 90 deg Elbow Outside	121	121
TF-L90E-1	TDC <90 deg Elbow Top	79	79
TF-L90E-2	TDC <90 deg Elbow Bottom	79	79

Figure 18.6   (a) Parts data for the sheet metal shop entered in the PFAST input file.

(Continued)

(b)

Work Center No.	Description	Area
39943	Stiffeners Chop Saw	1
90005	Palletizer	1
90040	Gecka	1
90041	Shear	1
90043	Box Brake	1
90045	Plasma Cutter	1
90046	Small Band Saw	1
90049	Big Band Saw	1
90058	Small Roller	1
90059	Crimping Station	1
90061	TDC Machine	1
90062	Roto Die	1
90067	Coil Line	1
90068	Drive Machine	1
90080	Small Brake	1
90081	Insulation Station	1
90082	Punch	1
90094	Drill Press	1
90107	Vanemaker	1
90108	Whisper Lock	1
90110	Brake	1
90114	Electrical Roller	1
90143	Ruoff Notcher	1
90144	Hobo Maker	1
90145	Pittsburgh/Hobo Maker	1
90149	Spot Welder	1
90151	Square to Round Maker	1
90152	Drivemaker	1
98582	Ward Flange Chop Saw	1

Figure 18.6 (CONTINUED) (b) Work centers data for the sheet metal shop entered in the PFAST input file.

Figure 18.6(c) shows the Routing of each component that was entered into the ROUTINGS spreadsheet in the PFAST Input File.

Figure 18.7(a) shows the part family for Cell #1 that was identified using the Product-Routing Analysis Type IV output produced by PFAST. Figure 18.7(b) shows the part family for Cell #2 that was identified using the Product-Routing Analysis Type IV output produced by PFAST. Figure 18.7(c) shows the part family for Cell #3 that was identified using the Product-Routing Analysis Type IV output produced by PFAST. Figure 18.7(d) shows the part family for Cell #4 that was identified using the Product-Routing Analysis Type IV output produced by PFAST.

(c)

Part No	Work Center No	Sequence No
TF-TRA-1	RACK1	1
TF-TRA-1	90045	2
TF-TRA-1	SORTT	3
TF-TRA-1	90145	4
TF-TRA-1	90110	5
TF-TRA-1	90061	6
TF-TRA-1	KNOCK	7
TF-TRA-1	BWRAP	8
TF-TRA-1	90005	9
TF-TRA-1	TRUCK	10
TF-TRA-2	RACK1	1
TF-TRA-2	90045	2
TF-TRA-2	SORTT	3
TF-TRA-2	90145	4
TF-TRA-2	90110	5
TF-TRA-2	90061	6
TF-TRA-2	KNOCK	7
TF-TRA-2	BWRAP	8
TF-TRA-2	90005	9
TF-TRA-2	TRUCK	10
TF-TRA-3	RACK1	1
TF-TRA-3	90045	2
TF-TRA-3	SORTT	3
TF-TRA-3	90145	4
TF-TRA-3	90110	5
TF-TRA-3	90061	6
TF-TRA-3	KNOCK	7
TF-TRA-3	BWRAP	8
TF-TRA-3	90005	9
TF-TRA-3	TRUCK	10

Figure 18.6 (CONTINUED) **(c) Routings data for the sheet metal shop entered in the PFAST input file.**

(a)

SF-RE90-1	RACK1	90045		SORTT		90144	90152		KNOCK	BWRAP	90005	TRUCK
SF-RE90-2	RACK1	90045		SORTT		90144	90152		KNOCK	BWRAP	90005	TRUCK
SF-REL90-1	RACK1	90045		SORTT		90144	90152		KNOCK	BWRAP	90005	TRUCK
SF-REL90-2	RACK1	90045		SORTT		90144	90152		KNOCK	BWRAP	90005	TRUCK
SF-RO-1	RACK1	90045		SORTT		90144	90152		KNOCK	BWRAP	90005	TRUCK
SF-RO-2	RACK1	90045		SORTT		90144	90152		KNOCK	BWRAP	90005	TRUCK
TF-RE90-1	RACK1	90045		SORTT		90144	90061		KNOCK	BWRAP	90005	TRUCK
TF-RE90-2	RACK1	90045		SORTT		90144	90061		KNOCK	BWRAP	90005	TRUCK
TF-REL90-1	RACK1	90045		SORTT		90144	90061		KNOCK	BWRAP	90005	TRUCK
TF-REL90-2	RACK1	90045		SORTT		90144	90061		KNOCK	BWRAP	90005	TRUCK
TF-RO-1	RACK1	90045		SORTT		90144	90061		KNOCK	BWRAP	90005	TRUCK
TF-RO-2	RACK1	90045		SORTT		90144	90061		KNOCK	BWRAP	90005	TRUCK

Figure 18.7 **Part family to design (a) cell #1.**

(*Continued*)

(b)

SF-90E-1	RACK1	90045	SORTT	90145	BARFOLDER	90152	KNOCK	BWRAP	90005	TRUCK
SF-90E-2	RACK1	90045	SORTT	90145	BARFOLDER	90152	KNOCK	BWRAP	90005	TRUCK
SF-L90E-1	RACK1	90045	SORTT	90145	BARFOLDER	90152	KNOCK	BWRAP	90005	TRUCK
SF-L90E-2	RACK1	90045	SORTT	90145	BARFOLDER	90152	KNOCK	BWRAP	90005	TRUCK
SF-SO-1	RACK1	90045	SORTT	90145	BARFOLDER	90152	KNOCK	BWRAP	90005	TRUCK
SF-SO-2	RACK1	90045	SORTT	90145	BARFOLDER	90152	KNOCK	BWRAP	90005	TRUCK
SF-90E-3	RACK1	90045	SORTT	90145	90110	90152	KNOCK	BWRAP	90005	TRUCK
SF-90E-4	RACK1	90045	SORTT	90145	90110	90152	KNOCK	BWRAP	90005	TRUCK
SF-L90E-3	RACK1	90045	SORTT	90145	90110	90152	KNOCK	BWRAP	90005	TRUCK
SF-L90E-4	RACK1	90045	SORTT	90145	90110	90152	KNOCK	BWRAP	90005	TRUCK
SF-SO-3	RACK1	90045	SORTT	90145	90110	90152	KNOCK	BWRAP	90005	TRUCK
SF-SO-4	RACK1	90045	SORTT	90145	90110	90152	KNOCK	BWRAP	90005	TRUCK
SF-TRA-1	RACK1	90045	SORTT	90145	90110	90152	KNOCK	BWRAP	90005	TRUCK
SF-TRA-2	RACK1	90045	SORTT	90145	90110	90152	KNOCK	BWRAP	90005	TRUCK
SF-TRA-3	RACK1	90045	SORTT	90145	90110	90152	KNOCK	BWRAP	90005	TRUCK
SF-TRA-4	RACK1	90045	SORTT	90145	90110	90152	KNOCK	BWRAP	90005	TRUCK
SF-RE90-3	RACK1	90045	SORTT	90145	90114	90152	KNOCK	BWRAP	90005	TRUCK
SF-RE90-4	RACK1	90045	SORTT	90145	90114	90152	KNOCK	BWRAP	90005	TRUCK
SF-REL90-3	RACK1	90045	SORTT	90145	90114	90152	KNOCK	BWRAP	90005	TRUCK
SF-REL90-4	RACK1	90045	SORTT	90145	90114	90152	KNOCK	BWRAP	90005	TRUCK
SF-RO-3	RACK1	90045	SORTT	90145	90114	90152	KNOCK	BWRAP	90005	TRUCK
SF-RO-4	RACK1	90045	SORTT	90145	90114	90152	KNOCK	BWRAP	90005	TRUCK
SS-NCL-1	RACK1	90045	SORTT	90145		90152	KNOCK	BWRAP	90005	TRUCK
SS-NCL-2	RACK1	90045	SORTT	90145		90152	KNOCK	BWRAP	90005	TRUCK

(c)

TF-EC-1	RACK1	90045	SORTT	90145						90005	TRUCK
TS-NCL-2	RACK1	90045	SORTT	90145		90061	LION	KNOCK	BWRAP	90005	TRUCK
TS-NCL-1	RACK1	90045	SORTT	90145		90061	LION	KNOCK	BWRAP	90005	TRUCK
TF-RO-4	RACK1	90045	SORTT	90145	90114	90061		KNOCK	BWRAP	90005	TRUCK
TF-RO-3	RACK1	90045	SORTT	90145	90114	90061		KNOCK	BWRAP	90005	TRUCK
TF-REL90-4	RACK1	90045	SORTT	90145	90114	90061		KNOCK	BWRAP	90005	TRUCK
TF-REL90-3	RACK1	90045	SORTT	90145	90114	90061		KNOCK	BWRAP	90005	TRUCK
TF-RE90-4	RACK1	90045	SORTT	90145	90114	90061		KNOCK	BWRAP	90005	TRUCK
TF-RE90-3	RACK1	90045	SORTT	90145	90114	90061		KNOCK	BWRAP	90005	TRUCK
TF-TRA-4	RACK1	90045	SORTT	90145	90110	90061		KNOCK	BWRAP	90005	TRUCK
TF-TRA-3	RACK1	90045	SORTT	90145	90110	90061		KNOCK	BWRAP	90005	TRUCK
TF-TRA-2	RACK1	90045	SORTT	90145	90110	90061		KNOCK	BWRAP	90005	TRUCK
TF-TRA-1	RACK1	90045	SORTT	90145	90110	90061		KNOCK	BWRAP	90005	TRUCK
TF-SO-4	RACK1	90045	SORTT	90145	90110	90061		KNOCK	BWRAP	90005	TRUCK
TF-SO-3	RACK1	90045	SORTT	90145	90110	90061		KNOCK	BWRAP	90005	TRUCK
TF-L90E-4	RACK1	90045	SORTT	90145	90110	90061		KNOCK	BWRAP	90005	TRUCK
TF-L90E-3	RACK1	90045	SORTT	90145	90110	90061		KNOCK	BWRAP	90005	TRUCK
TF-90E-4	RACK1	90045	SORTT	90145	90110	90061		KNOCK	BWRAP	90005	TRUCK
TF-90E-3	RACK1	90045	SORTT	90145	90110	90061		KNOCK	BWRAP	90005	TRUCK
TF-SO-2	RACK1	90045	SORTT	90145	BARFOLDER	90061		KNOCK	BWRAP	90005	TRUCK
TF-SO-1	RACK1	90045	SORTT	90145	BARFOLDER	90061		KNOCK	BWRAP	90005	TRUCK
TF-L90E-2	RACK1	90045	SORTT	90145	BARFOLDER	90061		KNOCK	BWRAP	90005	TRUCK
TF-L90E-1	RACK1	90045	SORTT	90145	BARFOLDER	90061		KNOCK	BWRAP	90005	TRUCK
TF-90E-2	RACK1	90045	SORTT	90145	BARFOLDER	90061		KNOCK	BWRAP	90005	TRUCK
TF-90E-1	RACK1	90045	SORTT	90145	BARFOLDER	90061		KNOCK	BWRAP	90005	TRUCK

Figure 18.7 (CONTINUED) Part family to design (b) cell #2, (c) cell #3.

(*Continued*)

(d)

SF-ST-1	RACK1	90045		90143	90047B	90047A	90110	90152	KNOCK	BWRAP	90005	TRUCK
SF-ST-2	RACK1	90045		90143	90047B	90047A	90110	90152	KNOCK	BWRAP	90005	TRUCK
TF-ST-1	RACK1	90045		90143	90047B	90047A	90110	LAYOUT	KNOCK	BWRAP	90005	TRUCK
TF-ST-2	RACK1	90045		90143	90047B	90047A	90110	LAYOUT	KNOCK	BWRAP	90005	TRUCK
SF-EC-1	RACK1	90045		SORTT			90152			90110	90005	TRUCK
TF-SR-2	RACK1	90045	LAYOUT	90046	90044B	90151	PIPE	90149	LAYOUT	BWRAP	90005	TRUCK
TF-SR-1	RACK1	90045	LAYOUT	90046	90044B	90151	PIPE	90149	LAYOUT	BWRAP	90005	TRUCK
SF-SR-2	RACK1	90045	LAYOUT	90046	90044B	90151	PIPE	90149	90152	BWRAP	90005	TRUCK
SF-SR-1	RACK1	90045	LAYOUT	90046	90044B	90151	PIPE	90149	90152	BWRAP	90005	TRUCK
SF-SR-3	RACK1	90045	LAYOUT				90058	90149	90152	BWRAP	90005	TRUCK
TF-SR-3	RACK1	90045	LAYOUT				90058	90149	LAYOUT	BWRAP	90005	TRUCK
O-BS-1	RACK1	90045	LAYOUT		90110						90005	TRUCK
O-SDP-1	RACK1	90045	LAYOUT		90110			LAYOUT			90005	TRUCK
O-SMP-1	RACK1	90045	LAYOUT		90110			LAYOUT			90005	TRUCK
O-WDP-1	RACK1	90045	LAYOUT		90110			WELD			90005	TRUCK
O-WMP-1	RACK1	90045	LAYOUT		90110			WELD			90005	TRUCK
SS-CL-1							90067	90108		BWRAP	90005	TRUCK
TS-CL-1							90067	90108	901405	BWRAP	90005	TRUCK
O-BS-2		MESH	LAYOUT		90110						90005	TRUCK
SF-CC-1			LAYOUT		90110		90149	90152			90005	TRUCK
TF-CC-1			LAYOUT		90110		90149	90061			90005	TRUCK

Figure 18.7 (CONTINUED)   Part family to design (d) cell #4.

Unfortunately, the Product-Routing Analysis Type I[10] output that was produced by PFAST showed that it was not advisable for this sheet metal fabrication shop to implement an independent cell to produce each of the four part families, as shown in Figures 18.8(b) and (c). Instead, the realistic alternative was to implement the flexible flow shop layout shown in Figure 18.8(b) based on the linear material flow patterns observed for Part Families #1, #2, and #3. Can you guess why Part Family #4 was ignored?☺

Unfortunately, neither part family formation nor facility layout eliminated the chaotic multi-directional material flows in the flexible flow shop layout displayed in Figures 18.8(b) and (c). However, that laid the foundations for exploring how some of the practices listed in Tables 18.3 and 18.4 could potentially simplify the overall material flow in this sheet metal shop. Specifically, their in-house CI engineer agreed to explore the following ideas for flow simplification: (i) Create a branched multi-line flexible flow shop for at least the types of ductwork being produced in Cells #1, #2, and #3;

---

[10] This is the standard Product-Process 0–1 Matrix Analysis that is used to identify product families in a product mix (*Source*: www.lean.org/lexicon_images/301.gif). Please watch this video *How to Identify Your Value Streams* on YouTube to understand the link between a product family and a "Value Stream" (*Source*: www.youtube.com/watch?v=CtT6hz3EZtU).

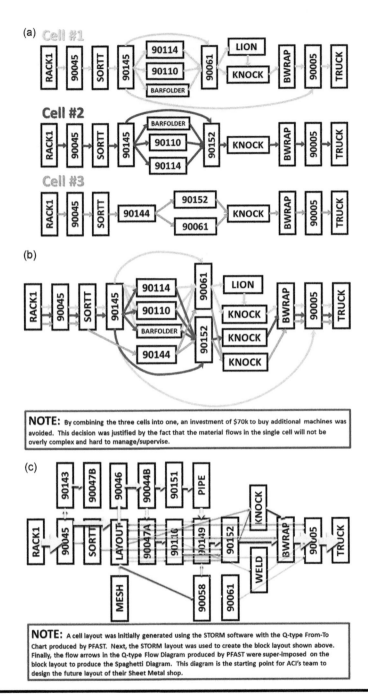

Figure 18.8 (a) Shop layout with an independent cell to produce the part families #1, #2, and #3. (b) Shop layout with an independent cell to produce the part families #1, #2, and #3. (c) Shop layout with an independent cell to produce part family #4.

Table 18.3 Strategies to Prevent Production Delays Due to a Cell's Dependence on Other Cells for Additional Capacity

Exploit the Constraint: Increase Value-Added Utilization of Existing Equipment, Especially for the Bottleneck Machines		
How?	**Men**	• Educate employees to overcome their age-old mindset of those who work in job shops to do batch production even when machines are adjacent to each other in any cell • Reduce absenteeism, discourage extended breaks, discourage chatting during a shift, prevent late start (and early end) of a shift, etc. • Prevent employee turnover by providing competitive pay and benefits • Overlap shift changes to keep machines running continuously • Teach/train one or more of the better employees to be Water Spiders who will handle all inter-cell flow logistics
	Machines	• Adopt a hybrid shape (instead of the standard U, L, S, W, and Z shapes) for each cell's layout in order to allow multi-machine tending by each operator which, in turn, will encourage transfer batch flow, possibly even single-piece flow • Reduce setup changeover times with SMED practices, use of flexible fixtures for different parts in the same part family, point-of-use storage of fixtures, lifting devices to facilitate rapid loading/unloading of fixtures on machines, etc. • Maximize use of common setups, tooling families, canned CNC programs, etc. for consecutive jobs run on the bottleneck machines, **if and only if** the schedule is showing that parts from the same family have to be produced in the same week • Minimize tool change times using pre-set tools, Automated Tool Changers, combination tools, large tool magazines, tool wear sensing technology with periodic replacement of tools before they fail, etc. • Reduce the number of tools needed for any part family by standardizing the dimensions, tolerances, filet radii, chamfer angles, thread types, bend radii, raw material sizes, etc. within a part family • Utilize in-process inspection devices (such as Renishaw probes or vision sensors), Poka-Yoke (mistake proofing), and other process sensing technology that eliminate the need to stop a machine one or more times during a cycle, possibly even take the part off the machine, to inspect it • Maximize use of real-time communications between the machine operators and the Water Spider(s) using (i) phones, two-way radios and tablets for electronic communications and (ii) electronic scheduling boards that display status of jobs on different machines, "hot jobs", machines that are down and need repair, electronic kanbans, etc.

(Continued)

Table 18.3 (*Continued*) Strategies to Prevent Production Delays Due to a Cell's Dependence on Other Cells for Additional Capacity

Elevate the Constraint: Increase the Available Capacity, Especially for the Bottleneck Machines, Especially the Bottleneck Machines		
How?		
Methods		**Materials**
• Support an aggressive TPM to increase operational availability of bottleneck machines • Coordinate with the Inspection department for rapid FAI by signaling them to send one of their inspectors to the cell for "JIT (Just-In-Time) inspection" • Make Quality the responsibility of the cell operators to eliminate dependence on the (external) Inspection department, i.e., absorb Inspection operations into the cell • Maintain Statistical Process Control (SPC) charts to monitor undesirable trends in quality of parts being produced • Prevent frequent schedule changes that necessitate multiple setups to complete the same order • Utilize Time Studies, Methods Analysis, Process Engineering, DFM, etc. to reduce setup times and cycle times for operations performed on the bottleneck machine(s)		• Reduce inflation of order batch sizes to compensate for scrap/re-work at each operation in any part's routing • Limit the proliferation of part designs within a part family by maintaining a comprehensive classification tree for features that impact machine choice (tolerances, material removal rates, finishes, raw material sizes, etc.)

(Continued)

Making a Fabrication Shop Lean and Flexible ■ 423

Table 18.3 (*Continued*) Strategies to Prevent Production Delays Due to a Cell's Dependence on Other Cells for Additional Capacity

Elevate the Constraint: Increase the Available Capacity, Especially for the Bottleneck Machines, Especially the Bottleneck Machines	How?	
	Men	• Cross-train cell operators so they can inspect each other's work, tend to multiple machines, perform support activities (5S, clean-up, etc.) if they are idle, etc. • Add another shift (if appropriate) • Acquire flexible automation to enable lights-out operation in the third shift • Outsource (if appropriate) • Use overtime (if appropriate)
	Methods	• **[See Chapter 7]** Implement a Hybrid Cellular Layout (HCL) that is intermediate between a Cellular and Functional Layout. To design an HCL, the product mix must be analyzed to discover the part families and the machines that must be included in any cell to produce a part family. However, at the time of HCL implementation, creative strategies are adopted to overlap the cells and locate all the shared machines as if they had been retained in functional departments ("process villages"). Examples of HCLs are (i) Cascading Cells (ii) Hybrid Flow Shop,, (iii) Remainder Cell[a], (iv) Layout Modules[b], and (v) Virtual Cells[c]. • Revise process plans for parts so they can be produced in a single cell or the cell that results in the least inter-cell flow delays
	Machines	• Purchase one or more multi-function machines that combine the capabilities of two or more machines in a cell, possibility automating machine loading/unloading, on-machine raw material storage, etc. • Purchase new machines that help to reduce setup times and cycle times for parts run on the bottleneck machine(s) • Purchase new machines but dedicate existing machine(s) that they replace to running certain parts that have steady and significant repeating demand • Explore cobots or other automated/semi-automated material handling devices to handle parts during setup and/or loading/unloading of machines, especially big and heavy parts

(Continued)

Table 18.3 (*Continued*)   Strategies to Prevent Production Delays Due to a Cell's Dependence on Other Cells for Additional Capacity

Elevate the Constraint: Increase the Available Capacity, Especially for the Bottleneck Machines, Especially the Bottleneck Machines		
How?		
Machines	• Design cells to be reconfigurable by investing in machines that are compact and mobile whereby they can be relocated quickly from one location to another in the same facility; thereby, the machines in a cell can be dynamically relocated when the mix and/or demand for any part family fluctuates. **EXAMPLE:** If a customer moves their business overseas and demand for that part family "dries up", the cell can be dismantled and the machines (and their operators) absorbed into other cells	
Materials	• Rationalize the part family produced in the cell to eliminate "cats and dogs", i.e., short run orders that do not repeat • Redesign the parts to eliminate those features that result in the "exception operations" that cannot be done on machines inside the cell; else investigate if other alternative machines inside the cell could perform those operations • Evaluate SS (Safety Stock) quantities for parts produced in the cell to reduce production lot sizes for replenishing on-hand inventory for those parts; else shorten Lead Times quoted to customers because they wish to buffer against erratic demand for those parts • Do a Product-Process Matrix Analysis of the product mix every year to detect changes in the compositions of the different part families; in particular, focus on detecting the outlier parts that necessitate inter-cell flows of parts to access machines not available in their host cells	

a   A Remainder Cell operates like a job shop and fulfills those orders that were too small and one-off to produce in any of the production cells.

b   In a Modular Layout, each layout module is a partial cell. The complete group of machines needed to produce any part family can be "cobbled together" with two or more modules.

c   In the case of a Virtual Cell, the machines that constitute the cell to produce a part family remain where they are in their departments (aka functional silos). However, they are assigned fixtures and tools to run only the parts in one part family or at most two part families. The Shop Logistics Lead (aka Water Spider) ensures that these machines are always producing orders for parts in these designated/assigned part families.

Table 18.4   Strategies to Prevent Production Delays Due to a Cell's Dependence on External Monuments and Shared Resources

Strategy	Details of Implementation
Implement a modular layout	1. Each layout module is a partial cell because it contains two or more machines that occur together in a significant number of routings, preferably the routings for a part family 2. Split the machines in the routing of each part into two sub-groups: (i) group those machines that occur prior to the monument (the "before" machines) in one partial cell and (ii) group those machines that occur after the monument (the "after" machines) in another partial cell 3. Locate both partial cells in close proximity to the monument
Outsource the process, especially if it is an environmentally unfriendly process that has to be isolated from the rest of the equipment (and people) in the facility, usually by placing it in a separate building or a corner of the facility	1. Qualify a local supplier who will supply the parts 2. Hold two buffers of the parts: (i) pre-shipping and (ii) post-shipping 3. Establish a milk run schedule for delivery of the parts by the supplier **EXAMPLES:** Painting, heat treatment, phosphating, black oxidation
Switch to right-sized equipment that can be included in the cell	1. For each cell, determine the process requirements for just the parts being produced in the cell 2. Based on that limited set of process requirements, build or purchase a smaller, possibly cheaper, machine **EXAMPLES:** Painting (Booth vs. Monolithic Conveyor Line), Heat Treatment (Induction Heating Furnace vs. Gas or Oil-fired Furnace), Washing (Dishwasher vs. Wash Tank), Deburring (Pedestal Grinder vs. Pneumatic Hand Tool)

(Continued)

Table 18.4 (*Continued*)   Strategies to Prevent Production Delays Due to a Cell's Dependence on External Monuments and Shared Resources

Strategy	*Details of Implementation*
Operate the monument like a service center	1. Segment the product mix using PQR$T Analysis to identify the Runners, Repeaters, and Strangers 2. Split the machines in the department whereby (i) some machines will only run orders for parts that are Runners and Repeaters, whereas (ii) other machines will do short runs of many different parts[a]
Operate the monument like a service center	3. Utilize an FCS tool[b] to generate a daily production schedule that shows when different cells will have their parts processed at the monument. The tool will use management-specified guidelines for customer service, such as EDD (Earliest Due Date) to set priorities and schedule the orders received from different cells 4. If their schedules allow it, the leaders of the different cells can negotiate with each other to adjust the original Month/Day/Hour (MM/DD/HH) when their parts will be processed at the monument and return to them 5. Utilize any and all modes of communication (electronic schedule boards, walkie-talkies, Water Spiders, morning huddles, etc.) to connect the cells to the monument in order that schedule changes are continuously communicated throughout the facility
Increase throughput using the standard strategies discussed in Table 18.3, such as reducing setup times on the machines using SMED methods, group scheduling parts with delivery dates in the same week(s), sequencing parts consecutively to exploit commonality of fixtures, tooling, materials, etc. between consecutive parts, storing the tools to produce each part family on a separate shadow board, etc.	
Rationalize the part design to eliminate the features that require the operation(s) needed on the monument process	
Switch to a radically new process that is "cell friendly" **EXAMPLE:** Manual Deburring vs. Cryogenic Deburring	

[a] This is similar to the concept of an HCL that consists of several Production Cells and one or more Remainder Cells aka Job Shop Cells.

[b] If applicable and viable, the reader is encouraged to adopt a simpler pull scheduling system like DBR, CONWIP (CONstant WIP), or POLCA (Paired-Cell Overlapping Loops of Cards with Authorization).

(ii) purchase additional equipment of the same type and distribute them at multiple locations to prevent backtracking; (iii) purchase multi-function equipment that could combine two or more work centers (RACK1 → 90045 → SORTT) used consecutively while continuing to use the existing conventional equipment; (iv) conduct a rigorous DFM) analysis of the routings, especially for the parts in Part Family #4, to eliminate or combine some operations in order to reduce the bypass or backtrack flows between work centers; (v) utilize a commercial FCS like Schedlyzer or Tactic to generate a daily shop schedule; and (vi) paint color-coded Kanban squares and pathways on the floor in order to guide the operators (or a dedicated Water Spider) to distinguish between orders for ductwork in different part families, e.g., in Cell #1, there are two bypass flows (90145 → 90061 and 90145 → 90005) and in Cell #2, there is one bypass flow (90145 → 90152).

Strategies to Improve OTD Performance Using Lean Principle #2

Visualize, analyze, and reduce delays in the material flow at every level of the enterprise[11]: The method of PFA can be used to visually assess how the layout of a factory contributes to flow delays that increase the Flow Time for fulfilling any order. PFA can be used to reduce flow delays at a single machine, within a cell, in an entire shop (or building), in a factory site composed of many shops (or buildings) or across an enterprise with multiple factories at different geographical locations. For example, if it was desired to do an Enterprise Flow Analysis to revise the supplier network, all that would be necessary to reuse the Sgetti app would be to (i) use a different layout that is a scaled geographical map showing the locations of the custom fabricator's facility and those of its suppliers and (ii) modify the routings in the product's BOM to replace the machine used for each operation in any routing with the city where it was done. Figure 18.9(a) is the Spaghetti Diagram for a complete fabricated product that consists of three large sub-assemblies that get assembled into the final product. The diagram was produced using the Sgetti app (www.Sgetti.com). Figure 18.9(b), which was also produced using the Sgetti app, shows a new layout with three fabrication cells that were designed to minimize travel distances between all "customer-supplier"

---

[11] **FURTHER READING: (1)** Burbidge, J.L. (1989). *Production Flow Analysis for Planning Group Technology.* Oxford: Oxford University Press.

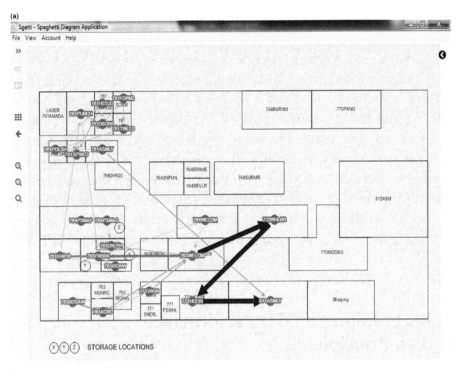

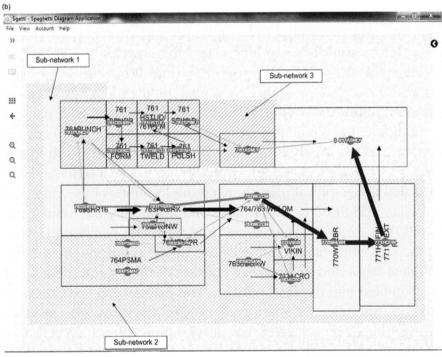

Figure 18.9 Production flow in a custom fabrication facility (a) *before* **and (b)** *after* **layout improvements.**

(Continued)

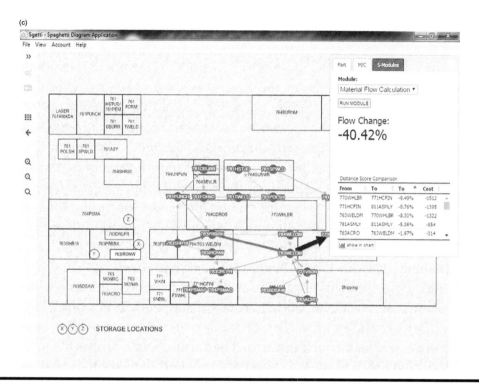

Figure 18.9 (CONTINUED)   Production flow in a custom fabrication facility (c) Improvement in production flow in a custom fabrication facility *after* layout improvements.

pairs of machines in the routings of all the components and sub-assemblies. Figure 18.9(c) shows that, per the assessment done by the Sgetti app, the new layout significantly reduced the machine-to-machine travel delays that impacted the production schedule for the complete product.

Strategies to Improve OTD Performance Using Lean Principle #3

Split the manufacturing facility in two: If the product mix can be divided into two segments – (Runners + Repeaters) and Strangers – then the existing facility of any custom fabricator should be split into at least two mini-factories. The resource sharing between the two mini-factories should be kept to a minimum. Each mini-factory will produce orders for products in the appropriate segment. In addition, the custom fabricator should (i) measure separately the OTD performance and (ii) use different order fulfillment strategies, rules for Customer Relationship Management (CRM), pricing practices, penalties for due date changes, etc. in the two segments. This practice is no different than the practice of triage in the ER of any hospital. As soon as a patient arrives, he/she is assessed by the hospital triage nurse. This nurse evaluates the patient's condition and determines their priority for admission to the Emergency Room and appropriate treatment that may/may not require being admitted to the hospital (*Source*: https://en.wikipedia.org/wiki/Triage).

Implement cells to produce part (or product) families[12]: As shown in Figures 18.4(b), 18.8(b), and 18.9(b), analysis of the routings of products in the (Runners + Repeaters) segment of their product mix will *surely* reveal to any custom fabricator that there are one or more part (or product) families. If that analysis proves fruitful, all efforts should be made to implement a stand-alone flexible cell to produce each part (or product) family.

For example, Factory Pipe (Ukiah, CA) is an extremely vertically integrated fabricator of exhaust systems for the power sports industry with fifty employees that serves OEMs and aftermarket suppliers. It not only designs and manufactures the product, but also makes its own deep-draw tooling, weld fixtures, and leak-check fixtures. The business has evolved from low volume and high mix to more of medium mix and high volume. A typical product run might be 2,000–3,000 for one type of exhaust assembly with the largest run being ≈20,000. Their 3D fiber laser robotic cutting cell sits between their stamping presses and robotic welding cells. The cell can be loaded with up to twenty different parts at any one time. If a welding job is completed on one of the robotic welding cells, the cell indicates a part has been finished, and the software initiates a trim cutting program in the fiber laser cutting cell. Only a specific exhaust stamping matched to firm demand from a customer is trimmed. When the trimming is completed, an

---

[12] **FURTHER READING: (1)** Davis, D. (2018, December). A Robotic Laser Cell Helps a Manufacturer Cut Time to Market: Automation Keeps Factory Pipe on Schedule as it Serves a Demanding Powersports Industry. *The Fabricator*, 54–56. **(2)** Bossard, B. (2017, May). Kitting it Right: How a Panel Bender and Press Brake Work Together in Kit-Based Part Flow. *The Fabricator*, 66–69. **(3)** LeGrand, J. (2018, December). 5 Ways to Improve Your Flow of Laser-Cut Parts: Planning Is Key. *The Fabricator*, 60–61. **(4)** *Cellular Manufacturing Evolves. Source*: www.metal-formingmagazine.com/magazine/article/?/2018/9/1/Cellular_Manufacturing_Evolves. **(5)** Heston, T. (2012, May). Steady Flow, Steady Profits: New England Contract Fabricator Keeps Quality Parts Moving. *The Fabricator*, 68–71. **(6)** Heston, T. (2010, November). Another Day, Another Economic Recovery: Jobshop Rebounds Quickly With Fiscal Conservatism, Pragmatism. *The Fabricator*, 52–54. **(7)** Irani, S.A. (2003, May). Understanding Families Is Key in High-Mix, Low Volume Facility. *Lean Manufacturing Advisor*, 4–5. **(8)** Irani, S.A. (2001, March). Software Solves Identify Crises for Parts from "Big" Families. *Lean Manufacturing Advisor*, 3–6. **(9)** Miller, D. (1999, June). Automating your end forming operation: How to maximize efficiency in the shop. *The Tube and Pipe Journal*, 26–30.

operator removes the exhaust components and sends them to the welding department. The cell can adjust to demand increases in the welding department, because, while the laser cutting head goes to work on one side of the table, the operator can be unloading the finished part on the other side of the table. After the introduction of this semi-automated cell, Factory Pipe has seen a 50% increase in productivity in laser trimming, a decrease in overall production costs decrease due to reduction in overtime, a decrease in rework in the welding department, and a decrease in energy consumption compared with the CO_2 lasers that were replaced.

Identify CI project opportunities driven by **one** *question, "Why must products have to leave their cells for any operations in their routings?"* Unfortunately, as Figures 18.4(b) and 18.8(b,c) illustrate, no custom fabricator will find it easy to accomplish a complete transformation into a cellular layout. Few part families can be identified that can be completely produced within a cell. In that case, creativity and innovation are needed to reduce flow delays caused by a cell's reliance on external resources to complete one or more parts being produced in the cell!

For example, having using the PFAST outputs to design factory layouts for many years, the choice of strategies to prevent one or more parts (or products) from leaving their host cell depends on the type of external equipment that is required. Specifically, is that outside resource a *monument*? A monument is any process equipment that *cannot* be included in the cell, such as a Coordinate Measuring Machine, a heat treatment furnace, a shot blasting machine, a paint line, a surface grinding machine, welding booths, an electroplating tank, a wash tank, an acid bath for rust removal, a galvanizing tank, etc. Table 18.3 shows different strategies for the case when a cell must send one or more of its parts to other cells because its internal capacity on a particular machine (or machines) is exceeded due to a surge in demand for one or more of the parts it produces. In contrast, Table 18.4 shows different strategies for the case when a cell **must** send one or more of its parts to an (external) monument that is not resident in any of the cells.

For example, Figures 18.10(a–c) are strategy maps based on Tables 18.3a and b that were suggested to achieve single-piece flow in a manual Printed Circuit Board (PCB) assembly cell.

For example, based on Tables 18.3(a) and (b), Figure 18.11 is a strategy map based on Tables 18.3(a) and (b) that was suggested to improve the operational performance of a machining cell that was implemented in a small CNC machine shop being relocated into a new building.

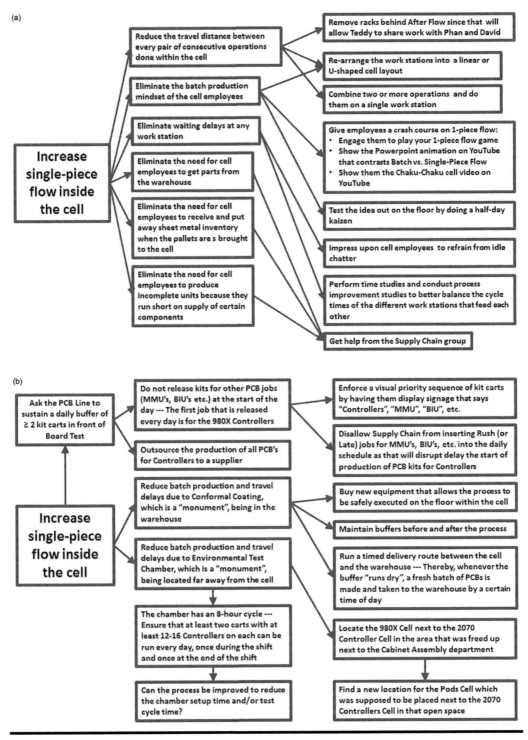

Figure 18.10 (a) Strategy map 1 (of 3) , (b) Strategy map 2 (of 3).

(Continued)

(c)

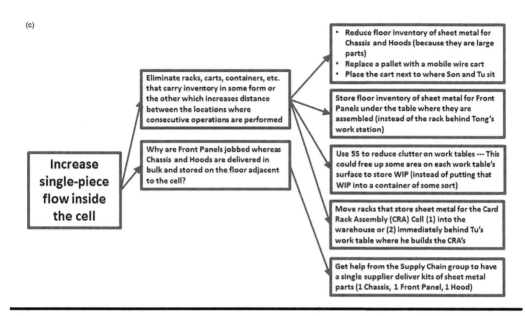

Figure 18.10 (CONTINUED) (c) strategy map 3 (of 3) to achieve single piece flow in a manual PCB assembly cell.

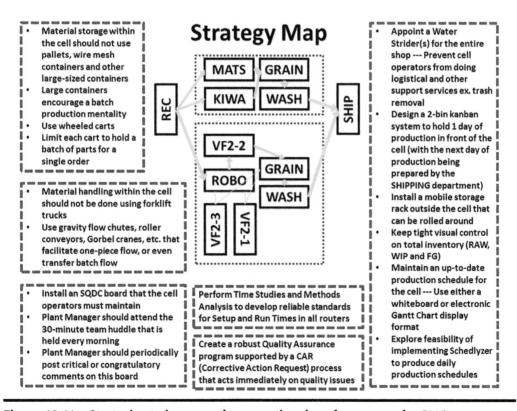

Figure 18.11 Strategies to improve the operational performance of a CNC machining cell.

Right-size as many monuments as possible[13]: Any equipment or process that is an external monument, such as heat treating, painting, washing, deburring, etc., usually processes parts from many cells. The cells will invariably produce these parts in batches sent to the monument(s). And most, if not all, batches will invariably have to wait in queue at the monument(s). This will *surely* increase the Flow Times for all parts that need to use the monument(s). When implementing Job Shop Lean in CNC machine shops, I have always asked my clients, "Could an Inspection department be dissolved and replaced by roving inspectors? Could quality be made the responsibility of every cell instead of the (external) Inspection department?" The responses I have received have ranged from "No!" to "Are you kidding?" to "Maybe but we will need to think about it!"

For example, in a recent client engagement with an aerospace MRO fabrication shop, I noticed that employees working at different benches would all walk to a cluster of pedestal grinders to deburr the parts they were working on. Naturally, my question to their Operations Manager was, "Could a pedestal grinder be placed near each work bench?" At first, his response was, "But they are all connected to one dust collector?" Then he looked closely at the dust collector and said, "Wait, that dust collector is not even plugged in!" So? Basically, every day for 250 working days every year, their employees had been walking back and forth between their work benches and those pedestal grinders! Instead, they could easily have (i) put a grinder adjacent to each bench and (ii) made the operator at each table responsible for sweeping the floor at the end of their shift. In fact, they could easily have purchased a shop vacuum and located it where the grinders stood. At the end of the day, every employee would use it to clean their workstation and return it to its designated location when they were done. Such right-sizing to eliminate a monument could be justified simply by showing the labor hours saved each year!

Employ multi-tasking machines to the maximum extent possible: A primary capability of multi-tasking machines is that they can produce parts on a single machine, possibly in a single setup. They eliminate the need for moving a part between different machines that could be located far apart in the facility. A multi-tasking machine will significantly reduce Flow Time for any part because it will eliminate the travel times, waiting times, setup times, etc. in the current multi-step process. In fact, the flexibility of a

---

[13] **FURTHER READING: (1)** Boeing Auburn Machine Fabrication. https://19january2017snapshot. epa.gov/lean/boeing-auburn-machine-fabrication-_.html#obstacles.

multi-tasking machine can be better determined if it replaces a pre-existing multi-machine cell that is producing a family of parts. The downside of these complex machines includes maintenance, operator skills, and a heavier workload due to aggregation of work that was done previously on separate machines.

Strategies to Improve OTD Performance Using Lean Principle #4

Get an ERP system that can generate and issue a feasible production schedule to the shop floor: Without a reliable schedule, how can the operator of a press brake or burn table or welding booth in any fabrication job shop know when to start a job and when to finish that job? Unfortunately, it is rare that an ERP system at any small-to-medium size custom fabricator (or any job shop for that matter!) benefits any department other than Human Resources, CRM, Purchasing, Accounting, and IT. It is puzzling to observe that, by default, a custom fabricator has an ERP system that uses an MRP engine to do the production planning, capacity planning, work order releases, shop floor control, etc. that are crucial for achieving world-class OTD performance. According to the TOC developed by Dr. Eliyahu Goldratt:

1. Bottlenecks govern both throughput and inventories.
2. Schedules should be established by looking at all of the constraints simultaneously.
3. Lead times are the result of a schedule and cannot be predetermined.

Unfortunately, scheduling based on MRP logic makes numerous wrong assumptions such as (i) infinite capacity on all resources, (ii) fixed lead times, and (iii) minimizing setup costs by combining orders for the same product that could be weeks apart. Instead of expecting their ERP systems to (ever!) produce feasible daily schedules, custom fabricators should evaluate the following FCSs that have a proven track record – Preactor (www.Preactor.com), Tactic (www.Waterloo-Software.com), and Schedlyzer (www.Optisol.biz). Alternatively, they could utilize "pseudo-schedulers" that use the Drum-Buffer-Rope (DBR) method based on the TOC – DBR+ (http://demanddriventech.com/home/solutions/dbr/), Visual ERP (www.visualbusiness.net/easy-lean), and Protected Flow Manufacturing (www.protectedflowmanufacturing.com/). Finally, between the true FCSs and the DBR pseudo-schedulers stands a unique Operations Analytics software, CSUITE (www.factoryphysics.com/quick-flow-benchmarking), that does Rough-Cut Capacity Requirements Planning to choke the release of orders into a capacity-constrained production system.

If a custom fabricator has *both* data *and* a competent scheduler, then they could use any of the three FCSs (Preactor, Tactic, or Schedlyzer) to generate (i) a feasible daily production schedule and (ii) timely alerts to the production floor to avoid the well-known causes for delays and disruptions that lead to poor OTD performance:

1. Shortage of raw materials (plate, pipe, bar, beam, etc.)
2. Incorrect capacity requirements calculated for each week's production plan
3. Late deliveries by vendors
4. High variability in week-by-week demand and product mix
5. Insufficient capacity at bottlenecks
6. Batching and sequence-dependent setup times at monuments (heat treat, paint, etc.)
7. Etc.

Manage with visual schedules displayed as Gantt Charts: So what would the Gantt Chart for a daily schedule look like? Figure 18.12(a) is the Operations Process Chart (aka Work Breakdown Structure) developed from the Indented Bill Of Routings of the fabricated product referenced earlier in Figures 18.9a–c. It provides the "goes-into" configuration for the components that become the sub-assemblies that become the final product. Figure 18.12(b) is the Gantt Chart that was generated using MS Project to obtain the shortest possible Flow Time to produce one unit of the final product referenced earlier in Figures 18.9(a–c). Academic textbooks teach the simple Critical Path Method for project scheduling. However, in this real-world case, MS Project determined a Critical Path after taking into consideration (i) finite resource constraints because there was only one machine in each work center and (ii) two or more components and sub-assemblies that had to wait in queue at one or more work centers because they all needed to use the same machine.

*Prioritize CI investments **always** to maximize throughput at the bottleneck of each manufacturing cell*: According to the TOC developed by Dr. Eliyahu Goldratt:

(a)

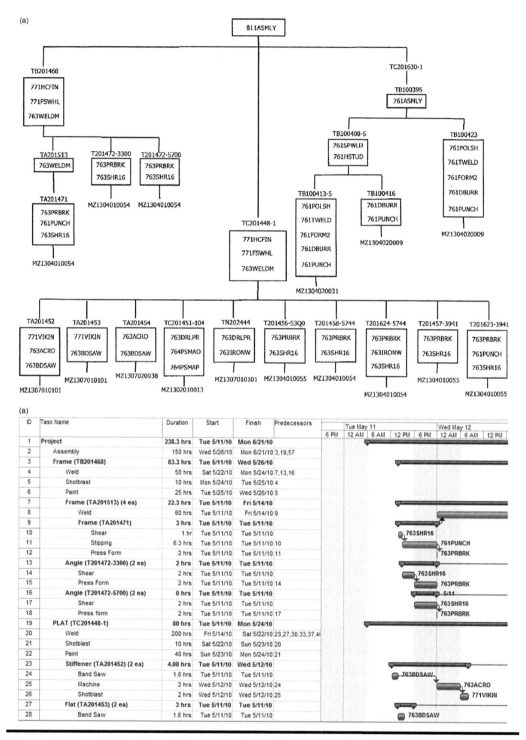

Figure 18.12 **(a)** Work breakdown structure for a (complete) fabricated product. **(b)** MS project Gantt Chart for building the (complete) fabricated product whose work breakdown structure is shown in (a).

1. An hour lost at a bottleneck is an hour lost for the total system.
2. The level of utilization of a non-bottleneck is not determined by its own potential but by some other constraint in the system.
3. An hour saved at a non-bottleneck is just a mirage.

The ideal manufacturing cell is (i) a stand-alone cell that can operate autonomously without dependence on external resource constraints and (ii) the value-added utilization of the bottleneck machine in the cell hovers in the range 80%–85%. Unfortunately, wasted capacity on the bottleneck will reduce throughput at the bottleneck in the cell. This, in turn, will delay the order being run (possibly even the orders to be run) on the bottleneck in the cell. Hence, top priority must be given to those CI projects that increase the value-added portion of the daily available capacity at/on the bottleneck(s) in every cell since that has significant impact on the OTD performance of the cell. So if it is desired to improve throughput and OTD performance of a cell, the five-step POOGI (Process Of Ongoing Improvement) used to implement TOC is as follows (*Source*: www.tocinstitute.org/five-focusing-steps.html):

1. Find the constraint in the cell.
2. Exploit the constraint.
3. Subordinate everything else to the constraint.
4. Elevate the constraint.
5. Prevent inertia from becoming the constraint; therefore, return to Step 1.

Use a one-cell-at-a-time approach to pursue CI using TOC's POOGI: If it is desired to improve OTD performance one-cell-at-a-time, then TOC should be used to drive all CI projects as shown in Figure 18.13. First, do Product-Process Matrix Analysis to identify potential product families, as demonstrated previously in Figures 18.4(a,b) and 18.7(a–d). Next, select a product family and, for that product family, develop a Value Network Map (VNM) to capture the Current State of the product family and its cell. Using the VNM, design and implement a manufacturing cell to produce orders for that part family. In order to identify the cell's bottleneck, develop a load profile for all machines in that cell using at least the past year's data for orders fulfilled by that cell. Finally, to maximize throughput at the cell's bottleneck, implement Step #2 (Exploit the Constraint) in the POOGI. If the cell needs to utilize external processes and support services, utilize the strategies listed

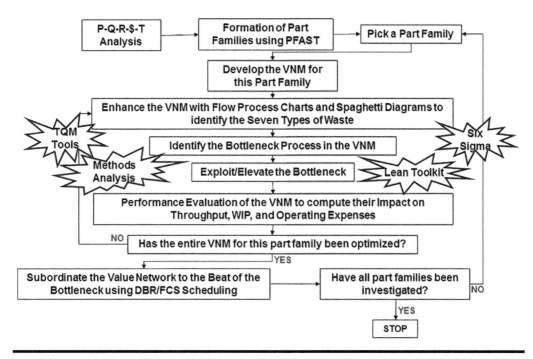

Figure 18.13   One-cell-at-a-time approach combined with TOC's POOGI.

in Tables 18.3(a) and b to mitigate the delays caused by the flow of parts (products) into and out of the cell.

Leverage the Data Collection Capabilities of Machine Monitoring Software[14]: The throughput of a fabrication cell could be poor for any number of reasons such as (i) the ERP system does not have good data to accurately calculate value-added utilization on the bottleneck machine, (ii) high setup changeover times override all other considerations when loading jobs on the bottleneck, (iii) production control allows customers to suddenly change the status of jobs to "Hot" or "No Longer Needed By Due Date", (iv) the ERP system releases jobs to the cell without consideration for available capacity and current workload on the bottleneck machine, (v) absenteeism and labor turnover in the cell leads to high variability in run times for the same job, (vi) an external (but in-house) monument that is shared by other cells frequently disrupts the cell's schedule, and (vii) a supplier's delivery schedule and quality frequently disrupts the cell's schedule, etc.

---

[14] **FURTHER READING: (1)** Heston, T. (2015, November). Why Machine Monitoring Matters. *The Fabricator*, 90–93. **(2)** Finnerty, J. (2013, September). Automating OEE for the Job Shop. *The Fabricator*, 84–87. **(3)** Finnerty, J. (2008, September). *Automated Collection of Real-Time Production Data: How to Get the Data, and What to Do with it Once You Have it. The Fabricator*, 66–69. **(4)** Schneider, R. (2004, July). Pushing Plate Processing Productivity. *The Fabricator*, 30–32.

And what about all the additional reasons for loss of cell throughput, either due to wasted capacity on the bottleneck machine in the cell, such as an arc welding robot, a waterjet cutting machine or a laser cutting machine, or an external monument, such as a powder coating line or a paint line? Nor does the open literature on TOC offer concrete guidelines for implementing the Lean tools in the different steps of the POOGI to increase Throughput by improving the Operational Availability of the bottleneck machine(s) in the cell (*Source*: www.leanproduction.com/theory-of-constraints.html).

So does management follow the well-traveled path and start conducting kaizen events where the Lean tools listed in the left-hand column of Table 18.1 are used to "win back" the lost capacity on the bottleneck machine(s) in the cell? Not without doing data analysis to avoid the willy-nilly use of the Lean tools which is equivalent to "CI by Whack-A-Mole"!

At least start by doing a Root Cause Analysis and produce a Fishbone Diagram (or Ishikawa Diagram) to identify all the M's (Men, Materials, Methods, Machines, Management, Metrics) that are the reason for wasted capacity on the bottleneck machine(s) in each cell during every 8-hour shift of operation. For example, the typical machine shop will swear that "Keep making chips" is a simple and profitable manufacturing strategy. Not if they are failing to first and foremost increase the operational availability of the bottleneck machine(s) in the cell! But will this be done by manually collecting the data that will drive the decision-making? Table 18.5 shows the six major categories of capacity loss on any equipment. Table 18.6 explodes the six categories in Table 18.5 into fifty-four specific loss codes based on maintenance records and operator input in a CNC machine shop. No skilled CNC machine operator will agree to manually record the type and duration of each and every instance of machine stoppage listed in Table 18.6 during their shift! In order to determine significant categories of lost capacity on a bottleneck machine in a cell during any 8-hour shift of operation, it is necessary to semi-automate (or automate) the collection of data on the operating states of the machine, possibly using a subset of the fifty-four loss codes in Table 18.6. This data collection can be done using machine monitoring software like Merlin (*Source*: www.MemexOEE.com) that is pre-installed on all fabrication shop equipment that is built by Mazak Optonics Corporation (*Source*: www.mazakoptonics.com/machines/mazak-ismart-factory/).[15] Now,

---

[15] There are numerous vendors of machine monitoring software, such as Scytec (*Source*: https://scytec.com/), FactoryWiz (*Source*: www.FactoryWiz.com), FORCAM (*Source*: www.FORCAM.com), and Machine Metrics (*Source*: www.machinemetrics.com/blog/epicor-erp-integration1).

Table 18.5 Common Causes for Loss of Productive Capacity on a Bottleneck Machine

Overall Equipment Effectiveness	Recommended Six Big Losses	Traditional Six Big Losses
Availability loss	Unplanned stops	Equipment failure
	Planned stops	Setup and adjustments
Performance loss	Small stops	Idling and minor stops
	Slow cycles	Reduced speed
Quality loss	Production rejects	Process defects
	Startup rejects	Reduced yield
Overall equipment effectiveness	Fully productive time	Valuable operating time

Source: www.oee.com/oee-six-big-losses.html.

Table 18.6 Examples of Capacity Loss Codes for CNC Machines

Category	Loss Code	Description of Problem	Category	Loss Code	Description of Problem
Idle	CL	Complete paperwork	Maint	SP	Spindle problem
Idle	CU	Cleanup	Maint	SW	Switch broken
Idle	GT	Go to tool crib (gauges and tools)	Maint	TM	Tool magazine/tool changer
Idle	MH	Material handling	Maint	TP	Turret
Idle	OC	Operator communications	Misc	EE	Prototype machining
Idle	OO	Operator on another machine	Misc	FA	First aid/dispensary visit
Idle	OT	Operator training operator	Misc	MT	Meeting (unscheduled)
Idle	WF	Waiting for fork lift	Misc	NP	No power
Idle	WK	Waiting for parts or raw material	Misc	PD	Part/process/program development

(Continued)

Table 18.6 (*Continued*)   Examples of Capacity Loss Codes for CNC Machines

Category	Loss Code	Description of Problem	Category	Loss Code	Description of Problem
Idle	WM	Waiting on maintenance	Misc	PE	Program error
Idle	WT	Waiting for tooling and fixtures	Misc	PR	Power loss recovery
Maint	AF	Add fluids (coolant, oils, etc.)	Misc	RB	Repair broken tooling
Maint	AL	Air leak/low pressure	Misc	VA	Vacation/personal time
Maint	CC	Chip conveyor chain	Quality	GP	Gauge problem
Maint	CP	Coolant leak/ pressure	Quality	QC	Quality check/lab time
Maint	EC	Electronic control problem	Quality	QO	Operator in-process part check
Maint	EP	Electrical problem	Quality	RW	Rework
Maint	FL	Filter change	Setup	AC	Axis check and align
Maint	FM	Fixture problem (or maintenance)	Setup	CR	Crash recovery
Maint	HL	Hydraulic leak/ pressure problem	Setup	CT	Change tooling/ inserts
Maint	IT	Table problem	Setup	SU	Setup changeover
Maint	MP	Mechanical problem	Speed	DC	Empty chips dumpster
Maint	OM	Operator maintenance tasks	Speed	DW	Dress grinding wheel
Maint	PF	Pallet change failure	Speed	PH	Parts holding/loading problems
Maint	PM	TPM-assigned tasks	Speed	TA	Tool adjustment
Maint	PP	Pump problem	Speed	TS	Startup/shutdown
Maint	RM	Relocate/move machine(s)	Speed	UNAC	Unaccounted time

Source: Dipak Sheth, Eaton Corporation (2006).

any custom fabricator using Mazak equipment can identify, track, and measure how much capacity is lost on their bottleneck machine(s). Once operational data is obtained from the machine's controller with additional inputs from the operator(s), just about any MMS (Machine Monitoring System) can generate a Pareto Analysis of the different types of capacity loss on a machine, as shown in Figure 18.14. The Pareto Analysis provides crystal clear guidance and prioritization of the appropriate Lean tools in the left-hand column of Table 18.1 that should be used to increase the value-added utilization of the bottleneck machine by eliminating (or mitigating) the most significant losses of capacity. No more "CI by Whack-A-Mole"! Figure 18.14 shows that the top three reasons for capacity loss on the particular CNC machine being monitored are "Bar Feeder Problem", "No Operator", and "Tool Change". The two machine-related issues would be addressed by the Maintenance department. But, as regards the "No Operator" issue, the MMS is a non-intrusive non-threatening alternative to the traditional methods that are resented by machine operators, such as vision-aided machine monitoring (*Source*: https://atollogy.com/products/), video-aided Time and Motion Study (*Source*: www.acsco.com/ or https://www.proplanner.com/), or "Taiichi Ohno's Chalk Circle" (*Source*: www.allaboutlean.com/chalk-circle/).

Utilize an MES to track all in-process orders: Practitioners and academics in the fields of Human Factors and Cognitive Ergonomics use the term "situation awareness" needed by decision-makers in highly dynamic high-risk work environments such as firefighting, air traffic control, emergency services, etc. (*Source*: https://en.wikipedia.org/wiki/Situation_awareness). By the same token, a custom fabricator must be able to check the status of all active orders (work in process (WIP)) either in their own facility or at a supplier's facility. The segment of a Value Stream Map shown in Figure 18.15 illustrates how delays get added to the Flow Time of any order either (i) at each processing step in its routing or (ii) at each transportation step between consecutive operations in its routing.

Similarly, for any custom fabricator to have situation awareness on any in-process order, they require timely and accurate knowledge of its geographical location to determine whether it is (i) in setup at a machine, (ii) in-process at a machine, (iii) in queue at a machine, (iv) complete at current machine but waiting to be moved to the next machine in its routing, (v) being moved to the next machine in its routing, (vi) waiting for the First Article Inspection (FAI) to be completed by the Inspection department with the rest of the batch waiting at current machine, and (vii) waiting at a machine (or kitting location) for other batches in the kit to arrive,

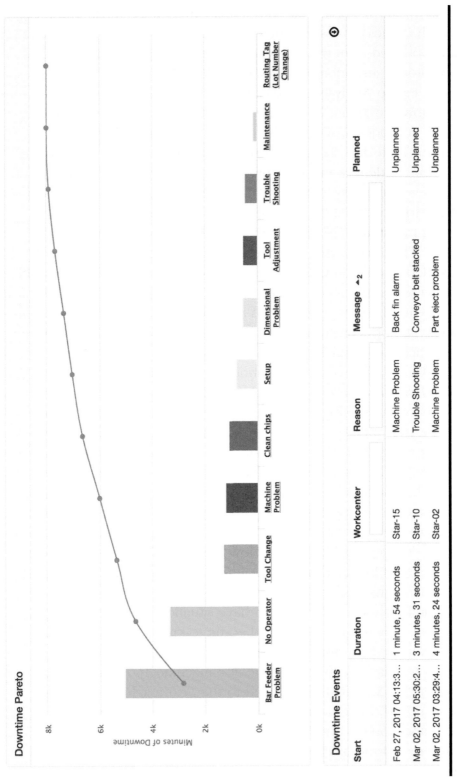

Figure 18.14   Pareto plot of capacity loss categories. (*Source*: www.MachineMetrics.com.)

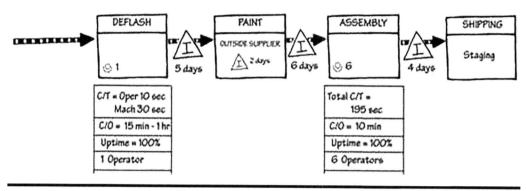

Figure 18.15 **Interoperation product flow complicates tracking and locating any order.**

and so on. Even a job shop can have situation awareness if they have a Manufacturing Execution System like Epicor Mattec (*Source*: www.epicor. com/business-need/production-management-systems/mattec-mes.aspx) that is complemented by practices and systems discussed in Tables 18.3a and b, such as Manufacturing Cells, Water Spiders, Daily Team Huddles, Mobile Communications (including two-way Radios), Machine Monitoring, Bar Code Scanners, and Electronic Scheduling Boards?

Strategies to Improve OTD Performance Using Lean Principle #5

Implementing the one-cell-at-a-time approach will take time: Figure 18.13 shows the roadmap that custom fabricators would use to implement the Principles of Lean in their HMLV manufacturing facilities. But, implementing even one cell will be beset with challenges such as (i) being able to place inside each cell all the equipment it needs to be self-sufficient, (ii) ensuring that the order pipeline for the part family assigned to each cell is sustained (else the cell would die), (iii) cross-training employees to run different machines in their cell, (iv) allowing the cell operators to manage their cell, and (v) planning for employee turnover in the cells due to retirement and other reasons, etc. Tables 18.3a and b provide an exhaustive list of the many ways in which to improve the performance of an individual cell or an entire facility that has a Cellular Layout.

Is management willing to let a cell's team operate autonomously? Each cell has the potential to become an Autonomous Business Unit (ABU). But this will require the team of employees in each cell to be empowered to manage day-to-day operations and make decisions about scheduling, assigning work to different operators, deciding who gets cross-trained on which machines, etc. The team would have to be allowed to determine the improvement projects to eliminate, or at least mitigate, all the constraints that force the cell to send its orders to external resources, either in-house or vendors. The team must be allowed to communicate directly with their customers concerning changes in delivery dates, questions about part drawings or routers, unforeseen quality problems, etc.

The Way Forward for Custom Fabricators

For custom fabricators to achieve world-class OTD performance, their priority should be to find and implement practical solutions to the age-old problems that remain to be solved effectively to this day even after the 2003 publication of the seminal book *Lean Thinking*: (i) Identify the product families in their product mix, (ii) design a flexible facility layout that fits the material flow inherent to their product mix, and (iii) issue a feasible daily production schedule that was generated after consideration of all known resource constraints. These three age-old problems are restated in the Principles of Lean that were introduced in the 2003 publication of the seminal book *Lean Thinking*! This chapter showed how custom fabricators can implement the Principles of Lean using the tools of Job Shop Lean at each step of implementation of a high-level conceptual framework for implementing the TPS.

Bibliography

Danford, M. (2010, November). From Job Shop Chaos to Lean Order. *Modern Machine Shop*, 60–67.

Heston, T. (2010a, August). Can Lean Manufacturing Work in the Job Shop? *The Fabricator*, 46–48.

Heston, T. (2010b, November). Another Day, Another Economic Recovery. *The Fabricator*, 52–54.

Heston, T. (2010c, October). How a Shop Devoted to Improvement Improved. *The Fabricator*, 32.

Heston, T. (2011, February). Continuous Improvement: No One Size Fits All. *The Fabricator*, 44–45.

Huskonen, W. (2003, January/February). Thinking Lean at TECT Cleveland. *Forging*, 16–19.

Huskonen, W. (2004, March/April). Ulven Forging Succeeds with Jobshop Lean. *Forging*, 26–28.

Irani, S.A. (2008, April). Starting Your Jobshop on its "Lean Journey". *Forge*, 34–37.

Irani, S.A. (2011, August). Choosing What Works. *Industrial Engineer*, 42–47.

Irani, S.A. (2012a, August). Adapting Lean for High-Mix Low-Volume Manufacturing Facilities. *Gear Technology*, 10–12.

Irani, S.A. (2012b, October). A Quick-Start Approach for Implementing Lean in Jobshops. *Gear Technology*, 10–16.

Irani, S.A. (2013a, August). Design of a Flexible and Lean (FLEAN) Machining Cell: Part 2 (Application). *Gear Technology*, 58–63.

Irani, S.A. (2013b, August). Solving the NDT Bottleneck at SIFCO. *Forge*, 17–20.

Irani, S.A. (2013c, July). Savvy Students Help Shipping Department Move. *Industrial Engineer*, 30–35.

Irani, S.A. (2013d, June/July). Design of a Flexible and Lean (FLEAN) Machining Cell: Part 1 (Theory). *Gear Technology*, 20–26.

Irani, S.A. (2013e, November/December). Educating the Workforce and Management about FLEAN (Flexible and Lean) Manufacturing Cells. *Gear Technology*, 82–92.

Irani, S.A. & Fischer, M.C. (2013, March). Recession-proof your shop the lean way. www.leanandflexible.com/wp-content/uploads/2017/08/Recession-proof_your_ Shop_the_Lean_Way.pdf.

Jaster, M. (2012, June). The Robust and Reliable Jobshop. *Gear Technology* www. geartechnology.com/newsletter/0612/lean.htm.

Lechleitner, D. & Irani, S A. (2013, September). Implementing lean manufacturing in a high-mix low-volume job shop. https://jobboss.com/lean-manufacturing.

Sabri, S. & Shayan, E. (2004). Lean strategies for furniture manufacturing. *Proceedings of the Fifth Asia Pacific Industrial Engineering and Management Systems Conference*, Gold Coast, Australia, 31.18.1–13.18.8.

Wang, B. (2007). The quick-start approach to JobshopLean: How to initiate the implementation of lean in a high-mix low-volume manufacturing facility.

Chapter 19

Introduction to Operations Scheduling for High-Mix Low-Volume Manufacturers

Acknowledgments

This chapter is based on the work that I did when I was the Director of IE (Industrial Engineering) Research at Hoerbiger Corporation of America. This was my first industry job and a golden opportunity given to me by Hannes Hunschofsky, who was then the President of Hoerbiger Corporation of America. He invited (and challenged!) me to pilot the implementation of Job Shop Lean in their Houston, TX, facility. Had it not been for this job, I would never be where I am today – in industry doing hands-on projects to put my research into practice. Thank you, Hannes!

In addition, I wish to thank Pranav Joshi who co-authored this chapter with me while I was the Director of IE Research at Hoerbiger Corporation of America. At that time, Pranav was pursuing his MSIE (Master of Science in Industrial Engineering) graduate degree in the Department of Integrated Systems Engineering at The Ohio State University. Subsequently, he did an internship at Hoerbiger Service Inc. from June 2013 to November 2013. Since November 2013, he has been a Quality Engineer at Honda of America Manufacturing Inc. (USA). Pranav can be reached by email (Pranav.Joshi18@gmail.com) or by phone (414-943-9193). Thank you, Pranav!

Scheduling Is the Weakness of ERP Systems *and* Lean

One of the major differences between an HMLV (high-mix low-volume) manufacturer and Toyota is that it is easier to schedule production on an assembly line. On an assembly line, FIFO (First In First Out) flow of orders is naturally enforced by the conveyor lines on which the products and major subassemblies move through a predetermined sequence of assembly stations. The speed of the conveyor line is synchronized with the Takt Time (TT) for that line (TT for the Line = Available Capacity on the Line ÷ Daily Demand for Products Built on the Line). And the TT for the line is synchronized with the daily production rate required to meet market demand for the mix of products coming off that line.

In contrast, the majority of HMLV manufacturers rely on the legacy MRP (Material Requirements Planning) engines for production planning, operations scheduling, and shop floor control that are embedded in their ERP (Enterprise Resource Planning) systems. MRP cannot plan production and schedule operations because (i) it assumes infinite capacity of resources such as machines, labor, and materials and (ii) it cannot sequence and schedule multiple orders that use one or more common resources. Therefore, the use of an MRP-driven ERP system will undoubtedly produce many of the Seven Types of Waste that Lean targets for elimination or reduction! For example, overproduction is due to basing production on MRP-generated demand forecasts, and WIP (work-in-process) is due to batching of several orders to reduce setup time losses and queues form when workload on a system bottleneck exceeds its available capacity. That happens when too many orders are released for production without any consideration for finite resource levels. The shortcomings of ERP systems are so many that the Lean community has a good reason to malign them for causing operational inefficiencies.

But, even as the Lean community maligns ERP systems, Lean has little to offer that can overcome the limitations of MRP to plan production and schedule operations in an HMLV non-assembly manufacturing environment. As seen in Table 19.1, only some of the popular Lean tools belong in the toolkit for implementing Job Shop Lean. The tools listed in the right-hand column of Table 19.1 have to do with Production Planning and Control, Inventory Control, Operations Scheduling, and Shop Floor Control. Those Lean tools would not work in the most challenging HMLV environment of all, a job shop, because they are primarily designed for Make-To-Stock (MTS) production on assembly lines. Unlike an assembly line, the typical

Table 19.1 Lean Tools That Will (or Will Not) Work in Most Job Shops

Tools That *Will* Work in Most Job Shops	Tools That May Not Work in Most Job Shops
Strategic planning	Value Stream Mapping (VSM)
Top-down leadership	Assembly line balancing
Employee involvement	One-piece flow cells
5S	Product-specific Kanbans
Total Productive Maintenance (TPM)	First In First Out (FIFO) sequencing at work centers
Setup reduction (SMED)	Pacemaker scheduling
Error-proofing (Poka-Yoke)	Inventory supermarkets
Quality at source	Work order release based on pitch
Visual controls/visual management	Production based on level loading (Heijunka)
Product and process standardization	Mixed model production with TT
Single-function (Inflexible) Machines	**Single-function (Inflexible) Machines**
Jidoka	Plan for Every Product (PFEP)
Right-sized machines	
Standard work	

job shop does not have a fixed production rate that drives the daily schedule for the assembly line. A job shop could experience daily changes in its order mix. Plus each order could have a different due date for delivery to its customer.

HMLV manufacturers need to turn their attention away from the standard Lean practices and tools suited for repetitive production. Instead, they need to focus on how to generate and execute a production schedule that could change from one day to the next! This chapter uses an academic job shop scheduling (JSS) software, LEKIN, to demonstrate how an HMLV manufacturer can "plan the work then work the plan" on a daily basis without using ERP or Lean tools for production planning and operations scheduling. The scheduling software helps to determine which orders to release into production, how to set priorities at individual work centers so they process orders in the right sequence, and utilizes performance metrics for on-time delivery performance **and** waste elimination.

LEKIN: A General Job Shop Scheduling System

LEKIN is a general JSS system developed by Prof. Michael Pinedo and his research colleagues. Originally, the LEKIN scheduling system was designed for teaching and research. In due course of time, several offshoots of the system were embedded in real world implementations. The academic version of the system is available on CD-ROM in Dr. Pinedo's book *Planning and Scheduling in Manufacturing and Service* (Pinedo, 2005). It can also be downloaded from this website: http://web-static.stern.nyu.edu/om/software/lekin/. The system contains a number of dispatching rules and heuristics for scheduling. It also allows the user to link and test his/her own heuristics and compare their performances with the heuristics and algorithms embedded in the system. This flexible interactive scheduling system can display different production schedules in the form of Gantt Charts. Prof. Pinedo's contact information is as follows:

Prof. Michael Pinedo
Department of Operations Management
Stern School of Business
New York University
Phone: 212-998-0287
Email: MPinedo@stern.nyu.edu.
Website: www.stern.nyu.edu/om/faculty/pinedo/.

Manufacturing Systems That Can Be Scheduled by LEKIN

The Main Menu of LEKIN is shown in Figure 19.1. LEKIN can schedule six different types of manufacturing systems. The user must select any one of the six available scheduling environments to access the heuristics programmed for that configuration. The six scheduling system configurations available in LEKIN are:

1. *Single machine:* Single machine scheduling problems have been thoroughly analyzed under all kinds of conditions with many different objective functions. The result is a collection of rules that often provide optimal solutions in the single machine environment, such as the Earliest Due Date (EDD) rule or the Shortest Processing Time (SPT) rule. In many multi-machine production systems, there is a single bottleneck

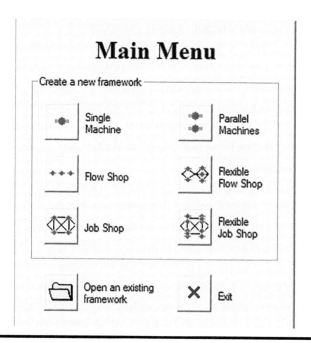

Figure 19.1   Scheduling environments available in LEKIN.

machine. In that case, the job sequence at the bottleneck typically determines the performance of the entire system. In such a case, it makes sense to schedule the bottleneck first and all other machines (upstream and downstream) afterward.

2. *Parallel machines:* Many production systems consist of several stages or work centers, each with a number of machines in parallel. All machines in a work center are assumed to have identical processing capabilities. Thereby, a job can be processed on the particular machine in that work center which has the earliest availability. Like in the case of a single machine, if one particular work center in the production system is a bottleneck, then the schedule that works best for that work center will determine the performance of the entire system.

3. *Flow shop:* In a flow shop, the routes of all jobs are identical; i.e., all jobs visit the same machines in the same sequence. The machines have a linear layout. So whenever a job completes its processing on one machine, it enters the queue at the next machine. If there is no conveyor to move jobs from one machine to the next in FIFO fashion, then jobs may be resequenced between machines. If the job sequence varies from machine to machine, this complicates the scheduling problem. However, if a conveyor transports the jobs from one machine to the next, then the same job sequence is maintained at very machine throughout the system.

4. *Flexible flow shop:* In a flexible flow shop, as in a flow shop, all the jobs follow the same sequence of operations through a series of stages. However, each stage has two or more parallel machines. So, in a flexible flow shop, a job may not have to wait to get processed at any stage. In some flexible flow shops, a job may bypass a machine (or stage) if it does not require any processing at that state. That way it goes ahead of the jobs that are being processed at that stage or waiting to be processed at that stage.

5. *Job shop:* In multi-operation shops that process a high product mix using different combinations of many different machines, the simplest case of a job shop is one where jobs have different routes and each job does not visit any of the machines in its route more than once. Also, their processing times on the different machines that they visit could be different from those for other jobs. The simplest case of a job shop that is dealt with in any scheduling textbook is still an extremely complex scheduling problem. Just about every job shop in the real world is more complicated!

6. *Flexible job shop:* In a flexible job shop, each work center has two or more machines that could process different jobs in parallel. For example, a semiconductor fab is a flexible job shop where the routes of the jobs are order-specific and require the job to visit the same work center several times for processing (aka "re-entrant flows").

LEKIN is also capable of dealing with sequence-dependent setup times in all the environments listed above.

Scheduling a Machining Cell Using LEKIN

Let us consider the case of a single sales order for ten different part #s. These ten parts comprise a kit ordered by a maintenance crew working at an oil refinery. They need all of these parts to be delivered by a specific due date in order for them to perform field repairs on one or more compressors. Since Maintenance, Repair, and Overhaul (MRO) is a non-repetitive business, these parts are produced in a stand-alone 10-machine cell that is separate from the rest of the machine shop that produces parts for assembling new compressors. Table 19.2 shows the (hypothetical) routings to capture the diversity of the machining requirements of these ten parts. Every operation (or step) in a routing is shown as X[##], where X represents the machine number used for that operation and ## represents the processing

Table 19.2 Routes and Processing Times for a Kit of Parts

Part #	Route for the Part
1249211	1[3]→2[3]→3[3]→4[18]→5[1]→6[1]→7[6]→8[1]→10[1]
1249452	4[55]→6[16]
1249498	1[3]→2[3]→3[3]→4[33]→6[3]→7[7]→8[3]→10[3]
1249538	1[3]→2[3]→3[3]→4[9]→5[12]→6[14]→7[7]→8[2]→10[2]
1249542	2[3]→3[7]→4[4]→7[9]
1250888	7[3]
1287501	1[1]→2[1]→3[1]→4[3]→6[5]→8[1]→10[1]
1287511	1[1]→2[1]→3[5]→7[4]→8[1]→10[1]
1287518	1[1]→2[1]→3[1]→4[4]→6[1]→7[4]→8[1]→10[1]
1288716	6[2]→7[4]→8[2]→10[2]

time on that machine. When scheduling the cell using LEKIN, the goal is to minimize the total time it takes to complete the entire kit of ten parts. In the academic scheduling literature, this metric is called the *Makespan* of a schedule. Note that in any such Make-To-Order situation, especially when due dates must be met, it is inadvisable to use assembly line scheduling strategies such as TT, Heijunka, Pitch, Pacemaker, etc.

The data in Table 19.2 clearly indicates that the flow of products in the machining cell corresponds to that of a job shop (and not an assembly line or flow shop). So, in order to initiate scheduling of the cell, we select the job shop environment from the LEKIN Main Menu (Figure 19.2).

Input Overall Size of the Job Shop

Once the selection *job shop* has been made, the *Number of work centers* (ten) and the *Number of jobs* (ten) need to be input in order to specify the size of the job shop that must be scheduled, as shown in Figure 19.3.

Input Work Center Data

Next, the data for each of the ten work centers in the job shop must be entered. Given the simplicity of the problem, we assumed that there is only one machine in each of the different work centers. Also, we used a default

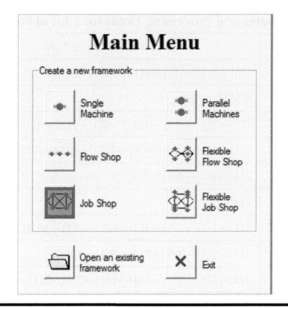

Figure 19.2   Job shop selection is made in the main menu of LEKIN.

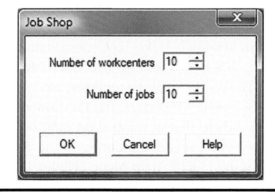

Figure 19.3   Parameters for the size of the job shop.

value of "0" for the *Availability date* for each of the ten machines. LEKIN being an academic scheduling package, it assumes a simple timeline starting at Time = 0.[1] Therefore, the *Availability date* for each machine was specified as 0 to indicate that all work centers were available to accept jobs at Time = 0 (Figure 19.4).

---

[1] Commercial FCS packages have detailed calendars with dates to indicate availability of any resource.

Figure 19.4   Work center data for each machine in the job shop.

Input Job Data

Figures 19.5 and 19.6 illustrate how to insert the data for any job in LEKIN. For example, Figure 19.5 shows the screen for entering the Header data for Part # 1249211 from the appropriate row in Table 19.2. Once that screen is complete, you click on the *Load Route* button to insert the details for the routing of that same part, as shown in Figure 19.6.

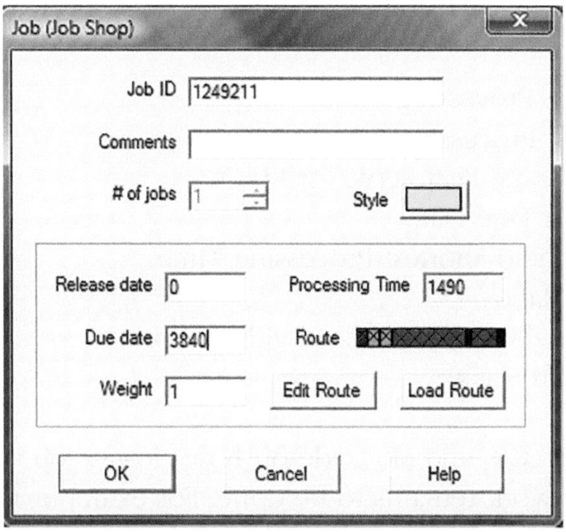

Figure 19.5   Header data for a job.

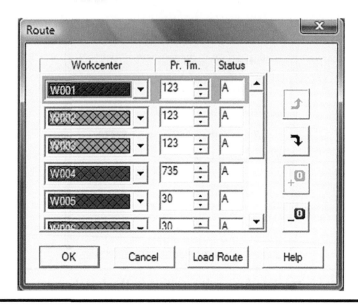

Figure 19.6 Complete route for a job.

Scheduling the Job Shop

After inserting the data for the Work centers and Jobs, you can proceed to schedule the job shop using the data that has been input to LEKIN using the simplest approach available – Dispatching Rules. A dispatching rule is an algorithm that is used to prioritize all the jobs that are queued at each machine. Whichever job is at the front of this ordered queue is chosen to be processed next. LEKIN offers various dispatching rules such as:

- SPT – Shortest Processing Time
- LPT – Longest Processing Time
- FCFS – First Come First Serve (or FIFO)
- EDD – Earliest Due Date
- WSPT – Weighted Shortest Processing Time
- CR – Critical Ratio
- ATCS – Apparent Tardiness Cost with Setup
- MS – Minimum Slack

Rules such as EDD, CR, and MS trade-off how close a job is to its Due Date versus how much work remains to be done. For example, the trade-off could be (i) just at the machine where the job is in queue or (ii) the total remaining work considering all incomplete steps in the routing, including

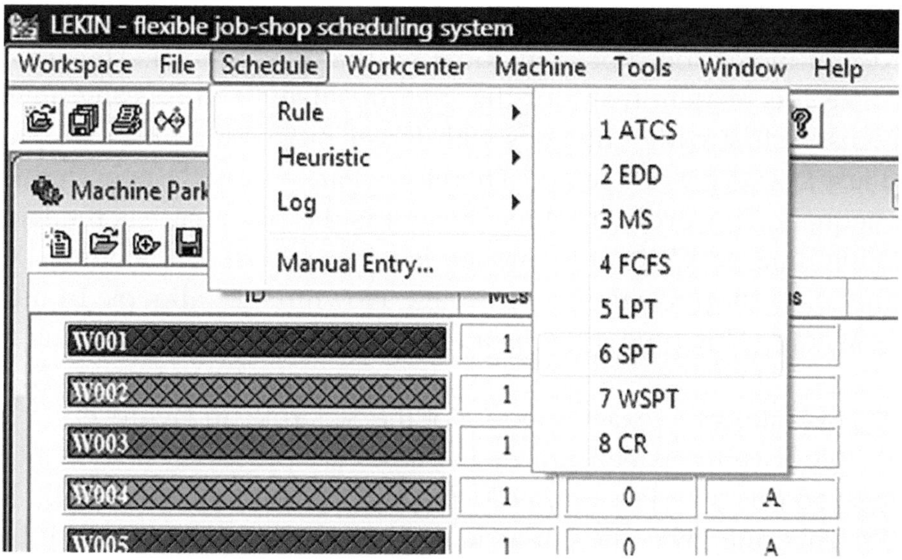

Figure 19.7   Scheduling using a dispatching rule.

the work to be done at the machine where the job is in queue. In contrast, rules such as SPT, LPT, and WSPT are based on the processing times for immediate operations that need to be done. Figure 19.7 shows how the sequence of steps to select the SPT rule for scheduling a job shop is implemented in LEKIN using the Drop Down Menu Bar for *Schedule*.

On selecting the SPT dispatching rule, LEKIN will generate a Gantt Chart showing the sequence in which jobs are processed on each of the ten machines in the job shop using that dispatching rule. Notice the option **Heuristic** in the Drop Down Menu Bar for *Schedule*? This option allows some of the more advanced scheduling heuristics available in LEKIN to be chosen instead of the notoriously "myopic" dispatching rules that are limited to a particular machine in the job shop.

Gantt Charts

A Gantt Chart is a visual display of the sequence in which jobs are processed at each and every work center. No job can start its next operation on any work center unless (i) it has completed its previous operation and (ii) the next work center is available to accept its next job. The Gantt Charts shown in this section demonstrate how different dispatching rules may or may not result in schedules that optimize the Makespan metric.

SPT: Per this rule, jobs queued at any work center are sequenced in the order of increasing processing time on that work center. Thus in Figure 19.8 it is evident that jobs that require smallest processing times are processed first while the ones with larger processing times are processed last at every work center. Therefore, Part # 1249211 is placed last in the sequence for every machine since it is the part that has the largest processing time on WC1. This rule tends to work well if it is desired to schedule a job shop to minimize Average Flowtime for all jobs. In minimizing Average Flowtime, there is a direct correlation to minimizing the WIP too.

LPT: This rule is the exact opposite of the SPT rule. In Figure 19.9 the jobs that have the largest processing times are processed first on all machines. So this time Part # 1249211 is now processed first on WC1.

FCFS: This rule gives the job arriving first at any workstation the highest priority. This scheduling rule is very simple to understand and implement, especially in the case of assembly lines and flow shops where every product flows through the same sequence of steps. But, in a job shop, it usually results in high waiting times (and therefore high WIP too) (Figure 19.10).

EDD: This rule gives highest priority to the job with the EDD compared with all other due dates assigned to jobs. In the case of our scheduling problem, since all the parts being produced constitute a single sales order, the due date for shipment of the kit of parts is the due date for every one of the ten jobs. Therefore, the Gantt Chart for this rule looks very similar to the one obtained using the FCFS rule (Figure 19.11).

CR: CR for a job is calculated by dividing the time remaining until a job's due date by the total time remaining for those operations that have not been completed for the job. The total time remaining for a job is defined as the sum of the setup, processing, move, and expected waiting times for all the operations that remain to be done on the job. Per this rule, the job with minimum value for CR is given the highest priority and selected first to be processed at the work center under consideration (Figure 19.12).

MS: Slack for a job is the difference between the time remaining until the job's due date and the total remaining time for all the operations that remain to be done for that job. Per this rule, the job with the least slack (MS) is given the highest priority and selected first to be processed at the work center (Figure 19.13).

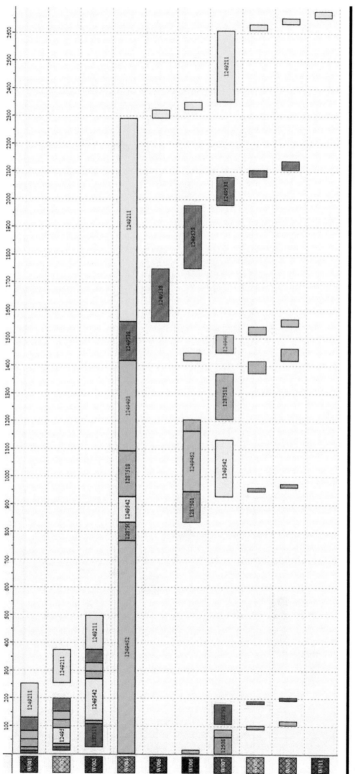

Figure 19.8 Gantt Chart using SPT dispatching rule.

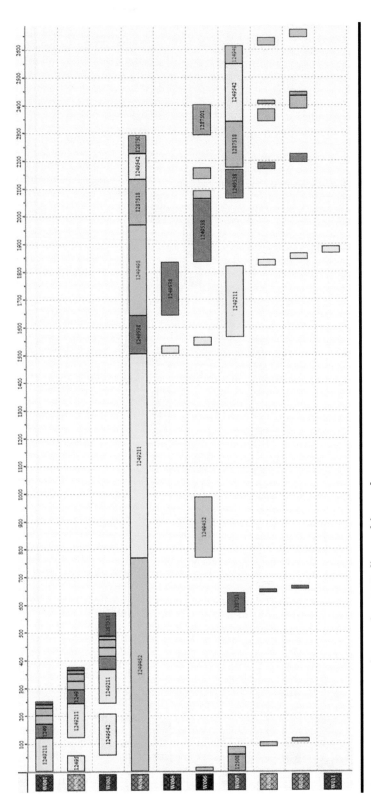

Figure 19.9 Gantt Chart using LPT dispatching rule.

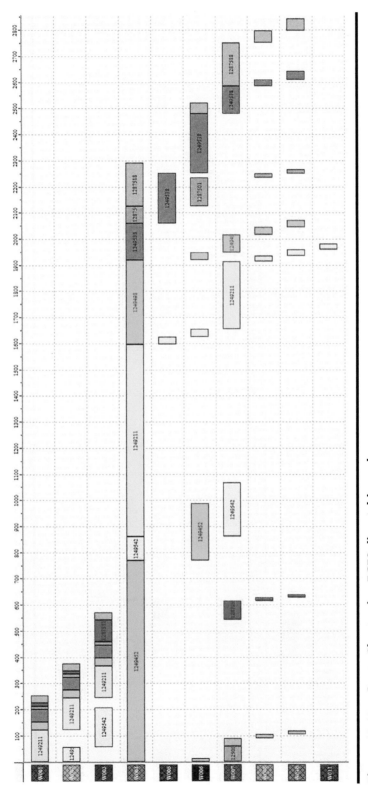

Figure 19.10 Gantt Chart using FCFS dispatching rule.

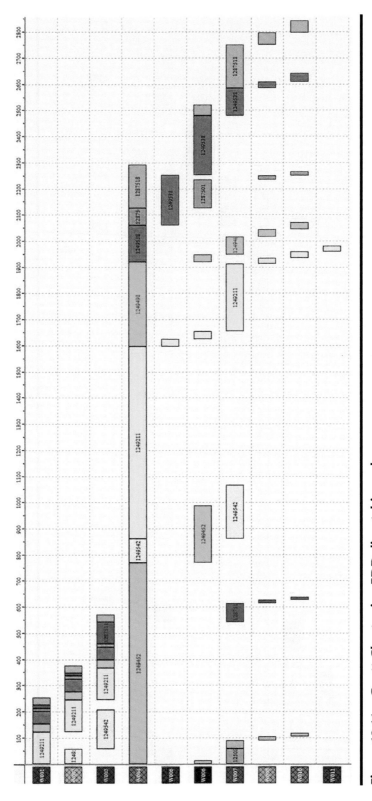

Figure 19.11 Gantt Chart using EDD dispatching rule.

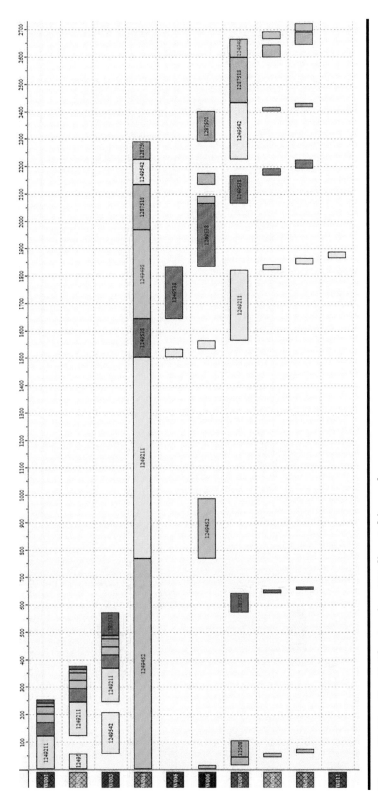

Figure 19.12   Gantt Chart using CR dispatching rule.

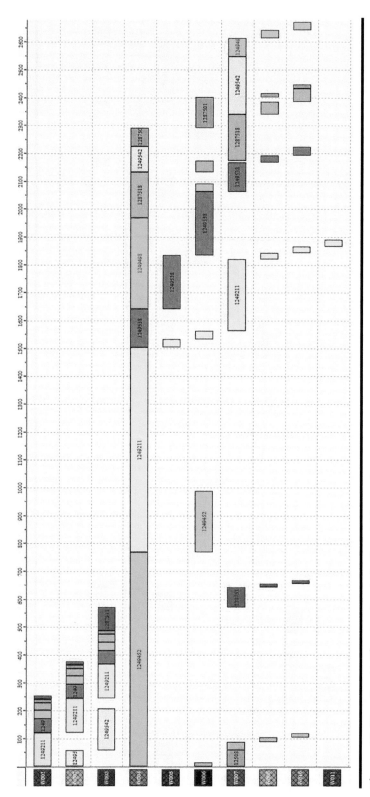

Figure 19.13   Gantt Chart using MS dispatching rule.

Performance Measures

In order to compare the performance of different dispatching rules and heuristics used to schedule the job shop, LEKIN offers a logbook feature to compare their performance using several performance measures such as:

1. *Job flow time* – Time a job completes minus the time when the job became available for processing on the first machine in its route.
2. *Makespan* – Time it takes to finish the entire set of jobs being scheduled. In the case of our scheduling problem, this is the metric that is of interest. It is the time when the last job in the kit of ten jobs completes, and the kit can be shipped to the customer.
3. *Job lateness* – Time that the job is completed ahead of, on, or behind schedule.
4. *Job tardiness* – Time that the job's completion time exceeds the due date for the job. Note that if a job is completed early, its tardiness is 0 (because it is not late).

Table 19.3 is a logbook that shows how the different dispatching rules performed on different performance measures.

Table 19.3   Logbook for Results from Different Dispatching Rules

	Performance Measure				
Dispatching Rule	Makespan C_{max}	Maximum Tardiness T_{max}	TFT ΣC_j	Number of Late Jobs ΣU_j	Total Tardiness ΣT_j
SPT	2,679	179	11,514	1	179
LPT	2,672	172	16,058	2	221
FCFS	2,844	344	14,688	2	486
EDD	2,844	344	14,688	2	486
CR	2,723	223	16,236	2	415
MS	2,672	172	16,058	2	221

Charts for Visual Comparison of Performance Measures

Figure 19.14 shows a Radar chart that LEKIN generates to display how different dispatching rules and heuristics performed on various performance metrics. Figure 19.15 shows a Line chart to compare the Tardiness, Makespan, and Total Flow Time (TFT) performance of different dispatching rules. Based on Figures 19.14 and 19.15, when Makespan is the metric under consideration, it appears that all the scheduling rules have comparable performance. Still SPT, LPT, and MS rules perform better than the other rules. In the case of Tardiness, the SPT, LPT, and MS rules still outperform the other scheduling rules. But when it comes to the TFT, the SPT rule clearly outperforms all the other rules and obtains the lowest value for TFT (which is the same as Average Flow Time). Thus, in the case of our scheduling problem, since all the parts being produced constitute a single sales order, the scheduler would advise the cell leader to advise the cell operators to use the SPT rule to select jobs at their individual machines whenever there are two or more jobs waiting to be processed at that machine.

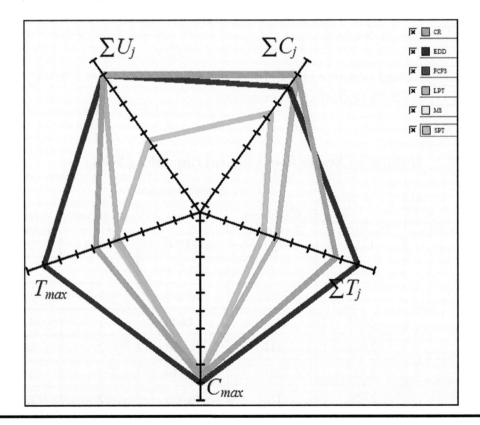

Figure 19.14 Radar Chart.

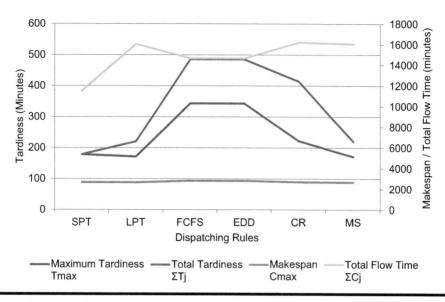

Figure 19.15   Line Chart.

How Scheduling Extends Lean in High-Mix Low-Volume (HMLV) Facilities

This chapter discussed the fundamentals of JSS. It used the LEKIN academic scheduling software to solve a simple JSS problem involving ten different parts that comprise a single sales order that had to be produced in a cell. In the real world, an HMLV manufacturer that has the data, in-house personnel, budget, and willingness to implement a commercial Finite Capacity Scheduler (FCS) would realize many benefits that otherwise cannot be gained by implementing the popular Lean tools like Value Stream Mapping (VSM), Heijunka, Inventory Supermarkets, and Kanban. What are some of these benefits?

A Gantt Chart can display the timelines for many products: VSM has absolutely no ability to visualize and evaluate any multi-product multi-machine production system where different resources are shared dynamically by different products. This is evident from Figure 19.16, which shows the Current State Map for a single product's Value Stream. In contrast, a Gantt Chart can highlight problems in the current production schedule for an assembly line, a flow shop, a job shop, a repair shop, and other Make-To-Order HMLV environments. Also, any commercial FCS tool can help to selectively display much more data about all of the active jobs than the data boxes featured in a manually prepared Value Stream Map.

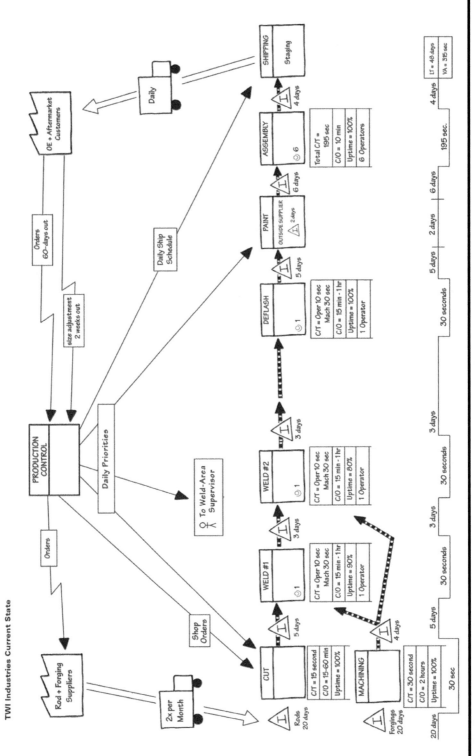

Figure 19.16   VSM for a *Single* product.

A Gantt Chart can suggest Continuous Improvement opportunities: The timeline that appears at the bottom of any VSM like the one shown in Figure 19.16 (Rother & Shook, 2003) is unfit for representing the flow efficiency (aka Value-Added Ratio in a VSM) of multiple products that are being simultaneously processed in a multi-machine flow shop, job shop, or project shop. Instead, a classical Gantt Chart like those shown in Figures 19.8–19.13 can provide visual guidance to improve the existing manufacturing system using a variety of product/process improvement strategies. For example, in the case of the scheduling problem in Table 19.2, it is obvious that the processing times are the highest on WC #4. In all the Gantt Charts (Figures 19.8–19.13) obtained using various dispatching rules, the large chunks of idle time in the timelines for WCs #5, #6, #7, #8, #9, and #10 indicate that these machines do not have high workloads compared with WC #4. Also, almost all the jobs in the sales order are processed on WC #4. Naturally, unless these processing times are reduced, subsequent work centers (WCs #5, #6, #7, #8, #9, and #10) that process the jobs that come off WC #4 will experience high waiting times besides the low utilization of their capacity.

Computer-Aided Scheduling of Mixed Model Value Streams (MMVS): It is important to not equate a multi-product assembly line to a flow shop or other variants of the basic flow shop. It is incorrect to equate an MMVS (Duggan, 2013) or a Mixed Model Production Line (Rahn & Leone, 2014) to a flow shop, job shop, or custom fabrication project shop. Similar to the assembly lines in any Toyota facility, either of these manufacturing systems is an assembly cell (or line) that is producing multiple orders for a family of similar products. Each is designed using a classical Assembly Line Balancing methodology. Both assume a steady production rate based on an annual, maybe quarterly, forecasted demand for each product. Both ignore due dates and operate in a Make-To-Stock (MTS) mode. Today, especially with the ready availability of several commercial software tools like FLEXSIM,[2] SIMIO,[3] SIMCAD,[4] CSUITE,[5] and FLOWLYTICS,[6] there is no need to rely on simplistic manual calculations for analysis and design of a single-product Value Stream (Rother & Shook, 2003) or an MMVS (Duggan, 2013). In particular, the academic research literature on simulation-aided enhancements

---

[2] *Source:* www.flexsim.com/value-stream-mapping/.
[3] *Source:* www.simio.com/software/production-scheduling-software.php.
[4] *Source:* www.createasoft.com/Industries/Value-Stream-Map-Simulation.
[5] *Source:* www.factoryphysics.com/flow-benchmarking.
[6] *Source:* www.invistics.com/?page_id=4734.

in the manual method of VSM is extensive (McDonald, Van Aken & Rentes, 2002; Lian & Van Landeghem, 2017).

If it is desired to implement Job Shop Lean, an MMVS is to an assembly line what the flow shop, the flexible flow shop, and hybrid flow shop producing a variety of similar (or dissimilar) products are to HMLV environments. Specifically, a *Flexible Flow Shop* consists of a flow line with several parallel machines on some or all production stages. Multiple products are produced in such a flow line. While all the products follow the same linear path through the system, all of them may not visit all the stages of production. On each of the stages, one of the parallel machines has to be selected for the production of a given product. The production of a product consists of multiple operations, one for each production stage. When an operation is started on a machine, it must be finished without interruption. And, a *Hybrid Flow Shop* is a multi-stage and sequential production system where each stage is composed of M parallel machines. Each machine is able to process one job at a time. A multi-stage flow shop would be considered to be a hybrid flow shop even if one stage at least is made up of more than one machine. All operations on every job have to be realized sequentially without overlapping between stages. Job preemption and job splitting are not allowed. Each job has a given processing time at each stage. Therefore, the simplifying assumptions and manual calculations used to design an MMVS are unsuitable for scheduling a flow shop or a hybrid flow shop or a flexible flow shop and, in the worst case, a job shop. It is not easy to predict the flow and completion times of production orders, bottlenecks, and inventories (over time) in production systems that are more complicated than an MMVS. It is also not easy to fix rational due dates for new orders, sequence multiple orders, predict delivery lead time, and minimize WIP in flow shops and job shops. Enter tools for analysis, planning, and control of a variety of production system FCS such as Preactor (www.Preactor.com), TACTIC (www.Waterloo-Software.com), Schedlyzer (www.Optisol.biz), Asprova (www.asprova.com/en/), and Simio (www.simio.com/software/production-scheduling-software.php). An FCS is a powerful software tool that helps in planning, scheduling, controlling, and managing flexible flow shops, job shops, and project shops. It facilitates fast and extensive what-if analysis of a variety of production systems. It enables users to simulate and analyze the workflow and measure the impact of any changes in the system on performance measures of the system. However, these tools require considerable and complete information including due dates, quantities, priorities and process requirements of orders, the resource requirements of operations, and resource available times.

Conclusion

This chapter discussed a simplified example of cell scheduling where ten different jobs that constitute a single sales order had to be produced in a cell. LEKIN, an academic scheduling software, was used to generate the best schedule that would minimize the total time to complete the entire kit of parts. LEKIN may lack the ability to consider many real-world scheduling scenarios such as transfer delays between operations, batch splitting (including one-piece flow), finite capacity constraints, etc. In fact, LEKIN does not separate processing time and setup time (for a batch) in the operation times, run time per piece in a batch of parts, sequence-dependent changeover times on a bottleneck machine, order quantities, etc. Yet, despite these limitations, LEKIN will help any interested individual learn the basic scheduling theory underlying the commercial scheduling software packages that are suitable for scheduling flow shops, flexible flow shops, job shops, and other multi-machine HMLV manufacturing environments that are not assembly lines. An HMLV manufacturer who is frustrated with their ERP systems and seeks more return from Lean should first gain sufficient knowledge of scheduling using a simplified scheduling package like LEKIN. Subsequently, they should start evaluating commercial scheduling software packages to find one that fits their particular HMLV environment **and** has current users in industry who vouch for that product.

Appendices

Appendices for this chapter are available for download at https://www.crcpress.com/9781498740692.

Supplementary Reading

Scheduling an M-machine Flow Shop to Minimize Makespan: This is my lecture on flow shop Scheduling in the course on Production Control and Scheduling that I taught at The Ohio State University.

An IE Student's Study Guide for Bottleneck Scheduling using Theory Of Constraints: This ebook was written in collaboration with an extremely bright undergraduate student, Sadono Djumin. He later became the Teaching Assistant for the course on Production Control and Scheduling that

I taught at The Ohio State University. This ebook is the result of his idea to develop a quantitative foundation for the Theory Of Constraints (TOC) using appropriate Operations Research models and Single Machine Scheduling theory. Also, this book contains an exhaustive Q&A to teach the numerous practical strategies for managing production systems that are taught in *The Goal* video. If you plan to incorporate TOC in your Lean Six Sigma training, then you could ask the attendees to answer some, preferably all, the questions in the Q&A. And if you come up with more questions to teach lessons for effective management of complex production systems embedded in this classic video, please share them with me. Thank you, Sadono!

Introduction to Flow Shop Scheduling: Trafficware Inc. is a Make-To-Order assembler of electromechanical assemblies. Each assembly requires a variety of printed circuit boards (PCBs) that are fabricated in-house on a manual assembly line. This folder contains the materials that I developed to conduct a simple training exercise to teach the basics of Flow Shop Scheduling to a team at Trafficware Inc. (www.trafficware.com/) *using hypothetical data.*

Case Study on Flow Shop Scheduling: Trafficware Inc. is a Make-To-Order assembler of electromechanical assemblies. Each assembly requires a variety of PCBs that are fabricated in-house on a manual assembly line. This folder contains the materials that I developed to conduct a simple training exercise to teach the basics of Flow Shop Scheduling to a team at Trafficware Inc. (www.trafficware.com/) *using actual time study data based on shop floor observation.*

Scheduling a 5-Machine Flow Shop: The primary purpose of this exercise to teach Flow Shop Scheduling is to demonstrate (i) the need for good data to do any scheduling and (ii) the essential role of software to schedule any real-world flow shop. Scheduling and producing Gantt Charts manually is out of the question! This folder contains the materials for a 5-machine flow shop producing ten different products.

Releasing Orders to a Cell with Capacity Constraints: This folder contains the solution key for the scheduling example discussed in Appendix 4 for this chapter which appears later in this book. It also includes blank Gantt Charts if you are interested in manually generating the schedules for different scenarios that result in a Makespan ≥ 400 minutes. For example, say you decided to produce the jobs in the cell using the sequence $4{\to}2{\to}3{\to}1$ and "did the MRP thing"; i.e., you release material to produce the Demand Lot Sizes for the four parts ($DLS_1 = 50$, $DLS_2 = 20$, $DLS_3 = 30$, $DLS_4 = 40$). You can rest assured that, even if you used one-piece flow to stream each batch from Machine #1 to #2 and setup each machine to run a batch well in advance before the first piece from that batch arrived at the machine, you will NOT be able to complete Part #1 on Machine #2 within 400 minutes! Just the workload on Machine #1 is (10 + 5*50 + 5 + 3*20 + 12 + 2*30 + 5 + 4*40) = 562 minutes! Next, there could be idle times on Machine #2 because, given the sequence in which the parts were run through the cell, the machine may be unable to immediately load and run the parts it receives from Machine #1.

Bibliography

Baker, K.R. & Trietsch, D. (2009). *Principles of Sequencing and Scheduling.* Hoboken, NJ: John Wiley.

> *Relevance of this book to the chapter:* The authors have programmed most of the fundamental scheduling problems in Excel. The Excel macros are available on their website. If you find LEKIN a challenge to learn and use, then these Excel macros would be easier to learn to get a flavor of operations scheduling in different manufacturing environments.

Duggan, K. (2013). *Creating Mixed Model Value Streams: Practical Lean Techniques for Building To Demand.* Boca Raton, FL: CRC Press.

Lian, Y.-H. & Van Landeghem, H. (2017). Analyzing the effects of Lean manufacturing using a value stream mapping-based simulation generator. *International Journal of Production Research*, 45(13), 3037–3058.

McDonald, T., Van Aken, E.M. & Rentes, A.F. (2002). Using simulation to enhance value stream mapping: A manufacturing case application. *International Journal of Logistics: Research and Applications*, 5(2), 213–232.

Pinedo, M. (2005). *Planning and Scheduling in Manufacturing and Services.* New York: Springer-Verlag.

Pound, E.S., Bell, J.H. & Spearman, M.L. (2014). *Factory Physics for Managers: How Leaders Improve Performance in a Post-Lean Six Sigma World.* New York: McGraw-Hill.

> *Relevance of this book to the chapter:*

> 1. Chapter 8 (Leadership, Measures, and Culture Change): This chapter presents an example of how the Factory Physics approach has been used by the leadership of Ace Precision (https://arc-precision.com/factory-physics/), a Minnesota company that offers a wide range of CNC (Computer Numerical Control) machining services to produce components and assemblies for medical devices, instruments, and implants. The company leadership accomplished very good control over their operations through its employees' application of Factory Physics science in operations design, daily shop floor control, and supplier management.

2. Chapter 9 (Examples from Industry): This chapter contains five case studies that demonstrate the use of the Factory Physics (www.FactoryPhysics.com) methodology in different industry sectors. In particular, the results of a Value Stream Mapping example from a famous book on Lean Manufacturing (Rother & Shook, 2003) are extended using Factory Physics science.

Rahn, R. & Leone, G. (2014). *The Complete Guide to Mixed Model Line Design: Designing the Perfect Value Stream*. Boulder, CO: Leonardo Group Americas LLC. (www.leonardogroupamericas.com).

Rother, M. & Shook, J. (2003, June). *Learning To See: Value Stream Mapping to Create Value and Eliminate Muda*. Cambridge, MA: Lean Enterprise Institute.

Sipper, D. & Bulfin, R.L. (1997). *Production: Planning, Control and Integration*. New York: McGraw-Hill.

Relevance of this book to the chapter: Chapter 8 (Operations Scheduling) was the basis for my lectures on scheduling in the course on Production Control and Scheduling that I used to teach at The Ohio State University. Section 7 (Finite Capacity Scheduling Systems) merits reading. Try to solve the scheduling problem in Section 10 (Mini Case: Ilana Designs) using LEKIN!

Sule, D.R. (1997). *Industrial Scheduling*. Boston, MA: PWS Publishing Co.

Relevance of this book to the chapter: Chapter 4 (Flow Shop Problems) discusses a real-world scenario involving travel time between the machines in a 2-machine cell.

Relevance of these YouTube videos to the chapter: These videos will introduce the reader to the fundamentals of multi-product multi-machine scheduling problems whose solutions have evaded HMLV manufacturers to this day:

1. Scheduling a 2-machine Flow Shop to Minimize Makespan (*Source*: www.youtube.com/watch?v=O3Zuq9-9Hu0)
2. Scheduling a 3-machine Flow Shop to Minimize Makespan (*Source*: www.youtube.com/watch?v=SSyGL8LTXXo)
3. JSS using Dispatching Rules (*Source*: www.youtube.com/watch?v=xZs7WsNPJXY)
4. JSS using Shifting Bottleneck Heuristic (*Source*: www.youtube.com/watch?v=JUz0pCG51DE)

Relevance of these YouTube videos to the chapter: These videos will give the reader a quick high-level overview on some of the leading commercial FCSs:

1. Why Production Scheduling Is Necessary (*Source*: www.youtube.com/watch?v=tEDbYkAJvms&list=PLx8-4MlxYCksZ8ZZzvb3hAIrEO8BUTB-d)
2. JSS/Machine Shop Scheduling (*Source*: www.youtube.com/watch?v=mmJuJoTsXQo)
3. Advanced Planning and Scheduling for Manufacturing (*Source*: www.youtube.com/watch?v=-zCfC_SUvSQ)

4. Preactor 11 in the Job Shop (Part 1 of 2) (*Source*: www.youtube.com/ watch?v=A5fq0pg6loY&t=38s), Preactor 11 in the Job Shop (Part 2 of 2) (*Source*: www.youtube.com/watch?v=ZVjDLbMJW4k&t=65s)
5. Finite Scheduling with Asprova (*Source*: www.youtube.com/ watch?v=FXr0K8GOZrY)

Case Studies and White Papers on Finite Capacity Scheduling:

1. *Source*: www.waterloo-software.com/case-studies/
2. *Source*: www.lean-manufacturing-japan.com/
3. *Source*: www.simio.com/case-studies/index.php

Chapter 20

Finite Capacity Scheduling of a Flexible and Lean (FLean) Machining Cell

Acknowledgment

This chapter is based on the work that I did when I was the Director of Industrial Engineering (IE) Research at Hoerbiger Corporation of America. This was my first industry job and a golden opportunity given to me by Hannes Hunschofsky, who was then the President of Hoerbiger Corporation of America. He invited (and challenged!) me to pilot the implementation of Job Shop Lean in their Houston, TX, facility. Had it not been for this job, I would never be where I am today – in industry doing hands-on projects to put my research into practice. Thank you, Hannes!

Background

Figure 20.1 gives an overview of a comprehensive approach that is followed for implementing Job Shop Lean in any high-mix low-volume discrete manufacturing facility, such as machine shops, forge shops, fabrication shops, mold shops, etc. At the core of this iterative approach is the expectation that a job shop (i) will utilize Production Flow Analysis and/or Group Technology to identify the stable part families in its product mix, (ii) will produce each part family that has a stable demand in an FLean (Flexible+Lean) manufacturing

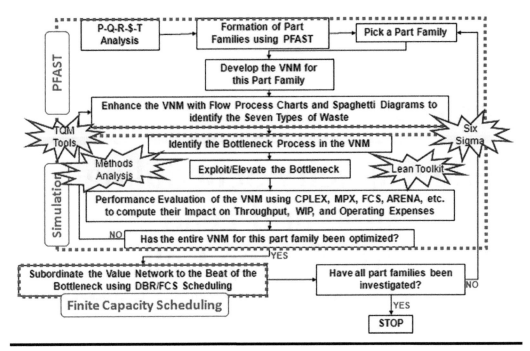

Figure 20.1   Comprehensive approach for implementing Job Shop Lean.

cell and (iii) utilize Finite Capacity Scheduling (FCS) to schedule each cell on a daily shift-by-shift basis. *In theory*, every time that one loop of the process shown in Figure 20.1 is completed, it will result in the implementation of a stand-alone FLean manufacturing cell dedicated to producing a family of parts whose manufacturing requirements are completely satisfied by the cell, except for in-house support services like Maintenance or Tool Room and (external) vendor operations that simply could not be absorbed into the cell. *In reality*, numerous constraints may need to be broken to the extent that is possible. For example, it **is** possible to train operators to run different machines in a cell and to offer group incentives to those who work in a cell so they begin to work as a team to achieve metrics like on-time delivery and first-time quality rather than machine utilization or labor efficiency. However, it **is not** possible to incorporate a heat treatment furnace inside a cell next to a CNC (Computer Numerical Control) grinder. Typically, after several iterations of the process in Figure 20.1, a job shop will get divided into at least two areas: (i) One area consists of several FLean manufacturing cells with each cell dedicated to a product family and (ii) the other area is a "remainder job shop" that produces parts in the product mix that are produced in small quantities, have low value and are ordered infrequently (aka "cats and dogs"), such as spare parts, prototypes for emergent business, and one-off orders. By dividing the job shop into these two areas, (i) the FLean cells provide unquestionable quick response, high quality, teamwork, and other benefits that are guaranteed by manufacturing cells and (ii) only a smaller non-cellular portion of the entire facility will continue to operate as a complex job shop which is always a challenge to schedule and control.

What Follows the Layout Design of an FLean Cell

Numerous job shops continue to rely on their ERP (Enterprise Resource Planning) systems to schedule (sic!) production, regardless of whether it is a single cell or the entire facility that is being scheduled. ERP systems are incapable of scheduling! Any ERP-generated schedule for a cell will have to be adjusted daily by experienced cell operators who can eyeball workloads (and capacity requirements) by just looking at the queue of parts in the cell. In the case of Hoerbiger Corporation of America in Pompano Beach, FL, Preactor (www.preactor.com) is the FCS tool being used in the main facility located in Pompano Beach, FL. The firm orders and their due dates quoted to customers are downloaded into Preactor from SAP (which is their ERP system). After the schedule is generated by Preactor, it is input to the MES (Manufacturing Execution System), FactoryViewer, which publishes twice daily a machine-by-machine sequence for producing orders loaded on every machine in the facility. Since every machine's operator must record the start/stop times for each order processed on their machine, the MES closes the loop between the daily schedule produced by Preactor and the real-time execution of that schedule. The complete daily schedule for a shop can be visualized using a Gantt Chart, such as the one shown in Figure 20.2 which was produced by Preactor.[1]

Scheduling a *Single* High-Mix Low-Volume Cell

Per the methodology for implementing Job Shop Lean outlined in Figure 20.1, if a cell can be implemented so all value-adding operations to produce its part family are performed inside it, then its operations can

---

[1] Computer-aided scheduling facilitates Visual Management! For our Power Rings Cell, our IT staff had developed a robust user interface between the FCS (Preactor) and the MES (FactoryViewer) to standardize how the employees in the cell interacted with the daily schedule displayed on their computer monitors.

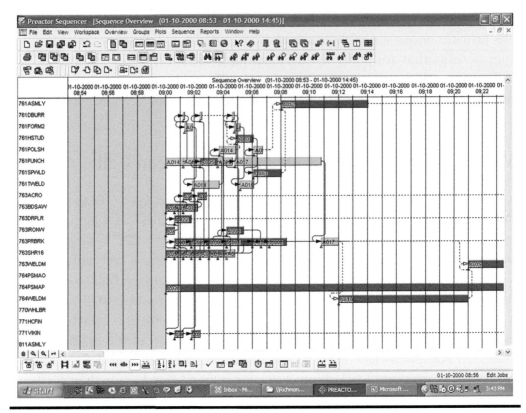

Figure 20.2 Gantt Chart representation of a production schedule for visual management.

be scheduled using an FCS running on a stand-alone desktop in the cell. Having implemented a new layout for the Manual Packings Cell (MPC) in the Houston, TX, facility of Hoerbiger Corporation of America, the next step was to schedule daily operations in the cell. Depending on the complexity of the part family and the fluctuations in demand for the parts produced in the cell, a manual/visual system for scheduling the cell may have sufficed. One of our own cells, the Quick Response Cell (QRC), used a manual scheduling board that was populated with orders by an office manager based on his estimates of workload and available cell capacity. But I did not wish to schedule the MPC cell using ad hoc manual cell scheduling methods. Because, if future cells had to share resources with this cell, then the schedules of those cells (and outside vendors too) would have to be coordinated with this cell's schedule.

Therefore, in this chapter, I will focus on the use of FCS software for computer-aided scheduling of the MPC cell. The cell was essentially a small job shop. Therefore, effective scheduling would improve its performance and employee utilization. The complexity of scheduling even a small job shop with four or more machines used in various combinations makes it hard to generate, revise, and maintain its daily schedule manually. Ask any IE graduate who has taken a course in Scheduling about how much time it took him/her to produce the schedule for a job shop consisting of just three machines producing 4 parts with different routings! In the case of the MPC cell, it had different equipment types, and in some cases, two machines of the same type that were capable of processing the same parts if the tools and fixtures were available. So, in order to complete the Job Shop Lean implementation process shown in Figure 20.1, we undertook an exploratory proof-of-concept project to demonstrate the following operational scenario for the cell:

If the daily schedule that was issued to the cell at the start of the day was subject to change due to changing order priorities, machine breakdowns, rush orders, operator(s) taken sick during the shift, due date changes forced by customers, etc., could we rapidly revise and regenerate a new schedule for the cell?

Why Schedlyzer Lite Was Chosen over Preactor

Like all other ERP systems on the market, SAP uses MRP (Material Requirements Planning) for production planning and operations scheduling. MRP uses assumptions of infinite capacity, backward scheduling from customer due dates using fixed lead times, batch production, etc. So there was no question of using SAP for scheduling the MPC.

Although Preactor was being used successfully in our Pompano Beach facility, our current license and implementation was for a factory-wide installation. This licensing structure had resulted in a less than desirable pilot implementation of the SAP+Preactor+FactoryViewer system to manage the day-to-day operations of the Power Rings Cell in our Houston, TX, facility. Also, our Director of Manufacturing Systems, who was the architect of the integrated system being used in Pompano Beach, FL, had prior commitments that made him unavailable during the period when we wanted to do this project. Due to his time constraints, it was difficult to obtain a standalone license that would run on a desktop computer dedicated to the MPC.

Therefore, we decided to work with another FCS vendor, Optisol Inc. (www.Optisol.biz), and used their Schedlyzer Lite tool for the project. Schedlyzer Lite is easy to learn and allows a user-friendly VBA (Visual Basic) interface to be developed for shop floor employees. Its price tag easily makes it affordable to purchase a single license for a computer that can be dedicated to a cell. Its vendor, who is resident in Bryan, TX, boasts a track record of successful implementations in several job shops.

Figure 20.3 shows the VBA interface between SAP and Schedlyzer Lite that was developed by the graduate intern we hired to work on this project. Since SAP query authorization was not allowed for our project, a macro in SAP was adapted to automatically generate data for daily orders. First you would click on the button highlighted in **red** then click on the button highlighted in **yellow**. Voila, the Input Data File for Schedlyzer, would be ready with data extracted from SAP!

Next, as shown in Figure 20.4, we would open the Input Data File for Schedlyzer that was produced from SAP and, with one click on the "Schedule" button, we would schedule all jobs for production in the cell. By default, Schedlyzer Lite releases all jobs to complete by Earliest Due Date (EDD) subject to capacity constraints. Queues of jobs at individual machines are prioritized using the same EDD dispatching rule.

Figure 20.5 shows the Cell Schedule Summary screen in Schedlyzer Lite with detailed information on every job (Job ID, Job Start Time, Job Finish Time, Relative Earliness/Lateness compared to Due Date, etc.). In the case of our pilot project, 30 jobs and 139 operations were scheduled to minimize the Average # of In-Process Jobs (WIP) to 8.2 orders. Some immediate benefits of this screen are that (i) it will help Customer Services to decide whether a new order could be finished by its customer-specified due date and (ii) it will tell the Shipping Department when to expect any order so it can be ready to start packaging it for shipment as soon as it arrived.

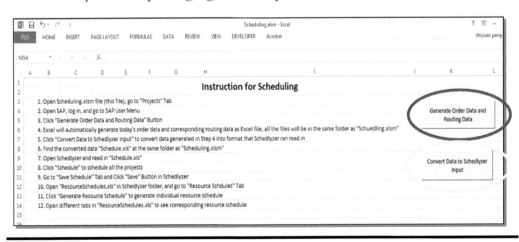

Figure 20.3 VBA interface between SAP and Schedlyzer Lite.

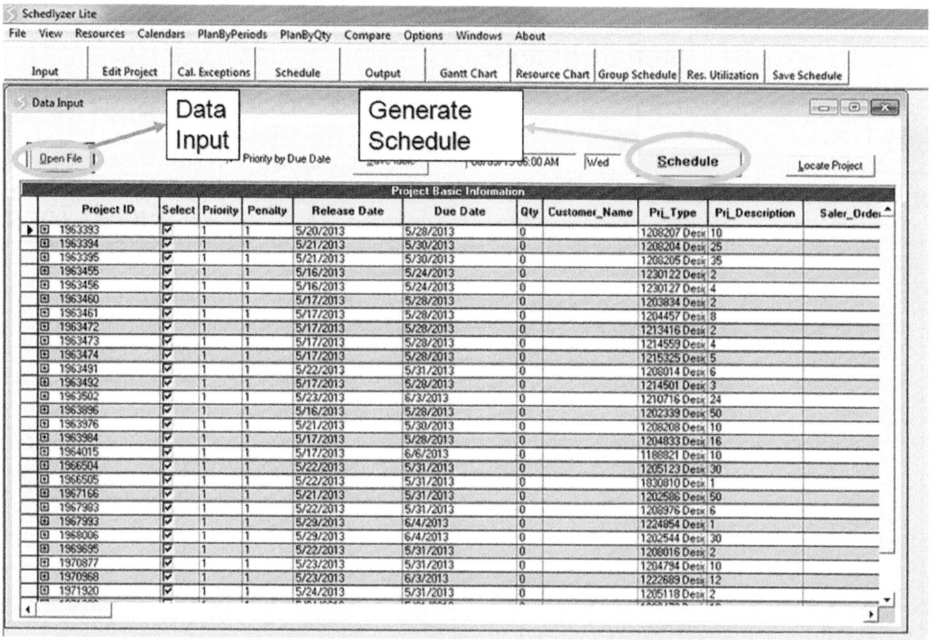

Figure 20.4   Schedlyzer screen for data input.

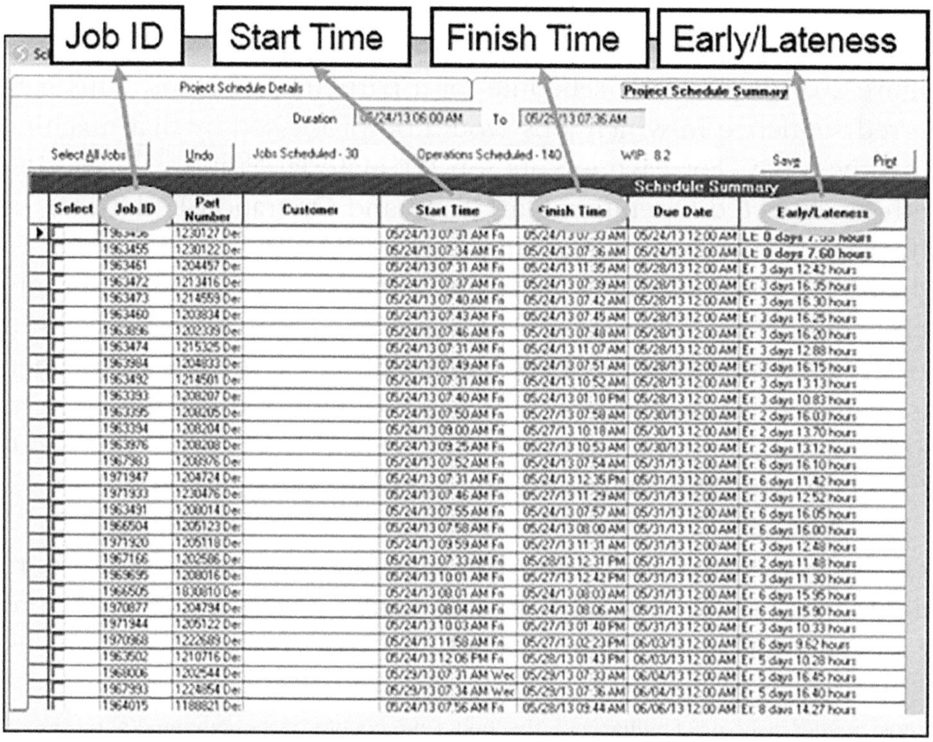

Figure 20.5   Cell Schedule Summary.

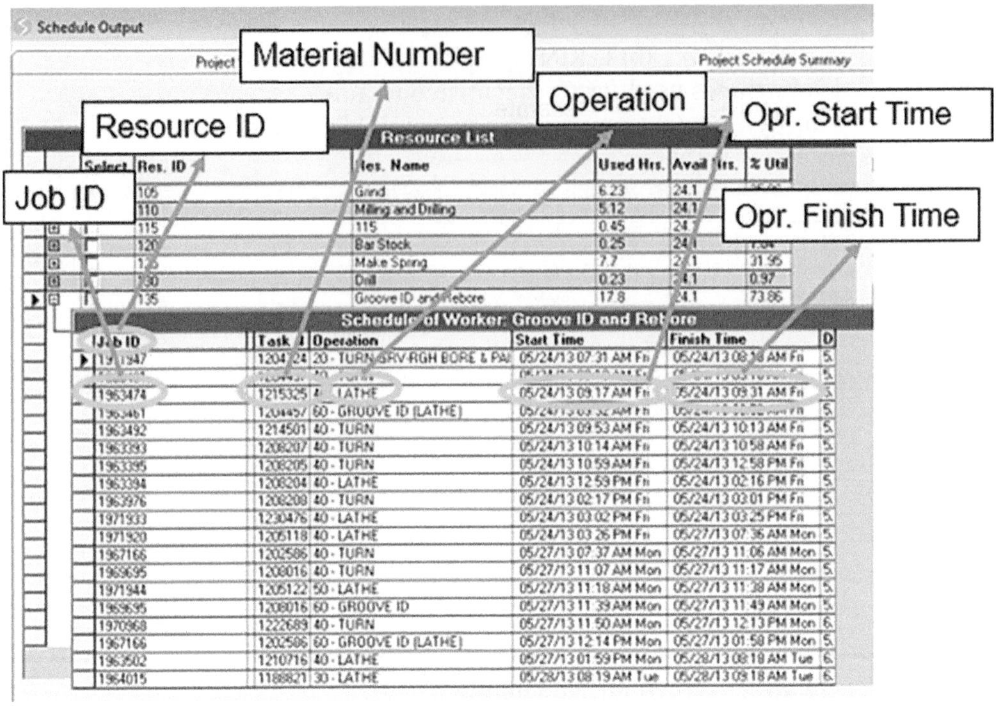

Figure 20.6   Schedule for a specific machine.

Figure 20.6 displays the schedule for a particular machine. This is the preferred sequence in which jobs would be processed by that machine on any given day. For each job, its Job ID, Material Number, Operation # (with its expected Operation Start Time and Operation End Time), etc. are displayed. Thereby, the machine operator would have no doubt as to which jobs absolutely must be ready to run before/after another job. This schedule is the "drum beat"[2] to which everyone associated with the cell, such as the machine operators, material handler(s), the cell leader, office manager, etc. would march! Every violation of this daily sequence could be noted and initiate a problem-solving event (kaizen) that would start with the question, "Why did this happen?" being asked five times (aka Five Why's).

Schedlyzer can also display the complete schedule for all active jobs run on all machines in the cell, either in a standard Gantt Chart format or produce an Excel spreadsheet equivalent of the Gantt Chart. Although not as

---

[2] For those readers who are familiar with the Takt Time counter that is mounted above an assembly line, the Gantt Chart display of the schedule for a high-mix low-volume cell serves the same purpose.

Resource ID	Project ID	Material Number	Operation Desciption	Start Time	Finish Time	Ring Type
105	1971947	120472	30 - GRIND	05/31/13 08:19 AM	05/31/13 08:53 AM	Design:PACKING RING
105	1963461	120445	50 - GRIND	05/31/13 09:17 AM	05/31/13 09:27 AM	Design:OIL SCRAPER
105	1963474	121532	50 - GRIND	05/31/13 09:32 AM	05/31/13 09:41 AM	Design:PACKING RING
105	1963393	120820	50 - GRIND	05/31/13 10:59 AM	05/31/13 11:18 AM	Design:PACKING RING
105	1963395	120820	50 - GRIND	05/31/13 12:59 PM	05/31/13 02:08 PM	Design:PACKING RING
105	1963394	120820	50 - GRIND	05/31/13 02:17 PM	05/31/13 03:06 PM	Design:PACKING RING
105	1963976	120820	50 - GRIND	05/31/13 03:07 PM	05/31/13 03:26 PM	Design:PACKING RING
105	1971933	123047	50 - GRIND	05/31/13 03:27 PM	06/03/13 07:43 AM	Design:PACKING RING
105	1971920	120511	50 - GRIND	06/03/13 07:44 AM	06/03/13 07:50 AM	Design:PACKING RING
105	1969695	120801	50 - GRIND	06/03/13 11:18 AM	06/03/13 11:24 AM	Design:PACKING RING
105	1971944	120512	60 - GRIND	06/03/13 11:39 AM	06/03/13 11:53 AM	Design:PACKING RING
105	1970968	122268	50 - GRIND	06/03/13 12:14 PM	06/03/13 12:19 PM	Design:PACKING RING
105	1963502	121071	50 - GRIND	06/04/13 08:19 AM	06/04/13 10:04 AM	Design:PACKING RING

| ▸ | Resource Schedules | 105 | 110 | 115 | 120 | 125 | 130 | 135 | 145 | 150 | 155 | 180 | ... | ⊕ |

Figure 20.7   Detailed machine schedule output.

visually pleasing, the spreadsheet showing the sequence of jobs, start/finish times, waiting times, etc. was preferred by the cell employees and Plant Manager! (Figure 20.7)

How FCS Facilitates Waste Elimination

Scheduling a cell's operations using an FCS tool[3] would help any cell to reduce WIP, minimize job waiting, plan on-hand inventories of raw materials, anticipate short-term overtime needs, etc. For example, in this pilot project involving the MPCcell, the Schedlyzer schedule projected that we could reduce the number of in-process orders (WIP) from fifty-nine orders to fifteen, which was equivalent to about $12,000 based on the prices of those orders. That is because a schedule based on *finite* capacity constraints

---

[3] The well-known FCS tools on the market are Preactor (www.PREACTOR.com), Tactic (www.WATERLOO-SOFTWARE.com), and Schedlyzer (www.OPTISOL.BIZ). But I know of at least one precision machine shop that uses a DBR (Drum-Buffer-Rope) scheduling tool (www.dbrplus.com/).

will never allow a pre-mature release of orders that will simply queue up in front of the bottleneck machine in the cell. This ability to check if an order will complete by its due date if released into a cell is especially useful if the current bottleneck machine is NOT the first machine used to process the orders. This is just one of many more benefits of effective scheduling using an FCS tool that are claimed by any FCS software vendor. But beware the hidden pitfalls and dangers of wanting to have those benefits when you **do not** (i) hire the personnel and (ii) complete the pre-requisite tasks essential for the success of an FCS implementation!

Ensuring the Success of an FCS Implementation

You *must* implement the new layout for the cell in order to co-locate **all** the machines and their operators who will be responsible for completing orders loaded on the cell. In my entire career, I have not visited a single high-mix low-volume facility that had a correctly designed layout! Due to a poorly designed cell layout, *whenever there is a distance of separation between two consecutive operations that exceeds 3 ft*, the inter-operation transfer delays can result in disorderly flow of jobs that could destroy the best schedules generated by any FCS software.

You *must* have good data to input to the FCS tool. Any software, be it an ERP, FCS, or MES, suffers from the GIGO (Garbage In Garbage Out) rule if it is provided bad data. You *have* to populate the routings for all the unique parts being produced in the cell with reasonably accurate setup and machining cycle times for all value-added operations performed in the cell. Instead of relying on Time Studies alone, you should use Group Technology and Pre-Determined Standard Times also to produce those standard times.

You need to have an in-house Production Controller and Scheduler to support the implementation. I firmly believe that this pilot project succeeded because of Clement Peng, the graduate intern from the Department of Industrial and Systems Engineering at Texas A&M University. He did most of the implementation work on this project in partnership with Dr. Prasad Velaga, who is the President of Optisol Inc. (www.optisol.biz), the vendor for Schedlyzer. Clement made the difference with his computer skills and prior IE coursework related to scheduling. He demonstrated an excellent work ethic, aptitude, and willingness to learn SAP and Schedlyzer on his own. He was determined to learn about and implement Job Shop Lean using computer tools like PFAST and Schedlyzer. Any company will need a full-time IE like him to make their FCS implementation a success!

Next, you need buy-in from the employees who will use the FCS. Software running on a cell computer, let alone someone's desktop in an office removed from the shop floor, will never be aware of all the disruptions that are bound to occur daily inside the cell.[4] No software could ever match the flexibility and response time that good cell operators can provide when any number of unscheduled disruptions, such as machine breakdowns, missing tools, defective parts requiring rework, scrapped parts, and vendor delivery failures, render useless the current computer-generated schedule for a cell.[5]

Then, there is the need for top-down leadership by an individual who understands the technical and IT aspects of an FCS implementation. He/she must also ensure disciplined use of the system by the entire company. For example, in our Pompano Beach, FL, facility, our Director of Manufacturing Systems teamed with the Plant Managers of Plants 1 and 3 to stress to the shop floor employees that the dispatch lists displayed at their machines *had* to be followed. Cell operators were forbidden to cherry-pick jobs out of the machine's dispatch list! Any FCS could quickly generate a new schedule after any disruption in a cell's day-to-day operations. Still, it would be the cell leader who must input the data to accommodate and/or override the existing schedule.

Conclusion

Lean, IT, and flexible automation can co-exist with a motivated, talented, and well-trained workforce in a cell, even more so in an entire high-mix low-volume manufacturing facility. Despite the incorporation of computer-aided data analysis and systems optimization, flexible automation, data analytics for production planning and control, etc., people and the standard Lean tools are going to be the foundation for successful implementation of Job Shop Lean. CIM (Computer Integrated Manufacturing) places an even greater reliance on employees and managers who can eliminate the myriad problems that arise when computer-generated shop schedules are disrupted by the vagaries of the dynamic shop floor.

---

[4] Do you forbid a machine operator from taking a restroom break just because the schedule generated by the FCS shows that he/she should be running Job X at that time?

[5] Will the computer be willing to report to work on a Saturday to get a rush order done and shipped to a key customer?

About the Co-Author

Zhiyuan (Clement) Peng is a data analytics professional at Wal-Mart, Global People Analytics, where he has implemented forecasting models for staffing planning in high-volume highly seasonal retail locations using integrated financial and workload information. He was a graduate student at the Texas A&M University, where he pursued his master's degree in IE. He worked as an IE intern at Hoerbiger Corporation of America, Houston, TX. During his internship, he supported a Continuous Improvement project and an Inventory Control project in the Shipping Department for whom he designed a new layout to improve their logistics. Previously, he had worked as a Quality Engineering Intern in TPT Electronics, where he used his Six Sigma skills to increase product quality. His other areas of expertise are data-driven justification of projects related to Lean Manufacturing, Inventory Control, and Quality Control.

Bibliography

Ellis, M. & Mittendorff, P. (2013, September 5). Integration of MES (Manufacturing Execution System) with material and inventory management. *Presentation made at the Second Lean and Flexible Conference* in Houston, TX.

Irani, S.A. (2012, October). A quick-start approach for implementing Lean in Jobshops. *Gear Technology*, 10–16.

Irani, S.A. (2013, April 1). What are the Wastes created by a Jobshop's ERP System? *Presentation made at the First Lean and Flexible Conference* in Houston, TX.

Irani, S.A. (2013, October). Computer-aided Finite Capacity Scheduling of a Flexible and Lean (FLEAN) Machining Cell. *Gear Technology*, 42–48.

Irani, S.A. & Velaga, P. (2013, September 5). Revisiting time and motion studies: Implementing Lean improvements for a high-mix low-volume flexible manufacturing cell. *Presentation made at the Second Lean and Flexible Conference* in Houston, TX.

Joshi, P. & Irani, S.A. (2013, April 1). A tutorial on Job Shop Scheduling (JSS) using LEKIN academic scheduling software. *Presentation made at the First Lean and Flexible Conference* in Houston, TX.

Lean Scheduling. (2011, August). *Preactor and Factory Viewer get Seal of Approval from Hoerbiger.* https://lean-scheduling.com/case-studies/hoerbiger/.

Mittendorff, P. (2013, April 1). The water strider: How to get the right material to the right machine at the right time per the daily schedule. *Presentation made at the First Lean and Flexible Conference* in Houston, TX.

Chapter 21

Classroom Tutorial on the Design of a Cellular Manufacturing System

Acknowledgment

I wish to thank Manvendra Singh Gehlot for his contributions to this chapter. Manvendra is a graduate student in the Department of Industrial Engineering at the University of Houston and will receive his MIE degree in 2019. For questions about system simulation using FlexSim, operations scheduling using LEKIN, project management and scheduling using MS Project, and real-time job tracking using SmartSheet, please contact him by email (Manvendra.Singh071996@gmail.com) or phone (209-242-1416).

I wish to thank Dr. Smart Khaewsukkho for his contributions to this chapter. He is the developer of the Sgetti application and helped me to incorporate Sgetti in the toolbox of software applications that are discussed in this tutorial. In addition, he contributed the section *Analysis of Machine Duplication Decisions in Hybrid Cellular Layouts Using Sgetti* in this chapter. For questions about Sgetti, please visit www.SGETTI. com or else contact him by email (Khaewsukkho.1@gmail.com) or phone (614-598-0642).

Table 21.1 Lessons on Factory Layout and Scheduling from over 100 Years Ago

Excerpt from the Article	*Relevance to this Tutorial*
Many industrial plants are seriously handicapped through the fact that the *arrangement* of their departments and equipment imposes operating expenses that are almost prohibitive. If errors are made in the selection of certain machines or other detail features, they can usually be corrected at comparatively small expense. On the other hand, if the arrangement of the departments and equipment, and therefore the character of the buildings, has been incorrectly solved, the resulting plant may be such as practically to prohibit the establishment of correct conditions unless a very great monetary loss is incurred…the efficiency of a given plant is governed primarily by the *manner* in which its layout is worked out.	The tutorial demonstrates how to transform the Process Layout of any HMLV discrete manufacturing facility into a Hybrid Cellular Layout based on the principles of Design For Flow (Chapter 4).

(Continued)

Background for This Tutorial

The tutorial discussed in this chapter was originally published as Chapter 20 in the *Handbook of Cellular Manufacturing Systems* (John Wiley, 1999, ISBN 0-471-12139-8). Nearly two decades later, the chapter continues to be an invaluable instructional resource and helps to teach students how the steps for implementing Cellular Manufacturing (CM) (Part Family Formation → Cell Layout → Shop Layout → Cell Scheduling → Shop Scheduling) can again be followed to implement the Principles of Lean in any job shop-type high-mix low-volume (HMLV) manufacturing facility.

Lessons on Factory Layout and Scheduling from Over 100 Years Ago

An article[1] published in 1910 (yes, 1910!) discusses the importance of a good factory layout to achieve efficient material flow **and** effective production scheduling. Table 21.1 contains key excerpts from the article that reinforce

---

[1] If you would like to receive an electronic copy of this article. (*Source*: Day, C. (1910). The routing diagram as a basis for laying out industrial plants. *The Engineering Magazine*, XXXIX(6), 809–821), please contact me at ShahrukhIrani1023@yahoo.com or 832-475-4447.

Table 21.1 (*Continued*) Lessons on Factory Layout and Scheduling from over 100 Years Ago

Excerpt from the Article	Relevance to this Tutorial
The first (routing) diagram prepared showed as accurately as was possible the manner in which the materials progressed through the plant at the time of the initial investigations and a study of this diagram formed the basis for a series of revised layouts... While a diagram which is carried out in no greater detail than Figure 21.1 gives comparatively little information that is of specific value as a basis for the design of buildings and installation of equipment, yet it is a *key* to the manufacturing problems as a whole and a useful and, in fact, a necessary step toward the final solution... One must make a thorough study of all the more important factors entering into the business that is to be housed, and on this account the diagram forms the logical basis upon which to develop and reconcile all (factory layout) detail considerations.	The tutorial uses Sgetti, a commercial tool for diagramming material flow in any HMLV discrete manufacturing facility, to design and evaluate a variety of layout options for a hypothetical machine shop.
Operation 6 is housed in the same building as Operations 1–5 because the (product) must be carried the least distance possible between Blowing and Forming (departments)... The locations of the various departments were worked out with a view to minimizing the travel of the (products) and at the same time making possible the use of but one Dry Room serving both (product families).	The tutorial demonstrates how the design of a Hybrid Cellular Layout helps to reduce some of the Seven Types of Waste (Transportation, Work-In-Process Inventory, Waiting, Operator Motion) by locating those work centers that have significant product flow between them adjacent to each other (or in close proximity to each other).
The Dry Room is located in the center of the building, and although (both product families) must go into this department four times before they pass to the third and last series of operations, this is accomplished with a minimum of handling. There are six means of entrance or exit to the Dry Room, allowing practically a continuous movement of material in well-defined directions and obviating the possibility of congestion.	Monuments are work centers such as heat treatment, painting, electroplating, etc. that are visited by parts from two or more different product families, or different batches of parts. Such shared departments in any factory should have multiple entrances/exits, FIFO (First In First Out) material flow lanes, and visual markers to separate WIP locations for different orders.

(*Continued*)

Table 21.1 (*Continued*) Lessons on Factory Layout and Scheduling from over 100 Years Ago

Excerpt from the Article	Relevance to this Tutorial
In the majority of industries work must be performed upon a great number of small parts which, of course, makes the routing problem a very more complex one. Under such circumstances there is almost sure to be a considerable amount of travel in a backward direction, and the arrangement of departments and equipment that is finally adopted will represent, at the best, but a compromise of many conflicting conditions... Nor has any attempt been made to route the individual parts, numbering several thousand, that enter into the construction of a complete gasoline automobile. The (routing) diagram is in reality but a "key" indicating the travel paths of travel of materials from the point where they are received until they reach the Shipping department in their completely assembled state.	This problem can be effectively solved using some of the commercially available software for *Part Family Formation* and *Facility Layout* that is listed in Table 21.3.
One of the principal factors entering into modern methods of industrial administration is that of scheduling the work from a central planning office in a manner that provides for the completion of each unit of work in a certain time... The importance of the schedule is best illustrated in connection with the operation of large railroad systems. They depend for their very existence upon the exact adherence to a train schedule that defines the arrival and departure of every train at every important point upon the system. Such a schedule, however, can be carried out only after the tracks, terminals, yards, and stations have been laid out in strict accordance with the requirements of the schedule itself. In other words, a Routing Diagram must be made of the entire system based upon the series of schedules that it is proposed to establish... Industrial managers now realize, as they never have before, that the scheduling of their work is one of the prime factors of economic production, and that operating expenses can be minimized only when the plant has been physically arranged in accordance with the requirements of the most efficient schedule.	The tutorial demonstrates how the decomposition of a Process Layout into a Hybrid Cellular Layout helps to schedule each cell and, if necessary, the entire shop which is comprised of multiple cells.

the learning objectives of this tutorial to teach a computer-aided approach to implement Job Shop Lean that is guided by the (five) Principles of Lean.

Introduction

CM is a strategy to reform job shop production system that attempts to break up a job shop into several self-sufficient production units called "cells". A manufacturing cell is a group of functionally dissimilar machines co-located on the shop floor. The group of machines and their operators working in the cell are dedicated to the manufacture of a family of similar parts. Like any other manufacturing improvement strategy (TOC (Theory Of Constraints), Six Sigma, OpEx), CM has both advantages and disadvantages. Some of the advantages of CM are:

1. Reduced material handling,
2. Reduced setup times,
3. Reduced work-in-process,
4. Increased speed of response to customer requests,
5. Effective employee cross-training,
6. Fostering of teamwork and friendship,
7. Simplified production control and operations scheduling.

Unfortunately, the disadvantages of CM are:

1. *Lower machine utilization due to volume changes*: With the machines in a cell being dedicated to a select family of parts, if demand for those parts reduces, then fewer orders will be loaded on the cell. Also, when a work center in a Process Layout is broken up and identical machines of the same type are allocated to several cells, there is bound to be a variation in the value-added utilization of those machines of the same type in the different cells. In addition, a cell is highly susceptible to unexpected machine breakdowns and operator absenteeism.
2. *Reduced flexibility to respond to mix changes*: If the part mix for which a cell is designed changes significantly with time, it is possible that the cell may have to send its orders to other cells for processing by machines it does not have. What if part designs change? Or the customers asking for those parts go away (or find other suppliers)?

However, using practices of the Toyota Production Systems (aka Lean Tools) such as Total Productive Maintenance, Water Spiders, and Employee Engagement, the above disadvantages of CM can be overcome.

Teaching Objectives of This Tutorial in 1999

The tutorial discussed in this chapter was originally published with the same title as Chapter 20 in the *Handbook of Cellular Manufacturing Systems* (John Wiley, 1999, ISBN 0-471-12139-8). It focused primarily on teaching how to transform the existing layout of a multi-product multi-machine job shop from a Process Layout into a Cellular Layout. Some of the major steps in the implementation of a CM System that the tutorial taught are:

1. Formation of part families
2. Identification of the manufacturing cell to produce each part family
3. Identification of exception operations that may result in inter-cell flows
4. Identification of shared machines that may result in inter-cell flows
5. Determination of capacity requirements for each machine type assigned to a cell
6. Allocation of shared machines to each cell based on their workloads
7. Design of the layout of each cell
8. Design of the layout for the entire facility
9. Operations scheduling for each cell.
10. Operations scheduling for the entire facility (including priority scheduling of pick-ups and drop-offs of parts to different cells to utilize available capacity on shared machines)[2]

Teaching Objectives of This Tutorial in 2019

This tutorial explains how to implement Principles of Lean #2, #3, and #4 in any HMLV discrete manufacturing facility. The implementation of a Cellular Layout is the foundation for implementing Job Shop Lean in any job shop or similar HMLV Make-To-Order (MTO) manufacturing facility by following the Principles of Lean, as discussed in Table 21.2.

---

[2] The dataset used in the tutorial did not consider the case of (external) Monuments and one or more Remainder Cells that contained expensive machines that could not be duplicated in every cell that needed them.

Table 21.2 How to Implement the Principles of Lean in Job Shops

Principle of Lean	*How to Implement the Principle in Any Job Shop*
Principle #1: Specify value from the standpoint of the end customer by product family	• Segment the product mix into Runners, Repeaters, and Strangers based on Production Volume, Revenue, and Demand Variability (Chapter 13) • Identify product families in each segment based on similar routings (Chapter 8)
Principle #2: Identify all the steps in the Value Stream for each product family, eliminating whenever possible those steps that do not create value	• Generate a Value Network Map for each product family (Chapter 27) • Analyze the Flow Process Charts for the parts that constitute each Value Network Map using Methods Analysis, Spaghetti Diagrams, Flow Process Charts, etc. • Identify opportunities to eliminate waste and production delays in each product family's Value Network
Principle #3: Make the value-creating steps occur in tight sequence so the product will flow smoothly toward the customer	• Implement work cells to produce stable product families (Chapter 16) • Organize the factory floor into a Hybrid Cellular Layout (Chapters 7 and 8) • Eliminate or reduce inter-cell flows (Chapter 18)
Principle #4: As flow is introduced, let customers pull value from the next upstream activity	• Level week-by-week production plans subject to available hours of capacity • Schedule operations using an FCS tool (Chapter 19) • Utilize a Manufacturing Execution System and Water Spiders to execute and monitor daily schedules (Chapters 17 and 18)
Principle #5: As value is specified, Value Streams are identified, wasted steps are removed, and Flow and Pull are introduced, begin the process again and continue it until a state of perfection is reached in which perfect value is created with no waste	• Selectively utilize Continuous Improvement strategies such as Setup Reduction, Cross-training, Inspection at Source, etc. in each cell (Chapters 17, 18, and 28) • Hire an IE to lead the Continuous Improvement projects and employee training programs (Chapters 17, 18, and 28) • Promote employee-led kaizen activities (Chapters 17, 18, and 28)

This tutorial has replaced the section on design of a 3-cell layout that appears in the 1999 book with a section on design of a Hybrid Flow Shop Layout. In 1999, the author had just read the book *Lean Thinking* and lacked the much-needed work experience in industry to understand that the 3-cell solution is impractical because significant inter-cell flows is a sign that the cells are not autonomous. Inter-cell flows rob a cell's team of the much-needed responsibility (and accountability) to process any order from start to finish. In the real world, inter-cell flows ought to be permitted only under special circumstances: (i) The cells have to send their parts to Monuments (heat treatment, welding, painting, electroplating) external to the cells and (ii) the cells have to send their parts to be processed by machines in a Remainder Cell that contains expensive equipment (a Coordinate Measuring Machine) that cannot be duplicated in every cell. In both cases, resources that cannot be resident in a cell necessitate inter-cell flows.

In 1999, almost all of the data analysis and system design in the tutorial had to be done manually. Fortunately, the tutorial uses a simple **and** small dataset for a hypothetical machine shop that was obtained from a research paper published in a peer-reviewed academic journal. Students felt overwhelmed because the key steps in the tutorial had to be done as follows:

1. PF Formation (Steps #1, #6, and #7) was done semi-manually using the STORM software.
2. Cell and Shop Layout (Steps #2, #3, #4, and #5) was done semi-manually using the STORM software and Excel.
3. Cell and Shop Scheduling (Steps #8 and #9) was done semi-manually using MS Project, with Excel being used to "draw" the Gantt Charts depicting the cell and shop schedules.

In stark contrast, in 2019, the key steps in the tutorial are done as follows:

1. PF Formation (Steps #1, #6, and #7) is done using PFAST (Production Flow Analysis and Simplification Toolkit) and Sgetti.
2. Cell and Shop Layout (Steps #2, #3, #4, and #5) is done using PFAST, Sgetti, and STORM.
3. Cell and Shop Scheduling (Steps #8 and #9) including the Gantt Charts is done using LEKIN.

After working through this tutorial, practitioners interested in real-world implementation of Job Shop Lean can refer to Table 21.3 for some of the

Table 21.3 Commercial Software to Implement Job Shop Lean

Task	Commercial Software to Perform This Task
PF Formation	• JMP (Website: www.jmp.com/en_us/home.html) • Minitab (Website: www.minitab.com/en-us/) • Sgetti (Website: www.sgetti.com/)
Facility Layout	• Flow Planner (Website: www.proplanner.com/solutions/material-logistics-planning/flow-planner/) • Sgetti (Website: www.sgetti.com/) • SIMOGGA (Website: www.amia-systems.com/)
Process and System Simulation	• FLEXSIM (Website: www.flexsim.com/) • SIMCAD (Website: www.createasoft.com/) • SIMIO (Website: www.simio.com/index.php)
FCS	• Preactor (Website: www.plm.automation.siemens.com/global/en/products/manufacturing-operations-center/preactor-aps.html) • Tactic (Website: www.waterloo-software.com/) • Schedlyzer (Website: https://optisol.biz/)

commercial software that is currently available to implement the (five) Principles of Lean.

Perhaps the biggest difference between 1999 and 2019 is that the tutorial now promotes the importance of the *Five Why's* questioning process. It teaches students (and practitioners!) to challenge the need for inter-cell flows by asking, "Why design a CM System that tolerates inter-cell flows? Why cannot a sufficient number of machines of Type X be assigned to Cell Y to satisfy its workload? Why be dogmatic about splitting a work center and distributing the machines in it into physically separate cells?" Specifically, in Chapter 18 of this book, Tables 18.3 and 18.4 explain how, instead of permitting inter-cell flows, a comprehensive Continuous Improvement program can be started to reduce reliance on machine capacity external to a cell by attacking the sources of capacity wastage that reduce machine availability (high setup times, long cycle times, inflated batch sizes due to wrong forecasts, high cycle times due to poor choice of processing parameters, idle time due to unscheduled machine stoppages, idle time due to non-arrival of raw materials, idle time because the machine operators exit the cell to get tools or gauges, setup changes due to frequent schedule changes, scrap/rework, etc.).[3]

---

[3] The interested reader is encouraged to see the video or read the book *The Goal* (*Source*: www.goldratt.com/store/tg).

A Tutorial on Implementing the Principles of Lean in a Job Shop

This tutorial uses data for a hypothetical machine shop. Table 21.4 lists the parts being produced, the batch size for each part, the sequence of machines visited by each part, and the total machining time for each operation. For example, Part #1 has a Batch Size = 2. Its Operation Sequence consists of four machines 1→4→8→9. For each operation, the Batch Machining Time = Batch Size * Cycle Time. So, the Cycle Time on Machine #1 is 96/2 = 48 minutes, the Cycle Time on Machine #4 is 36/2 = 18 minutes, the Cycle Time on Machine #8 is 36/2 = 18 minutes, and the Cycle Time on Machine #9 is 72/2 = 36 minutes.

Table 21.4   Routings for Parts Made in the Machine Shop

Part #	Batch Size	Sequence of Machines (Operation Sequence) for Part #						
		Batch Machining Time for Each Operation (minutes)						
1	2	1	4	8	9			
		96	36	36	72			
2	3	1	4	7	4	8	7	
		36	120	20	120	24	20	
3	1	1	2	4	7	8	9	
		96	48	36	120	36	72	
4	3	1	4	7	9			
		96	36	120	72			
5	2	1	6	10	7	9		
		96	72	200	120	72		
6	1	6	10	7	8	9		
		36	120	60	24	36		
7	2	6	4	8	9			
		72	36	48	48			
8	1	3	5	2	6	4	8	9
		144	120	48	72	36	48	48

(Continued)

Table 21.4 (*Continued*)   Routings for Parts Made in the Machine Shop

Part #	Batch Size	Sequence of Machines (Operation Sequence) for Part #					
		Batch Machining Time for Each Operation (minutes)					
9	**1**	3	5	6	4	8	9
		144	120	72	36	48	48
10	**2**	4	7	4	8		
		120	20	120	24		
11	**3**	6					
		72					
12	**1**	11	7	12			
		192	150	80			
13	**1**	11	12				
		192	60				
14	**3**	11	7	10			
		288	180	360			
15	**1**	1	7	11	10	11	12
		15	70	54	45	54	30
16	**2**	1	7	11	10	11	12
		15	70	54	45	54	30
17	**1**	11	7	12			
		192	150	80			
18	**3**	6	7	10			
		108	180	360			
19	**2**	12					
		60					

Table 21.5 shows the list of (12) Work Centers that comprise the machine shop. Each work center has one or more machines of the same type; e.g., Work Center #9 has two machines available, whereas Work Center #11 has 3 machines available. For the sake of simplicity, it is assumed that the machine shop is open for one shift (8 hours = 480 minutes). Except for highly

Table 21.5 Number of Machines Available in Different Work Centers in the Machine Shop

Work Center	Number of Machines Available in the Work Center
1	2
2	1
3	1
4	2
5	1
6	2
7	4
8	1
9	2
10	3
11	3
12	1
Production horizon = 1 shift = 480 minutes	
Machine availability = 80%	
Availability capacity on any machine = 384 minutes	

automated production lines or process plants, no machine in a machine shop is known to cut metal for the entire duration of a shift. Therefore, considering all types of non-value-added time, the Machine Availability of any machine in any work center was set at 80%. Thereby, any machine in any work center is doing value-added processing of parts for a maximum of 384 (0.8 * 480) minutes during the shift.

Input File for PFAST and Sgetti

Figure 21.1 shows the first of three spreadsheets that constitute a PFAST Input File. This spreadsheet provides the PQ$ data (P = Parts, Q = Quantity, $ = Revenue). Since Revenue data was not available, a surrogate measure for the Revenue earned by any part, Touch Time, was used to segment the

1	Part No	Description	Annual Quantity	Revenue	<== Revenue has been replaced by adding up Total Batch
2	1	Part 1	2	240	Machining Time for each and every operation in the entire
3	2	Part 2	3	336	routing. So, instead of Revenue, we are using the
4	3	Part 3	1	408	Batch Manufacturing Cost (= Touch Time X Labor Hour Rate).
5	4	Part 4	3	324	
6	5	Part 5	2	560	
7	6	Part 6	1	276	
8	7	Part 7	2	204	
9	8	Part 8	1	516	
10	9	Part 9	1	468	
11	10	Part 10	2	284	
12	11	Part 11	3	72	
13	12	Part 12	1	422	
14	13	Part 13	1	252	
15	14	Part 14	3	828	
16	15	Part 15	1	268	
17	16	Part 16	2	268	
18	17	Part 17	1	422	
19	18	Part 18	3	648	
20	19	Part 19	2	60	
21					

Figure 21.1 PFAST Input File: Parts.

product mix. Touch Time for a part is the total time that it was processed on the different work centers in its routing. For example, with reference to Table 21.4, the Touch Time for Part #1 is the sum of the Batch Machining Times on each of the four machines (1→4→8→9) in its routing = 96 + 36 + 36 + 72 = 240 minutes.

Figure 21.2 shows the second of three spreadsheets that constitute a PFAST Input File. This spreadsheet lists all the work centers that constitute the machine shop and feature in different part routings.

Finally, Figure 21.3 shows the last of three spreadsheets that constitute a PFAST Input File. This spreadsheet lists the routings of the different

1	Work Center No	Description	Area
2	1	Machine 1	1
3	10	Machine 10	1
4	11	Machine 11	1
5	12	Machine 12	1
6	2	Machine 2	1
7	3	Machine 3	1
8	4	Machine 4	1
9	5	Machine 5	1
10	6	Machine 6	1
11	7	Machine 7	1
12	8	Machine 8	1
13	9	Machine 9	1

Figure 21.2 PFAST Input File: Work centers.

1	Part No	Work Center No	Sequence No	Cycle Time	<== This column (Cycle Time) added to synchronize
2	1	1	1	48	PFAST Input File with SGETTI Input File
3	1	4	2	18	
4	1	8	3	18	
5	1	9	4	36	
6	2	1	1	12	
7	2	4	2	40	
8	2	7	3	7	
9	2	4	4	40	
10	2	8	5	8	
11	2	7	6	7	
12	3	1	1	96	
13	3	2	2	48	
14	3	4	3	36	
15	3	7	4	120	
16	3	8	5	36	
17	3	9	6	72	
18	4	1	1	32	
19	4	4	2	12	
20	4	7	3	40	
21	4	9	4	24	
22	5	1	1	48	
23	5	6	2	36	
24	5	10	3	100	
25	5	7	4	60	
26	5	9	5	36	
27	6	6	1	36	
28	6	10	2	120	
29	6	7	3	60	
30	6	8	4	24	
31	6	9	5	36	
32	7	6	1	36	
33	7	4	2	18	
34	7	8	3	24	
35	7	9	4	24	
36	8	3	1	144	
37	8	5	2	120	
38	8	2	3	48	
39	8	6	4	72	
40	8	4	5	36	

H ◄ ► H | Routing / Part / Workcenter / 🖉 /

Figure 21.3   PFAST Input File: Routings.

parts being produced in the machine shop. The column *Cycle Time* was added in this spreadsheet to enable Sgetti to utilize the (same) PFAST Input File.

Part Family Formation and Machine Grouping for Cell Design

Here we are implementing Lean Principles #1 and #2 which were described in Table 21.2 as follows:

Principle of Lean	How to Implement the Principle in Any Job Shop
Principle #1: Specify value from the standpoint of the end customer by product family	• Segment the product mix into Runners, Repeaters, and Strangers based on Production Volume, Revenue, and Demand Variability (Chapter 13) • Identify product families in each segment based on similar routings (Chapter 8)
Principle #2: Identify all the steps in the Value Stream for each product family, eliminating whenever possible those steps that do not create value	• Generate a Value Network Map for each product family (Chapter 27) • Analyze the Flow Process Charts for the parts that constitute each Value Network Map using Methods Analysis, Spaghetti Diagrams, Flow Process Charts, etc. • Identify opportunities to eliminate waste and production delays in each product family's Value Network

Figure 21.4 is a screen capture of the Product-Routing Analysis Type I (Product-Process Matrix Analysis) output from PFAST. If one draws a horizontal line between Parts # 4 and #14 to split the (vertical) permutation of parts, two part families can be formed:

1. PF #1 (11, 18, 5, 6, 8, 9, 7, 10, 2, 1, 3, 4)
2. PF #2 (14, 15, 16, 12, 17, 13, 19).

PR Analysis Type I

Parts	2	3	5	6	9	8	4	1	7	10	11	12
11			1									
18			1						1	1		
5			1	1				1	1	1		
6			1	1	1				1	1		
8	1	1	1	1	1	1	1	1				
9		1	1	1	1	1	1	1				
7			1	1	1	1						
10						1	1		1			
2							1	1	1	1		
1						1	1	1	1			
3	1					1	1	1	1	1		
4						1		1	1	1		
14									1	1	1	
15								1	1	1	1	1
16							1	1	1	1	1	1
12									1		1	1
17									1		1	1
13											1	1
19												1

Figure 21.4   Product-Routing Analysis Type I output from PFAST.

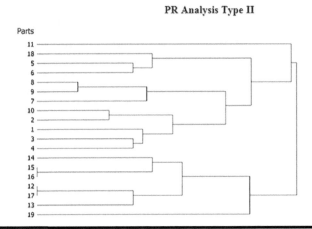

Figure 21.5 Product-Routing Analysis Type II output from PFAST.

Figure 21.5 is a screen capture of the Product-Routing Analysis Type II (Hierarchical Cluster Analysis) output from PFAST. Since the permutation of parts shown at the base of the dendrogram in the figure is identical to the permutation of parts in Figure 21.2(a), the compositions of the two-part families suggested by this analysis will be identical to those identified using Figure 21.4.

Figure 21.6 is a screen capture of the Product-Routing Analysis Type IV (Multiple Sequence Alignment) output from PFAST. The heuristic algorithm for this analysis does not use Similarity Coefficients as input data. Instead it uses the actual part routings in Table 21.4 as input data. Therefore, the compositions of the two-part families suggested by this analysis are not identical to those in Figures 21.2(a) and (b). Specifically, Part #18 whose routing is 6→7→10 was incorrectly assigned to PF #2 instead of PF #1. That is because, if sequence of visitation of machines is the basis for grouping parts, then the sequence of machines (6→7→10) is missing in the routing of Part #5 (1→6→10→7→9) as well as the routing of Part #6 (6→10→7→8→9). If one draws a horizontal line between Parts # 18 and #10 to split the (vertical) permutation of parts, two part families can be formed:

1. PF #1 (10, 2, 1, 3, 4, 5, 6, 7, 8, 9, 11)
2. PF #2 (19, 13, 17, 12, 14, 15, 16, **18**)

Author's Note: Part #18 does not belong in PF #2 and should be reassigned to PF #1. With reference to the input data and heuristic

PR Analysis Type IV

Parts											
19											12
13			11								12
17			11				7				12
12			11				7				12
14			11				7		10		
15			1				7	11	10	11	12
16			1				7	11	10	11	12
18			6				7		10		
10						4	7	4	8		
2			1			4	7	4	8	7	
1			1			4			8	9	
3			1		2	4	7		8	9	
4			1			4	7			9	
5			1	6	10		7			9	
6				6	10		7		8	9	
7				6		4			8	9	
8	3	5	2	6		4			8	9	
9	3	5		6		4			8	9	
11				6							

Figure 21.6   Product-Routing Analysis Type IV output from PFAST.

algorithms that produced Figures 21.2(a) and (b), if the sequence of machines is ignored and only usage of common machines is considered, Part #18 has a higher similarity to the parts in PF #1 than to the parts in PF #2.

Here is the justification for the proposed 2-cell layout option for the machine shop. Figure 21.2(a) suggests that, if only two cells are implemented, then the least number of work centers will need to be split up and their machines distributed among cells. Table 21.5 shows that Number of Machines Available in Work Center #1 = 2, Number of Machines Available in Work Center #7 = 4 and Number of Machines Available in Work Center #10 = 3. Figure 21.2(c) shows that Machine #1 is always the first machine in the routings of all parts in both part families that use it. Table 21.6 confirms that the workload on Work Center #1 in Cell #2 from PF #2 is insufficient to justify dedicating one of the two machines in that work center to Cell #2. Instead, either of the two machines could be setup to run orders for PF #2 on an as-needed basis driven by due dates. Clearly, PF#1 (and Cell #1) are the primary users of Machine #1. So, it is not necessary to break up Work Center #1. Both its machines could be co-located in a single location to retain flexibility in loading orders on either machine, especially if one machine breaks down.

Based on the workload calculations for the two cells in Table 21.6, the following decisions were made regarding how many machines from shared work centers to assign to either cell:

1. *Work Center #1*: Assign both machines to Cell #1 and route the parts from Cell #2 to use either of the two machines.
2. *Work Center #10*: This work center poses a problem because (i) only 3 machines are available in the work center and (ii) both cells need at least two machines. Here is where (practical) Lean Thinking beats academic rigor and lack of industry experience any day! Rather than purchase an extra machine for Work Center #10, the logical action would be to explore ways to reduce the setup times and cycle times on the parts in PF#2 that use Work Center #10. The workload on Work Center #10 due to the PF produced in Cell #2 should be reduced just enough that one machine from that work center would suffice for the cell.

Table 21.6 Machine Requirements in Cells #1 and #2 for Work Centers #1, #7, and #10

		Work Center #		
Cell #	Part #	1	7	10
1	18		180	360
1	5	96	120	200
1	6		60	120
1	10		20	
1	2	36	40	
1	1	96		
1	3	96	120	
1	4	96	120	
Workload		420	660	680

(Continued)

Table 21.6 (*Continued*) Machine Requirements in Cells #1 and #2 for Work Centers #1, #7, and #10

		Work Center #		
Cell #	Part #	1	7	10
# of Machines Assigned		1.094 ≈ 1	1.719 ≈ 2	1.771 ≈ 2
2	14		180	360
2	15	15	70	45
2	16	15	70	45
2	12		150	
2	17		150	
Workload		30	620	450
# of Machines Assigned		0.078 ≈ 1	1.615 ≈ 2	1.172 ≈ 2

Figure 21.7 is a screen capture of the *Workload Analysis* done by Sgetti for the machines in Cell #1. Figure 21.8 is a screen capture of the *Workload Analysis* done by Sgetti for the machines in Cell #2. The reader is encouraged to compare the calculations in the Sgetti outputs of Figures 21.7 and 21.8 with the calculations shown in Table 21.6.

Figure 21.9 is a screen capture of the PQ$ Analysis output from PFAST. Recall that Touch Time (Labor Hours) has replaced Revenue in the

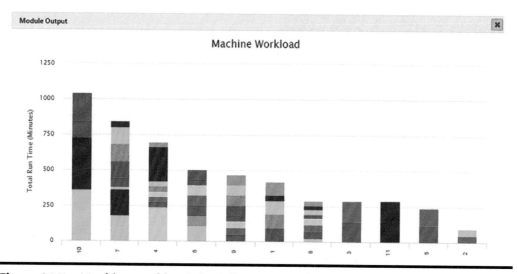

Figure 21.7 Machine workloads in Cell #1 output from Sgetti.

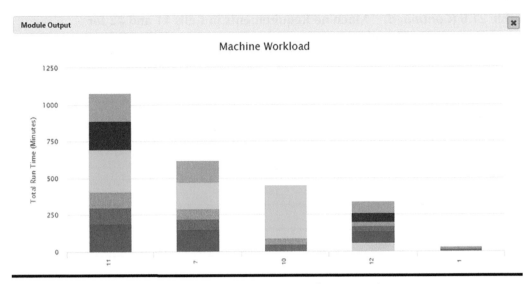

Figure 21.8   Machine workloads in Cell #2 output from Sgetti.

Part	Revenue	Quantity	Agg. Rev	Agg. Qty	Agg. Rev %	Agg. Qty %
14	828	3	828	3	12	8
18	648	3	1476	6	21	17
2	336	3	1812	9	26	25
4	324	3	2136	12	31	34
11	72	3	2208	15	32	42
5	560	2	2768	17	40	48
8	516	1	3284	18	47	51
10	284	2	3568	20	52	57
16	268	2	3836	22	56	62
1	240	2	4076	24	59	68
7	204	2	4280	26	62	74
9	468	1	4748	27	69	77
19	60	2	4808	29	70	82
12	422	1	5230	30	76	85
17	422	1	5652	31	82	88
3	408	1	6060	32	88	91
6	276	1	6336	33	92	94
15	268	1	6604	34	96	97
13	252	1	6856	35	100	100

Figure 21.9   Product mix segmentation using production batch size and touch time (Labor Hours).

Revenue (and therefore Aggregate Revenue and Aggregate Revenue %) columns. If a limited sample of parts is desired that accounts for ≈50% of the Total Labor Hours (52%) and Total Production Quantity (57%) for the product mix, that sample of parts (14, 18, 2, 4, 11, 5, 8, 10) is dominated by parts from PF #1.

Cell and Shop Layout

Here we are implementing Lean Principle #3 which was described in Table 21.2 as follows:

Principle of Lean	How to Implement the Principle in Any Job Shop
Principle #3: Make the value-creating steps occur in a tight sequence so the product will flow smoothly toward the customer	• Implement work cells to produce stable product families (Chapter 16) • Organize the factory floor into a Hybrid Cellular Layout (Chapter 7, Chapter 8) • Eliminate or reduce inter-cell flows (Chapter 18)

Figure 21.10 is a screen capture of the Q-type From-To Chart output from PFAST.

Figure 21.11 is a screen capture of the Q-type Flow Diagram output from PFAST. The thickness of the material flow arrows in Figure 21.11 is proportional to the values in the cells of the Q-type From-To Chart in Figure 21.10. This diagram corresponds to a classic Process Layout for the machine shop because none of the (12) work centers has been split. The reader is encouraged to compare the inter-departmental adjacencies in this layout with those shown in Figure 7.1 in Chapter 7.

Figure 21.12 is a screen capture of the $-type From-To Chart output from PFAST. Since Revenue data was not available in the dataset for this tutorial, a surrogate measure for the Revenue earned by any part, Touch Time (Labor Hours), was computed. Touch Time for a part is the total time that it was processed on the different work centers in its routing. For example, with

Q-Type From-To Chart

W/C	12	11	10	6	1	4	7	8	9	3	5	2
12												
11	4		3				5					
10		3					3					
6			3		4	3						
1				2		8	3					1
4							9	11				
7	2	3	6			5		2	5			
8							3		8			
9												
3										2		
5				1								1
2				1	1							

Figure 21.10   Q-type From-To Chart output from PFAST.

(Continued)

Q Type Flow Diagram

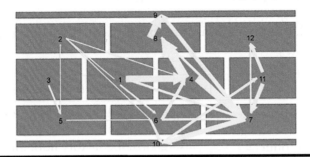

Figure 21.11 Q-type Flow Diagram output from PFAST.

$-Type From-To Chart

W/C	1	4	6	2	8	9	12	11	7	10	3	5
1		900	560	408					536			
4					2048				1352			
6		1188							648	836		
2		408	516									
8						2112			336			
9												
12												
11								788	1672	536		
7		620			684	884	844	536		1476		
10								536	836			
3												984
5			468	516								

Figure 21.12 $-type From-To Chart output from PFAST.

reference to Table 21.4, the Touch Time for Part #1 is the sum of the Batch Machining Times on each of the four machines (1→4→8→9) in its routing = 96 + 36 + 36 + 72 = 240 minutes. Assuming that a fixed Labor Hour Rate applies to all 19 parts in the product mix, (Touch Time * Labor Hour Rate) would serve as an estimate of the cost of producing the entire batch (= 2) for Part #1.

Figure 21.13 is a screen capture of the standard facility layout that is generated by STORM. This layout corresponds to a classic Process Layout for the machine shop because none of the (12) work centers has been split. In

```
Storm - [Process Layout for Machine Shop using From-To Charts]
  File  Edit  Window  Help

Process Layout for Machine Shop using From-To Charts
LAYOUT

         Col  1       Col  2       Col  3       Col  4       Col  5
       +-----------+-----------+-----------+-----------+-----------+
Row 1  |M12        |M10        |M6         |M2         |M5         |
       +-----------+-----------+-----------+-----------+-----------+
Row 2  |M11        |M7         |M4         |M1         |M3         |
       +-----------+-----------+-----------+-----------+-----------+
Row 3  |DUMMY 5    |M9         |M8         |DUMMY 8    |DUMMY 3    |
       +-----------+-----------+-----------+-----------+-----------+
Row 4  |DUMMY 2    |DUMMY 1    |DUMMY 6    |DUMMY 4    |DUMMY 7    |
       +-----------+-----------+-----------+-----------+-----------+

Total objective function value = 127120
```

Figure 21.13   Optimal Process Layout output from STORM based on Figures 21.10 and 21.12.

the input file for STORM, the Q-type From-To Chart shown in Figure 21.10 was used as the FLOW matrix and the $-type From-To Chart shown in Figure 21.12 was used as the COST matrix. The reader is encouraged to compare the inter-departmental adjacencies in this layout with Figure 7.1 in Chapter 7 and Figure 21.11.

The two facility layouts in Figures 21.11 and Figure 21.13 that were produced by PFAST and STORM, respectively, *cannot* be edited. However, both layouts were generated using a heuristic optimization algorithm. In stark contrast, Figure 21.14 is a screen capture of the Q-type Flow Diagram output from Sgetti. This layout corresponds to a classic Process Layout for the machine shop because none of the (12) work centers has been split. After Sgetti produced a (random) bubble diagram for the initial shop layout, the locations of the bubbles representing the different work centers were **manually** rearranged over several iterations. After each layout adjustment was manually made in the layout, a *Material Flow Calculation* was done by Sgetti to assess the extent to which the new layout was better than the initial layout. The reader is encouraged to compare the inter-departmental adjacencies in the layout of Figure 21.14 with the layouts in Figure 7.1 in Chapter 7 and Figure 21.11 and 21.13

Figure 21.15 is a screen capture of the Q-type Flow Diagram of Figure 21.14 for **only** Cell #1 **before** layout improvement. The reader is encouraged to verify that the parts listed in the *Part No.* column correspond to PF #1 and that all parts in PF #2 have been eliminated from the sample used to generate the material flows. Notice that this cell is a large cell that includes all but two of the twelve work centers in the shop (Work Centers #11 and #12).

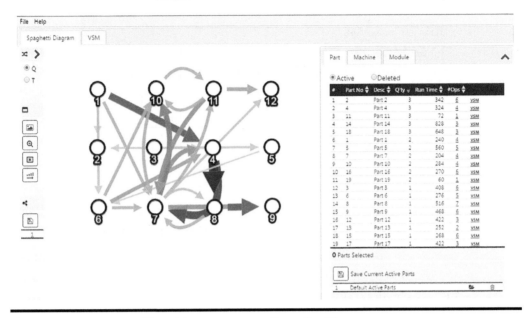

Figure 21.14   Q-type Flow Diagram output from Sgetti.

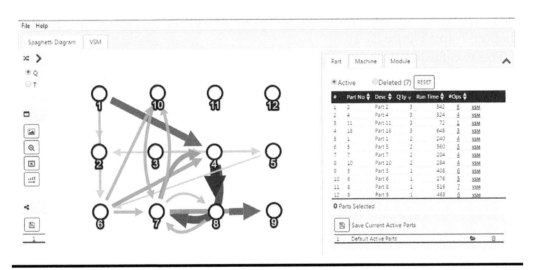

Figure 21.15   Q-type Flow Diagram for initial layout for Cell #1 output from Sgetti.

Figure 21.16 is a screen capture of the Q-type Flow Diagram for **only** Cell #1 **after** layout improvement.

Based on the *Material Flow Calculation* done by Sgetti, Figure 21.17 shows a significant reduction in travel distance achieved with the new layout for Cell #1.

Figure 21.18a is a screen capture of the Q-type Flow Diagram of Figure 21.14 for **only** Cell #2 **before** layout improvement. The reader is

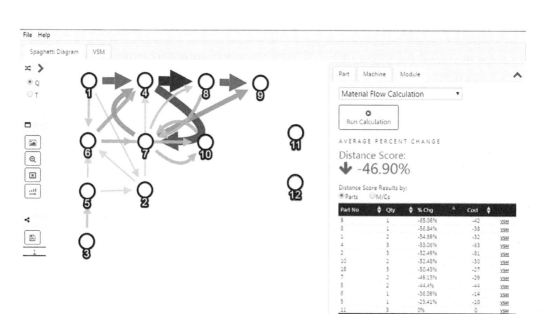

Figure 21.16   Q-type Flow Diagram for improved layout for Cell #1 output from Sgetti.

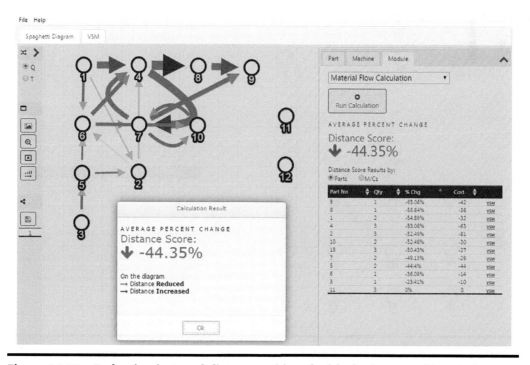

Figure 21.17   Reduction in travel distance achieved with the improved layout for Cell #1 output from Sgetti.

encouraged to verify that the parts listed in the *Part No.* column correspond to PF #2 and that all parts in PF #1 have been eliminated from the sample used to generate the material flows. Notice that this cell, unlike Cell #1, includes only five of the twelve work centers in the shop (Work Centers #1, #7, #10, #11, and #12).

Figure 21.18(b) is a screen capture of the Q-type Flow Diagram for **only** Cell #2 **after** layout improvement.

Based on the *Material Flow Calculation* done by Sgetti, Figure 21.18(c) shows a significant reduction in travel distance achieved with the new layout for Cell #2.

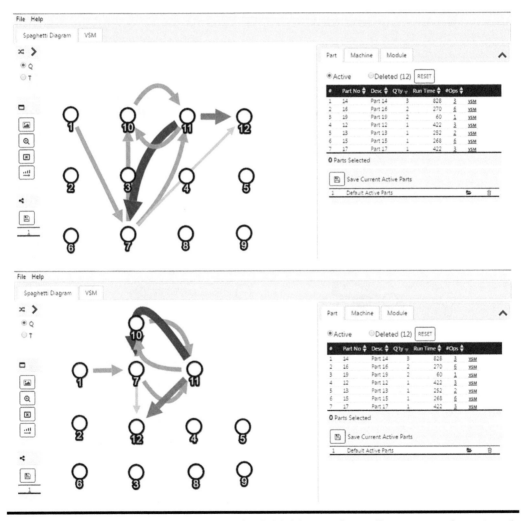

Figure 21.18 a) Q-type Flow Diagram for initial layout for Cell #2 output from Sgetti. b) Q-type Flow Diagram for improved layout for Cell #2 output from Sgetti.

(Continued)

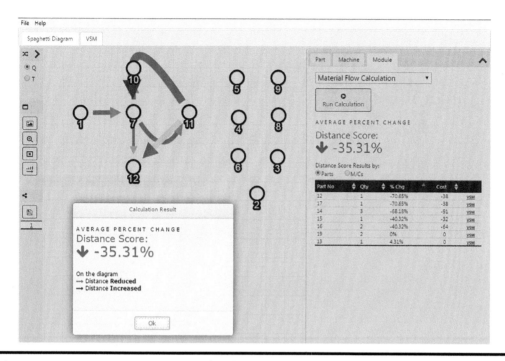

Figure 21.18 (CONTINUED)   c) Reduction in travel distance achieved with the improved layout for Cell #2 output from Sgetti.

Figure 21.19 is a screen capture from Sgetti that shows a Virtual Cellular Layout. It was designed by (i) taking the layout shown in Figure 21.14 and (ii) rearranging the relative locations of the twelve work centers per their locations in Cell #1, as shown in Figure 21.16, and Cell #2, as shown in Figure 21.18(b). None of the twelve work centers were broken up to distribute the machines in any of them to separate locations in the new layout. The reader is encouraged to compare this layout (Virtual Cellular Layout) with Figure 7.7 in Chapter 7. The *Material Flow Calculation* done by Sgetti shows a significant reduction in travel distance achieved with the new layout.

In Figure 21.9, none of the work centers were split up in order to distribute their machines in two or more cells. Figure 21.20 is a screen capture from Sgetti that shows a Hybrid Cellular Layout (Cellular Layout with Reorientation of Cells) in which (i) some of the work centers have been broken up and their machines distributed in the two cells, (ii) the machine compositions of the two cells were not changed, (iii) the orientations of the two cells were changed, (iv) the shapes of the cells were changed (Cell #1 has an L shape whereas Cell #2 has a linear shape), and (v) the shop layout was designed to maximize sharing of machines common to both cells. The reader is encouraged to compare the layout in Figure 21.19 with Figure 7.3 (Cellular Layout

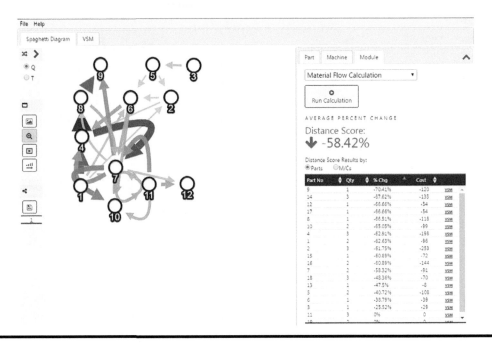

Figure 21.19   Virtual Cellular Layout for the shop.

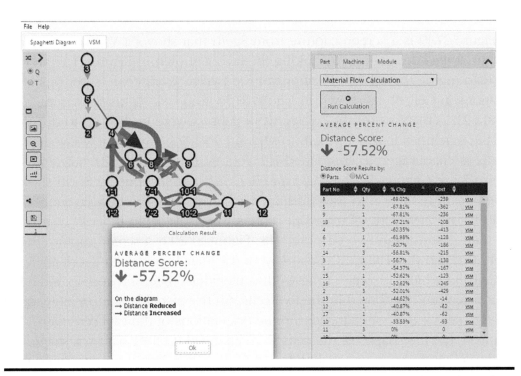

Figure 21.20   Hybrid Cellular Layout for the shop (Cellular Layout with reorientation of cells).

with Reorientation of Cells) in Chapter 7. In contrast to Figure 21.19, based on the calculations in Table 21.6, the layout in Figure 21.20 shows that three work centers have been broken up and their machines put in both cells – Work Center #1 (1-1 and 1-2), Work Center #7 (7-1 and 7-2), and Work Center #10 (10-1 and 10-2). Unlike a traditional Cellular Layout, the Hybrid Cellular Layout permits the machines from each of those three work centers to be duplicated in the two cells **BUT** still be located adjacent to each other. By allowing identical machines placed in the two cells to remain in proximity to each other as in the Process Layout of Figure 21.14, the shop has maximum loading flexibility because it can load orders on the same machine(s) available in either cell. Thereby, if demands for the parts in the two cells fluctuate, this Hybrid Cellular Layout is more flexible than a Cellular Layout. The *Material Flow Calculation* done by Sgetti shows a significant reduction in travel distance achieved with the new layout compared to the original layout in Figure 21.14.

In contrast to Figure 21.20 where Cell #1 has a U layout and Cell #2 has a linear layout, Figure 21.21 is a screen capture from Sgetti that shows a Hybrid Cellular Layout (Hybrid Flow Shop Layout) in which (i) the machine compositions of the cells were not changed, (ii) both cells were arranged side-by-side and meshed into a **linear** multi-stage flow shop, and (iii) the shop layout was

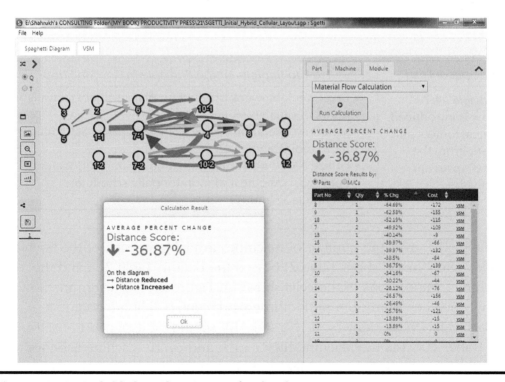

Figure 21.21   Hybrid Flow Shop Layout for the shop.

designed to maximize unidirectional material flow and proximity between identical machines in both cells (see Figure 4.14 in Chapter 4). The reader is encouraged to compare this layout (Hybrid Flow Shop Layout) with Figure 7.6 in Chapter 7. Like the Hybrid Cellular Layout in Figure 12.8, the Hybrid Cellular Layout in Figure 21.21 is more flexible than a Cellular Layout. Thereby, if demands for the parts in the two cells fluctuates, machines common to both cells are co-located in a work center. The *Material Flow Calculation* done by Sgetti shows a significant reduction in travel distance achieved with the new layout compared to the original layout in Figure 21.14.

Author's Note: The reader is encouraged to read the section *Analysis of Machine Duplication Decisions in Hybrid Cellular Layouts Using Sgetti* that appears at the end of the chapter. It was contributed by Dr. Smart Khaewsukkho, the developer of the Sgetti software. He describes how to use the *Lead Time Reduction* module in Sgetti to complement the analyses done using the *Material Flow Calculation* module in Sgetti.

Cell and Shop Scheduling

Here we are implementing Lean Principle #4 which was described in Table 21.2 as follows:

Principle of Lean	How to Implement the Principle in Any Job Shop
Principle #4: As flow is introduced, let customers pull value from the next upstream activity	• Level week-by-week production plans subject to available hours of capacity • Schedule operations using a Finite Capacity Scheduling (FCS) tool (Chapter 19) • Utilize a Manufacturing Execution System and Water Spiders to execute and monitor daily schedules (Chapters 17 and 18)

Table 21.5 gives the number of machines available in each of the twelve work centers in the shop. Table 21.6 used the data in Table 21.4 and the machine compositions of the cells shown in Figure 21.4 to determine how many machines from each of the three work centers that are common to both cells (Work Centers #1, #7, and #10) should be assigned to each cell. Table 21.7 lists the Machine ID for each and every machine assigned to Cell #1. Similarly, Table 21.8 lists the Machine ID for each and every machine assigned to Cell #2.

Table 21.7 Number of Machines from Different Work Centers Assigned to Cell #1

Work Center	Number of Machines Available in the Work Center
1	2 [M/C #1-1, M/C #1-2]
2	1 [M/C #2]
3	1 [M/C #3]
4	2 [M/C #4-1, M/C #4-2]
5	1 [M/C #5]
6	2 [M/C #6-1, M/C #6-2]
7	2 [M/C #7-1, M/C #7-2]
8	1 [M/C #8]
9	2 [M/C #9-1, M/C #9-2]
10	2 [M/C # 10-1, M/C #10-2]
Availability capacity on any machine = 384 minutes	

Table 21.8 Number of Machines from Different Work Centers Assigned to Cell #2

Work Center	Number of Machines Available in the Work Center
1	1 [M/C #1-2]
7	2 [M/C #7-3, M/C #7-4]
10	1 [M/C #10-3]
11	3 [M/C #11-1, M/C #11-2, M/C #11-3]
12	1 [M/C #12]
Availability capacity on any machine = 384 minutes	

Table 21.5 shows that several work centers have only one machine. Excluding them, for the remaining work centers listed in Tables 21.7 and 21.8, Table 21.9 shows how identical machines in a cell were assigned parts in order that their workloads were balanced. The reader is encouraged to use the data in Table 21.4 to verify the assignments in Table 21.9.

Table 21.9 Detailed Part-Machine Assignments in the Cells to Equalize Workloads on Identical Machines

Cell #	Part #							*Workload on Work Center # (minutes)*					
		2	3	5	6	9	8	4	1	7	10	11	12
1	11				72 [#6-1]								
1	18				108 [#6-2]					180 [#7-2]	360 [#10-2]		
1	5				72 [#6-2]	72			96 [#1-2]	120 [#7-2]	200 [#10-1]		
1	6				36 [#6-1]	36	24			60 [#7-1]	120 [#10-1]		
1	8	48	144	120	72 [#6-1]	48	48	36 [#4-1]					
1	9		144	120	72 [#6-1]	48	48	36 [#4-1]					
1	7				72 [#6-2]	48	48	36 [#4-1]					
1	10						24	240 [#4-1]		20 [#7-2]			
1	2						24	240 [#4-2]	36 [#1-1]	40 [#7-1]			

(Continued)

Table 21.9 (Continued) Detailed Part-Machine Assignments in the Cells to Equalize Workloads on Identical Machines

Cell #	Part #	2	3	5	6	9	8	4	1	7	10	11	12
						Workload on Work Center # (minutes)							
1	1					72	36	36 [#4-2]	96 [#1-1]				
1	3	48				72	36	36 [#4-2]	96 [#1-1]	120 [#7-1]			
1	4					72		36 [#4-2]	96 [#1-2]	120 [#7-1]			
2	14									180 [#7-3]	360 [#10-3]	288 [#11-1]	
2	15								15 [#1-2]	70 [#7-3]	45 [#10-3]	108 [#11-2]	30
2	16								15 [#1-2]	70 [#7-3]	45 [#10-3]	108 [#11-1]	30
2	12									150 [#7-4]		192 [#11-3]	80
2	17									150 [#7-4]		192 [#11-2]	80
2	13											192 [#11-3]	60
2	19												60

Using the data in Tables 21.7 and 21.9, the data that LEKIN used to schedule operations in Cell #1 is shown in Table 21.10. Similarly, using the data in Tables 21.8 and 21.9, the data that LEKIN used to schedule operations in Cell #2 is shown in Table 21.11.

LEKIN is an academic scheduling software[4] that does not have the scheduling capabilities of commercial FCSs like Preactor, Tactic, and Schedlyzer. But, these commercial packages were not available to the author. Also, the dataset used in the tutorial was not comprehensive enough to populate the

Table 21.10 Input Data About PF #1 That LEKIN Used to Schedule Operations in Cell #1

Part #	Batch Size	Sequence of Machines (Operation Sequence) for Part #						
		Batch Machining Time for Each Operation (minutes)						
1	2	#1-1	#4-2	#8	#9-1			
		96	36	36	72			
2	3	#1-1	#4-2	#7-1	#4-1	#8	#7-2	
		36	120	20	120	24	20	
3	1	#1-1	#2	#4-2	#7-1	#8	#9-1	
		96	48	36	120	36	72	
4	3	#1-2	#4-2	#7-1	#9-2			
		96	36	120	72			
5	2	#1-2	#6-2	#10-1	#7-2	#9-2		
		96	72	200	120	72		
6	1	#6-1	#10-1	#7-1	#8	#9-2		
		36	120	60	24	36		
7	2	#6-2	#4-1	#8	#9-2			
		72	36	48	48			
8	1	#3	#5	#2	#6-1	#4-1	#8	#9-1
		144	120	48	72	36	48	48

(Continued)

[4] The free (academic) version of LEKIN is available for download at http://web-static.stern.nyu.edu/om/software/lekin/.

Table 21.10 (*Continued*)   Input Data About PF #1 That LEKIN Used to Schedule Operations in Cell #1

Part #	Batch Size	Sequence of Machines (Operation Sequence) for Part #						
		Batch Machining Time for Each Operation (minutes)						
9	1	#3	#5	#6-1	#4-1	#8	#9-1	
		144	120	72	36	48	48	
10	2	#4-1	#7-2	#4-2	#8			
		120	20	120	24			
11	3	#6-1						
		72						
18	3	#6-2	#7-2	#10-2				
		108	180	360				

Table 21.11   Input Data About PF #2 That LEKIN Used to Schedule Operations in Cell #2

Part #	Batch Size	Sequence of Machines (Operation Sequence) for Part #					
		Batch Machining Time for Each Operation (minutes)					
12	1	#11-3	#7-4	#12			
		192	150	80			
13	1	#11-3	#12				
		192	60				
14	3	#11-1	#7-3	#10-3			
		288	180	360			
15	1	#1-2	#7-3	#11-1	#10-3	#11-2	#12
		15	70	54	45	54	30
16	2	#1-2	#7-3	#11-1	#10–3	#11-2	#12
		15	70	54	45	54	30
17	1	#11-2	#7-4	#12			
		192	150	80			
19	2	#12					
		60					

input data files that these commercial schedulers use. Fortunately, LEKIN was freely available to use to demonstrate how to implement Lean Principle #4 in this tutorial. Unfortunately, it has limitations that impacted the quality of the schedules that were produced. Table 21.12 lists the limitations of LEKIN that impacted the schedules for (i) each of the two cells and (ii) the entire machine shop.

(CASE 1) Scheduling the Entire Shop: In this case, the facility being scheduled is the entire shop that has a classic Process Layout shown in Figure 21.14. Table 21.4 provides the Batch Size and routing for each of the nineteen parts. For each operation in any part's routing, the Batch Machining Time (= Batch Size × Cycle Time) is the total time the machine will take to process the entire batch. Table 21.5 gives the number of machines in each of the twelve work centers in the shop. Since there is more than one machine in several work centers, the data in Tables 21.4 and 21.5 was run through the *Flexible Job Shop* module in LEKIN. Figure 21.22(a) shows the LEKIN screen for scheduling the entire shop. Figure 21.22(b) shows the LEKIN screen to specify a transfer delay of 20 minutes between the machines used for consecutive operations in every routing. Since the layout is a Process Layout, a reasonably high transfer delay between consecutive operations was chosen. The "20 minutes" corresponds to the lowest Batch Machining Time in the data which happens to be for the last operation in the routing of Part #2 in Table 21.4. Figure 21.22(c) provides a comparison of the different schedules based on standard scheduling metrics that are surrogate measures for Flow Time and WIP (work in progress). *For the Makespan (C_{max}) performance metric,* Figure 21.22(d) displays the Gantt Chart for the best of the five schedules that were generated using different heuristics that LEKIN ranked as follows: #1 General Shifting Bottleneck Routine/$C_{max,}$ #2 Longest Processing Time, #3 Weighted Shortest Processing Time, #4 First Come First Serve, and #5 Shortest Processing Time. Figure 21.22(e–g) are essentially a rewrite of the Gantt Chart in Figure 21.22(d) and specifies, for every individual machine in the schedule, the Start and End times for each job that is processed in chronological sequence on that machine. The reader is encouraged to map Figure 21.22(e–g) onto Figure 21.22(d).

(CASE 2) Scheduling only Cell #1: In this case, the facility being scheduled is Cell #1, which is an L-shaped cell in the Cellular Layout shown in Figure 21.20. Table 21.10 provides the Batch Size and routing for each of the twelve parts. For each operation in any part's routing, the Batch Machining Time (= Batch Size × Cycle Time) is the total time the machine will take to process the entire batch. Table 21.7 gives the number of machines in each

Table 21.12 How the Limitations of LEKIN Impacted the Cell and Shop Schedules

Limitation	Adjustments to Overcome the Limitation
LEKIN does not allow a batch of parts to be split into two or more transfer batches, much less single-piece flow aka "lot streaming". So, if the Batch Size for a part is >1, LEKIN will force all parts to be run consecutively as a single batch at each operation in the part's routing. For example, Table 21.4 shows that Part #1 has a Batch Size of 2 and its routing is 1→4→8→9. But the Cycle Time for each operation in the routing of the part that is input to LEKIN is actually the Batch Machining Time = Cycle Time × Batch Size.	Nothing can be done to eliminate this limitation.
If the Batch Size for a part is >1, LEKIN will force all parts to be run consecutively as a single batch at each and every operation in the part's routing. LEKIN will **not** allow one-piece flow between two machines inside a cell even if the machines needed for consecutive operations in the routing of a part are located adjacent to each other. For example, in the case of Part #1 which is processed in Cell #1, as soon as one part in the batch for Part #1 is completed on Machine #1, it ought to be immediately transferred into the queue at Machine #4.	Nothing can be done to eliminate this limitation. But, a schedule produced by LEKIN could be improved by **manually** implementing one-piece flow between consecutive operations for each and every one of the parts that have a Batch Size >1. This "left shifting of the entire schedule" is guaranteed to reduce the waiting times that inflate the values for the Makespan, Total Flow Time, and Weighted Total Flow Time for any LEKIN schedule.
If the Batch Size for a part is >1, LEKIN will force all parts to be run consecutively as a single batch on a single machine, even when there are two or more machines of the same type available in the cell. LEKIN will **not** allow a batch to be split and for each sub-batch to be run in parallel on identical machines in a cell or work center. For example, in the case of Part #1 which is processed in Cell #1, the batch could be split and a part processed on each of the two machines that are in Work Centers #1, #4, and #9.	Nothing can be done to eliminate this limitation. However, the *Flexible Job Shop* module in LEKIN at least allows two jobs to be run in parallel on separate machines of the same type if they are available in a cell or work center.

(*Continued*)

Table 21.12 (*Continued*)   How the Limitations of LEKIN Impacted the Cell and Shop Schedules

Limitation	Adjustments to Overcome the Limitation
LEKIN does not allow backtrack flows to allow a part to visit the same work center multiple times if it is required for two or more non-consecutive operations in the part's routing. For example, in the case of Part #2 which has a routing 1→4→7→4→8→7, LEKIN would not allow this routing to be input as-is because the part would backtrack twice, once to Work Center #4 and once to Work Center #7.	Nothing can be done to eliminate this limitation if the work center has only one machine (See Table 21.5). However, in the case where there are two or more machines of the same type available inside a cell, as shown in Tables 21.10 and 21.11, then the routing of a part could be modified to use a different machine of the same type for successive operations requiring the same machine. For example, see the routings for Parts #2 and #10 in Table 21.10 and the routings for Parts #15 and #16 in Table 21.11 that were input to the *Flexible Job Shop* module in LEKIN.
	In the *Flexible Job Shop* module of LEKIN, if any work center has more than one machine, LEKIN automatically numbers them to distinguish one from the other in the Gantt Charts. For example, Table 21.5 shows that Work Center #1 has two machines. Therefore, in the Gantt Chart displayed in Figure 21.22(d), there are two timelines, one for Work Center "W/C #1.01" and another for Work Center "W/C #1.02". **This automatic numbering of the machines in a work center that LEKIN does can get complicated!** For example, Table 21.4 shows that Work Center #11 features twice in the routings for Parts #15 and #16. Since LEKIN does not allow backtracking, for scheduling the entire shop (Case 1), Work Center #11 was broken up into two Work Centers, W/C #11-1 and W/C #11-2. Table 21.5 shows that Work Center #11 has 3 machines; therefore, two of those machines were assigned to W/C #11-1 and the third one was assigned to W/C #11-2. Therefore, in the Gantt Chart displayed in Figure 21.22d, LEKIN created three timelines for Work Center "W/C #11-1.01", "W/C #11-1.02", and "W/C #11-2.01".

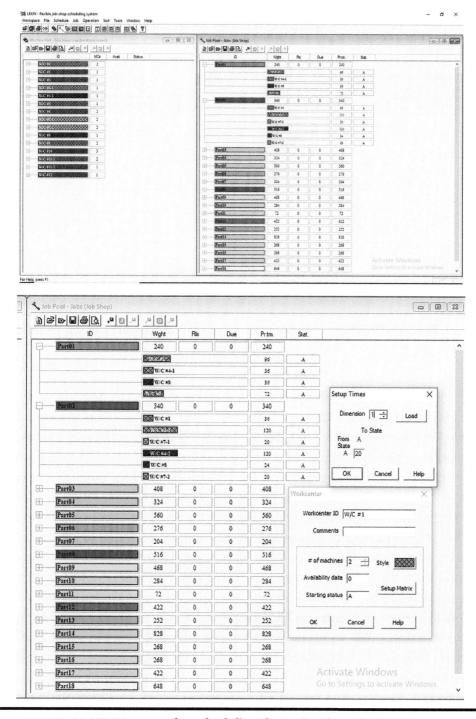

Figure 21.22 (a) LEKIN screen for scheduling the entire shop. (b) LEKIN screen to specify a transfer delay of 20 minutes between the machines used for consecutive operations in every routing in the Process Layout for the shop.

(Continued)

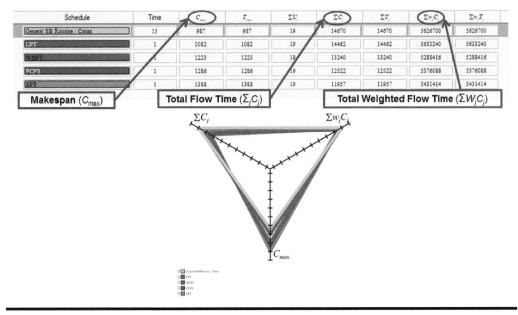

Schedule	Time	C_{max}	T_{max}	ΣU_j	ΣC_j	ΣT_j	$\Sigma w_j C_j$	$\Sigma w_j T_j$
General SB Routine / Cmax	15	987	987	19	14670	14670	5626700	5626700
LPT	1	1082	1082	19	14462	14462	5633240	5633240
WSPT	1	1223	1223	19	13240	13240	5288416	5288416
FCFS	1	1286	1286	19	12522	12522	5376088	5376088
SPT	1	1388	1388	19	11957	11957	5431414	5431414

Makespan (C_{max})   **Total Flow Time ($\Sigma_j C_j$)**   **Total Weighted Flow Time ($\Sigma W_j C_j$)**

Figure 21.22 (CONTINUED) **(c) Comparison of several schedules based on different metrics.**

(Continued)

of the 10 work centers in the cell. Since there is more than one machine in several work centers, the data in Tables 21.7 and 21.10 was run through the *Flexible Job Shop* module in LEKIN. Figure 21.23(a) shows the LEKIN screen for scheduling the cell. Figure 21.23(b) shows the LEKIN screen to specify a transfer delay of 6 minutes between the machines used for consecutive operations in every routing. Since the layout is a Cellular Layout, a lower transfer delay between consecutive operations was chosen. The "6 minutes" corresponds to the lowest Cycle Time in the data, which happens to be for the last operation in the routing of Part #2 in Table 21.4. Figure 21.23(c) provides a comparison of the different schedules based on standard scheduling metrics that are surrogate measures for Flow Time and WIP. *For the Makespan (C_{max}) performance metric,* Figure 21.23(d) displays the Gantt Chart for the best of the five schedules that were generated using different heuristics that LEKIN ranked as follows: #1 General Shifting Bottleneck Routine/C_{max}, #2 Longest Processing Time, #3 First Come First Serve, #4 Weighted Shortest Processing Time, and #5 Shortest Processing Time. Figure 21.23(e–g) is essentially a rewrite of the Gantt Chart in Figure 21.23(d) and specifies, for every individual machine in the schedule, the Start and End times for each job that is processed in chronological sequence on that machine. The reader is encouraged to map Figure 21.23(e–g) onto Figure 21.23(d).

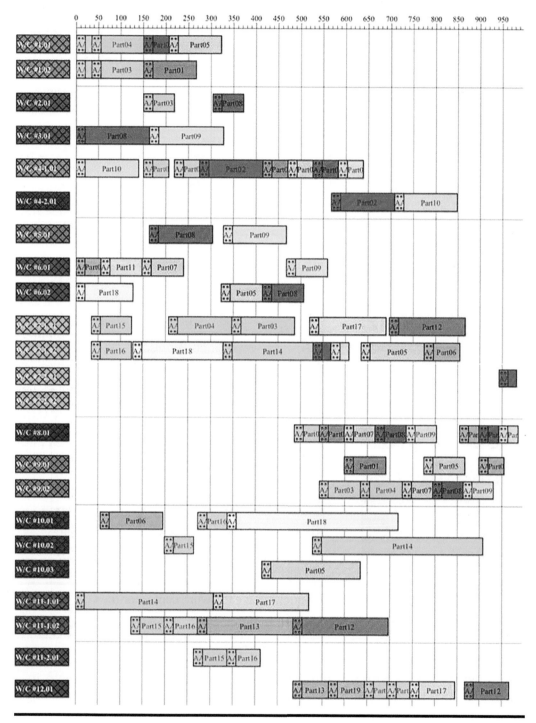

Figure 21.22 (CONTINUED)   (d) Gantt Chart for the C$_{max}$ schedule

(*Continued*)

Mch/Job	Setup	Start	Stop	Pr.tm
W/C #1.01	80			243
Part16	20	20	35	15
Part04	20	55	151	96
Part02	20	171	207	36
Part05	20	227	323	96
W/C #1.02	60			207
Part15	20	20	35	15
Part03	20	55	151	96
Part01	20	171	267	96
W/C #2.01	40			96
Part03	20	171	219	48
Part08	20	324	372	48
W/C #3.01	40			288
Part08	20	20	164	144
Part09	20	184	328	144
W/C #4-1.01	160			456
Part10	20	20	140	120
Part04	20	171	207	36
Part03	20	239	275	36
Part02	20	295	415	120
Part01	20	435	471	36
Part07	20	491	527	36
Part08	20	547	583	36
Part09	20	603	639	36
W/C #4-2.01	40			240
Part02	20	588	708	120
Part10	20	728	848	120
W/C #5.01	40			240
Part08	20	184	304	120
Part09	20	348	468	120

Figure 21.22 (CONTINUED) **(e) Job sequence on each work center for the C_{max} schedule.**

(Continued)

(CASE 3) Scheduling only Cell #2: In this case, the facility being scheduled is Cell #2 which is the linear cell in the Cellular Layout shown in Figure 21.20. Table 21.11 provides the Batch Size and routing for each of the seven parts. For each operation in any part's routing, the Batch Machining Time (= Batch Size × Cycle Time) is the total time the machine will take to process the entire batch. Table 21.8 gives the number of machines in each of the 5 work centers in the cell. Since there is more than one machine in

W/C #6.01	80			252
Part06	20	20	56	36
Part11	20	76	148	72
Part07	20	168	240	72
Part09	20	488	560	72
W/C #6.02	60			252
Part18	20	20	128	108
Part05	20	343	415	72
Part08	20	435	507	72
W/C #7.1.01	100			610
Part15	20	55	125	70
Part04	20	227	347	120
Part03	20	367	487	120
Part17	20	540	690	150
Part12	20	717	867	150
W/C #7.1.02	140			650
Part16	20	55	125	70
Part18	20	148	328	180
Part14	20	348	528	180
Part02	20	548	568	20
Part10	20	588	608	20
Part05	20	655	775	120
Part06	20	795	855	60
W/C #7.2.01	20			20
Part02	20	963	983	20
W/C #7.2.02	0			0

Figure 21.22 (CONTINUED) **(f) Job sequence on each work center for the C_{max} schedule.**

(Continued)

several work centers, the data in Tables 21.8 and 21.11 was run through the *Flexible Job Shop* module in LEKIN. Figure 21.24(a) shows the LEKIN screen for scheduling the cell. Figure 21.24(b) shows the LEKIN screen to specify a transfer delay of 6 minutes between the machines used for consecutive operations in every routing. Since the layout is a Cellular Layout, a lower transfer delay between consecutive operations was chosen. The "6 minutes" corresponds to the lowest Cycle Time in the data which happens to be for the last operation in the routing of Part #2 in Table 21.4. Figure 21.24(c) provides a comparison of the different schedules based on standard scheduling metrics that are surrogate measures for Flow Time and WIPc. *For the Makespan (C_{max}) performance metric,* Figure 21.24(d) displays the Gantt Chart for the best of the five schedules that were generated using different

Mch/Job	Setup	Start	Stop	Pr.tm
W/C #8.01	160			288
Part03	20	507	543	36
Part01	20	563	599	36
Part07	20	619	667	48
Part08	20	687	735	48
Part09	20	755	803	48
Part06	20	875	899	24
Part02	20	919	943	24
Part10	20	963	987	24
W/C #9.01	60			180
Part01	20	619	691	72
Part05	20	795	867	72
Part06	20	919	955	36
W/C #9.02	100			288
Part03	20	563	635	72
Part04	20	655	727	72
Part07	20	747	795	48
Part08	20	815	863	48
Part09	20	883	931	48
W/C #10.01	60			525
Part06	20	76	196	120
Part16	20	293	338	45
Part18	20	358	718	360
W/C #10.02	40			405
Part15	20	219	264	45
Part14	20	548	908	360
W/C #10.03	20			200
Part05	20	435	635	200
W/C #11-1.01	40			480
Part14	20	20	308	288
Part17	20	328	520	192
W/C #11-1.02	80			492
Part15	20	145	199	54
Part16	20	219	273	54
Part13	20	293	485	192
Part12	20	505	697	192
W/C #11-2.01	40			108
Part15	20	284	338	54
Part16	20	358	412	54
W/C #12.01	120			340
Part13	20	505	565	60
Part19	20	585	645	60
Part15	20	665	695	30
Part16	20	715	745	30
Part17	20	765	845	80
Part12	20	887	967	80

Figure 21.22 (CONTINUED) **(g) Job sequence on each work center for the C_{max} schedule.**

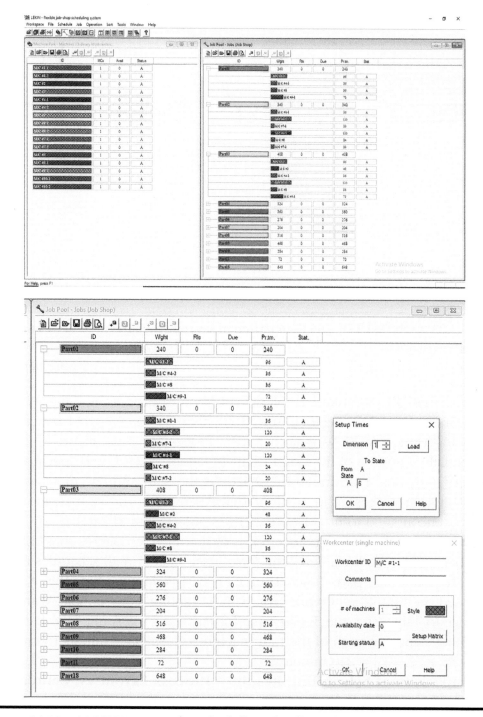

Figure 21.23 (a) LEKIN screen for scheduling of Cell #1. (b) LEKIN screen to specify a transfer delay of 6 minutes between the machines used for consecutive operations in every routing in the Cellular Layout for Cell #1.

(Continued)

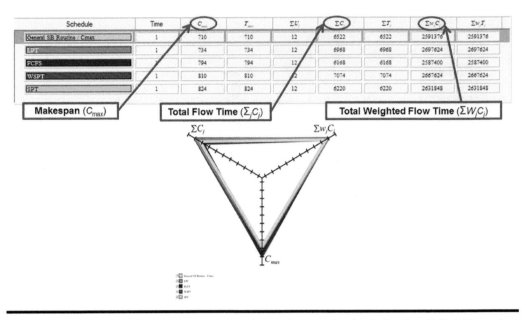

Schedule	Time	C_{max}	T_{max}	ΣU_j	ΣC_j	ΣT_j	$\Sigma w_j C_j$	$\Sigma w_j T_j$
General SB Routine / Cmax	1	710	710	12	6522	6522	2591376	2591376
LPT	1	734	734	12	6968	6968	2697624	2697624
FCFS		794	794	12	6168	6168	2587400	2587400
WSPT	1	810	810	2	7074	7074	2667624	2667624
SPT	1	824	824	12	6220	6220	2631848	2631848

Makespan (C_{max})   **Total Flow Time ($\Sigma_j C_j$)**   **Total Weighted Flow Time ($\Sigma W_j C_j$)**

Figure 21.23 (CONTINUED)   (c) Comparison of several schedules for Cell #1 based on different metrics.

(Continued)

heuristics that LEKIN ranked as follows: #1 Shortest Processing Time, #2 First Come First Serve, #3 General Shifting Bottleneck Routine/C_{max}, #4 Longest Processing Time, and #5 Weighted Shortest Processing Time. Figure 21.24(e) is essentially a rewrite of the Gantt Chart in Figure 21.24(d) and specifies, for every individual machine in the schedule, the Start and End times for each job that is processed in a chronological sequence on that machine. The reader is encouraged to map Figure 21.24(e) onto Figure 21.24(e).

Author's Note: The weights for each of the nineteen part #s that LEKIN used to compute the Weighted Total Flow Time metric in all schedules is the Touch Time for each part. Touch Time for a part is the total time that it was processed on the different work centers in its routing. For example, with reference to Table 21.4, the Touch Time for Part #1 is the sum of the Batch Machining Times on each of the four machines (1→4→8→9) in its routing = 96 + 36 + 36 + 72 = 240 minutes.

Comparison of Scheduling Results – Process Layout vs. Cellular Layout: The conversion from a Process Layout to a Cellular Layout does not eliminate the complexity of the Job Shop Scheduling Problem (JSSP). However, splitting up the entire shop into two separate cells has a divide-and-conquer effect! The Process Layout operates as a single job shop, whereas each of the two cells in the Cellular Layout operates as a

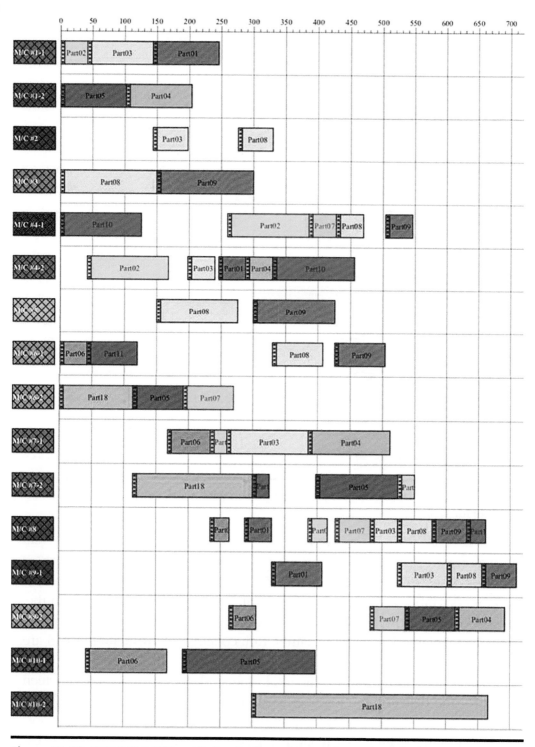

Figure 21.23 (CONTINUED) **(d)** Gantt Chart for the C_{max} schedule for Cell #1. **(e)** Job sequence on each work center for the C_{max} schedule for Cell #1.

(Continued)

Mch/Job	Setup	Start	Stop	Pr.tm
M/C #1-1	18			228
Part02	6	6	42	36
Part03	6	48	144	96
Part01	6	150	246	96
M/C #1-2	12			192
Part05	6	6	102	96
Part04	6	108	204	96
M/C #2	12			96
Part03	6	150	198	48
Part08	6	282	330	48
M/C #3	12			288
Part08	6	6	150	144
Part09	6	156	300	144
M/C #4-1	30			348
Part10	6	6	126	120
Part02	6	266	386	120
Part07	6	392	428	36
Part08	6	434	470	36
Part09	6	510	546	36
M/C #4-2	30			348
Part02	6	48	168	120
Part03	6	204	240	36
Part01	6	252	288	36
Part04	6	294	330	36
Part10	6	336	456	120

Figure 21.23 (CONTINUED)   (e) Job sequence on each work center for the C_{max} schedule for Cell #1.

(Continued)

stand-alone **and** smaller job shop which, in principle, makes each of the two cells easier to manage. Therefore, it should come as no surprise that, according to Table 21.13, the 2-cell Cellular Layout performs better than the entire shop on all three schedule performance criteria (Makespan, Total Flow Time, and Weighted Total Flow Time). Key conclusions from Table 21.13 are:

1. If it is desired to minimize the total time it takes to complete all nineteen parts and deliver them together as an assembly kit, then the schedule performance criterion, **Makespan**, indicates that the Cellular Layout does better than the Process Layout. Per Table 21.13, Makespan for the Process Layout is 987, whereas Makespan for the Cellular Layout is 846 (Makespan for Cell #1 = 710 which is less than Makespan for Cell #2 = 846).

M/C #5	12			240
Part08	6	156	276	120
Part09	6	306	426	120
M/C #6-1	24			252
Part06	6	6	42	36
Part11	6	48	120	72
Part08	6	336	408	72
Part09	6	432	504	72
M/C #6-2	18			252
Part18	6	6	114	108
Part05	6	120	192	72
Part07	6	198	270	72
M/C #7-1	24			320
Part06	6	174	234	60
Part02	6	240	260	20
Part03	6	266	386	120
Part04	6	392	512	120
M/C #7-2	24			340
Part18	6	120	300	180
Part10	6	306	326	20
Part05	6	404	524	120
Part02	6	530	550	20
M/C #8	48			288
Part06	6	240	264	24
Part01	6	294	330	36
Part02	6	392	416	24
Part07	6	434	482	48
Part03	6	488	524	36
Part08	6	530	578	48
Part09	6	584	632	48
Part10	6	638	662	24

Figure 21.23 (CONTINUED) (f) Job sequence on each work center for the C_{max} schedule for Cell #1.

2. If it is desired to minimize WIP in the shop, then the other two schedule performance criteria, **Total Flow Time** and **Weighted Total Flow Time**, indicate that the Cellular Layout (again) does better than the Process Layout. The reader is encouraged to verify this by comparing the numbers in the *Entire Shop* column versus the numbers in the *Cell #1* **and** *Cell #2* columns in Table 21.13.

Mch/Job	Setup	Start	Stop	Pr.tm
M/C #9-1	24			240
Part01	6	336	408	72
Part03	6	530	602	72
Part08	6	608	656	48
Part09	6	662	710	48
M/C #9-2	24			228
Part06	6	270	306	36
Part07	6	488	536	48
Part05	6	542	614	72
Part04	6	620	692	72
M/C #10-1	12			320
Part06	6	48	168	120
Part05	6	198	398	200
M/C #10-2	6			360
Part18	6	306	666	360

Figure 21.23 (CONTINUED) **(g) Job sequence on each work center for the C_{max} schedule for Cell #1.**

(a)

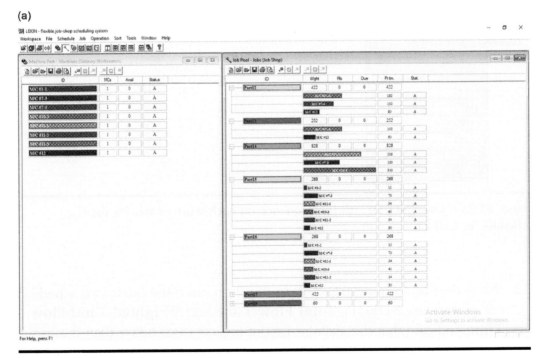

Figure 21.24 **(a) LEKIN screen for scheduling of Cell #2.**

(Continued)

(b)

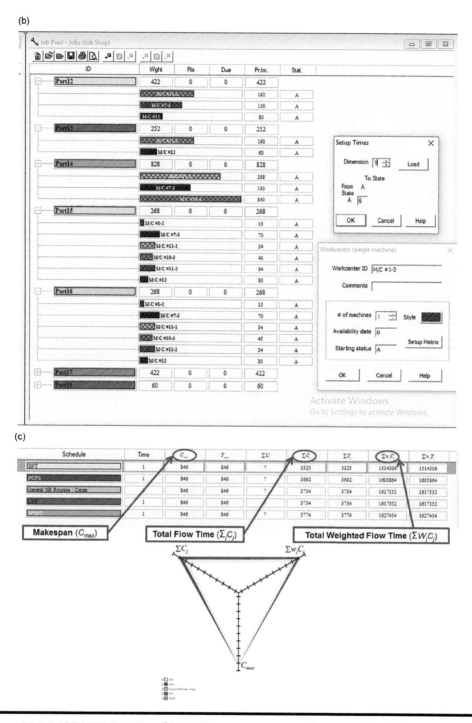

(c)

Figure 21.24 (CONTINUED) **(b)** LEKIN screen to specify a transfer delay of 6 minutes between the machines used for Consecutive operations in every routing in the Cellular Layout for Cell #2. **(c)** Comparison of several schedules for Cell #2 based on different metrics.

(Continued)

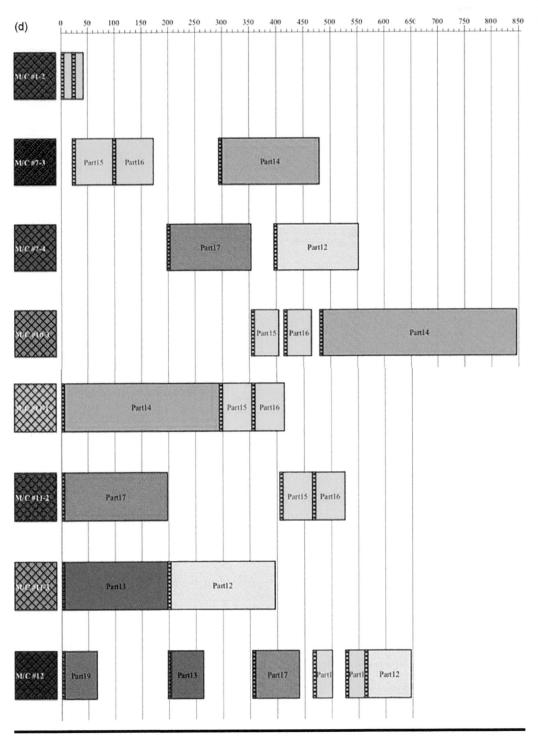

Figure 21.24 (CONTINUED) (d) Gantt Chart for the C_{max} schedule for Cell #2.

(Continued)

(e)

Mch/Job	Setup	Start	Stop	Pr.tm
M/C #1-2	12			30
Part15	6	6	21	15
Part16	6	27	42	15
M/C #7-3	18			320
Part15	6	27	97	70
Part16	6	103	173	70
Part14	6	300	480	180
M/C #7-4	12			300
Part17	6	204	354	150
Part12	6	402	552	150
M/C #10-3	18			450
Part15	6	360	405	45
Part16	6	420	465	45
Part14	6	486	846	360
M/C #11-1	18			396
Part14	6	6	294	288
Part15	6	300	354	54
Part16	6	360	414	54
M/C #11-2	18			300
Part17	6	6	198	192
Part15	6	411	465	54
Part16	6	471	525	54
M/C #11-3	12			384
Part13	6	6	198	192
Part12	6	204	396	192
M/C #12	36			340
Part19	6	6	66	60
Part13	6	204	264	60
Part17	6	360	440	80
Part15	6	471	501	30
Part16	6	531	561	30
Part12	6	567	647	80

Figure 21.24 (CONTINUED)   (e) Job sequence on each work center for the C_{max} schedule for Cell #2.

Table 21.13 Comparison of Scheduling Results

Scheduling Heuristic Used	Entire Shop			Cell #1			Cell #2		
	Makespan	*Total Flow Time*	*Total Weighted Flow Time*	*Makespan*	*Total Flow Time*	*Total Weighted Flow Time*	*Makespan*	*Total Flow Time*	*Total Weighted Flow Time*
General SB (Shifting Bottleneck) routine for C_{max}	987	14,670	5,626,700	710	6,522	2,591,376	846	3,754	1,617,552
Longest processing Time	1,082	14,462	5,633,240	734	6,968	2,697,624	846	3,754	1,617,552
Shortest processing time	1,388	11,957	5,431,414	824	6,220	2,631,848	846	3,325	1,514,306
Weighted shortest processing time	1,223	13,240	5,288,416	810	7,074	2,667,624	846	3,774	1,627,454
First come first serve	1,286	12,522	5,376,088	794	6,168	2,587,400	846	3,692	1,605,864

What About Lean Principle #5?

Until this point, this tutorial has discussed the first four of the five Principles of Lean that guide the implementation of Job Shop Lean in any HMLV facility. Essentially, the implementation of the first four principles helps to:

1. Focus implementation (and improvement) efforts on one part (or product) family-at-a-time (instead of tackling the entire product mix in one shot).
2. Change the existing layout of the facility one-cell-at-a-time so that the facility logistics, supporting services, HR training programs to develop a team-based work culture, etc. can be developed to support execution and monitoring of the daily production schedule.

3. Schedule daily operations in each cell using formal scheduling methods. It is absolutely not a must that a full-blown commercial FCS tool be purchased at the get go. It is more important to display a daily schedule that at least serves as a "ball park" so every cell operator knows their work assignments and the cell knows their delivery goals for that day!

In practice, if the above sequence of three steps is fully executed in a disciplined manner, then that will help to implement Lean Principle #5 which was described in Table 21.2 as follows:

Principle of Lean	How to Implement the Principle in Any Job Shop
Principle #5: As value is specified, Value Streams are identified, wasted steps are removed, and Flow and Pull are introduced, begin the process again and continue it until a state of perfection is reached in which perfect value is created with no waste	• Selectively utilize Continuous Improvement strategies such as Setup Reduction, Cross-training, Inspection at Source, etc. in each cell (Chapters 17, 18, and 28) • Hire an IE (Industrial Engineer) to lead the Continuous Improvement projects and employee training programs (Chapters 17, 18, and 28) • Promote employee-led kaizen activities (Chapters 17, 18, and 28)

Conclusion

The reader will recall that this chapter began with the following paragraph *An article published in 1910 (yes, 1910!) discusses the importance of a good factory layout to achieve efficient material flow **and** effective production scheduling. Table 21.1 contains key excerpts from the article that reinforce the learning objectives of this tutorial to teach a computer-aided approach to implement Job Shop Lean that is guided by the (five) Principles of Lean.* This tutorial demonstrated how to do this using software tools instead of the manual methods that were used over a century ago.

Contributed Section

Dr. Smart Khaewsukkho, PhD
Founder: www.Sgetti.com
Email: Khaewsukkho.1@gmail.com
Phone: 614-598-0642

Analysis of Machine Duplication Decisions in Hybrid Cellular Layouts Using Sgetti

Part 1 of 2: Material Flow Reduction

Figure 21.25(a) shows the Flow Diagram for all parts produced by the machine shop. If there is more than one machine in a work center, it is shown as *Qty: X* above the bubble for that work center. Figure 21.25(b) shows the workload on each of the twelve work centers in the machine shop.

Figure 21.26(a) shows the Flow Diagram for all parts that are produced in Cell #1. PF #1 contains the following parts: (1, 2, 3, 4, 5, 6, 7, 8, 9, 10, 11, 18). Figure 21.26(b) shows the workload on the work centers in Cell #1.

Figure 21.27(a) shows the Flow Diagram for all parts that are produced in Cell #2. PF #2 contains the following parts: (12, 13, 14, 15, 16, 17, 19). Figure 21.27(b) shows the workload on the work centers in Cell #2.

Figure 21.28 is the same Flow Diagram as in Figure 21.25(a) but the material flows for Cell #1 (which produces the parts in PF #1) and Cell #2 (which produces the parts in PF #2) have been superimposed on the same layout by

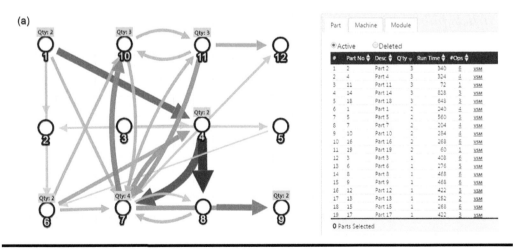

Figure 21.25   (a) Flow Diagram for all parts produced by the machine shop.

(Continued)

(b)

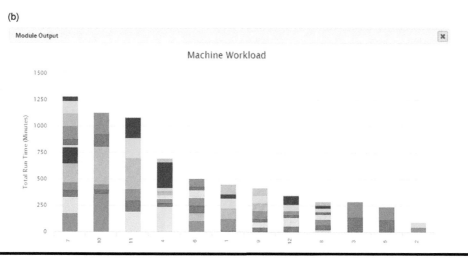

Figure 21.25 (CONTINUED) **(b) Workload on the twelve work centers in the machine shop.**

using colors (**green** for PF #1 and **purple** for PF#2) to distinguish between the two part families. Recall that Table 21.6 listed Work Centers #1, #7, and #10 as being required to produce parts in both cells. This is verified in Figure 21.28 because only these three work centers have flow arrows of both colors (**green** and **purple**) leaving or entering them. In contrast, other work centers that have significant to/from traffic, such as Work Centers #4 and #6 which belong in Cell #1, only have material flow arrows colored **purple** entering or leaving them. In particular, based on the number and thickness of the material flow arrows, Work Centers #7 and #10 have heavy workload in

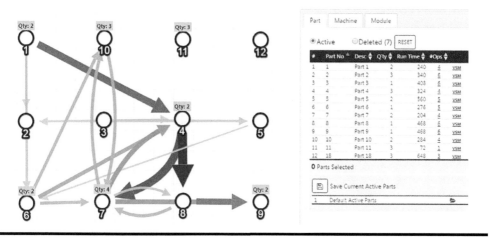

Figure 21.26 **(a) Flow Diagram for Cell #1.**

(Continued)

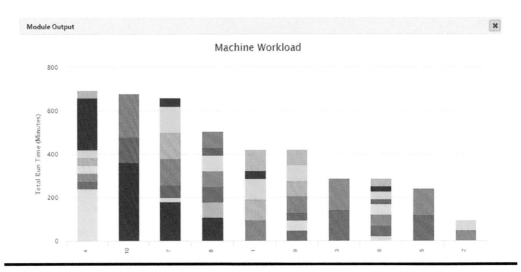

Figure 21.26 (CONTINUED) **(b) Workload on the work centers in Cell #1.**

both cells, whereas Work Center #1 is primarily loaded with work from PF #1 and has negligible workload from PF #2.

Based on the visual assessment of workloads on Work Centers #1, #7, and #10 in both the cells, it was decided to duplicate each of these three work centers in both cells. After the work centers were duplicated, Figure 21.29(a) shows the two independent cells that were implemented. As shown in the figure, in Cell #1 the parts in PF #1 are routed to Work Centers # 1, 7, and 10, whereas in Cell #2 the parts in PF #2 are routed to Work Centers # 1(**1**), 7(**1**), and 10(**1**).

Based on the data in Table 21.4, Figure 21.29(b) provides a comparison of the workloads on the work centers that occur in both cells, i.e., 7

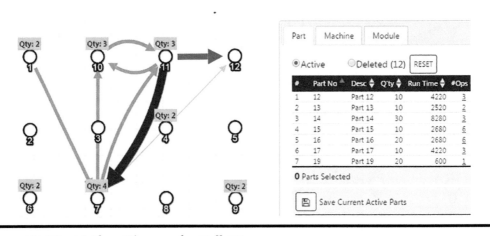

Figure 21.27 **(a) Flow Diagram for Cell #2**

(Continued)

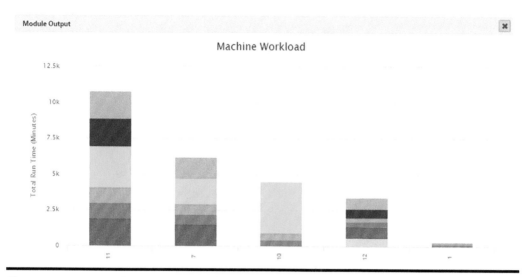

Figure 21.27 (CONTINUED)   (b) Workload on the work centers in Cell #2.

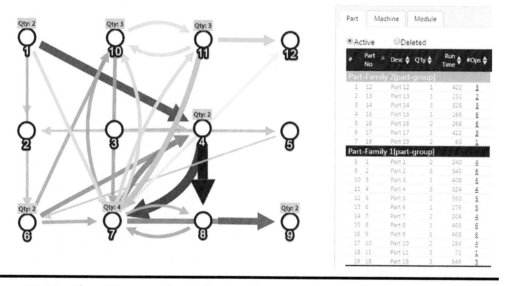

Figure 21.28   Flow Diagrams for Cells #1 and #2 superimposed on same layout.

vs. 7(1), 10 vs. 10(1), and 1 vs. 1(1). From the workloads and the cal-culations in Table 21.6, we can justify the number of machines from each of the three shared work centers that were assigned to either cell as follows:

1. The workload on Work Center #7 is about the same for the two fami-lies. There are 4 machines in this work center. So, putting two machines apiece in both Cells #1 and #2 is appropriate.

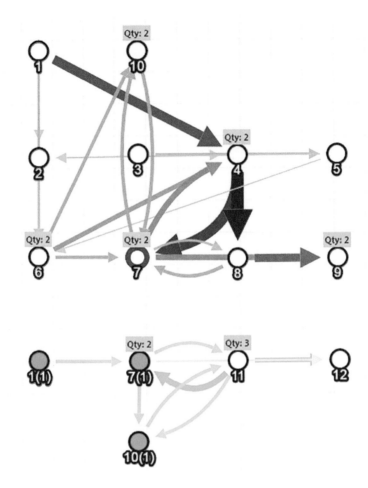

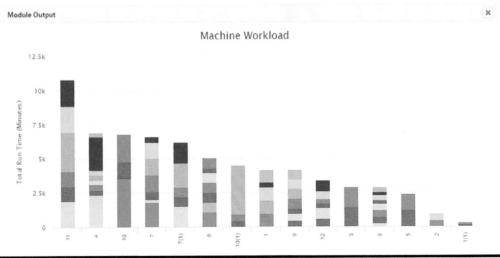

Figure 21.29 (a) Flow Diagrams for Cells #1 and Cell #2 are shown separately. (b) The comparison of workloads on the work centers in both cells.

2. The workload on Work Center #10 is slightly higher in Cell #1 than it is in Cell #2. There are 3 machines in this work center. So, putting two machines in Cell #1 and 1 machine in Cell #2 is appropriate.

3. The workload on Work Center #1 is significant in Cell #1 and almost negligible in Cell #2. There are 2 machines in this work center. Unfortunately, if it is desired to make the two cells independent with zero inter-cell flows between them, then putting one machine apiece in Cells #1 and #2 is appropriate.

Author's Note: Prior to discussing the results in the next section, it is important to mention that, for the sake of simplicity, the batch sizes for the different part numbers in the original dataset shown in Table 21.4 were really small (they ranged in the interval [1, 3]). Unfortunately, if it is desired to use simulation to compare the performance of different layouts for a facility obtained by rearranging machines in the current layout, splitting work centers or adding extra machines, then those values for the batch sizes are too small to use as sample sizes in the simulation runs. Why can a small sample size be a problem for running a simulation? For example, say that Part A has a batch size of 10 and its processing time on Machine M1 is 10 minutes per piece. If we have only one copy of the machine, it will take 100 minutes to process the entire batch, whereas, if we have 2 copies of the machine, it will take 50 minutes to produce the entire batch because it can be split and run in parallel on both machines. On the other hand, if Part A has a batch size of 1, then one copy of Machine M1 would complete the batch in 10 minutes. Unfortunately, even if there were 10 copies of Machine M1, *since the batch cannot be split*, it would still take the (same) 10 minutes to complete the batch. **Therefore**, for the Sgetti simulations that were run to generate the results reported in this section, the original values in the *Batch Size* column in Table 21.4 have (all) been increased by multiplying each of them by 10.

Part 2 of 2: Lead Time Reduction

The fundamental premise of Job Shop Lean (and Lean) is that a Cellular Layout is always going to perform better than a Process Layout. But is a Cellular Layout like the one shown in Figure 21.29(a) always better than a Process Layout like the one shown in Figure 21.25(a)? *Not necessarily!* Recall that the Cellular Layout with two cells was obtained by (i) separating identical machines that were co-located in the Work Centers #1, #7, and #10 and (ii) distributing them into two stand-alone cells. Both the academic research literature and empirical evidence from industry suggest that there are pros **and** cons from breaking any work center in a Process Layout and distributing the machines in that work center into two or more cells in a Cellular Layout. The advantages of dissolving a work center and distributing its machines into two or more cells are (i) reduced material handling costs, (ii) reduced flow times for parts produced in any cell, (iii) better communication between all members of any cell's team regarding quality issues, (iv) improved cooperation between members of each cell's team, etc. However, a **major** disadvantage of dissolving a work center and distributing its machines into two or more cells is the reduction in machine availability and loading flexibility. For example, in the Process layout shown in Figure 21.25(a), any part arriving to Work Center #7 can be processed on any one of four identical machines. Plus, there could be four different part #s being processed in parallel in that work center. Unfortunately, after changing to a Cellular Layout, since each cell has only 2 machines from the original Work Center #7, the rate at which either cell processes parts at that work center will reduce. Here is where the rough-cut simulation capabilities of Sgetti can help to gain greater insights on whether a complete transformation from a Process Layout to a Cellular Layout is justifiable on a case-by-case basis. Based on the *Lead Time Simulation* done by Sgetti, Figure 21.30 suggests that the change to the Cellular Layout in Figure 21.29(a) from the original Process Layout in Figure 21.25(a) increased the average lead time (ALT) to complete the product mix in Table 21.4.[5]

Based on the results of Figure 21.30, it does not seem advisable to implement a pure Cellular Layout with two stand-alone independent cells (Cells #1 and #2) that each produces PFs #1 and #2. Instead, it was decided to implement a Hybrid Cellular Layout like the one in Figure 21.20. In Figure 21.31, compared with the Cellular Layout in Figure 21.29(a), the following modifications were made: (i) Work Centers #1 and #1(1) have been merged into a single work center, (ii) Work Centers #7 and #7(1) have been merged into a single work center, and (iii) an additional Machine #10 has been added to Cell #2 as shown by the *Qty: 2* above the bubble for Work Center #19(1).[6] Based on the *Lead Time Simulation* done by Sgetti, Figure 21.31 suggests that, unlike the Cellular Layout in Figure 21.29(a), a change from the original

---

[5] Note that the ALT is simply the average of the (individual) lead times for the nineteen part #s in the product mix obtained from the simulation.

[6] This can be confirmed in Table 21.6, which shows that more than one machine from Work Center #10 is needed in that cell.

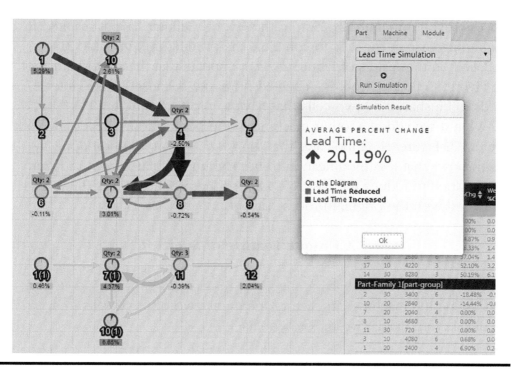

Figure 21.30 Performance of the Cellular Layout in Figure 21.29(a).

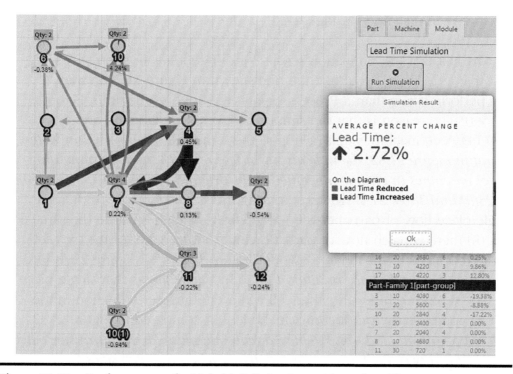

Figure 21.31 Performance of a Hybrid Cellular Layout based on Figure 21.20.

Process Layout in Figure 21.25(a) to the Hybrid Cellular Layout resulted in a smaller increase in the ALT to complete the product mix in Table 21.4.

Based on the results of Figure 21.31, it appears that the performance of the Hybrid Cellular Layout is impacted primarily because Work Center #7 needs to be shared by two cells that have to produce different PFs #1 and #2. What if we added another machine to the pool of four already in Work Center #7? Figure 21.32 indicates that the *Lead Time Simulation* done by Sgetti shows that this modification to the Hybrid Cellular Layout in Figure 21.31 helped to reduce the ALT to complete the product mix in Table 21.4 compared with the original Process Layout in Figure 21.25(a).

A Unique Feature of Sgetti

It is well known that dissolving the work centers in a Process Layout and distributing the machines in each of them into two or more cells in a Cellular Layout yields two major benefits:

1. Short delays when a part (or batch of parts) is transferred from one machine to some other machine inside a cell.
2. Single-piece flow (or at least transfer batch flow instead of batch flow) between machines inside a cell.

So why is it that the simulation results for different layout alternatives suggest that a Cellular Layout like the one shown in Figure 21.29(a) **may not** perform better than a Process Layout like the one shown in Figure 21.25(a)? The reason is that the simulations were not allowing one-piece flow between machines that belong to the same cell! *Therefore, unlike the layout in Figure 21.32, the new layout in Figure 21.33 used the same number of machines in each work center as the original Process Layout in Figure 21.25(a) and Table 21.5.* However, during the simulation run, (i) there is single-piece flow of parts between any pair of machines inside the same cell and (ii) there is batch flow of parts flowing from/to either of the two cells to the machines in the (shared) Work Centers #1 and #7. Figure 21.33 indicates that the *Lead Time Simulation* done by Sgetti shows that single-piece flow between machines in either cell achieved a greater reduction in the ALT to complete the product mix in Table 21.4 compared to Figure 21.32. *The reductions in lead times achieved with one-piece (or even transfer batch) flow inside any cell will become even greater when (i) batch sizes for the parts being produced are large or (ii) cycle times for the parts being produced are*

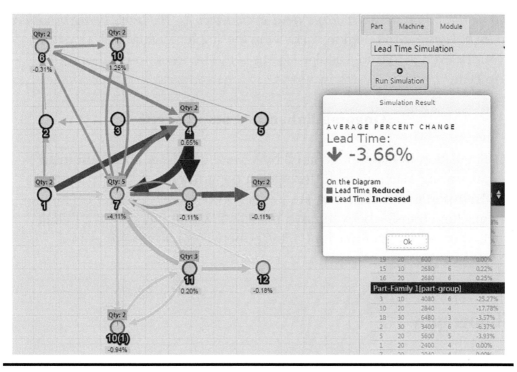

Figure 21.32   Impact on lead times when a fifth machine is added to Work Center #7.

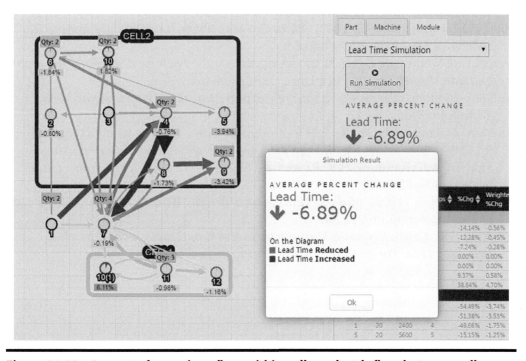

Figure 21.33   Impact of one-piece flow within cells vs. batch flow between cells.

*high or (iii) batch sizes are large **and** cycle times for the parts being produced are high.* Figure 21.33 demonstrates why the implementation of a Cellular Layout or even a Hybrid Cellular Layout is the bedrock foundation of Job Shop Lean.

Ongoing Enhancements in Sgetti

1. Simulation of machines shared by several cells, e.g., the Coordinate Measuring Machine in an Inspection department
2. Transportation delays that are a function of travel distance, e.g., inter-machine transfer between two machines within any cell in a Cellular Layout versus inter-machine transfer between two machines in a Process Layout

Bibliography

Arvindh, B. & Irani, S.A. (1994). Cell formation: The need for integrated solution of the sub-problems. *International Journal of Production Research*, 32(5), 1197–1218.

Burbidge, J.L. (1989). *Production Flow Analysis for Planning Group Technology*. Oxford, UK: Oxford University Press.

Hales, H.L. & Anderson, B. (2002). *Planning Manufacturing Cells*. Dearborn, MI: Society of Manufacturing Engineers.

Hyer, N.L. & Wemmerlov, U. (2002). *Reorganizing the Factory: Competing through Cellular Manufacturing*. Portland, OR: Productivity Press.

Irani, S.A. (Editor). (1999). *Handbook of Cellular Manufacturing Systems*. New York: John Wiley.

Irani, S.A. & Ramakrishnan, R. (1995). Production flow analysis using STORM. pp. 299–349 in *Planning, Design and Analysis of Cellular Manufacturing Systems*, A.K. Kamrani, H.R. Parsaei & D.H. Liles (Editors) York, Amsterdam, Netherlands: Elsevier.

Lee, R.N. (Editor). (1992). *Making Manufacturing Cells Work*. Dearborn, MI: Society of Manufacturing Engineers.

Suri, R. (1998). *Quick Response Manufacturing: A Company-wide Approach to Reducing Lead Times*. Portland, OR: Productivity Press.

Chapter 22

Teaming Industrial Engineers with Employees to Improve a Shipping Department

Acknowledgment

This chapter is based on the work that I did when I was the Director of Industrial Engineering (IE) Research at Hoerbiger Corporation of America. This was my first industry job and a golden opportunity given to me by Hannes Hunschofsky, who was then the President of Hoerbiger Corporation of America. He invited (and challenged!) me to pilot the implementation of Job Shop Lean in their Houston, TX, facility. Had it not been for this job, I would never be where I am today – in industry doing hands-on projects to put my research into practice. Thank you, Hannes!

Right-Sizing the Expertise of Problem-Solving Teams

The organizational hierarchy of any company has executives in the C-Suite, Vice Presidents, managers, engineers, supervisors, employees, etc. Yet, when it comes to Continuous Improvement (CI), the media literature on Lean suggests that CI is primarily something that only shop floor and office employees do by conducting a large number of short events (kaizens). Typically, a kaizen will involve the supervisor and employees who work in the department (or line or work cell) where the kaizen is done. Does this mean that the engineers and managers in the company are not contributing their share of effort to improve the bottom line of their company? Popular wisdom seems to dictate that all CI work should be thought about and implemented only by the employees themselves. Otherwise, the improvement(s) may not be accepted and the CI idea(s) will be implemented in a half-hearted fashion at best. But shop floor and office employees may not be aware of the problems that are technically demanding, and necessitate the use of Information Technology (IT), data mining, and other engineering expertise. In that case, should we avoid solving those "sticky" problems of production planning and operations scheduling that have plagued manufacturers for decades yet have not been solved effectively since time immemorial? Should we not expand our choice of who we put on a problem-solving team so that maturity and work experience **combined with** computer skills and analytical ability **together** help to solve a complex problem? In this chapter I will argue that, even if a problem is hard or complex, it is best solved by assembling a team composed of employees whose skills and experience are best suited to the work that must be done.

"Team Shipping"

All of the CI projects in the Shipping department that are reported in this chapter were done by teams drawn from the following pool of willing and capable employees:

- Charlotte P. (Supervisor, Shipping)
- Juan N., Shafel C., Robert L., Darrion W. (Employees, Shipping)
- Armando G. (Co-Team Leader, Power Rings Cell)
- Francisco S. (Leader, Maintenance)
- Andrew R. (Supervisor, Warehouse and Inventory)
- Anthony H. (Manager, Materials)
- John S. (Manager, Facilities and Maintenance)
- Shalini G. (In-house IE)

Industrial Engineering (IE) Students Who Helped "Team Shipping"

- *Thomas L.:* An undergraduate intern from Austria who was studying for his BSc in Industrial Management in the Department of Industrial Management at the FH-Joanneum University of Applied Sciences.

- *Pranav J.:* A graduate student from the Department of Integrated Systems Engineering at The Ohio State University who did a non-thesis project at Hoerbiger Corporation of America, Texas, for his Master of Science in IE.
- *Clement P.:* A graduate student from the Department of Industrial and Systems Engineering at Texas A&M University who did an Independent Study Project at HCA-TX for his Master of Science in IE.

A Project That Involved the Entire Team

Soon after I started my job at HCA-TX, on the urging of our COO, I met with Charlotte P. to explore the possibility of introducing Lean in her department, Shipping. She enthusiastically welcomed the opportunity to have the intern (Thomas L.) and I work with her team to implement 5S in the department. This department was the closest to the customer and its main objective was to maximize $ of shipped orders every month. When asked what contributed to various inefficiencies that impacted work most in the department, Charlotte P. unhesitatingly said, "We do not have space. It is too crowded in here! I see my guys running from one end to the other between the tables, workstations, computers, and printers. It is chaotic!" Figures 22.1a and b show the initial condition of various areas in the shipping. Would you be surprised that the first video I showed them during our first training session on Lean was about 5S?

We wanted to show the employees that the lack of space, workstations that were cramped, and the time they wasted[1] walking about the department throughout the day were problems that could be solved. A workstation could "be cramped" only because it held items that should not be in that location in the first place! First, Thomas L. and I generated a department layout to visualize how much of the current floor space in the Shipping department was "dead" and therefore could easily be reclaimed. Next, we took the team for a walk through the department to point out examples of areas that were VA (value-added), NNVA (necessary-but-not-value-added), and NVA (wasted). They realized that it was the NVA areas occupied by junk ("dead assets") that, if cleaned up, would free up the much-needed floor space! So that is how we began implementing Lean in the Shipping department – a

---

[1] In one of the training sessions on Lean, I had shown them the *Toast Kaizen* video (*Source*: www. GBMP.org). The video does a great job of explaining the Seven Types of Waste.

(a)

(b)

Figure 22.1 (a) Current state of the dock door side of the Shipping department.
(b) Current state of other areas of the Shipping department.

Figure 22.2   Items removed after a "First S of the 5S" (Sorting) event.

simple housekeeping project that lasted about 2 hours. We handed everybody a few red stickers and asked them to go around the department and affix their stickers to items that they were confident nobody had any use for. Figure 22.2 shows the items that were eliminated from the Shipping department after this project was complete. This pile of junk (and the area that was freed up after it was removed) convinced everyone on the team that there was more to be done for their own benefit.

A One-Employee Project

After the "First S of the 5S" (Sorting) event was complete, the intern and I again did a walk-through with Team Shipping to point out the remaining instances of wasted floor space in the current layout. One of the areas we showed them had three shelves carrying dead inventory, unused bins, and incomplete orders that had not been shipped (Figure 22.3a). In addition, there was a rack outside the Shipping department (Figure 22.3b) that was also carrying the dead inventory of corrugated materials used to make shipping cartons.

After watching the video during the week, Juan N. came in on a Saturday to do a solo project. First, he emptied the outside rack by (i) moving some of the dead inventory to the topmost shelf and (ii) placing some of the dead inventory on pallets that he relocated to the Barn using a forklift. He did

(a)

(b)

Figure 22.3 (a) Shelves inside the Shipping department (BEFORE). (b) Rack outside the Shipping department (BEFORE).

the same with the dead inventory on the pallet on the floor next to the rack. Next, he categorized all the incomplete orders waiting to be shipped that were on the inside shelves, i.e., GE (General Electric), Rings, Packings, QRC (Quick Response Cell), etc. The orders corresponding to each category of shipments were placed on a particular shelf on the outside rack. The QRC parts, which were shipped in the small white boxes, were moved to a separate multi-shelf wheeled cart placed next to the rack (See Figure 22.4b). Next, he printed paper labels for each category and taped them to the

(a)

(b)

Figure 22.4   (a) Shelves inside the Shipping department (AFTER). (b) Rack outside the Shipping department (AFTER).

appropriate shelf on the outside rack. Later, on the advising of Armando G., who had done 5S in the Power Rings Cell, he replaced these paper labels with magnetic labels that Armando had made using the machine and materials available in-house.[2] Figures 22.4a and b show the inside shelves and outside rack, respectively, after Juan N. completed his solo project. He did all this on his own initiative!

---

[2] It turned out that for quite some time we had been using a vendor for the same label-making services!

But Juan N. was not done at this point! Subsequently, he eliminated a large table inside the department by finding a "new home" for it elsewhere in the shop where it was put to good use. Finally, along the opposite wall, where there were many shelves carrying bins that stored a large variety of Packing Rings, he did another "First S of the 5S" (Sorting) to consolidate inventory of the same part numbers that were being stored in two or more bins. This emptied an entire rack and the bins it carried. Thomas L., who was also conducting time studies in the Power Rings Cell, advised him to send this rack and its bins to the Power Rings Cell. There Armando G. used them for machine-side storage of scrapped metallic rings.[3]

A Project That Involved the IE Graduate Students

Our Shipping department was essentially a job shop because (i) each of the five cells in our Machine Shop was a high-mix low-volume job shop and (ii) both molding cells – Cold Compression Molding and Hot Compression Molding – were high-mix low-volume flow shops. Also, we shipped different products to different customers in different countries. This resulted in a variety of workflow routings in the Shipping department. In addition, the orders had different packaging requirements due to carton size, container type (corrugated or wooden crate), labeling specific to the customer, country of destination, etc.

Given her experience and knowledge of the diverse workflows in her department, Charlotte P. listed the following products whose workflows dominated the material, person, and information flows in the Shipping department:

1. Packing Rings
2. Piston & Rider Rings
3. QRC Packing Rings
4. Bushings and Cases
5. GE Kits

Using the routings for the workflows provided by Charlotte P., Thomas L. developed the PFAST Input File, an Excel spreadsheet that would be

---

[3] These rings, when placed on the magnetic table of either of the Blanchard Grinders in the cell, helped to "enclose" non-metallic rings that would otherwise fly off the machine table during the grinding cycle.

submitted to the PFAST (Production Flow Analysis and Simplification Toolkit) software. He emailed the file to Pranav J. at The Ohio State University who processed the data and emailed the PFAST Analysis Report back to us. We used these outputs to generate five new alternative layouts for the Shipping department. These layouts were designed using different criteria and priorities specified by Team Shipping, such as a separate cell for each customer, a central location for all computers and printers, etc. Figure 22.5a shows the current layout. Figure 22.5b shows Layout #3 that was selected by Team Shipping as the new layout for their department.

At this stage, the graduate student from Texas A&M, Clement P., started assisting Team Shipping on this project. For his Independent Study Project during the Spring 2013 semester, he decided to develop a detailed blueprint for the final layout, including a budget and implementation timeline. He visited HCA-TX every Friday to observe and document the daily work routines of the employees. Since he was developing a detailed layout for the department, he spent considerable time developing the essential footprint[4] for each workstation. That was because every workstation, table, aisle, rack, container, etc. in the layout appeared to be occupying more floor space than it should have! For example, on the packaging table, the employee would carefully place all the parts that were going to be shrink-wrapped on a skin board (cardboard backing) provided by GE. Next, he would carefully pick up the skin board, slowly turn around to prevent parts falling off the skin board, and place the board on the table of the shrink-wrap machine. During one of our team meetings, we challenged the team to eliminate the need for the station-to-station transfer. On the same table on which the parts were first put on the skin board, the team cleared up surface space for the shrink-wrap machine to be put on it. As always, all that Clement P., Thomas L. and I were doing was encouraging the employee(s) who shrink-wrapped the parts to challenge themselves, "So why am I doing that? Is there a better way that I could do that?"

A Project That Teamed the In-House IE with the IE Intern

Earlier, Figures 22.1a and b showed how inventory was stored and organized inside and outside the Shipping department before Team Shipping began their Lean implementation projects. While the Sort phase of a full-fledged

---

[4] This is the area of the rectangle (or square) that it occupied on the floor.

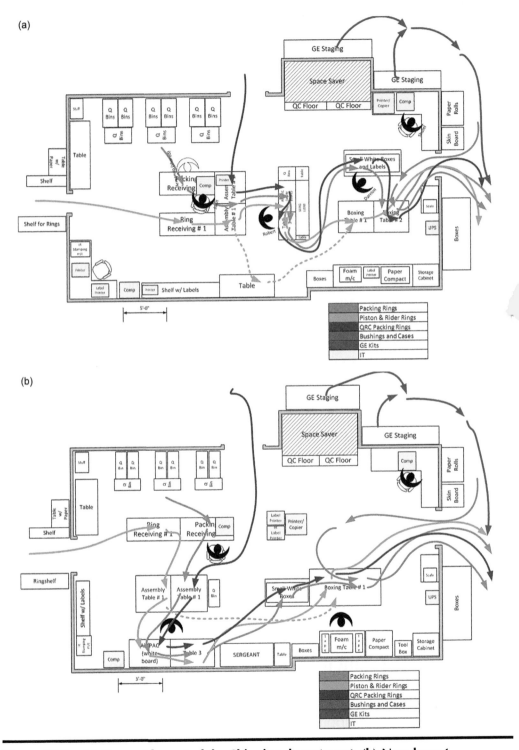

Figure 22.5   (a) Current layout of the Shipping department. (b) New layout implemented for the Shipping department.

5S program usually yields quick visible results, the real benefits to be gained from doing 5S were (i) reduction of inventory costs, (ii) reduction of time that employees waste doing non-value-added work, and (iii) elimination of un-ergonomic material handling tasks and injury risks. So, it was the pursuit of these benefits that made us address the issues indicated in Figure 22.6. Since inventory is visual and measurable, we implemented a visual two-bin inventory control system for the packaging materials, especially the corrugated materials used to make the shipping cartons that were used to ship our products all over the world, often to sister plants. From a financial perspective, this helped to reduce and control the purchasing costs for the different types and sizes of materials shown in Figure 22.6.

In Figure 22.6, it is easy to see that there is excessive inventory of several Stock Keeping Units (SKUs) of corrugated inventory. Thomas L., with the help of Charlotte P., collected data on the purchases that were made between June 20, 2012, and November 7, 2012 of the different SKUs (See Figure 22.7a). This time series plot of the data did not yield any insights. Instead, when we plotted the same data using the classical Pareto Rule of 80-20 (see Figure 22.7b), some valuable insights were gained. In addition, Charlotte P. pointed out that the high inventory of the GE skin boards was unavoidable because (i) we used that item to package shipments to sister divisions and (ii) the supplier would ship only full pallets instead

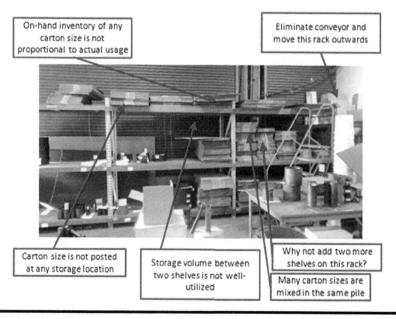

Figure 22.6 Current storage of inventory for different Shipping cartons.

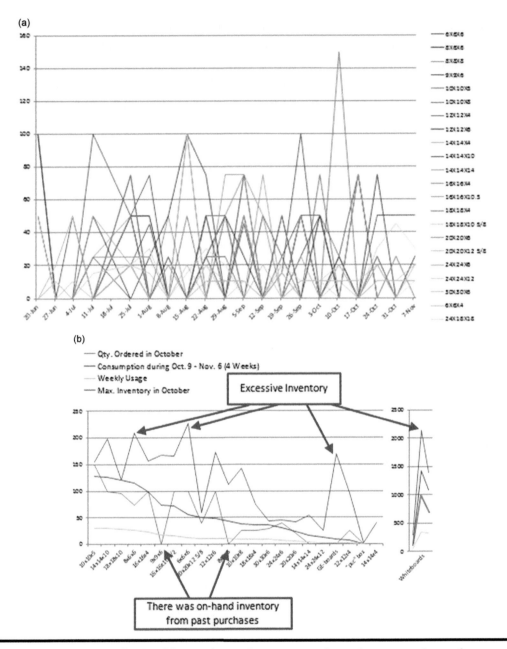

Figure 22.7 **(a) Purchasing history for various carton sizes. (b) Comparison of usage vs. purchased quantities for various carton sizes.**

of partials. For these reasons, what appeared to be excessive inventory was unavoidable. But it was these discussions that helped Anthony H. and Charlotte P. to later decide on weekly replenishments with the purchase quantity of every SKU set equal to (Demand Forecast for that

Week + Buffer Stock). Our in-house IE, Shalini G., developed the Demand Forecasting model that used the past few weeks' consumption for any SKU to forecast the requirement for next week. Of course, this forecast was adjusted by Charlotte P. who had the best knowledge of the shipment schedule for next week. Charlotte P. would provide the weekly usage and receipts data for each SKU to Shalini G. who would enter the data into her forecasting model.

The data that Thomas L. collected also helped to sort the SKUs by volume into Runners (high weekly usage) and Strangers (low weekly usage). This, in turn, helped us to implement a one-bin kanban system for any SKU that was a slow mover.[5] All on-hand inventory for that SKU was stored in the outside rack, whereas a two-bin kanban system was used for the Runners. All in-house inventory for each of these SKUs was split between a mobile carton stand (Inventory = 2 days usage) kept right next to the table on which the cartons were filled and the outside rack (Inventory = 3 days usage). Charlotte P. followed up with a supplier (www.stackbin.com/categories/carton-racks/) to inquire about a mobile carton stand that had been brought to our attention by Anthony H.

The Demand Forecasting model developed by Shalini G. helped to size the inventory in each bin of a two-bin kanban system to manage the corrugated inventory. Instead of buying a carton rack, Figures 22.8a and b show the carton rack that was fabricated and installed by three employees – Francisco S., Armando G., and Juan N. – on a Saturday! The design of the rack (i) exploited the natural shape and size of how these items were delivered to us and rested even when they were cut loose, (ii) compacted all of the inventory shown in Figure 22.6 into a smaller volume, and (iii) made it easy for an employee to simply eyeball each slot to know how much on-hand inventory we had for that particular SKU in case it was necessary to order more.

Do you see the wooden crates on the top shelf in Figure 22.8a? They used to be stored in the Barn! Shafel C. used to drive the forklift back and forth between the Barn and the Shipping department to get these crates. Now, once the corrugated inventory was removed from the top shelf, he used it to store the crates at point-of-use near where kits of parts were packed in them for shipment.

---

[5] The entire inventory for that SKU was stored in the outside rack.

Figure 22.8 (a) Bicycle rack for compact storage of corrugated inventory. (b) Detailed view of the bicycle rack.

A Project That Involved a Key Supplier's Rep

I would often see Inmer G. onsite replenishing inventories of shop and office supplies. One day I observed him using his iPhone to swipe bar codes for office and lunch room supplies that were stored in the cabinets in our lunch room. That was my first introduction to a VMI (Vendor Managed Inventory) system that started with a bar code swipe and ended as an order for that item being placed in their ERP (Enterprise Resource Planning) system. Ivan and I discovered that we had a mutual interest in Lean. So I explained to him the two-bin Kanban system that we had implemented in the Shipping department to control the on-hand inventory of corrugated materials for building shipping cartons. So he walked me out on the shop floor to explain one of his ongoing projects – an e-kanban system to manage supplies in the First Aid cabinets at multiple locations on the shop floor. Figure 22.9a shows the First Aid cabinet before he started his project. Figure 22.9b shows the new automated replenishment system that he implemented. The numbers on the labels stuck on each red bin reference the bar code for those items on a laminated sheet that was stuck inside the glass door of every cabinet. Immediately after that conversation with Ivan, I met with Anthony H. to explain how Inmer's system could reduce the manual work involved in maintaining the two-bin Kanban system in the Shipping department. Anthony liked the idea and authorized a pilot system to automate the weekly replenishment of three of the SKUs stored in the carton rack.[6]

Challenging Projects Undertaken by the Industrial Engineering Students

The downside with employee-led Lean implementation is that 5S helps to quickly "pluck many of the low-hanging fruits". This is all well and good. What next? Most Lean tools are simple manual IE methods. These tools are incapable of solving complex problems that necessitate data analysis and decision-support analytics. For example, had it not been for the IE undergraduate intern and IE graduate students, we could not have undertaken the following improvement projects:

■ *Reducing the number of corrugated SKUs that we purchased:* We decided to reduce the number of different carton sizes that we used. Because if we reduced the number of unique sizes that we had in stock, then we could increase the purchase quantities for the remaining sizes. Also, employees packing orders would not have to ask "Do I use this box size or do I use that box size?" For example, the carton sizes **8** × 6 × 6 and **6** × 6 × 6 differ by a cubic volume of only (**2** × 6 × 6 = 72)

---

[6] The long-term plan was to debug this system and make it fully operational for those three SKUs. Then, we would expand this data-driven computerized inventory control system to other SKUs, such as QRC Packing Boxes, GE Skin Boards, Wooden Cartons, Packing Rings, Powders (for the Molding departments), and Bar Stock (for the cells in the Machine Shop).

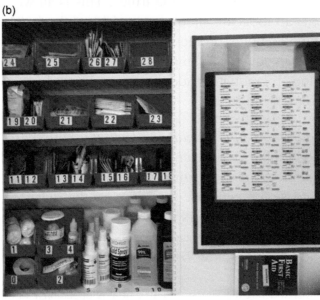

Figure 22.9   (a) Previous condition of First Aid cabinet. (b) Current state of First Aid cabinet.

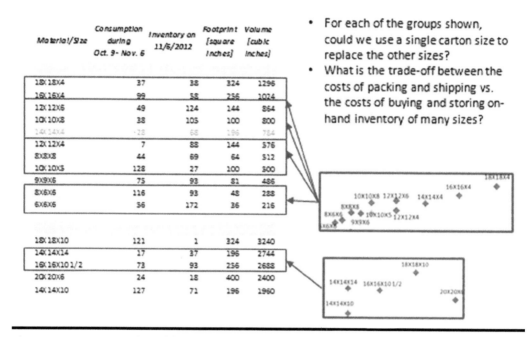

Material/Size	Consumption during Oct. 9– Nov. 6	Inventory on 11/6/2012	Footprint [square Inches]	Volume [cubic Inches]
18X18X4	37	38	324	1296
18X18X4	99	58	256	1024
12X12X6	49	124	144	864
10X10X8	38	105	100	800
14X14X4	-28	68	196	784
12X12X4	7	88	144	576
8X8X8	44	69	64	512
10X10X5	128	27	100	500
9X9X6	75	93	81	486
8X6X6	116	93	48	288
6X6X6	56	172	36	216
18X18X10	121	1	324	3240
14X14X14	17	37	196	2744
16X16X10 1/2	73	93	256	2688
20X20X6	24	18	400	2400
14X14X10	127	71	196	1960

- For each of the groups shown, could we use a single carton size to replace the other sizes?
- What is the trade-off between the costs of packing and shipping vs. the costs of buying and storing on-hand inventory of many sizes?

Figure 22.10 Grouping Shipping cartons with similar packing volume.

cubic inches. We studied the data shown in Figure 22.10 for the usage of these two sizes during the period October 9–November 6. Say we decided to use only the 8 × 6 × 6 size. Since we shipped 56 boxes built from the 6 × 6 × 6 size, now we would ship a total empty volume of (**2** × 6 × 6 × **56**) cubic inches filled with crumpled paper or foam padding. So the cost of using the extra paper and foam padding would be traded off against the cost of no longer buying the 6 × 6 × 6 size. Unfortunately, due to factors beyond our control, we could not pursue this project after the initial meeting with the team. Still there was a happy ending! Later, Charlotte P. informed us that she had eliminated the four SKUs.

■ *Implementing best practices of warehouse management:* This project was done by HCA-TX employee, Andrew R., with remote assistance (including a visit to Houston) from the OSU (Ohio State University) graduate student, Pranav J. Figure 22.11 shows how the on-hand inventory of the many different Packing Rings that we sold to our customers was distributed in bins kept in floor-mounted racks (Q-bins) and the Space Saver (an older generation Vertical Lift Module). We felt that the packing density of both storage areas could be improved, especially in the case of 38 kits of parts where each kit consisted of a set of different rings. In the case of these kits, it was decided that kits with heavy

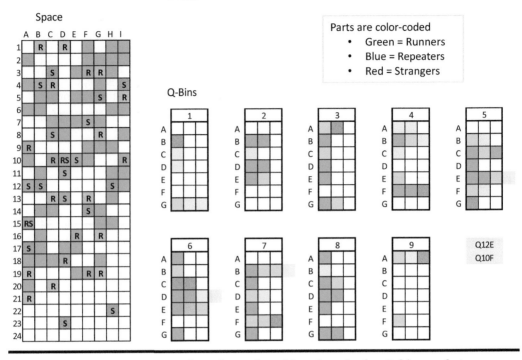

Figure 22.11 Current storage locations of packing rings in the Q-bins and storage saver.

metallic rings would be stored in the Q-bins, whereas the kits with the lighter nonmetallic rings would be stored in the Space Saver. In either storage area, based on past demand, it was decided to group the high-volume kits (Runners) and locate them closest to the shrink-wrap machine, then fill the next band of locations with medium-volume kits (Repeaters), and place the low-volume kits (Strangers) furthest away. The new location scheme helped to (i) reduce the average pick time to collect the different rings included in an order, and (ii) ensure that all inventory for a particular type of ring would be found in a single bin, or more bins adjacent to each other.

A Tribute to Team Shipping

The Shipping department was a high-pressure work environment. Its employees had just one goal every day – receive the "stuff" coming in from the door that faced the shop floor and get it out the other door where a truck was waiting in one day. They knew that would make the customers (and management) of HCA-TX happy! If operational problems arose, they solved them using common sense, firefighting, thumb rules, resignation, brute force, overtime, team work, negotiations, patience, determination, and prayers too. I taught them the Seven Types of Waste and some simple Lean tools that they used to effect several improvements in their department. Together, the three IE students, our in-house IE (Shalini G.) and I helped them to eliminate daily frustrations and delays that hampered their work.

Lessons Learned

Set up the first project's team for success: First, hold a brainstorming session with everyone at the outset. Have the entire team lay out a priority sequence in which the first few projects will be done. Then, decide on the first project that will be done *after which* you plan the composition of the team to suit the scope and complexity of the problem. When forming the team, do not hesitate to insist that some employees *must* work on the team. Volunteers are not necessarily best equipped to solve the problem that the project will tackle! Select Key Performance Indicators (KPIs) for the project but choose one KPI that will clearly drive all effort.[7] Finally, let the team know that they have your full support. Maybe you could enlist the help of your in-house IE and/or MfgE to support the team?

Develop a strong partnership with an IE department: There is considerable benefit for any business that establishes a partnership with one or more IE departments to involve IE students and faculty in their Lean implementation. The students of the IE department are experts in the use of IE software tools for statistical analysis, system simulation, etc. And you can be sure that they are keen to get hands-on experience in implementing Lean in applying the IE tools that they have learned in the real world. At HCA-TX, I was very fortunate that the upper management allowed me to engage students from The Ohio State University, Texas A&M University, University of Texas at Arlington, and the University of Houston.

Earn the support of the employees[8]: Training of employees is key to the success of any Lean implementation. However, it is essential that (i) the

---

[7] Avoid burdening the team with a KPI for Safety and one for Quality and one for On-Time Delivery and one for Cost Reduction. I am sure you get my drift! ☺

[8] Even the training seminars must have hands-on content that engages the employees constantly. And if a training session extends beyond a couple of hours, say a 1-day workshop, then use a half-and-half format – use the morning for instruction and use the afternoon for an activity on the floor or applying what was taught in the morning using actual data.

employees be given training that relates to the work they do and (ii) that the trainer then works side-by-side with them to show how to put that training to work. Avoid having the employees sit through a PowerPoint presentation in a training room and then asking *them* to figure out how to put that training to work *on their own*! Instead, immediately after the training session, get together with them and apply what was taught to the project, regardless of success or failure on the first try. If employees see that the training resulted in tangible improvements in their workplace, then they will undertake future improvements on their own initiative. If someone from upper management can make the time to expressed appreciation to them for the results they achieve, that would be preferable.

Every small improvement that gets implemented is worthwhile: Yes, the Shipping department could have benefitted from every Lean and Six Sigma tool in the book! There was even a need for Total Productive Maintenance in that department. But, it was important to not overburden the employees with improvement projects when their primary responsibility was to pack and ship orders. So the training we gave them focused on personal productivity tools like Five Why's, Spaghetti Diagrams, 5S, etc. As for the more challenging projects, they were assigned to the IEs.

Communicate and appreciate! Communicate and appreciate! Communicate and appreciate! The weekly team meeting for about an hour in the afternoon on Thursday was a must. Else, I would just walk over to the Shipping department and chat with a couple of team members to get quick feedback if the work we were doing was producing results. Periodically, the efforts of Team Shipping would be mentioned in the all-hands production meetings every Friday morning.

Gauge the commitment and support of upper management for "big bang" changes: Recall that the Shipping department was assessed on just one KPI – Total $ shipped per month. Please refer to Figure 22.4b. Per this metric, all the incomplete orders stored on that rack should not have been there in the first place! Sure, the initial flurry of 5S projects helped to organize the WIP and highlight the extent of shortages that held up shipments. But, the "big bang" goal was to not have any shortages! So the intern and I had a meeting with a cross-functional team composed of Anthony H., Andrew R., Charlotte P., Shane B. (Customer Service), and Greg O. (Machine Shop Supervisor). The discussions helped us to identify the different reasons for shortages that forced orders to end up on that rack. Most of the time, the shortages were due to one or other shortcomings of the ERP system we had! But a request to corporate to allow us to investigate the ERP system's shortcomings got no response.

Chapter 23

Implementation of Job Shop Lean in a Forge Shop

In this chapter, we describe a project to introduce Job Shop Lean in a custom forge shop by implementing a Modular Layout that was designed using PFA (Production Flow Analysis). The strategy for designing a flexible layout for this forge shop was to (i) group as many machines required to produce a part family that could be relocated into Layout Modules,[1] (ii) locate these modules in close proximity to the monuments, and (iii) coordinate workflows between the layout modules using visual triggers, such as designated WIP (work-in-process) locations and roving forklift operators who had daily production schedules issued to them.

About Ulven Forging

Ulven Forging was founded in 1971. The company began with open die forging, then gradually added closed die hammer forging, press forging, and upset forging. Today it is one of the most versatile forge shops in the US. The forging operation is one of six companies in the Ulven Group. The other companies include a steel foundry, a CNC (Computer Numerical Control) machining facility, and three companies with proprietary product

---

[1] A Layout Module is a small group of machines that could be operated by a single associate, or at least a smaller number of associates than the number of machines. A module is an incomplete cell because all the machines required for the cell could not be moved and co-located into a cell.

lines for construction and related industries. The CNC division offers both lathe and mill CNC and manual machining services.

Ulven uses *open die forging* to produce larger-size products, as well as prototypes and short-run quantities. *Closed die hammers* are used to produce longer runs of forgings ranging in weight from ½ lb. to 100 lb. Ulven's *closed die forging* business first exceeded its open die volume in 1996. *Press forging* is used for medium- to high-volume runs and is set up with automatic bar feed systems and induction heating. *Upset forging* is used for both low- to high-volume runs. Parts are forged in a horizontal position where the workpiece is gripped between two grooved dies and deformed by a heading die that exerts force to the end of the stock. Examples of upset forgings include axles, rod ends, eye bolts, and shafts.

Being a military/government contractor, this custom forge shop had a critical need to be flexible and respond to significant product mix changes without any increase in lead times. A poorly designed facility layout and high variety of parts resulted in complex material flow control in the shop. This was the primary reason for high manufacturing lead times for delivery of mission-critical parts to defense customers. Some equipment in this forge shop, such as hammers, had significant foundations that made it economically infeasible to relocate them, which made them "monuments". However, the support equipment, such as induction heating and flash trimming, were somewhat more mobile, as were other support operations such as material storage, tool and die storage/repair, material cutting (shear and saw), shot blasting, and magnetic particle inspection. Their CNC machine shop was at a separate location.

Data Collection and Preliminary Machine-Part Matrix Analysis

The sample data provided by the company consisted of 530 products and 57 pieces of equipment. To do the PFA analyses, the P-Q-R-$ (P = Product, Q = Quantity, R = Routing, $ = Sales) information for each product and the attributes for each piece of equipment were collected, as shown in Tables 23.1 and 23.2, respectively. Next, the traditional Machine-Part Matrix Clustering (aka Product-Process Matrix Analysis) method was used to find the part families and their corresponding machine groups that are the basis for forming cells. The optimized 0–1

Table 23.1   P-Q-R-$ Information for Each Product

Product No.	6-Month Quantity	Sell Price	6-Month Total $	Product Routings															
				1	2	3	4	5	6	7	8	9	10	11	12	13	14	15	16
80-D70865-004				17	21	22	26	29	27	48									
80-A138–1000				17	3	7	12	4	58	55									
80-A138–1001				17	3	7	12	4	53	55									
80-U104–1009				17	3	7	12	4	53	55									
80-U104–1010				17	3	7	12	4	53	55									
80–2303611				17	16	11	10	29	4	55									
80-37B				17	3	7	12	4	55										
80-37C				17	3	7	12	29	28	4	55								
80-A117–1002				17	2	55													
80-A117–1003				17	2	55													
80-A117–1004				17	2	55													
80-A117–1005				17	2	55													
80-A139–1000				17	16	11	10	15	29	53	4	55							
80–13334X				17	39	40	21	22	53	29	4	55							
80-SC300–0417-00				1	16	53	55												
80-B131–1000				17	3	7	12	4	53	55									
80-B131–1005				17	3	7	12	4	53	55									
80-B00909				1	15	54	55												
80-B00910				1	15	54	55												
80-B137–1000				17	39	40	21	22	53	26	29	4	48						
80-B107–1004				17	21	22	48												
80-A37353				17	6	2	11	10	29	54	55								
80-C27416-1				17	6	2	11	10	29	54	55								
80-C27416-2				17	6	2	11	10	29	54	55								

(*Continued*)

Table 23.1 (*Continued*)   P-Q-R-$ Information for Each Product

Product No.	6-Month Quantity	Sell Price	6-Month Total $	Product Routings															
				1	2	3	4	5	6	7	8	9	10	11	12	13	14	15	16
80-C46806-1				17	6	2	11	10	29	54	55								
80-C55581				17	6	2	11	10	29	54	55								
80-C558-1				17	6	2	11	10	29	54	55								
80-D8097				17	6	2	11	10	29	54	55								
80-B113–1001				17	56	57	54												
80-B136–1000				17	3	7	12	4	53	55									
80–200130996N				17	3	7	12	53	55										
80–2016685993				17	39	40	21	24	55										
80–201685993N				17	39	40	21	24	55										
80–202990010N				17	16	11	10	55											
80–204760151N				17	3	7	12	53	55										
80-C153–1000				17	39	40	26	4	55										
80-C150–1000				17	39	40	29	28	53	55									
80-C150–1001				17	3	7	12	4	53	55									
80-C150–1002				17	3	7	12	4	53	55									
80-11SIL				17	21	22	53	26	29	28	48								
80-126600030000				17	39	40	29	53	55										
80-C106-1002				17	39	40	29	28	55										
80-C07E1002-3				17	16	11	10	15	29	28	4	55							
80-100FH				17	21	22	26	53	29	28	48								
80-125FH				17	21	22	26	53	29	28	48								
80-175FH				17	42	41	26	53	29	28	48								
80-C115-1000				17	21	22	26	53	29	28	48								
80-MC860				17	6	2	7	12	42	33	41	57	54	55					
80-MC860AG				17	6	2	7	12	42	33	41	57	54	55					
80-C116-1006				17	43	35	48												

(Continued)

Table 23.1 (*Continued*)   P-Q-R-$ Information for Each Product

Product No.	6-Month Quantity	Sell Price	6-Month Total $	Product Routings															
				1	2	3	4	5	6	7	8	9	10	11	12	13	14	15	16
80-C151-1000				17	3	7	12	4	53	55									
80-C151-1001				17	3	7	12	4	53	55									
80-D122-1000				17	39	40	53	57	54	55									
80-D122-1001				17	39	40	53	57	54	55									
80-C0122-P				17	32	31	53	29	28	27	48								
80-D118-ULC0122				17	39	40	21	22	53	29	28	27	48						
80-16-108				17	16	11	10	4	55										
80-E126-1000				17	39	40	29	53	27	48									
80-4003111				1	57	25	52	48	55										
80-4009121				1	57	25	52	48	55										
80-4009262				1	57	25	52	48	55										
80-4009263				1	57	25	52	48	55										
80-4009270				1	57	25	52	48	55										
80-4010346				1	57	25	52	48	55										
80-4010348				1	57	25	52	48	55										
80-4010349				1	57	25	52	48	55										
80-4010350				1	57	25	52	48	55										
80-4010351				1	57	25	52	48	55										
80-4010352				1	57	25	52	48	55										
80-4010809				17	39	40	26	57	55										
80-4010965				17	39	40	26	57	55										
80-4011714				1	26	57	52	48	55										
80-4011725				1	57	25	52	48	55										
80-4012169				1	26	57	52	48	55										
80-4012174				1	26	57	52	48	55										
80-4012179				1	26	57	52	48	55										

(Continued)

Table 23.1 (*Continued*)   P-Q-R-$ Information for Each Product

Product No.	6-Month Quantity	Sell Price	6-Month Total $	Product Routings															
				1	2	3	4	5	6	7	8	9	10	11	12	13	14	15	16
80-4012212				1	26	57	52	48	55										
80-4012213				1	26	57	52	48	55										
80-4030339				1	27	9	57	48											
80-4030341				1	27	9	57	48											
80-4035144				1	28	50	27	48	55										
80-4035149				1	28	50	27	48	55										
80-4039260				1	28	50	27	48	55										
80-4041707				1	57	25	52	48	55										
80-4049822				17	39	40	21	22	53	29	28	27	48						
80-4049823				17	39	40	21	22	53	29	28	27	48						
80-4056191				17	39	40	21	22	53	29	28	27	48						
80-4059989				1	26	57	52	48	55										
80-4067179				17	39	40	26	57	54	57	55								
80-4103404				17	42	41	26	53	29	28	27	48							
80-4104280				56	1	26	57	55											
80-4123817				17	16	11	10	26	57	55									
80-8001394				17	21	22	57	29	28	57	48								
80-8005665				17	21	22	26	29	28	27	48								
80-8005667				17	21	22	26	29	28	27	48								
80-8005669				17	21	22	26	29	28	27	48								
80-8005911				17	21	22	26	29	28	27	48								
80-E111-1007				17	21	22	26	29	28	27	48								
80-F121-1000				17	3	7	5	57	8	55									
80-F112-1000				17	39	40	26	53	29	28	48								
80-20NV500				17	3	7	5	57	8	55									

(Continued)

Table 23.1 (*Continued*)   P-Q-R-$ Information for Each Product

Product No.	6-Month Quantity	Sell Price	6-Month Total $	1	2	3	4	5	6	7	8	9	10	11	12	13	14	15	16
80-4030011870964				17	39	40	21	22	53	29	28	4	55						
80-150T084LT				17	6	2	7	12	8	42	41	57	55						
80-G121-1002				17	6	2	7	12	8	42	41	57	55						
80-NL150T060LT				17	6	2	7	12	8	42	41	57	55						
80-NL150T072LT				17	6	2	7	12	8	42	41	57	55						
80-NL150T084LT				17	6	2	7	12	8	42	41	57	55						
80-NL150T096LT				17	6	2	7	12	8	42	41	57	55						
80-NL150T120LT				17	6	2	7	12	8	42	41	57	55						
80-70-2				17	32	31	53	4	55										
80-G122-1000				17	39	40	29	53	4	55									
80-G104-1001				17	39	40	42	41	53	29	28	27	48						
80-G104-1002				17	39	40	42	41	53	29	28	27	48						
80-G104-1003				17	39	40	42	41	53	29	28	27	48						
80-3249869				17	56	1	17	29	26	54	57	48							
80-121009-00				17	39	40	21	22	55										
80-121188-002				17	39	40	21	22	55										
80-121189				17	39	40	21	22	55										
80-671391				17	16	11	10	26	4	55									
80-121018-00				17	39	40	21	22	55										
80-121052-00				17	16	11	10	53	4	55									
80-121148				1	50	26	27	55											
80-121387				17	39	40	21	22	55										
80-ULC0200				17	39	40	21	22	55										
80-35123				17	39	40	26	53	29	28	27	48							
80-36551				17	21	22	53	29	28	27	48								

(Continued)

Table 23.1 (*Continued*) P-Q-R-$ Information for Each Product

Product No.	6-Month Quantity	Sell Price	6-Month Total $	Product Routings															
				1	2	3	4	5	6	7	8	9	10	11	12	13	14	15	16
80-9033704				54	57	48	55												
80-H128-1000				17	3	7	12	57	53	55									
80-1896-9057C-1				17	39	40	8	4	55										
80-6547J				17	39	40	42	41	30	29	14	57	55						
80-8567615				17	14	13	57	55											
80-8567621				17	14	13	57	55											
80-8567636				17	53	13	57	55											
80-C125086G				17	53	13	57	55											
80-C137587G				17	53	13	57	55											
80-C175090G				17	53	13	57	55											
80-C2250936				17	14	13	57	55											
80-C225093G				17	14	13	57	55											
80-C250096G				17	14	13	57	55											
80-H119-25				17	39	40	53	42	41	30	53	57	55						
80-H119-1000				17	39	40	42	41	30	29	14	57	55						
80-H119-1083				17	39	40	53	42	41	30	53	57	55						
80-H119-1099				17	39	40	42	41	30	14	57	55							
80-H119-1143				17	39	40	42	41	30	14	57	55							
80-H119-1151				17	53	21	24	57	48										
80-H119-1152				17	14	13	57	55											
80-H119-2000				17	14	13	57	55											
80-H119-2001				17	53	14	13	57	55										
80-H119-2002				17	53	14	13	57	55										
80-H119-2005				17	53	14	13	57	55										

(Continued)

Table 23.1 (*Continued*)   P-Q-R-$ Information for Each Product

Product No.	6-Month Quantity	Sell Price	6-Month Total $	Product Routings															
				1	2	3	4	5	6	7	8	9	10	11	12	13	14	15	16
80-H119-2006				17	14	13	57	55											
80-H119-2007				17	14	13	57	55											
80-H119-2008				17	3	7	12	8	4	55									
80-H119-2009				17	3	7	12	8	4	55									
80-H119-2010				17	39	40	42	41	26	27	53	55							
80-H119-3.25X62				17	6	2	42	41	30	14	8	57	55						
80-H119-3.75				17	3	7	12	8	4	55									
80-H119-3.75X66				17	6	2	42	41	30	14	8	55							
80-T6430W				17	39	40	53	42	41	30	53	57	55						
80-T6547G				17	39	40	42	41	30	14	8	4	55						
80-26621				17	3	7	12	29	48										
80-26622				17	3	7	12	29	48										
80-D10-517RCH				17	3	7	12	29	48										
80-90001033				17	21	22	26	53	29	28	27	48							
80-B155				17	16	11	10	4	53	55									
80-J110-1013				17	16	11	27	55											
80-J110-1014				17	16	11	27	55											
80-J110-1015				17	16	11	27	55											
80-J110-1016				17	16	11	27	55											
80-PDR42-F03				17	16	11	10	29	27	55									
80-PDR48-F02				17	16	11	10	29	27	55									
80-PDR48-F03				17	16	11	10	29	27	55									
80-PDR50-F01				17	16	11	10	29	27	55									
80-TR310-F01				17	16	11	10	29	27	55									

(*Continued*)

Table 23.1 (*Continued*)   P-Q-R-$ Information for Each Product

Product No.	6-Month Quantity	Sell Price	6-Month Total $	Product Routings															
				1	2	3	4	5	6	7	8	9	10	11	12	13	14	15	16
80-TR310-F02				17	16	11	10	29	27	55									
80-TR310-F07				17	16	11	10	29	27	55									
80-B107-1000				17	21	22	26	53	29	28	51	48							
80-B107-1001				17	21	22	48												
80-B107-1002				17	21	22	26	53	29	28	51	48							
80-J116-1000				17	39	40	26	53	29	28	27	48							
80-66007				17	39	40	26	53	48										
80-J117-1000				17	39	40	42	41	53	14	26	29	4	55					
80-K110-1000				17	16	11	10	15	53	29	4	55							
80-K108-1003				17	39	40	31	26	53	55									
80-K109-1001				17	16	11	10	15	29	4	55								
80-C0120				17	21	22	26	53	29	28	27	48							
80-C0122				17	39	40	21	22	53	29	28	27	48						
80-19542				17	39	40	21	22	53	29	28	27	48						
80-62695				17	39	40	42	41	53	29	28	27	48						
80-63006				17	39	40	21	22	53	29	28	27	48						
80-63231				17	42	41	26	53	48										
80-6761342				17	39	40	21	22	53	57	55								
80-J62124				17	39	40	21	22	53	57	55								
80-L104-1015				17	39	40	21	22	53	29	28	27	48						
80-L104-1016				17	39	40	21	22	53	29	28	27	48						
80-L104-1028				17	39	40	42	41	53	29	28	27	48						
80-L104-1054				17	39	40	42	41	53	29	28	27	48						
80-L104-1055				17	39	40	42	41	53	29	28	27	48						
80-L104-63244				17	39	40	42	41	53	29	28	27	48						

(*Continued*)

Table 23.1 (*Continued*)   P-Q-R-$ Information for Each Product

Product No.	6-Month Quantity	Sell Price	6-Month Total $	Product Routings															
				1	2	3	4	5	6	7	8	9	10	11	12	13	14	15	16
80-RS25				17	16	11	10	15	53	57	55								
80-RS38				17	16	11	10	15	53	57	55								
80-ULD-0151				17	13	42	41	53	8	4	55								
80-L119-81426				17	6	2	42	41	8	55									
80-L108-1001				17	39	40	21	22	53	29	28	27	48						
80-L108-1003				17	39	40	21	22	53	29	28	27	48						
80-0101295A				17	5	57	4	55											
80-L116-1000				17	39	40	17	26	4	55									
80-L116-1004				17	5	57	4	55											
80-L111-1004				17	3	7	12	57	53	4	55								
80-L111-1008				17	6	2	7	12	42	41	33	57	55						
80-L111-1014				17	3	7	12	57	53	4	55								
80-L125-1000				17	3	7	12	57	4	8	53	55							
80-A140-1000				17	39	40	42	41	53	29	28	26	27	48					
80-501386-0100				17	39	40	42	41	53	29	28	26	27	48					
80-BU7A-516				17	39	40	16	11	10	29	4	55							
80-2776118				17	16	11	10	55											
80-35-B357				17	1	57	4	54	55										
80-M106-1000				17	39	40	42	41	26	29	28	27							
80-M112-1005				17	39	40	21	22	26	53	57	55							
80-M112-1006				17	39	40	21	22	26	53	29	28	27	48					
80-M134-1000				17	3	7	12	8	4	53	55								
80-N103-1008				17	39	40	42	41	53	26	29	28	4	55					
80-N119-1000				17	39	40	42	41	53	26	29	28	27	48					
80-6-064288-001				17	53	55													

(*Continued*)

Table 23.1 (*Continued*) P-Q-R-$ Information for Each Product

Product No.	6-Month Quantity	Sell Price	6-Month Total $	1	2	3	4	5	6	7	8	9	10	11	12	13	14	15	16
								Product Routings											
80-O100-1002				17	6	2	7	12	42	33	41	29	28	4	54	55			
80-O100-1005				17	39	40	26	29	28	55									
80-O100-1009				17	6	2	7	12	42	33	41	29	28	4	54	55			
80-O100-1011				17	6	2	7	12	42	33	41	29	28	4	54	55			
80-O100-1012				17	6	2	7	12	42	33	41	29	28	4	54	55			
80-O100-1015				17	6	2	7	12	42	33	41	29	28	4	54	55			
80-O100-1018				17	42	41	26	53	29	28	27	48							
80-O100-1019				17	39	40	17	4	53	29	28	55							
80-O100-1020				17	39	40	17	4	53	29	28	55							
80-O101-1000				17	6	2	7	12	42	33	41	29	28	4	54	55			
80-O101-1001				17	39	40	21	22	26	53	29	28	27	48					
80-O101-1002				17	39	40	21	22	26	53	29	28	27	48					
80-O101-1004				17	39	40	42	41	26	29	28	27	53	57	55				
80-27750-01				17	39	40	42	41	3	7	12	57	54	55					
80-37355-1072				17	6	2	7	12	8	42	41	57	55						
80-37355-1084				17	6	2	7	12	8	42	41	57	55						
80-O104-1008				17	42	41	26	53	29	28	48								
80-135692209D				17	39	40	26	29	28	48									
80-325-921-02C-15"				17	39	40	26	29	28	48									
80-717692209D				17	39	40	26	29	28	48									
80-C5010040				17	39	40	26	29	28	48									
80-LB0492207C				17	39	40	26	29	28	48									
80-P101-1000				17	39	40	26	29	28	48									
80-P101-1001				17	39	40	26	29	28	48									
80-746100010				17	21	22	26	53	21	22	26	29	28	48					

(*Continued*)

Table 23.1 (*Continued*)   P-Q-R-$ Information for Each Product

Product No.	6-Month Quantity	Sell Price	6-Month Total $	Product Routings															
				1	2	3	4	5	6	7	8	9	10	11	12	13	14	15	16
80-P128-1000				17	39	40	42	41	53	29	28	27	57	55					
80-U104-1011				17	3	7	12	8	57	4	53	57	55						
80-051-1				17	1	26	4	54	55										
80-071-50M				1	26	4	54	57	55										
80-071-54				1	4	54	55												
80-8051400053				17	56	1	26	48											
80-R100-1014				17	1	57	26	48											
80-R100-1016				17	1	57	26	48											
80-R100-1017				17	1	57	26	48											
80-R100-1018				17	56	1	26	54	57	26	55								
80-R100-1031				17	1	57	26	48											
80-R100-1032				17	1	57	26	48											
80-R100-1033				17	1	57	26	48											
80-R103-1014				17	1	57	26	48											
80-4707-01				17	3	7	12	57	54	57	55								
80-R-23004				17	1	15	57	54	55										
80-REL-15500				17	3	7	12	57	54	57	55								
80-R134-1000				17	39	40	42	41	29	28	27	53	57	55					
80-R132-480001				17	16	11	10	29	28	4	55								
80-9610320				1	19	20	53	29	28	27	57	48							
80-9610400				17	39	40	19	20	53	29	28	27	57	48					
80-9610680				17	39	40	21	22	53	29	28	27	57	48					
80-9610840				17	39	40	21	22	53	29	28	27	57	48					
80-961260				17	39	40	21	22	53	29	28	27	57	48					
80-9651680				17	53	27	57	48											

(Continued)

Table 23.1 (*Continued*)   P-Q-R-$ Information for Each Product

Product No.	6-Month Quantity	Sell Price	6-Month Total $	Product Routings															
				1	2	3	4	5	6	7	8	9	10	11	12	13	14	15	16
80-9652080				17	53	27	57	48											
80-S100-1003				17	39	40	21	22	53	29	28	27	57	48					
80-S141-1003				17	3	7	12	8	53	55									
80-S121-1002				17	39	40	21	22	26	53	29	28	27	48					
80-S121-1003				17	39	40	21	22	26	53	29	28	27	48					
80-12123				17	16	11	10	57	54	55									
80-8653				17	16	11	10	57	54	55									
80-99-327				17	16	11	10	57	54	55									
80-S136-1004				17	39	40	29	28	27	53	55								
80-010401-0				17	39	40	21	22	26	53	29	28	27	48					
80-101011				17	32	31	26	53	29	28	27	48							
80-101991				17	39	40	21	22	26	53	29	28	27	48					
80-102008				17	32	31	26	53	29	28	27	48							
80-102010				17	32	31	26	53	29	28	27	48							
80-102012				17	32	31	26	53	29	28	27	48							
80-103247				17	32	31	26	29	28	27	48								
80-103250				17	39	40	17	26	29	28	4	55							
80-103267				17	39	40	17	4	53	29	28	4	55						
80-103356				17	39	40	17	4	53	29	28	4	55						
80-108513				17	42	41	26	53	29	28	27	48							
80-109014				17	42	41	26	53	29	28	27	48							
80-110006				17	32	31	26	53	29	28	27	48							
80-110012				17	32	31	26	53	29	28	27	48							
80-157000B				1	26	29	28	27	48										
80-191820				17	16	11	10	26	29	28	27	48							

(Continued)

Table 23.1 (*Continued*)   P-Q-R-$ Information for Each Product

Product No.	6-Month Quantity	Sell Price	6-Month Total $	Product Routings															
				1	2	3	4	5	6	7	8	9	10	11	12	13	14	15	16
80-191832				17	3	7	12	26	29	28	27	48							
80-191850				17	32	31	29	26	27	48									
80-308070				17	16	11	10	29	28	27	48								
80-308513				17	3	7	12	29	28	27	48								
80-312069				17	42	41	26	53	29	28	27	48							
80-522500				17	16	11	10	26	29	28	27	48							
80-533140				17	3	7	12	29	28	27	48								
80-551500				17	16	11	10	26	29	28	27	48							
80-551611				17	42	41	26	53	29	28	27	48							
80-551616				17	42	41	26	53	29	28	27	48							
80-551652				17	42	41	26	53	29	28	27	48							
80-551703				17	42	41	26	29	28	27	48								
80-551706				17	42	41	26	29	28	27	48								
80-553607				17	42	41	26	53	29	28	27	48							
80-605908A				17	39	40	42	41	26	53	29	28	27	48					
80-605909A				17	39	40	42	41	26	53	29	28	27	48					
80-605910A				17	39	40	42	41	26	53	29	28	27	48					
80-605912A				17	39	40	42	41	26	53	29	28	27	48					
80-609020SP				17	42	41	26	53	29	28	27	48							
80-611007B				17	32	31	26	53	29	28	27	48							
80-611007P				17	32	31	26	53	29	28	27	48							
80-611008B				17	32	31	26	53	29	28	27	48							
80-611008P				17	32	31	26	53	29	28	27	48							
80-611009B				17	32	31	26	53	29	28	27	48							
80-611009P				17	32	31	26	53	29	28	27	48							

(Continued)

Table 23.1 (*Continued*) P-Q-R-$ Information for Each Product

Product No.	6-Month Quantity	Sell Price	6-Month Total $	Product Routings															
				1	2	3	4	5	6	7	8	9	10	11	12	13	14	15	16
80-611010B				17	39	40	26	53	29	28	27	48							
80-611010P				17	32	31	26	53	29	28	27	48							
80-611012B				17	39	40	26	53	29	28	27	48							
80-611012P				17	32	31	26	53	29	28	27	48							
80-611056B				17	39	40	26	53	29	28	27	48							
80-611056P				17	32	31	26	53	29	28	27	48							
80-611057B				17	39	40	26	53	29	28	27	48							
80-611058B				17	39	40	26	21	22	53	29	28	27	48					
80-611605				17	21	22	26	29	28	27	48								
80-611606				17	21	22	26	29	28	27	48								
80-611711				17	21	22	26	53	29	28	27	48							
80-612008A				17	41	42	26	29	28	27	48								
80-612328				17	41	42	26	53	41	42	29	28	48						
80-612337				17	41	42	26	53	41	42	29	28	48						
80-612418				17	21	22	26	53	21	22	29	28	48						
80-612804				17	16	11	10	51	48										
80-613106				1	50	26	57	55											
80-613107				1	50	26	57	55											
80-616318				17	21	22	26	53	21	22	29	28	48						
80-616321				17	21	22	26	53	21	22	29	28	42						
80-616505A				17	41	42	26	29	28	48									
80-632014B				17	39	40	26	41	42	53	29	28	27	48					
80-632014P				17	39	40	17	27	53	29	28	27	48						
80-632020B				17	6	2	7	12	42	33	29	28	53	48					
80-632020P				17	39	40	17	27	53	29	28	27	48						

(Continued)

Table 23.1 (*Continued*)   P-Q-R-$ Information for Each Product

Product No.	6-Month Quantity	Sell Price	6-Month Total $	Product Routings															
				1	2	3	4	5	6	7	8	9	10	11	12	13	14	15	16
80-632028B				17	6	2	7	12	42	33	29	28	53	48					
80-632028P				17	39	40	17	27	53	29	28	27	48						
80-632122B				17	6	2	7	12	42	33	29	28	53	48					
80-632122P				17	39	40	17	27	53	29	28	27	48						
80-784000				17	21	22	26	53	29	28	27	48							
80-784300				17	16	11	10	26	53	29	28	27	48						
80-793410				17	39	40	31	21	22	53	29	28	27	48					
80-793411				17	39	40	31	21	22	53	29	28	27	48					
80-793412				17	39	40	31	21	22	53	29	28	27	48					
80-793416				17	39	40	31	41	42	53	29	28	27	48					
80-793504				17	16	11	10	29	27	48									
80-793508				17	16	11	10	29	27	48									
80-793609				17	39	40	31	21	22	53	29	28	27	48					
80-793610				17	39	40	31	21	22	53	29	28	27	48					
80-793611				17	39	40	31	21	22	53	29	28	27	48					
80-797009				17	39	40	31	21	22	53	29	28	27	48					
80-797109				17	39	40	31	21	22	53	29	28	27	48					
80-810105				17	39	40	31	21	22	53	29	28	27	48					
80-810107				17	39	40	31	21	22	53	29	28	27	48					
80-810108				17	39	40	31	21	22	53	29	28	27	48					
80-810109				17	39	40	31	21	22	53	29	28	27	48					
80-810110				17	39	40	31	21	22	53	29	28	27	48					
80-810112				17	39	40	31	21	22	53	29	28	27	48					
80-810206				17	39	40	31	21	22	53	29	28	27	48					
80-810211				17	39	40	31	21	22	53	29	28	27	48					

(*Continued*)

Table 23.1 (*Continued*) P-Q-R-$ Information for Each Product

Product No.	6-Month Quantity	Sell Price	6-Month Total $	1	2	3	4	5	6	7	8	9	10	11	12	13	14	15	16
80-810212				17	39	40	31	21	22	53	29	28	27	48					
80-810306				17	39	40	31	21	22	53	29	28	27	48					
80-810512				17	39	40	31	21	22	53	29	28	27	48					
80-810806				17	39	40	31	21	22	53	29	28	27	48					
80-810807				17	39	40	31	21	22	53	29	28	27	48					
80-810808				17	39	40	31	21	22	53	29	28	27	48					
80-810809				17	39	40	31	21	22	53	29	28	27	48					
80-810810				17	39	40	31	21	22	53	29	28	27	48					
80-810812				17	39	40	31	21	22	53	29	28	27	48					
80-810814				17	39	40	31	21	22	53	29	28	27	48					
80-811206				17	39	40	31	21	22	53	29	28	27	48					
80-811208				17	39	40	31	21	22	53	29	28	27	48					
80-811210				17	39	40	31	21	22	53	29	28	27	48					
80-811211				17	39	40	31	21	22	53	29	28	27	48					
80-812611				17	42	41	26	29	28	27	48								
80-817406				17	39	40	31	21	22	53	29	28	27	48					
80-817410				17	39	40	31	21	22	53	29	28	27	48					
80-817411				17	39	40	31	21	22	53	29	28	27	48					
80-817413				17	39	40	31	21	22	53	29	28	27	48					
80-8337138				42	41	48													
80-932022A				17	6	2	7	12	42	33	57	53	48						
80-961165				17	42	41	53	26	29	28	27	48							
80-R109-1049				17	39	40	31	42	41	53	29	28	27	48					
80-R109-1050				17	39	40	31	21	22	53	29	28	27	48					
80-R109-1051				17	39	40	31	42	41	53	29	28	27	48					

(*Continued*)

Table 23.1 (*Continued*)   P-Q-R-$ Information for Each Product

Product No.	6-Month Quantity	Sell Price	6-Month Total $	Product Routings														
				1	2	3	4	5	6	7	8	9	10	11	12	13	14	15	16
80-R109-1052				17	39	40	31	42	41	53	29	28	27	48					
80-S109-1004				17	39	40	31	21	22	53	29	28	27	48					
80-S109-1005				17	39	40	31	21	22	53	29	28	27	48					
80-S114-1000				17	3	7	12	4	53	55									
80-S111-1001				17	6	2	7	12	42	33	29	28	4	55					
80-S113-1000				57	53	57	48												
80-S113-1001				17	16	11	10	57	53	55									
80-S113-1004				17	16	11	10	57	53	55									
80-S113-1012				17	6	2	7	12	42	33	29	28	4	55					
80-S113--1012				17	6	2	7	12	42	33	29	28	4	57	55				
80-957-21				17	54	57	55												
80-23193				17	16	11	10	29	4	55									
80-30311				17	16	11	10	29	4	55									
80-34673				17	56	1	57	54	55										
80-37914				17	56	1	57	54	55										
80-27708-302UP				17	39	40	16	9	11	10	39	40	57	54					
80-9033023-303				57	54	57	55												
80-9033704UP				57	55														
80-9434913-301UP				17	16	11	10	57	54	55									
80-9434913-303UP				17	16	11	10	57	54	55									
80-9434913-307UP				17	16	11	10	57	54	55									
80-9434913-309UP				17	16	11	10	57	54	55									
80-9434913-311UP				17	16	11	10	57	54	55									
80-9627637-3UP				17	3	7	12	57	54	57	55								
80-9627637-4UP				17	3	7	12	57	54	57	55								

(*Continued*)

Table 23.1 (*Continued*)   P-Q-R-$ Information for Each Product

Product No.	6-Month Quantity	Sell Price	6-Month Total $	Product Routings															
				1	2	3	4	5	6	7	8	9	10	11	12	13	14	15	16
80-9627637-5UP				17	3	7	12	57	54	57	55								
80-9627637-6UP				17	3	7	12	57	54	57	55								
80-9627712-301UP				17	6	56	16	11	10	6	7	12	8	54	57	54	53	8	55
80-9627713-301UP				17	6	56	16	11	10	6	7	12	8	54	57	54	53	8	55
80-9627714-301UP				17	6	56	16	11	10	6	7	12	8	54	57	54	53	8	55
80-9627715-301UP				17	6	56	16	11	10	6	7	12	8	54	57	54	53	8	55
80-9627716-301UP				17	6	56	16	11	10	6	7	12	8	54	57	54	53	8	55
80-9627787-1F				17	3	7	12	8	57	55									
80-SW25085JI				57	55														
80-SW25435JI				57	55														
80-SW25473JI				57	55														
80-SW27049JI				57	55														
80-SW28173-1UP				17	40	39	16	11	10	40	39	26	57	54					
80-SW32217JI				57	55														
80-SW32972JI				57	55														
80-WP32969-5JI				57	55														
80-3260-041				17	6	2	11	10	29	28	54	57	55						
80-3260-0980				17	6	2	11	10	29	28	54	57	55						
80-3260-503				17	6	2	11	10	29	28	54	57	55						
80-W131-1000				17	3	7	12	4	53	55									
80-W131-1001				17	3	7	12	4	53	55									
80-U104-1012				17	3	7	12	4	53	55									
80-U104-1013				17	3	7	12	4	53	55									
80-U104-1016				17	3	7	12	4	53	55									
80-U104-1017				17	3	7	12	4	53	55									

(*Continued*)

Table 23.1 (*Continued*) P-Q-R-$ Information for Each Product

Product No.	6-Month Quantity	Sell Price	6-Month Total $	| Product Routings															
				1	2	3	4	5	6	7	8	9	10	11	12	13	14	15	16
80-U104-1018				17	3	7	12		4	53	55								
80-671635-00				17	3	7	12	26	4	55									
80-4030007296089				17	3	7	12	8	4	54	29	4	55						
80-4030007296090				17	3	7	12	8	4	54	29	4	55						
80-4030007296091				17	3	7	12	8	4	54	29	4	55						
80-4030007296094				17	3	7	12	8	4	54	29	4	55						
80-U110-1000				17	6	9	57	4	55										
80-V104-1000				17	3	7	12		4	53	55								
80-V104-1002				17	3	7	12		4	53	55								
80-27377				17	16	11	10	26	4	55									
80-36318				17	3	7	12	29	4	55									
80-36892				17	3	7	12	29	4	55									
80-37626				17	3	7	12	29	4	55									
80-37772				17	40	39	6	11	10	29	4	55							
80-37773				17	40	39	6	11	10	29	4	55							
80-39320				17	40	39	6	11	10	29	4	55							
80-39321				17	40	39	6	11	10	29	4	55							
80-7549				17	16	11	10	29	4	55									
80-7551				17	3	7	12	29	4	55									
80-7633				17	16	11	10	29	4	55									
80-13217E7085				17	40	39	21	22	26	50	53	29	28	27	48				
80-921790				17	3	7	12	8	54	29	28	4	55						
80-W101-1001A				17	6	2	7	12	42	41	33	29	28	51	54	55			
80-W101-1003				17	6	2	7	12	42	41	33	29	28	51	54	55			
80-W101-1006				17	6	2	7	12	42	41	33	29	28	51	54	55			

(Continued)

Table 23.1 (*Continued*)   P-Q-R-$ Information for Each Product

Product No.	6-Month Quantity	Sell Price	6-Month Total $	Product Routings															
				1	2	3	4	5	6	7	8	9	10	11	12	13	14	15	16
80-W101-1019				17	6	2	7	12	42	41	33	29	28	51	54	55			
80-W101-1019P				17	6	2	7	12	42	41	33	29	28	51	54	55			
80-W101-1020				17	6	2	7	12	42	41	33	29	28	51	54	55			
80-W101-1022				17	6	2	7	12	42	41	33	29	28	51	54	55			
80-W101-1028				17	6	2	7	12	42	41	33	29	28	51	54	55			
80-W101-1030				17	6	2	7	12	42	41	33	29	28	51	54	55			
80-W101-1036				17	6	2	7	12	42	41	33	29	28	51	54	55			
80-W101-1037				17	6	2	7	12	42	41	33	29	28	51	54	55			
80-W101-1058				17	6	2	7	12	42	41	33	29	28	51	54	55			
80-W101-1060				17	6	2	7	12	42	41	33	29	28	51	54	55			
80-W101-1083				17	40	39	21	22	26	50	53	29	28	27	48				
80-W101-1116				17	6	2	7	12	42	41	33	29	28	51	54	55			
80-W101-1120				17	6	2	7	12	42	41	33	29	28	51	54	55			
80-W101-1153				17	40	39	29	28	4	54	55								
80-W101-1154				17	40	39	29	28	4	55									
80-W101-1155				17	40	39	21	22	26	50	53	29	28	27	48				
80-W101-1156				17	57	55													
80-W101-1157				17	57	55													
80-W101-1158				17	57	55													
80-W101-2000				17	40	39	21	22	26	50	53	29	28	27	48				
80-W101-2001				17	40	39	21	22	26	50	53	29	28	27	48				
80-W101-2002				17	40	39	21	22	26	50	53	29	28	27	48				
80-W101-2003				17	40	39	21	22	26	50	53	29	28	27	48				
80-W101-2004				17	40	39	29	28	4	54	55								
80-W101-2005				17	6	2	7	12	42	41	33	29	28	51	54	55			

(*Continued*)

Table 23.1 (*Continued*) P-Q-R-$ Information for Each Product

Product No.	6-Month Quantity	Sell Price	6-Month Total $	Product Routings															
				1	2	3	4	5	6	7	8	9	10	11	12	13	14	15	16
80-W101-2006				17	6	2	42	33	41	54	57	4	55						
80-W101-2007				17	40	39	42	41	51	53	29	28	27	48					
80-W101-2008				17	40	39	21	22	26	50	53	29	28	27	48				
80-W101-2009				17	6	2	7	12	42	41	33	29	28	51	54	55			
80-150SLA				17	6	2	7	12	42	41	33	29	28	51	54	55			
80-150SLAW				17	6	2	7	12	42	41	33	29	28	51	54	55			
80-175SLAW				17	6	2	7	12	42	41	33	29	28	51	54	55			
80-175SLC				17	6	2	7	12	42	41	33	29	28	51	54	55			
80-175SLCW				17	6	2	7	12	42	41	33	29	28	51	54	55			
80-200SLA				17	6	2	7	12	42	41	33	29	28	51	54	55			
80-200SLAW				17	6	2	7	12	42	41	33	29	28	51	54	55			
80-200SLCW				17	6	2	7	12	42	41	33	29	28	51	54	55			
80-225SLA				17	6	2	7	12	42	41	33	29	28	51	54	55			
80-225SLC				17	6	2	7	12	42	41	33	29	28	51	54	55			
80-250SLA				17	6	2	7	12	42	41	33	29	28	51	54	55			
80-250SLAW				17	6	2	7	12	42	41	33	29	28	51	54	55			
80-250SLC				17	6	2	7	12	42	41	33	29	28	51	54	55			
80-2687				17	6	2	7	12	42	41	33	29	28	51	54	55			
80-W102-1006				17	6	2	7	12	42	41	33	29	28	51	54	55			
80-W102-1007				17	6	2	7	12	42	41	33	29	28	51	54	55			
80-W102-1008				17	6	2	7	12	42	41	33	29	28	51	54	55			
80-W102-1063				17	6	2	42	41	33	54	57	4	55						
80-W102-1063B				17	6	2	42	41	33	54	57	4	55						
80-W103-1000				17	42	41	57	26	54	57	48								
80-ULC0078				17	3	7	12	29	4	55									

(Continued)

Table 23.1 (*Continued*) P-Q-R-$ Information for Each Product

Product No.	6-Month Quantity	Sell Price	6-Month Total $	Product Routings															
				1	2	3	4	5	6	7	8	9	10	11	12	13	14	15	16
80-W120-1000				17	42	41	51	53	29	28	48								
80-575V87				17	21	22	51	53	29	28	48								
80-V1280				17	21	22	51	53	21	22	29	28	48						
80-111199				17	42	41	51	53	29	28	48								
80-12706-D				17	42	41	53	29	28	27	48								
80-Y102-1001				17	6	2	42	41	53	57	55								

matrix (Figure 23.1) with "1"s colored to make them visible indicated a considerable overlap in the machine requirements of the different part families. This is typical of job shops and other Make-To-Order manufacturing facilities that make a large variety of products in low-to-medium quantities. Based on this analysis, it was felt necessary to do P-Q Analysis and P-Q-$ Analysis to segment the product mix. Product Mix Segmentation helped to select a subset of parts from the original population of 530 for more detailed analysis.

Product Mix Segmentation

The results of both P-Q Analysis and P-Q-$ Analysis were generated, as shown in Figures 23.2 and 23.3, respectively. Based on these analyses (and indicated by the dotted line circling the sample of products selected in Figure 23.3), only those products produced in quantities greater than 1,800 and earning revenues higher than $30,000 were selected in the sample of products (Table 23.3) on which to base the facility layout design. The number of products included in this sample is 44, which is only about 8% of the total number of products in the complete population. However, this sample of products accounts for 68% of the Total Production Volume and 46% of the Total Revenue for the company.

Table 23.2 Attributes for Each Equipment Type

Number	Equipment	Moveable	Cost of Duplication
1	700-ton press	Yes	Expensive
2	5″ upsetter	No	Expensive
3	5,000# area furnace	Yes	
4	Large rotoblaster	Yes	
5	350-ton press	Yes	Expensive
6	5″ upsetter furnace	Yes	
7	5,000# area hammer	No	Expensive
8	Grinding table	Yes	
9	60-ton press	Yes	
10	150-ton trim press	Yes	Expensive
11	3,000# area hammer	No	Expensive
12	158-ton trim press	Yes	Expensive
13	Hydraulic bender	Yes	
14	4″ Threader	Yes	
15	4″ Belt grinder	Yes	
16	3,000# area furnace	Yes	
17	Band saws	Yes	
18	200# area open die hammer	No	Expensive
19	400# area furnace	Yes	
20	400# area open die hammer	No	Expensive
21	600# area furnace	Yes	
22	600# area open die hammer	No	Expensive
23	Stone grinder	Yes	
24	Hydraulic bender	Yes	
25	Dual belt grinder	Yes	
26	Belt grinder	Yes	

(Continued)

Table 23.2 (*Continued*)   Attributes for Each Equipment Type

Number	Equipment	Moveable	Cost of Duplication
27	Small rotoblaster	Yes	
28	Temper furnace	Yes	
29	Quench furnace	Yes	
30	Horizontal boring machine	Yes	
31	3 Post-hydraulic press	Yes	
32	Induction heater	Yes	
33	3 Post-hydraulic bender	Yes	
34	Die milling machine	No	
35	Drill press	Yes	
36	Vertical lathe	Yes	
37	Vertical mill	Yes	
38	Tool grinder	Yes	
39	Slot furnace	Yes	
40	2.5″ upsetter	Yes	Expensive
41	1,500# area open die hammer	No	Expensive
42	1,500# area furnace	Yes	
43	Die milling machine	Yes	
44	EDM machine	Yes	
45	Vertical mill	Yes	
46	Turret lathe	Yes	
47	Engine lathe	Yes	
48	Shipping desk	Yes	
49	H.T. (Heat Treat) testing area	Yes	
50	Small tumbler	Yes	
51	Large tumbler	Yes	
52	Clear coat dip tank	Yes	

(*Continued*)

Table 23.2 (*Continued*)   Attributes for Each Equipment Type

Number	Equipment	Moveable	Cost of Duplication
53	Manual machine shop	Yes	Expensive
54	CNC machine shop	Yes	Expensive
55	Shipping area	Yes	
56	5″ Upsetter	Yes	Expensive
57	Outside processing	Yes	

MACHINES

PARTS

Figure 23.1   Optimized machine-part Matrix Clustering for 500+ routings.

Among the 486 products that were excluded from the sample, there were 35 products with routings identical to the 44 selected products. That is, they belonged to the same product families as these 44 products do, and

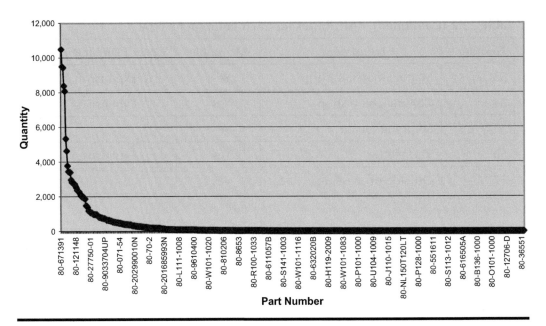

Figure 23.2 P-Q Analysis.

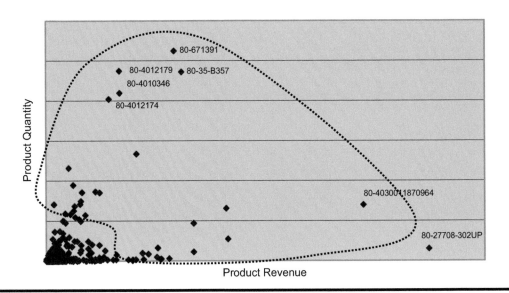

Figure 23.3 P-Q-$ Analysis.

thus could be included in the Working Sample. After the inclusion of those additional 35 products, the final Working Sample of products (Table 23.4) now included about 15% of the total number of products in the original sample, yet accounted for 74% of the Total Production Volume and 54% of the Total Revenue earned by the company.

Table 23.3   Initial Working Sample of Products

Product No.	6-Month Quantity	Sell Price	6-Month Total $	1	2	3	4	5	6	7	8	9	10	11	12	13	14	15	16
80-4011714				1	26	57	52	48	55										
80-4012169				1	26	57	52	48	55										
80-4012174				1	26	57	52	48	55										
80-4012179				1	26	57	52	48	55										
80-4030339				1	27	9	57	48											
80-4030341				1	27	9	57	48											
80-4035149				1	28	50	27	48	55										
80-121148				1	50	26	27	55											
80-4009121				1	57	25	52	48	55										
80-4009263				1	57	25	52	48	55										
80-4009270				1	57	25	52	48	55										
80-4010346				1	57	25	52	48	55										
80-4010348				1	57	25	52	48	55										
80-4010350				1	57	25	52	48	55										
80-4041707				1	57	25	52	48	55										
80-051-1				17	1	26	4	54	55										
80-35-B357				17	1	57	4	54	55										
80-671635-00				17	3	7	12	26	4	55									
80-4030007296091				17	3	7	12	8	4	54	29	4	55						
80-4030007296094				17	3	7	12	8	4	54	29	4	55						
80-921790				17	3	7	12	8	54	29	28	4	55						
80-C27416-2				17	6	2	11	10	29	54	55								
80-150T084LT				17	6	2	7	12	8	42	41	57	55						
80-NL150T060LT				17	6	2	7	12	8	42	41	57	55						
80-NL150T072LT				17	6	2	7	12	8	42	41	57	55						

(Continued)

Table 23.3 (*Continued*)   Initial Working Sample of Products

Product No.	6-Month Quantity	Sell Price	6-Month Total $	Product Routings															
				1	2	3	4	5	6	7	8	9	10	11	12	13	14	15	16
80-37355-1072				17	6	2	7	12	8	42	41	57	55						
80-37355-1084				17	6	2	7	12	8	42	41	57	55						
80-3260-041				17	6	2	11	10	29	28	54	57	55						
80-W101-2006				17	6	2	42	33	41	54	57	4	55						
80-9627713-301UP				17	6	56	16	11	10	6	7	12	8	54	57	54	53	8	55
80-9627715-301UP				17	6	56	16	11	10	6	7	12	8	54	57	54	53	8	55
80-671391				17	16	11	10	26	4	55									
80-191820				17	16	11	10	26	29	28	27	48							
80-S113-1001				17	16	11	10	57	53	55									
80-4067179				17	39	40	26	57	54	57	55								
80-4030011870964				17	39	40	21	22	53	29	28	4	55						
80-121009-00				17	39	40	21	22	55										
80-121188-002				17	39	40	21	22	55										
80-121018-00				17	39	40	21	22	55										
80-27750-01				17	39	40	42	41	3	7	12	57	54	55					
80-27708-302UP				17	39	40	16	9	11	10	39	40	57	54					
80-3249869				17	56	1	17	29	26	54	57	48							
80-B113-1001				17	56	57	54												
80-9033023-303				57	54	57	55												

Machine-Part Matrix Clustering

The Machine-Product Matrix Clustering result (Figure 23.4) for the Working Sample of products showed that there would still be considerable machine sharing and overlap if it was desired to design stand-alone manufacturing cells. Since the blocks of operations (indicated by "1"s) could not be isolated into independent clusters, it was concluded that independent product-focused (or product family-based) manufacturing

Table 23.4 Final Working Sample of Products

Product No.	6-Month Quantity	Sell Price	6-Month Total $	Product Routings															
				1	2	3	4	5	6	7	8	9	10	11	12	13	14	15	16
80-A37353				17	6	2	11	10	29	54	55								
80-C27416-1				17	6	2	11	10	29	54	55								
80-C27416-2				17	6	2	11	10	29	54	55								
80-C46806-1				17	6	2	11	10	29	54	55								
80-C55581				17	6	2	11	10	29	54	55								
80-C558-1				17	6	2	11	10	29	54	55								
80-D8097				17	6	2	11	10	29	54	55								
80-B113-1001				17	56	57	54												
80-4003111				1	57	25	52	48	55										
80-4009121				1	57	25	52	48	55										
80-4009262				1	57	25	52	48	55										
80-4009263				1	57	25	52	48	55										
80-4009270				1	57	25	52	48	55										
80-4010346				1	57	25	52	48	55										
80-4010348				1	57	25	52	48	55										
80-4010349				1	57	25	52	48	55										
80-4010350				1	57	25	52	48	55										
80-4010351				1	57	25	52	48	55										
80-4010352				1	57	25	52	48	55										
80-4011714				1	26	57	52	48	55										
80-4011725				1	57	25	52	48	55										
80-4012169				1	26	57	52	48	55										
80-4012174				1	26	57	52	48	55										
80-4012179				1	26	57	52	48	55										
80-4012212				1	26	57	52	48	55										

(Continued)

Table 23.4   Final Working Sample of Products

Product No.	6-Month Quantity	Sell Price	6-Month Total $	Product Routings															
				1	2	3	4	5	6	7	8	9	10	11	12	13	14	15	16
80-4012213				1	26	57	52	48	55										
80-4030339				1	27	9	57	48											
80-4030341				1	27	9	57	48											
80-4035144				1	28	50	27	48	55										
80-4035149				1	28	50	27	48	55										
80-4039260				1	28	50	27	48	55										
80-4041707				1	57	25	52	48	55										
80-4059989				1	26	57	52	48	55										
80-4067179				17	39	40	26	57	54	57	55								
80-4030011870964				17	39	40	21	22	53	29	28	4	55						
80-150T084LT				17	6	2	7	12	8	42	41	57	55						
80-G121-1002				17	6	2	7	12	8	42	41	57	55						
80-NL150T060LT				17	6	2	7	12	8	42	41	57	55						
80-NL150T072LT				17	6	2	7	12	8	42	41	57	55						
80-NL150T084LT				17	6	2	7	12	8	42	41	57	55						
80-NL150T096LT				17	6	2	7	12	8	42	41	57	55						
80-NL150T120LT				17	6	2	7	12	8	42	41	57	55						
80-3249869				17	56	1	17	29	26	54	57	48							
80-121009-00				17	39	40	21	22	55										
80-121188-002				17	39	40	21	22	55										
80-121189				17	39	40	21	22	55										
80-671391				17	16	11	10	26	4	55									
80-121018-00				17	39	40	21	22	55										
80-121148				1	50	26	27	55											
80-121387				17	39	40	21	22	55										
80-ULC0200				17	39	40	21	22	55										

(Continued)

Table 23.4 Final Working Sample of Products

Product No.	6-Month Quantity	Sell Price	6-Month Total $	Product Routings															
				1	2	3	4	5	6	7	8	9	10	11	12	13	14	15	16
80-35-B357				17	1	57	4	54	55										
80-27750-01				17	39	40	42	41	3	7	12	57	54	55					
80-37355-1072				17	6	2	7	12	8	42	41	57	55						
80-37355-1084				17	6	2	7	12	8	42	41	57	55						
80-051-1				17	1	26	4	54	55										
80-191820				17	16	11	10	26	29	28	27	48							
80-522500				17	16	11	10	26	29	28	27	48							
80-551500				17	16	11	10	26	29	28	27	48							
80-S113-1001				17	16	11	10	57	53	55									
80-S113-1004				17	16	11	10	57	53	55									
80-27708-302UP				17	39	40	16	9	11	10	39	40	57	54					
80-9033023-303				57	54	57	55												
80-9627712-301UP				17	6	56	16	11	10	6	7	12	8	54	57	54	53	8	55
80-9627713-301UP				17	6	56	16	11	10	6	7	12	8	54	57	54	53	8	55
80-9627714-301UP				17	6	56	16	11	10	6	7	12	8	54	57	54	53	8	55
80-9627715-301UP				17	6	56	16	11	10	6	7	12	8	54	57	54	53	8	55
80-9627716-301UP				17	6	56	16	11	10	6	7	12	8	54	57	54	53	8	55
80-3260-041				17	6	2	11	10	29	28	54	57	55						
80-3260-0980				17	6	2	11	10	29	28	54	57	55						
80-3260-503				17	6	2	11	10	29	28	54	57	55						
80-671635-00				17	3	7	12	26	4	55									
80-4030007296089				17	3	7	12	8	4	54	29	4	55						
80-4030007296090				17	3	7	12	8	4	54	29	4	55						
80-4030007296091				17	3	7	12	8	4	54	29	4	55						
80-4030007296094				17	3	7	12	8	4	54	29	4	55						
80-27377				17	16	11	10	26	4	55									

(*Continued*)

Table 23.4 Final Working Sample of Products

Product No.	6-Month Quantity	Sell Price	6-Month Total $	Product Routings															
				1	2	3	4	5	6	7	8	9	10	11	12	13	14	15	16
80-921790				17	3	7	12	8	54	29	28	4	55						
80-W101-2006				17	6	2	42	33	41	54	57	4	55						

cells were infeasible for the custom forge shop. Therefore, it was decided to explore a Hybrid Cellular Layout to achieve a streamlined flow for the diverse sample of products.

Design of Modular Layout

To design a Modular Layout for the forge shop, the Modified Multi-Product Process Chart (MM-PPC) (Figure 23.5) was generated for the final Working Sample of products. Based on the MM-PPC, seven layout modules (Figure 23.6) were identified. Using the routings of parts in the final Working Sample, the Modular From-To Chart (Table 23.5) was generated. In Table 23.5, "M1-M7" are the layout modules, "56" is an individual machine, "IN" is the Receiving area, "OUT" is the Shipping area (or office location), and "External" is a group of machines – #53, #54, #55, and #57 – located off-site, including the Machine Shop which is located nearly 10 miles away from the forge shop. Using the Modular From-To Chart, the flow diagram for the Modular Layout (Figure 23.7) was generated.

Evaluation of the Proposed Layout

To evaluate the proposed Modular Layout, it was compared to the existing facility layout of the forge shop. The From-To Chart for the final Working Sample (Table 23.6) was generated. The flow diagram of the existing layout (Figure 23.8) shows the flows in the current layout due to the existing locations of various machines and support equipment in the forge shop. The flow path of any product starts from Receiving (IN), goes through the sequence of machines per its routing, and ends in Shipping (OUT). Yellow-colored rectangles represent machines that occur in the product routings of the final Working Sample used to design the layout,

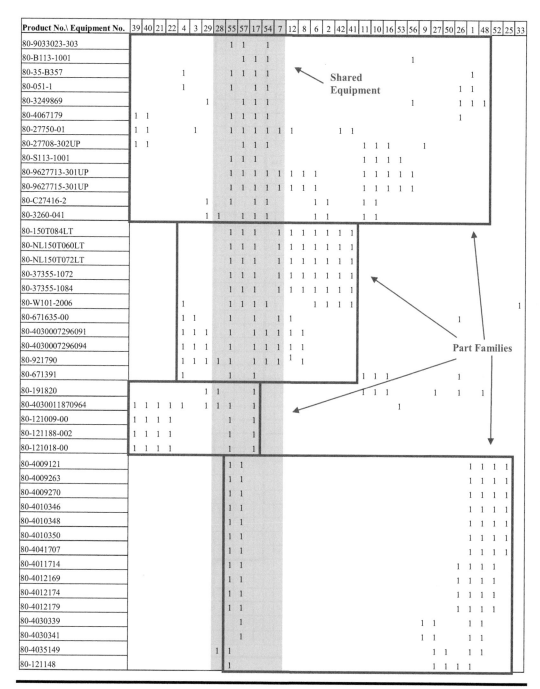

Figure 23.4 Machine-Product Matrix Clustering for the Final Working Sample

Product No.	Product Routings
80-9627713-301UP	17, 6, 56, 16, 11, 10, 6, 7, 12, 8, 54, 57, 54, 53, 8, 55
80-9627715-301UP	17, 6, 56, 16, 11, 10, 6, 7, 12, 8, 54, 57, 54, 53, 8, 55
80-3260-041	17, 6, 2, 11, 10, 29, 28, 54, 57, 55
80-C27416-2	17, 6, 2, 11, 10, 29, 54, 55
80-121009-00	17, 39, 40, 21, 22, 55
80-121188-002	17, 39, 40, 21, 22, 55
80-121018-00	17, 39, 40, 21, 22, M3, 55
80-4030011870964	17, 39, 40, 21, 22, 53, 29, 28, 4, 55
80-921790	17, 3, 7, 12, 8, 54, 29, 28, 4, 55
80-4030007296091	17, M4, 3, 7, 12, 8, 4, 54, 29, 4, 55
80-4030007296094	17, 3, 7, 12, 8, 4, 54, 29, 4, 55
80-671635-00	17, M2, 3, 7, 12, 26, 4, 55
80-671391	17, 16, 11, 10, 26, 4, 54, 55
80-051-1	17, 1, 26, 4, M5, 55
80-121148	1, 50, 26, 27, 55
80-4035149	1, 28, 50, 27, 48, 55
80-4030339	1, 27, 9, 57, 48
80-4030341	1, 27, 9, 57, 48
80-4009121	1, 57, 25, 52, 48, 55
80-4009263	1, M1, 57, 25, 52, 48, 55
80-4009270	1, 57, M7, 25, 52, 48, 55
80-4010346	1, 57, 25, 52, 48, 55
80-4010348	1, 57, 25, 52, 48, 55
80-4010350	1, 57, 25, 52, 48, 55
80-4041707	1, 57, 25, 52, 48, 55
80-4011714	1, 26, 57, 52, 48, 55
80-4012169	1, 26, 57, 52, 48, 55
80-4012174	1, 26, 57, 52, 48, 55
80-4012179	1, 26, 57, 52, 48, 55
80-9033023-303	57, 54, 57, 55
80-4067179	17, 39, 40, 26, 57, 54, 57, 55
80-27750-01	17, 39, 40, 42, 41, 3, 7, 12, M6, 57, 54, 55
80-150T084LT	17, 6, 2, 7, 12, 8, 42, 41, 57, 55
80-NL150T060LT	17, 6, 2, 7, 12, 8, 42, 41, 57, 55
80-NL150T072LT	17, 6, 2, 7, 12, 8, 42, 41, 57, 55
80-37355-1072	17, 6, 2, 7, 12, 8, 42, 41, 57, 55
80-37355-1084	17, 6, 2, 7, 12, 8, 42, 41, 57, 55
80-W101-2006	17, 6, 2, 42, 33, 41, 54, 57, 4, 55
80-35-B357	17, 1, 57, 4, 54, 55
80-B113-1001	17, 56, 57, 54
80-3249869	17, 56, 1, 17, 29, 26, 54, 57, 48
80-191820	17, 16, 11, 10, 26, 29, 28, 27, 48
80-S113-1001	17, 16, 11, 10, 57, 53, 55
80-27708-302UP	17, 39, 40, 16, 9, 11, 10, 39, 40, 57, 54

Figure 23.5 MM-PPC for the Final Working Sample

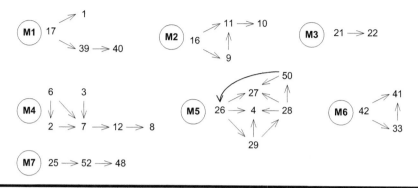

Figure 23.6   Layout modules identified based on the MM-PPC.

Table 23.5   Modular From-To Chart

Module	M1	M2	M3	M4	M5	M6	M7	56	External	In	Out
M1	-	1,034	940	4,041	1,209	1		5	2,791		
M2	610	-		371	1,875				35		
M3			-						940		
M4		1,497		-	1,235	605		371	1,094		
M5		7			-		887		5,050		
M6						-			605		
M7							-		3,366		12,377
56	2	371						-	3		
External				371	1,625		2,873		-		104,229
In	113,974								2,632	-	
Out											-

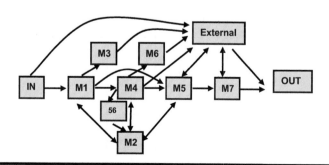

Figure 23.7   Modular Layout.

Table 23.6 From-To Chart for the Final Working Sample

Machine	17	6	2	11	10	29	54	55	56	57	1	25	52	48	26	27	9	28	50	39	40	21	22	53	4	7	12	8	42	41	16	3	33
17		1,270				2			5		12									621											13	1,470	
6			1,122						148																	148							
2				603																						486			33				
11			603		1,374																												
10		148				603				2					11					610													
29							401								2			556							1,114								
54						1,465		414		388														148									
55																																	
56								691		3	2																				148		
57							765					20	21	9		24		2	2					2	42								
1	2									29																							
25													20																				
52														41																			
48								43																									
26						1	2			22						2									18								
27								2		7					3		7																
9				610												1			2						353								
28							202																										

(Continued)

Table 23.6 (Continued)   From-To Chart for the Final Working Sample

Machine	17	6	2	11	10	29	54	55	56	57	1	25	52	48	26	27	9	28	50	39	40	21	22	53	4	7	12	8	42	41	16	3	33
50															2	2																	
39																					1,231												
40										610					1							9							1		610		
21																							9										
22								7																2									
53						2		2																				148					
4							1,126	1,515																									
7																											2,105						
12										1					5													2,099					
8							499	148																	1,114				486				
42																														487			33
41							33			486																						1	
16				161													610																
3																										1,471							
33																														33			

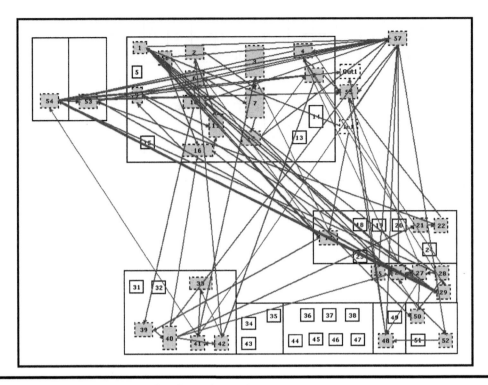

Figure 23.8   Flow diagram for the existing layout.

whereas the machines represented by white rectangles are not used by the products in this sample.

The flow diagram for the proposed Modular Layout (Figure 23.9) shows the recommended relocation and grouping of various sets of machines into layout modules. Figure 23.9 shows the flows in the Modular From-To Chart superimposed on the proposed layout. Also, the different modules have been assigned to new locations in order to minimize the total distance (and time) of travel between different pairs of modules. Machines represented by white rectangles are the "monuments" that could not be relocated in any new layout that the company decided to implement.

A comparison of the two flow diagrams shows that the new layout would (i) increase the speed of material flows between the modules, (ii) increase visual connectivity and communication among inter-dependent machines and (iii) allow multi-machine operation by a single cross-trained operator inside any module. Had it been possible to relocate some of the monuments per the improved material flow network, then even more significant reductions in order completion time, material handling costs, and labor hours would have been possible.

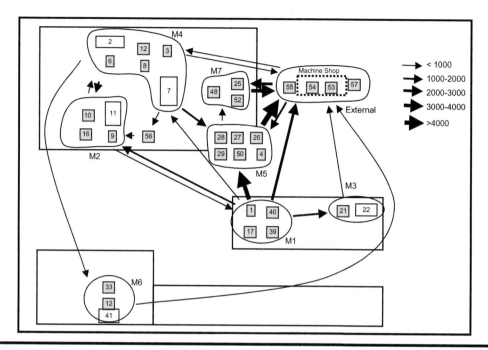

Figure 23.9 Flow diagram for the Modular Layout.

Implementation and Results

Recommendations were made to the forge shop to make significant layout changes and to invest capital to acquire additional equipment. Their implementation team evaluated and ranked each of the recommendations based on cost and time savings, feasibility, affordability, and ease of implementation. The following changes were made:

- An additional processing area was created in the Drop Hammer building where cleaning, finishing, packaging, and shipping were consolidated. This reduced order flow times and increased throughput.
- The 158-ton Trim Press was replaced by a 440-ton press that was positioned next to the 5,000 lb. Hammer to form an Upset Forging cell. This eliminated the transportation of large forgings to a distant 350-ton Trim Press. Also, a 350 kW induction heater and conveyor were purchased and co-located in the cell.
- A new 2.5″ Upsetter was purchased and positioned next to the 3,000 lb. Hammer to form an Upset Forging cell. The benefits included a reduction in part travel distance and increased throughput at the Hammer.

- The 1.5″ Upsetter was replaced with a faster machine for shearing the same size of bar stock and positioned next to the 700-ton Press to form an Upset Forging cell. With its faster upsetting/forging cycle time, it drastically increased throughput at the 700-ton press.
- An overhead crane was installed at the 5,000 lb. Hammer to reduce piston change-out time, reduce die key tightening time, and improve product flow in the area.
- A portable Marvel Hacksaw and 1.5″ Bar Shear were acquired.
- In their machine shop, a CNC Mill was acquired and positioned next to the EDM (Electric Discharge Machine) to reduce outsourcing costs and lead times because the company could make its own die sets.
- A new Magnaflux test machine was purchased and installed. This eliminated costs and reduced lead times associated with outside testing.

Based on implementing four of the above layout changes that were recommended to them, the forge shop reported a Total Annual Savings of $137,000. The savings from the individual projects are itemized below:

- 2.5″ Upsetter installed next to the 3,000 lb. Hammer (Annual Savings = $37,000)
- 350 kW Induction Heater installed next to the 3,000 lb. Hammer (Annual Savings = $49,000)
- Crane installed at the 5,000 lb. Hammer (Annual Savings = $17,000)
- Addition of CNC Mill for die sinking (Annual Savings = $34,000)

Other results that were achieved:

- The cost of one group of upset-and-forge parts was reduced by 10%–15%
- Savings in handling, finishing, and shipping were estimated at 10%–12%. More significant savings were expected as a result of future projects to implement additional manufacturing cells.
- Several jobs took less time to move through the plant due to the speed of handling, processing, and finishing. This netted the company more open production time for additional jobs.

For further information on financial benefits realized from this project, please contact Mike Ulven (MikeU@ulvencompanies.com, (503) 651-2101).

Conclusion

Custom forge shops that are suppliers to defense organizations, such as the Defense Logistics Agency, are typically high-mix low-volume (HMLV) job shops. It is inadvisable to use the standard tools in the Lean Toolkit based on the Toyota Production System for implementing Lean in job shops. A majority of those tools either need significant modification to be applicable, or they must be replaced by alternative methods that address the complexities of a job shop, such as diverse product mix, variable demand, process layout, different due dates set by many different customers. Production Flow Analysis, with its emphasis on material flow analysis, part family formation, and facility layout, proved to be a reliable and effective tool for implementing Lean in this custom forge shop.

Chapter 24

Implementation of Job Shop Lean in a CNC Machine Shop

Acknowledgment

This chapter's content is adapted from the original article titled *From Job Shop Chaos to Lean Order* (Modern Machine Shop, November 2010, 61–67) with permission from the main author, Matt Danford (Senior Editor, Modern Machine Shop), and the original copyright owners, Gardner Publications Inc. and Modern Machine Shop. Classic Lean principles are practically taken as gospel, but benefits can be elusive for manufacturers that produce a variety of parts in low volumes. G&G Mfg. Co. took a different approach to Lean – one aided by software that helped identify patterns in part routings that were used to design a more efficient layout for their machine shop. This chapter describes work that was done in partnership with Jeffrey Gleich (President/Owner, G&G Mfg. Co.) and Dr. Smart Khaewsukkho, who was a core member of the team at The Ohio State University that developed the PFAST (Production Flow Analysis and Simplification Toolkit) software. After completing his PhD at The Ohio State University, Dr. Khaewsukkho worked briefly at G&G Mfg. Co. to support their implementation of Job Shop Lean.

Background

Jeff Gleich was frustrated. The year was 2007, and Mr. Gleich had done everything he thought he was supposed to do to implement Lean principles two years after coming back onboard at The G&G Mfg. Co., a job shop founded by his grandfather, Kurt Gleich. A Kaizen program was well underway, setup teams had been put in place to improve spindle uptime, and 5S and other Lean programs had helped identify and reduce waste. Nonetheless, the shop had hit a wall when it came to continuing the efficiency gains realized at the start of its Lean journey. "It seemed like we'd taken a step forward only to take another step back", Mr. Gleich recalls.

Getting out of the slump required two key insights about the nature of Lean and how it applies to the job shop, as opposed to production environments (Toyota is the classic example). First was the understanding that the vast majority of generally accepted Lean practices are designed to optimize flow, i.e., how product is routed through the manufacturing operation. Second, and most critical, was the realization that the most effective way to streamline flow in a high-mix, low-volume (HMLV) operation is to organize jobs into families of parts with similar manufacturing routings.

Armed with these notions and a software analysis tool that helped identify patterns in job routings, G&G realized improvements in productivity and lead times ranging to 25% and 50%, respectively. Of course, implementing what Mr. Gleich calls "flexible flow cells" and other Lean strategies associated Flow was easier said than done. Likewise, the insights described above certainly didn't spring from his brain unprompted. The chapter offers a glimpse into the evolution of G&G's Lean thinking, the challenges it faced, and the software that propelled its transformation into an exemplary model of how Lean can be adapted to a job shop environment.

The Journey of a 1,000 Miles...

...begins with a single step, as the saying goes, and G&G had come a long way since its first tentative steps toward Lean implementation in 1998. That year, a top-tier customer introduced Mr. Gleich's father, Kurt Gleich II, the company's owner and president at the time, to a book called *Lean Thinking* by James T. Womack and Daniel T. Jones. It was essentially a demand to "get lean or else". Mr. Gleich recalls how his father dropped the book on his lap and said, "I need you to read this and figure out how we can get this done!".

After reading the book, Mr. Gleich put together some training material and set out to start his Shop's Lean journey. G&G moved away from departmentalizing machines and other equipment by type and toward its first cellular layouts. The shop realized some benefits, but ultimately, its commitment to Lean faltered. The new cells, which were organized to complete specific jobs as efficiently as possible, lacked the flexibility required to accommodate inevitable changes in demand and in the shop's product mix. If a contract was not renewed, the cell became useless and would be broken up.

The Job Shop Difference

G&G's initial efforts with cellular production illustrate the difficulty of applying a "one-size-fits-all" approach to Lean practices. An HMLV operation like G&G isn't exactly what Toyota engineers had in mind when they developed their famous production system in the wake of World War II to streamline the production of automobiles. Rather, the Toyota Production System (TPS), which forms the basis for much of today's Lean thinking, is geared toward large assembly plants dedicated to high production processing of a relatively limited number of parts or part families. In contrast, a typical job shop tries to be "all things to all people", Mr. Gleich says.

That is somewhat true of G&G, which serves a wide variety of industries with all manner of part sizes and shapes from its 30,000-sq. ft facility in Cincinnati, Ohio. In addition to an array of mills, lathes, machining centers, and screw machines, the shop floor is home to equipment used for secondary processes such as grinding, lapping, and honing. The company produces approximately 1,000 different parts in batch sizes ranging from the 100s to the 1,000s for more than 120 regular customers. Figure 24.1 displays an illustrative sample of parts to demonstrate the diversity of work

Figure 24.1   Diversity of parts machined by G&G Mfg. Co.

Figure 24.2 Diversity of materials machined by G&G Mfg. Co.

that G&G Mfg. Co. takes on from year to year. Depending on their annual volume, parts are classified as "runners", "repeaters", and "strangers". In addition to an assortment of part geometries and sizes, G&G contends with the challenge of machining materials ranging from plastic to all types of metals and alloys, as shown in Figure 24.2. Materials machined include steel and stainless steel; harder alloys such as titanium and Inconel; and copper, bronze, and plastic, to name a few.

Pursuing such a dynamic mix of jobs presents a number of Lean implementation hurdles that would be completely foreign to a large, assembly-type operation. Many parts share relatively few machining resources. Design changes are common, demand fluctuates, and contracts can change from year to year. Delivery dates, lot sizes, equipment requirements, and cycle times are also highly variable. As a result of these and other factors, dedicated cells, Pull Production based on Kanban visual aids, and other practices designed for continuous flow simply do not translate easily to G&G's environment.

As such, it is no wonder so many job shops have floundered in their attempts at Lean. This is not to say that the central philosophy of Lean – improving efficiency by doing away with all processes or practices that do not add value for the customer – does not apply to the job shop. Rather, the issue is a lack of well-defined methods for implementing that philosophy in a HMLV operation.

Mapping Job Shop DNA

Dr. Shahrukh Irani, Associate Professor at The Ohio State University's Department of Integrated Systems Engineering, has been attempting to change that. One recent project in his Job Shop Lean research was the development of the PFAST. PFAST is a library of software programs designed to evaluate and simplify material flows in order to help HMLV manufacturers develop part families and machine groupings.

In a job shop, it might appear that no two parts are alike in terms of how they proceed through the process chain. However, in the end, all move through a relatively limited number of workstations. PFAST helps identify common patterns in these routings. Paired with data regarding the frequency of a job, its volume, and the revenue it generates, these patterns help manufacturers design efficient shop layouts that facilitate optimum flow and prioritize the most important work.

Mr. Gleich credits this software tool for helping G&G overcome a key hurdle in its Lean journey. However, he never would have met Dr. Irani or discovered PFAST if he had not come to a key realization about why his shop needed such a tool. That is, when boiled down to its essence, Lean is really all about flow. If a job shop were a living organism, part routings would be its DNA – the genetic blueprint for how it functions. Addressing operations on this basic level is imperative to changing a shop's essential makeup and getting the most out of Lean. Without optimizing routings, a shop can go only so far with alternative efficiency-boosting strategies, useful as they may be.

Reaching an Epiphany

Of course, Mr. Gleich came to this realization the hard way. By the time he met Dr. Irani at the Annual Job Shop Lean Conference that was hosted by The Ohio State University in November 2007, the shop had pursued Lean on and off for about a decade. After failures with cellular layouts in the 1990s, those efforts began again in earnest in 2005, when Mr. Gleich returned to his family's business to spearhead Lean efforts after working as a dot-com entrepreneur.

A year later, the company hired outside consultant Definity Partners to assist with implementing a comprehensive Kaizen system. For the first time, G&G began to track and review metrics critical to making and understanding the impact of changes. Setup Reduction programs and 5S organization further contributed to efficiency. Figure 24.3 shows Wayne Reeves, who has performed setups on G&G's screw machines for 26 years, standing in front of a 5S board implemented after the Shop's Lean project with Definity Partners in 2005. G&G wanted to ensure that Lean efforts were driven from the bottom up rather than the top down. In keeping with that philosophy, Mr. Reeves and other employees would use these boards to document waste, downtime, and other issues, which were then discussed with management at weekly huddles. At first, all this paid off – big time. "My mandate was '10 years in 2'. We needed to make up for 10 years of faltering at Lean that fast to stay relevant", Mr. Gleich noted. During that time period, productivity increased 20%, lead times were cut by 40% and scrap and rework were halved.

Figure 24.3   5S Board used to track performance metrics discussed in weekly huddles.

However, by the fall of 2007, the shop had essentially reached a plateau. After these significant initial gains, productivity had inched up by only about 2%. As mentioned above, it all came back to Flow. Tracking metrics and streamlining processes did little to alleviate inconsistencies and bottlenecks resulting from the fact that workloads on the shop's machines, each of which is responsible for a variety of jobs, tended to change with demand.

Mr. Gleich recalls staring at the schedule board, thinking there had to be some simple, common denominator underlying all of the machine shop's work that would provide a basis for more efficient part routings. He was suddenly struck by the notion that perhaps the business was not so complicated and unpredictable after all. In fact, the entire operation could be boiled down to about eight core process flows that involved various sequences of milling, turning, and the like. Rather than organizing 1,000s of different jobs into 1,000s of part families, would it not be more efficient to organize work according to the comparatively few machining processes required to produce that diverse product mix?

Mr. Gleich thought so. But even after entering the routings for about 100 parts into an Excel spreadsheet – a time-consuming endeavor, to say the least – he had difficulty determining the best way to organize the machines on the shop floor. While he had gained a better understanding of the varying workloads on each machine and how parts moved between machines, identifying similarities among so many different routings seemed an insurmountable task.

Decrypting the Product Mix

That was in August 2007, 3 months before Mr. Gleich attended the Job Shop Lean Conference at The Ohio State University where he would meet Dr. Irani, the organizer of the 3-day event. Afterwards, Mr. Gleich was convinced that he was on the right track with his idea of process families. "Dr. Irani's presentation crystallized everything in my mind, and we really hit it off".

The relationship paid dividends. By February of 2008, Dr. Irani had visited G&G multiple times to evaluate the operation and conduct Lean seminars for employees and managers. By Spring, the shop had implemented PFAST and begun the process of organizing its machines into hybrid flow cells to ensure efficient routing of its diverse parts. The PFAST outputs helped to prioritize the most important jobs and segment the product mix into routing families – this was the essential information that was key for developing an efficient shop floor layout for G&G's machine shop. The first step is to input the necessary data into PFAST, including each part's number, routing sequence, annual production quantity, and annual revenue.

In a case like G&G's involving large numbers of different jobs, PFAST analyzes a representative sample of parts that prioritizes the most important work, as opposed to the entire mix. To aid in selecting such a sample, the software segments the part mix via a process known as PQ$ Analysis, where "P" represents the part, "Q" represents Annual Production Quantity, and "$" represents Annual Revenue. Each part is displayed in its appropriate position on a scatter plot, with Quantity plotted along the X axis and Revenue plotted along the Y axis. Dividing the plot into four quadrants reveals which parts are high quantity/high revenue, which are low quantity/high revenue, and so on. Each segment of the product mix merits a different layout and manufacturing strategy.

Then, PFAST uses a series of algorithms to compare the routing sequences of each part within the PQ$ Analysis sample. The software groups clusters of parts that share similar routings into potential process families that could be produced more efficiently by co-locating certain machines or workstations together in a cellular configuration. The PFAST Analysis Report supports analysis to suggest whether a shop would be best served by a traditional cellular or hybrid cellular layout (more on that below). If there is significant overlap among the potential cells, and if that overlap involves expensive machines that must be shared between them, hybrid cells are likely the best choice. This is typically the case for HMLV job shops, as it was for G&G.

Focusing on Value

Nonetheless, even in a job shop like G&G, some jobs do occur with enough frequency to merit production in a traditional, U-shaped cell composed of dedicated resources that could be justified because the part (or parts) it produces are in sufficiently high volumes throughout the year. For example, Figure 24.4 shows one such cell that is dedicated solely to production of one of G&G's "runners", a forged, silicate iron component for the rail industry. Parts like this, which typically involve 35 weeks per year or more of production time, are classified as "runners". It consists of VMCs (Vertical Machining Centers) from Miyano and Mori Seiki, as well as a lathe from Intertech.

Figure 24.4   U-shaped cell dedicated solely to one of G&G's "Runners".

However, runners are rare at G&G. These jobs at the other end of the spectrum, known as "strangers", are characterized by erratic, unpredictable demand and are ill-suited for extensive efficiency boosting efforts. The backbone of the shop's work – and the primary focus of its Lean efforts – are "repeaters", jobs for which demand is somewhat regular but not sufficiently periodic to justify dedicated cells.

As such, repeaters made up the majority of the part sample G&G selected with the aid of PQ$ Analysis. The shop's hybrid cells, organized around the most frequent part routings within the sample, standardized the process for producing these jobs. The fact that G&G emphasized that improving the process for repeaters illustrates a key point: The sample selected for PFAST analysis should consist of parts that represent the highest value for the shop. Any layout change should be geared toward streamlining production of parts that generate the most profit. "Sometimes, Lean practices can force you to do all the right things around all the wrong stuff", Mr. Gleich says. "It's not just about Lean, it's about running a business and providing a compelling offer for the market".

On the surface, basing facility layout on only a portion of the total product mix might seem counterintuitive. Would not comparing routings for all parts result in a more efficient overall layout for any machine shop? What this logic fails to take into account is the fact that the selected sample of high-value jobs typically represents a disproportionate share of both total production volume and total revenue. That was certainly the case at G&G. Moreover, products not included in the sample might have similar or identical routings to their higher-priority cousins. G&G could have pursued the customers who ordered those parts to increase purchased quantities, possibly by making them a preferred vendor to outsource to.

A Different Kind of Cell

The end result of G&G's efforts to streamline flow was the implementation of hybrid cells. A hybrid cell combines the flexibility of a process layout, in which machines of similar types are grouped together, with the low throughput times and work-in-process levels of dedicated cells. The idea is to realize the advantages of producing part families identified by PFAST in cells while also maintaining flexibility by keeping shared machine types close to one another. G&G's shop now contains six of these flexible cells, each arranged for a separate process family identified by PFAST.

One such cell used for G&G's higher-value, medium-sized, and large-sized turning and milling work is perhaps the best example. The most obvious difference between this cell and its more common, dedicated brethren is that the cell isn't shaped like a "U". Rather, it consists of two parallel lines of machines, each containing identical equipment (in all, the cell contains two opposing VMCs and two opposing lathes, and the part family shares a single Horizontal Machining Center). Rather than being bunched together, as is the case in most dedicated cells, the machines are spaced far enough apart to allow parts to flow in and out at various points along the perimeter of the cell.

The logic behind this design is to avoid the set "in" and "out" points common to most U-shaped cells. This cell shape enables streamlined production of various parts that share similar, but not necessarily identical, routings. For example, one part might flow from the lathe to the mill, while another might flow from the mill to the lathe. If one of those machines is occupied, the part can be processed on the identical machine on the opposing side of the cell. Enabling work to enter the cell at any point, flow down one side or the other, and cross the aisle as-needed helps ensure timely, efficient production of a variety of parts with only one thing in common: the processes used to produce them.

Another example of a hybrid cell is shown in Figure 24.5, which is a cell for smaller turn and mill work. This cell consists of two bar-fed lathes

Figure 24.5 **Hybrid cell to machine smaller turned and milled parts.**

on either end with one milling machine and one chucking lathe in the middle. Similar to the "mirror" cell described above, work can enter and exit from either side. A variety of such mini-cells can be created on demand. Having multiple types of the same kinds of machines helps ensure that, if one machine in the cell is occupied, then an order can be loaded on other machines of the same type that are all located in close proximity within a compact space. "Whether we're turning or milling, it's set up to flow parts between each machine in the area with a minimal amount of work stoppage", Mr. Gleich says. This hybrid cell enables the shop's smaller turning and milling work to flow in and out at any point, depending on the machining requirements of each order. Also, the compact footprint of the cell minimizes walking times for the operator(s) and ensures that a machine will be open even if others are occupied.

Figure 24.6 illustrates how G&G had designed their hybrid cells to be reconfigurable by having minimum equipment that is bolted to the ground. The sign INCOMING MATERIAL is mounted on a pedestal that is light and easy to move. Also, the rack behind it is on wheels. Thereby, work can flow in and out of the cell at any point according to the requirements of a given job, especially if a customer sends a large order that necessitate the use of a 3′ × 3′ wooden pallet to be kept on the floor or on a wheeled table.

Figure 24.6   Mobile accessories that promote flexible workflow inside a hybrid cell.

Quoting Intelligently

Organizing hybrid cells around process families based on similar part routings has led to lead time improvements ranging from 40% to 50% and productivity improvements ranging from 20% to 25%, depending on the job. However, G&G's Lean reorganization has led to more intangible benefits, as well. A prime example is the fact that the shop has greater assurance that it can produce incoming work just as efficiently as long-standing jobs. That is because G&G's hybrid cells are sufficiently flexible to produce a wide range of parts, as evidenced by the benefits already realized on current and past work. Considering the limited number of machining operations around which these cells are based, any new job will likely fit into an existing process family. With this in mind, the company has endeavored to teach its sales force how to evaluate potential jobs in light of the Lean cells it has implemented. In addition to helping develop an appropriate quote, this can keep the cells fed with work that is likely to be the right cost for the customer and the right profit margin for G&G, even when demand for jobs in certain process families drops off.

Of course, this also ensures that the shop sticks to work it feels it can produce at a competitive advantage while still providing the flexibility to pursue a diverse mix of jobs. "The more work we find that we can successfully produce in these cells, the better", Mr. Gleich says. "Know thyself! It is just as important to be good at 'no' quoting and rejecting jobs that do not fit the cells' capabilities – it keeps us focused on what we do best".

Beyond Flow

Organizing parts into process families and implementing hybrid cells to streamline routings has fundamentally transformed G&G's business. There is no reason why other contract manufacturers cannot pursue similar Lean implementation strategies. However, while optimizing flow is the foundation of Job Shop Lean, further efficiency gains are available to shops that are willing to take the next step, says Andy Glaser of Ellison Technologies (West Chester, Ohio).

Mr. Glaser says that the next step after implementing a cell is automation. At first glance, automation might appear to be beneficial only for similar parts produced in high quantities. Mr. Glaser points out that, similar to Lean, this is not necessarily the case. The implementation might be different than in a large, assembly-type operation, but the essential goals of automating processes still apply. "Automation does not have to involve a 6-axis robot", he explains. "It can be anything that limits operator involvement, such as incorporating part probing within a machining process, changing from manual to hydraulic fixturing, or installing a bar feeder to an existing turning center, to name a few examples".

However, he emphasized that flow should come first. Automating a process would provide limited benefit if a bottleneck occurred during a part's journey to or from that stage in its production. That said, once a shop has streamlined its part flows, it can set about identifying such manual tasks as deburring, welding, gaging, and the like that might be good candidates for automation. Another option might be incorporating multi-tasking machine tools to combine operations currently being performed on separate machines.

Like Mr. Gleich at G&G, Mr. Glaser met Dr. Irani at one of the Annual Job Shop Lean Conferences that he held at The Ohio State University. He would end up collaborating with Dr. Irani to present his ideas about implementing automation as a follow-up to optimizing flow at future Job Shop Lean conferences.

Perhaps more significantly, Mr. Glaser strove to bring the Job Shop Lean message to customers in his role at Ellison, which distributes and services equipment from Mori Seiki and Fanuc Robotics. This was in keeping with a core principle guiding the distributor's business. "Ellison is committed to educating manufacturers about strategies to improve productivity before selling them on new equipment", he says. "Once they get the fundamental message, then we talk about new equipment and automation".

Appendices

Appendices for this chapter are available for download at https://www.crcpress.com/9781498740692

Supplementary Reading

The PowerPoint presentation titled *Introducing JobshopLean at Hardy Machine & Design Inc.* describes work that I did in 2014 for Hardy Machine & Design Inc., a CNC (Computer Numerical Control) machine shop located in Houston, TX. I was ably assisted by a graduate IE (Industrial Engineering) student intern from the University of Houston. Unlike G&G Mfg. Co., the co-owners of this job shop felt that their product mix and demand were too volatile to merit the implementation of cells to produce fixed part families. Their marching orders to us were as follows, "Go and find any and every opportunity that you can find that merits our consideration (and investment). Then we will decide if any idea is something that we wish to immediately implement or defer to the future". In particular, they were interested in consolidating the existing two buildings into one and leasing the vacated building to another business.

Chapter 25

Implementation of Job Shop Lean Using a One-Cell-at-a-Time Approach

Acknowledgment

This chapter is based on the work that I did when I was the Director of IE (Industrial Engineering) Research at Hoerbiger Corporation of America. This was my first industry job and a golden opportunity given to me by Hannes Hunschofsky, who was then the President of Hoerbiger Corporation of America. He invited (and challenged!) me to pilot the implementation of Job Shop Lean in their Houston, TX, facility. Had it not been for this job, I would never be where I am today – in industry doing hands-on projects to put my research into practice. Thank you, Hannes!

Background

The initial approach to give Lean training to employees consisted of a weekly 1-hour training session delivered to the following group of employees:

- Supervisors of these departments: Machining and Molding
- Team leader from each of these manufacturing cells: QRC (Quick Response Cell), Power Rings, CNC (Computer Numerical Control)-machined Packings, Manual Packings, and Piston Rider Rings

- Team leader of each of these support departments: Maintenance, Receiving, and Shipping.

This approach was ineffective. It assumed that employees would automatically get engaged and voluntarily undertake improvement projects of their choice. Wrong! Between meeting daily production goals set by their supervisor versus working on a side project with an unknown WIIIFM (What Is In It For Me?), you can guess what they preferred to do. Also, it took me considerable time to conduct weekly audits of each department/cell to assess if the attendees had put to work what they had been taught. A different approach was needed! This led to the creation of the Tiger Team. Why "Tiger"? Because we wanted to take big bites out of the waste that existed in the shop and in the front office!

Initial Composition of the Tiger Team

The team was designed to include (i) managers who were well-versed in the concepts, methods, and Continuous Improvement (CI) tools and had prior experience with Lean implementation, (ii) shop employees who had demonstrated an enthusiasm and some prior exposure to Lean or other variation of CI, and (iii) office staff from departments in the front office, such as Customer Service, Purchasing, Design, Engineering, and Sales/Marketing, who wanted to learn about Lean. Based on these criteria, the following employees were selected initially to be on the team:

- Andrew R. (Warehouse and Inventory Supervisor): Team Leader
- Shahrukh Irani (Director, IE Research): Team Facilitator, Subject Matter Expert (SME)
- Anthony H.(Materials Manager): Team Facilitator, SME
- Guenther B. (Global Project Manager): SME
- Shane B. (Customer Service): Volunteer from his/her department
- James "Rojo" B. (Molding Department): Volunteer from his/her department
- Kenny P. (Power Ring Cell): Volunteer from his/her department
- Shafel C. (Shipping): Volunteer from his/her department.

Later, the above composition of the Tiger Team was revised. The SMEs were retained. However, some of the original members were replaced by other employees from the shop and office. They went through the same foundation training and process of learn-by-doing often in a different cell or department. The results obtained and the feedback we got from several team members suggested that this new approach to rapidly teach employees to undertake CI projects was viable!

Schedule of Activities

The initial plan called for the Tiger Team to meet at least once a week for a period of 3 months. Each meeting usually consisted of two parts:

- First, an SME would make a presentation to the rest of the team on a basic problem-solving method/tool that is frequently used by CI teams.
- Next, the team would go to a particular area in the shop. There they would engage and collaborate with the employees in that area to apply the method/tool they had just learned. The goal was to improve the workspace and/or the work processes performed in that area.
- After each meeting, the team members would continue to do their "homework" leading up to the next week's meeting.

This weekly routine continued in that particular area for the entire period of 3 months, or until sufficient improvements had been made in that area to justify ceasing work there.

The Tiger Team's First Project

Our group was a mix of talented individuals drawn from different departments who wanted the team's first project to benefit the company at many levels. The team was confident that it could (i) reengineer daily work processes and (ii) redesign the work system to eliminate waste in any manufacturing cell or department. But where to do our first project in order to have a clear-cut impact on business performance also? That dilemma was soon solved for us. As part of a massive supply chain reorganization, corporate decided that Hoerbiger Corporation of Texas (HCA-TX) would build a certain family of products in the existing "CA Cell". This cell built assemblies using machined parts that were being sourced from our sister plant in Pompano Beach, FL. Now that HCA-TX would be responsible for the entire

Value Stream of the "CA Assembly", the Tiger Team's project had the right focus! Our goal would be to understand how the CA Cell worked, document how it currently operated, and determine what it would take to design a more efficient and effective assembly cell.

Ground Rules for the Tiger Team

- Everyone has an equal say – No pulling rank or position.
- There is no single answer for any problem.
- Learn by doing – It is okay to fail as long as you try and try again to get a better result.
- Every idea is good – Just prove that it *really* is good.
- Ask five Why?'s if you think that the work system cannot be improved.
- Maintain a positive attitude – Avoid blaming anyone or anything.
- Keep an open mind to change.
- Practice mutual respect – Treat others the same way that you would have them treat you.

What We Did in the Team's Weekly Meetings

On November 13, 2012, the Tiger Team met for the first time in the upstairs training room. The COO (Chief Operating Officer) led off with a presentation explaining the rationale and strategic reasons for formation of the team. Next, Anthony H. and I explained the objectives and ground rules for team governance. Although ROI (Return On Investment) was not stressed as a metric, we did emphasize that the team should keep an eye out for improvement ideas that had tangible impact on Safety, Ergonomics, Quality, and Operating Cost. The choice of the CA Cell as the first area where the team would go to work was revealed. The meeting ended with a Q&A (Question & Answer) session during which time the COO, Team Leader (Andrew R.), and Co-Facilitators addressed the doubts, concerns, etc. of the other members.

On November 16, 2012, the Tiger Team met again. They received a 30-minute lecture on the basics of kaizen (What does it mean to "do a kaizen?" Why is it important that a kaizen be done in the "gemba" where the actual work is being done? and so on). The Plan-Do-Check-Act cycle of CI was also mentioned to put the team at ease that it was okay if any idea did not pan out. At the same time, simple ideas that could quickly be implemented were definitely encouraged. Next, the team was shown the *Toast Kaizen* video (source: www.gbmp.org) which is extremely effective for explaining key concepts: (i) Work is a process that consists of discrete steps; (ii) these steps can be value-adding, necessary-but-not-value-adding, and non-value-adding; and (iii) every step that is producing one or more of the Seven Types of Waste should be scrutinized for improvement. It was stressed that results could be achieved *simply* by recognizing and eliminating or reducing the wastes in the CA Cell (see Figure 25.1). After the lecture was over, the team walked to the CA Cell. Every member had received a notepad and was asked to quietly observe the employees working in the cell, assess the overall layout of the cell, etc. Their assignment was to record each and every instance of waste that they observed. They were clearly instructed that, while they were welcome to communicate with the employees in the cell, that they could not discuss/communicate anything with another member of the Tiger Team. After about 15 minutes inside the CA Cell, the entire team returned to the meeting room upstairs. Each member was invited to write on the whiteboard the different instances of waste that they had noted (see Figure 25.2).

In subsequent meetings, the SMEs taught the team about Value Stream Mapping, Process Mapping, Flow Diagrams, Assembly Operations Process

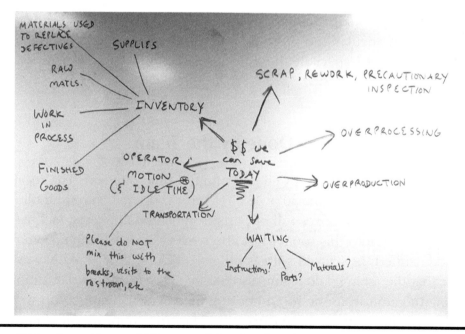

Figure 25.1 Seven Types of Waste explained to the Tiger Team.

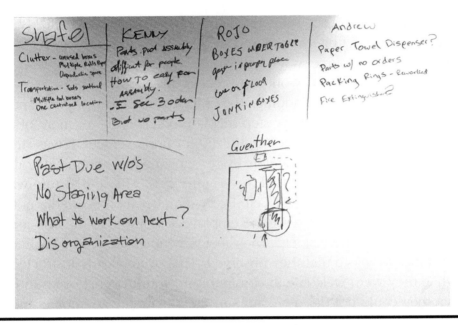

Figure 25.2 Wastes in the CA Cell recorded by the Tiger Team.

Charts, BOM (Bill Of Material), Five Whys, Ishikawa Diagrams, Cellular Manufacturing, etc. After each tool was taught, it was used for analysis of the Current State of the CA Cell. Every one of these tools yielded a wealth of information on the current condition of the CA Cell and helped to identify opportunities to streamline the work being done by the two employees in the cell. In particular, the potential for worker injury due to handling of heavy components, especially the fully assembled unit, was immediately recognized.

Improvement Projects Done by the Team

Sort (the first S in 5S): The CA Cell had one full-time operator. The room that housed it measured just 30′ × 15′! Yet, over the years, several toolboxes, cabinets, tables, racks, boxes full of parts from various projects, etc. had "found their way into this room". Just about every surface in the room was crammed, stuffed, or stacked with "stuff" (see Figure 25.3). It really was no wonder that the team could claim resounding success on that day simply by removing the junk from the room housing the CA Cell. Teaming up with the full-time operator and the floater from the Machine Shop, we filled numerous trashcans and quarantined items for other departments to review before

Figure 25.3 "Stuff" that covered *Every* surface in the CA Cell.

disposal. If any item was owned by a person still working at the company, it was placed outside the CA Cell with that person's name written all over it. An email was sent to him/her to kindly collect their property from that location outside the cell. This phase of 5S was sorely needed to clear the mess in the cell and ensure that other departments (or individuals) did not continue to use it as a dumping ground! The removal of unused or unneeded tooling helped to consolidate the remaining tooling that would be used in the cell into a single mobile toolbox that was purchased for the cell.

Shine (the second S in 5S): We wanted the cell to impress customers and visitors touring our facility as soon as they entered from the lobby onto the production floor. Among the many enhancements that our Maintenance department made were several coats of epoxy for the floor, fresh new paint for the walls, the ceiling tiles were fixed, and an array of bright ceiling lights were mounted right above the assembly tables after they were repositioned in the new layout. Later, we planned to install a digital clock inside the cell, and outside its entrance, mount a framed photograph of the main product that the cell assembled. Beside that product's photograph, we planned to post the autographed photographs of the two employees who worked in the cell, in order to reinforce their pride and identity working in the cell.

Set (the third S in 5S): There is a reason why the success of Lean in any production system depends on the layout, regardless of whether it is a single workstation, a single machine, a cell, a machine shop, or an entire factory. Flow is achieved (or not achieved) because of a good (or bad) layout, respectively. In the case of our CA Cell, the initial layout of the cell had tables and shelves lined along the walls. A large table with lighting and racks on it sat in the middle of the room. Several small tables and benches were scattered all over the room. Assembly was not done on a single table; instead, several incomplete assemblies, rework, and other projects in differing phases of completion were strewn throughout the room. The Tiger Team spent several consecutive weeks just standing around the cell and watching how work was done (or delayed) in the cell. During one meeting, we mapped the movements of the main assembly operator from start to finish of a complete assembly cycle (Spaghetti Diagram). After every session inside the cell, the team would reconvene upstairs. The good ideas started pouring out! The large table in the middle had become a crutch. It had good lighting and that was the only reason it was being used. Next, we found that about half of the assembly steps were being performed along one wall, and the rest of the assembly steps along the other wall. A couple of steps were even being done on the small tables in the middle of the room! All of these problems were solved simply by implementing an assembly line flow that required placement of two tables side-by-side and moving the toolbox, fixtures, and gauges onto them, or adjacent to them at point-of-use (POU) locations. In turn, this freed up the space inside the cell. Now, material that was earlier staged in carts kept outside the cell could be positioned in a two-cart queue just inside the entrance to the cell. Also, we knew that other departments, particularly our supervisors, needed an area inside the cell to work on special projects. To address this need, we added a rework/project table, as well as a staging rack for jobs and parts needing further attention. Thereby, anyone doing support work inside the CA Cell no longer needed to worry about interfering with the core assembly work being done in the cell. Figure 25.4 shows the Before and After layouts for the CA Cell.

Safety and ergonomics in the workplace: Watching the operator lift each heavy final assembly and hold it up during shrink-wrapping, often turning it around while doing that, raised a red flag. So the new layout included a jib crane and an automatic shrink-wrapping machine to wrap each final assembly before it was placed on a cart, and the cart was rolled into the Shipping department. Anti-fatigue mats were bought to reduce standing fatigue for the operator. The ceiling drop for the air hose was repositioned to reduce both the travel and exertion by the operator to pull the hose when he wanted to blow air into the product assembly to expel metal chips and other debris.

Inventory rationalization: The cell carried inventory of many items that were used in the final product (see Figure 25.5). We found that the inventory

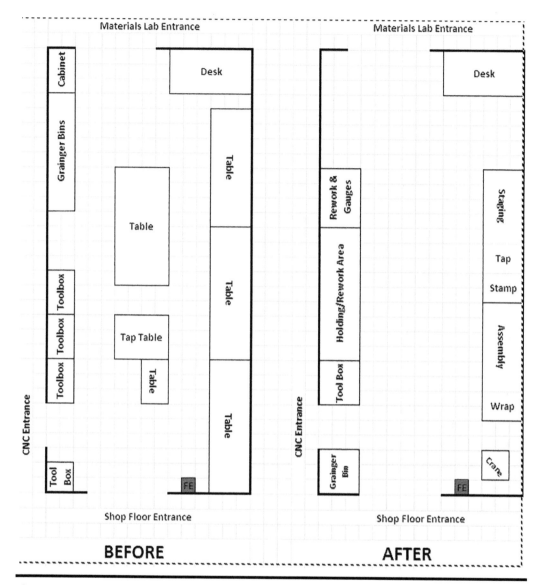

Figure 25.4   Before vs. After layouts for the CA Cell.

of these items was poorly maintained and controlled. BOMs and/or drawings for an order would be wrong. Fortunately, our expert operator was himself correcting these issues. To ensure accuracy and quality we pulled all of our gaskets, O-rings, and tie rod stock out of the cell into a controlled environment. Now, only kits of the correct items were delivered to the cell at the time of assembly. This also allowed the operator to inform if a BOM or drawing was incorrect which permitted the front office to fix the problems immediately. This also resulted in an accurate and complete BOM for reuse

Figure 25.5 Inventory of gaskets, rings, etc., used in the final product.

when the particular product configuration was ordered again. After a few months not only were our inventories accurate but we could ensure better quality of our final product.

The product(s) assembled in the CA Cell also required fasteners. Our part number Rolodex contained about fifty different nuts, bolts, washers, and plugs. What we found was that we were actually stocking 150 different part numbers. Obviously something was wrong! To eliminate this issue, we teamed up with our MRO (Maintenance, Repair and Overhaul) supplier (Grainger). We started from scratch and planned our inventory levels based on current drawings. This ensured that the engineering group was included in the feedback loop if drawing revisions were made to include new types of fasteners. We set reasonable minimum/maximum inventory levels for each fastener and labeled each fastener bin with a picture of the part, dimensions, Grainger reference number, and most importantly, our ERP (Enterprise Resource Planning) Reference Number. This way there was no room left for error, ensuring that we procured and used the correct fasteners.

Figure 25.6 shows the new layout for the CA Cell after all upgrades were completed.

Integrated product and process design (IPPD): Each CA assembly used threaded tie rods for shipping and installation purposes. We found that we were procuring smooth rods, threading them ourselves, and then cutting them down to size. This was all being done during assembly and wasted

Figure 25.6 New layout for CA Cell.

the operator's time. He would start assembly, see that he needed tie rods, stop work, thread the rods, and cut each to specification, then complete the assembly. Initially, we relocated the saw used to cut the tie rods to size adjacent to the CA Cell. Since this reduced the walking time for the operator, he used this time to make tie rods to fill the buffer kept in the cell. The buffer allowed him to work uninterrupted on the assembling product for a significant portion of the shift. Later, per a team member's idea, we decided to procure the threaded tie rods, which eliminated the threading and sawing operations. Also, the threaded rod was less expensive than the smooth variant that we used to buy.

Splitting a large order batch into transfer batches: We found that most of our order quantities for the CA product were small (less than ten units). On occasion, we received large orders of fifty or more. Why do you think we had all those tables packed into the single room that housed the CA Cell? They had been placed there to hold the entire batch for that occasional large order! Why was this the case? Because the traditional approach to batch assembly is to do the assembly of ALL the assembled units in batch mode one part at a time! After the Tiger Team implemented their changes, now instead of running a large order as a single batch, we would use our ERP system to split an order and issue multiple transfer batches linked to the same order. For starters, we simply split a large order into (smaller) transfer batches. Each transfer batch was one half, sometimes even one quarter, the order quantity that was shipped. This use of transfer batches made all in-house activities related to the Value Stream for the "CA Cell" more manageable. If a large order batch was to be assembled, we would start the order using on-hand inventory of components and issue a production request for the additional components early enough so they arrived in time to complete the order batch. Even the Shipping department got an early start on packaging a particular CA order. They allocated a table specifically for packaging CA Cell product. As soon as the CA Cell pushed one cart loaded with a transfer batch into Shipping, those assemblies would get packaged for shipment. Meanwhile, the next cart full of assemblies would be getting filled across the aisle that separated the CA Cell from the Shipping department.

Kit carts: Each cart would carry the entire kit of parts needed to assemble a single CA assembly, or a transfer batch for the same product. If there were shortages on the cart, the stores personnel could visually detect them. In the short term, we had to continue to receive machined parts (the cups and flanges that go into the final product assembly) from Florida. Each case is built from a specific list of parts, i.e., X pieces of Cup X and 1 piece of Flange Y. However, analysis of our ERP records showed that we may get one cup on Monday, one cup on Tuesday, another on Thursday, and the last one next Monday. Guess when assembly began? Only when that last cup in the complete kit per the product's assembly BOM would arrive next Monday! So we discussed with our sister plant in Florida how their machining cells could coordinate the completion times of the components in order to ship a complete kit of components for a CA assembly. We wanted the complete kit to arrive at our facility on a date that left enough days for us to fully assemble the final product leaving a 1-day buffer for the Shipping department. Figure 25.7 shows a kit cart placed outside the CA Cell. Appendix 1 for this chapter presents more examples of kit carts that we have implemented in several different client companies.

In the future, the CA Cell was expected to be more flexible and assemble a larger number of variants of the CA product. To achieve this mixed model production, the cell would pull from a parts supermarket that would be sized and configured to carry min/max inventories of parts used in the popular product configurations. In turn, the parts taken from this supermarket would be pulled from a supermarket in our Florida facility. That supermarket was replenished by different machining cells in that facility. Soon, to eliminate the supermarket in FL, we repurposed some of the machines in our TX facility to in-source work from the machining cells in FL.

Figure 25.7 Kit cart for a CA unit outside the CA Cell.

Lessons Learned

How much training to give employees? Management agreed that the Tiger Team members be given an in-depth training on Lean and Six Sigma. The basic curriculum that I had designed had at its core the Lean and Six Sigma tools used when implementing the *Quick-Start Approach to Job Shop Lean*. The plan was for all Tiger Team members to go through this in-house Lean Six Sigma curriculum. But, a half-day per week was simply not sufficient to do both the training and the floor application of that training. Plus, the employees in the team had the standard question, "WIIIFM?" They expected "something more" than the learning and a Certificate of Achievement to enroll in and complete this training program.

Key performance indicators (KPIs): The failure to have a higher goal of achieving financially meaningful metrics was our biggest failing. In our defense, this project that the team undertook was the first ever Lean implementation that had been attempted at HCA-TX! So we did the right thing by avoiding vague/subjective goals, such as "Improve Quality, Cost, and Delivery" or "Improve the 5Ss of our Business" (**S**atisfaction of customers, employees, and suppliers, **S**afety of employees, customers, and the environment, **S**peed with which orders are fulfilled, **S**ales, and **S**avings from cost reduction without workforce reduction). Looking back, we should have defined metrics like the ones that our COO, Don Y., shared with us that he had set for the company:

■ Reduce total value of late orders below $100k per month.
■ Reduce scrap and rework costs by 50%.
■ Improve or maintain production efficiency (=Worked Hours/Earned Hours) at our bottlenecks.
■ Increase monthly shipments to $2 million without increasing Direct and/or Indirect Labor.

Cell performance display board: The plan was to have a whiteboard on which would be mounted SQDIC charts (S = Safety, Q = Quality, D = Delivery, I = Inventory, Cost = Cost), A3 Reports on improvement ideas, and a photograph of each cell member. But should the cell operators be marking up charts or assembling product that could be shipped out the door? Besides, the cell's performance was at the mercy of on-time delivery of parts from FL. So we did the right thing by doing the basic improvements to first stabilize cell performance after which its performance could be tracked using financial metrics.

Compensation for team members: Surprisingly, while we offered low-cost ideas for rewards (T-shirts, lunches, reserved parking spots for a month, etc.), senior management wanted to link selection to the Tiger Team and significance of project results to promotions, overtime pay, and bonuses. The idea was socialized with Human Resources for approval. But there was a happy ending to this project because senior management made a mention about the Tiger Team at the company's Global Production Conference that was held later that year!

What comes first – Lean or Job Shop Lean? It really does not matter! This project was my first Job Shop Lean implementation in industry. We did some things right and we did some things wrong. Still, we made tangible improvements in the performance of a cell. Above all, the two employees who worked in the cell really appreciated the changes that were made, especially related to ergonomics and layout. My epiphany was that it does not matter whether what was implemented was "Lean" or "Job Shop Lean". All that mattered was that beneficial changes were made using methods that worked and solved the problems that they were applied to! I will unhesitatingly say this today – If you desire to improve an existing assembly cell, let alone design and implement a new work cell in a machine shop, expect to

Table 25.1   Lean Tools That Will (or Will Not) Work in Most Job Shops

Tools That Will *Work in Most Job Shops*	*Tools That* May Not *Work in Most Job Shops*
Strategic planning	Value Stream Mapping
Top-down leadership	Assembly line balancing
Employee involvement	One-piece flow cells
5S	Product-specific Kanbans
Total productive maintenance (TPM)	FIFO (First In First Out) sequencing at work centers
Setup reduction (SMED)	Pacemaker scheduling
Error-proofing (Poka-Yoke)	Inventory supermarkets
Quality at source	Work order release based on pitch
Visual controls/visual management	Production based on level loading (Heijunka)
Product and process standardization	Mixed model production with Takt Time
Single-function (inflexible) machines	**Single-function (inflexible) machines**
Jidoka	Plan for Every Product (PFEP)
Right-sized machines	
Standard work	

first use (i) Value Stream Mapping and (ii) all the Lean tools in the left-hand column of Table 25.1. Yes, there could be a need for sophisticated computer models down the road. But, at the outset, when it is most important to "sell changes" to employees and management, just do the basics really well!

The Next Cell That the Tiger Team Worked On

The Manual Packings Cell (MPC Cell) was selected for the next Tiger Team project. Of the four employees on the original Tiger Team, only Kenny P. was retained. Dhananjay P. (a graduate intern from the University of Texas at Arlington) and Phillip N. (he was the floater employee who worked part-time in the CA Cell) were added to the team. This time around, it was decided to include key employees from the MPC Cell in the Tiger Team. Our project began with the Sort and Shine phases of 5S in the week of April 15, 2013. The three managers – Andrew R., Anthony H., and Guenther B. – worked with us during the afternoon every week.

Appendices

Appendices for this chapter are available for download at https://www. crcpress.com/9781498740692

Chapter 26

Educational and Training Resources for Job Shop Lean

Background

FLean (Flexible+Lean) cells are the foundation for implementing Job Shop Lean in any complex high-mix low-volume (HMLV) facility. The core steps in the process for implementing Job Shop Lean in any HMLV facility requires its leadership to (i) identify the stable part families in their product mix, (ii) implement an FLean manufacturing cell to produce each part family that has a stable demand, and (iii) utilize Finite Capacity Scheduling to schedule the daily operations in each cell. But, after they are done with the design and implementation of each FLean cell and its support systems, the real challenge of implementing the cell lies in educating and training cell employees and company managers to embrace a new way of working together. For example, if a cell is to operate as an Autonomous Business Unit (ABU), the cell's team must be given the full responsibility for fulfilling all customer orders loaded on their cell. Is company management prepared to allow that? This chapter describes strategies and examples of the available resources that can be used to educate and train people (i) about Lean (in general) and (ii) FLean cells (in particular).

Learning Lean from Other Manufacturers

Sometimes all that it takes to get the people in your own company fired up about Lean is for them to see how other companies have succeeded with Lean. Successful implementation of Lean does not always have to be a complete bolt-by-bolt rearrangement of the entire facility! Even seeing the results of Continuous Improvement (CI) events done by employees in another company can get your own employees fired up.

Learning Lean from Videos

Some of the inspirational videos that create a basic awareness about Lean are:

- The Society of Manufacturing Engineers (www.SME.org) offers several videos such as *Introduction to Lean Manufacturing* (DV03PUB46), *Lean Manufacturing at Miller SQA* (DV03PUB47), and *Lean Manufacturing at TAC* (DV03PUB48)
- The Greater Boston Manufacturing Partnership (GBMP, www.gbmp.org) has developed a mini-library of videos that feature some of their successful clients, such as Jotul, Madico, The Gem Group, VIBCO, AbioMed, etc.

Please do not rely solely only on videos to educate and train people in your company about Lean. At some point, you have to demonstrate that you, the in-house Lean expert, know a lot more than what is taught in those videos. So be prepared to frequently stop any video and explain details that are not displayed or verbalized in the video. For example, when a video shows a shadow board for tools, stop the video and explain that, for a shadow board to fulfill its purpose, every operator should commit to never return a broken tool on the board and walk away.

Learning Lean from Doing Facility Walkthroughs

Nothing is better than seeing actual examples of the Seven Types of Waste[1,2] in your own facility. Just take along a video camera to record your entire facility walkthrough![3] However, it is important that you plan this walk based on the routing of a key component (or product), or better yet, an entire part family that you make. Figure 26.1a shows the manufacturing path followed

---

[1] If you are interested in free videos on how to do a facility walkthrough and conduct an effective morning meeting to report your observations, you may find helpful these YouTube videos with the following titles: (i) *Morning Improvement Walk* and (ii) *Lean, The Morning Meeting at FastCap.*

[2] There are numerous forms of waste but I have found that most of them can be reduced to the original Seven Types of Waste – Overproduction, Transportation, Scrap/Rework, Operator Motion, Overprocessing, Waiting, and Inventory.

[3] A more advanced version of a facility walkthrough is the Gemba Walk.

by a forged part. The locations of the different machines that feature in that part's routing and the sequence in which they are used are shown on the Spaghetti Diagram that depicts the actual travel of the forging. *To capture the wastes **between** all pairs of consecutive operations*, stand at the location of each operation, look in the direction of the location where the next operation will be done, and take a photograph. For example, Figure 26.1b captures the distance of travel and the absence of Line Of Sight (LOS = 0) between the locations of Operation #1 (the partially shown building on the right in the photo) and Operation #2 (the building on the left in the photo). How many of the Seven Types of Waste are caused by the transportation between these two consecutive operations to produce the forging?

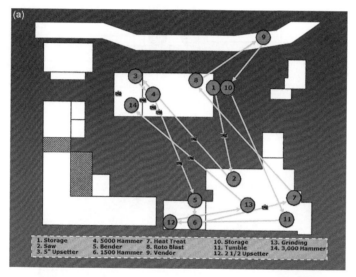

Figure 26.1 **(a) Spaghetti Diagram for a single forged component. (b) Wastes due to transportation between consecutive operations.**

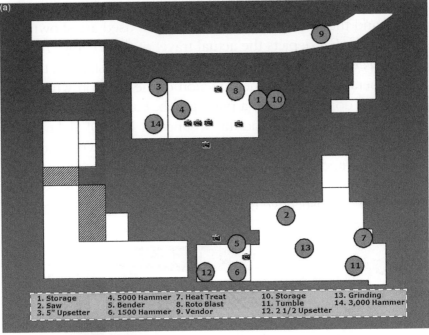

Figure 26.2   (a) Locations at or near different machines where wastes were photographed. (b) Wastes due to inefficient storage of raw materials.

Next, *to capture the wastes **at** the location of every operation*, stand at the location of each operation and take a wide-angle photograph[4] of the machine and its vicinity. Figure 26.2a shows different locations in the facility where I took photographs related to the machines used to make the

---

[4] It would be preferable to also place a video camera that can record a continuous period of operation at key machines. Yes, the operators of these machines will feel that they are being spied upon. But, their concerns can be laid to rest by simply explaining to them the purpose of the video. Better yet, organize a pizza lunch during which time they can also watch the video and learn how the Seven Types of Waste could be reduced at the different machines.

forging. For example, Figure 26.2b shows how bar stock delivered by the suppliers was stored outside the building that housed the presses. Which of the Seven Types of Waste are caused by the absence of any visual indicators to distinguish the different types of bar stock stored on the racks? The success of Lean easily depends on employee engagement and open communications.

Lean Assessment of an Operational Cell

There comes a time when it is important to demonstrate how to bring together all this education and training on Lean to design and operate an actual cell! Figures 26.3-26.9 capture the Current State of an actual operational cell. In the case of this forging cell, the bar stock was stored in a different building (LOC #1 in Figure 26.3 and transported in large tubs to the cell by a forklift (Material Handling Equipment ("MHE") in Figure 26.3. Notice that the large tubs were put down a considerable distance away from the Oven by the forklift driver? From where the cell operator stood in front of the Drop Hammer, he would walk to the tubs, pick up and cradle several billets in his hands, walk back behind the Oven, and place them one-by-one on the conveyor. Then he would walk around the Oven and wait for a heated billet to emerge from the Oven. As soon as a heated billet emerged from the oven, he would pick it up with a pair of tongs, load it into the Drop Hammer, and forge the part.

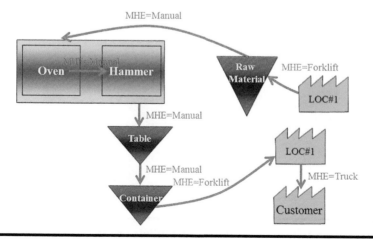

Figure 26.3   Factory-level material flow for the cell.

Figure 26.3 presents a high-level visualization of the material flow of each forging produced in this cell. Figure 26.4 is a simplified Value Stream Map to display the operational parameters for all the activities performed in the cell. Figure 26.5 shows the location where tubs full of sawn billets are delivered from another facility. Do you think that the current inter-facility logistics is wasteful? Can you point out specific instances of the traditional Seven Types of Waste in Figure 26.5? Figure 26.6 shows two tubs full of

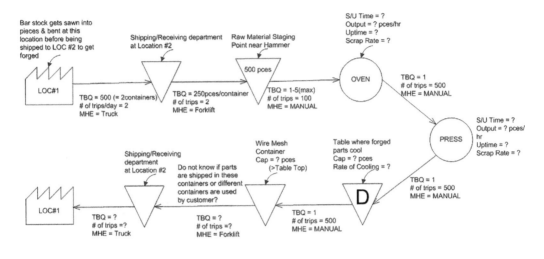

NOTE: Parts get inspected, counted, packed at location #1 from where they are shipped to the Customer!!??!!

Figure 26.4   Shopfloor-level value stream map for the cell.

Figure 26.5   Location where tubs full of sawn billets are delivered from another facility.

sawn billets that are delivered to the cell. Would you know how many billets are contained in each tub? And does that quantity relate to the daily demand that should pace the production rate of the cell? And will it be easy for the operator to reach into the tub to pick the last few billets off the bottom? Figure 26.5 shows the relative locations of two key pieces of equipment in the forging cell. The Oven needs to be used first before the Drop Hammer. But aren't their positions opposite of what the material flow dictate (because the two tubs full of billets are dropped off to the right of

Figure 26.6   Tubs full of sawn billets delivered to the cell.

Figure 26.7   Relative positions of oven and hammer in the cell.

Figure 26.8 Relative locations of WIP and finished forgings in the cell.

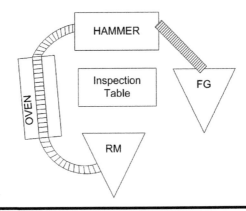

Figure 26.9 Improved layout for the cell.

the hammer)? Figure 26.8 shows the relative locations of in-process and finished forgings produced in the cell. Why do they put the forgings coming hot off the hammer to cool down on a table, and then expend labor to pick them off that table one by one and drop them into the wire mesh container. Later, they empty that wire mesh container into a sturdier tub that would be used to transport the entire batch of finished forgings to the facility that supplied the billets. **QUESTION:** Could a fixture be designed that would serve as the surface of the table but could be placed on top of the wire mesh container? That way, the operator would take hot forgings from the hammer and drop them on this surface. Then, with the palm of his hand he would sense if the hot forgings had cooled off. Once they had cooled down, he would simply tilt the fixture to drop the forgings into the container. Why unnecessarily accept the delays and costs of Waiting and Inventory wastes in the Current State? Figure 26.9 presents the improved layout that was designed for the cell to eliminate NVA (non-value added) activities. How does the circular layout of the cell eliminate Operator Motion waste?

Figures 26.3–9 should be the basis for discussion during meetings attended by all employees and managers who "touch" the cell. Indicate the "unLean" practices captured in each photo. Quantify the costs and delays due to the different wastes captured in each photo. Give everyone a chance to air their observations! Allow them to defend their actions but also encourage constructive argument to challenge those who take an "unLean" stance. If suggestions for improvement are voiced, note each idea on a Post-It and assign each idea to a person who will follow through and implement it. Seeing is believing! Believing is doing! Doing is changing (for the better)!

Videos That Provide More In-Depth Training

Having completed the preliminary Lean training, next you can teach specific Lean tools and best practices that are essential to make a cell operate like an ABU. While there are numerous commercial videos on individual Lean tools such as 5S, Setup Reduction, Cross-Training, Visual Control, Continuous Flow, etc., I know of only the following videos that I have consistently used to discuss what it will take to implement a cell that can operate as an ABU[5]:

■ *Customer Focused Manufacturing* (**Vendor:** www.sme.org, DV03PUB53): I use this video to emphasize that CI efforts must be made by everybody at all levels of the organizational hierarchy – Business → Factory → Shop → Cell → Machine. For example, at the *Business* level, this video has segments that show top executives

---

[5] If you are interested in free videos on work cells, you may find helpful these videos posted on YouTube: (i) *Why Do You Use "U" Shape Cells at FastCap?* (ii) *Manufacturing Work Cell Optimization* and (iii) *Subway is a Lean Work Cell – Be a Money Belt!*

receiving training on strategic planning to help them decide that manufacturing cells were a key component of their strategy to be globally competitive. Similarly, at the *Machine* level, this video shows error-proofing (Poka-Yoke) devices for quickly checking product quality, tools hanging within easy reach of every operator, wheeled containers designed to hold a specific number of parts ("*cart*ban"), the ergonomical (and therefore safe) way to lift heavy containers from a cart onto a rack, etc.

■ *Single-piece flow* (**Vendor:** www.sme.org, DV06PUB13): I use this video in conjunction with notes I took to document every Lean best practice that is demonstrated in the video. For example, the digital counter on the assembly machine displays the Takt Time (TT) for the cell. Although TT may not be relevant in a high-mix machining or fabrication cell, it is far more important that (i) the LED (Light Emitting Diode) display is clearly visible both to the cell operator and anyone outside the cell and (ii) it displays a single metric to evaluate cell performance. I especially like the segment on the Water Strider in this video. This person is not just a material handler but also an expeditor who ensures that orders are on-time, that replenishments signaled by kanban cards are made in time, etc.[6] Once again, I will stress that you cannot just rely on videos to teach and train your employees and managers about Lean or Job Shop Lean. Either you or someone else has to become good enough to at least be the in-house expert who will repeatedly stop these videos to offer more details about a useful tool or a best practice or a behavior trait! Personally, I find it okay to put myself under this pressure because it forces me to keep learning. And that makes me a better teacher! To date, I have never hesitated to borrow every relevant concept, tool, and system from the Lean body of knowledge and embed it into the Job Shop Lean body of knowledge. I have realized that Toyota has pioneered and continues to practice to this day an IE curriculum that we are simply not teaching in the 100+ IE departments in the United States! Even though Job Shop Lean is built on IE science, I find the proven, simple, practical tools of Lean to be invaluable.

---

[6] Please email me at ShahrukhIrani1023@yahoo.com if you are interested in the notes I have developed on this video.

Do Not Ignore *The Goal* Video!

While it never mentions Lean and despite its intimidating price tag, a video that I highly recommend to every Lean trainer, is *The Goal* (**Vendor:** www. goldratt.com). It introduced the world to Eliyahu Goldratt's Theory Of Constraints (TOC). The trouble I have with Lean's overemphasis on waste elimination pursued with employee-led kaizens is that it is very easy to unleash a frenzy of factory-wide waste elimination efforts with no overarching goal. Instead, I favor integrating TOC and Lean as follows: (i) Select a key Value Stream (or part family) and (ii) focus on eliminating waste first and foremost on the bottleneck in the Value Stream (or Value Network for the part family). Every time that I show *The Goal*, I stop the video and challenge the group to answer a question that I pick from a comprehensive list of questions that I have prepared about the video. Over the years, I have continued to check the original answer that I had written for each question in my question bank. It amazes me that others have helped me to improve almost every answer! In addition, I have added a question every time I found a new nugget of knowledge to be gained from this classic educational video.[7]

Advanced Workshops on Lean/Job Shop Lean

I find that games and simulations on Job Shop Lean are entertaining and effective for explaining concepts and strategies. But, they are incapable of teaching the methods and tools that actually *solve* the operational issues that plague HMLV manufacturers! This is why I have developed the following workshops to teach Job Shop Lean and IE enhancements of Lean tools:

- (5-day workshop) *Fundamental Methods and Tools of Lean Manufacturing*
- (1-day workshop) *IE Software to Extend the Lean Tools*
- (3-day workshop) *Fundamentals of Finite Capacity Scheduling*
- (1-day workshop) *Practical Cell Scheduling Using Scheduling Algorithms, Lean, and TOC*
- (5-day workshop) *Building an HMLV Manufacturing Facility Using Production Flow Analysis.*

---

[7] Please email me at ShahrukhIrani1023@yahoo.com if you are interested in the list of questions on the video.

If you are interested in the subject matter that is taught in any of these workshops, please email me at ShahrukhIrani1023@yahoo.com.

Conclusion

Nobody taught Toyota how to develop the revolutionary Toyota Production System on the pillars of *Just in Time* and *Respect for People*. They did it on their own! They had the confidence and internal experts who were courageous enough to learn novel problem-solving tools via a try-and-try-again process. And that is what should drive you to implement, improve, and enhance the implementation of Job Shop Lean in your HMLV manufacturing facility. Yes, it is not easy to implement Job Shop Lean. If Lean takes years to embed into a large company's culture, it takes a similar amount of time, if not more time, to truly convince the owner of a small or medium manufacturer to invest time and money, especially their own, to implement Job Shop Lean.

Supplementary Reading

How a Job Shop Developed Their In-House Training Video on Waste Elimination: One of the ways to instill desire and motivation among your employees could be to try and develop an internal video on waste elimination based on your own operations. Find an interested employee in your company and let him/her loose on this video project to kick-start your company's Lean training curriculum! The CD contains a folder that carries the video and related training materials that we developed for PR Machine Works (www.prmachineworks.com). All the content in the folder is based entirely on the video recording of a facility walkthrough that was led by their President, Mark Romanchuk, himself. The step-by-step tutorial on waste identification and elimination that was later taught to the manager team at PRMachineWorks is based entirely on this video. **Now**, what if you do not find any takers for this challenge within your employee ranks? No problem! Hire an IE intern from a local university with the necessary skills. I cannot say enough about one of my all-time favorite videos titled *A Program to Initiate Job Shop Lean at Bula Forge & Machine Inc.* that was made by Bryan Wang, a former IE graduate student at The Ohio State University. They had hired him to do a pilot project to implement Job Shop Lean in their facility. He single-handedly produced the video that documented his 3-month summer internship in a custom forge shop. Please click on this link https://vimeo.com/91520874 to see the video online.

Toast Kaizen: The *Toast Kaizen* video (**Vendor:** www.gbmp.org) is one of the best educational videos ever made on Lean. I use this video to teach the Seven Types of Waste at the start of every client engagement. In addition, I have developed a complete teaching package on problem-solving tools and production system design methodology based on this video. This teaching package shows how to utilize a variety of CI tools, such as Flow Process Chart, Spaghetti Diagram, Five Why's, Ishikawa (Cause-and-Effect) Diagram, Constraint-Driven Thinking, Tree Diagram, and Gantt Chart to improve the Toast Production System (ToPS). And now a cautionary note about this video! It is easy to conclude that the toaster is the bottleneck. But, in reality, the butter could very well be the bottleneck. That is why the teaching package includes several Gantt Charts that were produced using MS Project. The reason for doing so is because the toast-making process is a parallel process and **not** a linear process! Therefore, it is important to teach the fundamentals of Project Activity Scheduling to emphasize that waste elimination involves fundamental IE skills such as (i) reduction of the time it takes to setup and execute certain tasks, (ii) determining the best sequence in which to perform the steps in a process and (iii) investigating the possibility of executing tasks in parallel to the extent possible.

The *Single-Piece Flow*© Simulation: One of the key reasons for implementing cells is to reduce the tendency for batch production. It may not be possible to have a one-piece flow between machines in each and every cell that is implemented. But surely an Order Batch could be split into at least two (smaller) Transfer Batches in many cases? That is the primary goal of this simulation! Prior to developing this simulation, I went on YouTube and found a video titled *One-Piece Flow Versus Batch Production – Lean Manufacturing*. Please set aside some time to watch this video! Maybe you will not need to use my simulation thereafter. The complete details of the game are described in the overview that I have written for this game. Figure 26.10 provides a template for the part's route sheet that you could use for this game. Be sure to make each square a large 1″ by 1″ square so it takes time to X each square out!

Now let me share with you a little history about what happened when I first ran this simulation to train a group of employees at the Milby, TX, facility of Hoerbiger Corporation of America. One of the employees in that group was Luong D. He worked in the MPC Cell where an IE graduate

Part XXX	Lot Size: 6	Part # of 6	
Operation #	Machine Used	Operation Time	
1	M1	5	☐☐☐☐☐
2	M2	5	☐☐☐☐☐
3	M3	5	☐☐☐☐☐
4	M4	5	☐☐☐☐☐
5	M5	5	☐☐☐☐☐

Figure 26.10   Route sheet for the part.

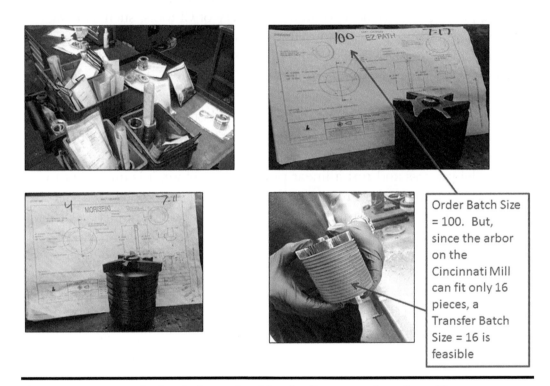

Order Batch Size = 100. But, since the arbor on the Cincinnati Mill can fit only 16 pieces, a Transfer Batch Size = 16 is feasible

Figure 26.11   Transfer batch determined by the fixture used on the mill.

intern was working with me to completely redesign that cell. The three of us discussed (and argued a lot too!) why one-piece flow ought to be implemented between the Haas Mill and the group of three Cincinnati Mills that Luong D. operated. The intern and I maintained that it was unacceptable that operators at two machines which were a few steps apart continued to use a batch-and-queue policy instead of using transfer batches! A few days after this training, Luong D. gestured to us and showed us what he had implemented. Figure 26.11 shows his idea to start pulling just enough pieces off the Haas Mill that he could pack on the arbor used on each of his three mills. Thereby, the same order could be split up and each batch run in parallel on all three machines. This is just one instance of the economic benefits of (i) implementing cells, (ii) giving Lean education to the cell operators, **and** (iii) empowering the cell operators to exercise their creativity!

The *Stamping Out Chaos*© **Simulation:** This simulation teaches the layout and day-to-day operations of a cell. The cell needs to produce a number of different license plates. The group is asked to design a cell that must be (i) flexible, (ii) fast, and (iii) cost-effective to operate. The cell consists of six stamping presses and a location "R/S". The location "R/S" is the combination of two departments: "R" = Receiving (for receipt and storage of raw materials) and "S" = Shipping (for receipt and shipping of finished products). Six volunteers are chosen to role-play as the "stamping presses". They each receive an inkpad and a stamp with one of the six letters – W, E, T, A, H, C. They would stamp their letter on each license plate that has a word with that letter in it. The set of license plates that must be produced is as follows:

Wheat	Thaw	Etch
Cheat	What	Whet
Teach	Chew	Each
Chat	Hate	Ache
Watch	Heat	

Each license plate is assigned to a different person in the group. Each license plate will start at the location "R/S", visit the appropriate sequence of presses one by one, get the sequence of letters stamped on it at the different presses, and after all the needed letters have been stamped on their plate, they return to the location "R/S". When a license plate reaches a particular press to get their next letter stamped, they wait their turn in the queue to get stamped before they can move to the next press to collect the next letter stamp, and so on. The person carrying a license plate *must* keep a count of the total number of steps that he/she walked on their route, beginning and ending at the location "R/S". On completion of his/her manufacturing route, each person reports the total number of steps that they walked to the person acting as the R/S clerk sitting near the cell.

My goal is to provide the attendees insights into some of the key differentiators between Job Shop Lean and Lean. Here are some of the challenging questions that I ask the group after we are done playing this seemingly simple game:

- Which of the 720 possible layouts for the cell would minimize the total distance traveled by all the license plates?
- Where should the R/S station be located with respect to the six presses in the cell?
- What is the sequence in which the plates should be released to the cell to minimize the total time it takes the cell to complete all the license plates?[8]
- Would they release all the plates for production at the same time? If not, would they release similar plates such as WHEAT, WHAT, and HEAT one after the other? Or would they prefer to release dissimilar plates such as WATCH, HEAT, and CHAT one after the other?

A Step-By-Step Approach for Implementing Job Shop Lean: I developed this case study while I was at the University of Minnesota to teach total facility reorganization into cells, and appropriate support systems and operational strategies to manage the individual cells as well as interactions between them. It was originally published as Chapter 20 ("A Classroom Tutorial on the Design of a Cellular Manufacturing System") in the *Handbook of Cellular Manufacturing Systems* (John Wiley, 1999, ISBN 0-471-12139-8). It has been reproduced in this book with the permission of the publishers, John Wiley & Sons, Inc. Special thanks are due to Bob Argentieri for facilitating the permissions process that allows me to disseminate this one chapter from the handbook. At the time, he was with John Wiley and managed the handbook project.

This case study uses data for a hypothetical machine shop to illustrate how the PFAST (Production Flow Analysis and Simplification Toolkit) software can perform some of the basic analyses for the design of Cellular Layouts (or Hybrid Cellular Layouts) such as product mix segmentation, material flow mapping, part family formation, and block layout design. However, these are *just* the preliminary analyses to design a detailed facility layout. PFAST *does not* perform many of the subsequent steps to relayout a job shop. Therefore, this case study explains *in full detail* the following activities that are essential for implementing an FLean facility layout:

---

[8] If you wish to answer this question, you may want to learn about Job Shop Scheduling and download the free *LEKIN Academic Scheduling Software*. Please visit http://community.stern.nyu.edu/om/software/lekin/ to download the software.

- Product-Process Matrix Analysis to form part families
- Capacity Requirements Analysis to determine how many machines of each type are required in a particular cell (Machine Loading)
- Distribution of shared machines among competing cells (Machine Allocation Analysis)
- Strategies for limiting inter-cell flows, e.g., elimination of Exception Operations
- Design of the layout of each cell (Intra-Cell Layout)
- Design of the overall layout of the entire facility (Inter-Cell Layout)
- Scheduling operations inside each cell (Intra-Cell Scheduling)
- Synchronizing cell schedules with the inter-cell flows to complete operations on parts that visit (i) other cells, (ii) Monument(s) (if any), and (iii) Remainder Cell(s) (if any) that are external to the cells (Inter-Cell Scheduling).[9]

I urge you to work through these steps as that will help you to understand what data you will need to extract from your ERP system if you decide to implement Job Shop Lean using the methods described in this book! **Please email me at ShahrukhIrani1023@yahoo.com if you have questions.**

The *JobshopLean*© **Simulation:** This low-cost interactive simulation is based on the *Classroom Tutorial on the Design of a Cellular Manufacturing System*. While the classroom tutorial may be better suited to IE students, I realized that industry practitioners needed something more dynamic and hands-on without sacrificing the learning content. This simulation teaches the following Job Shop Lean practices:

- Segment the parts into multiple segments based on Volume, Value, and Complexity (*and not just Volume using the 80–20 Pareto Rule!*).
- Identify part families in the product mix.
- Implement manufacturing cells but also consider other layout options, such as Hybrid Cellular Layouts or Virtual Cells.
- Plan the equipment allocations to the cells based on Workload vs. Available Capacity.
- Cull the low-value low-volume products from the existing product mix.
- Try to reengineer certain routings to eliminate "misfit routings" and "exception routings".

---

[9] This coordination of cell schedules is to be done jointly by Production Control and the Water Strider(s) on the factory floor.

- Train material handlers to become "Water Striders" who have complete "situational awareness" on the shop floor.
- Cross-train employees to attend to multiple machines within a cell (or even if they were distributed across the facility in Virtual Cells).
- Introduce multi-function flexible automation to compact the facility.
- Schedule with finite capacity constraints in order to manage work releases into the shop so as to maintain sufficient WIP (work-in-process) in Time (*not* Inventory) Buffers.
- Use appropriate sequencing/dispatching rules to prioritize jobs at different machines, especially the bottleneck(s).
- Use performance measures, such as Cash Flow Velocity, instead of Cost Reduction (aka Seven Types of Waste).
- Encourage feedback and ideas from the employees.
- Implement a visual queue management system to facilitate Pull scheduling.

In addition, you can incorporate into this simulation **some** of the standard Lean tools as follows:

- *Quality at source:* You can issue help cards that show how the squares on the route sheets should be X'ed out else rework will be called for.
- *5S:* You can have the players who represent the different machines go to a central tool storage rack to get the particular colored pencil they must use to mark up the route sheets.
- *Visual management:* You can mount a whiteboard on which the specific sequence in which jobs must be done at certain work centers is announced.

The first run of the simulation demonstrates the Current State of a hypothetical machine shop with twelve different machines making approximately fifteen parts with routings that use different combinations of those machines. Please click on this link https://vimeo.com/5425379 to see the online video titled *JobshopLean Simulation – Current State of the Jobshop*. The second run of the simulation demonstrates the Future State of the same machine shop after implementing some of the Job Shop Lean strategies listed earlier. Please click on this link https://vimeo.com/5537406 to see the online video titled *JobshopLean Simulation – Future State of the Jobshop*. In both videos, I play the role of the Water Strider moving jobs between different machines. This allows me to have fun while I entertain and instruct the class.

Chapter 27

Introduction to Value Network Mapping

Complex problems do not have simple solutions

When all you have is a hammer, everything looks like a nail

Don't try to hammer a nail with a monkey wrench

Don't use a screwdriver to pound nails. It takes forever and wrecks the screwdriver

It is important to find the right tool for the job

Introduction

I read the Bible on Value Stream Mapping (VSM) – Rother, M. & Shook, J. (2009). *Learning to See: Value Stream Mapping to Create Value and Eliminate Muda*. Brookline, MA: The Lean Enterprise Institute – when I was still on the faculty of the Department of Integrated Systems Engineering at The Ohio State University. I taught VSM in three IE (Industrial Engineering) undergraduate courses (Methods Analysis, Facilities Planning, and Production Control). VSM enriches and enhances classical manual IE tools like Process Maps, Flow Process Charts, and Flow Diagrams. A Current State Map is a clear visual guide to which specific departments (or processes) in a company ought to be improved using Lean best practices, such as Setup Reduction, Total Productive Maintenance, Work Cells, etc. VSM is easy to learn and implement using an 11 × 17 sheet of paper or Post-It notes plastered on a wall.

High-Mix Low-Volume Manufacturers Are Different from Toyota

Unlike an OEM (Original Equipment Manufacturer) like Toyota, there are numerous **high**-mix **low**-volume (HMLV) manufacturers such as:

- Any job shop that does fabrication, machining, forging, molding, tool and die, casting, maintenance/repair/overhaul, etc.
- Any production shop that serves a diverse mix of aerospace and defense customers
- Any vertically integrated Make-To-Order facility that makes customized versions of a large and complex fabricated product such as a crane or heat exchanger for different customers
- Any shipyard that builds an aircraft carrier
- Any MRO (Maintenance, Repair and Overhaul) facility
- Any collision repair shop
- etc.

The fundamental difference between any HMLV manufacturing facility and any Toyota facility is that an HMLV manufacturing facility, such as a forge shop, fabrication shop, or machine shop, produces a large number of different components. In many cases, these components are used to build subassemblies that comprise a large and complex fabricated product. In either case, VSM is incapable of simultaneously displaying the large number of Value Streams that are processed in any HMLV facility on a single day, let alone any week, month, or year!

Value Stream Mapping Is Ill-Suited for HMLV Manufacturers

Based on my past career in academia and current industry experience as an IE consultant whose clients are primarily HMLV manufacturers, I find that VSM is ill-suited for guiding the implementation of Lean in any HMLV manufacturing facility. VSM is at best a macro-level tool that helps management to gain a high-level visualization of their operations. A map developing using VSM is unable to represent anything more complex than a repetitive high-volume production system, such as an assembly line (or cell). *Every* VSM on record usually represents a single product, or a family of similar products with little, if any, significant differences in their routings. From an IE viewpoint, some major shortcomings of VSM are:

- VSM cannot handle variety. It cannot map a large number of dissimilar manufacturing routings involving dozens of different work centers. Nor can it map the complete BOM (Bill Of Material) of any complex product. This is supported by what Rother and Shook state in their book "… (when) any value streams have multiple flows that merge….draw such flows over one another…but do not try to draw every branch if there are too many. Choose the few components first, and get the others later if you need to….just draw the flow for one or two main materials".

- VSM cannot handle variation. It provides a single day's snapshot of a dynamic system; thereby, it fails to capture time-dependent variability in the performance of the system. This is supported by what Martin and Osterling state in their book[1] "… The current *state value stream map* represents how the value stream is performing on the day the map is created. Because the current state map represents a snapshot in time, the observations the team makes and the metrics it collects reflect value stream performance on that specific day. For value streams with high variation, it may be helpful to revisit the value stream on a different day to explore how it operates in different conditions".

- VSM lacks the analytics to show how the performance of the Value Stream could be impacted by changing transfer batch sizes, scheduling priorities, OEE (Overall Equipment Effectiveness) at different work centers, etc. VSM simply cannot evaluate multiple "what if" options for improving any system!

- VSM misleads a Lean implementer to consider *only* those practices that work in high-volume low-mix (HVLM) assembly facilities, such as kanban-based inventory replenishment, First In First Out (FIFO) scheduling and single-piece flow cells.

- VSM is slow, cumbersome, and error-prone when used to map and visualize a collection of Value Streams.

Some of the shortcomings of VSM are shown in Figures 27.1 and 27.2.

---

[1] The new Bible on VSM is – Martin, K. & Osterling, M. (2014). *Value Stream Mapping: How to Visualize Work and Align Leadership for Organizational Transformation.* New York: McGraw-Hill.

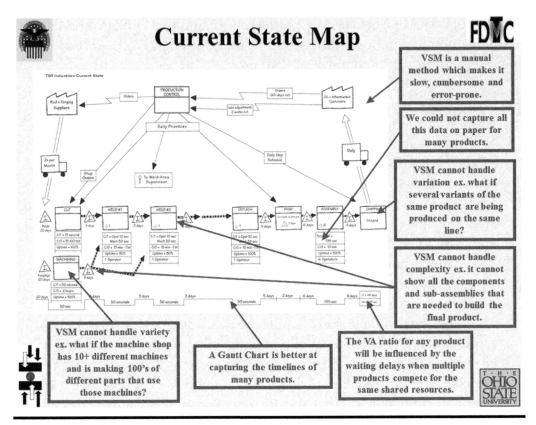

Figure 27.1 Shortcomings of Value Stream Mapping (Current State Map).

Theoretical Foundations of Value Network Mapping

An IE working in any manufacturing or service facility has to perform functions such as Facility Layout, Production Planning, Operations Scheduling, Materials Handling, Inventory Control, Warehouse Management, etc. All of these functions are embedded in a rudimentary form in any VSM. A VSM consists of three layers: (i) The top layer deals with production planning and scheduling, (ii) the middle layer deals with material flow, and (iii) the bottom layer deals with performance measurement using the Value-Added Ratio (VAR) metric to measure the efficiency of order completion.

Next, I will summarize a research paper[2] published in 1978 that gave ideas on how to implement Value Network Mapping (VNM) using IE methods such as Group Technology (GT), Material Requirements Planning (MRP),

[2] Sato, N., Ignizio, J.P. & Ham, I. (1978). *Group technology and material requirements planning: An integrated methodology for production control. Annals of the CIRP,* 27(1), 471–473.

Future State Map

FD⚙C

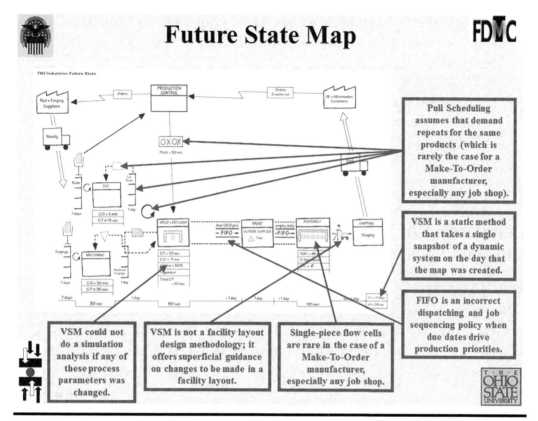

Pull Scheduling assumes that demand repeats for the same products (which is rarely the case for a Make-To-Order manufacturer, especially any job shop).

VSM is a static method that takes a single snapshot of a dynamic system on the day that the map was created.

FIFO is an incorrect dispatching and job sequencing policy when due dates drive production priorities.

VSM could not do a simulation analysis if any of these process parameters was changed.

VSM is not a facility layout design methodology; it offers superficial guidance on changes to be made in a facility layout.

Single-piece flow cells are rare in the case of a Make-To-Order manufacturer, especially any job shop.

Figure 27.2   Shortcomings of Value Stream Mapping (Future State Map).

and Flow Shop Scheduling. The authors proposed an integrated methodology for production control of any HMLV production system that assembles a variety of products using a large variety of components. The sequence of steps that they followed is described below:

1. Use GT to segregate the large variety of components being produced in the facility into a relatively small number of part families. A part family is a group of parts that pass through identical/similar process flow sequences (aka routings).[3]
2. Use the routings of the parts in each family to identify a "machine group" (aka cell). Each cell is dedicated to the production of a part family.
3. Use MRP to determine the week-by-week production of all the parts needed to assemble different products per the delivery dates for those products that were quoted to their customers.

---

[3] A part family corresponds to a single Value Stream!

4. For each week, load the batch for each component that has been scheduled for production on the cell which has all the equipment specified in its routing.

5. For each week, schedule production of all the components that have been loaded on each cell using a Flow Shop (or Job Shop) Scheduling heuristic. The choice of heuristic will depend on whether the routings are identical (Flow Shop) or the routings do not use the same combination and sequence of machines in the cell (job shop).

Comparison of Value *Stream* Mapping and Value *Network* Mapping

How does an HMLV manufacturer map and analyze a large number of value streams on a single map to determine what improvements to make in their production system? Table 27.1 outlines how a VNM is developed using IE methods to implement the same steps taken to develop a VSM as follows:

Table 27.1   Comparison of Value Stream Mapping and Value Network Mapping

Steps in VSM	*How the Same Step Is Implemented in VNM*

Identify value: Specify value from the standpoint of the end customer by product family.	• The same metrics (Quality, Cost, and Delivery) that drive a manufacturer like Toyota also drive an HMLV manufacturer. However, unlike high-volume repetitive production, HMLV manufacturers need to be able to produce a wide variety of products (flexibility), be able to modify their facilities as product mix and demand change (reconfigurability), and adapt to changes in customer base (adaptability).
	• Product (or component) families are formed using methods such as GT or Production Flow Analysis (PFA) as follows:
	  • GT can be implemented using a statistical analysis package.
	  • PFA can be implemented using the Production Flow Analysis and Simplification Toolkit (PFAST) software.

(Continued)

Table 27.1 (*Continued*) Comparison of Value Stream Mapping and Value Network Mapping

Steps in VSM	*How the Same Step Is Implemented in VNM*
Map the value stream: Identify all the steps in the value stream for each product family, eliminating whenever possible those steps that do not create value.	• In the case of components manufacturers, such as machine shops, forge shops, and foundries, use a Product-Process Matrix Analysis or Multi-Product Process Chart to map the value streams for all the products in any family. • In the case of product assembly manufacturers, develop the Operations Process Chart for each product assembly, including the components and subassemblies that are listed in its BOM.
Create flow: Make the value-creating steps occur in tight sequence so the product will flow smoothly toward the customer.	It is well known that flow is best achieved in a focused factory with a cellular layout. Each cell produces a part family or variants of the same product. And, if excessive equipment sharing occurs between the cells and many external monuments force delivery constraints on the cells, then hybrid factory layouts and virtual cells are preferable.
Establish pull: As flow is introduced, let customers pull value from the next upstream activity.	• Production capacity is not infinite, even though every ERP (Enterprise Resource Planning) system in the world assumes that. How to plan production and schedule operations subject to finite capacity? In order to control the release of new orders into a production system subject to available capacity on the bottleneck work centers, we can use a variety of proven strategies such as Finite Capacity Scheduling (www.Preactor.com, www.Waterloo-Software.com), Constant Work In Progress (CONWIP) (www.FactoryPhysics.com), and Drum-Buffer-Rope (www.DBRPlus.com) • Although lacking the VSM icons, a Gantt Chart produced by a scheduling tool, such as the Work Status Gantt produced by TACTIC (from Waterloo Manufacturing Software Inc., www.Waterloo-Software.com), is an effective visualization of the work center-by-work center progress of multiple Value Streams that need to share common resources.

(Continued)

Table 27.1 (*Continued*)   Comparison of Value Stream Mapping and Value Network Mapping

Steps in VSM	*How the Same Step Is Implemented in VNM*
Seek perfection: As value is specified, value streams are identified, wasted steps are removed, and flow and pull are introduced, begin the process again and continue it until a state of perfection is reached in which perfect value is created with no waste.	• Since each cell is analogous to a value stream, it is sensible to implement cells one at a time. It is not easy for employees and managers to accept self-managing autonomous teams, especially in union facilities. • Cells are not always immediately feasible. It takes time to break the constraints that initially prevent their implementation. "Breaking the constraints" requires implementing best practices such as Setup Reduction, Total Productive Maintenance, Right-sized Equipment, etc.

Example: Developing a Value Network Map for a Fabricated Product

1. From the ERP system, extract the BOM for the product as shown in Figure 27.3.
2. In the BOM, identify the components and subassemblies that are made in-house.
3. From the ERP system, obtain the manufacturing routings of the components and subassemblies (and final product too!) that are made in-house.
4. From the ERP system, identify the specific stations on the final assembly line to which each of the in-house components and subassemblies is delivered to.
5. Transform the data collected in Steps 1–4 into an Operations Process Chart for the complete product as shown in Figure 27.4.
6. Analyze all the value streams in the Operations Process Chart to find part families and the work cell (or line) to produce each part family as shown in Figure 27.5.
7. Use the Future State material flow map obtained from Step 6 to modify the existing facility layout *to the extent possible* in order to align the factory layout with the product flow as shown in Figure 27.6.
8. Designate locations in the facility that will receive components and/or subassemblies from the different cells to build kits of components for different subassemblies.

```
 .5:44:14                                                              PAGE:    1
FUNCTION: MBIL                  MULTI-LEVEL BILL INQUIRY              07/21/1999

    PARENT: 2158002065-A       DESC: 2158, ●,20K,5X7,4KD
        RV:        UM:EA       RUN LT:     1  FIXED LT:   3
      PLNR: 3KB                PLN POL: N           DRWG: TC202034

     LEVEL     PT                     C PARTIAL                   Q M LT    SCR
     1...5...10 USE SEQN COMPONENT    T DESCRIPTION      QTY UM   T B OFF   PCT
     1          0   010 WC[R]811ASMLY R ASSEMBLY, F/S     1.5 HR I M  0    0.0
     1          0   900 TB201990      N 2158,FRAME,CS,      1 EA I M  0    0.0
     2          0   010 WC[R]763WELDM R WELD,MANUAL WE    .5 HR I M  0    0.0
     2          0   020 WC[R]770WHLBR R SHOTBLAST,WHEE    .1 HR I M  0    0.0
     2          0   030 WC[R]771HCFIN R PAINT,HEAVY-CA    .5 HR I M  0    0.0
     2          0   900 T201972-4300  P ANGLE,CS,7GAX2     2 EA I M  0    0.0
     3          0   010 WC[R]763SHR16 R SHEAR 16'        .01 HR I M  0    0.0
     3          0   020 WC[R]763PRBRK R FORM,PRESS BRA   .01 HR I M  0    0.0
     3          0   900 MZ1304010054  N SHEET,7GAX48.7 11.96 LB I B  0    0.0
     2          0   900 T201972-6700  P ANGLE,CS,7GAX2     2 EA I M  0    0.0
     3          0   010 WC[R]763SHR16 R SHEAR 16'        .01 HR I M  0    0.0
     3          0   020 WC[R]763PRBRK R FORM,PRESS BRA   .01 HR I M  0    0.0
     3          0   900 MZ1304010054  N SHEET,7GAX48.7 18.63 LB I B  0    0.0
     2          0   900 TA201974      N 2158,BEARING,L     4 EA I B  0    0.0
     2          0   900 TB201971      P 2158,FRAME COR     4 EA I M  0    0.0
     3          0   010 WC[R]764WELDM R WELD,MANUAL WE   .15 HR I M  0    0.0
     3          0   900 TB201970      P 2158,FRAME COR     1 EA I M  0    0.0
     4          0   010 WC[R]763SHR16 R SHEAR 16'        .01 HR I M  0    0.0
     4          0   020 WC[R]761PUNCH R STRIPPIT          .1 HR I M  0    0.0
     4          0   030 WC[R]763PRBRK R FORM,PRESS BRA   .02 HR I M  0    0.0
     4          0   900 MZ1301010034  N PLATE,1/4X72X1 10.05 LB I B  0    0.0
     3          0   900 TN201973      N 2158,BUMPER,CS     2 EA I B  0    0.0
     1          0   900 TB600364-1    N LC,745,10K,5KD     4 EA I B  0    0.0
     1          0   900 TC201989-1    N 2158,PLAT,MT,2     1 EA I M  0    0.0
     2          0   010 WC[R]763WELDM R WELD,MANUAL WE   2.5 HR I M  0    0.0
     2          0   020 WC[R]770WHLBR R SHOTBLAST,WHEE    .1 HR I M  0    0.0
     2          0   030 WC[R]771HCFIN R PAINT,HEAVY-CA   .75 HR I M  0    0.0
     2          0   900 MZ0901020056  N NUT,3/4-10,HEX     4 EA I B  0    0.0
     2          0   900 T201962-6544  P CHAN,CS,1/4X2.     1 EA I M  0    0.0
     3          0   010 WC[R]763SHR16 R SHEAR 16'        .01 HR I M  0    0.0
     3          0   020 WC[R]763PRBRK R FORM,PRESS BRA   .02 HR I M  0    0.0
     3          0   900 MZ1301010034  N PLATE,1/4X72X1 43.41 LB I B  0    0.0
     2          0   900 T201963-6431  P CHAN,CS,1/4X2.     3 EA I M  0    0.0
     3          0   010 WC[R]763SHR16 R SHEAR 16'        .01 HR I M  0    0.0
     3          0   020 WC[R]763PRBRK R FORM,PRESS BRA   .02 HR I M  0    0.0
     3          0   900 MZ1301010034  N PLATE,1/4X72X1 68.12 LB I B  0    0.0
     2          0   900 T201965-4738  P CHAN,CS,1/4X2.     1 EA I M  0    0.0
     3          0   010 WC[R]763SHR16 R SHEAR 16'        .01 HR I M  0    0.0
     3          0   020 WC[R]763PRBRK R FORM,PRESS BRA   .02 HR I M  0    0.0
     3          0   900 MZ1301010034  N PLATE,1/4X72X1 50.19 LB I B  0    0.0
     2          0   900 T201966-4738  P CHAN,CS,1/4X2.     1 EA I M  0    0.0
     3          0   010 WC[R]763SHR16 R SHEAR 16'        .01 HR I M  0    0.0
     3          0   020 WC[R]761PUNCH R STRIPPIT          .02 HR I M  0    0.0
     3          0   030 WC[R]763PRBRK R FORM,PRESS BRA   .03 HR I M  0    0.0
     3          0   900 MZ1301010034  N PLATE,1/4X72X1 50.19 LB I B  0    0.0
     2          0   900 TA201967      P FLAT,CS,3/4X3X     2 EA I M  0    0.0
     3          0   010 WC[R]763BDSAW R SAW,BAND SAW     .01 HR I M  0    0.0
     3          0   020 WC[R]771VIKIN R SHOTBLAST,VIKI   .01 HR I M  0    0.0
     3          0   900 MZ1307010089  N FLAT,3/4X3X20'  10.9 LB I B  0    0.0
     2          0   900 TA201968      P 2158,STIFFNR W     2 EA I M  0    0.0
     3          0   010 WC[R]763BDSAW R SAW,BAND SAW     .01 HR I M  0    0.0
     3          0   020 WC[R]763ACRO  R MACHINE,ACROLO   .01 HR I M  0    0.0

                    *** continued on next page ***
```

Figure 27.3   Indented BOM for a fabricated product.

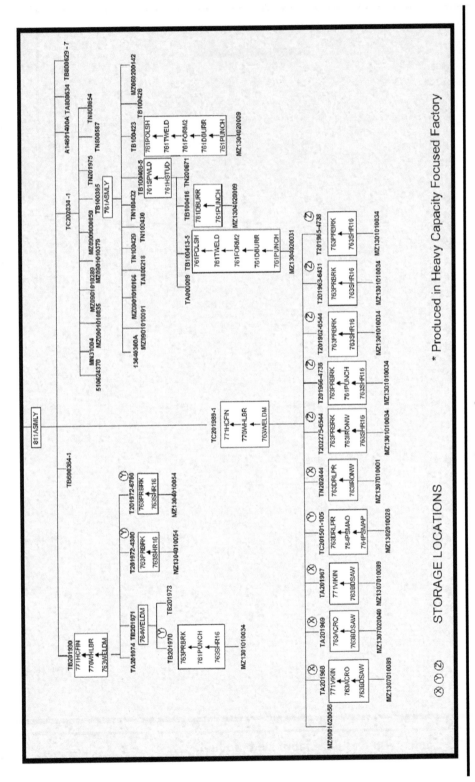

Figure 27.4   Operations Process Chart for the complete product.

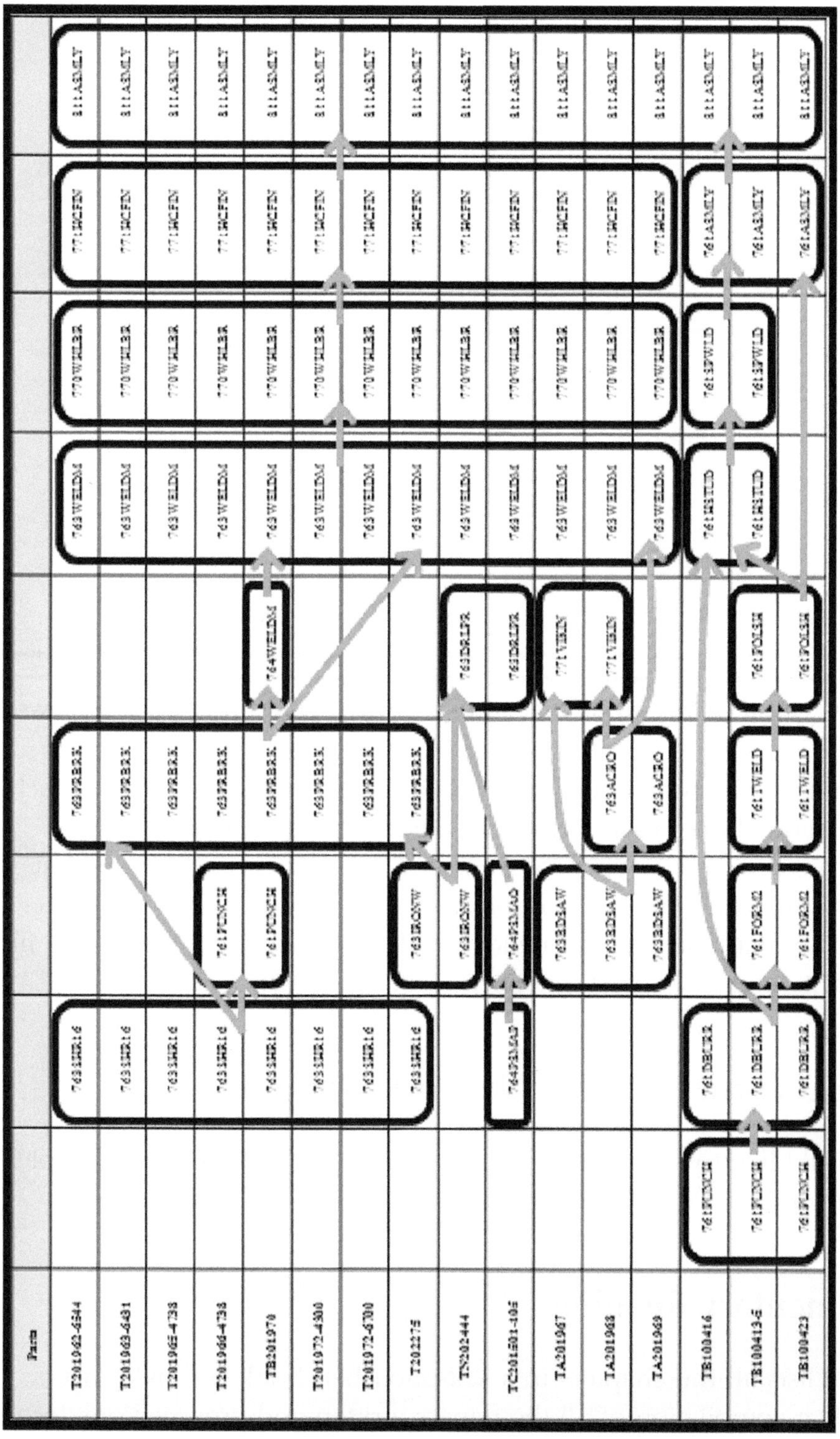

Figure 27.5 Finding part families by comparing routings in the Operations Process Chart.

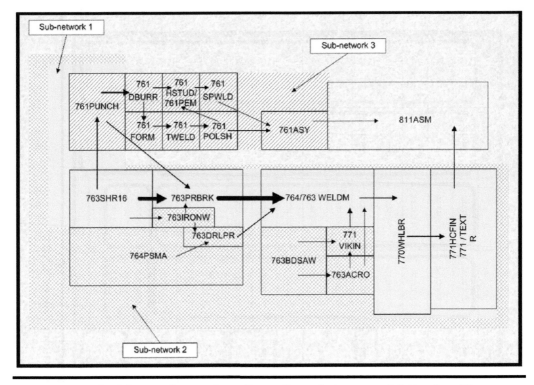

Figure 27.6   Ideal factory layout that aligns all Work Centers with Product Flows.

9. From the ERP system, extract the setup time and cycle time for each value-added operation in the Operations Process Chart.
10. Use the data from Step 9 to generate a visual project schedule that shows the Start/Finish Time for every operation in the Operations Process Chart, subject to queueing delays at shared resources and finite capacity constraints at bottleneck resources as shown in Figure 27.7.

Online Lecture on Value Network Mapping

If you would like to listen to a video recording of a lecture on VNM, please follow this link: https://vimeo.com/89422376

Supplementary Reading

Table 27.2 lists all the chapters in a self-published book on VNM that is essentially a compilation of all the papers written and presentations/lectures delivered on my method.

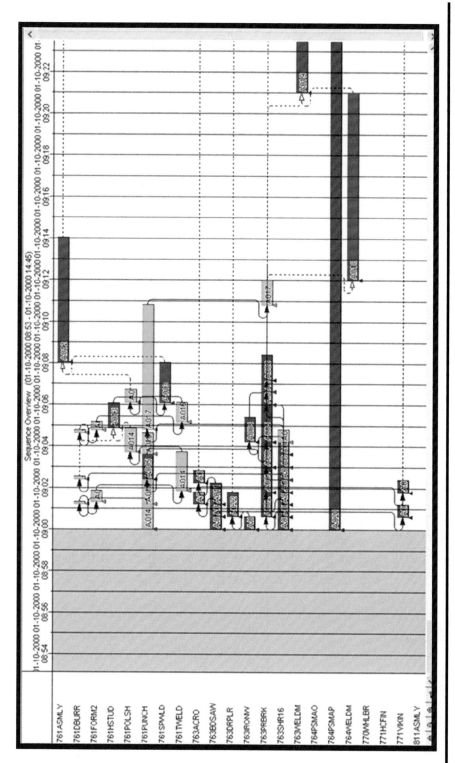

Figure 27.7 Visual project schedule for *All* operations in the Operations Process Chart.

Table 27.2 Supplementary Reading

Title of the Chapter	Overview of the Chapter
Value Stream Mapping: A Foundation Step for Lean Manufacturing	• This chapter is a PowerPoint presentation that summarizes the book – Rother, M. & Shook, J. (2009). *Learning To See: Value Stream Mapping to Create Value and Eliminate Muda*. Brookline, MA: The Lean Enterprise Institute. ISBN 978-0-9667843-0-5. • It provides specifics about a difficult challenge – *Selecting a product family* (Pages 9–11) – when defining the boundaries of the Value Stream that will be improved. • It offers guidelines on how to estimate the costs due to the Seven Types of Waste exposed in a Current State Map (Pages 17–25). • It lists in a single table well-established practices that could be used in combination to eliminate each of the Seven Types of Waste (Page 33). • The chapter ends with helpful advice to use the Process Of Ongoing Improvement (POOGI) based on the Theory Of Constraints (Page 41) in order to select improvement projects.
Value Stream Mapping from an IE Viewpoint: Ideas for Enhancement and Extension	• This chapter is a PowerPoint presentation that explains how VSM is at best helpful for macro-analysis of production and service systems. VSM is incapable of micro-analysis of production and service systems, especially systems that involve many value streams that dynamically share resources. • VNM was inspired by the difficulties I ran into on industry projects where the clients insisted that I develop VSMs for them. I found that a manual mapping method like Value Stream Mapping is unsuitable for implementing Lean in any real-world HMLV production system! • The chapter explains how IE tools like Multi-Product Process Chart, Cluster Analysis, Operations Process Chart, From-To Chart, Gantt Chart, Simulation, Economic Production Quantity, Scheduling, etc. could enhance a slow, error-prone and static method like VSM. • The latter half of the chapter introduces the methodology and new icons to implement VNM as described in the following conference paper published in 2001 – Khaswala, Z. & Irani, S.A. (2001, September 10–11). Value network mapping: Visualization and analysis of multiple flows in value stream maps. *Proceedings of the Lean Management Solutions Conference*: Institute of Industrial Engineers and University of Missouri-Rolla, St. Louis, MO, 47–63. • The chapter concludes with a summary of the pros and cons of VNM.

(Continued)

Table 27.2 (*Continued*) Supplementary Reading

Title of the Chapter	*Overview of the Chapter*		
Value Stream Mapping from an Industrial Engineering Viewpoint	This chapter expands on the previous chapter by comparing the icons used in classical IE tools (Process Mapping, Flow Charting, etc.) with the richer template of icons used in VSM, especially in modern-day graphics software tools like eVSM and iGrafx.		
Evaluation of the Value Stream Mapping Icons for Use in Job Shop-Type Facilities	This chapter assesses whether each of the icons used to create VSMs could be used in VNMs. The assessment is presented in a table with the following columns:		
	VSM Icon	**Applicability As-Is for VNM**	**New Icon Proposed for VNM**

Value Network Mapping (VNM): Visualization and Analysis of Multiple Interacting Value Streams in Job Shops	• This chapter is a PowerPoint presentation that expands on the original conference paper published in 2001 that introduced VNM.
	• It summarizes the advantages and disadvantages of VSM (Pages 128–131), provides the inspiration for VNM (Pages 312–134), and compares the two mapping methods (Page 135).
	• It illustrates the sequence of steps for implementing VNM using two different cases of HMLV manufacturing: (i) a machine shop and (ii) a fabrication facility.
	• The chapter illustrates the use of IE software tools to implement these core steps in the method:
	  1. Formation of part families[a],
	  2. Design of a flexible facility layout,
	  3. Generation of a daily production schedule based on finite resource constraints (instead of relying on an MRP system).		

(Continued)

Table 27.2 (Continued) **Supplementary Reading**

Title of the Chapter	Overview of the Chapter
Value Stream Mapping of a Complete Product	• This chapter describes a method to map on a **single** sheet of paper all the Value Streams that comprise the components, subassemblies, and final assembly for a fabricated product. Two examples of fabricated products are discussed: (i) a Gate Valve Assembly and (ii) an Industrial Weighing Scale. • The problem of manually drawing a VNM on a *single* sheet of paper is as hard as trying to *manually* design a factory layout! Therefore, VNM is implemented using IE software tools.
Integration of Lean Thinking and Theory Of Constraints in a Custom Forge Shop	• This chapter is a PowerPoint presentation that has a simple message – no single method, whether it is VSM or VNM or Six Sigma or Theory Of Constraints, ought to be used in isolation to improve any production or service system. • This chapter describes a case study where an entire forge shop was approximated as a single multi-product Value Stream, as is typically done when the Theory Of Constraints is used to improve any production or service system. • It was not necessary to develop a VNM! • It was sufficient to find the bottleneck in the forge shop by drawing a Multi-Product Spaghetti Diagram showing material flow in the entire facility and seeking input from the shop employees. Having identified the bottleneck in the forge shop, we focused on improving Throughput, Quality, and Efficiency at the bottleneck.

[a] Each part family is the basis for a VNM.

Current Status of VNM

At the present time, the status of VNM is as follows:

What the Method Can *Do*	*What the Method* Cannot *Do*
• Draw a large number of different Value Streams on the map • Locate a large number of process boxes representing the different work centers on the map • Retain the routing of each and every Value Stream to be included in the map • Group Value Streams with similar routings into part families • Design manufacturing cells to produce part families • Schedule and synchronize the production of all Value Streams and display the schedule as a Gantt Chart • Compute a Production Lead Time that accounts for queuing delays and capacity constraints (because several Value Streams use the same work centers)	• There is no detailed map with a large number of icons. But is a map at all necessary in the first place? And are icons really needed to visually identify areas of improvement in a complex HMLV production system? • Data is not displayed. But, given the sheer volume of data for a large number of Value Streams, is it at all necessary to have data displayed? Instead, this data ought to be exported from the ERP system as spreadsheets on an as-needed basis. • There is no commercial software available for GT and PFA. • Isn't a commercial Finite Capacity Scheduling package such as PREACTOR or TACTIC sufficient for computing the Value-Added Ratio for a large number of Value Streams using many common work centers? Else, in the case of a single large fabricated product, a commercial Project Scheduling package like MS PROJECT is sufficient to compute the Critical Path Duration subject to resource sharing.

Appendices

Appendices for this chapter are available for download at https://www.crcpress.com/9781498740692

Bibliography

Heston, T. (2015, November). How SWOT and Lean go together: Good planning should be grounded in real data, not assumptions. *The Fabricator*, 94–96.
Heston, T. and Irani, S.A. (2011, April). Developing the value network map: Value stream mapping alternative shows promise in job shops. *The Fabricator*, 37–39.

Irani, S.A. (2004). *Value Network Mapping (VNM): Extending Value Stream Mapping to Enable Lean Manufacturing in Jobshop-Type Custom Manufacturing Facilities.* Sugar Land, TX: Lean & Flexible, LLC.

Irani, S.A. (2018, March). 5 steps to building a value network map. *The Fabricator,* 76–78.

Khaswala, Z. & Irani, S.A. (2001, September 10–11). Value network mapping: Visualization and analysis of multiple flows in value stream maps. *Proceedings of the Lean Management Solutions Conference.* Sponsored by Institute of Industrial Engineers and University of Missouri-Rolla, St. Louis, MO.

Lechleitner, D. & Irani, S. A. (2015, November 9–12). Improving flow through practical lean technologies and tools. *Proceedings of the FABTECH 2105 Conference* held on November 9–12 at the McCormick Place in Chicago, IL. Sponsored by Society of Manufacturing Engineers (SME) & Fabricators and Manufacturers Association (FMA).

Chapter 28

Starter Advice for Implementing Job Shop Lean

Learn about the Toyota Production System

I was still an Industrial Engineer (IE) faculty at The Ohio State University during the years when I developed Job Shop Lean. I never had the opportunity to learn from a Toyota sensei about their revolutionary production system and management practices. I did not even know about Ohno's "Stand on the X" practice of forcing managers to stand at a location and observe work being done in an area! So, my only recourse was to read a slew of books about TPS (Toyota Production System)/Lean! In Chapter 1, I have listed books on TPS/Lean that I read because those books are by authors who have worked at Toyota or been guided by a Toyota sensei. Any individual or team seeking to implement Job Shop Lean ought to read at least a subset of these books. Given my IE education and applied research on practical IE problems, I quickly realized that the TPS/Lean tools are simple derivatives of the classical IE tools. But, I was ignorant about the "soft" elements of the TPS such as culture development, top-down leadership, employee engagement, employee training, etc.[1] The books by Ohno

---

[1] I humbly say this from personal experience after succeeding and failing in my own efforts to implement Job Shop Lean. I had spent my entire career in academia! Every IE educator needs to take a job in industry and work for at least 2–3 years to get personal hands-on experience in implementing TPS/Lean. It does not matter how simple or advanced their improvement projects are! All that matters is that they get hands-on experience and first-hand experience in implementing/leading/participating in TPS/Lean implementation projects at a local company. Current IE curricula are loaded with courses that mislead students that the operation of the factory floor can be optimized using quantitative models developed by researchers with no industry experience.

helped me to appreciate the tremendous importance of engagement with/by both employees and management. For example, at Toyota the CEO has risen through the ranks so he is intimately aware about the TPS/Lean practices. That is far from the case in most US companies!

Will Company Leaders Lead Your Transformation?

The primary reason why Lean will fail to "stick" in most organizations is the lack of sustained involvement by senior management who have sufficient knowledge about Lean. This is the conclusion I drew after reading some of the online articles I found when I Googled "Why Lean Programs Fail". In any organization, people with titles like Owner, President, CEO (Chief Executive Officer), COO (Chief Operating Officer), or VP (Vice President) Operations are the most powerful people in the best position to ensure the success of their Lean transformation. Unfortunately, they usually are never seen walking the floor talking to their employees, participating in kaizens, attending progress meetings, and questioning their middle managers about their projects. For example, in a CNC (Computer Numerical Control) machine shop that I worked with, I would see either of the two owners on the floor only when they had to ask Shipping about the status of an order or worse, they were themselves hunting for the order! So, instead of trying to implement Job Shop Lean there, which would have required them to invest time in implementing a pilot cell, I decided to limit what we attempted to "Lean basics" such as 5S to improve WIP (work-in-process) organization, Setup Reduction on a large CNC lathe, and a whiteboard that displayed the daily schedule in the Shipping department. In addition, most executives lack patience. They have an incorrect perception about Lean that astounding results will be achieved in no time with little if any active involvement on their part! In fact, the opposite was the case at one of my client companies. Both their CFO (Chief Financial Officer) and Director of Operations had been actively involved in the implementation of Lean at previous companies where they had worked. The CFO would make it a point to attend the daily morning huddles on the shop floor. He would ask questions of the department managers that demonstrated his grasp of Lean metrics. I reported to the Director of Operations, who was later promoted to VP Operations. He would scrutinize every project I did by asking the employees in the area where it was done if they were benefitted by the work that was done. That is executive-level involvement!

James Gatto, III, a Value Stream Manager/Engineer at Robinson Fans Inc., was one of the reviewers of an earlier draft of this chapter. He had this to say about the role of leadership in a Lean transformation, "From our perspective of being beginners and far from perfect, we would have benefited from additional advice. Based on our starts and stops at attempting to implement Lean, we have learned that it was necessary to have our leadership team create and communicate a shared vision of the future state and be able to communicate how we are moving along this path. We agree that leaders must do gemba walks, but only if they have a purpose that supports moving us toward the future state. In order to enhance their skill in moving the organization ahead, leaders must be willing to have the humility to realize that they themselves may need coaching as this cannot be delegated to others. Furthermore, we realized that we could not drop 'Lean' onto our existing organizational structure. If moving information and material across an organization is the goal, why are we so unwilling to consider the need to realign our organization(s)? Ultimately an organization can be inspired or disengaged by their leaders' words. But in order for organizations to create new habits and beliefs they must see leaders participating and truly caring for and celebrating their teams. Regardless of any advice you may be given, the real learning only occurs when you try".

To-Do's for Executives Who Want to Implement Job Shop Lean

- Read two books by former CEOs, Art Byrne[2] and George Koenigsaeker,[3] because each was the champion and driver for their company's Lean transformation.
- Start doing Gemba Walks ("Gemba" is Japanese for "where the actual work is done") to see and learn first-hand about the "state of their production floor".[4] Set aside time every week for these walks and vary your schedule to visit different departments. Make it a point to talk with the employees about their concerns and ask for *their* ideas/suggestions to improve their workplaces.

---

[2] Byrne, A. (2013). *The Lean Turnaround: How Business Leaders Use Lean Principles to Create Value and Transform Their Business.* New York: McGraw-Hill.

[3] Koenigsaecker, G. (2013). *Leading the Lean Enterprise Transformation.* Boca Raton, FL: CRC Press.

[4] I found excellent (and free!) information on *Gemba Walks* available online, including YouTube videos.

- Remain in constant communication with the team to which you have delegated the actual implementation of Lean.
- Entrust the implementation of Job Shop Lean to someone who understands the fundamental differences between Lean and Job Shop Lean.
- Be patient! Implementing Lean is like embarking on a never-ending journey with many stops and detours. Each stop is a better state of your company that you achieve (or hope to achieve) by improving the current state. Each detour is a change of the original route for the journey which increases the time it takes to reach the final destination. Toyota is the epitome of a company that has made CI (Continuous Improvement) an effective and self-sustaining long-term business strategy.
- Strive to demonstrate to your employees that you genuinely intend to make *how to work better, faster, and cheaper* the DNA of your company.

Engage All Departments

At one of my clients, we started by implementing an *Order Status Tracking Board* to monitor the daily production schedule and highlight problems/issues associated with all active orders. The Lean Champion conducted a daily Production Meeting at 1 p.m. in the lunch room with every manager in attendance whose department touched an order – Production, Purchasing, Material Control, Engineering, Sales, Quality Control, etc. The Lean Champion would affix Post-It's of different colors on the board to indicate which department must address a particular problem/issue with one or more orders. Every meeting saw the managers from all departments talking to each other, chiding each other, offering to help one another, etc. At the end of each meeting, the spreadsheet containing all the current problems/issues would be updated with a stated date for resolution of each issue by the manager responsible for it and emailed to everybody in the room. Yes, the board was a visual crutch for expediting! Yes, expediting is wasteful! But, at least it was a start for the Lean Champion to talk face-to-face with all managers. We replaced standoff and remote communications by email or phone with face-to-face communications. The board will continue to facilitate and coordinate everybody's efforts to get orders out the door. *Next*, we planned to install a *CI Project Status Tracking Board* next to the *Order Status Tracking Board*. The projects will address those problems/issues that the group collectively determines as impacting their company's ability to deliver orders on time and on budget. We will locate this project noticeboard in the same lunch room. On this board the different managers will post progress milestones and key results for their project(s). On a regular basis, the team will recognize the manager (and employees that assisted him) whose projects produced "wow" results. This "living" noticeboard, or maybe even a company newsletter published by the team, is expected to sustain interest in Lean/Job Shop Lean.

Get the Employees Involved!

An ant colony collectively executes and completes challenging tasks because of three characteristics[5]:

- Flexibility (the colony can adapt to a changing environment)
- Robustness (even when one or more individuals fail, the group can still perform its tasks)
- Self-organization (activities are neither centrally controlled nor locally supervised).

It is important to first and foremost encourage *all* employees to undertake improvement projects of *their* choice. Allow them to choose what to improve, where to improve, how much to improve, etc. Do not impose any constraints on them. Have expectations (but not hallucinations!) for results. Much can be achieved simply by asking and empowering each and every employee to offer improvement ideas.

Focus on Workplace Safety and Ergonomics

In my previous job, the very first improvement idea came from a shop employee who was concerned about his safety. Ly N. worked in the QRC (Quick Response Cell) cell. One day, after my Lean training session that he attended, he walked me over to one of the T-lathes that he operated and demonstrated how loading/unloading heavy parts off the machine could lead to injury. Very soon after this safety hazard was communicated to higher-ups, the Plant Manager (Keith F.), the Maintenance Manager (John S.),

---

[5] Bonabeau, E. & Meyer, C. (2001, May). Swarm intelligence: A whole new way to think about business. *Harvard Business Review, 79,* 106–114.

the Director of Safety (Frank O.), and the VP of HR (Bruce D.) authorized the repair of a jib crane that could load/unload that machine. Recall that the Toyota Production System was founded on the two pillars : (i) Just In Time (JIT) Production and (ii) Respect for People!

Hire a Lean-Savvy Plant Manager Who Cares about Profits *and* People

Soon after I started on my previous job, they hired a new Plant Manager, Keith F., who was a well-respected individual and very knowledgeable about Lean. He respected each and every employee who reported to him. He started having a weekly all-hands meeting with the shop employees at 7:00 a.m. every Friday. The employees on both shifts were organized into teams. These teams were basically the employees who worked in a manufacturing cell (Quick Response Cell, CNC Packings Cell, Power Rings Cell, Piston Rings Cell, Manual Packings Cell) or a support department (Quality, Maintenance, Shipping, Receiving). He appointed a Lead for each team. At each Friday meeting, he would invite the Leads to report any improvement ideas that they had implemented. I recall doing a simple calculation back then. If every week, each team in each of the two shifts per day implemented one improvement idea in their cell or department, this would result in 18 improvements every week. Assuming approx. fifty working weeks in the year, we would have 900 improvements that would impact our core business goals – Workplace Safety, Job Satisfaction, Speed of Customer Service, Waste Reduction, and Sales. If you put a $ value on the savings from each of those improvements, what would the total savings amount to?

Besides Kaizens, Do "Big Bang" Improvement Projects Also

The media would have us believe that all CI work ought to be implemented only by the employees themselves. Their justification is that this will ensure that the improvement(s) will get implemented and are sustained. I will respectfully disagree. Sometimes the project is technically demanding, and involves IT, data mining, and other engineering skills. In my previous job, our Director of Manufacturing Systems (Paul M.) personally led a pilot project in one of our cells to assess if the cell's team was ready for the introduction of computer-aided shop scheduling and order tracking. He was assisted by one of our Planners, Russell I., who helped to implement the software in the cell. In parallel, the employees in the cell team undertook complementary improvement projects and provided feedback to Paul and Irvine about the user-friendliness of their software. For example, they helped to determine the best way to mount the dual-monitor display at each of their workstations, the display format for the active sequence of jobs that the cell should be running, etc. This helped to speed up adoption of the computerized shop floor control system!

Hire Industrial Engineers

I owe the success of Job Shop Lean to the IE students I taught at The Ohio State University! It was those students who did Job Shop Lean projects and internships in industry over the years that helped me to validate Job Shop Lean.[6] A surefire way for an HMLV manufacturer to get ambitious projects done, including Six Sigma projects, is to have as many IEs on staff as you can. In my previous job, I was very lucky to be able to work with the following IEs:

■ *Full-time shop supervisor:* Leonel S. was the Supervisor of both Molding departments. He had BS and MS degrees in Manufacturing Engineering from the University of Texas – Pan American. Previously, he had worked at Seimens where he got to learn and implement Lean. If you were to walk past his departments, you would see considerable evidence that Lean was being practiced. Both departments were clean and well-organized. He would do weekly production huddles with the employees in both departments to address pressing issues. Often, I would see him on the floor assisting his employees. He would write up some of the employees' projects and recommend them for Employee Achievement Awards. Most noteworthy was the fact that he recognized that the work in either department involved heavy loading/unloading.

---

[6] Please email me at ShahrukhIrani1023@yahoo.com if you would be interested in a systematic approach to leverage the different co-curricular or extra-curricular programs of an IE department that allow their students to work in industry.

So he allowed rest breaks that, to outside observers, would make it appear as if the employees were slacking off at their workstations. Finally, the fact that he was Hispanic as were all the employees who worked in both departments (except James "Rojo" B.), definitely facilitated communications!

■ *Full-time industrial engineer:* Our CI Engineer (Shalini G.) had an MS degree in IE from the University of Houston. It helped to have a detail-oriented IE like her assisting on some of my projects. In particular, the time studies she did in several work cells helped cost accounting, scheduling and level loading of production. If you have an Enterprise Resource Planning (ERP) system, then at the barest minimum you need an IE to populate it with good data!

■ *Part-time interns:* Every year student interns from the Department of Industrial Management at the FH-Joanneum University of Applied Sciences in Austria would spend 4–6 months at one of our US facilities. I was especially fortunate to work with one of them, Thomas L., an undergraduate student who was studying for his BSc in Industrial Management. The two of us became facilitators and assisted several employees with their CI projects. In addition, we did technical projects on production scheduling and design of a flexible layout for the Shipping department. Thomas brought to our company a great work ethic and solid IE preparation. Our company gave him valuable OJT (On the Job Training) by assigning him several meaningful projects and a senior executive as his mentor. Many interns eventually chose to work at our company!

Get Going with the Quick-Start Approach for Job Shop Lean

If you desire to implement the *Comprehensive Approach for Job Shop Lean*, then you will need data mining software that would be able to identify the part families in your product mix. But, if you are an HMLV manufacturer and just getting started with Job Shop Lean, I think that you can achieve much. Now that I have worked in industry full-time for 7+ years, I understand how difficult it is for most small and medium manufacturers to access advanced software that is easily available to students and faculty at any university. Plus there is so much pressure on those tasked with implementing Lean in their companies to show results in a jiffy! So I urge you to get going with a simple approach, the *Quick-Start Approach for Job Shop Lean*.[7] It integrates Lean tools (like Value Stream Mapping) with Theory Of Constraints (TOC) and IE tools like Time Studies and Methods Analysis. With Value Stream Mapping, you focus on a particular product (or product family). But where to start improving the Value Stream? This is where TOC, with its focus on improving operational performance at the bottleneck in the system, proves its worth. Have you read *The Goal* (Eliyahu Goldratt, 2004, ISBN 0884271781)?[8] Goldratt lists three objectives for running a business: *Maximize Throughput, Minimize Inventories,* and *Minimize Operating Costs.* Recall that Profit Margin = Throughput − (Cost of Inventories + Operating Costs). This metric is far superior to Lean which focuses on cost reduction through waste elimination. TOC even helps to implement a simple scheduling method to ensure on-time delivery! So would you invest $1,000 to purchase a copy of *The Goal* DVD from The Goldratt Institute (www.goldratt.com)? That would be a true measure of your commitment to education and training of your employees on ideas and methods that are directly relevant to a job shop's operating conditions. Ask key managers and employees in your company to watch this video over and over again. Maybe you can have them answer a detailed list of questions that I have developed to test their learning from the video?[9] Ideally, key managers and shop supervisors should know how to implement *Value Stream Mapping* (Lean) and the *POOGI (Process of Ongoing Improvement)* that is central to the TOCs.

Do Not Ignore Six Sigma

There is a tendency among manufacturers to fault Six Sigma for its extensive use of statistics. But, for any manufacturer to stay competitive, Quality Control, Statistical Analysis of Data, and Design Of Experiments are essential! However,

---

[7] Please email me at ShahrukhIrani1023@yahoo.com for a copy of a prize-winning paper titled *The Quick-Start Approach to JobshopLean: How to Initiate the Implementation of Lean in a High-Mix Low-Volume Manufacturing Facility* that former Ohio State University graduate student, Byran Wang, wrote for a competition sponsored by the Lean Division of the Institute of Industrial Engineers.

[8] If you feel that *The Goal* is dated, then you may want to read a new book: Jacob, D., Bergland, C. & Cox, J. *Combining Lean, Six Sigma and the Theory Of Constraints to achieve breakthrough performance.* New York: Free Press.

[9] Please email me at ShahrukhIrani1023@yahoo.com if you are interested in my list of questions on *The Goal* video that I used in the Production Control and Scheduling course that I taught at The Ohio State University.

I have misgivings about a CI strategy when (i) every improvement project has to be cast in an Six Sigma framework, (ii) the actual problem is sliced and diced to fit the SS framework, (iii) the toolkit is limited, and (iv) other more pressing problems are ignored and a secondary problem is selected because it fits the SS framework.

Put Your ERP Vendor's "Feet to the Fire"

For decades, HMLV manufacturers have relied on "Lean Production" methods to plan production and schedule their production systems. They have no choice because their ERP system cannot produce a daily schedule subject to **finite** capacity constraints. In reality, if state-of-the-art software (Finite Capacity Scheduling, Manufacturing Execution Systems) and hardware (RFID (Radio Frequency Identification), smart phones, mobile computers mounted on forklift trucks, electronic displays for dynamic visual communications) are placed in the hands of employees who are tech-savvy and motivated, these age-old limitations of ERP could be overcome. Besides, there are Lean practices such as daily production meetings, water striders, etc. to complement the technology and the people using that technology. Every HMLV manufacturer needs to challenge their ERP vendor by asking, "Why do we not get a working schedule from our ERP?" and demand that the vendor eliminate the limitations of their ERP!

Determine How Many Businesses You Are Trying to Manage

This is important because a job shop needs to see their business in its entirety, and confirm whether one or more businesses are being run under the same roof. This is essential if they wish to plan to improve one, or all, of them. If they do not do this, they run the risk of financing a large number of kaizens with no focus on the key problems ailing their business! Use the method of *Product Mix Segmentation* to break up your product mix into different business segments based on Volume, Revenue, Demand Repetition, and Routing Similarity. Segmenting the product mix based only on Volume and Demand Stability will identify segments such as *Runners, Repeaters,* and *Strangers.* Segmenting the product mix based only on Revenue will identify segments such as *Stars, Questions, Cash Cows,* and *Dogs* (aka Growth-Share

Matrix). But what about the product families based on Routing Similarities? Ideally, each segment of the product mix should be managed as a separate business, maybe even produced in a separate area of the same facility. In the typical job shop, two or more businesses are allowed to intermingle, so they tend to interfere and compete with each other. *This* is what makes it much harder to implement Lean in a job shop, as compared to any Toyota factory!

Explore the Role of Group Technology

Group Technology (GT) is based on a general principle that many problems are similar, and by grouping similar problems, a single solution can be found to a set of problems, thus saving time and effort. The concept of the *part family* based on similarities in design and manufacturing is central to GT. GT has universal applications across an enterprise, such as design of manufacturing cells, design of flexible automation, employee cross-training, cost estimation, RFQ (Request For Quote) generation, etc. If you are an HMLV manufacturer, I urge you to develop a GT Classification and Coding system suited to your product mix!

Is Your Facility Layout Able to Support Flow?

You need to know if your facility layout is a problem. As soon as you can, have a team meeting to do this assessment. Simply update your facility layout, take a full-scale printout of your CAD (Computer Aided Design) printer and mount this drawing on a conference wall. Bring to that meeting a set of at least 20+ multi-color marker pens. Ask your team to make a list of 20–25 different part numbers that are Runners or Repeaters. For each of these parts, agree on the current routing for making that part. Then have a volunteer trace that complete routing on the facility layout. Repeat the process for all the part numbers that the team selected. Does the resulting Flow Diagram look like a bowl of spaghetti?

Do Not Ignore "Naturally UnLean" Processes – Think Right-Sized Equipment!

Heat treatment, extrusion, plating, etching, painting, washing – these are the so-called "naturally unLean" processes that, unlike machining or stamping, defy the standard Lean practices of Single-Piece Flow and Cellular

Manufacturing. If you have these processes, please do not ignore the changeover times, idle times, reject rates, etc. on them. This brings to mind a project we did for a high-mix pipe fabricator. They had 1,000's of SKUs (Stock Keeping Units) in inventory (by diameter, thickness, material, length, shape, etc.). They had three warehouses that were full of inventory and were building another one at the time they decided to investigate Job Shop Lean. *They had a single wash tank located in the middle of their facility.* **Every** batch of pipes they produced **had** to be washed in that tank. The tank was undoubtedly a monument, the obvious "Herbie" (aka bottleneck) in their system. Operators continually changed cleaning solutions between batches. And it was a common practice to group orders for the same type of pipe into a single batch in order to save changeover time (even if they always saw large batches in queue at the tank for days!). We went blue in the face advising their management to "right-size" that tank and replace it with several smaller tanks based on size of the parts, order quantity, type of washing needed based on oils used on the benders, etc. We even showed them the chapter in Lean Thinking where James Womack and Daniel Jones contrast how Toyota bought two commercial dishwashers to do the same washing that one of their Big Three competitors opted to do using an extremely complicated flexible washing "monument" that had an OEE (Overall Equipment Effectiveness) of only about 60%. We even found out that the Sales department had made no attempt to show their agents how uncontrolled diversity of incoming orders was creating a production bottleneck at the wash tank. All to no avail![10]

Invest in Employee Training and Development

I hope that you have on staff (or will hire) an IE from a recognized IE department whose curriculum incorporates a Lean Six Sigma Green Belt Certification. An IE (or MfgE) who understands the theory and practice of Lean, TOC, and Six Sigma can benefit a manufacturer regardless of company size![11] If hiring a full-time IE is unacceptable, then at least hire an IE intern on a semester-by-semester basis. A good IE ought not to find it too difficult

[10] Zelinski, P. (2006). Why Boeing is Big on Right-Size Machine Tools. *Modern Machine Shop.* www. mmsonline.com/articles/why-boeing-is-big-on-right-size-machine-tools.

[11] Please Google "Integrated TOC Lean Six Sigma" to access considerable online literature on how to integrate the three well-known improvement strategies – TOC, Lean, and Six Sigma – because they are complementary to each other.

to help their employer save, or earn, every year new business that is equal to his/her annual salary with benefits.

Having hired this IE, nurture him/her to become your company's full-time Lean Champion. His/her responsibility will be to support kaizen events, develop training materials, develop spreadsheets for automating mundane processes, mine data to support complex projects, etc. Put aside a travel budget for the IE to attend annual conferences and cutting-edge workshops. Accompany him/her on benchmarking visits to local companies that have successfully implemented Lean in their high-mix low-volume operations. **Above all**, put the IE in charge of a Lean Resource Office (LRO) that will support employees on their CI projects and help your employees learn the Why?, How? What? about Lean. Equip this office with resources such as CDs, books, posters, an annual subscription to the learning resources of www. GembaAcademy.com or www.ToolingU.com or www.Enna.com or www. gbmp.org, DVDs that feature learning games, a catalog of (free!) information available online at websites like www.TOCforMe.com and http://www. strategosinc.com/, etc. Be sure to keep enhancing the learning and training resources housed in the LRO with materials developed from the projects and implementations that your own employees do and/or the project reports submitted by interns. Nothing breeds a thirst for more success than seeing one's own success being recognized! Lastly, you may want to consider the TWI (Training Within Industry) Program for employee training and development. The TWI workforce training program was developed by US manufacturers and taught to Toyota soon after World War II. Toyota mastered it, improved it, and built their Toyota Production System on it. Somewhere I read that at Toyota every employee, from the President down to the line operator, comes to work thinking how they could make improvements in their current work processes. If you desire more information on TWI, please visit the website of The TWI Institute (http://www.twi-institute.org/).

Appendices

Appendices for this chapter are available for download at https://www. crcpress.com/9781498740692

Index

For Product Safety Concerns and Information please contact our EU
representative GPSR@taylorandfrancis.com Taylor & Francis Verlag GmbH,
Kaufingerstraße 24, 80331 München, Germany

Printed and bound by CPI Group (UK) Ltd, Croydon, CR0 4YY
08/05/2025
01864483-0001